Croatia

the Bradt Travel Guide

Piers Letcher

with Rudolf Abraham

edition
6

www.bradtguides.com

Bradt Travel Guides Ltd, UK
The Globe Pequot Press Inc, USA

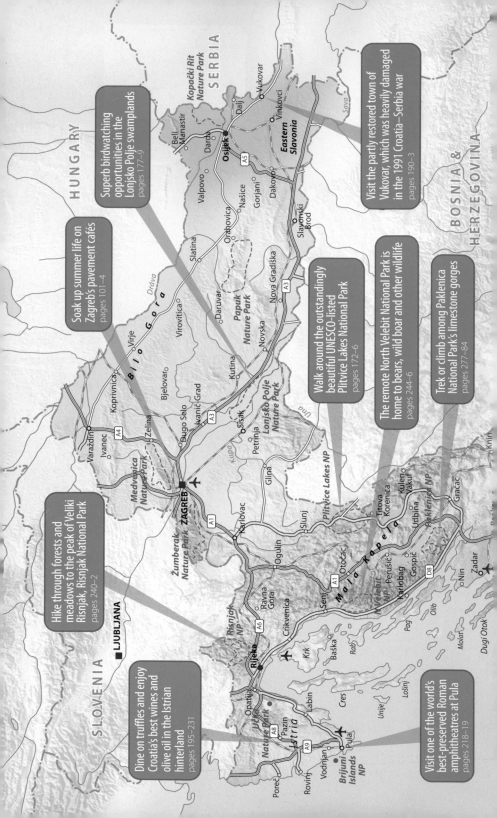

Superb birdwatching opportunities in the Lonjsko Polje swamplands
pages 177–9

Soak up summer life on Zagreb's pavement cafés
pages 101–4

Visit the partly restored town of Vukovar, which was heavily damaged in the 1991 Croatia–Serbia war
pages 190–3

Walk around the outstandingly beautiful UNESCO-listed Plitvice Lakes National Park
pages 172–6

The remote North Velebit National Park is home to bears, wild boar and other wildlife
pages 244–6

Trek or climb among Paklenica National Park's limestone gorges
pages 277–84

Hike through forests and meadows to the peak of Veliki Risnjak, Risnjak National Park
pages 240–2

Dine on truffles and enjoy Croatia's best wines and olive oil in the Istrian hinterland
pages 195–231

Visit one of the world's best-preserved Roman amphitheatres at Pula
pages 218–19

SLOVENIA
HUNGARY
SERBIA
BOSNIA & HERZEGOVINA

LJUBLJANA
ZAGREB
Rijeka
Osijek
Pula
Zadar

Kopački Rit Nature Park
Eastern Slavonia
Papuk Nature Park
Lonjsko Polje Nature Park
Plitvice Lakes NP
Medvednica Nature Park
Žumberak Nature Park
Risnjak NP
Učka Nature Park
Brijuni Islands NP
Velebit NP
Paklenica NP
Mala Kapela
Bilo Gora

Beli Manastir, Darda, Dalj, Vukovar, Vinkovci, Valpovo, Našice, Gorjani, Đakovo, Slavonski Brod, Slatina, Orahovica, Virovitica, Daruvar, Novska, Nova Gradiška, Kutina, Bjelovar, Koprivnica, Virje, Ivanec, Varaždin, Zelina, Dugo Selo, Ivanić-Grad, Sisak, Petrinja, Glina, Karlovac, Slunj, Ogulin, Otočac, Titova Korenica, Udbina, Kuleno Vakuf, Gospić, Karlobag, Gračac, Knin, Nin, Ravna Gora, Crikvenica, Senj, Perušić, Krk, Baška, Rab, Pag, Olib, Molat, Dugi Otok, Cres, Lošinj, Unije, Opatija, Labin, Pazin, Poreč, Rovinj, Vodnjan

Drava, Sava, Una, Kupa

A1, A3, A4, A5, A6, A8, A9, D8

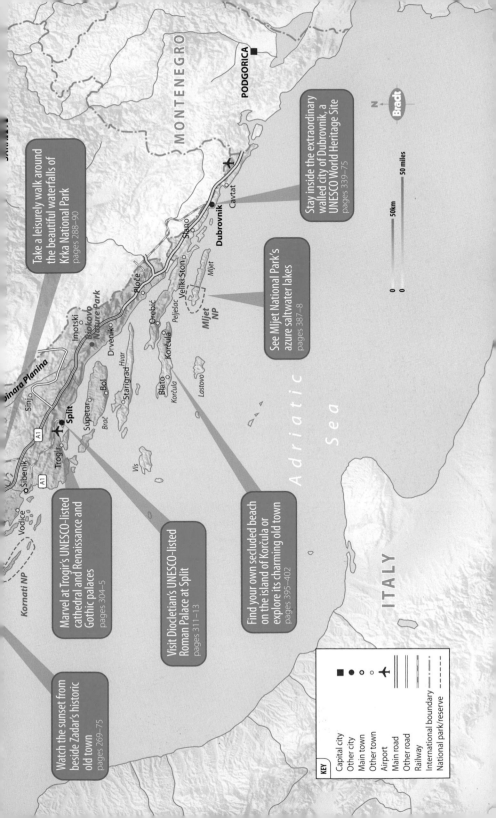

Watch the sunset from
beside Zadar's historic
old town
pages 269–75

Marvel at Trogir's UNESCO-listed
cathedral and Renaissance and
Gothic palaces
pages 304–5

Visit Diocletian's UNESCO-listed
Roman Palace at Split
pages 311–13

Find your own secluded beach
on the island of Korčula or
explore its charming old town
pages 395–402

Take a leisurely walk around
the beautiful waterfalls of
Krka National Park
pages 288–90

Stay inside the extraordinary
walled city of Dubrovnik, a
UNESCO World Heritage Site
pages 339–75

See Mljet National Park's
azure saltwater lakes
pages 387–8

MONTENEGRO

PODGORICA

Dubrovnik

Cavtat

Ston

Veliki Ston

Mljet
NP

Mljet

Pelješac

Orebić

Korčula
Korčula

Blato

Lastovo

Ploče

Biokovo
Nature Park

Imotski

Drvenik

Hvar

Starigrad

Bol

Brač

Supetar

Vis

Split

Trogir

A1

Šibenik

Vodice

A1

Kornati NP

Dinara Planina

Sinj

Adriatic

Sea

ITALY

KEY

■ Capital city
● Other city
○ Main town
○ Other town
✈ Airport
    Main road
    Other road
    Railway
    International boundary
    National park/reserve

Bradt

N

0   50km
0   50 miles

Croatia
Don't
miss...

Traditional culture and festivals
A young woman in traditional folk costume at the prestigious Brodsko Kolo in Slavonski Brod
(RA) page 183

National parks
The waterfalls of Krka National Park make a great day trip from Šibenik or Zadar
(SV/S) pages 288–90

Islands

Krk, one of Croatia's largest islands, has a surprisingly low-key feel to it
(MK/S) pages 255–60

Zagreb

The Croatian National Theatre isn't just a theatre, it's an entire experience
(RA) page 106

Medieval cities

Split is a lively, modern city, but with a gorgeous old town; pictured here, the Cathedral of St Domnius with the Ethnographic Museum in the foreground
(S/S) pages 311–15

Croatia in colour

left With its red-roofed stone houses and time-polished marble streets, Dubrovnik is a truly mesmerising city. Pictured, Stradun with the Franciscan Monastery on the left (SC/S) page 364

below Surrounded by vineyards, the medieval hilltop town of Motovun is exemplary of interior Istria's charm (SH/CTB) pages 223–4

above   Šibenik itself is lovely, but its 15th-/16th-century cathedral — a UNESCO World Heritage Site and Croatia's most important Renaissance monument — is terrific (RA) page 286

right   Zadar is an unpretentious, partially walled old town of fine churches and excellent museums. Here, the 9th-century St Donat's Church (D/S) page 273

below   The traffic-free old town of Trogir is one of the most charming on the whole Adriatic coast (DP/AWL) pages 301–5

above   The statue of Ban Jelačić stands
         proud on Zagreb's main square (RA)
         page 110

left   Zagreb's 13th-century St Mark's Church
         has a distinctive, brightly tiled roof
         which finally emerged from beneath
         scaffolding after years of restoration
         in 2009 (AL/S) page 113

below   The beautiful, non-denominational
         Mirogoj Cemetery is the work of
         architect Hermann Bollé
         (ZA/S) pages 131–2

AUTHOR

Born and educated in the UK, **Piers Letcher** has lived in France for over 30 years. He has published 17 books, more than a thousand newspaper and magazine articles and hundreds of photographs. He is currently Senior Speechwriter at the International Telecommunication Union, the United Nations specialised agency for information and communication technologies. Piers is the author of *Eccentric France* and *Dubrovnik: The Bradt City Guide*, and co-author of *Zagreb: The Bradt City Guide*.

UPDATER

Rudolf Abraham (*www.rudolfabraham.co.uk*) is an award-winning travel writer and photographer specialising in Croatia and eastern Europe. He first visited Croatia in the late 1990s, lived in Zagreb from 1999 to 2001, and continues to spend several weeks a year based in his favourite country in Europe. His books include *Istria: The Bradt Travel Guide*, *The Islands of Croatia*, *Walking in Croatia*, *The Alpe Adria Trail* and *The Mountains of Montenegro*.

AUTHOR'S STORY

I was enormously fortunate to meet Hilary Bradt in 1986, as it gave me the excuse to spend a year writing the Bradt guide to Yugoslavia. Back in those days, Hilary still marked up all the proofs herself, and it was a red-faced moment for a young writer to have to deal with comments in the margin such as 'Purple prose!'. It was a learning experience, and one I've been very grateful for over the past two million words or so: thank you, Hilary.

After a long interval – paying rent, starting a family, marrying Sarah, getting a dog – I returned to the Bradt stable in 2002 and spent several years researching, writing about and travelling in Croatia. It's a highly addictive place, not just for tourism but for what makes any country worth visiting: the people, the unexpected details, the moments of pure wonder.

As a guidebook author, it's never as much fun as people imagine. Which is why – in the name of research – I've done things in Croatia such as breaking a tooth trying to eat a decorative gingerbread heart; being escorted around an all-naturist hotel; or bursting into a family's front room, on the assumption that their simple dwelling was part of an anthropological museum village.

On one occasion I was trying to get back into Croatia – having somehow slipped into Slovenia on a back road – when I was caught at an illegal border crossing. It didn't help that excessive heat had caused a bottle of home-distilled spirits to explode in the boot of the car. Fortunately, every guidebook writer's most useful local language phrase – 'I am writing a book about your wonderful country' – did the trick and got me off the hook. While none of these things should happen to you, I hope you'll get as much pleasure from Croatia as it's given me over the years.

PUBLISHER'S FOREWORD   *Adrian Phillips, Managing Director*

Croatia has come a long way since Piers Letcher wrote the Bradt guide to Yugoslavia back in 1989. A country as popular as Croatia needs an expert author – or in our case two. Piers is one of our most-praised writers: travellers love his informal style combined with meticulous research and insider observations. Rudolf Abraham knows Croatia equally well, so we were delighted he could team up with Piers to update this sixth edition.

Sixth edition March 2016   First published 2003

Bradt Travel Guides Ltd
IDC House, The Vale, Chalfont St Peter, Bucks SL9 9RZ, England
www.bradtguides.com
Print edition published in the USA by The Globe Pequot Press Inc,
PO Box 480, Guilford, Connecticut 06437-0480

Text copyright © 2016 Piers Letcher
Maps copyright © 2016 Bradt Travel Guides Ltd
Photographs copyright © 2016 Individual photographers (see below)
Project Manager: Laura Pidgley
Cover image research: Pepi Bluck, Perfect Picture

British Library Cataloguing in Publication Data
A catalogue record for this book is available from the British Library

ISBN: 978 1 78477 008 2 (print)
e-ISBN: 978 1 78477 153 9 (e-pub)
e-ISBN: 978 1 78477 253 6 (mobi)

Photographs
AWL Images: Doug Pearson (DP/AWL), Peter Adams (PA/AWL); Croatian National Tourist Board: Luka Tambača (LT/CTB), Saša Halambek (SH/CTB); Dreamstime: Pozezan (P/D), Tuomaslehtinen (T/D); Greg Dickinson (GD); Rudolf Abraham (RA); Shutterstock: Alberto Loyo (AL/S), andras_csontos (AS/S), Dziewul (D/S), Matej Kastelic (MK/S), Nadezhda1906 (N/S), OPIS Zagreb (OZ/S), stepmorem (S/S), Simun Ascic (SA/S), Sorin Colac (SC/S), Simone Simone (SS/S), Syrota Vadym (SV/S), YingHui Liu (YL/S), Zvonimir Atletic (ZA/S)
Front cover Vis town (PA/AWL)
Back cover Folk musician, Dakovo (ZA/S); St Mary's Church, Zagreb (RA)
Title page Sumartin, on the eastern tip of Brač (OZ/S); Pula amphitheatre (YL/S); Plitvice Lakes National Park (CTB)

Maps David McCutcheon FBCart.S; colour map relief base by Nick Rowland FRGS; includes map data © OpenStreetMap contributors

Typeset by Wakewing, High Wycombe and Ian Spick, Bradt Travel Guides
Production managed by Jellyfish Print Solutions; printed in India
Digital conversion by www.dataworks.co.in

Acknowledgements

PIERS LETCHER For this sixth edition, first and sincerest thanks must go to Rudolf Abraham, whose unrivalled knowledge of the country and tremendous efforts on the ground ensured that this edition of the guide is as up to date as it can possibly be.

For their help in Croatia, thanks must go to Dubravka Mičić and Iva Čaleta at the Zagreb Tourist Board; Lidija Miščin and Vlatka Marić at the Zagreb County Tourist Board; and Ingrid Lovrić and Krešo Jakubak at the Medvednica Nature Park. For their assistance, I'd also like to thank Silvija Berković, Vladimir Crnković, Ivana Čukvina Nikolić, David Frayer, Vladimir Fumić, Gary Jarvis and Renata, Edo Kletečki, Deana Kovačec, Sanjin Mihelić, Mario Mirković, Stuart Panes, Borivoj Popovčak, Jakov Radovčić, Mirjana Randić, Ivana Rončević, Darinka Širola, Sanda Sokol, Petra Tramiščak and Vesna Vrabec in Zagreb; Duda Dravica Modriča in Velika Gorica; Krešimir Režek and Želko Škiljan in Plešivica; Dina Begić, Anđđdelka Mađd-đar and Dubravka Lapčić in Karlovac; Branka Tropp, Tanja Bunjevac and Elizabeta Dolenc in Varaždin; Sandra Bojić in Krapina; and Kristijan Kovačić and Rudi Gruba in the Međimurje.

For their feedback and input, I'm grateful to Zeljka Jelavić (Etnografski Muzej Zagreb), Zoran Sadaić and Vlasta Krklec (Museum of Krapina Neanderthal Man), Emilio Mendušić (Sokolarski Centar Dubrava), Rudi Grula (Međimurje County Tourist Board), Aleksandra Kolić Puškarić (Turistička Zajednica Grada Ogulina), Turistička Zajednica Grad Karlovac, Nina Rusković at War Photo Limited, Ilijana Cvetković, Richard Ellis, Fritz Frigan, Judy Johnson, Katherine Ljubojević, John Lobb, Joško Matušan, Professor Paul Richardson, Romuald Vučetić and Rajko Zorić.

A heartfelt thank you, too, to all the people whose names I never caught, who offered help, hospitality and kindness along the way.

I'd also like to thank Brice and Alec for being such fine and upstanding sons.

Finally, as always, I am indebted to Sarah Parkes (my sun and moon) for her kindness and thoughtfulness, her company and help, and her endlessly generous spirit.

RUDOLF ABRAHAM I would especially like to thank Sara Sabadin at the Croatian National Tourist Board in London; Nina Štohera of the Zadar County Tourist Board; Ante Galić of the Zadar City Tourist Board; Zrinka Badurina of the Lošinj Tourist Board; Renata Vincek of the Kvarner Tourist Office; Željka Stašić at the Opatija Tourist Board; Darja Juzbašić at the Zagreb City Tourist Board; Marija Burek at the Đakovo Tourist Board; Jelena Bilić of the Sinj Tourist Board; Aleksandra at the Ogulin Tourist Board; Josip Perčević in Slavonski Brod; Thammy Evans; Ivana Abraham; my daughter Tamara for testing the child-friendliness of many places in this guide; and Piers for letting me update his excellent book once again.

Contents

LIST OF MAPS

FEEDBACK REQUEST AND UPDATES WEBSITE

At Bradt Travel Guides we're aware that guidebooks start to go out of date on the day they're published – and that you, our readers, are out there in the field doing research of your own. You'll find out before us when a fine new family-run hotel opens or a favourite restaurant changes hands and goes downhill. So why not write and tell us about your experiences? Contact us on 01753 893444 or e info@bradtguides.com. We will forward emails to the author who may post updates on the Bradt website at www.bradtupdates.com/croatia. Alternatively you can add a review of the book to www.bradtguides.com or Amazon.

Introduction

I've had a love affair with Croatia for over 30 years, ever since I first InterRailed around Europe in 1982 and got stranded in Split for four days, waiting for someone to show up who never showed. It wasn't difficult to find my way out to the islands of Brač and Hvar, and from there to Korčula and on to Dubrovnik, by which time I was off the InterRail map, and into a different place altogether.

Next time out I got diverted in Trieste and ended up in Pula instead of Athens, and worked my way down the coast as far as Split again, stopping at Rab, and then for a week at the lovely Paklenica National Park (still a Croatian favourite). To get back to where I was going, I went up through the country to Zagreb, and saw the Plitvice Lakes for the first time. I travelled inland and visited the pretty, Baroque town of Vukovar, then wandered up through Osijek into Hungary.

It wasn't long before I was hammering at Bradt's door and clamouring to write about (what was then) Yugoslavia. That book came out in 1989, just in time to be washed away by the war – I spent 1991 glued to the television set, watching in horror as Vukovar fell and Dubrovnik was shelled, and had to wait a decade for my second chance.

My guide to Croatia was published in 2003, with a second edition in 2005, a third in 2007, a fourth in 2010, a fifth in 2013 and now this sixth edition – the most comprehensive and (I hope) useful guide to the country, and the only one that covers all the national parks and nature reserves.

HOW TO USE THIS GUIDE

AUTHOR'S FAVOURITES Finding genuinely characterful accommodation or that unmissable off-the-beaten-track café can be difficult, so the author has chosen a few of his favourite places throughout the country to point you in the right direction. These 'author's favourites' are marked with a ✳.

MAPS
Keys and symbols Maps include alphabetical keys covering the locations of those places to stay, eat or drink that are featured in the book. Note that regional maps may not show all hotels and restaurants in the area: other establishments may be located in towns shown on the map.

Grids and grid references Several maps use gridlines to allow easy location of sites. Map grid references are listed in square brackets after the name of the place or sight of interest in the text, with page number followed by grid number, eg: [103 C3].

OPENING TIMES Church opening hours can be erratic, so they are only listed when they are fixed.

SEND US YOUR SNAPS!

We'd love to follow your adventures using our *Croatia* guide – why not send us your photos and stories via Twitter (@BradtGuides) and Instagram (@bradtguides) using the hashtag #croatia. Alternatively, you can upload your photos directly to the gallery on the Croatia destination page via our website (*www.bradtguides.com*).

Part One

GENERAL INFORMATION

CROATIA AT A GLANCE

Country name Republic of Croatia (Republika Hrvatska)
Border countries Slovenia, Hungary, Serbia, Bosnia and Herzegovina, Montenegro
Language Croatian
Population 4.29 million (2011 census)
Religion Roman Catholic (87.8%), Orthodox Christian (4.4%), Muslim (1.3%) (2011)
President Kolinda Grabar-Kitarović
Capital Zagreb (population 793,000, 2011 census)
Other major cities and towns Split, Rijeka, Osijek, Zadar, Slavonski Brod, Karlovac, Pula, Sisak, Varaždin, Dubrovnik
Size 56,542km^2
Islands, reefs and islets 1,185
Inhabited islands 67
Coastline 5,835km (1,777km mainland and 4,058km islands)
High point Mount Dinara, 1,831m
National parks Eight
Nature parks 11
Protected species 380 (fauna), 44 (flora)
Time GMT + 1
Currency Kuna (abbreviated kn or HRK)
Exchange rate €1 = 7.62kn, £1 = 10.8kn, US$1 = 7.2kn (December 2015)
International telephone code +385
Tourist board website www.croatia.hr
Public holidays 1 January (New Year's Day); 3 February (St Blaise's Day); Easter (27 March 2016, 16 April 2017, 1 April 2018); 1 May (Labour Day); Corpus Christi (60 days after Easter Sunday, and taken seriously in Croatia, with processions and lots of first communions. Corpus Christi falls on 26 May 2016, 15 June 2017, 31 May 2018); 22 June (Day of Antifascist Struggle); 25 June (Statehood Day); 5 August (Homeland Thanksgiving Day); 15 August (Assumption of the Virgin Mary); 8 October (Independence Day); 1 November (All Saints' Day); 25 and 26 December (Christmas).

Background Information

FACTS AND FIGURES

Croatia's curious shape – wishbone, boomerang, croissant, or what you will – tells you immediately about its historical past. Between the Austro-Hungarian Empire to the north and the Ottoman Empire to the southeast, Byzantium to the east and Rome and Venice to the west, Croatia sits at the crossroads of Europe.

NAME It's one of those countries like Finland or Albania whose name appears quite differently to foreigners from the way it appears to locals. For us, it's the Republic of Croatia – for them, it's Republika Hrvatska. That is why the top-level domain name (TLD) for Croatia on the internet is .hr.

AREA The country covers 56,542km² of southeastern Europe. It also claims 31,067km² of territorial waters in the Adriatic Sea.

LOCATION Southeastern Europe bordered by the Adriatic Sea and Italy to the west and southwest, Slovenia and Hungary to the north, Serbia to the east, Bosnia & Herzegovina along Croatia's inside arc, and Montenegro for 25km in the far south.

A Bosnian corridor to the sea cuts Dubrovnik and the south coast off from the rest of the country – though now Bosnia has harmonised its visa requirements with Croatia, this shouldn't cause any problems (see box on page 341 for further details).

The westernmost point of Croatia is the settlement of Bašanija near Umag, at 13°30'E; the easternmost point is Ilok, in Slavonia, at 19°27'E. Croatia also stretches from Žabnik in the Međimurje in the north (46°33'N) to Lastovo in the south (42°23'N).

POPULATION The 2011 census measured a population of 4.29 million people, down from the previous (2001) result of 4.44 million.

CITIES Croatia's administrative, cultural, academic and communications centre is the city of Zagreb, with a little under 793,000 inhabitants in town – though over a million people live in and around the capital.

The next largest city, Split, is only a quarter of the size of Zagreb, with 178,000 inhabitants. This is followed (2011 census) by Rijeka (128,000), Osijek (107,000), Zadar (75,000), Slavonski Brod (59,000), Pula (57,000), Karlovac (56,000), Sisak (47,000), Varaždin (47,000) and Dubrovnik (42,000).

COAST AND ISLANDS Croatia has 5,835km of coastline, including 4,058km on the 1,185 islands, islets and reefs. There are 67 inhabited islands, the largest of which are Krk (the largest island in the Adriatic, at 409km², population 16,400) and Cres (404km², population 3,200).

MOUNTAIN HIGHS Croatia starts at sea level and peaks at Dinara (1,831m, near the Bosnian border, inland from Šibenik), the highest point on the eponymous Dinara range, which runs down almost the whole length of the coast. Some of the other peaks over 1,500m are: Kamešnica (1,809m), Sv Jure (Biokovo, 1,762m), Vaganski vrh (Paklenica, Velebit, 1,758m), Sveto brdo (Paklenica, Velebit, 1,753m), Mali Rajinac (northern Velebit, 1,699m), Lička Plješevica (Ozeblin, 1,657m), Bjelolasica (Velika Kapela, 1,534m), Risnjak (Gorski Kotar, 1,528m), Svilaja (Dalmatia, 1,508m) and Snježnik (Gorski Kotar, 1,505m).

GEOGRAPHY

The country is perhaps most famous for its enormous – relative to the country's size – coastline and wealth of islands, but away from the beaches it's also geographically diverse. A long ridge of mountains – or rather series of ridges, peaking at Dinara – stretches from the northwest to the southeast of the country, while the plains of Pannonia dominate the Hungarian border to the north. Rolling hills characterise much of the rest of the country from behind the Dinara mountains to the Pannonian plain, while the Adriatic islands can be surprisingly mountainous, with peaks up to 778m (Brač), and Cres, Hvar, Lošinj, Vis, Krk, Korčula and Mljet all rising to over 500m.

The coast and islands are Croatia's natural selling point (especially when it comes to tourism), and they provide the country with an astonishing 5,835km coastline. Although it's only about 500km in a straight line from Trieste, the last town in Italy, to Herceg Novi, the first town in Montenegro, the Croatian coast itself is 1,777km long, with the remaining 4,058km accounted for by 1,185 islands, islets and reefs. See also page 3.

CLIMATE

If you're seeking an escape from a wet winter, then Croatia's probably not for you – most of the rain here falls in the cooler months, making it chilly and damp in the interior and mild but drippy along the coast. Outside the long, dry summers, Croatia is wetter than you might think, with an average annual countrywide precipitation of close to 1,100mm (compared to about 600mm on average for London and 1,400mm for Scotland as a whole), but the humid winters are more than compensated for by warm, early springs, hot, dry summers and prolonged autumns.

Croatia's climate falls into three distinct patterns, varying from northern to central Croatia, and different again for the coast and islands.

The **north** has a moderate continental climate, equating to hot, dry summers and cold, damp winters. Average daily winter temperatures vary from around –1 to +3°C, while in summer they range from 22 to 26°C. The capital, Zagreb, is coldest in January, when the daily average barely creeps above freezing, and warmest in August, when it's 21°C, and often much higher. You can expect about 24mm of rainfall a month in the capital in August, but closer to 100mm from September through to November.

Central Croatia has a semi-highland and highland climate, making for cool summers and hard winters, with plenty of snow. Average daily winter temperatures run from –5 to 0°C, while in summer they bounce up to 15–20°C.

The geological term 'karst' came from the rock formations of neighbouring Slovenia (Kras), and is now used to describe any similar terrain – very useful as that includes most of the limestone mountains along Croatia's coast and on its islands.

Karst is grey, wild and very dry. It is formed by the absorption of water into porous limestone, which then corrodes and finally erodes the harder limestone underneath – this, combined with a history of earthquakes, is the geological reason for the shape of the Adriatic and its islands.

Young karst is typically characterised by small fissures in the rock, while more developed areas contain long underground caves, rivers that appear from the rock and then disappear again almost immediately, and highly porous limestone that is completely dry only a few minutes after rain has fallen. Karst is irregularly sculptured into sharp and wild shapes, and is extremely abrasive.

Croatia's karst was once almost entirely covered in vegetation, but large parts, particularly along the coast and on the islands, were deforested (the Venetians, in particular, needed a lot of wood) and then lost their soil from wind, erosion and over-grazing. This is known as naked karst, and can be seen at its most spectacular and barren on the island of Pag and on some of the islands of the Kornati archipelago. It's incredibly poor land, on which it seems unlikely that anything could survive – but people do live here, and somehow eke out a living from the wilderness.

When an underground cave collapses, the surface is flattened, and soil gradually accumulates. Usually, this is then cleared of rocks, walled in, and cultivated. One of the hazards of this type of field (known as polje) is that they don't always drain as quickly as they fill up, creating lakes of a few days' or weeks' duration. Every so often, you'll be surprised by a boat at the edge of a field or pasture, even in the mountains. It's also the reason why you'll never see houses built on the polje itself, but always to one side.

Up in the **mountains**, you need to be well equipped for the weather. In Risnjak National Park, at around 1,500m, you can expect precipitation in the sort of quantities you'd be unlucky to find even in the wettest parts of England's Lake District – though here much of the annual 3,579mm falls as snow. At the mountain lodge in the park, at 1,418m, snow stays on the ground for an average of 157 days a year, and can be up to 4m deep. Weather in the mountains is unpredictable all year round, so plan accordingly. Snow can fall in every month of the year at 1,700m, and I've been caught in terrible hail in June on the Velebit massif at 1,200m, just a few kilometres inland from the coast. It has even been known to snow in coastal resorts like Trogir.

Down at sea level, of course, the **coast and islands** have a Mediterranean climate, with wet, mild winters, and long, hot and very dry summers. Daily averages range from 5 to 10°C in winter and from 25 to 30°C in summer, though almost never exceed 35°C – and daily maximums in Dubrovnik never fall below 12°C. The coast gets most of its precipitation in the autumn, with 508mm falling in Rijeka and 377mm falling in Dubrovnik from October to December, but only 10mm of rainfall expected in Split in July. However, that's not to say that it won't rain during the summer months – August 2014 for example saw severe storms and flooding in some areas of the Dalmatian coast and islands – though such conditions are thankfully quite rare.

The sea is for many the main attraction, so you should remember that it cools down to a chilly 8°C at Pula in winter, although from mid-June to early September it stays above 20°C, making for pleasant swimming (especially in August, when the water reaches its maximum temperature of 26°C).

There's also no shortage of sunshine on the Adriatic – Pula's pleased with its 2,480 hours annually, while Brač brags about its 2,700 sunny hours per year, and Hvar claims to have more hours of sunshine than anywhere else on the coast. Bring plenty of suncream.

NATURAL HISTORY AND CONSERVATION

For more on wildlife in Croatia check out Bradt's Central and Eastern European Wildlife. *See page vii for a special 30% offer.*

Croatia is blessed with unpolluted lakes, spectacular limestone scenery, and the cleanest coastline on the Mediterranean. During Tito's days, Yugoslavia embarked on a progressive programme of tourist development, and although some of the resorts along the coast might be considered overdeveloped, there's also a wealth of national parks and other protected areas.

FLORA AND FAUNA In the remoter forests of the interior and in the inland national parks, there are still bears and wolves at large, though you're unlikely to see them – bears are notoriously cautious, while wolves only come down from the mountains to raid villages for scraps during the depths of winter. Wild boar, however, are still common in the northern and eastern forests, along with red, fallow and roe deer. You might also be lucky enough to see chamois and mouflon in the mountains along the Slovenian border and through Dalmatia. But you're more likely to see eagles than griffon vultures or lynxes – lynx being almost shyer than bears, and griffon vultures now being confined to a small colony on the island of Cres (which you can visit – see pages 249–50).

Snakes are reasonably common, but there are very few that are poisonous (admittedly one of these, the nose-horned viper or *poskok*, is very poisonous), and the old saying is worth repeating: they're much more frightened of you than you are of them. Snakes will mostly avoid regularly walked paths or roads, but if you're heading across country, it's as well to wear sensible shoes or boots. In accumulated months of walking in Croatia, I've seen several dozen snakes of four or five species, but never anything dangerous, so please don't kill them out of ignorance or fear.

You'll see a number of charming species of lizard if you're out walking, or even sightseeing – they love to bask on warm stone the moment the sun's shining. Look out, too, for frogs if you're near water, and several varieties of toad that are peculiar to the woods which grow on limestone mountains. Martens, wild cats and squirrels also live in these forests, but they're pretty shy.

From early summer onwards, Croatia features several species of butterfly you won't see often in the UK – look out for swallowtails in the mountains, white admirals on the islands, and hosts of butterflies of all species if you're here in late spring or early summer.

A total of 44 species of vegetation and 380 species of animal are protected in Croatia. Most endangered of all is the fast-disappearing Mediterranean monk seal, with only one sighting within the past dozen years or so, off Rt Kamenjak in Istria. These elegant dark brown seals grow to around 2.4m in length and weigh up to

300kg or more. There are also a surprising number of dolphins along the coast, and notably around the island of Cres, as well as further south.

Croatia's flora is also delightful. Along the coast and on the islands, you'll find aromatic herbs and abundant bougainvillea. In the woods and forests, there's a wide variety of plants and trees ranging from orchids to holm oak to pine and beech, while higher up in the mountains, you'll find beautiful summer pastures, home to tiny flowers and fragrant herbs.

As the summer wears on, the colours fade and everything dries out, leaving an arid impression across much of the country, which doesn't really wear off until the leaves change to their superb autumnal colours.

ENVIRONMENTAL ISSUES In spite of the long-standing promotion of ecotourism, the creation and maintenance of a whole crop of national parks and protected areas (see below), and its pride in having the cleanest waters of the Mediterranean, Croatia hasn't entirely escaped the blights of the modern world. Metal works, refineries and other factories have damaged some forests with acid rain, while coastal pollution from industrial and domestic waste has been experienced in some areas, and new roads continue to chew a path through forests on mountains such as Velebit.

Much more significant, in environmental terms, however, has been the destruction of both infrastructure and natural resources by the civil strife of the early 1990s. In spite of the quick repairs in tourist centres like Dubrovnik, it will take some time before the damage is entirely fixed countrywide, and longer still before the countryside returns to its natural state – there are still a handful of minefields that haven't yet been fully cleared.

Fire is another environmental hazard – a landscape that quickly absorbs what little water there is and a hot dry summer is a recipe for accidental combustion. The starting of any fire in Croatia in summer is strongly discouraged in most areas, and is forbidden in the national parks. If you're going to be barbecuing, do so carefully, and be sure you have what it takes to put the flames out if things get out of control.

Croatia is also strongly exposed to one other environmental risk: earthquakes. A major and active earthquake fault network runs through Italy and the Balkans, and it was an earthquake in 1667 that killed more than 5,000 people in Dubrovnik and levelled most of the public buildings. In 1880, another major earthquake destroyed much of Zagreb, and most of what you see in the capital today dates from the post-1880 reconstruction of the city.

The most recent serious earthquake in Croatia occurred in 1996, with its epicentre in the area of Slano and Ston, 50km up the coast from Dubrovnik. The historical town of Ston – now famous for its excellent oysters – was almost completely destroyed. Although there were no fatalities, around 2,000 people in the area lost their homes to the earthquake damage.

NATIONAL PARKS, NATURE PARKS AND OTHER PROTECTED AREAS Croatia has an impressive range of national parks, nature parks and other protected areas. Below, you'll find a summary of what's on offer – more detail can be found in the relevant chapters.

National parks Croatia has eight national parks covering a total of 98,697ha (987km²).

The Brijuni Islands Often written 'Brioni' in English, these islands were the government's (ie: Tito's) private retreat for decades, off limits to the general public

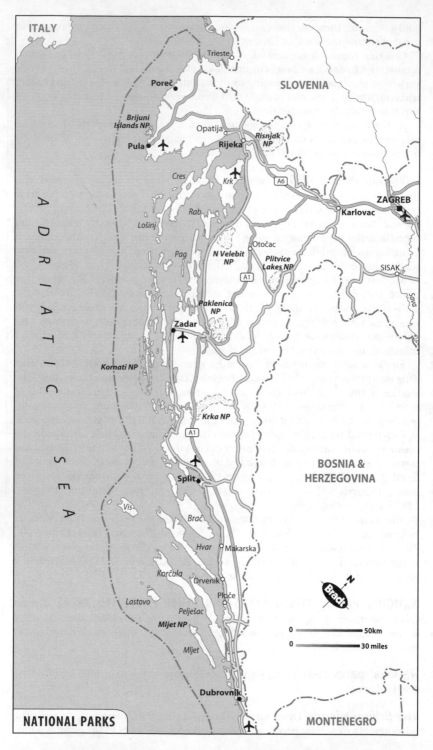

ITALY

Trieste

SLOVENIA

Poreč

Brijuni
Islands NP

Opatija

Risnjak
NP

Pula

Rijeka

ZAGREB

Cres

Krk

A6

Karlovac

Rab

Lošinj

Otočac

SISAK

Pag

N Velebit
NP

Plitvice
Lakes NP

A1

A
D
R
I
A
T
I
C

Paklenica
NP

Zadar

Kornati NP

S
E
A

Krka NP

A1

BOSNIA &
HERZEGOVINA

Split

Vis

Brač

Hvar

Makarska

Korčula

Drvenik

Lastovo

Ploče

Pelješac

Mljet NP

Bradt

N

0 ——————— 50km

0 ——————— 30 miles

Mljet

Dubrovnik

NATIONAL PARKS

MONTENEGRO

and used for entertaining heads of state and the like. The group of two larger and 12 smaller islands lies off the west coast of Istria, and was once a fashionable holiday destination for the upper classes. Now it's a pretty national park featuring ruins from antiquity and a large open-air zoo – many of the animals are the descendants of gifts to the former Yugoslavia. Be warned, however, that it's on the package-tour circuit – it's the closest and most accessible park to Croatia's busiest stretch of coast. See pages 208–12.

The Kornati archipelago This is a scattered group of 147 uninhabited islands, islets and reefs south of Zadar; 89 of the islands were declared a national park in 1980. Popular with the yachting community, it's relatively difficult to access for other visitors to Croatia, but is nonetheless one of the most striking national parks I've ever seen, with sheer cliffs, unusually indented coastlines, clear seas and no water sources at all. See pages 299–300.

The Krka River and waterfalls The Krka River runs from Knin to Skradin, just inland from Šibenik. The park – which is mainly visited by boat – features stunning karst scenery of lakes, waterfalls, canyons and deep forests. At the river's widest point, you'll find a lovely Franciscan monastery on an island. See pages 288–90.

Mljet The western part of the island of Mljet, between Korčula and Dubrovnik, has been designated a national park with good reason. Home to Europe's only wild mongooses, lush vegetation, and a former monastery on an island on one of two saltwater lakes, Mljet is a delight. See pages 383–9.

North Velebit Between Senj and Karlobag, where the Kvarner Bay turns into northern Dalmatia, lies the forbidding ridge of North Velebit National Park. Here, you'll find some of the remotest hiking in Croatia just inland from one of the most deserted parts of the coast. There's a good reason for that, of course – there's little room along the narrow coast for development, while the massif behind it can be a wild, unwelcoming place, cold in spring and autumn and baking hot in summer. It's not for the faint-hearted, but it is your best chance of seeing a bear in the wild – many of Croatia's population of around 400 live up here. See pages 244–6.

Paklenica This pair of fabulous limestone gorges runs up from the sea into the Velebit massif not far from Zadar. Popular with Croatian climbers and walkers, it's one of my personal favourites and offers hiking from the merely gentle to the seriously strenuous. See pages 277–84.

The Plitvice Lakes These are one of Croatia's best-known and biggest draws. Situated inland, halfway between Zagreb and Zadar, the national park contains 16 lakes at different levels, interconnected by waterfalls. Excellent walking trails keep you away from the crowds, but fun can be had too on the mini-train and organised boat rides. See pages 172–7.

Risnjak Situated north of Rijeka, where the Alps and the Dinara meet, Risnjak is the perfect national park for mountaineers and naturalists alike, featuring as it does Croatia's biggest diversity of flora and fauna. The beautiful forests and magnificent views here are understandably popular with locals, but you're surprisingly unlikely to bump into foreign visitors. See pages 240–2.

Nature parks Croatia also boasts 11 designated nature parks covering a further 424,285ha (4,242km²) of the country.

Biokovo This is the name of the massif overhanging the Makarska Riviera, between Split and Dubrovnik, and although it's a hard walk to the summit, it offers the most breathtaking views out over the islands of Brač and Hvar. See pages 317–20.

Kopački Rit On Croatia's eastern border, where the River Drava flows into the Danube, this area of swampland features superb bird and plant life, along with plenty of deer and wild boar. It's a birdwatcher's paradise, but take serious mosquito repellent. See pages 188–9.

Lastovsko Otočje Croatia's newest nature park comprises the islands of the Lastovo archipelago. See pages 402–4.

Lonjsko Polje Running along the River Sava in Slavonia, this is one of the biggest swamps in Europe, featuring huge oak forests and excellent birdlife (some 240 species) – and, in particular, storks. It's still well off the tourist trail. See pages 177–80.

Medvednica Just north of Zagreb, this low-key mountainous area provides the capital's nearest refuge from city life for the locals. Pleasant beech and fir forests, steep-sided valleys, and well-maintained walking paths make this a lovely and quiet alternative to some of the more strenuous parks, and it's very easy to get to. See pages 132–5.

Papuk At under 1,000m high, this is eastern Slavonia's biggest mountain and its forested slopes make for some lovely summer walking, with well-marked and well-maintained trails, burbling brooks, and even thermal baths to swim in. See page 181.

Telašćica Bordering on the northern end of the Kornati archipelago, and hogging the cleft-stick inlet at the southern end of Dugi Otok (Long Island), Telašćica has Croatia's biggest cliffs, rising a dramatic 180m out of the sea. It's naturally popular with anyone lucky enough to be on a sailing holiday. See page 299.

Učka This is the name given to the massif above Opatija, in Istria. Rising to 1,400m, the park provides excellent views out over Rijeka and the islands of the Kvarner Bay, and a welcome relief from the crowds along the shore. Well-marked trails and pleasant oak and beech forests make this an excellent day trip from the coast. See page 231.

Velebit Stretching for more than 100km, from Senj to Zadar, the 2,000km² Velebit Park includes both the Paklenica and North Velebit National Parks, the latter being home to the **Velebitski Botanički Vrt** botanical gardens and the strictly protected Hajdučki Kukovi nature reserve. The gardens, established in 1967, are some of the remotest in Croatia, being situated at around 1,500m in the most inaccessible part of the Velebit, and feature flora unique to the region. See pages 244–6.

Vransko Jezero Between Zadar and Šibenik, in northern Dalmatia, lies Croatia's largest natural lake, famous for its mix of sea and freshwater fish, and an ornithological reserve, which is home to a wide variety of wading birds and a colony of rare purple herons. See pages 276–7.

Žumberak-Samoborsko Gorje West of Zagreb, across the Sava River and nestled up against the Slovenian border, lies this protected area of pretty villages connected by well-marked trails, and popular with weekend hikers from the capital. See pages 161–4.

Other protected areas
This section wouldn't be complete without a brief mention of some of Croatia's other protected areas.

Probably the most famous – and the one you may have seen photographed from the air – is **Zlatni Rat** (Golden Cape), at Bol, on the island of Brač, one of the prettiest beaches on the Adriatic. The 600m spit of fine gravel, backed by pine forests, changes shape according to the sea currents and seasonal winds.

Hajdučki Kukovi nature reserve shelters one of the dozen deepest caves in the world, **Lukina Jama**, which was only discovered in 1993, and has now been explored to a depth of around 1,400m. In the same area, you'll find **Patkov Gust**, the second deepest vertical shaft in the world, dropping a dizzying 553m. You would need a special permit – and a very good reason – to access either of these.

Apart from the famous Krka (pages 288–90), six other rivers in Croatia deserve a mention. The **Danube** (called the Dunav here) roughly delineates the eastern border with Serbia, while the great **Sava** runs past Zagreb, the capital, and then through Lonjsko Polje before marking the long border with Bosnia and Herzegovina. The **Drava**, for its part, starts in Slovenia and runs along the border between Croatia and Hungary, and forms part of the transborder Mura-Drava-Danube UNESCO World Biosphere Reserve, over 395,000ha of which lies in Croatia. The fast-flowing **Dobra**, near Karlovac (50km west of Zagreb), is popular for rafting, kayaking and canoeing, while the **Mrežnica**, nearby – a tributary of the Kupa River – is all the rage with bathers. Finally, the 30km-long **Gacka**, near Otočac, inland from Senj, is a trout-fisher's paradise, with clear waters flowing past picturesque old watermills.

On the west coast of Istria is the fjord-like 10km inlet of **Limski Zaljev**. A nature reserve since 1979, it's an important haven for fish overwintering or spawning. The low salinity and high plankton count make it popular too with mussel and oyster farmers – and eaters.

Down at the other end of the coast, between Makarska and Dubrovnik, is the **Neretva Delta**, one of the Adriatic's most important waterfowl reserves, featuring swampy salt marshes, lagoons, reeds and meadows. Inland from Makarska, near Imotski, are the **Red and Blue Lakes** (Crveno Jezero and Modro Jezero), a pair of unusually deep water-filled holes in the karst. The bottom of Red Lake is only 19m above sea level, with a depth varying from 280 to 320m, and Blue Lake really is blue. As indeed is the **Blue Cave** (Modra Špilja), of course, on the island of Biševo, off the western end of Vis. The cave – like the Blue Grotto on Capri – is visitable only by boat, and many rate it as highly as its Capri counterpart.

Finally, a mention should be given to **Gorski Kotar**, the mountainous area east of Rijeka, which contains Risnjak National Park (pages 240–2). In the forests here, which are among Europe's most unspoiled, wolves, brown bear, lynx and wild boar can still be found in the wild, along with a wide variety of bird species and plant life. Gorski Kotar also features such striking natural phenomena as the extraordinary karst rock formations at Bijele and Samarske Stijene, or Vražji Prolaz (the Devil's Pass) near Skrad, a narrow canyon with a perilous footpath running through it.

1

Croatia is at once a very old country and a very young one. Inhabited since the early Stone Age, and a linchpin of the Roman Empire, it only became a modern nation in 1991, and parts of the country were still under UN control – following the war – until 1998. And while it was a respectable kingdom of its own in medieval times, Croatia has spent most of the past millennium attached to (or subjugated by) its near neighbours. As a result, the country's history is unbelievably turbulent; fraught with foreign intervention, plagued by constant strife from pre-Roman times on, and richly textured with assassinations, intrigues, piracy and treachery.

Over the past 2,500 years, a succession of empires invaded, annexed or occupied Croatia, and each left its mark. For example, islands along the Adriatic coast that were deforested by the Venetians in the 18th century are still barren, yet the coastal towns and cities wouldn't be half as lovely if it weren't for the Venetian Gothic architecture.

Croatian independence today is remarkable given the sheer numbers of land grabs it's been subjected to, with Greeks, Romans, Ostrogoths, Avars, Slavs, Franks, Byzantines, Venetians, Hungarians, Tartars, Austrians, French, Italians, Turks, Germans and Serbs all having had their eye on a piece of the Croatian action.

Which is hardly surprising: the Adriatic has been the most practical trade route between Europe and the East since trade began there, around 3,000 years ago. Croatia has also been a buffer zone between east and west and between north and south for centuries.

ILLYRIANS, GREEKS AND ROMANS In spite of lots of early Stone Age finds, recorded history in Croatia starts with the Illyrians, a group of tribes that shared techniques for building and burying their dead, but not much else, it seems. By the 7th century BC, they were trading with the ancient Greeks, and within two centuries the Greeks had established colonies in the area, notably at Pharos (now Stari Grad, on the island of Hvar) and Salona, and on the island of Vis.

By 229BC the Greeks were calling on Rome to help them in their quest to dominate the Illyrians, and the Romans pitched in with enthusiasm – though it took them more than two centuries to complete the job. In AD9, five years before becoming emperor, Tiberius finally annexed the area for Rome, thereby becoming the first (and last, until 1918) person to unify this bit of the Balkans.

Under Roman rule, the Balkans – and Dalmatia in particular – prospered, providing the empire with troops and provisions and receiving the protection of a major world power in return, setting something of a pattern for the region. The Romans built (or reinforced) many of the existing settlements, with their principal cities being Pola (Pula), Jadera (Zadar) and Salona (Solin). As was their wont, they also constructed summer palaces along the coast and on the islands, and reinforced trade links all the way from Pula to Cavtat.

The most famous Dalmatians to make it big at this time were the three who went on to become Roman emperors, most notably Diocletian, who ruled from AD284 to 305 – an astonishingly long period given that more than a dozen emperors had come and gone in the generation before he came to power. Diocletian ruled from Nicomedia (now Izmít, in Turkey), but started building himself a fabulously swanky retirement home just along the coast from his native Salona within months of taking the purple. Diocletian's palace in Split remains one of Croatia's most impressive monuments, with its corridors today being streets and its rooms entire houses.

In AD293 Diocletian partitioned the empire into the western and eastern parts, with the River Drina being the boundary, thus sealing Croatia's fate forever as a province on the front line. Diocletian's frontier ran through the cities of Budva and Belgrade, and a rough approximation of this can still be seen on maps today, marking the eastern border of Slavonia in Croatia, and running down the eastern side of Bosnia & Herzegovina and Albania. Everything east of this line ultimately became Byzantium, and Orthodox, while everything west became part of Rome (and the eventual Holy Roman Empire), and Catholic. The division is also clearly visible today in the use of the Latin alphabet to the west and Cyrillic to the east.

Diocletian abdicated in AD305 and retired to Split, spending the last 11 years of his life in palatial splendour, rousing himself only to have Christians thrown to the lions; having tolerated the religion for most of his reign, he spent the rest of his life in relentless persecution of it.

ARRIVAL OF THE SLAVS The Roman Empire imploded in the 5th century, leaving the way clear for invasions by Huns, Goths, Vlachs, Avars, Bulgars and – most importantly for this guide – Slavs.

One group of Slavs, coming from what is now Poland, was the Croats. They conquered Roman Pannonia (now roughly the area known as Slavonia) and much of Dalmatia, and drove the inhabitants from the Dalmatian capital, Salona, to the nearby islands of Šolta, Brač, Hvar, Vis and Korčula.

During the same period, other Slavic ethnic groups, the Slovenes and the Serbs, settled the areas roughly corresponding to Slovenia and Serbia.

After a series of tussles with the Franks, Avars and Byzantines, the Croats finally managed to unite Dalmatian and Pannonian Croatia in AD925, under the crown of King Tomislav. For more than a century, the kingdom prospered, with the greatest Croatian king being Petar Krešimir IV, who ruled over Bosnia, Slavonia and the Dalmatian towns and islands from 1058 to 1074.

Byzantium and Venice were already encroaching on the southern and northern coastlands, however, and Hungary soon captured most of the interior, driving a

WESTERN TIES

Most men dressing for work in the morning don't spare a thought for Croatia – which is a pity, as the ubiquitous tie they put on not only originated there, but is also named after the country.

The origins of one of fashion's most durable accessories date back to the Thirty Years War in Europe, which ran from 1618 to 1648. The story goes that Croatian mercenaries of the period wore a colourful silk scarf tied around the neck. Some of their number were stationed in Paris, and were presented to the court (whether that of Louis XIII, who died in 1643, or Louis XIV, who succeeded him, is debatable), triggering off a copycat craze for cravats – the word coming from dressing *à la Croat* (or Hrvat, in Croatian).

During the dandyish reign of Louis XIV, the wearing of cravats by French men became widespread, and the new fashion soon spread right across Europe – indeed the French word *'cravate'* exists in one form or another in almost every European language, from *gravata* in Greek to *krawatte* in German.

Today, businessmen across the whole world consider the tie a basic part of their wardrobe, though for the most part they probably aren't wearing the enormously expensive long and floppy silk scarves favoured by Croatian soldiers, but the rather more sober ties launched in England at the end of the 19th century.

corridor through to the sea by 1089. After the death of King Stjepan II in 1091, it all fell apart. A decade later, in 1102, the Hungarian King Kalman knocked together the heads of the 12 most powerful Croatian clans, persuading them to sign up to the Pacta Conventa, under which they would accept the Hungarian monarch's rule, but were able to maintain Croatia's traditions and customs. Amazingly, the treaty held until 1918.

VENETIANS, AUSTRO-HUNGARIANS AND THE ILLYRIAN PROVINCES Over the next 700 years, Croatian history largely depended on which of its neighbours was the most powerful at the time, with Hungary/Austria driving down from the north, the Ottoman Empire steaming in from the southeast, and Venice ever expansive from its corner of the Adriatic. Much of the architectural heritage of the country dates from this period, with the coast and islands still looking remarkably Venetian, and the interior retaining a monumental Habsburg feel.

During the 16th century, Austria created the Krajina (literally 'zone'), as a buffer against the advance of the Ottoman Turks, and Serbs who had escaped Ottoman rule were given land in the Krajina in exchange for military service.

In 1558, the Croatian and Slavonian diets were united, and Zagreb became Croatia's capital. Just 15 years later, the peasants revolted and – as you'd expect – were ruthlessly suppressed. Their leader, Matija Gubec, was executed in Zagreb (page 113).

A century later, in 1671, another rebellion was set in motion against the Habsburgs, this time led by the aristocratic Petar Zrinski and Fran Krsto Frankopan. Expecting help from abroad that never materialised, they were swiftly brought to task, and they too were executed (page 78).

USKOKS For much of the 16th century, the regional balance of power along the coast had been in the hands of a small third party, the Uskoks, who were pirates, based in the port of Senj from the 1530s until the Uskok War of 1615–17.

The Uskoks (from the Croatian word *uskočiti*, to 'jump in' or 'to board') were refugees who had been driven north by the advancing Ottoman Turks, but as their swashbuckling exploits grew, they attracted rebels from all quarters. When a party of Uskoks was hanged in Venice in 1618, nine of them turned out to be English – of whom six were apparently of noble birth.

At first, until the mid-1560s, the Uskoks attacked the Ottoman Turks on land and sea, but after this anyone appears to have been fair game, especially the Venetians, who were accused by the Uskoks of being un-Christian. This suited the Habsburgs just fine. Even though they paid lip service to condemning piratical exploits (they were after all the nominal rulers of Senj at the time) anyone that was harassing their enemies was a friend rather than a foe.

The Uskoks, however, appear to have been reluctant pirates, and pleas for tillable land in the interior fell on deaf ears for more than 50 years. They also had an honourable reputation among their immediate neighbours, the Kvarner Bay islanders of Krk, Cres, Rab and Pag, redistributing their booty whenever possible and paying for provisions when they had the money to do so.

The unwilling pirates were finally crushed during the eponymously named Uskok War in 1615–17, after which the Habsburgs agreed to a military occupation of Senj. The surviving Uskoks were banished inland, disappearing without trace – though Uskok surnames survive in the villages of Samoborsko Gorje, among other areas.

RAGUSA At the same time, another city, Ragusa, was at the height of its fame and powers. Ragusa was one of the most important – and independent – of the

14

Dalmatian cities, fending off unwanted interference by successfully paying off the Ottoman Turks and the Hungarians. Ragusa, in fact, remains one of Croatia's most fashionable tourist attractions today … under its Croatian name, Dubrovnik.

THE ILLYRIAN PROVINCES Venice and Ragusa alike were swept aside by Napoleon, who created the Illyrian Provinces, a region running all the way from Trieste and Slovenia in the north to Dubrovnik in the south. The region was administered by Marshal Marmont, and for a few years benefited from the French passion for building roads, fortifying towns and encouraging the local south Slav culture – in a bid to create a buffer against undue Russian and Austro-Hungarian ambitions. 'Though Marmont was a self-satisfied prig, he was an extremely competent and honourable man, and he loved Dalmatia,' as Rebecca West (author of *Black Lamb and Grey Falcon: A journey through Yugoslavia*) so succinctly put it when she came through in 1937.

AUSTRO-HUNGARIANS It was for nought; Napoleon fell, and Habsburg rule was restored in 1815, albeit within a separate Kingdom of Croatia and Slavonia. By the middle of the 19th century, an educated elite, led by Ljudevit Gaj, started defending Croatian nationality and sovereignty and worked towards a national revival, under the moniker of the Illyrian Movement. Count Janko Drašković helped the movement along in 1832 by publishing the first political pamphlet in Croatian.

KARAĐORĐEVIĆ ROYALTY

Having been born in the Royal Palace in Belgrade in September 1923 and been pronounced king at the age of 11 after his father's assassination, it must have been a shock for the 17-year-old monarch, King Petar II, to find himself sitting out the war in London.

Fortunately for the Karađorđević dynasty, Petar married Princess Aleksandra of Greece (the daughter of King Alexander) at the Yugoslav Embassy in London in 1944, and on 17 July the following year she bore him a son, Crown Prince Aleksandar II of Yugoslavia.

Parliament, under the orders of Winston Churchill, stepped in quickly and proclaimed Suite 212 of Claridge's as Yugoslav territory, so that the putative heir would have the right to be king some day, and the child was baptised in Westminster Abbey by the Patriarch of Serbia. No prizes for guessing the godparents: King George VI and his daughter Princess Elizabeth (QE II to you).

An auspicious start to Aleksandar's life, perhaps, but, in November 1945, the Yugoslav monarchy was abolished by the communists under the leadership of Tito, and although King Petar II never abdicated, he never saw Yugoslavia again, either.

He died after a long illness at the Colorado General Hospital, in Denver, in 1970, only a year older than his father had been when he was assassinated in Marseille in 1934.

Since the summer of 2001, post-Slobodan Milošević, Crown Prince Aleksandar has been living with his family in the Royal Palace in Belgrade having returned from lifelong exile. As the great-great-grandson of Queen Victoria and the cousin of King Juan Carlos of Spain, he half expects to see the monarchy restored – on constitutional lines, of course – but he has one major disadvantage: he apparently speaks very poor Serbian.

In 1848, the viceroy of Croatia, Ban Josip Jelačić, led an army of 50,000 soldiers towards Hungary, but, instead of winning independence for his country, he unfortunately allowed Austria to take over both countries. Nonetheless, he was a great hero, having abolished feudalism and brought in reforms allowing elected officials to join the nobility in parliament (the Sabor). After his death in 1859, a great statue of him on horseback was raised in Zagreb's central square. A year later, a new constitution allowed Croatian to become the national language.

The Kingdom of Croatia and Slavonia continued under Austro-Hungarian rule until the 525th anniversary of the Ottoman defeat of Lazar, last of the independent Serbian rulers, at the battle of Kosovo Polje in 1389.

On that day (28 June 1914), Archduke Franz Ferdinand, heir to the Austro-Hungarian Empire – in a remarkable display of hubris, given that it was a day of national mourning – ignored all warnings and paid an official visit to Sarajevo. And with his wife, Sophie Chotek, was shot dead by a 19-year-old student called Gavrilo Princip, thus kicking off World War I. Austria had long been looking to declare war on Serbia, and this provided the perfect excuse. Russia took offence; Germany supported Austria; Britain and France piled in with Russia; and the world's bloodiest war to date was underway.

THE KINGDOM OF THE SERBS, CROATS AND SLOVENES Aware that the Austro-Hungarian Empire was going to come out of the war at best badly diminished, Slovenia and Croatia threw in their lot with Serbia in 1918, resulting in the creation of the Kingdom of Serbs, Croats and Slovenes, under the Crown of King Petar I from the dynastic Karađorđević family (see box, page 15).

Petar was succeeded on his death, three years later, by his son, King Aleksandar I, in the face of increasing irritation by the Croats that they had so little power in Belgrade. The Croatian Republican Peasant Party, led by firebrand Stjepan Radić, had won local elections in 1920, but this wasn't of any use to the party in the capital.

Tension remained high through the 1920s until, on 20 June 1928, Radić was shot in Belgrade's parliamentary chamber by a Montenegrin deputy. Six weeks later, Radić died and more than 100,000 turned up to his funeral in Zagreb. The king suspended parliament 'reluctantly' at the beginning of 1929 and established a dictatorship in its place, promising to restore democracy once unity had been achieved. In October that year, however, he did finally manage to put diplomats and letter-writers out of their misery by changing the country's name to the much more manageable Yugoslavia – Land of the South Slavs.

So much for the good news: 1929 also saw the founding of the Ustaše by Ante Pavelić, a party dedicated to the violent overthrow of the Yugoslav state, and one that would later have a dramatic effect on Croatia's future.

Croatian national sentiment continued to run high and, in 1934, King Aleksandar, aged 46, was assassinated in Marseille, in a plot sponsored by the Ustaše, but executed by a Macedonian with Italian support. Aleksandar's death left the ill-equipped Prince Petar to run the country – aged only 11. His uncle, Prince Pavle, was drafted in to help, but Yugoslavia was in no state to prosper. And war was once again on the horizon.

WORLD WAR II By the time World War II broke out – not the Balkans' fault this time around – the country was in a mess. The Ustaše fascists wanted independence for Croatia, Macedonia was trying to secede, and only the Yugoslav Communist Party, founded in 1919 and outlawed nine years later, had any countrywide support.

Yugoslavia managed to remain neutral for the first year and a half of the war, but increasing axis pressure resulted in Prince Pavle signing a pact on 25 March 1941, aligning Yugoslavia with fascist Germany and Italy, in spite of his personal pro-British sentiments. Two days later, a group of air force officers, backed by both the communists and the Orthodox Church, staged a coup d'état, deposed Prince Pavle and installed King Petar II, now aged 17½, in his place.

The pact was annulled and Yugoslavia reaffirmed its neutrality; Hitler responded by bombing Belgrade on 6 April. On the same day, massive German and Italian armies entered the country, and Yugoslavia capitulated ten days later. King Petar II escaped to London with the Yugoslav government and set up house in Claridge's, never to return to his former kingdom.

THE USTAŠE Once Yugoslavia had thrown in the towel in 1941, the Ustaše declared the Independent State of Croatia (Nezavisna Država Hrvatska, NDH), leaving the rest of Yugoslavia to be carved up between Germany, Hungary, Bulgaria and Italy – something for which the Ustaše has never really been forgiven by many. Contrary to what has been claimed by some, resistance to the Ustaše was strong across Croatia throughout the war, but it was often the subject of ruthless suppression.

From the start, the Ustaše tried to clear the Serbs out of Croatia. When this proved impossible, they set up a number of concentration camps, the most notorious being the Jasenovac complex, a string of five camps on the bank of the Sava River, about 100km south of Zagreb. The camps were used from 1942 to 1945 to eliminate not just Serbs, but also religious minorities (including thousands of Jews) and political opponents of the Ustaše, and reports are that they were just as bad as the more notorious German camps at Auschwitz, Belsen or Treblinka. Scenes of unbelievable barbarism were reported at the Jasenovac 'death factory', including contests to see who could kill the most people in a single night.

Nobody will ever know for sure how many people were killed by the Ustaše, but it's now thought that between 300,000 and 400,000 Serbs were killed in total, with 40,000–50,000 being murdered at Jasenovac alone. One of the unfortunate reasons for the confusion over the numbers is that Jasenovac has long been used by both sides in a propaganda war between Serbia and Croatia, with some Croatians calling the Serbian numbers (up to a million) inflated, while many Serbs feel that Croats have tried to whitewash the past.

THE RESISTANCE After the fall of Yugoslavia, in April 1941, resistance was immediately organised, but divided into two fiercely opposed groups, the Četniks and the partisans. The royalist, pro-Serbian, Četniks supported the government in exile in London, and hated just about everybody else – Croats (both Ustaše and resistance), Germans, Italians, communists, and a host of non-Serb minorities.

As anti-Germans, the Četniks were aided at first by the Allies, but they were regarded with distrust by many Yugoslavs. The partisans, on the other hand, led by Josip Broz 'Tito', were the army of the Communist Party, and although only 42,000 strong at the outset, their effective resistance and daring attacks earned them wide support from communists and non-communists alike.

Unfortunately, however, the desire of the two resistance groups to rid Yugoslavia of invaders – and indeed the Ustaše – was at times exceeded by their determination to kill each other, resulting in a long and bloody civil war being run in parallel with the greater conflict. The partisans themselves are thought to have murdered up to 100,000 of their opponents at the end of the war, interring them in caves, never to be mentioned again.

When the end of the war was close, Ustaše founder Ante Pavelić mobilised large numbers of Croat reservists and civilians and persuaded them to go to Bleiburg, in Austria (the British HQ), to surrender to the Allies. The British, to whom they surrendered, immediately handed them back (against American orders) to Tito's troops, who had some shot and buried in mass graves on the spot and marched the rest to the other end of Yugoslavia along what Croats now call the Križni Put (Way of the Cross). Contemporary Croat history tells us that at least 50,000 died along the way. Ante Pavelić wasn't one of them: he escaped to South America (Pavelić and many of his closest allies were helped by Argentina's leader, Juan Peron, who offered them blank passports) and then on to Franco's Spain, where he died in 1959.

Yugoslavia paid a terrible price during World War II, with more than a tenth of its citizens being killed. Among them were at least 300,000 Croats, 300,000 partisans and nearly 400,000 Bosnians. But the resistance had successfully tied up enormous numbers of Axis soldiers, and it's quite possible that the Allies couldn't have won the war without Yugoslavia.

With the help of the British (aid was transferred from the Četniks to the partisans in 1943), and the Red Army, Belgrade was finally liberated in 1944, and by 1945 a provisional government, in temporary accord with the government in exile, was in force.

TITO AND A NON-ALIGNED YUGOSLAVIA Post-war elections not surprisingly gave the communists 90% of the vote – with separate ballot boxes provided for those who cared to vote against Tito. That gave the government the freedom to set up on the lines adopted by Stalinist Russia, and to embark on a disastrous experiment with collectivisation.

Stalin, however, was wary of Yugoslavia, as it was the only country in the Eastern Bloc to have made its way entirely independently. And indeed, in 1948, Tito broke with the Cominform, the economic ground base for the countries allied to the Soviet Union. This declaration of non-alignment was arguably the greatest political act of Tito's career, allowing Yugoslavia to develop its own brand of communism. And it's the main reason why Serbs, Croats, Slovenes, Montenegrins and Macedonians get huffy even today if you lump them in with the Eastern Bloc.

Tito's was a brave political move, for sure, but it brought hard times for Yugoslavia in the 1950s, starting with an economic blockade by the Soviet Union. Credits from the West and the launch of mass tourism in the 1960s saved the country, however. Tito introduced the idea of workers' self-management, putting the country's hospitals, schools and factories in the hands of those who staffed them, and despite leading to sometimes excessive decentralisation, it allowed competition within the framework of communism, proving reasonably effective during the 1960s and 1970s.

In an attempt to solve Yugoslavia's nationalist problems, Tito had also decentralised the state itself, giving each of the six republics complete control over its internal affairs. While Tito lived, this was a remarkably effective strategy, mainly because he was ruthless in suppressing opposition. Croatian writers and intellectuals had issued a declaration in 1967 stating that Croatian was a different language from Serbian, and Croatian Serbs had quickly counter-declared their right to be taught in Serbian, but Tito would have none of it, and was quick to quash the so-called 'Croatian Spring' in 1971.

After being declared President for Life in 1974, Tito died in 1980, three days before his 88th birthday. His body made one more trip around the country in the Blue Train made famous during the early post-war days when he toured the country tirelessly promoting his programme of Brotherhood and Unity. This time it was mourners who lined the tracks in their thousands, and it's difficult now to conjure up just how important Tito's funeral was. It still stands as one of the best attended ever, from an international perspective, with official mourners coming from more than 120 countries, including four kings, 32 presidents and other heads of state, 22 prime ministers, and more than 100 representatives or secretaries of communist and workers' parties.

POST-TITO Like so many singularly powerful men, Tito left his country with a weak succession. Each of the republics would, in theory, get a year as head man, but without Tito's personal charisma and unifying strength it was never going to work. It wasn't long before the old problems of nationalism, unfair distribution of wealth between the republics, and corruption in government resurfaced.

FRANJO TUĐMAN – CROATIA'S FIRST PRESIDENT

Franjo Tuđman was born in 1922 and, at the age of 19, joined Tito's partisans, becoming a decorated hero by the end of World War II. His youngest brother was killed as a partisan in 1943, and his depressed father is said to have shot himself and his second wife in 1946 – though Tuđman himself claimed first that they were victims of the Ustaše and, later, that they had been killed by the communists. (As a curious parallel, both of Milošević's parents committed suicide; his mother when Milošević was a child; his father when he was 18.)

After the war, Tuđman was sent to the advanced military academy in Belgrade, and he stayed in the army until 1961, when he retired at the age of 38, with the rank of major-general. During the 1960s, as a historian, Tuđman gradually began to fall out of favour with the communists, and in 1971, following the suppression of the 'Croatian Spring', he was jailed for a short time, escaping a longer sentence only through an intervention by Tito and the support of the respected Croatian writer Miroslav Krleža. He served nine months in prison in 1972.

A decade later and more strongly nationalistic than ever, Tuđman was sentenced in 1981 to a three-year sentence and banned from all public activity for his dissident/revisionist views on history and for advocating a pluralist democracy. He served about half of this before being released because of failing health.

In 1987, having finally got his passport back after 17 years, he travelled widely in the West, promoting the cause of Croatian independence, and in 1989 he founded the Croatian Democratic Union (HDZ), which became the dominant political force in the first multi-party parliamentary election in the spring of 1990. The tenor of the campaign can be measured by Tuđman's reportedly having said 'Thank God my wife is neither a Serb nor a Jew.'

In spite of the strong words, Tuđman nonetheless found time for a secret meeting with Milošević in March 1991, to discuss how Croatia and Serbia might best carve up Bosnia & Herzegovina for themselves. Tuđman was hugely popular among most Croatians, as the first person since the Middle Ages to gain international recognition for Croatia as an independent state. At his funeral, in December 1999, thousands filed past his coffin – but only his death may have saved him from being indicted, like Milošević, by the Tribunal in The Hague.

On to this scene arrived Slobodan Milošević, who rapidly gained popularity in Serbia after defending Serb protestors against mostly ethnic Albanian police in Kosovo in 1987. Two years later, on 28 June 1989 – that date, again (see page 16) – Milošević addressed a million Serbs at Kosovo Polje and was elected President of Serbia in the autumn.

This was the beginning of the end for a united Yugoslavia. Milošević's talk of an ethnically pure Greater Serbia was never going to sit well with Slovenes, Croats, Bosnians, Macedonians – or indeed most Kosovars.

WAR – AND CROATIAN INDEPENDENCE The fall of the Berlin Wall in 1989 and the collapse of communist governments across Europe encouraged several republics, led by Slovenia and Croatia, to try to change the political structure of Yugoslavia.

In 1990, led by former army general and dissident (some would prefer revisionist) historian Franjo Tuđman (see box, page 19), the Croatian Democratic Union (HDZ) won elections. Once in power, the HDZ pushed parliament to drop the word 'Socialist' from the Croatian republic's name, and the red star was quietly removed from public symbols. The HDZ also put Croatia's 600,000 Serbs on the defensive by changing their status from 'constituent nation' in Croatia to 'national minority', and many Serbs in government lost their jobs. The HDZ didn't improve matters by making itself an easy target for Serb propaganda, party members playing straight into Serb hands by attempting to rehabilitate the Ustaše or by saying that the numbers of people killed at Jasenovac were inflated (whether or not that was true).

At the same time, most of the republics tried to negotiate a transition to a confederation, on the Swiss model, but this went completely against the Milošević view of a Greater Serbia, with money and power concentrated in Belgrade. As a result, the rebellious republics raised their sights, aiming for independent statehood instead. Trouble was inevitable.

During the summer of 1990, encouraged by Belgrade into fearing real danger, Croatia's Serbs (armed by the Yugoslav People's Army, the JNA) declared an autonomous region around Knin, 50km inland from Šibenik. Croatian police helicopters, sent in to sort out the trouble, were soon scuttled by Yugoslav air force MIGs. Tension continued to mount until March 1991, when Knin paramilitaries took control of the Plitvice Lakes, resulting in the first casualties of the conflict.

Slovenia, meanwhile, had unilaterally decided to declare independence on 25 June 1991, so Croatia declared independence on the same day – after a referendum held in May had delivered a 94% verdict in favour of a sovereign and independent Croatian state. Milošević immediately sent tanks into Ljubljana, in Slovenia (and I'll never forget the phone call I had from a friend in the Slovene Mountain Association, who had a tank outside his office), and to the Italian and Austrian borders. The world sat up and took notice, and the EU introduced sanctions; within a week, Serbia realised it didn't stand a chance (with Italy and Austria so close) and the war in Slovenia was over. Within a month, the army had left the country – though it only retreated as far as Croatia, and later distributed many weapons to the local Serb population.

Croatia, with a significant Serb minority, wasn't as fortunate as Slovenia. As soon as it proclaimed independence, the Serbs countered by proclaiming the independent state of Republika Srpska Krajina (RSK) within Croatia, declaring loyalty to Belgrade and Milošević (the commander of the army), and choosing Knin as its capital.

In six months at the end of 1991 – with the help of the JNA, and heavy fighting, bombardments and air strikes – the Serbs ethnically 'cleansed' nearly a third of

Croatia, reawakening memories of the brutality of the 1940s. Thousands of Croats were forced to leave their homes and many were killed by the JNA or loosely associated paramilitary forces.

Many towns were besieged and bombarded for months, with wholesale destruction and local suffering involved. Worst of all was the siege of Vukovar, which ended with appalling atrocities being carried out on the local Croatian population. Dubrovnik was also besieged, suffering huge damage and considerable loss of life.

Local industry across the country was effectively destroyed, and Croatia was paralysed by the RSK, which controlled most of the country's oil resources, the land routes to the Dalmatian coastal cities, and the main access road from Zagreb into Slavonia. The tourist trade – one of Croatia's main sources of foreign earnings – came to a complete halt.

By the time the UN was able to broker a ceasefire in January 1992, thousands of people had died, tens of thousands of homes had been destroyed, and Croatia had hundreds of thousands of local refugees, placing a huge burden on the main cities. Only then did the European Union (in spite of French and British reluctance) recognise Slovenian and Croatian independence. In May, after amending its constitution to protect minority groups and human rights, Croatia joined the United Nations.

It was not a happy country, however. Croatia was all but impossible to administrate with its newly fragmented borders, and from 1994 it lobbied hard, against intense European opposition, to end the UN policing of the ceasefire line. Failing on that front, it took matters into its own hands. From June 1995, Croatia 'liberated' the Krajina in a series of lightning assaults, first reclaiming the main road into Slavonia, and then focusing on the main part of the RSK in August.

In just three days, fuelled both by fear and by propaganda from Belgrade, most of the civilian Serb population fled the land they had lived on for centuries, in perhaps the biggest example of ethnic cleansing in the war so far. The leaders of the RSK launched rocket attacks on Zagreb and Sisak as a parting shot, before retreating to Serbia. In the vacuum left in the Krajina, however, Serb houses across the RSK were looted and destroyed, while the authorities turned a blind eye.

The December 1995 Dayton Peace Agreement finally helped to restore stability to the region, reinforced at the end of 1996 by the signing of a peace treaty between Croatia and Yugoslavia, although the last bit of eastern Slavonia that was still in Serb hands was only returned to Croatia, under UN supervision, in January 1998.

A vast reconstruction programme has meant that most houses have now been rebuilt, and Serbs have been encouraged to return – though nobody's sure quite how many have actually done so. What is clear is that with so much bloodshed, anguish and suffering across the region, reconciliation is a painful process, and it's not surprising that some people are still bitter about the failure – of Britain in particular – to support Croatia early on during the conflict.

POLITICS

Independence brought Croatia a new constitution (online in English at www. constitution.org/cons/croatia.htm if you're interested) and a new political system that – as the Ministry of Foreign and European Affairs says on its website (*www. mvep.hr*) – is now 'democratic and based on a respect for human rights, law, national equality, social justice and multiple political parties'. The last part is certainly true enough, with a bewildering array of three- and four-letter acronyms to deal with. At the elections in the year 2000, following the death of Franjo Tuđman (see box, page 19), more than 4,000 candidates from 55 political parties stood for office. As Rebecca West said witheringly, when she was here in 1937: 'There is no end to political disputation in Croatia. None.'

Croatia's independence also brought it a new flag, known locally, irreverently, as the 'zoo' – above the chequerboard of the main flag are the old coats of arms from the regions, featuring Dalmatia's three crowned leopards, Istria's goat, and Slavonia's marten.

Croatia's legislature consists of a parliament, the Sabor, with 151 MPs elected for a four-year period. Croatia's second president, the popular centrist Stjepan (Stipe) Mesić – a former Secretary of the HDZ, who was also Croatia's first prime minister in 1990 – was in office from 2000 to 2010. See www.president.hr for more information.

Like Tuđman, Mesić had also been condemned in the repression of the 'Croatian Spring' in 1971, and he served a one-year jail sentence at the notorious Stara Gradiška prison. Later, however, he went on to be elected to the Sabor (parliament), the body from which Yugoslav presidents were appointed in rotation, following Tito's death in 1980. As a result, Mesić also became the last president of a united Yugoslavia, until his resignation in December 1991.

In 1994, disagreeing with the HDZ policy on Bosnia & Herzegovina – Tuđman still appearing to be keen to carve it up between Serbia and Croatia – Mesić left the party and set up the rival Croatian Independent Democrats (HND). Three years later, he joined the Croatian People's Party (HNS) and became the HNS executive vice president.

In the parliamentary elections of 2003, the HDZ saw a return to form, winning 66 of the 151 seats available in the Sabor, and forming a government via an informal coalition with other smaller parties, with Ivo Sanader as prime minister. Quite suddenly in July 2009, Ivo Sanader resigned – he has since been at the centre of a major scandal involving the 'disappearance' of vast amounts of government funds during his time in office – and Jadranka Kosor, Croatia's first female prime minister, was elected in his place. Mesić was succeeded by the SDP candidate Ivo Josipović, who became president in February 2010. A former lawyer (and lecturer at Zagreb's Academy of Music), Josipović had earlier been a member of the SDP, though left politics in 1994 before returning as an independent MP in 2003, and renewing his membership of the SDP in 2008. Jadranka Kosor was succeeded as prime minister by the SDP's Zoran Milanović (who holds a Master's degree in EU law from the Flemish University in Brussels) in 2011.

Josipović lost the presidential election of January 2015, which saw the HDZ's Kolinda Grabar-Kitarović voted in as Croatia's new president – the first woman to hold this office. Grabar-Kitarović was formerly Minister of Foreign Affairs from 2005 to 2008, Croatian Ambassador to the United States from 2008 to 2011, and Assistant Secretary General for Public Diplomacy for NATO from 2011 to 2014.

Croatia joined NATO in 2009, and after long anticipation finally joined the EU in the summer of 2013.

ECONOMY

Progress towards economic reform after the war in the 1990s was hampered by coalition politics and resistance on the street, mainly from trade unions, but significant reform in recent years has since led to EU membership (in 2013), and the huge boom in tourism over the past decade has helped ensure that the economy is now in better shape than it has been for years.

Inflation was 0.2% in 2015 (down from 6% in 2008), and GDP per capita in 2014 was estimated at €10,561 – still under half that in the UK or France. Average net salary had risen to 5,697kn per month (around €750) in 2015, though unemployment stood at 16.1%, a figure which has risen due to the global downturn in 2009.

Vital to the economy – especially along the coast – is tourism. In the year 2000, revenue from tourism finally exceeded the 1990 figures for the first time, and is now worth something like US$8 billion annually.

TOURISM

In 1990, more than 16 million tourist nights were spent in Istria alone, and 3.5 million nights were spent in Dubrovnik – more than 814,000 of them by the British. The following year, people stayed away in droves. In Istria – one of the parts of the country least affected by the war – tourist nights plummeted by more than three-quarters, to below four million.

Since 1998, however, the recovery has been rapid and continuous, and the number of tourist nights in Croatia as a whole grew from 47.8 million in 2004 to just over 57 million in 2008, before dropping very slightly to around 56.4 million in 2010, and climbing to a whopping 74.7 million in 2014. The number of foreign visitors to the country over the same period grew from 7.9 million to more than 9.4 million in 2008, and reached 12.1 million in 2014. The number of domestic tourists in 2014 was 1.5 million.

Istria is Croatia's undisputed tourist capital, registering a staggering 22.2 million tourist nights from 3.2 million visitors in 2014. In the same year, Dubrovnik county, one of the next busiest places on the tourist map, registered just under 1.3 million overseas visitors.

The vast majority of tourists in Croatia are foreign visitors (around 90%) mainly coming in search of sea and sunshine. The most numerous among them in 2014 were Germans (two million) and Italians (just under one million), with the UK some way down the list but climbing steadily with 450,100.

PEOPLE

In spite of the large displacement of people – both Serbs and Croats – during the war of the 1990s, Croatia's total population has remained fairly stable (at around 4.4 million) over the past 20 years. Ethnic demographics have changed, however.

In the 1991 census, around three-quarters of people considered themselves Croats, while 12.2% said they were Serbs. A decade later, the 2001 census showed that almost 90% of people thought of themselves as Croats, while Serbs only accounted for 4.5% of the population. There are a number of reasons for the decline in Serb numbers, including the introduction of a new category, 'ethnically uncommitted' (which attracted 2% of the population in 2001), changes in the census methodology, especially relating to Croatians living abroad (ethnic Croats were counted; ethnic Serbs weren't), and the exodus of Serbs from Croatia during 1995. The 2011 census showed the Croatian population to have fallen slightly, to 4.29 million; the percentage of people calling themselves Croats was still around 90%, those calling themselves Serbs 4.5%.

Croatia also has a whole host of other tiny national minority populations – all of them well below 1% each of the total population (2001 and 2011 censuses) – including Bosnians (the highest figure at 0.5%) as well as Hungarians, Italians, Slovenians, Albanians, Czechs, Montenegrins, Macedonians and Slovaks.

However they describe themselves, I've always found the people of Croatia to be warm, hospitable and generous, though inevitably this varies from place to place and person to person. In the interior, and especially in the national parks and nature reserves, people tend to have more time for you, whereas along the coast you might sometimes find a certain brusqueness, especially at the height of the season. But in Croatia, as everywhere, you'll find that if you treat them right, people on the whole will treat you right too.

LANGUAGE

The official language is Croatian, written using a Latin alphabet. Though comparatively unfamiliar to most, it is not as difficult as it might seem – it's a phonetic language, for a start, so letters are always pronounced in the same way (unlike English) – and it's well worth making the effort to learn a few words and phrases. English is widely spoken in Zagreb, on the coast and in major tourist centres – less so off the beaten track. See pages 421–7 for more details and vocabulary.

RELIGION

In the 2011 census, some 87.8% of the population labelled themselves as Roman Catholics (up from three-quarters in 1991), and Catholicism has long been tied to national identity here – it's as much a statement against Tito's brand of socialism or Serbia's Orthodox Church as it's a credo in itself. As a result, church attendance was hugely popular in the first years of Croatian independence, though has tailed off somewhat in recent years.

Outside of church service times, there are often people worshipping privately at the bigger churches and cathedrals, and their peace and privacy should of course be respected. Smaller churches – and even some of the bigger ones – may well be closed outside of the periods immediately before and after mass.

Beyond Catholicism, 4.4% of the population say they're Orthodox Christians, while Muslims account for 1.3% of the population.

EDUCATION

Children in Croatia begin school at the age of six or seven, attending primary school (*osnovna škola*) and then from age 14 secondary school (*srednja škola*). Secondary schools can take the form of *gimnazija* (similar to a grammar school), vocational or art schools. Zagreb also has an American and a French international school (*www.aisz.hr, www.efz.hr*). In recent years the secondary school leaving examination (*matura*) has started to replace entrance exams at some universities. Zagreb's university is the oldest in Croatia (first founded in 1669); other universities include Zadar, Split, Osijek and Dubrovnik, and there are also a fair number of polytechnics and other accredited schools of higher education. The standard is high, and the syllabus demanding – as anyone who has worked their way through the reading lists for literature courses will happily tell you.

CULTURE

Thousands of years of foreign occupiers have left Croatia with an impressive architectural heritage, ranging from Greek and Roman ruins to a wealth of Venetian

Gothic to the Habsburg splendour of the cities in the north. See the individual chapters for specific sights (and sites).

By contrast, there are very few Croatian artists, writers or composers who are well known outside the country, the most famous probably being the sculptor Ivan Meštrović. Which is not to say the Croats are an uncultured lot; on the contrary, it's simply that most of the country's culture hasn't been exported.

What you can see – and hear – is Croatia's abundant folk music, often as *klapa*, the quite beautiful Dalmatian a cappella singing, or sometimes as the somewhat eclectic mix known as 'turbofolk'. Tito's communist government was unusual in encouraging people to retain their folk tradition, and as a result most of the popular tourist destinations – notably Dubrovnik and Split, and many of the islands – have summer music festivals that highlight the best in folk songs and dancing, along with jazz and classical music too.

Croatia now has no less than a dozen traditions inscribed on the **UNESCO Intangible Cultural Heritage List**, including the Zvončari from Kastav (page 239), lacemaking at Lepoglava and on the islands of Hvar and Pag, the Procession of the Cross on Hvar and the Sinjska Alka (page 315).

CROATIA ONLINE

For additional online content, articles, photos and more on Croatia, why not visit www.bradtguides.com/croatia.

2

Practical Information

High summer is a great time to be in the higher parks, such as Risnjak, in the north, or to visit the capital and other towns away from the coast, as lots of locals are themselves on holiday then. But bear in mind that inland Croatia can get pretty hot and sweaty in the absence of sea breezes – and you'll need to book tickets on public transport in advance.

If you have a choice, September is the best month to be on the coast or visit the islands. The weather is fine, the school holidays are over and the sea is still easily warm enough for swimming. October is also fine, but by November the sunshine hours are down and the rainfall hours up. May and early June, too, are absolutely gorgeous along the coast, though there's an increasing tendency for accommodation and ferries to fill up as June progresses.

September and June are the best months for walkers and hikers, closely followed by October and May, and autumn in the inland parks provides stunning visuals as the leaves change colour. Earlier than May and you may find it damp in the lowlands and freezing higher up; later than October and you run the risk of being caught by the first snows.

Yachting, sailing and motor-cruising have a season running from the beginning of May to the first week of October. Outside this period, charters won't be possible and you'll find the weather in any case less pleasant, with a more frequent gale-force *bura* (the gusty northeasterly wind that can blow at gale-force from September to May for anything from four days to a fortnight).

July and August are easily the most popular months with all types of visitor, so you may want to leave well alone, unless you're absolutely set on clubbing, or that deep suntan. These are the months when you'll be competing for rooms with several million others, and, if you're travelling by car, you'll find parking a hassle, and queues for the car ferries measured in hours. That said, July and August are easily the best months for being on the beach, and Croatia's coastal nightlife only really comes alive in summer.

If you're not bothered by the damp and cold, winter is a great time for cultural exploration – the coast and islands are deserted and you'll have museums and churches to yourself. Waiters and hoteliers will be delighted you're there rather than hassled by the next customer, and while you may have to wait a day for the next ferry, you won't have to queue. If you're in inland Croatia in winter, however, do wrap up warm. Finally, if you're planning winter trips to any islands, especially the smaller and remoter ones, bear in mind that from November until Easter they're simply not expecting you. That means accommodation can be hard or impossible to find and restaurants may be closed for the duration – even such otherwise popular spots as Hvar town – so check ahead before you catch the ferry.

HIGHLIGHTS

SCENIC INTEREST For wild karst scenery right on the seashore, you can't beat the Velebit massif, at its most accessible in Paklenica National Park, which has well-marked trails for all grades of walking. Less rugged scenery, punctuated by falling water, is provided by the rightly famous Plitvice Lakes National Park and the Krka River and Falls, both of which easily outshine the crowds.

Offshore, the island of Mljet is a personal favourite, with its saltwater lake and roaming mongooses, while if you have no time to do anything at all, you'll still have time to take the ten-minute ride from Dubrovnik to the island of Lokrum. The country's most famous beach is Zlatni Rat, near Bol, on the island of Brač, though if it's sand not shingle you're after then head to Šunj on the island of Lopud, and if you have your own boat then you'll find the exquisite Kornati archipelago irresistible.

Inland, there's little to match the rugged beauty of the Istrian interior, with its hilltop villages, or the Zagorje and Žumberak regions to the north and southwest

FIFTEEN OF THE BEST

This list isn't in any particular order, but represents the places I've been most taken with in Croatia.

PLITVICE LAKES Much-hyped, these 16 lakes interconnected by waterfalls never fail to impress, and deserve their UNESCO classification as a World Heritage Site. See pages 172–6.

DIOCLETIAN'S PALACE, SPLIT Spreading out from the peristyle, the streets of the old town of Split were once palatial corridors and the houses huge reception rooms for the former Roman emperor in retirement. It's difficult not to be captivated. See pages 311–13.

RISNJAK NATIONAL PARK Situated within the confines of Gorski Kotar, and featuring Croatia's biggest diversity of flora and fauna, this is the perfect park for mountaineers and naturalists alike. See pages 240–2.

ŠIBENIK CATHEDRAL Šibenik itself is lovely, but the 15th-/16th-century cathedral here – Croatia's most important Renaissance monument – is terrific. See page 286.

BIOKOVO Overhanging the Makarska Riviera, Biokovo is Croatia's answer to Cape Town's Table Mountain, offering fabulous views out over the islands of Brač and Hvar. See pages 317–20.

LOKRUM This is a haven, just a short boat ride away from the bustle of Dubrovnik, offering rocks to swim from, woods to picnic in, and a small café set in a ruined Benedictine monastery. See pages 375–6.

ROMAN AMPHITHEATRE, PULA It may look like a cliché on a postcard, but the world's sixth biggest extant Roman amphitheatre is a wonderful monument all the same. See pages 218–19.

of Zagreb, where rolling hills are home to vineyards and dozens of castles from the late Middle Ages onwards.

WILDLIFE AND BOTANY Gorski Kotar, the mountainous area to the east of Rijeka, has the country's rarest fauna, with bear, lynx, wild boar and wolves on the hoof, and various species of eagle and vulture in the air. In the Velebit, you'll also find chamois and mouflon, along with red, fallow and roe deer. Rt Kamenjak in Istria is a great place to see orchids and butterflies.

Ornithologists really are spoiled for choice, from the waterfowl and wading birds on the Neretva Delta, south of Split, and Vransko Jezero, near Zadar, to the storks at Lonjsko Polje and the abundant birdlife at Kopački Rit, in Slavonia.

Botanists, for their part, can head up to the remote Velebitski Botanički Vrt gardens and their unique mountain flora.

BY BOAT Croatia's section of the Adriatic is a sailor's paradise, with more than a thousand islands to choose from, and spectacular scenery all along the way. Remote,

ZAGREB My number one European capital city; a happening mix of bars and alfresco terraces, lovely architecture and excellent museums and galleries. See pages 75–136.

LONJSKO POLJE One of Europe's largest concentrations of storks – more than 500 pairs – makes this wetland park a stunning place to visit. Go by boat, when it floods in spring. See pages 177–9.

KRKA RIVER AND FALLS Several sets of travertine waterfalls you can walk over, across and around, a monastery on an island in the river, and boat trips up and down, along with the chance to swim at the base of the falls, make Krka a delight. See pages 288–90.

TROGIR The traffic-free old town of Trogir is one of the most charming on the whole Adriatic coast. A medieval island settlement, it's astonishingly well preserved and well deserving of its classification as a UNESCO World Heritage Site. See pages 301–5.

PAKLENICA NATIONAL PARK Twin karst canyons running up from the sea into the Velebit massif offer some of the best and most accessible walking and hiking in Croatia. See pages 277–84.

DUBROVNIK Clichéd, over-busy and over-priced (relatively speaking, anyway), there's still nowhere else on earth like Dubrovnik, and I keep going back, and miss it when I'm away. See pages 339–76.

ROVINJ The site that has graced a million postcards is Istria's jewel. The organically medieval historic centre of Croatia's most Italian town stands on a former island, with red-tiled roofs crowned by a Venetian campanile. See pages 202–8.

MLJET Lush vegetation, an abandoned monastery on an island on a lake on an island, Europe's only wild mongooses and relatively few visitors make Mljet a treasure not to be missed. See pages 383–9.

Practical Information HIGHLIGHTS

2

uninhabited islands compete with the charm of old towns like Hvar, Korčula and Rab on the islands and Rovinj and Zadar along the coast. With a boat, you can sail alongside Croatia's most spectacular cliffs at Telašćica (on the island of Dugi Otok), or lose yourself among the thousands of inlets and harbours of the islands of the Kvarner Bay. And there are few greater pleasures than being thrown a mooring line from a private jetty belonging to a tiny restaurant, with an evening of eating, drinking and music ahead of you.

ART AND ARCHITECTURE From the Austro-Hungarian magnificence of the northern cities like Zagreb and Osijek to the Venetian Gothic of towns along the coast and islands, visitors to Croatia are spoilt for choice. Add one-offs like Roman Pula, medieval Dubrovnik, palatial Split, Renaissance Šibenik and Baroque Varaždin, and you'll find yourself having to pick and choose – or come back again next year. Croatia's place at the crossroads of Europe means you can find anything here, from Habsburg palaces to Greek and Roman ruins, from fortified churches to Venetian loggias and from Byzantine mosaics to medieval frescoes.

PUBLIC TRANSPORT Almost everything in this guide can be reached on public transport, which in Croatia mostly means by the regular and inexpensive buses. A good train network also connects the main cities together, but doesn't go as far as Dubrovnik. Some parts of the mountains, obviously, are a whole lot easier to reach by car than by bus, but having a car won't solve all your problems, as driving in Croatia can be pretty hard going – though it's improving every year as the road network gets upgraded. If you can't easily reach something on public transport, we'll tell you in the text.

SUGGESTED ITINERARIES

WEEKEND TRIP For a weekend break, the top of your list should really be the Croatian capital, Zagreb, which you'll find has more than enough to keep you busy for at least two to three days – if not longer. Alternatively, you could take advantage of budget fares to Dubrovnik, Split or Pula – or Osijek, which might just give you enough time to visit Kopački Rit as well.

ONE WEEK A one-week visit would give you enough time to base yourself on the coast, visiting some of the islands, or to start from Zagreb and explore some of

---

BEST BEACHES

Arguably the best beach in Croatia is that hidden cove you discover all by yourself – however, here are five of the best sand/shingle beaches the Croatian coast and islands have to offer, all of them well-known and extremely popular.

Zlatni Rat (Golden Cape) Possibly Croatia's most iconic beach, a long spit of fine shingle at Bol on the island of Brač (page 325).
Vela plaža (Big Beach) Around 1.8km of fine golden shingle at Baška, on the island of Krk (page 259).
Rajska plaža (Paradise Beach) This pale sand/shingle beach stretches for 1.5km at Lopar, on the island of Rab (page 266).
Sakarun A pale sand/shingle and pebble beach on Dugi otok (page 299).
Sunj Nice little sand/shingle beach on the island of Lopud (page 381).

inland Croatia. Budget flights make it easy to fly into one city and out of another, with two single tickets not necessarily costing any more than a return – so you can potentially cover a lot more new ground.

TWO TO THREE WEEKS If you have two or three weeks, you can see quite a bit of Croatia without having to rush – although there's always the temptation to rent an apartment and spend a whole week in one place. In either case, you can work your way up or down the coast making the most of the excellent ferry network, visit Istria, and head inland to Zagreb and Slavonia. A two- or three-week stay also gives you plenty of scope to include a decent hiking trip on Velebit or Gorski kotar.

ONE MONTH Those with a month in Croatia should count themselves lucky indeed, and as with a two- or three-week visit can divide their time between travelling along the coast and visiting Istria, Zagreb and inland Croatia.

TOUR OPERATORS

IN THE UK There's a long history of package tourism as well as independent travel from the UK to Croatia, and there are plenty of operators to choose from – beyond those listed below, it's worth seeing what your local travel agent has to offer, as well as visiting www.visit-croatia.co.uk/index.php/tour-operators-croatia.

Activities Abroad ☎01670 789 991; www.activitiesabroad.com. Offering family & adult activity holidays in Croatia, & perfect for those wanting to get close to Croatia's nature.

Activity Yachting ☎01243 641 304; www.activityyachting.com. Small company offering sailing holidays in Croatia, mainly based on the flotilla concept.

Adriatic Holidays ☎01865 339 481; www.adriaticholidaysonline.com. Specialises in sailing in the Croatian Adriatic with boats out of every major port in the country – sailing boats or motor boats. Based in Britain, the company is staffed primarily by Croatians & prides itself on its unrivalled local knowledge.

Balkan Holidays ☎020 7543 5555; www.balkanholidays.co.uk. Has a wide variety of package destinations on offer along the coast & on the islands.

Cosmos Holidays (Monarch Holidays) ☎0333 777 4740; www.cosmos.co.uk. Claims to be the UK's largest independent tour operator; flights from London, Manchester & Birmingham.

Croatia For Travellers ☎01825 766896; www.croatiafortravellers.co.uk. Aimed squarely at independent travellers, it can tailor a holiday to your precise requirements, or just book flights & hotels.

Croatia Gems ☎0117 973 2643; www.croatiagems.co.uk. Hand-picked villas & apartments.

Croatian Villas ☎020 8888 6655; www.croatianvillas.com. Offering a wide selection of villas & apartments in good locations, & specialists in multi-centre holidays within Croatia & neighbouring countries.

Discovery Travel ☎01904 632 226; www.discoverytravel.co.uk. Outdoor specialist offering 1-week self-guided cycling holidays in Istria.

First Choice www.firstchoice.co.uk. Specialises in southern Dalmatia, with packages to Koločep & Cavtat as well as Dubrovnik.

Freedom Treks ☎01273 224 066; www.freedomtreks.co.uk. Hiking, cycling & sailing specialist.

Headwater Holidays ☎01606 828 561; www.headwater.com. Specialises in walking & cycling holidays, including Istria & Dalmatia.

Nautilus Yachting ☎01732 867 445; www.nautilus-yachting.com. Well-established company offering good learning-to-sail & flotilla holidays.

Responsible Travel ☎01273 823 700; www.responsibletravel.com. Active & outdoor specialist.

Saga Holidays ☎0800 096 0074; www.saga.co.uk. Aimed at the over-50s, Saga has a range of Croatian destinations on offer along the coast & a loyal following.

Thomson Lakes and Mountains ☎0871 230 8181; www.thomsonlakes.co.uk. A subsidiary of the UK's biggest tour operator.

2

31

Trafalgar Tours ✆01481 754 799; www. trafalgartours.com. One of the world's largest & best-known tour operators.

Vamos Travel ✆01926 330 223; www. vamostravel.com. A central & eastern Europe specialist offering a range of city breaks, adventure holidays & active family holiday packages.

IN NORTH AMERICA A growing number of North American operators now include Croatia in package tours. You can contact the New York office of the Croatia National Tourist Board (✆ +1 212 279 8672) though a quicker route to a Croatian holiday is often to simply contact one of the UK operators listed on page 31. It's also a good idea to check what's available at your local travel agent, since new tour itineraries are being developed all the time to meet evolving demand. Ever since Croatia was voted National Geographic Adventure 'Destination of the Year 2006', more US operators have included the country in their European packages.

Friendly Planet Travel ✆+1 800 555 5765; www.friendlyplanet.com. Efficient family-run Philadelphia-based operator with an emphasis on upper-end hotels & luxury coach touring.
Homeric Tours ✆+1 800 223 5570 (within US), +1 212 753 1100 (outside US); www. homerictours.com. A Mediterranean-focused operator founded in 1969.

Kurtrubes Travel ✆617 426 5668; www. kutrubestravel.com; see ad, page 72. Family-run, Boston-based outfit specialising in the Balkans. Offers several Croatia tours inc cycling in Istria, an Istrian food & wine tour & several cruises, plus a 9-day 'Discover Croatia' itinerary.
Picasso Tours ✆+1 212 486 0533; www. picassotours.com. A Washington DC-based boutique operator that includes several itineraries for Croatia.

IN CROATIA There are a number of well-established tour operators and travel agents within Croatia who can organise holidays from abroad, including the travel to and from your home country. Unless you're coming from the particularly well-served UK, you may want to try one of the following. For details of tour operators in Zagreb, see pages 89–90.

Atlas ✆+385 1 2415 611; www.atlas-croatia. com. The Dubrovnik-based company offers everything from tailor-made holidays to coach tours, though its website is less than user-friendly.

Marco Polo ✆+385 52 830 978; www. marcopolo.hr. Rovinj-based operator, specialising in individual & activity-based holidays in the northern Adriatic.

RED TAPE

PASSPORTS/VISAS Nationals of most English-speaking and EU countries only need a valid passport to visit Croatia for up to three months within a six-month period starting from the first day of entry. If you want to stay for longer, you'll need to apply for a temporary residence permit (*privremeni borovak*) at the Croatian embassy in your home country. This is supposed to take up to 12 weeks, but don't be surprised if it takes almost as many months.

Full details of who does and doesn't need a visa for Croatia, as well as up-to-date addresses and phone numbers of all the Croatia diplomatic missions worldwide – and foreign diplomatic missions in Croatia – can be found on the Ministry of Foreign Affairs' website (*www.mvp.hr*).

Make sure you keep your passport with you at all times, as the failure to produce an identity document for a police officer can incur a fine or imprisonment – although having said this, if it's behind the reception desk at your hotel you're hardly likely to get into any trouble.

POLICE REGISTRATION The Law on Aliens governs the stay of foreigners in the country. It is essentially based on the old Yugoslav law and is similar in all the former Yugoslav republics. Under Article 150 a foreigner must be registered with the police at the latest within 48 hours of arriving in Croatia. If you are staying in a hotel or other licensed accommodation, then the hotelier will do this for you and must register you within 24 hours of your arrival at the hotel. The hotel will fill out the necessary *potvrda* (certificate) for you and you need do nothing except provide your passport for your identification details. You are entitled to keep your section of the potvrda (normally returned with your passport at the end of your stay) and it is advisable to make sure you keep your copy, because if you can't prove your official registration for any part of your stay in Croatia then you could be subject to deportation and a restriction on your return to Croatia.

If you are staying in private accommodation, with friends or in your own home bought in Croatia, then your host must register you within 24 hours of arrival at the accommodation. Your host should register you at the nearest tourist office if there is one in the local town, or at the nearest police station. Registration costs 10kn per stay throughout the year, and in addition there is a sliding scale of tourism tax per day ranging from 4kn to 8kn per day depending on the time of year. This is included in your accommodation costs if you are renting. Foreigner homeowners in Croatia staying in their own home (*korisčenje nekretnine*) are exempt from the tourist tax outside the peak tourism season (15 June–15 September) and pay a reduced tourist tax during the peak tourism season. If as a homeowner you will be using your property a lot during the summer season, you can pay a reduced lump sum for the entire period, saving you the hassle of going in and out of the tourist office. This will register you in the country for 90 days, however, and you will then not be able to return for a further three months. You will need to bring proof of your ownership of the property in order to qualify for home ownership exemptions/reductions to the tourist tax.

In the unlikely case that you first read this section while waiting for a delayed bus after you've already been in Croatia a while and therefore have not yet registered, you'll find that most unregistered tourists will probably get away with just a discretionary warning. Application of the law is, however, much stricter. The Law on Aliens is available at the Ministry of Interior's website (*www.mup.hr*).

EMBASSIES

CROATIAN DIPLOMATIC MISSIONS ABROAD There is a useful list of contact details for Croatian diplomatic missions abroad at www.mvep.hr/en – click 'Diplomatic Directory'.

FOREIGN DIPLOMATIC MISSIONS IN CROATIA Most English-speaking countries have embassies or consulates in the capital, Zagreb, while the UK also has consulates in Dubrovnik and Split. For a comprehensive click-through list of all embassies and consulates in the Croatian capital, go to www.zagreb-touristinfo.hr, and select 'Diplomatic Institutions' from 'Useful Information' in the sidebar menu, or see www.mvep.hr/en and click 'Diplomatic Directory'.

CUSTOMS There are no restrictions on the personal belongings you can bring into Croatia, though the government recommends you declare big-ticket items (boats, laptop computers, expensive camera or movie equipment, etc) to be sure of being able to re-export them hassle-free. Crossing into or out of Croatia in your own non-

2

Balkan registered vehicle, it's incredibly rare to be stopped or seriously questioned for any length of time, however.

Standard customs allowances apply for duty-free – 200 cigarettes, 1 litre of spirits, 2 litres of table wine and 250ml of perfume per person – and large amounts of some products, such as coffee and non-alcoholic drinks, also attract a special tax and should be declared. If you're taking your pets, then make sure they have an international veterinary certificate showing that it's been at least two weeks, but not more than six months, since they've had their rabies shot.

You can take as much foreign currency as you want in and out of the country (though you're expected to declare amounts larger than 40,000kn), but you can't export more than 15,000kn worth of local currency. For goods purchased in Croatia costing over 500kn, you can claim a VAT refund on the way out of the country on presentation of the PDV-P 'tax cheque' the merchant will have given you for this purpose – but it can be a giddyingly long procedure. Any questions you have can be answered by the helpful staff at the Customs Administration in Zagreb (\ 0800 1222 (general information); www.carina.hr).

GETTING THERE AND AWAY

There are five main ways of travelling to Croatia: plane, train, bus, car or boat. You could also arrive on foot, by bicycle or by hitching a lift (but see pages 52–3).

BY AIR
From the UK Flying to Croatia is easily the quickest way of arriving – Zagreb is just 2 hours from London, Zadar, Split and Dubrovnik only half an hour further, Pula and Rijeka somewhere in between. Both Croatia Airlines (www.croatiaairlines.hr) and British Airways (www.britishairways.com) fly to Croatia. Expect to pay anything between £100 and £500 for a scheduled return flight, including taxes.

These days a whole slew of budget airlines also fly to Croatia from the UK, but some of these routes only operate during the summer, and routes and timetables tend to change, so check the websites.

There are also various charter flights available, including First Choice (www.firstchoice.co.uk), Newmarket Holidays (www.newmarket-group.co.uk) and Thomson Holidays (www.thomson.co.uk).

You can also shop around for flights through sites such as www.whichbudget.com, as well as UK sites such as www.cheapflights.co.uk, www.lastminute.co.uk, www.opodo.co.uk, www.skyscanner.net, or US sites like www.expedia.com. But don't automatically assume that these are always the cheapest – these sites don't necessarily include fares from low-cost carriers or charter operators, where the cheapest fares are found on the company's own websites.

✈ **easyJet** www.easyjet.com. To Pula, Split & Dubrovnik (easyJet also operates flights to Ljubljana, which is a possibility for Zagreb).
✈ **Flybe** www.flybe.com. Flights to Zagreb.
✈ **Germanwings** www.germanwings.com. Operates routes to Zagreb, Zadar, Split, Dubrovnik, Pula & Rijeka to London airports via Cologne/Bonn (or sometimes Stuttgart), although this tends to make it a long flight.

✈ **Jet2** www.jet2.com. To Pula, Split & Dubrovnik.
✈ **Monarch** www.monarch.co.uk. To Dubrovnik.
✈ **Ryanair** www.ryanair.com. To Pula, Rijeka, Zadar & Osijek.
✈ **Thomsonfly** www.thomsonfly.com. To Dubrovnik & Pula.
✈ **Wizz Air** www.wizzair.com. To Split.

From outside Europe There are no direct flights from the USA, Canada, Australia or New Zealand, but most airlines will be able to route you through a European hub, usually in conjunction with Croatia Airlines. Prices from New York to Zagreb start at around US$1,000, but can rise to over US$2,000 depending on the time of year and your choice of airline. From Australia and New Zealand, standard tickets are US$2,500+, but with some judicious searching you can usually get a much better deal by choosing to route your Europe-bound flight through one of the hubs served by low-cost carriers such as easyJet, Germanwings or Ryanair.

If you're having trouble finding a reasonably priced flight through the usual channels (newspapers, travel agents etc), there are a number of alternatives. One is to take a package tour – see the list of tour operators on pages 31–2. If you want to sort out your own accommodation, some operators will be happy to arrange a 'flights-only' package for you. Even if this isn't the case, it can sometimes still work out cheaper to book yourself on a package and then not use the entire accommodation segment – though if you do this, you should check the conditions very carefully to ensure you still have a return flight home. Charter operators flying to Croatia from the UK are listed on page 34.

BY RAIL The train is a slow and difficult way of getting to Croatia, and not significantly cheaper than the plane. The journey from London to Zagreb or Rijeka takes over 24 hours non-stop, and involves at least three or four changes – and there's no railway to Dubrovnik. But if you're a train lover, have access to a cheap ticket or are planning on stopping off at various places on the way, it's nonetheless a great way of travelling.

If you're roving round Europe, Croatia can be included on an InterRail (*www. raileurope.co.uk*) or a Eurail pass (bought outside Europe – see www.eurail.com) – and InterRail tickets, once the privilege of those under 26, are now available to all age groups. International connections come in to Zagreb from Ljubljana (*2½hrs*), Belgrade (*6–7hrs*), Budapest (*5–7hrs*), Munich (*9hrs*), Trieste (*5½hrs*), Venice (*7–8hrs*), Innsbruck, Salzburg and Vienna (*9, 8½ & 6½hrs*), Sarajevo (*9hrs*) and Skopje (*9hrs*).

BY BUS Luxury coaches cruise between most cities in Europe, but it's a long journey (London to Zagreb takes between 30 and 40 hours) and buses aren't as cheap as they used to be (sample fares, without student discount, range from £120 upwards). That said, if you can get a discount, this may be a viable way to go – though if you're going to forego the convenience of a direct flight, the train is obviously a much more pleasant option for a long trans-European journey. A vast range of bus-related websites are available from www.budgettravel.com, while from the UK, National Express (*www.nationalexpress.com*) is the principal operator.

BY CAR In spite of the long drive (London to Zagreb is 1,640km by road; London to Dubrovnik 2,175km) and the expense (tolls and fuel in Europe are pricey), having your own car in Croatia can certainly be an advantage, especially if you're travelling as a family, or planning on moving around a great deal and wanting to visit remote places. Unless you're wedded to the idea of touring in your own vehicle, it can be much more cost effective to rent a car once you get there rather than take your own, and all the big companies have agencies in the main cities and airports. If you're doing this, make sure you book the car before you arrive in Croatia, as it's much more expensive once you get there if you haven't reserved ahead. Note that traffic on the coast – and on the motorways between Zagreb and the coast, especially at weekends – can be extremely busy in the summer.

If you do decide to drive all the way, you'll find a good motorway between Ljubljana and Zagreb (though the tolls in Slovenia are surprisingly expensive), and good motorways from Zagreb to the coast, making Istria and Dalmatia a whole lot faster to get to than they used to be. The motorway is planned to run all the way to Dubrovnik, although at the time of writing (2015) it hadn't got that far south yet.

An alternative – slower, but with its merits – is to drive down through Italy and then take the car ferry across. At around €90 for the passage (car + driver), it's more pricey than coming through Slovenia and Croatia – especially if you take a cabin – but it does mean you can take a break in Italy on the way. Ferries run from Ancona, Pescara and Bari, in Italy, direct to Zadar, Split and Dubrovnik, as well as to some of the larger islands. There are also services from Venice to Pula, Poreč and Rovinj. If you're doing this in summer (and some of these lines only run in the summer), it's essential to have a ferry booking – Italians simply love Croatia, and tend to bring their cars with them. See below and pages 53–4 for details of ferry routes.

In truth, however, if you're only going to main tourist centres – especially in high season, when coastal traffic can be terrible – why not just forget about driving altogether and stick to public transport?

BY BOAT You can travel across and up and down the Adriatic on one of the many ferries that ply the Croatian coast all the way from Pula and Rijeka in the north to Split and Dubrovnik in the south. The ferries are a slow but very attractive way of getting around, and a reminder of the only way people travelled any distance here as recently as the 1930s.

The are now several companies plying the Adriatic between Italy and Croatia, including: Jadrolinija (*www.jadrolinija.hr*) between Ancona and Split, Ancona and Zadar, and Bari and Dubrovnik; Sanmar (*www.sanmar.it*) between Pescara, Hvar and Split; SNAV (*www.snav.it*) from Pescara to Hvar and Vela Luka; Trieste Lines (*www.triestelines.it*) from Trieste to Rovinj and Pula; and Venezia Lines (*www.venezialines.com*) between Venice and Poreč, Rovinj, Pula and Mali Lošinj.

International ferries aren't especially cheap, with a typical passenger fare across the Adriatic in summer starting at €40 – see the previous section for details of the various ferry companies operating between Italy and Croatia. If you're travelling down through Italy by train and planning to cross the Adriatic from Ancona, also make sure you get off at the Ancona Maritime stop rather than the main train station. And if you're coming via Bari airport, bear in mind that the seaport is a long way distant, and you'll need to factor in moderately expensive taxi rides (or inconvenient buses).

Ferry travel is the only way to get between the coast and islands (with the exception of a couple of islands connected to the mainland by road bridge), and the main centres are well connected all year round, though ferries are generally more frequent in summer. If you're on foot, there's no need to book (on the whole – fast catamaran routes are an exception), and the short-hop ferries are inexpensive.

One of the most attractive ways of seeing the Adriatic and the Croatian coast and islands of course is from your own – or a chartered – boat. There is an extensive network of around 50 marinas offering around 12,500 berths, while a whole raft of companies offers charters, from skippered motor launches to self-sail yachts. Prices vary enormously depending on what you're looking for (see page 54 for more details), and you should book well ahead, as it's becoming increasingly popular.

TOURIST INFORMATION AND MAPS

Croatia has an active national tourist board and dozens of tourist organisations locally, so there's usually no shortage of information available. Maps, while often great at the town or regional level, are less satisfactory when it comes to providing for hikers – for these, search out the two series of excellent local hiking maps published by the HGSS and SMAND (see below).

TOURIST INFORMATION The Croatian National Tourist Board is an excellent source of information and can provide you with maps, brochures and accommodation details. The www.croatia.hr website is a great place to start, but if you don't have easy access to the internet you may want to contact one of the offices listed below for information. Note that these are the only English-language offices. For a full list of European regional offices, see www.croatia.hr.

i **Head office** Croatian National Tourist Board, Iblerov trg 10/IV, 10000 Zagreb; www.croatia.hr
i **UK office** Croatian National Tourist Office, 77 Fulham Palace Rd, London W6 8JA; 20 8563 7979; e info@croatia-london.co.uk; www.croatia.hr

i **USA office** Croatian National Tourist Office Inc, 350 Fifth Av, Suite 4003, New York 10118; +1 212 279 8672/8674; e cntony@earthlink.net; www.croatia.hr

Once in Croatia, you're likely to find that some tourist or information offices – in reality and on the map – are actually closer to travel agents; they'll be keen to help you find accommodation and arrange excursions, but may not be so useful when it comes to maps or finding local information. Official tourist information offices are listed throughout this guide.

MAPS The national tourist board can provide you with a useful reversible 1:1,000,000 (1cm = 10km) road map/tourist map that is good for situating yourself and planning an itinerary, and is perfectly acceptable for most users.

More detail – at a higher price – is provided by Freytag and Berndt's 1:250,000 Croatia/Slovenia road atlases, or the separate maps covering the various parts of the country, available from the Austrian publisher in 1:250,000, 1:500,000 and 1:600,000 sections. Two chunks of the Dalmatian coast are even covered at 1:100,000.

Kümmerly and Frey, the Swiss publisher, also does a reasonable 1:500,000 map covering Slovenia, Croatia and Bosnia & Herzegovina; Belletti Editore has a similar offering, but only covering Croatia and Slovenia; and Nelles has a good driving map of the Croatian Adriatic Coast with Istria at 1:225,000 and the rest of the coast at 1:525,000, and includes town plans for the main centres. You may also see the Hungarian Cartographia (1:850,000) on offer, but it's not great, to be honest.

Far and away the best map for drivers is the 1:300,000 two-sided map of 'Bosnia Erzegovina', which is published by Studio FMB Bologna – it covers all of Croatia except eastern Slavonia, and is a good deal more accurate than any of the others, though unfolding it and turning it over on the move is no joke, as it's enormous.

Finally, there's a pretty good 1:100,000 scale map of Istria published by Bruno Fachin Editore in Trieste, which also includes the most accurate map of the island of Krk I've ever seen.

None of these of course is much use for walkers or hikers looking to stretch their legs in the national parks or nature reserves. The best hiking maps by far are the detailed local (usually 1:25,000) maps published by the HGSS (*www.gss.hr*), SMAND (*www.smand.hr*) and national park offices. These cover most of the

Practical Information TOURIST INFORMATION AND MAPS

2

37

main hiking areas (Velebit, Gorski Kotar, Bjelolasica, Biokovo, Medvednica, etc) as well as an increasing number of the islands (Cres, Lošinj, Rab, Brač, Hvar, Vis, Lastovo, Mljet). They are available through some of the larger bookshops in Zagreb and other main cities, and usually sell for about 35kn–55kn. Hiking maps produced by local tourist offices are generally far less detailed and therefore much less useful if you actually try to hike with them. An exception is the local hiking map produced by the Baška tourist office which is excellent, and extremely detailed and accurate.

There is also a good series of maps published under the Trsat Polo imprint of the Geodetski zavod Slovinje (Slovenian Institute of Surveyors), which covers the whole coast at 1:100,000, with separate maps for Istria, Kvarner and Dalmatia 1–4. They're available in most Croatian bookshops. The series is aimed at sailors and drivers, and includes plans of the marinas as well as sea and mooring guidance, along with contours and clearly marked footpaths – however, the latter are in general *not* accurate, and for hiking you really should not use these but stick with the SMAND and HGSS maps.

If you're planning a walking holiday, it's also well worth getting hold of Rudolf Abraham's books *The Islands of Croatia* and *Walking in Croatia*, or Sandra Bardwell's *Croatia: Car Tours and Walks* (page 429). The former is the most recent of these, covering day walks on the islands and is the only book available which includes sections of the relevant HGSS and SMAND maps. The latter two cover a range of walks on the coast and islands.

Town and city plans are generally available cheaply or for free at local tourist offices, and will get you round the main sights, though they may not be all that much help if it's a particular street address you're looking for.

HEALTH *with Dr Felicity Nicholson*

The chances are you'll never need them, but here are four phone numbers worth knowing: ℡ 92 for the police, ℡ 93 for fire, ℡ 94 for an ambulance and ℡ 9155 for search and rescue at sea.

It is always important to purchase proper health insurance prior to travel, in case of a medical emergency. Travellers from EU countries or Switzerland can use their EHIC in Croatia, which allows you to access public healthcare at a reduced cost (or free). Normally hospital treatment and some other medical and dental treatments are free. If you are travelling from the UK then you will need to show your passport, but if you are a UK resident but not a UK national then you will need a certificate of insurance from HM Customs Centre for Non-Residents. Prescribed medicines are not free and are often no cheaper than they would be at home. In practice, you may well be told that the service you need (and that should be free) isn't available, and that you can only obtain it privately. Another reason for that all-important health insurance!

If you have a pre-existing medical condition, are pregnant or are travelling with children then you would be wise to establish healthcare facilities before arriving in Croatia. Larger hotels and tour company representatives are often able to assist, but failing that then contact the nearest British embassy or consulate for advice. A list of clinics is also provided by the International Society of Travel Medicine and can be found on its website (*www.istm.org*).

For minor treatments, a visit to one of the ubiquitous pharmacies (*ljekarna*) should sort you out, and there's very often someone who speaks some English. For more serious problems, get yourself to a clinic or hospital (*klinika* or *bolnica*).

There are no legal requirements for vaccinations for Croatia, but most doctors would advise immunisation against diphtheria, tetanus and polio (given as an all-in-one ten-yearly vaccine – Revaxis), and hepatitis A (e.g. Havrix Monodose or Avaxim). For longer trips (four weeks or more), or for those working in the medical field or with children, vaccination against hepatitis B is advised. Ideally, a course of three injections is required, the minimum time for which is over 21 days if you are 16 or over. For younger travellers the minimum course of three vaccinations is over two months.

Similarly, a course of rabies injections (three doses over a minimum of three weeks) is advisable for those working with animals, or spending a longer time in Croatia. Tuberculosis (TB) is spread through close respiratory contact in crowded conditions and may occasionally be spread through infected milk and milk products. Experts differ over whether a BCG vaccination against tuberculosis is useful in adults; discuss with your travel clinic.

Travellers planning to go rambling or trekking in the countryside during the spring–autumn period are at risk of tick-borne encephalitis. The ticks that transmit this potentially fatal disease live in long grass and overhanging tree branches. Precautions include wearing long trousers tucked into boots, and a hat. Using tick repellents and checking for ticks at the end of the day can also help. If you do find ticks, remove them as soon as possible (see box, page 40) and go to a doctor for treatment. Pre-exposure vaccine is in short supply in the UK, but if you do manage to track some down, it's worth having. Three doses can be given over two weeks if time is short. However, it's still important to seek medical help in the event of a tick bite.

If you use needles for any reason, you should bring a doctor's note explaining why, and if you wear contact lenses or glasses, bring spares; repairs and replacements aren't a problem, but can take time. It also does no harm at all to have a doctor's and dentist's check-up before you go – far easier at home than abroad.

You can drink the water if it's from a public supply; however, the mineral content may well be different so could cause stomach upsets. It is always safer to drink and clean your teeth with bottled water.

TRAVEL CLINICS AND HEALTH INFORMATION A full list of current travel clinic websites worldwide is available on www.istm.org. For other journey preparation information, consult www.nathnac.org/ds/map_world.aspx. Information about various medications may be found on www.netdoctor.co.uk/travel.

FITNESS Many a walking, hiking or cycling holiday has been ruined by a lack of form, so if you're planning one, try to get fit before you go. The best exercises are cycling and hill walking – far preferable to running or jogging. If you're surrounded by a dearth of hills to practise on, ordinary stairs make for easily the best substitute.

COMMON PROBLEMS You're less resistant to disease during your first weeks abroad, so make sure your diet contains enough vitamins – take supplements if you're not sure. Drink bottled water if the source is suspect – publicly supplied water is fine, but in the mountains, rivers and streams should be treated with caution; use chlorine-based water purification tablets if you're a long way off the beaten track, or buy yourself one of the amazing little water filters made by Sawyer (*www.sawyer. com*), which are incredibly lightweight and easy to use. You may also want to bring with you a mild laxative and something for diarrhoea, although both problems can normally be fixed with a change in diet (soft fruit for the first; dry-skinned fruits for the second). If you're afflicted with diarrhoea, your biggest danger is dehydration, so make sure you drink plenty – soft drinks are good.

Even if you're not heading into the wilds, it's a good idea to bring along a small supply of sticking plasters (band-aids), antiseptic cream and mild painkillers (aspirin or paracetamol) – you can top up your supplies of these at any pharmacy.

From May onwards, you should think about protecting yourself against mosquitoes. Along the coast and on the islands all you'll need is a gizmo that plugs into a wall socket at night (with the screw-in bottle of fluid; the ones that take tablets aren't effective) and you can buy these anywhere mosquitoes are present. It is also wise to use insect repellents whenever you are outside of your accommodation. This is even more important in other parts of the country – and notably in the wetlands of the Lonjsko Polje and Kopački Rit – where you'll be confronted with evil, savage beasts, which will attack you day or night, and are perfectly capable of puncturing light clothing. Use the gizmo at night, but double up with an effective spray-on repellent during the day.

Finally, don't hesitate to see a pharmacist or doctor if you're even slightly unsure about a diagnosis or cure. But know your source if you need a blood transfusion – HIV/AIDS is less prevalent in Croatia than in many countries, but you can't be too careful. Occasionally immigrants or long-term expatriates may be asked for proof that they are free from HIV infection. Check if you need this when applying for visas or work permits.

MOUNTAIN HEALTH Prevention being far better than cure, walkers and hikers should be conversant with first aid – or at the very least carry a booklet covering the basics. It's especially important to know how to deal with injuries and hypothermia. If you're in real trouble, call the police or alert the mountain rescue service (see *Mountain safety*, page 53).

Hypothermia This is responsible for the deaths of more walkers, hikers and climbers than any other cause. It occurs when the body loses heat faster than it can be generated, and the commonest cause is a combination of wet or inadequate clothing, and cold wind. It's easily avoided by making sure you always have a waterproof, a sweater or fleece, and a survival bag with you – even if you're hiking with only a daypack.

TICK REMOVAL

Ticks should ideally be removed as soon as possible, as leaving ticks on the body increases the chance of infection. They should be removed with special tick 'tweezers' that can be bought in good travel shops. Failing that you can use your finger nails by grasping the tick as close to your body as possible and pulling steadily and firmly away at right angles to your skin. The tick will then come away complete as long as you do not jerk or twist. If possible, douse the wound with alcohol (any spirit will do) or iodine. Irritants (eg: Olbas oil) or lit cigarettes are to be discouraged since they can cause the ticks to regurgitate and therefore increase the risk of disease. It is best to get a travelling companion to check you for ticks and if you are travelling with small children remember to check their heads, and particularly behind the ears. An area of spreading redness around the bite site, or a rash or fever coming on a few days or more after the bite, should stimulate a trip to the doctor.

If one of your party shows signs of hypothermia – uncomfortable shivering, followed by drowsiness or confusion – it's essential that he or she is warmed up immediately. Exercise is not the way to do this. Wrap the victim in warm clothing, or even better a sleeping bag, then increase blood-sugar levels with food and hot, sweet drinks.

Injury Again, prevention is much better than cure. Try to avoid walking or climbing beyond your limits – the majority of accidents happen when you're tired. If scrambling or bouldering, avoid using your knees or elbows, and keep at least three points of contact with the rock (two hands and a foot, or vice versa). In the event of being injured, use surgical tape for cuts that would normally be stitched, and then bind the wound laterally with zinc-oxide tape. If you're going a long way off the trail, take an inflatable splint.

Altitude sickness Croatia's lack of very high mountains means this is one problem you're unlikely to face, but if you've trekked up from sea level to 1,500m and feel dizzy or confused you should stop and rest. If this doesn't work, return to a lower altitude. And remember, altitude sickness doesn't discriminate – youth and fitness don't help at all.

SNAKES In the extremely unlikely event of being bitten by a snake, try not to panic, as a racing heart speeds up the spread of venom – much easier said than done, of course. Most first-aid techniques do more harm than good. If possible, splint the bitten limb and keep below the height of the heart, then get the victim to hospital immediately.

RABIES Rabies is present throughout the country and is spread by the saliva of any warm-blooded mammal – most commonly dogs. If you are bitten, scratched or licked over an open wound then wash the wound with soap and running water and apply an antiseptic – even alcohol will do. This helps stop the rabies virus entering the body and will guard against wound infections, including tetanus. Go as soon as possible to a doctor for treatment. You should still go for treatment even if you have had the pre-exposure course, but it does make treatment easier and less expensive than if you have not. Pre-exposure vaccinations for rabies are particularly important if you intend to have contact with animals and/or are likely to be more than 24 hours away from medical help. Ideally three doses should be taken over a minimum of 21 days. Contrary to popular belief these vaccinations are relatively painless.

If you think you have been exposed, then post-exposure prophylaxis should be given as soon as possible, though it is never too late to seek help, as the incubation period for rabies can be very long. Those who have not been immunised will need a full course of injections. The vast majority of travel health advisors including WHO recommend rabies immunoglobulin (RIG), but this product is expensive and may be hard to come by – another reason why pre-exposure vaccination should be encouraged.

Tell the doctor if you have had a pre-exposure vaccine, as this should change the treatment you receive. And remember that, if you develop rabies, mortality is 100% and death from rabies is probably one of the worst ways to go.

INSURANCE A good idea – it's reassuring to know you can be flown home if necessary. Read the fine print and make sure it covers what you'll be doing (walking in the mountains, for example). A general policy, covering health, theft and third party insurance, is usually cheaper and less hassle than multiple policies, though you may find you're already covered for some or all of the risks by existing insurance, such as private healthcare (which sometimes includes foreign travel) or that provided to holders of credit cards.

If you need to claim, you'll have to provide supporting evidence in the form of medical bills, in the case of health, or a police statement, in the case of theft. Obtaining the latter can be very hard work, but essential if you're hoping for reimbursement.

Travel policies are issued by banks, travel agents and others, and it's worth shopping around among reputable providers, as the price varies considerably. Arrange for the insurance to cover your full journey time, and keep the policy safe with your other travel documents.

SAFETY

Croatia is safer and freer of crime than most EU countries, though the normal precautions you'd apply at home apply here, too – don't be showy with money, jewellery or flashy possessions, and avoid the seedier or ill-lit parts of cities at night. You're more likely to be robbed by fellow travellers than by Croats, so be especially careful in hostels, campsites and overnight trains or buses, and keep your valuables close to you and separate from the rest of your luggage.

Car theft, however, is increasingly prevalent, and foreign-registered cars – and especially expensive foreign-registered cars, such as Audis, BMWs and Mercedes – are attractive to thieves. Generally speaking, you wouldn't expect problems along the coast, though be careful where you leave your car in any big city, and don't leave your vehicle unattended for more than a day anywhere – it's tantamount to painting a 'Steal Me' notice on it.

You'll see lots of police around, and they have rather fearsome powers – freedom of dissension shouldn't be taken for granted. The police carry out occasional spot checks on locals and foreigners alike for identification, so make sure you have your passport or identity card with you at all times. Otherwise, you'll find the police friendly and helpful, though, apart from along the coast and in the capital, few speak any English.

If you're driving, keep to the speed limits. There are an astonishing number of speed traps – especially along the Magistrala, the coast road running all the way from Opatija to Dubrovnik. If you're stopped for a traffic violation, you may find the police negotiate a lower penalty with you – the heavier fine for speeding, for example, may be traded down to the lower fine (payable in cash) for not wearing your seat belt.

Turning into a one-way street the wrong way in Dubrovnik, I was immediately stopped by the police and told to park the car in a spot reserved for the disabled. I was then given a choice of having my licence taken away and a 1,500kn fine (for driving the wrong way down a one-way street – unmarked as such, I might add), or paying the 150kn fine for parking in a disabled spot. I'll leave you to guess which I chose (clue: I still have my licence).

If you do get closely involved with the police, stay courteous, even (especially) when it's difficult to do so. Stand, rather than sit, if you can (it puts you on an even footing), and establish eye contact – if you can do so without being brazen or offensive about it. Some people recommend shaking hands with officialdom, but it depends very much on the circumstances. Wait until an interpreter arrives (or anyone who understands you clearly) rather than be misunderstood, though this may not happen on the same day. And remember that you can be held at a police station for up to 24 hours without being charged. Your consulate will be informed of your arrest, normally within the first day.

MINEFIELDS Along the frontlines of the war of the early 1990s – and that means in about a third of the country – minefields were laid down, and a handful still haven't been completely cleared. Most are clearly marked off with barbed wire and skull-and-crossbones signs saying 'Mine', and it would be plainly stupid to explore further.

Not every minefield is labelled, however. If you see villages that seem to have been abandoned for ten years or more, or fields that haven't been cultivated for a long while, there's a real risk of uncleared mines, and it's best to leave well alone – I was going to say 'tread carefully', but that hardly seems appropriate.

There are uncleared mines in parts of southern Velebit and Paklenica – all the more reason to carry a decent map or guidebook.

Finally, if you're travelling in the former war zone – most of Slavonia, and pretty much anywhere inland between Karlovac and Split, as well as some areas inland from Zadar – it's wise to stick to roads and tracks that carry regular traffic, or to marked footpaths in the national parks and nature reserves.

SMOKING Non-smokers beware: with more than a million smokers (and one of Europe's highest rates of lung cancer), Croatia is one of the last bastions of the 40-a-day habit.

However, in May 2009, Croatia introduced a ban on smoking in indoor public spaces – including cafés, bars and restaurants. Needless to say, this was a vast improvement, but it caused such an uproar (among café owners and smokers) that it was at least partially revoked, the ruling now being that bars and cafés smaller than 50m² which do not serve food have the choice of whether to be smoking or non-smoking (guess which most choose), whereas larger establishments (again, not serving food) may only have a smoking area (less than 30% of the total area) if it is properly ventilated. Restaurants at least seem destined to remain smoke-free – though the nice terrace outside, which is obviously where you'll want to sit, won't be.

Regardless of the outcome, most of the upper-end hotels have offered non-smoking rooms, and even non-smoking floors, for some time, so it's worth asking when you make your booking. Likewise, the bars and restaurants in these hotels – and some of the more upmarket establishments – have smoke-free sections, though you're still inevitably going to get some exposure to the smoke drifting over from the main area. In such cases, with smoking very much the norm, it may still be difficult to ask local people to refrain.

WOMEN TRAVELLERS Croatia is a safe country for women travellers, though, like anywhere with a big influx of holidaymakers, it has its fair share of local men on the make. This tends to come in the form of courteous persistence rather than aggression, and is usually easily rebuffed. Speaking firmly – in any language – should make your intentions clear.

People dress here the same way as they do anywhere in Europe, so there's nothing to worry about as far as dressing modestly is concerned – though wandering around churches in beachwear is likely to offend. If you want to get your kit off, head for the nearest naturist beach (usually marked FKK) – you won't be pestered.

GAY AND LESBIAN TRAVELLERS Homosexuality may have been legalised a generation ago in Croatia, but you won't find people particularly tolerant or open about it. Zagreb's first-ever gay parade wasn't held until June 2002, and only a few hundred people took part – heavily protected from hecklers by a slew of riot police.

Most activity is still very much underground, and even in Dubrovnik, one of Croatia's most tolerant and liberal cities, there is only a small gay/lesbian scene – though Zagreb does now finally have some good gay clubs, bars, video stores and saunas, and some hotels in the city have earned a reputation for being gay-friendly.

Elsewhere, same-sex couples (men in particular) can still raise eyebrows (or even hackles) when checking into hotels, though, as everywhere, younger people tend to be more tolerant than their elders. How you handle it will be up to you – some may be happy with a plausible cover story; others might find this too hypocritical.

For further information on gay-friendly places in Croatia, see www.croatia-gay.com.

TRAVELLING WITH KIDS Though perhaps not as children-friendly as the UK in terms of facilities at museums, etc, Croatia is nevertheless a great place to travel with kids, who will love the endless coastline, warm sea, ferry-hopping and mountainous ice creams. You'll find decent playgrounds (*igralice*) in most towns or cities of any size (for Zagreb, see box, page 111), and a whole slew of bouncy castles on the coast. Zagreb has a good zoo, Pula a decent aquarium (Dubrovnik's is best avoided), and there's the chance to see dolphins off some of the islands (especially Lošinj and Lastovo). Many of the larger resorts cater for families with children, and with the new smoking ban (at least, if it stays in place – see page 43), cafés and restaurants are no longer as smoke-ridden as they once were. See Will Gray's excellent *Travel with Kids* for inspiration (page 429).

TRAVELLERS WITH A DISABILITY Croatia has done a great deal to introduce active programmes and legislation to support those with disabilities. The country's main airports, train stations and bus stations are disabled-friendly, with ramps and lifts where needed, and good disabled toilets.

There are also ramps and lifts in all buildings with public access across the country, and most of the better hotels and restaurants are also equipped for the disabled.

In the capital, Zagreb, you'll find lowered public phones, and an ongoing curb-lowering initiative that makes the pavements more wheelchair-friendly. Most street crossings are equipped with pedestrian tracks and sound signals for the visually impaired. City public transport is free for the disabled, and a good number of the city's trams and buses, as well as the funicular up to the old town, are wheelchair-friendly too. Trams are equipped with displays for the deaf and spoken announcements for the blind – though these are in Croatian only.

In Dubrovnik, there's no disabled access on to the famous city walls, but you can get in and around most of the old town with no major problems – though the crowds at particularly busy times of year (or day) can be oppressive if you're wheelchair-bound.

Access for those with disabilities in other cities and tourist destinations is generally pretty good, but obviously less easy where there are cobbled streets in old towns or through the narrow streets and lanes of hilltop villages.

There are disabled parking spaces across the country, and these are generally well respected, particularly following a campaign based around the immediate towing away of improperly parked vehicles combined with signs carrying the message 'If you take my place, take my disability'.

The best way for packing for anywhere – and Croatia's no exception – is to set out all the things you think you'll need and then take only about a third of it. How much you eventually end up taking will depend to a large extent on whether you have your own transport (everyone takes more in their own car) and whether or not you're planning on camping (camping comes with a list of irreducibles – see below). But be realistic, especially if you're going to have to carry all your own stuff – what feels like an easy 15kg pack in your living room can be more like a sack of rocks halfway up a mountainside, or even getting from the bus station to a hotel in the heat of summer.

If you're coming to Croatia for a beach holiday, it's worth remembering that the majority of the beaches are rocks or pebbles, so bring appropriate beach footwear – along with the usual hat, sunglasses, suncream, etc. Summer evenings along the coast can be cool, but are rarely cold, so a light sweater should be sufficient; but if you're coming here in winter, bring warm clothes, especially if you're going inland or into the mountains.

Don't forget the usual range of documents you'll need – passport, tickets, travellers' cheques, cash, insurance papers, credit card, driving licence – and something to carry them in. A belt-bag or pouch is practical, but also draws attention to where you're keeping your valuables; I prefer a zipped pocket for the essentials, whether that's in a daypack or trousers, but it's a personal choice.

A small adaptor (to a standard European two-pin plug) or even two is essential if you're carrying anything which needs charging (phone, camera battery recharger, laptop, hairdryer).

And bring any books you want to read – except in the major cities and tourist centres, you'll have trouble finding much more than yesterday's papers.

Also, bring spare glasses if you wear them, along with any special medicines you need. You may also find it handy to have a tube of travel detergent with you for rinsing out your smalls, and a travel alarm for those early starts. And last but not least, if you're bringing any electrical appliances – even just a hairdryer or a phone charger – remember an adaptor. Croatian sockets are the same round two-pinned variety you find all across Europe.

WALKERS AND HIKERS Walkers and hikers need adequate clothes from the ground up, so make sure you have decent footwear – light, waterproof boots with good ankle support and a strong sole can make the difference between comfort and misery. But bring another pair of lighter, more flexible shoes or sandals, too, as you can get seriously fed up with wearing boots night and day (the updater swears by Keen's hardwearing but amazingly comfortable Newport H2 sandals, see www.keenfootwear.com). Proper hiking socks, while expensive, are worth every penny, but, again, make sure you have alternatives, not just for washing, but for those evenings out or for travelling to and from your hiking destination.

For hiking in the mountains, you'll need hard-wearing trousers, especially if you come into contact with karst. Jeans are tough, but useless in the mountains, as they're heavy and uncomfortable when wet and take ages to dry. Unless you're travelling in winter, you'll also need shorts, as it can warm up quickly during the day.

Take a variety of tops, so you can wear more thin layers rather than fewer thicker ones, and don't forget the all-important fleece and waterproof jacket (Goretex or similar material). It's definitely worth spending more on these last items – breathable, workable clothes are the difference between being warm and dry and cold and wet. In the summer – in fact, for all but winter use – bring a waterproof jacket that packs small, such as the nifty little Minimus made by Montane (*www. montane.co.uk*), which is lightweight, waterproof, incredibly breathable, and packs down to the size of an apple.

If you're using a rucksack as your main luggage you might prefer to go for tall and narrow rather than short and wide – not only is this easier for walking but it's also a whole lot more manageable for going through doorways and along narrow corridors. Outside pockets can be useful but are also just another zip to break.

Whatever your luggage, make sure you also have a good daypack, with adequate space for everything you might need on a full day's walk – extra clothing, survival bag, water bottle(s), food, camera, maps, compass, penknife, medical kit, sunglasses, etc (see also page 40). If you're going high into the steeper national parks (notably Paklenica), you should definitely have walking poles or a stick with you, as the paths can be slippery. The best sort are retractable poles, which can fit into your main bag or pack when checking your bag in at the airport.

CAMPING It sounds obvious, but if you're camping, take a tent that's easy to pitch (and practise at home before you leave) – trying to assemble an unfamiliar model on a windy and rainy night is suffering itself. I know: I've been there. Bring tent sealant and repair material; both are hard to find outside rare specialist shops.

What you have in the way of a sleeping bag and sleeping mat will define the shape of your nights – and, again, it's worth testing these before you leave home. Buy a down-filled bag if you can afford it, as they're warmer and more comfortable in use, and more compact when rolled, although care should be taken to keep them dry, as they lose their insulating properties when wet and take a long time to dry. However, having said that, if you're camping on the coast in the summer, anything but the lightest summer bag is likely to feel unbearably hot.

It can be worth dispensing with cooking materials, eating utensils and pre-packed food altogether. Given that freelance camping is illegal, you're generally going to be close to both restaurants and supermarkets, and in summer three hot meals a day aren't essential. Again, it's a personal choice, but the business of finding fuel, the weight and bulk, and the overriding cheapness and cheerfulness of cafés and restaurants, has always put me off doing my own cooking while camping in Croatia.

MONEY

Since May 1994, Croatia's currency has been the kuna – literally a marten, named after the trade in marten skins in Roman times, and first struck as a Croatian coin in AD1256. It's one of the few currencies in the world still officially named after an animal (the American buck was never legal tender, even if the word's still in fashion an awful long time since trading in deer skins was a measure of anything in the USA).

The **kuna** (HRK is the international three-letter code) is divided up into 100 lipa (literally lime tree, or linden). There are 1, 2, 5, 10, 20 and 50 lipa coins (the 1 and 2 lipa coins aren't used much these days, and if you buy something for 4.99, ie 4 kuna 99 lipa, it'll probably be rounded up to 5 kuna at the till), 1, 2 and 5 kuna coins and 5, 10, 20, 50, 100, 200, 500 and 1,000 kuna banknotes. There's also a 25-kuna coin, but the chances are you'll never see one. On the whole, people aren't comfortable with the two largest notes, and you may have trouble breaking them – ask for 100s and 200s when you're changing money.

The **euro** has also increasingly been used as a semi-parallel currency – the vast majority of Zagreb's visitors switched to the euro in 2002. Most people are comfortable with euro pricing, and you can usually pay with euros if you need to – but don't necessarily expect the right (or complete) change. You're much better off changing enough money for a couple of days at a time and getting used to the kuna. The kuna is pretty stable, averaging around 7.57 to the euro and 10.36 to the pound.

Finding a place to buy kuna is a doddle – all banks, exchange offices and post offices, and most travel agencies and hotels, will happily let you turn in your money, though you're better off with euros or sterling than US dollars, as there are so many dollar forgeries in circulation. Exchange rates are (remarkably) almost the same wherever you choose to change your money – fractionally worse at hotels, perhaps, but the difference is minimal. The black market for currency exchange – which thrived in the former Yugoslavia in spite of being one of the least efficient known to man – was mercifully put out of its misery.

Banks – unusually for Europe – are often open from 07.00 to 19.00 on weekdays and until 13.00 on Saturdays, though many close for lunch. At major train stations and airports, and in the bigger cities, some banks even open on Sundays.

Major **credit cards** (notably Visa, Eurocard/MasterCard and American Express) are accepted by most big hotels, restaurants and shops, though away from the coast their use isn't ubiquitous – and if you're staying in private rooms (page 58), you'll find cash is king. Credit and debit cards can also be used for raiding cash dispensers (ATMs) – widespread on the mainland and main islands, less so on the smaller islands.

Most people use **ATMs and exchange offices** to get kunas these days, but money can still be brought in the form of travellers' cheques, which are a safe way to travel and are worth the small commission you pay for the peace of mind – though changing them is a greater hassle than just turning up at an ATM. You lose about the same percentage of your money if you use a credit card, but it's easier to keep track of cheques. American Express cheques are still the most widely used, easily recognised and most quickly refunded in case of loss or theft, and your local bank will issue them to you (though you may have to insist).

Finally, have enough money/resources with you – having money wired to you from home is an expensive hassle.

BUDGETING

How much you'll spend will depend mostly on what level of luxury you're looking for, and to some extent on the season and where you're going.

Camping and using public transport is going to cost a lot less, obviously, than staying in swanky hotels and cabbing it around town. That said, Croatia is neither particularly cheap nor expensive – broadly speaking you should expect to pay about the same as in western Europe. Hotel accommodation and restaurants are on average slightly cheaper than in the UK, but about the same as in France – though house wine can be considerably cheaper than in either. Supermarket prices are slightly higher than they would be in the UK.

After the cost of getting to Croatia, your biggest single expense will be **accommodation**. Expect to pay €40–100 per night for a double room in private accommodation in summer, while doubles in hotels start at around €40 and rise beyond €500 (room prices are usually quoted in euros though paid in kuna). Single rooms are relatively scarce, but when available go for about 70% of the cost of a double. Off season along the coast those establishments (both hotels and private rooms) that don't close up altogether will discount by up to 20% in spring and autumn, and as much as 50% in winter.

For a couple, daily **food and drink** costs from around 250kn for picnic food bought in supermarkets and maybe eating out once a day in a cheap restaurant or pizzeria, to 600kn for breakfast in a café and lunch and dinner with wine in more upmarket restaurants. An average *konoba-* or grill-type restaurant meal for two, with salad, risotto or grilled meat and wine, averages around 100kn a head. A good quality fish dinner on the Adriatic, on the other hand, can easily set two of you back 750kn or more. White fish (sea bass, sea bream, etc) is priced by weight – around a hefty 270kn per kilo is not unusual – whereas dark-fleshed fish such as mackerel is much cheaper (not to mention more nutritious and usually more sustainable).

Public transport is inexpensive, with a single-zone Zagreb bus ticket costing 10kn. Typical bus fares in autumn 2015 were 110–140kn for the 285km from Zagreb to Zadar, and 205–255kn for the 565km from Zagreb to Dubrovnik.

If you're really eking out the kuna (camping or basic private rooms, picnic food) you could get away with a budget of 150kn per person per day. Twice that would get you into nicer private rooms and cheap restaurants, while 500kn would buy you a nice holiday, but not fish every day. For that, and upper-end hotels, you'd need to count on 1,000kn or more per person per day.

For two weeks in the shoulder season (May and October) using public transport and staying in private rooms, expect to spend upwards of 600kn a day for two people. Travelling 4,000km in a fortnight in June with your own car and staying in a mix of small hotels and private rooms will cost around 1,000kn a day – in both cases this doesn't include the cost of getting to Croatia.

Entry fees for attractions are reasonably inexpensive, but in a constant state of flux, so haven't been specifically included with each site here – in late 2015, however, you could expect to pay anything from 20kn to visit some of the smaller museums and galleries, to over 100kn to walk around the walls of Dubrovnik. Entry to the national parks ranges from 45kn (North Velebit) to 180kn (Plitvice).

TIPPING A service charge isn't included in your restaurant bill, so – assuming the service has been good – it's appropriate to round up the bill to the nearest 10kn or so (although waiting staff in places like Dubrovnik increasingly expect 10%). Don't be afraid not to tip if you think the service has been terrible, but equally don't be too stingy or extravagant – people appreciate a little extra, since they're generally less well off than their customers, but leaving a huge tip can tend to rub it in (as well as spoil things for future diners). Taxi drivers the world over expect fares to be rounded up, and Croatia's no exception.

OPENING TIMES

Croats are industrious and hard working, but like to knock off early and enjoy the evening. So you'll find people up at dawn, and many offices and shops open from 07.30 or even 07.00, but you may well find businesses shut after 16.00. Supermarkets and pharmacies have fairly long hours, and tend to be open all day, while smaller shops may take an extended lunch hour.

Generally speaking, things tend to be open when they're needed – if there's a real demand, then it'll be met. So you'll find **tourist agencies** in the main resorts open from early in the morning until late at night, seven days a week, in summer, but probably only open in the morning and on weekdays for the rest of the year. To be sure of finding a **tourist office** open, the 08.00–11.00 slot is far and away the most reliable time, all year round.

If everything's closed and you're looking for **accommodation**, you can almost always find something by asking at the nearest bar or café – there's usually someone who knows somebody with a spare room.

Museums are usually closed at least one day a week – normally Monday, but see individual listings for details – and many close for the day at 13.00 or 14.00.

Restaurants generally serve lunch between noon and 15.00, and dinner from 18.00 to 22.00, though cheaper places like pizzerias, and almost everywhere on the coast in summer, will have more extended hours.

Many **churches** – even some of the bigger ones – are only opened for services, and the periods just before and after them. The tourist office can sometimes help you find the person with the key, if there's something you absolutely must see.

GETTING AROUND

You can get around Croatia by plane, train, bus, car, bicycle and hitchhiking – or on foot – and around the Adriatic by ferry, or on your own (or a rented) boat. The train network is good to points connected to Zagreb, but poor (non-existent) along much of the coast, where you'll find yourself on the ubiquitous buses or ferries. Public transport is regular, effective and good value for money, but can be slow and is sometimes overcrowded – notably in summer.

BY AIR Croatia Airlines' (*www.croatiaairlines.hr*) domestic flights are pretty good value, and a great way of getting from one end of the country to the other, especially if you've already seen it all from the bus. A one-way, online fare from Zagreb to Dubrovnik went for as little as 338kn in October 2015; the flight takes around 55 minutes, compared with the 12- to 14-hour, around 250kn bus ride. Buy tickets from any travel agent or online at the website, but if you're planning on flying in summer make sure you book well ahead and bear in mind that if you do so from a travel agent outside Croatia, the price could be considerably higher.

BY RAIL Trains have greatly improved in the past decade, and cover the north and east of the country fairly comprehensively. They're about the same price as buses or slightly cheaper, for any given distance, but can be faster (inter-city, *brzi*) or slower (local trains, *putnički*). Trains can get very crowded, especially in summer, but they tend to be reasonably punctual. Local trains (the ones not marked in red on timetables) are usually much less crowded, and much less punctual. The high-speed line between Zagreb and Split has been dogged with problems (including a major accident in 2009), but has reduced the journey time between the two cities to around 5½ hours.

For all trains, buy tickets in advance (unless there's no ticket office); you'll pay a surcharge if you wait until you're on board. *Dolazak* means arrivals, while both *odlazak* and *polazak* mean departures. *Blagajna* is where you buy your tickets.

Major railway stations all have left-luggage facilities, normally costing around 15kn a day per piece of luggage. Don't lose your receipts or you'll have a terrible time recovering your bags.

If you have access to the internet, you'll find all the timetables at the Croatia Railways website (*www.hznet.hr*), recently revamped and now less user-friendly than it was before. Ho hum.

BY BUS The bus network is wide-ranging, reliable and regular, and operated – as in Switzerland – by a well-organised federated system of interconnected small companies. Buses offer the best way of coming into contact with local people, and are the only way of travelling on public transport along the coast and on the islands. The hourly average speed clocks in at about 45km/h on the coast, though much faster on motorways, and costs somewhere around 50kn per 100km, though prices and speeds vary quite a bit depending on the route. Buses that go on ferries to the islands include the ferry fare in the cost of the ticket.

On major routes – such as Zagreb to Rijeka or Zadar, for example – buses leave every hour or even more frequently; in more remote areas, they may only run once or twice a day, or even once or twice a week, to coincide with local needs.

If a bus originates in the town you're leaving from, then you can buy tickets and make reservations at the bus station, and you should do this a day or more ahead if you can. Otherwise, wait for the bus to arrive and either pay the conductor as you get on or pay once you're underway. If you can't get a reservation, don't buy a ticket – with several companies often plying each route, it's sensible not to lock yourself in to any particular one until you're sure of being able to travel.

Luggage is stored in the holds under the bus, and you'll pay a small supplement (often around 10kn) for this. The price seems to be entirely arbitrary and provides you with paltry insurance, but it's an amount sufficiently large for the bus company not to want to lose, however, so your luggage should be guarded safely.

If your bus breaks down – it happens – the chances are someone will be called to come and repair it on the roadside, and if necessary you'll be transferred to another bus – in which case, you should obviously take all your bags with you.

Buses stop every two hours or so for a *pausa*, and the conductor shouts out the duration of this above the din: *pet*, *deset*, *petnaest* and *dvadeset minuta* are the commonest break lengths (5, 10, 15 and 20 minutes). These invariably occur where you can grab a quick drink/snack/meal. Watch the driver and you won't go far wrong, but be warned that the bus will go without you if you've made a mistake. Buses sometimes change drivers at these stops – this would have caught me out on a couple of occasions, were it not for the helpfulness of fellow passengers.

It's sometimes difficult – particularly inland – to obtain reliable information on bus departures. Sometimes this is out of helpful ignorance, sometimes from a willingness to please. If it's known you want a bus at 11.00, you may be told there is one, just to make you feel better. Ask several sources open rather than closed questions (ie: 'What time is the bus to Koprivnica?' as opposed to 'Is there a bus to Koprivnica early tomorrow morning?') and you may find a consensus building up.

Another problem you may encounter is localised information, meaning that if you have to change buses to get to your destination, you may not be able to find out the timings for the second part of the journey before you get there. There's not much you can do about this.

For bus timetables see www.autobusni-kolodvor.com, or if travelling to/from Zagreb, the excellent www.akz.hr.

BY CAR The most comfortable and often quickest way of travelling is by car, and sometimes it's the only way to get somewhere really remote. Road quality has improved enormously in the 25-odd years since I first drove in Croatia, and there are now several good sections of motorway open – you'll pay tolls on these, though they're not excessive (for prices see http://hac.hr/en/toll-rates/pricelist). The most expensive stretch, the 380km from Zagreb to Split (Dugopolje exit), costs 174kn, while the 40km bit of motorway from Karlovac to Zagreb is 19kn, and the toll bridge across to the island of Krk costs 35kn. For more on Croatian motorways and tolls see www.hac.hr. Fuel costs around 11kn per litre.

Inland, the roads are less well maintained than you'd expect in western Europe (and often unpaved in really remote areas), while along the coast the single-lane Magistrala, running from Rijeka to Dubrovnik, inevitably clogs up in summer with holiday traffic – though the opening of the new motorway from Zagreb to Zadar and Split has alleviated the problem to some extent, and at some point soon (though nobody can say when – it was still incomplete in autumn 2015) the fast road should extend all the way to Dubrovnik.

Street parking in cities is a non-starter (pay instead for public parking) and parking anywhere along the coast can be a major hassle in high season.

You may find Croatian drivers rather ambitious – to the extent that blind corners and oncoming traffic aren't seen as a natural impediment to overtaking – but don't be competitive; the omnipresent (and omnipotent) traffic police are quick to keep drivers in line with steep fines and worse. Speed limits – 50km/h in built-up areas; 90km/h out of town (locally variable; keep your eyes peeled) and 130km/h on the motorway – are strictly enforced.

In the event of an accident or breakdown, you can call the Croatian Automobile Club's hotline (↺ 987; *www.hak.hr*). If you see someone else in need of assistance, you're legally obliged to stop and help. And remember: it's illegal for drunks or children under 12 to sit in the front of the car; the blood alcohol limit is 0.05%, or zero for drivers under the age of 24 (it was zero for all drivers until recently); all passengers must wear seat belts; it's illegal to drive while using a mobile phone; and headlights must be on at all times.

IN THE EVENT OF AN ACCIDENT

If you have an accident – even a small one – there's a 99% chance the police will be called, and (just my opinion, this) a 95% chance that you'll be found to be in the wrong. When I had a minor crash in Đakovo, admittedly back in 2002. I was told by the only English speaker in town (a 14-year-old boy) that I would be charged, and then taken to court the following day and punished. He was right – but he hadn't seen the accident, or assessed the damage.

If you're away from the coast (as I was) and a non-Croatian speaker, the police process after an accident can be long, confusing and traumatic – probably for the police, as well; it can't be easy when even the simplest questions aren't eliciting responses.

From the time of the accident, until the court hearing 24 hours later, I had no idea what was going on, through hours of questioning and the confiscation of my passport. I wasn't allowed to phone anyone myself (any of my Croatian friends would have been able to help me) and the police wouldn't call anyone for me, though it's important to say that they were courteous at all times. I wasn't allowed to go to the hotel until I'd signed various incomprehensible statements – and although these turned out to be anodyne, I didn't know this until the following day.

At the court, an English-speaking interpreter was provided, and she talked me through the accusation, and translated my responses to the judge. After some reflection, the judge explained that if I pleaded guilty I would probably get the minimum fine, but that if I pleaded not guilty I would have to wait for the full court to be in session. Given that it was a Saturday, I pleaded guilty, was fined €100 plus (very reasonable) court costs, and was soon on my way.

To source car parts or fix problems, your first port of call should be a petrol station – these are usually open from dawn until dusk, though on some main roads and in big cities there are 24-hour outlets. Try to ensure your car's roadworthy and insured against fatal breakdown, however. Although parts are in better supply and repairs more quickly effected than they used to be, it can still be an expensive and time-consuming business.

Car hire Car hire in Croatia isn't especially expensive, as long as you book ahead, from outside the country – count on spending from €300 a week with full insurance and unlimited mileage. The major companies are represented in all the main population centres and the most popular tourist destinations, as well as at airports, and increasingly don't hit you for a huge penalty if you pick up and drop off at different places – and there are some good, cheap local companies as well. For details of car hire companies in Zagreb, see page 83.

BY BICYCLE
Sadly, as a keen cyclist, I have to report that (with a few exceptions listed below) the main roads of mainland Croatia are still not very cycle-friendly. Courtesy is in short supply, traffic density is too high for comfort, and along the coast there isn't even the alternative of small roads or cycle paths to choose from. You should do anything you possibly can to avoid the Magistrala – it's not just busy, but downright dangerous, particularly in summer.

One way of doing this is to be clever with ferries and the islands, which are absolutely superb for cyclists. Central Dalmatia, in particular, has taken an excellent initiative in publishing a great series of maps entitled 'Central Dalmatia by Bike', which covers the islands of Šolta, Brač, Hvar and Vis, with suggested routes and route-profiles provided. Zagreb County has also published a fine series of cycle routes/maps and there's a fine 'Bike and Bed' initiative (*http://mojbicikl.hr/bike-bed*), which lists cycle-friendly places that aren't too far apart from one another. Other good cycling maps include the HGSS map of Brač. Top prize for cycle initiatives however must go to Istria, which has a wealth of information online at www.istria-bike.com, a series of maps, and the excellent (and increasingly well-known internationally) Parenzana route.

Cycle touring can also be a great way of visiting the interior, and remains an excellent way of getting to meet local people. There are innumerable little Croatian villages connected by roads that aren't even on the map because they don't carry any traffic, but you do need to be good at navigating, and well provisioned, as road signs are in short supply. Make sure you have decent off-road tyres, too, as surfaces are highly variable (and often gravel rather than tar). The 4x4 tracks and forest roads of Velebit and Gorski kotar are a good place for mountain biking, as is the Kalifron Peninsula on Rab and the Kabal Peninsula on Hvar.

HITCHHIKING
Definitely not a recommended option. Tourists are unlikely to pick you up and locals tend to be travelling very short distances.

WALKING AND HIKING
Walking is the slowest but most interesting way of getting around – you could follow in the footsteps of Patrick Leigh Fermor, who walked from the Hook of Holland to Constantinople in 18 months in 1933 and 1934. Plan on taking more money than he did though – he survived on a pound a week.

Croatia is a country ideally suited to the walker, with lots of national parks and nature reserves, and marked trails that range from the gentle stroll to the strenuous hike. A network of local and national walking, climbing and mountain associations keeps the paths in good repair, and staffs and maintains the mountain huts and lodges.

Hiking in the Velebit karst is a lot like walking in the Alps or the Dolomites. Even though Velebit is considerably lower, it shares the fairly hard climate and there's generally not much surface water around, winter or summer. You need to be well equipped and have plenty of food and water with you if you're hiking here, but it is some of the most rewarding walking I've ever done.

North of Velebit, the mountains are lower and less harsh (in Gorski Kotar, for example) and more heavily forested, while the mountains of Slavonia, between the Drava and Sava rivers, are different altogether. Here, you can find rich vegetation and plenty of water, and the softer, older mountains make for excellent hillwalking.

If you're going to focus on walking, consider getting hold of Rudolf Abraham's *The Islands of Croatia* or *Walking in Croatia*, or Sandra Bardwell's *Croatia: Car Tours and Walks*, which have a whole range of hikes from the easy to the demanding, covering most of the coast and islands (page 429).

Mountain safety Up in the mountains, in regions where the regular emergency services don't operate, you can call on the help of Croatia's mountain rescue service, the GSS (Gorska Služba Spašavanja, *www.gss.hr*), if you're in real trouble. Like mountain rescue people anywhere, the volunteers who staff the service won't be amused if you call them out for no good reason, but will willingly risk life and limb to bring you to safety if needed.

You can reach the GSS through the nearest information point or via a police station (call ✆ 92), or by calling ✆ 112. You can also contact the GSS through one of its local offices, which are listed on its website (*Gospić* ✆ *091 721 0007; Split* ✆ *091 721 0001; Rijeka* ✆ *091 721 0000; Delnice* ✆ *091 721 0004; Zadar* ✆ *091 721 0010; Zagreb* ✆ *091 721 0002*), or through the head office of the Croatian Mountaineering Association (*Hrvatski Planinarski Savez or HPS;* ✆ *01 482 3624; www.hps.hr*). If you're well equipped with enough clothing, food, water, maps and a compass, the chances are you won't need to make that call.

Marked trails Most of the trails in the national parks and nature reserves are well marked using a painted red circle with a white dot in the middle, or two red lines separated by a white line. The markings are maintained by local hiking and mountaineering associations, and are usually very clear, but if you're in a remote or rarely accessed part of the mountains, then you may find markings worn or damaged, especially if there's no mountain lodge nearby. Occasionally, you'll find trails where trees have been cut down, leaving the way ahead uncertain – try to make sure you have a local map (pages 37–8) and a compass with you in any case.

BY FERRY There are few experiences more pleasant than a ferry ride on the Adriatic, and in Croatia they're plentiful, economical, regular and reliable. Most domestic services are run by state-owned Jadrolinija (*www.jadrolinija.hr*), though in summer other local operators provide supplementary services.

Services vary from the roll-on, roll-off ferries used for very short hops between the coast and the nearest islands, to fast hydrofoils and catamarans, to the huge ships that ply the whole length of the coast from Rijeka to Split and Dubrovnik, once a day in each direction.

Local ferries are inexpensive – typical passenger fares are usually between 10kn and 60kn, while catamaran prices are normally a little higher, with prices dropping

2

around 20% in low season. Sample (high season) passenger fares include: 33kn Split–Supetar; 47kn Split–Stari Grad; 54kn Split–Vis; 59kn Zadar–Mali Lošinj; 55kn Split–Bol (catamaran); and 80kn Rijeka–Novalja (catamaran).

Taking your car to the islands needn't break the bank. Short hops are charged at under 100kn, while medium-length journeys cost from 160–530kn (eg: 160kn Split–Supetar; 370kn Split–Vis; 530kn Split–Vela Luka). Trailers and camper vans increase the price more.

However, many of the islands have perfectly serviceable local bus routes, and it's worth asking yourself whether taking your own car to the islands is really necessary (the updater has been managing just fine on the islands without a car for over 15 years).

BY BOAT: SAILING, YACHTING AND MOTOR-CRUISING Whether you have your own boat or whether you've chartered one, and whether you're travelling by steam or by sail, there's really no better way of seeing Croatia's wealth of islands. Once you've swallowed the costs associated with the boat itself (and here the sky really is the limit), a sailing or boating holiday is (or can be) quite reasonable, with the only significant outlays being food, drink and marina expenses.

The coast and islands between Split and Dubrovnik are on the whole less crowded than the north, and are most popular with English speakers – though English is widely spoken among the whole sailing community. The Kvarner Bay is understandably preferred by Germans and Austrians, being much closer to home, while the Italians love it all, from north to south. Friends who sailed here compared it to sailing in Greece 20 years earlier, with uncrowded waters, hospitable marinas and local restaurants, and wonderfully picturesque villages and fortified historical towns – though the 'uncrowded' part of this statement, at least when it comes to marinas, is not as true today.

Sailing and yachting experience The type of sailing or yachting holiday you embark on will depend at least to some extent on your level of experience. Beginners can be catered for either by a pre-arranged package (page 31) or by having more experienced friends, but bear in mind that a week on board in a confined space can strain even close friendships, so choose carefully. Once you're on board, the captain's word really is final – if he or she says jump, you jump.

Learning-to-sail holidays cost from around £500–650 per person for a week, or £700–1,000 for a fortnight, including flights from London.

If you're at an intermediate level, and at least one member of your crew is reasonably experienced, then sailing in a flotilla is an excellent way of improving your sailing skills, while not having to worry too much about navigation or the *bura* (that gusty northeasterly wind) around the corner. Boats can be chartered by between two and eight people, with the cost decreasing as the numbers go up. Expect to pay upwards of £1,000 per person for a week at the height of the season if there are just two of you, but around £500 per person if you're a party of eight in May or September, both including flights from London.

Take the experience requirements for renting a boat seriously, even if not all the charter companies are diligent about checking. Sailing is a tremendous activity, but it's also potentially hazardous and even life-threatening, so make sure you – or people in your party – have the necessary skills. Most charter companies won't need to see certificates (not all countries issue them anyway), but you may be asked to demonstrate your ability before heading out into open waters unaccompanied.

An alternative is to hire a local skipper with your boat – a good idea if no one in your group has the requisite experience, and a great way of finding hidden nooks and crannies in the islands. Expect to pay £400–500 a week for the services of a skipper.

Charters Most people will end up chartering a boat, and there are plenty of charter companies to choose from – over 150 at the time of writing. Around 14,000 vessels are available in total, with 10,000 of these being sailing boats and the rest motorboats. One recommended outfit is Gardelin Charters in Zadar (m *098 378 082; www.gardelin.hr*).

During the war of the early 1990s, many boats left Croatia for havens in Italy and Greece, and some have yet to return, so there's a greater demand than supply for charters. Even if you do book early, you may find boats in less good condition than you were expecting, with the charter business still somewhat in recovery mode.

Price depends on model, size, capacity and season, starting from around £500 a week for a three- to four-berth boat in low season and escalating rapidly up to the thousands for an eight-berth yacht in August. In the summer of 2015, you could expect to pay €1,000 per week for a six-berth, 12.35m Bavaria 40 sailing boat, and €1,750 per week for an eight-berth, 12.35m Bavaria 41.

Mooring Croatia's Association of Nautical Tourism, based in Rijeka, has a total of 48 marinas with some 12,500 sea moorings. The full list, along with all their facilities and individual websites (where available), can be found on the tourist board's new but woefully confusing website. Go to www.croatia.hr, then select Nautical. The Adriatic Croatia International Club (known everywhere as ACI), based in Opatija, runs 22 of these (the majority of them all year around) and has an excellent website (*www.aci-marinas.com*) listing fees, locations and facilities.

Marinas tend to be well equipped, with restaurants, bars and shops either on-site or nearby, and good technical services. Be aware that not all charter boats have shore power installations, even though electricity is usually available. Many marinas also have hot showers and some have laundry facilities. Sample ACI day rates in high season run from 92kn for small craft in Pula to 307kn in Split, and around two thirds this amount during the winter.

An alternative to marinas is mooring 'stern-to' in the smaller ports. You can also find mooring lines in some harbours, while remoter restaurants seeking sea-trade will put out mooring lines to encourage you in. Ports and bays are sometimes free, but can charge variable fees depending on the length of the boat and how much jetty you're occupying – they're meant to provide services (such as rubbish collection, and the supply of groceries), and a receipt, in return.

Provisions/restaurants Keeping yourself in food and drink shouldn't be a problem. You can stock up on speciality items in supermarkets in towns, but you'll also find plenty of street markets and small shops in the villages on the islands. If there's been a prolonged spell of bad weather and there isn't a ferry service you may find it hard to get bread or fresh fruit, but it's very unlikely to affect you during the summer sailing season.

Restaurants, especially on the smaller islands, tend to be good value, with local wines and cheeses recommended, and you're more likely to find the homely *konoba* (low-key restaurant) here than on the mainland.

Water and fuel Watering and fuelling isn't usually a problem, with all marinas and most ports having abundant supplies of both, though you may have to scout

2

around to find the right person responsible for supplying water to boats. Some islands, however, have no water supply of their own, so don't expect to fill up here.

Charts and guides Croatian waters are very well charted, and Croatian, English, German and Italian charts are available. The Croatian sea charts come well recommended, and can be bought in most marinas and harbours once you're there. If you want to do some advance reconnoitring, you should be able to order charts from Kelvin Hughes Charts & Maritime Supplies (\ *+44 19 9280 5300; www.kelvinhughes.com*), which has offices in London, Copenhagen, New Orleans, Rotterdam, Singapore and elsewhere.

If that doesn't work out, you can go direct to the publisher (*Hrvatski Hidrografski Institut, Zrinsko-Frankopanska 161, 21000 Split;* \ *021 308 800;* e *office@hhi.hr; www.hhi.hr*), or Plovput, the government agency that looks after all the lighthouses, beacons etc (*Plovput, Obala Lazareta 1, 21000 Split;* \ *021 390 600;* e *plovput@ plovput.hr; www.plovput.hr*).

Also highly recommended comes the *Adriatic Pilot*, which is now in its sixth edition. This 500-page nautical guide to the Adriatic comes in at £32.50, and is well worth the expense. Another useful book is *777 Harbours and Anchorages: Croatia, Slovenia & Montenegro*, now in its fifth edition. Both are available through Imray (\ *+44 1480 462 114;* e *ilnw@imray.com; www.imray.com*).

Winds If you're sailing outside the summer months, you'll need to keep a weather-eye out for the bura, and the jugo (a warm, humid, east-southeasterly, accompanied by heavy clouds and rain). Once winter's over, you can expect lighter winds and better weather, though during July and August storms are more frequent, and during September winds strengthen again.

Summer is characterised by the prevailing mistral (maestral), which is no relation of the Provençal horror. The mistral here is a sailor's dream, a fair-weather wind that springs up locally mid-morning, strengthens until the early afternoon and then dies down at sunset.

The summer bura is more localised and much less persistent than the winter version, springing up in sudden squalls and capable of gale-force strength, particularly in the Gulf of Trieste and the Velebit Channel. Fortunately, it's very reliably forecast, so listen carefully to the weather bulletins on the radio and head for a well-sheltered port if a bura's on the way.

The summer jugo is also mostly a local wind, and is more frequent in the south than the north. Be warned it can switch quickly to a bura – something to be borne in mind if you're in a mooring exposed to the northeast.

Weather forecasts/safety Marinas always have the latest forecasts available, but Croatia also has three coastal radio stations that broadcast excellent weather reports – particularly for the bura – and warning announcements in both Croatian and English, several times a day. They receive radio-telephone messages round the clock and re-broadcast these, so stay tuned to whichever station is nearest. All operate on VHF channel 17. They also operate on the following channels, with weather updates at the following times:

Dubrovnik Radio VHF channels 04, 07 – at 06.25, 13.20 & 21.20
Rijeka Radio VHF channel 24 – at 05.35, 14.35 & 19.35

Split Radio VHF channels 07, 21, 23, 28 – at 05.45, 12.45 & 19.45

After the weather, the coastal radio stations broadcast nautical warning messages, with information on obstacles to navigation, lighthouse failures, prohibited areas etc. Continuous weather forecasts are also issued by harbour offices and at www.meteo.hr.

During the day, you can usually contact marinas on VHF channel 17, while harbourmasters' offices are on channel 10. Harbourmasters tend to have their own patrol boats, which can be used to help boats in distress, and (as elsewhere) they can also call on the help of any suitable ship in the vicinity, including foreign boats. For a list of harbourmasters' offices and port authorities, with contact details, see www.mppi.hr.

If you run into trouble, it's worth knowing that the radio-telephone is more likely to get you help than a CB-radio distress signal, as the authorities aren't usually tuned into CB channels.

ACCOMMODATION

Thanks to its popularity with tourists in the 1970s and 1980s, Croatia has a good supply of accommodation, coming in a range of flavours – private rooms and apartments, hotels, family-run pensions and B&Bs, farmsteads, campsites, hostels and mountain lodges.

Private rooms and apartments offer the best value for money, but if you're in the mood to splash out there's little to beat the old-fashioned luxury of the grand hotels of the Austro-Hungarian era in old resorts like Opatija. Most hotels on the coast and islands were built in the tourist boom of the 1970s, though the great majority have been upgraded and well restored since the war of the early 1990s, and there's a whole wealth of smaller, smarter hotels and swish five-star establishments opening up around the country.

Hotel accommodation and campsites in the main resorts fill up fast in summer, so you need to reserve well ahead of time (phone ahead – weekdays between 08.00 and 14.00 are your best bet – and confirm by email). Turning up on the fly in high season in Poreč can be a disappointing experience.

These days there are also plenty of hostels to choose from, providing another good budget option.

In a category all of its own, you could also choose to holiday in a lighthouse, of which there are 11. Pictures and descriptions are available at www.croatia.hr or

NOTE ON PRICES

Accommodation prices in this guide are given in price brackets, which represent the price of a standard double room (hotel, pansion, etc) in high season (July/August); expect prices to drop by something like 10–15% in June/September, and considerably more off season. Accommodation prices are given in euros, as this is often the currency used in pre-negotiations, reservations and official accommodation quotations – although your final bill usually will be in kuna. All prices were correct as of autumn 2015.

Exclusive	€€€€€	€150+	1,145kn+
Upmarket	€€€€	€90–150	690–1,137kn
Mid-range	€€€	€60–90	462–682kn
Budget	€€	€40–60	310–455kn
Shoestring	€	up to €40	< 302kn

www.lighthouses-croatia.com – for further information and bookings, you should contact Hrvoje Mandekić at Plovput (☎ *021 390 609;* e *turizam@plovput.hr; www. lighthouses-croatia.com*).

PRIVATE ROOMS/APARTMENTS Anywhere that sees regular tourists has a supply of private rooms (*privatne sobe*) available, and for most independent travellers these represent the best-value accommodation option. They are the equivalent of B&Bs in the UK (though usually without breakfast), and are generally clean, comfortable and friendly. Their big advantage over hotels – other than reduced cost (many private rooms go for under €50 a night) – is that they offer you a chance to meet local people, though in the most popular places families are showing a tendency to insulate themselves from their lodgers.

Rooms can be sourced through local travel agencies (or through the tourist office, where there aren't agencies), but you can often save money by stopping anywhere you see signs saying *sobe/zimmer/chambres/camere/rooms/privat*.

Where buses, trains and ferries arrive in the main destinations – and notably in Split and Dubrovnik – gaggles of touts will be on hand to offer you rooms. Check both the price and location carefully, but these can be a good bargain, especially if you're staying for only a couple of nights. Through official channels, a 30–50% surcharge is usually applied for stays of only one or two nights, but if you're negotiating direct with the owner a lot will depend on the time of year and how busy a place is. Singles in theory get a double room for around 70% of the full price, but in a seller's market you may end up paying the full whack.

Private rooms are classified by the local tourist office and come in three categories: I, II and III. Category I rooms will be clean and functional, but you'll almost certainly be sharing a bathroom. In Category II, you'll be bathing en suite and may even have a TV, while in Category III you'll be in some luxury.

Private accommodation also includes apartments, which can be great value for families or small groups, but check how many beds have been crammed into each room before you buy. More expensive apartments tend to be better located rather than roomier.

Inland, there's also a healthy move towards eco- or agro-tourism, with rooms being available in farmhouses and small villages. This is a nascent trend and not yet well established, but look out for signs if you're in the countryside.

Finally, with both private rooms and apartments don't be afraid to say no if you don't like the look of the place – staying somewhere that doesn't suit you can really spoil your holiday.

A couple of good places to look for private rooms and apartments are www. gdjenamore.com and www.apartmanija.hr, many places are listed on Booking.com and an increasing number are also being offered through AirBnB (*www.airbnb.com*).

HOTELS Croatia's numerous hotels are classified by the standard international one- to five-star system, though at the lower end they don't represent very good value for money when compared with the better private rooms, which generally cost around half the price of the worst hotel in any particular town (though notably not in Zagreb and Dubrovnik).

Many establishments are still of the large, modern and functional variety, though there is a groundswell of smaller, family-run hotels and top-end five-star places appearing. Assuming you can't afford the Habsburg opulence of one of the few pre-World War I hotels still in operation, the smaller hotels are often the nicest places to stay, though rooms need to be booked well in advance. Most of the bigger hotels

– which is where you're likely to be if you're on a package – have been substantially upgraded since 1995, so you're unlikely to experience the cracked plaster, 1970s light fittings and intermittent hot water that made Croatian accommodation such an unlucky dip in the 1980s.

Breakfast is almost invariably included in the room price, and ranges from rolls, butter and jam to a full buffet, with a strong correlation between the quality of the food and the number of stars. You can save a fair amount of money by opting for half or full board – the supplement is usually only small, under €10 – but bear in mind you'd be limiting yourself to eating meals in the hotel, rather than getting out and about.

CAMPING In a country with fine weather and beautiful countryside, camping ought to be the ideal option. It ought to be, but it isn't always. Campsites are not especially cheap (usually not far behind a private room), and sites are often huge and far removed from easy access by public transport. Some of the places you're most likely to visit – notably Split – don't have campsites at all.

The explanation is a simple one – camping is mainly aimed at northern Europeans with their own transport, who come for a week or two and set up a temporary base on the beach. And if that's what you want to do, then you'll find Croatia's campsites friendly, clean and very well equipped. Expect to pay upwards of €25 a night for two people, a pitch and a parking space at an *autokamp*.

Freelance camping in Croatia is illegal and, if you're caught, you'll be subject to an immediate and fairly hefty fine. If you're off the beaten track and camping independently, however, then please, please don't let it be you that starts off the forest fire. Many areas of the country, especially in the mountains and on the islands, have no free water supply, and fires are a major hazard – so much so that in some areas even smoking is forbidden (in a country that is smoking-mad). Huge areas of forest – and more than one mountain lodge – have been devastated by fire.

YOUTH HOSTELS AND STUDENT DORMITORIES Croatia has only a handful of officially recognised youth hostels (*www.hfhs.hr*), but with summer prices averaging under €15 a head it can be easily the most economical option for single travellers (if you're in Zagreb, Pula, Rijeka, Zadar, Dubrovnik, Veli Lošinj, Krk or Punat). In recent years a new breed of smart, user-friendly hostels have started springing up all over the place (Zagreb, Pula, Zadar, Dubrovnik, Karlovac, to name just a few places), which in many cases offer several double rooms with en suites. For two or more people travelling together, however, private accommodation can still be both more convenient – no daytime lockout, for example – and competitive on price, so shop around.

At Zagreb University, there's some access to student accommodation in summer, but it's not especially good value unless you're travelling alone. Rooms go for around €20 a head, and can be organised via the tourist office.

MOUNTAIN LODGES Croatia has over 100 mountain huts and lodges, with facilities ranging from the basic (roof and walls) to the positively hotel-like. They're excellent value for money and are usually run by the local mountain associations under the auspices of the Croatian Mountaineering Association (*Hrvatski Planinarski Savez, HPS, Kozarčeva 22, Zagreb;* ☏ *01 482 4142 or 01 482 3624;* e *hps@plsavez.hr; www. hps.hr/info/planinarske-kuce*) where you'll find a full list of the accommodation available, along with altitudes and contact numbers. You can also ask at the various park offices around the country.

Huts usually fall into the following three categories: *planinarski/dom* (staffed mountain hut), *planinarska kuća* (hut open only by prior arrangement), and *sklonište* (basic unstaffed shelter, usually open all year).

EATING AND DRINKING

What you eat and drink in Croatia will depend on where you are – in Slavonia, along the Hungarian border, you can expect to find spicy sausages and heavy, meaty soups, while along the coast you'll find an Italian flavour to the food, with plentiful pizza, pasta and fish dishes, followed by lashings of ice cream. What you're unlikely to find these days, sadly, is Hoppel Poppel on the menu. According to my trusty 1966 Gateway Guide, 'Hoppel Poppel, which the visitor feels inclined to tackle straight away because the name sounds so amusing and exotic, turns out to be a well-known international dish – hash.' Each region has its own wines and beers to be proud of, and across the country you'll find a range of fearsome spirits, designed to warm the cockles and cement friendships.

FOOD If you're in a hotel, then breakfast of some sort will invariably be included in the price – usually in the form of a self-service buffet, with the quality and variety of fare on offer closely correlating to the number of stars.

If you're in a private room, you can rely on cafés and cake shops (*slastičarnice*) to sell you pastries and cakes for breakfast, and if you're outside the most touristed areas you may still find *burek*, a pastry filled with cheese (*sa sirom*), meat (*sa mesom*) and just occasionally spinach (*špinat*). Burek is cheap, filling and usually delicious – if occasionally too greasy for comfort.

You'll also find cheap restaurants and **snack bars** everywhere – often billed as *bife* (bar) or *roštilj* (grill bar) – serving up lunch or dinner of *ćevapčići* (spiced meatballs or small sausages, usually accompanied by spring onions and spicy green peppers), *pljeskavica* (a wad of minced meat often served in pitta bread – the Croatian hamburger), or *ražnjići* (kebab). Try any of these dishes with rich, smoky *ajvar*, a sauce made from tomatoes, peppers and aubergines.

Bakeries (*pekarnica*) sell a wide variety of breads (though occasionally only powdery white rolls and plain loaves) and sometimes offer ready-made sandwiches (*sendvići*) available with cheese (*sir*) or ham (*šunka*) fillings. Street markets (*tržnica*) will provide you with the usual fare for picnics, and you can ask for sandwiches to be made up to order at any deli counter in a supermarket (*samospluga*) – just point at the type of bread you want filled, say '*sendvič*' and point at your choice of filling.

Pizzerias are the next step up the food chain, and represent great value for money – though on the coast and islands, you can expect them to be significantly more expensive than inland. Pizza here is close to what you get in Italy, with a thin crust and a variety of toppings. Pizzerias also tend to do good (and keenly priced) pasta dishes – though personally, I tend to find Croatian pasta cooked closer to soggy than al dente.

Restaurants (*restoran*, *konoba* or *gostiona*) tend to focus on meat and/or fish dishes. Meat isn't especially exciting, leaning towards pork and lamb chops and cutlets, pan-fried veal, or steak, but it's generally tasty enough. Fish for its part is ubiquitous and delicious – but can turn out to be pricey. For most white fish, you'll pay by the raw weight, and a decent-sized fish for two can come in at as much as 400kn on its own. Whitebait, blue fish (sardines, mackerel, etc) and squid are, on the other hand, a lot cheaper.

Shellfish is especially popular on the coast, with steamed mussels on many menus and cockles appearing in pasta dishes and starters, and in winter (through to mid-May) you can get great oysters in the south (from Ston). You may also see crab and lobster on the menu – but mind the price tag (and watch out for mis-translations; crayfish is often billed as lobster). Finally, you'll see plenty of *škampi* (grilled or cooked in a tomato '*buzzara*' sauce, though you may get shrimps rather than scampi or king prawns) and *crni rižot* (literally black risotto) on offer; the latter is a delicious, pungent dish, made with cuttlefish ink, and though it's popular it's not to everyone's taste.

You'll see the term *ispod peka* on many menus – this is a delicious traditional method of cooking octopus or lamb, by slow roasting it under an iron bowl over hot coals. You'll also see lots of *pršut*, Croatia's answer to Italy's prosciutto, and pronounced (and produced) in almost exactly the same way. The air-dried ham is an Istrian and Dalmatian speciality and practically melts in the mouth when sliced thinly enough – which generally it isn't.

Of course if you're **vegetarian**, *pršut*, like much else on the menu, is a non-starter – indeed it's a non-main and a non-dessert, too. However, vegetarian options have improved greatly in recent years, and there are now some excellent vegetarian and vegan restaurants to choose from, such as Zrno and Vegehop (both in Zagreb; pages 99 and 100) and Makrovega (Split; page 311). Two good places to search for vegetarian and/or vegan dining options are www.happycow.net/europe/croatia and www.prijatelji-zivotinja.hr/index.en. Even where restaurants don't offer specific vegetarian options, you can always get a cheese omelette (*omlet sa sirom*), a meat-free pasta dish, or a pizza, along with a range of salads. There are also a number of homemade cheeses, which vary from the tastily pungent to the surprisingly bland (though these, like most cheeses, will in most cases be made with rennet, which will of course be off the menu for strict vegetarians). A must-try is the slightly salty, hard sheep cheese from the island of Pag, *Paški sir*.

For basic restaurant vocabulary, see pages 424–7.

DRINK The most important thing you need to know is that you can drink the water – all publicly supplied water is safe unless it explicitly says otherwise. The next piece of good news for drinkers is that alcohol is pretty inexpensive when compared to northern Europe, with a half-litre of draught beer (pivo) costing anything from 10 to 20kn, depending on the establishment. Premium brands go for a little more, but local beers are just great, our personal favourites being Ožujsko (from Zagreb) and Karlovačko (from Karlovac) – although the quality of the latter seems to have dropped in the past couple of years. The best beer in Croatia is brewed by Pivnica Medvedgrad in Zagreb, a small brewery producing some outstanding beers which are available in its two restaurants in Zagreb (page 98).

Wine Croatia makes lots of wine (*vino*), and the quality – drinkable at worst – continues to improve. Almost the entire production is guzzled down domestically, however, so you're very unlikely to see it on the supermarket shelves at home – though reds have long been imported into Germany, and Istrian whites are increasingly making an appearance in the UK. Equally, you won't see much in the way of non-local wine on menus or in the shops, so you're pretty much obliged to go the Croatian way.

In shops, you can pay anything from 35 to 500kn for a bottle, while in most pizzerias and restaurants a litre of the house red or white goes for 50–100kn and bottled wines start at around 80kn and head rapidly up from there. Swankier establishments don't always sell house wine (it's worth asking, however, even if it's not on the menu), and you can easily find yourself spending upwards of 200kn a bottle. Istrian Malvazija is excellent and you'll have no trouble finding this in Istria and increasingly elsewhere. Otherwise, Graševina (a white grape variety from Slavonia) tends to dominate local restaurant tables, and in most cases makes a good table wine. If given a choice it's worth making the effort to try some of the local Rieslings or Chardonnays too – or the excellent Vrbnička Zlahtina from the island of Krk, or Grk from Korčula. If you like your reds, try the sublime Dingač, which is made from *plavac mali* grapes grown on the Pelješac peninsula – but prepare to pay upwards of 150kn a bottle in a supermarket or 250kn in a restaurant.

Spirits (*rakija*)

Spirits are common, dangerous, and fairly cheap. In supermarkets you'll find brandies and other spirits at around 70–100kn a bottle, but you can also buy fiery and frequently excellent home-distilled spirits – especially *travarica*, a drink featuring a lot of alcohol and a few herbs – in the markets for anything from 50 to 100kn a bottle. The quality of spirits varies enormously and can't usually be determined from the label – price is a reasonable (but far from infallible) indicator. A personal favourite is Velebitska Travarica, which is made by monks up in the mountains and comes in an especially attractive bottle. On the other hand do anything you can to avoid a drink called Pelinkovac. I once had three in a row in Zagreb, convinced that at some point the apparently rebottled wood stain would become palatable – but it never did. It brings a bad taste to the mouth even now, just writing about it.

Friendships, business deals and meetings are all cemented with rakija, and it's surprising how often you'll find yourself expected to down lethal drinks. If you don't drink at all, then it's not a bad idea to come up with a plausible reason why not (health is always a reliable standby), as Croatians tend to be suspicious of anyone who won't join in.

Soft drinks

In marked contrast to the abundance of alcoholic choice, there are surprisingly few soft drinks available. Cola is of course mind-numbingly popular and bottles of sweet fizzy orange are ubiquitous. In the most popular tourist spots along the coast there's a better range of drinks now available – largely due to the presence of Italians here – but otherwise the most exotic thing you'll find will be the delicious homemade lemonade sometimes available with your morning pastry.

Coffee and tea

Coffee is as popular here as everywhere, and in cafés tends to be excellent – though what you'll be served with breakfast in the lower-end hotels can be frankly disgusting. Tea is most often of the fruit variety or comes in dodgy-looking bags that tend to work better with lemon than milk. Ordinary 'English' tea is known as black tea (*crni čaj*), but don't expect to find anything you'll be able to stand a spoon in unless you bring your own. Tea and coffee will cost anything from 7kn to 20kn in a café, depending on the upmarketness (or otherwise) of the establishment. If you want a latte-style coffee ask for a bijela *kava*; for decaf – increasingly available – ask for *bez kofeina*.

PUBLIC HOLIDAYS AND FESTIVALS

Croatia has the usual mix of religious and secular public holidays, as well as innumerable feast days, folk festivals and annual cultural events. Specifics are covered in the relevant sections, but the national holidays and a few of the festivals are included here.

NATIONAL HOLIDAYS You should expect banks and shops to be closed on Croatia's national holidays, which fall as follows:

1 January	New Year's Day
3 February	St Blaise's Day
Easter	27 March 2016, 16 April 2017, 1 April 2018
1 May	Labour Day
Corpus Christi	60 days after Easter Sunday, and taken seriously in Croatia, with processions and lots of first communions. Corpus Christi falls on 26 May 2016, 15 June 2017, 31 May 2018
22 June	Day of Antifascist Struggle
25 June	Statehood Day
5 August	Homeland Thanksgiving Day
15 August	Assumption of the Virgin Mary
8 October	Independence Day
1 November	All Saints' Day
25 & 26 December	Christmas

FESTIVALS Croatia's robust Catholic heritage was built on the back of a strong pagan culture, and you'll find lots of the festivals and celebrations here owing more than a little to each. The calendar of festivities is based around both Christian (Easter, Corpus Christi, saints' days) and seasonal (spring, solstices, harvest) events, with Croats ready and willing to celebrate them all.

On religious holidays and feast days – not to mention the local patron saint's day – villagers and townspeople will hold processions, masses and major celebrations, and they're a great thing to be a part of if you're in the neighbourhood.

There are also innumerable festivals relating to the business of survival on the land or sea. Most seaside towns, villages and ports have at least one annual fisherman's festival (where the sea is treated with the usual mix of fear and due respect, and blessed by the local priest), while inland you can still find people casting away bad luck after the winter (using bells or branches as talismans against misfortune).

Pretty much every island and town along the coast now has a 'cultural summer' and 'musical nights' which keep things lively once the sun's gone down, with Dubrovnik's summer festival being the largest and most famous. Concerts and theatre productions are held most evenings in the old town, through six weeks of July and August, and the festival culminates in spectacular fireworks.

You'll also find two main types of folk music on show. First off are the big festivals that bring together hundreds – or even thousands – of performers. The most celebrated of these is the **Zagreb Folk Festival** (*www.msf.hr*) in July, a five-day extravaganza drawing huge crowds and mirrored on a smaller scale across much of Slavonia. The second is the lower-key folk entertainments put on wherever tourists are to be found. While these certainly shouldn't be scorned, neither do they have the originality or the authenticity of the big festivals inland. You may be better off keeping your ears pricked for a wedding party, almost invariably featuring vibrant local costumes and music.

The festival year kicks off (or closes, depending on your viewpoint) with the **New Year's Regatta** on the island of Hvar, held annually and running from 28 to 31 December, and featuring seriously competitive dinghy racing.

Things are reasonably quiet from then until the wildly popular carnival season gets under way in February, culminating on **Shrove Tuesday** – or sometimes on the weekend before. Masked parades and gaudy floats can be found in many Croatian towns, but Rijeka takes the biscuit for the biggest and most showy event. Rijeka's **carnival** is now second only in Europe to the one in Venice, attracting more than 10,000 active participants and 100,000 spectators (page 239). At the same time men wearing sheepskins drive evil spirits away from Rijeka's hinterland villages, using bells.

In April, in odd-numbered years, Zagreb holds its *biennale*, the **International Festival of Contemporary Music**. This draws the biggest names in contemporary classical music (past stars have included Stravinsky, Stockhausen, Cage and Shostakovich) and is an absolute must for those trailing music's leading edge. Check out www.mbz.hr for more information.

Film festivals kick off in July, in Pula and Motovun. By the end of July, bikers across the continent will be revving up and heading towards Pula for the annual **Istria Bikers' Rally**, which draws not just rock musicians and heavy-metal bands but also more than 10,000 leathered motorcyclists. Barely a week later, on the first Sunday in August, 18th-century-uniformed cavalrymen charge around the town of Sinj, inland from Split, on horseback with lances, in the colourful **Sinjska Alka** festival (*www. alka.hr*) which celebrates the town's 1715 victory over an army of Turks.

August sees snow as well – or at least the celebration of it – in the village of Kukljica, on the island of Ugljan, where the **Feast of Our Lady of the Snows** features both a parade and a flotilla of fishing boats setting off in honour of the snow said to have fallen there one August centuries ago. Throughout July and August on the islands you'll also have the chance to see one of the festivals of sword dances. The most famous of these is the **Moreška** on the island of Korčula, which continues a tradition dating back at least 1,000 years.

In the autumn, once the harvest is in, the biggest festival is **All Saints' Day**, when every graveyard and cemetery in the country becomes a mass of flowers. The year then closes with **Christmas**, which is much as you'd expect, though a big fish rather than a turkey is the thing to have during the main celebration on **Christmas Eve**.

SHOPPING

Croatia's not a great place for bargain hunters, with prices for most goods pretty much in line with those across the EU, though you'll find an unbelievable number of shoe shops and people selling beachwear, both at prices a wee bit lower than in London or Milan. If you've forgotten to bring something with you, it'll be fairly easy to replace, but you're probably not going to need to buy extra suitcases for all the things you bought here on the cheap. Shops generally open from 07.30 until 17.00 or 18.00, with larger supermarkets staying open until 20.00 or 21.00. Most smaller shops close on Sundays.

PDV (VAT) Purchase tax (PDV, or VAT) is set at a flat rate of 22% on all goods except essentials and books. In theory foreigners can get this reimbursed on single-ticket items costing over 500kn, but you have to really want the money. Fill in the PDV-P form at the point of sale and get it stamped, so that when you leave Croatia, you can have the goods, receipts and forms certified by the Croatian Customs Service – not a process for the impatient.

And that's the easy part. You then post back the certified receipts etc to the shop, along with your bank account details. Within a year or so, bingo: the money reappears. It's worth the hassle, of course, on really big-ticket items, but bear in mind when you're bringing goods back into your home country you may in any case be subject to import duties or asked to prove you've actually paid the VAT.

BOOKS If you run out of holiday reading along the coast or in the capital, you shouldn't have too much trouble finding something to read, though expect to pay about 20% over the cover price. Inland, and especially in eastern Slavonia, it's a different matter, with school textbooks often being the only English-language reading material available.

MUSIC If you get hooked on the local music – and it happens – make sure you buy before you leave the country. There's a whole Croatian pop and rock music scene, as well as traditional folk music and the curiously popular 'turbofolk', but even in an online world Croatian music is pretty hard to come by once you're out of the country. CDs are about the same price (that's full price, not discounted) as in most of the EU.

HANDICRAFTS When Rebecca West travelled round Croatia in 1937, she spent a good part of her trip buying up antique peasant costumes, while noting that fewer and fewer people were wearing them. This trend has continued unabated to the present day, meaning you're unlikely to see traditional dress at anything other than folk festivals or weddings. The beautifully embroidered waistcoats and skirts are still being made, but with a few exceptions (the procession of the Ljelje in Gorjani, the Brodsko Kolo in Slavonski Brod) mostly fill a tourist need. Genuinely old costumes are now sufficiently hard to find – and precious – that you'd have to treat anything 'original' for sale with more than a dash of scepticism.

ARTS AND ENTERTAINMENT

With more than a nod to Austria in the north and Italy to the west, Croats love going to the theatre, and there are excellent productions to be seen at the professional theatres in Zagreb, Osijek, Rijeka, Split and Dubrovnik.

The **Croatian National Theatre** in Zagreb isn't just a theatre, it's an entire experience (page 106). The fabulous building sees more than 200 performances annually, in a season that runs all year except August, and includes excellent **ballet**, **opera** and **theatre** productions in a mix of premieres and revivals. Theatre productions tend to be in Croatian, but all opera is put on in the original language, and of course ballet is universal. Tickets can be hard to get (though some are kept aside for sale on the day), partly because – by the standards of most countries, and especially for opera – they're inexpensive, costing 30–200kn apiece. The current programme can be found in English at the theatre's website at www.hnk.hr.

Croats are also great **cinema**-goers. Fortunately for English-speakers, most of the films are subtitled rather than dubbed, straight from Hollywood. This makes going to the cinema easy enough, and tickets are cheap, but you'll be lucky to find films made outside the USA/UK that you'll be able to understand without good language skills. I once sat through the full six hours of Bertolucci's *Novocento* in Italian, with Croatian subtitles, but it's not something I'd necessarily recommend.

Croatia has more than its fair share of **concerts** and **festivals**, too. See pages 63–4 as well as individual entries throughout the guide for more information.

Most towns of any size have at least one **museum** or **gallery**, though the quality of these varies greatly – there are few modern art galleries, for example (though Zagreb's and Dubrovnik's are excellent). Mostly, too, galleries and museums reflect Croatia's long history of attachment to one empire or another, so you'll see a lot of Austro-Hungarian and Venetian influences in the art and architecture. The most notable exception is the sculptor Ivan Meštrović, whose work you'll see everywhere, and in particular at eponymous collections in both Zagreb and Split.

PHOTOGRAPHY

Croatia has some of the best photo opportunities you'll find anywhere, with great weather, good light, and a wide variety of photogenic subjects. While there are lots of opportunities to shoot wild flowers and the like, wildlife photography itself can be difficult, since the most interesting animals (bear, wolves, lynx, eagles etc) tend to shy well clear of people (though you can easily improve your chances of seeing wildlife by joining a photo safari).

With a long history of tourism, you're unlikely to run into people problems with photography in Croatia – they're used to it – but that doesn't mean you shouldn't apply the usual ethical standards. Respect people's privacy, don't take pictures you know will offend, and especially don't take pictures when you're asked not to. The one thing you should be aware of, however, is that with war memories still fresh, don't even think of photographing places that might have military significance. Spending the rest of your holiday being questioned by the authorities is no fun at all.

MEDIA AND COMMUNICATIONS

For a country of under 4.5 million people, Croatia has a surprisingly vigorous and wide-ranging press, though it's only very recently that the main newspapers, TV and radio stations have been anything other than a mouthpiece for the state.

Communications also suffered from the heritage of state communism, but the rapid uptake of mobile telephony and the internet in the new millennium, and the increased integration of Croatia with the rest of Europe, means Croatia now has services worthy of its status as an EU supplicant. Electricity comes in the European standard size and shape, at 220V and 50Hz, and twin round-pinned plugs are used.

MEDIA Croatian independence in 1991 did little to bring freedom to the media, and it was only with the election of Stipe Mesić (in 2000) that any real efforts were made to liberate editors and journalists from half a century of government puppethood. Since then the president himself has spoken out in favour of keeping the media free from politics, and has encouraged journalists to practise their profession independently, as public servants rather than government acolytes.

The dominant media provider is Croatian Radio and Television, HRT, which attracts an audience in excess of two million a day to its three TV channels and its national and local radio stations. HRT 1 and 2 produce the usual mix of news, documentaries, entertainment and game shows, while HRT 3 is dedicated almost exclusively to sport. The website, at www.hrt.hr, has an English-language site-map that will help you find the various web-streamed audio services on offer.

The most popular daily newspapers include *Jutarnji list* (*www.jutarnji.hr*) and *Večernji list* (*www.vecernji.hr*), published in the morning and evening respectively, while two of the most prominent magazines are *Globus* (*http://globus.jutarnji.hr*) and *Nacional* (*www.nacional.hr*). Right at the other end of the publishing spectrum – though it has now sadly gone out of circulation – was the satirical weekly *Feral Tribune*, which even used a fake *Herald Tribune* masthead (some of the archive's still online at www.feral.hr). Originally a satirical supplement to Dalmatia's largest daily, *Slobodna Dalmacija*, before the mother paper was closed down by the government in 1992, *Feral Tribune* gradually became more serious, and was a regular thorn in the side of the Tuđman government.

For news in English, the internet's your best bet, either by going through paper-specific websites like www.guardian.co.uk, the Croatian news portal www.hic.hr, or by tuning in directly to the BBC or another English-language news provider (*http://news.bbc.co.uk*, *www.cnn.com*, *www.abcnews.go.com*, etc). Alternatively, you can tune in to the BBC World Service on a short-wave radio, or – if you're lucky – catch one of the intermittent English-language news bulletins on HRT radio. In the bigger centres, you can pick up the main English papers a day or two (or more) out of date.

POST Mail out of the former Yugoslavia used to take anything from two weeks to three months, and frankly post out of 21st-century Croatia isn't all that much better – postcards within Europe tend to drift home in around two to three weeks, while airmail letters are quicker, but not enormously so. Just occasionally, something slips through a hole in the space-time continuum – a letter once arrived home in three days, and a card sent to Australia got there in eight – but you should reckon on post being fairly slow unless you pay for a premium, guaranteed-delivery service.

Post offices (*pošta*, or HPT) have long opening hours, usually from 07.00 to 19.00 (or 08.00 to 20.00), and until 13.00 on Saturdays, and parcels are reasonably cheap to send, but don't seal them until you've given the cashier time to check you're not posting bombs or contraband. If you send anything valuable you may have to pay duty on it when you get home.

If you want mail sent to you, have it addressed to Poste Restante, Pošta, postcode, town name. It will be delivered to the town's main post office if there's more than one – and remember you'll need photo ID, such as a passport, to recover your mail. If your family name is underlined and/or in capitals your mail is more likely to be filed correctly – but if there's nothing for you it's always worth asking them to look under your first name as well. Incoming post takes around ten days from most

WRONG NUMBER?

There's nothing worse than buying a guidebook and then finding out some of the phone numbers are wrong – but the sad truth is that (even though every single number is checked before going to print) numbers do change. So what to do? Your best option when we fail you (my apologies) is to log on to http://imenik.tportal.hr/?lang=en, Croatia's outstanding online phone directory. It's fast, efficient and up to date, and there are even links to other online directories worldwide. Another option is to call the tourist office – assuming their number hasn't changed in the meantime ...

European destinations, and about two weeks from North America – but can be quicker, or indeed slower.

Stamps (*marke*) are also sold at news stands, tobacconists and anywhere you can buy postcards, which can save you queuing at the post office. Expect to pay around 4kn to send a postcard or 7kn to send a letter to Europe, and 7.50kn to send a postcard to the USA, Australia or New Zealand.

For branch locations and other information, see www.posta.hr.

PHONE Croatia's phone network has vastly improved in the last 15 years, and you'll no longer be faced with multiple attempts to get access to the outside world. The international access code is 00, so for international calls simply dial 00 (or +) followed by your country code (+44 for the UK, +1 for the USA and Canada, +61 for Australia and +64 for New Zealand) followed by the local phone number (without the leading zero in most cases, but not in Italy or Russia, for example).

The international code for calls into Croatia is +385. Area codes within Croatia are for the most part refreshingly simple, covering large geographical areas (the whole of central Dalmatia is within the 021 area code, for example), though there are one or two anomalies, with the island of Pag being cut in two (served by 023 in the south and 053 in the north), and a whole clutch of codes used in the north. The codes are included at the beginning of each chapter.

Partial privatisation of the former state-owned telephone operator Hrvatski Telekom (HT) has seen the company rebranded as T-Com/T-Mobile by majority shareholder Deutsche Telekom (*www.hrvatskitelekom.hr*). Finding a telephone box is usually easy enough – they are plentiful, and operated by 25- to 500-unit phone cards, with the 25-unit card costing 15kn and the 100-unit card costing 40kn. Local calls normally cost one unit, with long distance calls being quite a bit more expensive, especially at peak time (07.00–19.00 Mon–Sat). International calls can also be made from main post offices. The cost of making an overseas call is not normally exorbitant, but it does depend on the destination.

There are three mobile operators in Croatia: T-Mobile, Tele-2, and VIP – though it's worth checking geographical coverage with Tele-2 as it is poor in some areas. The network is comprehensive and the local operators have roaming agreements with their foreign counterparts, so you'll almost certainly find your own phone works just fine – and with Croatia now part of the EU, calls and texts within the EU should cost the same as they would at home (and therefore be included in your provider's monthly allowance).

Otherwise, if you're not from and calling within the EU, using your own mobile for international calls will be expensive. Remember if you're calling your travelling companions that you need to make an international call: to dial a UK-registered mobile being used in Croatia for example you need to dial 0044 or +44 first.

If you're going to be glued to the phone, one option is to buy a local pre-paid subscription and then top up your SIM card as needed – if you do this, keep the SIM card for your home subscription in a safe place. Not only is a local pre-paid number convenient for your outgoing calls, but it also means you can easily be called from home. Local SIM cards become deactivated if not used for three months, so if you come to Croatia every year (for example) and don't use the SIM card in between (and why would you), you'll need to get a new one each year.

A local SIM card (T-Mobile, Tele-2, etc) costs very little and the price will include a certain amount of pre-paid credit, which can easily be topped up when needed at many supermarkets and kiosks, as well as mobile phone shops.

One final word about phones – like everywhere else in the world, you should aim to avoid calling long distance or international from your hotel room. Tariffs for fixed and mobile calls may have fallen, but hotel rates certainly haven't. The cost of a 15-minute call home from a decent hotel room can spoil your entire trip.

Some useful phone numbers:

Emergencies
☎112 or:
Police ☎92
Fire ☎93
Ambulance ☎94
Search and rescue at sea ☎9155
Roadside assistance ☎1987

General
Croatian Airlines ☎01 667 6555 or 01 616 0152
Weather forecast ☎060 520 520
General information ☎18981

Telecoms
International directory enquiries ☎11802
Local operator ☎11880
Long-distance operator ☎11888

INTERNET Internet uptake has been rapid in Croatia, and there's an enormous amount of information now available online. You'll find an increasing number of major towns offering free Wi-Fi across the city centre, most hotels have Wi-Fi, and many cafés and bars offer Wi-Fi for their customers. Failing that, most towns and resorts have an internet café of some sort.

Where Croatia has been slower on the uptake is in the regular use of email. While some people are instantly responsive, there's unfortunately barely a hotel or tourist board in the country that will reply to an initial email. During the research for this book (and its subsequent updates, right through to the present edition), many hundreds of emails were sent, the vast majority into the void. The frustrating thing is that when you do follow up with a phone call, the first response is all too often: 'Ah, yes, we saw your email!'

BUSINESS/TIME

Most Croatian businesses operate from 08.30 to 16.30, Monday to Friday. If you're calling ahead of your journey – or having people call you in Croatia – it's useful to know that Croatia's on Central European Time (CET). That's an hour ahead of GMT, six hours ahead of New York and Washington, nine hours ahead of California, and eight hours behind Sydney and Melbourne (ten in the European winter). Summer time dates in Croatia are the same as in most other European countries, with the clocks going forward an hour in spring and back an hour in autumn.

The working environment – dress, culture, etc – is similar to that in most European countries, but if you're doing business don't be surprised if you're expected to cement deals or friendships with a shot (or several) of rakija. If you don't drink out of choice, you need to invent a good reason why – the culture isn't particularly tolerant of non-drinkers.

BUYING PROPERTY

Although prices have risen sharply over the past few years (particularly in Dubrovnik), Croatia still represents good value when it comes to buying property, whether an old stone house or a new apartment. Rules for foreigners buying property as an individual eased up in 2009, and even further with Croatia's entry into the EU in 2013. However, there is still a certain amount of red tape – and it is particularly important that land registry and other documentation is in order – so make sure you choose a reputable estate agent, and keep up to date with the current value for the area you are interested in (calculated in euros per square metre). Try Ozana Real Estate (*www.ozana.hr*) or Milenka Real Estate (*www.milenkarealestate.com*).

CULTURAL ETIQUETTE

All visitors have an effect not just on a country but on its people, too. There are plenty of arguments for and against this that don't need to be enumerated here – suffice to say that it's worth considering both the environmental and sociological effects of your visit.

INTERACTING WITH LOCAL PEOPLE Croatia has been affected hugely by tourism, which has brought an improved standard of living to the country as a whole and to hundreds of thousands of individuals along the coast and on the islands. Tourism has also destroyed a way of life that was poorer and harsher and yet, paradoxically, is often fondly remembered. Your surly, inattentive waiter at the dog-end of the summer season is probably dreaming of being the fisherman his father was – even though he knows how hard a fisherman's life really is. Don't expect to be able to unravel this contradiction.

Away from the tourist spots – and especially in the mountains, and in smaller communities inland – there are plenty of opportunities to build bridges between foreigners and local people. Take the time to talk to those you meet, show people what life's like back home (photographs and postcards say more than words ever can, even if you do speak the language) and share in a cup of coffee, or a drink and a cigarette, if invited. Off the beaten track in Croatia I've been asked into the homes of people who have virtually nothing, only to be offered the little they do. Bring pictures to show, perhaps a frisbee or sketchbook to share with the children, and Western cigarettes for the adults – most Croatians smoke and, whatever your feelings, cigarettes are appreciated everywhere. There are good arguments against giving gifts to kids on the street, or handing out largesse to beggars – both encourage dependence – but in people's homes, there's very little else you can do to return hospitality.

In Croatia as a whole – and especially in the parts of the country directly affected – it's a good idea not to discuss the recent war. It's a conversational minefield, and the last thing you want is to step on a conversational landmine. Even with a population that's now over 90% Croat, you won't always know immediately whether you're talking to a Croat or a Serb and, even if you are sure, opinions are sufficiently divergent to be dangerous. The only really safe thing you can say, if you're asked directly, is that you're pleased it's all over, and that peace is clearly bringing prosperity.

ENVIRONMENT Croatia's environment is in good shape (page 7), so don't spoil it – preserving it is in everyone's interests.

The biggest impact you personally can have on the environment is to start a fire. There's almost nothing that can be done once a fire's out of control in Croatia's drier areas, so be especially careful here. Unless there's a plentiful supply of water nearby, in fact, it's advisable to avoid fires, or even naked flames, altogether.

Litter, by comparison, is a simple question of ugliness. Paper tissues take months to deteriorate, orange peel positively glows, and tin cans always look horrible. Take your litter with you – and if you collect any you find along the way you can feel suitably saintly about yourself. If you're in the wilds, and you can't find a toilet, do at least bury your doings – there are few sights (or sensations) more unpleasant than coming across someone else's.

DRESS/NATURISM In summer you won't look out of place in shorts and a T-shirt, but you won't be able to visit churches if you're too skimpily dressed – there are signs outside churches along the coast and islands giving you a pretty good idea of the dress code. Seaside topless sunbathing won't offend, but you shouldn't really be anywhere off the beach in your swimsuit (or indeed out of it).

Inland, you'll find local people more modestly dressed, though things have changed a lot in the last 20 years or so – you'll no longer look or feel out of place dressing the way you do back home (well, it depends on how outrageous you are back home, of course), or attract unwanted attention if you don't make an effort to conform. Quite the opposite is true these days – as a visitor you'll probably get strange looks if you're a woman in your fifties dressed all in black, or decked out entirely in retro denim if you're a man.

Back on the coast, Croatia is the main homing ground for the great European naturist – hundreds of thousands come here every year just to get their kit off. There are entire naturist resorts (the most popular are in Istria, page 202), campsites and apartment complexes, and most towns have a dedicated beach. Just look out for the FKK signs if you're interested. Croatia's also the only place I've been where you can go on a naturist sailing holiday. Mind your tackle.

DRUGS Illegal drugs are best avoided in Croatia. They're available, but the penalties are stiff, and harsher still for smuggling – don't be tempted or tricked into carrying anything across borders. Split in particular has something of a reputation with the authorities for being part of a drugs corridor from Asia to the West, so be especially vigilant, and – without excessive paranoia – make sure you know exactly what's in your bags.

TRAVELLING POSITIVELY

After travelling in Croatia (and possibly even before you go) you may want to do something for the country – the two obvious ways you can help are through voluntary work or through supporting a Croatian charity.

VOLUNTARY WORK There are a number of well-established voluntary programmes operating in Croatia, though happily they're all popular and you need to book well ahead if you want to participate. Below are a few, but you can find many more if you do your own research.

Croatian Heritage Foundation Hrvatska Matica Iseljenika; Trg Stjepana Radića 3, 10000 Zagreb; ☏ 01 611 5116; e hmi-info@matis.hr; www.matis.hr [in English]. This caters mainly for the Croatian diaspora of 3.5 million people around the world. The foundation organises a summer 'Task Force', which focuses on a different project each year, such as restoring medieval town walls, replanting damaged botanical gardens, or rebuilding paths in the national parks.

Croatian Red Cross Hrvatski Crveni Kriz; Vulinčeva 30; 10000 Zagreb; ☏ 01 3876 062; www.hck.hr. It is worth getting in touch with this organisation, as it is not just active in its own right but also works with many other partners.
Volunteers Centre Zagreb Volonterski Centar Zagreb, VCZ; Ilica 29, 10000 Zagreb; ☏ 01 3013 058; e vcz@vcz.hr; www.vcz.hr. This well-established organisation was started in 1996, & has been working to promote peace & human rights since the war ended. VCZ organises working camps in Croatia.

CHARITIES The single most important thing you can do to improve life in Croatia is to support any of the many organisations involved in mine clearance. In the UK, Heather Mills has done a lot in getting prosthetic limbs and financial aid to mine victims in Croatia, and has also been instrumental in setting up the Adopt-A-Minefield programme. Visit the website at www.adoptaminefield.org which co-ordinates anti-landmine activity and fundraising, and is directly involved in Croatia, raising money for mine clearance and for the survivors of landmine accidents. The Croatian Mine Action Centre or 'CROMAC' for short (Hrvatski Centar za Razminiranje, HCR) does a huge amount of work on the ground and keeps up-to-date statistics and maps on mine clearance at its website at www.hcr.hr.

Another active organisation is the **American Chamber of Commerce in Croatia** (*AmCham Croatia; www.amcham.hr*). Founded in 1998, and based in Zagreb, AmCham Croatia stresses its independence from the US government, and has various fundraising programmes for Croatian charities, in addition to its main mandate of promoting mutual co-operation and friendship between Croatia and the USA.

Part Two

THE GUIDE

3

Zagreb

Telephone code 01 (+385 1 from abroad)

Rebecca West sized up Croatia's capital nicely when she was here in 1937: 'Zagreb makes from its featureless handsomeness something that pleases like a Schubert song, a delight that begins quietly and never definitely ends. It has the endearing characteristic noticeable in many French towns of remaining a small town when it is in fact quite large.' Indeed, today, with a population of a million, Zagreb is easily Croatia's largest and most cosmopolitan city, though the centre is still delightfully manageable on foot.

Zagreb's heart is a fine, clean example of solid Habsburg architecture, tending towards palatial elegance, and large squares from which to view it – though if you move away from the city centre you'll find sprawling suburbs and high rises, thrown up to accommodate waves of incoming workers over the past 60 years.

For much of the year Zagreb is a lively outdoor city, with café tables spilling out across the pavements and flowers everywhere. In winter it can be cold, with snow on the ground for an average of over 50 days annually and the streets of the lower town seeming too large for their occupants – but with a big university and heaps of bars, clubs and nightlife on offer, the locals certainly know how to have a good time, and the café culture simply moves indoors. Perhaps not surprisingly as the Croatian capital, Zagreb is particularly strong on culture, with regular performances of

WHAT'S IN A NAME?

There are several conflicting theories about why Zagreb should be so-called, but everyone agrees that the name was first recorded in 1094, when Hungary's King Ladislav founded the bishopric here.

The most logical hypothesis is that 'Zagreb' means 'in the ditch', because of its geographic situation – a theory backed up by the old German name for the city being Agram, a contraction of '*am Graben*', meaning the same thing. Another supposition is that the city was named after efforts to scrape and dig away the soil in search of water here – though I'm sceptical about how much water that theory can hold, with the great River Sava a stone's throw away.

The name could also – if the word is Slavonian, which is itself doubtful – come from '*za grebom*', meaning 'behind the tomb', though which tomb also seems to be a well-shrouded mystery.

My favourite explanation, however, is that 'Zagreb' is a corruption of '*za breg*', meaning 'behind the hill'. Quite apart from anything else, it reflects an elegantly Austro-Hungarian-centric view of the world; anyone else would describe Zagreb as being 'in front of the hill'.

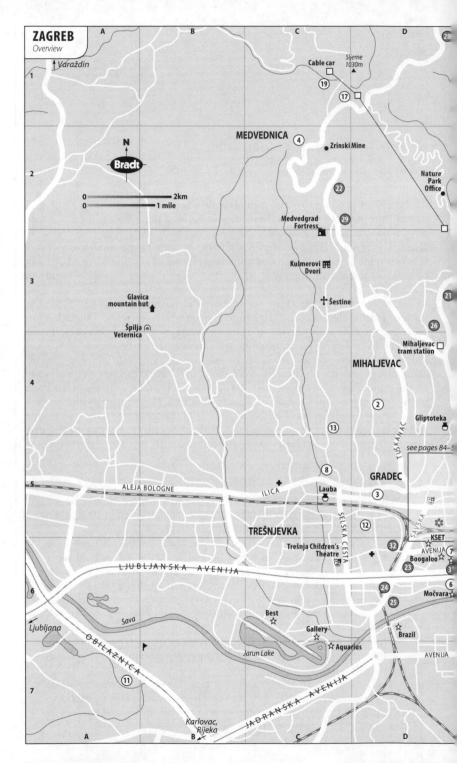

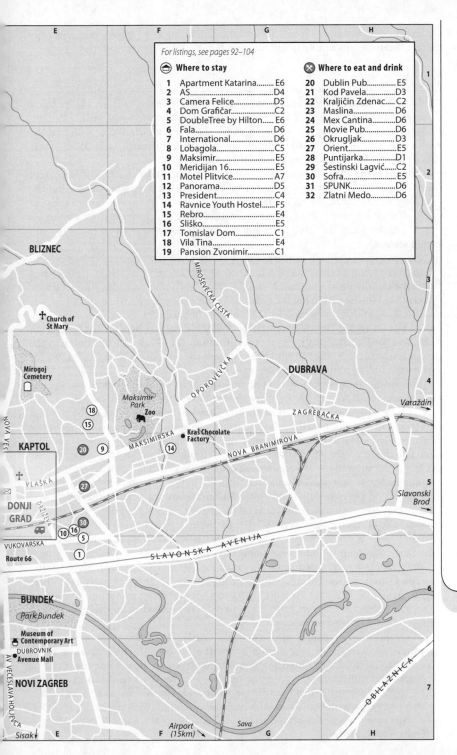

For listings, see pages 92–104

⌂ Where to stay

1	Apartment Katarina	E6
2	AS	D4
3	Camera Felice	D5
4	Dom Grafičar	C2
5	DoubleTree by Hilton	E6
6	Fala	D6
7	International	D6
8	Lobagola	C5
9	Maksimir	E5
10	Meridijan 16	E5
11	Motel Plitvice	A7
12	Panorama	D5
13	President	C4
14	Ravnice Youth Hostel	F5
15	Rebro	E4
16	Sliško	E5
17	Tomislav Dom	C1
18	Vila Tina	E4
19	Pansion Zvonimir	C1

⊗ Where to eat and drink

20	Dublin Pub	E5
21	Kod Pavela	D3
22	Kraljičin Zdenac	C2
23	Maslina	D6
24	Mex Cantina	D6
25	Movie Pub	D6
26	Okrugljak	D3
27	Orient	E5
28	Puntijarka	D1
29	Šestinski Lagvić	C2
30	Sofra	E5
31	SPUNK	D6
32	Zlatni Medo	D6

BLIZNEC

✝ Church of St Mary

Mirogoj Cemetery

NOVA VES

Maksimir Park
Zoo

MAKSIMIRSKA

MIROŠEVEČKA CESTA

OPOROVEČKA

DUBRAVA

ZAGREBAČKA

Varaždin

Kraš Chocolate Factory

NOVA BRANIMIROVA

KAPTOL

VLAŠKA

DRŽIĆEVA

DONJI GRAD

VUKOVARSKA

Route 66

SLAVONSKA AVENIJA

Slavonski Brod

BUNDEK

Park Bundek

Museum of Contemporary Art

DUBROVNIK
Avenue Mall

AV VEĆESLAVA HOLJEVCA

NOVI ZAGREB

Sisak

Airport (15km)

Sava

OBILAZNICA

Zagreb

3

international standard – from classical opera and ballet to smoky jazz and edgy street theatre – and a quite staggering number of museums and galleries.

HISTORY

Judging by the remains found in the Veternica Cave (page 134) on Medvednica, people have been living in the Zagreb area for at least 35,000 years. Modern history here doesn't begin until much, much more recently, however – around the 4th century BC – when Celtic tribes poured in from the north, only to be swiftly mopped up by Romans arriving from the south.

The Romans created several settlements in the area, which was important then, as now, as a crossroads on east–west and north–south trade routes. After the decline of the empire, the region faded back into obscurity, however, until the year 879, when it became part of the first Croatian state, which reached its apotheosis in 925 under King Tomislav – the guy on the big horse in front of Zagreb's main train station.

At the end of the 11th century, a lack of heirs saw the Croatian crown pass to Hungary, paving the way for the creation of the Zagreb diocese in 1094. It was nonetheless the rival communities of Kaptol (with the cathedral) and Gradec (today's old town) that made the running for several centuries thereafter.

The first cathedral was built in 1217, only to be trashed – along with everything else – by rampaging Tartars 25 years later. As a consequence, **Bela IV**, the Hungarian king, authorised the construction of fortifications for Gradec (it was home to the Hungarian garrison, after all) in 1242, and gave the settlement 'Free City' status for its part in hiding him from the enemy.

Solid ramparts and walls were built around Gradec by 1266. Today, however, the only signs you'll see are the Lotrščak Tower (where the noonday cannon is fired from, page 110) and the Stone Gate (Porta Lapidea, page 113), one of the original entrances to the old town, though the current version is 18th century. Up above the city, on Medvednica, meanwhile, work started in 1254 on what would eventually become the imposing Medvedgrad Fortress – though from the 16th century to its pricey restoration in the 1990s, there wasn't much more to it than a few ruins.

Kaptol, for its part, was only allowed to fortify in the 15th century, with the Turks practically on the doorstep. In 1469, the **Sultan's army** got as far as the Sava River, where they were miraculously scared off by a single cannon shot from the Lotrščak Tower. No, of course they weren't – but that's the legend behind the cannon still fired towards the Sava every day at noon. What actually repulsed the Turks was the Sava conveniently and spectacularly bursting its banks (something that would happen regularly, and catastrophically, until the current dykes were built in 1971).

The Ottomans went on being uppity for another century, though even their great victory of 1525, which led Croatia to seek Habsburg protection, didn't see Zagreb directly invaded, and the Turks were finally routed definitively in 1593 at Sisak, 50km southeast of the city.

With no common enemy to divert them, Gradec and Kaptol were now free to continue their rivalrous relationship across the Medveščak creek dividing them (now Tkalčićeva). The painted wooden bridge across the brook was the scene of frequent and violent conflicts – most famously in 1667, when drunken soldiers loyal to the powerful **Zrinski family** were persuaded by Kaptol to attack Gradec, with bloody results on both sides. Although today neither creek nor bridge remains, the short street where the bridge once stood still bears the name 'Krvavi Most' – literally 'Blood Bridge'.

It was only in the 19th century that the ancient rivalry between Gradec and Kaptol began to ease, with common interests finally prevailing – Zagreb was, after all, an important regional staging post on the routes from Vienna and Budapest to the sea. They were also brought together by the resurgence of Croatian nationalism, driven in large part by **Ljudevit Gaj**, who oversaw the publication of the first Croatian newspapers in 1835. New institutions flourished, with the founding of the Music Society in 1826, Croatian (originally Illyrian) Heritage in 1839, the Academy of Arts and Sciences in 1866, and the University in 1874. Key to this burgeoning scene was Josip Jelačić, the guy on the big horse in Zagreb's eponymously named Main Square. Jelačić was made 'ban' (viceroy) of Croatia in 1848.

Two years later, **Franz Josef I**, the Habsburg emperor, proclaimed Zagreb as a single city, and ushered in a whole new architectural era – particularly after 1857, when new building regulations came in stipulating streets at least 13m wide intersecting at right angles, and prescribing the heights and shapes of all new buildings (Habsburg, basically).

Everything was going swimmingly for Zagreb until 9 November 1880, when a **devastating earthquake** almost totally destroyed the city. The massive rebuilding programme that followed explains the uniform late 19th-century architecture that characterises Zagreb today, and was particularly noteworthy for the achievements of two men, the architect Hermann Bollé, and the urban planner Milan Lenuci. Bollé was responsible for the new neo-Gothic façade on the cathedral, the lovely Mirogoj Cemetery north of the city and the solid elegance of the Arts and Crafts Museum, while Lenuci designed the so-called 'Green Horseshoe', a series of grand, green squares that dominate the lower town between the train station and the central square.

During the 20th century, Zagreb's history closely followed Croatia's (pages 12–21), though the city was fortunate during the homeland war in largely avoiding direct conflict. The Ban's Palace (the official president's residence) was successfully targeted by a rogue rocket attack (you can see a reconstruction in the City Museum of what happened, page 120) in 1991, and seven people lost their lives during the last shellings of the city in 1995, but compared to what happened elsewhere, the damage was minimal.

PENKALA THE INVENTOR

Largely forgotten now, but enormously influential at the time, was a man called Eduard Slavoljub Penkala (1871–1922). An inveterate inventor, he was forever looking for ways to improve day-to-day life. In 1906, he patented the world's first 'mechanical pencil', the pioneer in a whole range of writing devices that actually worked, and from 1914 to 1926, as a direct result, Zagreb became the European capital for the production of writing instruments.

Penkala himself never gave up his job at the Ministry of Finance (where he was Royal Technical Controller), but seems to have had plenty of time to work on his inventions, leaving him free to become Croatia's first aviator, in 1909, and the inventor of its first two-seater aircraft the following year. He also patented a hovercraft design in 1908, half a century ahead of Christopher Cockerell's antics on the Isle of Wight, and a rotating toothbrush the same year, when dental hygiene was still barely a blip on the horizon.

In a short life – he died of pneumonia, aged only 50 – Penkala came up with hundreds of inventions and registered over 70 patents.

The city was spared, but the people of Zagreb were scarred, and from 1993 a touching raw brick monument to lost and missing soldiers and civilians was built by their mothers and relatives around the UN Peace Mission headquarters (on the corner of Ilica and Selska) – with each brick representing a dead or missing person. The monument has been replaced by a new formal memorial in Mirogoj Cemetery, though relatives were upset that the original bricks aren't visible.

In 1994, while the war was still on, **Pope John Paul II** visited Zagreb as part of the city's 900th anniversary celebrations, and a million people turned out to see him.

Zagreb people are proud of their city and those of its natives who go on to achieve world fame; so expect at least to be able to name local sporting celebrities if you're here. Clue: former AC Milan player Zvonimir Boban owns a restaurant in town, and skiing star Janica Kostelić, who came home with three golds and a silver from the 2002 Winter Olympics, is fêted wherever she goes.

GETTING THERE AND AWAY

As the capital, Zagreb is well served by both international and domestic transport routes, and has an international airport, as well as major rail and bus terminals.

BY AIR Zagreb's diminutive Pleso Airport is 17km southeast of the city centre (for details of getting to Zagreb, see page 34). As soon as you come out of International Arrivals you'll see the airport bus stop – shuttles to the main bus station in Zagreb run hourly or half-hourly (depending on the time of day) from 07.00 to 20.00, seven days a week. Outside the standard times, buses will also run whenever new flights arrive.

The trip takes about 30 minutes, and costs 30kn. A return (valid only on the same day) is 40kn. For full schedule information, check with Pleso Transport Company – it has an easy-to-follow English language website (*www.plesoprijevoz.hr*), and you can also get ticket and schedule information over the phone at ☎ 633 1982.

Airport shuttles from the main bus station back to the airport run every 30 minutes from 05.00 to 20.00, seven days a week, as well as outside these times whenever a plane lands. Buses leave from their own small terminal (rather than main long-distance bus departure gates), which is located on the ground floor level on the north side of the bus station. Buses are marked Zračna Luka Zagreb/Zagreb Airport, seating is first come, first served, and you buy your ticket on board. Don't worry if the driver isn't around when you get on – you can get your ticket when he or she does a round of the bus, just before departing.

With such an efficient bus service you're unlikely to need a taxi, but if you do, call Cammeo (*www.taxi-cammeo.net*) or EkoTaxi (*www.ekotaxi.hr*) as they are by far the cheapest companies operating (page 88). Otherwise, the stand is right next to the airport bus stop (note that Cammeo and EkoTaxi do not use taxi stands – you need to call/email and book – and recently, in 2015, EkoTaxi was prevented from picking up passengers at the airport, though it can still run you out to the airport from town. Zagreb taxi drivers have a good reputation, but it does no harm to make sure the meter's switched on when you set off. Expect to pay upwards of 150–200kn to the main Zagreb hotels, bearing in mind you'll also pay a few kuna extra per piece of luggage, and that there's a 20% surcharge at night, as well as on Sundays and public holidays (with Cammeo or EkoTaxi, this figure falls to about 120kn, and there's no charge for baggage or surcharge at night).

More information on the airport, including real-time flight arrival and departure times, can be found at www.zagreb-airport.hr (look under 'Timetable' on the home page).

BY RAIL The railway originally linked Zagreb to its Habsburg rulers in the north, before assuming a more glamorous international role as one of the stops on the Simplon Orient Express line from Paris to Istanbul in the 1920s.

When you arrive, make sure you get off at the central station, Zagreb Glavni Kolodvor; there are two other stations at which trains may stop (but which you don't want): Zagreb Klara and Zagreb Zapadni Kolodvor.

The station itself – Glavni Kolodvor [85 E7] – is an imposing Neoclassical edifice completed in 1891 by the Hungarian architect Ferenc Pfaff (who presumably had to endure a lifetime of wags telling him to stop faffing about). It's also known as Željeznički Kolodvor, just meaning 'railway station', but as it's a bit of a mouthful you're safer sticking with 'Glavni', meaning 'main'. It's located at the southern end of the city, a straight kilometre down from Zagreb's main square, Jelačić Square – trams #6 and #13 connect the two, or it's a ten-minute walk. From the train station it's a little over 1km east to the main bus station, which can be comfortably shortened by three stops on tram #2 or #6.

The station has good facilities, including large Arrival (*Dolazak*) and Departure (*Odlazak*) boards in the main hall, and a website in English providing information on timetables, ticket prices, journey duration, etc – see www.hzpp.hr/timetable. For trains to and from Zagreb, select Zagreb Gl. kol as your departure or arrival station from the drop-down menu.

Lockers are available at 15kn per 24 hours, with extra-large ones for 20kn per 24 hours, making this a cheaper and more convenient place to store your stuff than the main bus station (see below). Coins for the lockers and information on timetables are available at the Croatia Express office (\ 457 3253), which also has a foreign exchange service.

The kiosks in the central hall offer a limited selection of foreign-language newspapers and magazines, as well as selling stamps and postcards. The station bistro has its own outdoor terrace; it's conveniently open for drinks, snacks and more substantial meals from 05.00 to 23.00. Public toilets and shower facilities are available at the west end of the main platform, beyond the bistro.

BY BUS Zagreb's main bus station – Autobusni Kolodvor [85 H7] – is the largest and busiest in the country, as you'd expect, with around 200 arrivals a day, from destinations both domestic and international. Like bus stations everywhere, it's a bit shabby, but has good facilities, including a small supermarket, several cafés, various fast food outlets and newsagents. Up on the second floor there's also a post office and a bank, while down on the ground floor (at platforms 1 and 6) you'll find 24-hour left-luggage facilities – though at 5kn per hour per bag up to 4 hours and 2.50kn per hour thereafter, it's quite a bit more expensive than those at the train station (see above).

If you're planning on leaving by bus (not counting the airport transfer; page 80), you should try and buy your ticket as early as possible – from the main ticket office on the first floor – as long-distance buses tend to be booked out ahead of time, especially in summer.

The bus station is 1.5km east of the main train station, which would make for a dull 15-minute walk were it not for the fact that it takes you alongside some of the best street art in Zagreb (from the bus station, cross under the railway lines, then walk west along Branimirova) or a three-stop ride on the #2 or #6 tram. Tram #6 also continues on past the station two stops to Jelačić Square, Zagreb's central square.

Like the train station, the bus station also has a good website in English, at www. akz.hr. Be warned, however, that if your computer doesn't support Croatian accents,

3

the database won't always find your requested destination – the best way to avoid frustration is simply to type in the first two or three letters, and then use the drop-down menu of possibilities, from which you can quickly select your destination (though this doesn't work for places that start with accented letters, like Šibenik).

BY CAR If you can find a way of avoiding driving in town, then do so. Zagreb is compact enough to manage easily on foot or using public transport, and having your own car with you is, frankly, a bit of a liability – I speak as one who knows. A government credit on new cars, while good for the economy, has helped to further clog up Zagreb's arteries, while negotiating your way around the busy centre or the old town is made even harder by a tricky one-way system. Many streets are also car-free, designated for pedestrians or trams only, and these days taxi fares are much, much more reasonable than they used to be (page 88). So do yourself a favour – use your legs and Zagreb's charming and reliable network of trams, and you'll enjoy the city at its best.

If driving is a nightmare, parking is worse. Legitimate street parking spaces are a good deal scarcer than hen's teeth, but if you park illegally it's likely that the infamous 'spider' (*pauk*) impounding service will take your car away. If your car does disappear, try calling the spider on ☎ 631 1888, ☎ 631 1884, or ☎ 631 1881, before you panic and report its disappearance to the police – it might save you a lot of time and hassle. The pound – where you can pay the hefty fine and recover your car – is at Strojarska 14, just west of the bus station (it's the first right on Branimira heading east from the train station, after about 1km).

Street parking (I hardly know why I'm bothering to tell you this – but I suppose you might find a space) is divided into three zones – red, yellow and green – corresponding to one-, two- and three-hour maximum stay respectively. You pay 10kn per hour in the red zone, 5kn per hour in the yellow zone and 2kn per hour in the green zone. Payment is easy as pie; either by getting vouchers (*Parkirna Karta*) at kiosks, paying in cash at automatic ticket dispensers, or – best by far – sending an SMS with your registration number (no spaces) from your mobile phone. Send it to 101 for the red zone, 102 for the yellow zone and 103 for the green zone. One SMS equals an hour's worth of parking, and you get a return SMS to confirm you've paid, and another SMS 5–10 minutes before your parking time expires. See www.zagrebparking.hr.

There are also a growing number of underground car parks, which are safe and secure, though even here, at 7kn per hour (that's 08.00–18.00 Monday to Saturday; 18.00–08.00 Monday to Saturday; and 24 hours Sunday costs 4kn per hour), you can end up with a hefty bill if you're in the city for any length of time. The best-located are at the Sheraton Hotel, the Branimir Centre, the Kaptol Centre (at Nova Ves), a block and a half east of Jelačić Square (on the corner of Vlaška), and at the Importanne shopping centre near the train station – though the entrances can be hard to find and easy to miss, what with the one-way system and heavy traffic.

You could also consider leaving your car in the suburbs, where there's ample daytime parking, and catching a tram or bus into town – but, with car theft a real possibility, this may not be a great decision if you plan on leaving your vehicle unattended for days at a time. A safer option – though not a cheaper one; prices vary from 60–120kn per day – is to choose a hotel with its own parking, where you'll have the peace of mind of knowing your car will be secure for the duration of your stay. You might even want to consider staying somewhere out of town for the Zagreb part of your trip if you have a car with you (Samobor, for example) and making the short journey into the city on the regular bus service – another advantage being that out-of-town hotels can offer excellent value for money – but then you'd miss the heady charm of wandering the city's café- and bar-filled streets on a balmy late summer evening, which would be a shame.

Car hire Car hire is easy to organise direct through any of the main agencies, which can all be found at the airport.

🚗 **Avis** Pleso Airport; 📞626 5190; www.avis. com; ⏰ 07.00–23.00 Mon–Fri, 08.00–23.00 Sat–Sun. Also an office in town at Oreskoviceva 21; 📞615 8858; ⏰ 08.00–16.00 Mon–Fri

🚗 **Budget** Pleso Airport; 📞626 5193; www. budget.hr; ⏰ 07.00–23.00 Mon–Fri

🚗 **Dollar & Thrifty** Pleso Airport; 📞626 5333; www.subrosa.hr; ⏰ 07.00–21.00 Mon–Sun. Also downtown at Sub Rosa, Petrinjska 83; 📞483 6466

🚗 **Hertz** Pleso Airport; 📞456 2635; www. hertz.hr; ⏰ 08.00–21.00 daily. Also at Grada

Vukovara 274; 📞484 6777; ⏰ 08.00–18.00 Mon– Fri, 09.00–13.00 Sat–Sun

🚗 **National** Pleso Airport; 📞222 9058; www. nationalcar.com; 08.00–20.00 daily. Serviced by Europcar.

🚗 **Sixt** Pleso Airport; 📞621 9900; www.hr.sixt. com; ⏰ 07.00–22.00 daily. Also at Sheraton Four Points Hotel, Sportova Trg 9; 📞301 5303; ⏰ 08.00–19.00 Mon–Fri, 08.00–18.00 Sat, 08.00–noon Sun

ORIENTATION

Zagreb is 'pleasantly situated between the north bank of the Sava and the mountains which culminate in Sljeme' (according to my trusty 1911 *Encyclopaedia Britannica*) – and the mountain and the river are the two principal landmarks you'll still find on the larger city maps today, along with the railway line that separates the main city centre and old town to the north from the suburbs to the south.

The vast main square, **Jelačić Square** (Trg Bana Jelačića) [91 C4], sits on the northern side of the city centre, and is the main rendezvous point in town – for decades the exact spot was under the tail of Jelačić's horse, but people now seem to prefer meeting under the modern clock, about 50m away.

A series of great leafy squares run south to the main **train station** [85 E7], and these form the eastern arm of the so-called 'green horseshoe' – which then continues west from the station to the Esplanade Hotel and the Botanical Gardens, before turning north for another three blocks.

North of Jelačić Square you'll find **Dolac** [91 C3], the city's huge daily market, with fruit, vegetables, fish and flowers upstairs, and meat, cheese and all the rest downstairs. To the northeast stands the twin-spired, partly scaffolding-clad cathedral, at the heart of **Kaptol**, which was formerly a separate religious centre, while to the northwest is the old town, **Gradec** (also known as Gornji Grad, meaning 'upper town'), home to the president's palace and the parliament building (Sabor), along with several of the city's museums. Kaptol and Gradec are separated by **Tkalčićeva**, a café- and restaurant-filled pedestrian street running north, and **Radićeva**, a cobbled street parallel to and above it.

Running west from Jelačić Square is **Ilica**, Zagreb's main shopping area (along with the streets running off it), while to the south and southwest are the regular blocks and streets of **Donji Grad**, the lower town, where you'll find most of the remaining museums and other sights, and which was made possible by the construction of the railway embankment in 1860.

South of the railway are the suburbs built between the two world wars, while across the River Sava is **Novi Zagreb**, the residential area that sprang up in the 1950s and 1960s to house incoming labour. Just south of the railway line, a kilometre or

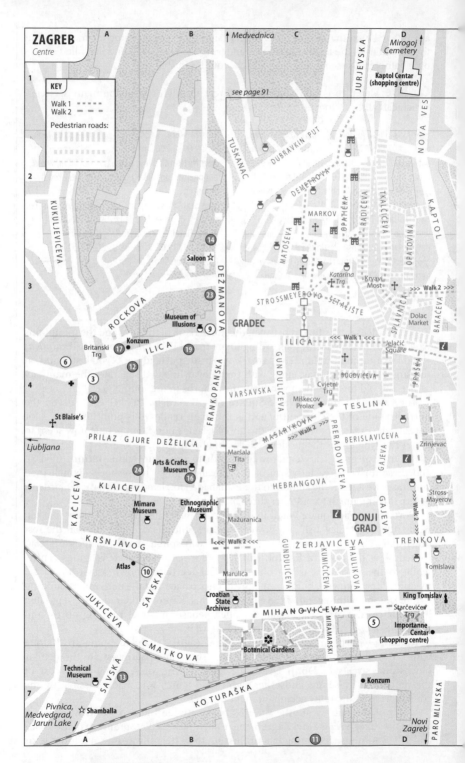

see page 91

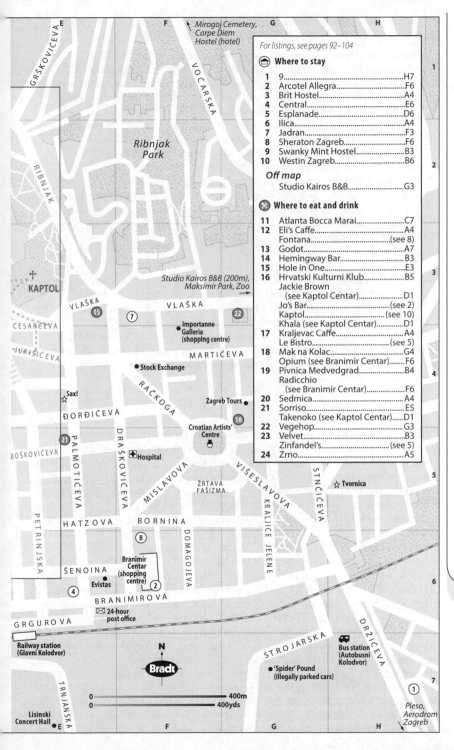

For listings, see pages 92–104

Where to stay

1 9...H7
2 Arcotel Allegra...................................F6
3 Brit Hostel..A4
4 Central..E6
5 Esplanade..D6
6 Ilica...A4
7 Jadran...F3
8 Sheraton Zagreb................................F6
9 Swanky Mint Hostel...........................B3
10 Westin Zagreb.....................................B6

Off map
   Studio Kairos B&B...............................G3

Where to eat and drink

11 Atlanta Bocca Marai...........................C7
12 Eli's Caffe..A4
   Fontana..(see 8)
13 Godot...A7
14 Hemingway Bar....................................B3
15 Hole in One..E3
16 Hrvatski Kulturni Klub........................B5
   Jackie Brown
     (see Kaptol Centar)........................D1
   Jo's Bar...(see 2)
   Kaptol...(see 10)
   Khala (see Kaptol Centar)................D1
17 Kraljevac Caffe.....................................A4
   Le Bistro..(see 5)
18 Mak na Kolac..G4
   Opium (see Branimir Centar).........F6
19 Pivnica Medvedgrad...........................B4
   Radicchio
     (see Branimir Centar)....................F6
20 Sedmica...A4
21 Sorriso..E5
   Takenoko (see Kaptol Centar)........D1
22 Vegehop...G3
23 Velvet..B3
   Zinfandel's......................................(see 5)
24 Zrno...A5

Zagreb ORIENTATION

3

85

It won't take sharp-eyed readers long to notice that what's written on Zagreb's street signs isn't quite the same as what we've used in this guide, both in the text and on the maps. That's because mapmakers and guidebook writers always use the spoken form of street names rather than the written form, which varies because of the subtleties of the Croatian language. The names we use here are the ones generally used in conversation and therefore best for obtaining any kind of directions, or what you'd ask a taxi or tram driver. As a result, if you want the square which is in reality Trg Svetog Marka (St Mark's Square), you'll be directed to Markov Trg, while if you're walking down Ulica Pavla Radića, it's Radićeva you'll see on the map – and that late-night drink will be on Tkalčićeva, not Ulica Ivana Tkalčića. If that's not confusing enough, a couple of important squares have their own colloquial names – Trg Petra Preradovićeva is generally known as Cvjetni Trg (Flower Square), while the place universally referred to as Zrinjevac is officially Trg Nikole Šubića Zrinskog.

so east of the main train station, is the main **bus station**, which is where the shuttle comes in from **Pleso Airport**, itself 15km further southeast.

The bus station, train station and Jelačić Square – and indeed the whole city centre – are well connected by a regular and efficient tram network (page 87).

Zagreb's weekend playgrounds – beyond the obvious bulk of Mount Medvednica to the north – are the **Jarun Lake** [76 C6], to the southwest, with its summer beaches, and the enormous forested **Maksimir Park** [77 F4] (where you'll also find the zoo) to the northeast.

GETTING AROUND

PUBLIC TRANSPORT Zagreb has excellent public transport, based around trams (and a tiny funicular) in the city centre, and a wide-ranging network of buses running to the inner and outer suburbs, all managed by ZET, Zagrebački Električni Tramvaj (www.zet.hr – in Croatian only) and all running from 05.00 to midnight – with a selection of night trams and buses as well. Maps of the network are published at most tram stops, making the system extremely easy to navigate.

There's a **flat fare ticket** that now costs a budget-friendly 10kn (which by the way is actually less than it used to be, a wonderfully refreshing change if you're used to price hikes on public transport in the UK) from news stands or on board (you'll be expected to have the right money). This is valid for 90 minutes from the time you punch it on board, for travel in the same direction on any number or combination of trams and buses. Tickets are also available on plastic pre-pay cards (making the ticket price cheaper than the paper tickets), which can be bought from newspaper kiosks. You can buy a single ticket by texting 'ZG' to ☏ 8585 just before boarding a tram; you'll receive a confirmation saying you've paid – and will need to show the message to a ticket inspector if one boards the tram (and they *do* board trams, so don't get caught out). On night-time services, tickets are 15kn.

Trips far into the suburbs also cost more. For a full list of fares, see www.zet. hr and click on 'Services'; in the unlikely event that you're stuck trying to find a newsagent or kiosk to buy a pre-pay or other ticket, there's also list of vendors and opening times on the website. The on-the-spot fine for travelling without a ticket is 150kn (and yes, there are inspectors and they do check). Note that travel on trams within central Zagreb is no longer free (as it was for a few years in the noughties), and requires a ticket.

A great-value **day pass** is available at 30kn, which is valid until 04.00 the following morning, or 70kn for three days. Much better value if you're here for three days or more however is the 90kn **Zagreb Card** (page 89), which covers not just all the public transport for 72 hours, it also gives numerous discounts to boot.

Trams Trams have been part of the very fabric of Zagreb since the first horse-drawn variety was introduced in 1892, and particularly since the electric tram started up in 1910. Today there are 15 day routes, and another four night routes, which run from midnight to 04.00. It's a good gag to get people to meet you at a #10 or #16 tram stop, as these routes don't exist.

The network is extremely efficient, though trams can get pretty crowded around the rush hour. All day routes run at least six times an hour, though as routes run in parallel you'll rarely find yourself waiting even five minutes for a ride. Night routes (#31, #32, #33, #34) go from the same stops as the day routes and are serviced about every 45 minutes, but take routes that even locals consider abstruse. When the tracks are being repaired, night trams are substituted by buses.

For quick reference, these are the stops you're most likely to use, and the trams that service them. See the map in the 2nd colour section for the full network.

Jelačić Square #1, #6, #11, #12, #13, #14, #17
Glavni Kolodvor (train station) #2, #4, #6, #9, #13
Autobusni Kolodvor (bus station) #2, #5, #6, #7, #8
Bukovačka (Maksimir Park, zoo) #4, #7, #11, #12

Local buses Anywhere there isn't a tram you'll find a bus, with ZET operating some 120 routes in total (70 within the city and 50 to the outer suburbs); almost all of them connect neatly into the tram network. Frequency varies enormously, with some routes running up to eight times an hour and others operating every half hour or hour; a few routes only run during the rush hour. Where specific buses will be useful to you I've provided details in the text.

Funicular There's a charming little funicular that runs from the main shopping street, Ilica, up to Gradec, the old town. Originally opened in 1891, as a steam-powered affair, the funicular was electrified in the 1930s. It's said to be the shortest in Europe, and at just 66m in length it's certainly a plausible claim; it's also one of the steepest funiculars in the world, with a vertical gain of 30m (which makes you wonder, though, at what degree of steepness a railway becomes a funicular, and a funicular becomes a plain old-fashioned lift). Anyway, it's a bit of fun, and well worth the 4kn fare, and it takes the legwork out of schlepping up to the Lotrščak Tower.

Cable car If the funicular isn't enough of a thrill for you, then you can try the cable car that climbs up towards the highest peak on Mount Medvednica, Sljeme (1,030m) – or at least you could, until it went out of service to be upgraded a few years ago, and still hasn't reopened at the time of writing in 2015. Built in the early 1960s, it covers a horizontal distance of 4km and a vertical one of nearly 700m. Until it stopped running it cost 11kn one-way/17kn return, ran every hour on the hour (but not at all if windy), and the journey took about 25 minutes. For more details on both the cable car and Medvednica, see pages 132–3.

Taxis By local standards, taxis were an expensive way of getting around until the arrival of Cammeo Taxis a few years ago, which introduced cheaper fares, causing outrage among other taxi firms and leading to strikes, and eventually forcing them to lower their fares somewhat as well (though Cammeo and now EkoTaxi remain the cheapest, for absolutely no loss in service or reliability). EkoTaxi (☎ *1414 or 060 7777; www.ekotaxi.hr*) fares – clearly listed on the website – are 8kn (well, 8.80kn to be precise) plus 6kn per kilometre thereafter, with no extra charges for baggage, and no increase in fares at night. Cammeo (☎ *060 700 700 or 1212; www.taxi-cammeo. net*) fares are similar, though not listed so clearly on its website. Fares for other taxi firms are higher, though even Zagreb Radio Taxis (once much more expensive) has now dropped its fares to 10kn start and 6kn per kilometre. You can pick up a taxi fairly easily in a number of public locations, including Trg Maršala Tita, by the theatre, or near the cathedral at Kaptol, as well as at any of the bigger hotels. If you're calling a taxi yourself, try EkoTaxi, Cammeo, or Zagreb Radio Taxi (☎ *1777 or 060 800 800; www.radio-taksi-zagreb.hr*).

Bicycles As a keen cyclist myself, I'd love to rave about what a fabulously cycle-friendly city Zagreb is, but the truth is that even though it ought to be perfect (mostly flat terrain, wide streets, large leafy squares, and 135km of cycle paths), it just isn't. City drivers aren't used to sharing their roads with cyclists, and can be somewhat aggressive, if not downright dangerous, so you're pretty much forced to use the pavements – which you then have to share not just with pedestrian traffic but also illegally parked cars.

That said, continuous efforts are being made to make Zagreb a better place for cyclists, and, ironically, cycling on some of the city's biggest thoroughfares, especially south of the railway line, is great, as the dedicated cycle paths there are kept well away from the traffic – notably along Vukovarska and Slavonska/Ljubljanska, and across both the central and eastern bridges over the Sava to Bundek and Novi Zagreb.

For the more athletic, there's fantastic cycling up on Mount Medvednica, and good cycle maps available which cover the trails through the woods, while a more leisurely spin can be had down on Lake Jarun or at Bundek – though both can get very busy on a summer Sunday afternoon. There's also excellent cycling available in Zagreb County, and you can pick up a whole raft of first-rate maps from the county tourist office (page 89), which detail not just the routes along with profiles, etc, but also places to stay and eat, and useful stuff like the locations of the nearest bike repair shops. Be warned, though, that you'll need a sturdy bike as quite a few trails take advantage of traffic-free gravel roads.

There are an increasing number of places where you can rent bikes, including **Blue Bike Zagreb** (m *098 246 320; www.zagrebbybike.com; €13/day, or €9 after 15.00*), which also offers cycle tours. If you have your own bike in Zagreb and need repairs, I can wholeheartedly recommend Vladimir Fumić, former pro and Croatian champion, who has a shop on the southwestern edge of town (*Dr Luje Naletilića 30c;* ☎ *466 4233; e bicikli.fumic@gmail.com; www.biciklifumic.hr*). This is also the place to head if you stay longer and want to buy a bike in Zagreb – it happens – or check out the locally designed and built **Mondo** (*http://mondobicikli.com*).

There's also a busy cycling association in Zagreb, which sponsors activities across Croatia, and is working notably on the major Danube cycle path project, as well as the excellent 'Bike and Bed' initiative, which promotes cycle-tourism (*http://mojbicikl.hr/bike-bed*). Alternatively, you can hire a **Segway** from Segway City Tour Zagreb (*www.segway.hr; tours €33–65*).

Zagreb has excellent tourist information, with a number of good free guides and maps available along with an information-packed website (*www.zagreb-touristinfo.hr*). The main **tourist information office** [91 D4] (✆ 481 4051/2/4; e info@zagreb-touristinfo.hr; ☉ summer *08.30–21.00 Mon–Fri, 09.00–18.00 Sat–Sun, winter 08.30–20.00 Mon–Fri, 09.00–18.00 Sat, 10.00–16.00 Sun*) is at Jelačić Square, less than ten minutes' walk from the railway station heading towards the town centre. There are also smaller offices at the airport and main railway and bus station, and at Lotrščak Tower – for a full list of tourist offices, contact details and opening times, see www.zagreb-touristinfo.hr. You can also get information by email.

Ask the friendly staff for a city map, and the **City Walks** and monthly **Events and Performances** brochures. They'll also be able to give you advice on (but not – officially, anyway – help in) finding accommodation, and can sell you the 72-hour **Zagreb Card**. This is tremendous value at 90kn, with unlimited city transport for the duration, half-price entry to the city's museums, 20% off most theatre tickets, and discounts on a huge range of goods and services, from restaurants and hotels to medical, dental and beauty treatments – ask for the Zagreb Card Guide for full details, or visit www.zagrebcard.fivestars.hr. There's a 24-hour version of the card priced at 60kn. The tourist office also has a good walking map of Mount Medvednica for sale and, if you're here for more than half a day, the bi-monthly *Zagreb: In Your Pocket* guide is a superb resource which you should definitely pick up a copy of.

For information on sights immediately outside the Zagreb metropolitan area, you'll need to contact the **Zagreb County Tourist Office** [89 B6] (*Turistička Zajednica Zagrebačke Županije*, which is at Preradovićeva 42; ✆ 487 3665; ✆ 487 3670; www.tzzz.hr; ☉ 08.00–16.00 Mon–Fri). The office has friendly, English-speaking staff, as well as everything you need to know about local attractions such as the picturesque town of Samobor, local wineries, rural accommodation and country restaurants, as well as free cycling and walking maps for those keen to enjoy the great outdoors.

MAPS There are about half a dozen different Zagreb maps in circulation, mostly with the old town on one side and the surrounding city on the other. Given the modest size and scale of the place, any of these should be more than adequate – despite the frequent lack of helpful information like scale, footpaths, bike tracks and so on.

If you're into cycling or walking, and planning to take a trip out of town, get hold of the Zagreb County Tourist Board's excellent maps, which show biking and walking trails along with suggested touring itineraries that take you through some of the county's prettiest countryside on smaller, mostly traffic-free roads.

LOCAL TOUR OPERATORS AND TRAVEL AGENCIES

There's a host of local tour operators and travel agencies in Zagreb; of these the following list includes the best known and longest established, as well as some excellent newer agencies. Most can organise entire holidays for you, including travel to and from your home country, as well as excursions and accommodation. You can also book air tickets by phone through the Croatia Airlines office, listed overleaf. For a full list of travel agencies in Zagreb, www.zagreb-touristinfo.hr/travel-plan/turist-information/travel-agencies.

Zagreb **LOCAL TOUR OPERATORS AND TRAVEL AGENCIES**

3

Atlas [84 A6] Izidora Kršnjavog 1; 241 5611; www.atlas-croatia.com; ① 08.00–21.00 Mon–Fri, 08.00–16.00 Sat. Zagreb office of the Dubrovnik-based company established in 1923 offering a wide range of coast-focused services, from flights & coach tours to accommodation, & also the Croatian representative for American Express. In the Hotel Westin.

Croatia Express [91 C5] Teslina 4; 481 1842; and Tomislav Trg 17; 492 2224; www.croatia-express.com; ① 09.00–17.00 Mon–Fri, 09.00–13.00 Sat. Specialising in rail, bus, ferry & airline bookings; also luxury coach charter & excursions.

Croatian Youth Hostel Association (HFHS) Savska 5/1; 482 9296, www.hfhs.hr. Advance bookings for Croatia's (few) youth hostels. You can also get an ISIC student card here (proof of student status required).

Kompas [91 C5] Gajeva 6; 481 1536; www.kompas.hr; ① 08.00–20.00 Mon–Fri, 09.00–13.30 Sat. Day excursions, bus tours, accommodation in Zagreb & on the coast, & a range of outdoor activities.

Plitvice Lakes National Park [91 C7] Tomislava 19; 461 3586/492 2274/487 0111; www.np-plitvicka-jezera.hr; ① 08.00–16.00 Mon–Fri. The park office can arrange excursions & accommodation to the national park.

STA Zagreb [91 B6] Andrije Hebrangova 22; 488 6340; www.staputovanja.com; ① 09.00–17.00 Mon–Fri. Part of the STA Travel group; specialises in student & discount travel.

ZagrebTours [85 G4] Lopasiceva 12a; 482 5035; www.zagreb-tours.com. New agency offering tours throughout Croatia.

WHERE TO STAY

As a bustling, business-oriented capital city, Zagreb has no shortage of accommodation, though until quite recently finding budget accommodation presented something of a challenge. Happily, however, the variety of accommodation on offer – both in terms of type and price – has expanded considerably over the past few years, and there's now something for most tastes and budgets.

Zagreb has plenty of **hotels**, though most still don't come especially cheap; there's nowhere within easy reach where you'll find a room for under €60 a night, and most upmarket establishments charge upwards of €120 per night for a double, all

---

ZAGREB *Gornji Grad, Kaptol & Donji Grad*
For listings, see pages 92–104

Where to stay

1	Best Western Premier Astoria...D7	3	Dubrovnik...C4	6	Taban...C1
2	Chillout Hostel...B4	4	Jaegerhorn...B4	7	Youth Hostel...D7
		5	Palace...C6	8	Zigzag...D5

Where to eat and drink

9	Agava...C3	26	Gulliver...C3	42	Nokturno...C3
10	Art Paviljon...D7	27	Hemingway...A5	43	Old Pharmacy Pub...C6
11	Asia...D7	28	Ivica i Marica...C2	44	Oliver Twist...C2
12	Baltazar...C1		Jaegerhorn...(see 4)	45	Oranž...B4
13	Ban Caffe...C4	29	Juice&Juice...A5		Palace...(see 5)
14	Boban...C5	30	K&K...D4	46	Piccolo Mondo...C4
15	Bulldog Pub...B4	31	Kaptolska Klet...C3	47	Pif...B5
16	Caffe Palainovka...C1		Kazališka	48	Pivnica Mali Medo...C2
17	Capuciner...C3		Kavana...(see 27)	49	Pivnica Tomislav...C7
18	Centar...D4	32	Katedralis...C3	50	Pod Gričkim Topom...B4
19	Charlie's...C4	33	Kerempuh...C3	51	Purger...D5
20	Cica...C3	34	Korčula...B5	52	Škola...B4
21	Čvenk...B3	35	La Bodega Pub...B4	53	Stari Fijaker...A3
22	Dubravkin Put...B1	36	Lari i Penati...D7	54	Strossmayer Bar...B3
	Dubrovnik Hotel Café...(see 3)	37	Lav...D4	55	Tolkein's House...C2
23	Gallo...B6		Mala Kavana...(see 12)		Trakošćan...(see 40)
	Gašpar...(see 11)	38	Maraschino...B4	56	Trilogija...B3
24	Giardino...C2	39	Mašklin i Lata...B6	57	Vallis Aurea...B4
25	Gradska Kavana...D4	40	Millennium...B4	58	Vincek...B4
		41	Mimice...D4	59	Žabica...B2

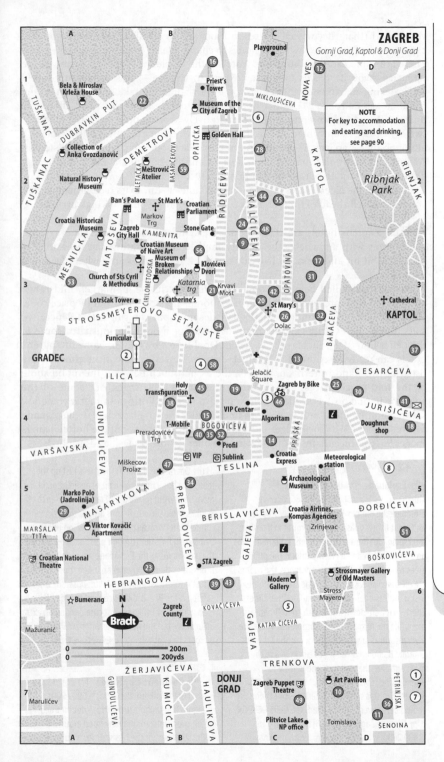

A   B   C   D

Playground

16

Priest's
Tower

Bela & Miroslav
Krleža House

22

Museum of the
City of Zagreb

6

12

NOVA VES

MIKLOUŠIĆEVA

Golden Hall

Collection of
Anka Gvozdanović

Meštrović
Atelier

59

Natural History
Museum

Ban's Palace   St Mark's

Croatia Historical
Museum

Markov
Trg

Croatian
Parliament

Zagreb
City Hall

KAMENITA

Stone Gate

Croatian Museum
of Naïve Art

56

Museum of
Broken
Relationships

Klovićevi
Dvori

Church of Sts Cyril
& Methodius

53

Katarnia
trg

Lotrščak Tower

St Catherine's

Krvavi
Most

21

STROSSMAYEROVO ŠETALIŠTE

Funicular

2

57

54

50

GRADEC

ILICA

4   58

44   55

24

48

9

RADIĆEVA

TKALĆIĆEVA

KAPTOL

Ribnjak
Park

RIBNJAK

17

31

42   33

OPATOVINA

20   St Mary's

26   32

Dolac

13

BAKAĆEVA

Cathedral

KAPTOL

37

Jelačić
Square   Zagreb by Bike

3   46

CESARĆEVA

25   30

JURIŠIĆEVA

41

Doughnut
shop

18

Holy
Transfiguration

45   19

VIP Centar

Algoritam

38

T-Mobile

15

BOGOVIĆEVA

Preradovićev
Trg

40   35   52

Profil

VIP

Sublink

TESLINA

14

Croatia
Express

PRAŠKA

Meteorological
station

8

Miškecov
Prolaz

47

VARŠAVSKA

GUNDULIĆEVA

MASARYKOVA

Marko Polo
(Jadrolinija)

29

34

PRERADOVIĆEVA

Archaeological
Museum

BERISLAVIĆEVA

Croatia Airlines,
Kompas Agencies

Zrinjevac

GAJEVA

ĐORĐIĆEVA

51

MARŠALA
TITA

27

Viktor Kovačić
Apartment

Croatian National
Theatre

STA Zagreb

23

HEBRANGOVA

39   43

BOŠKOVIĆEVA

Strossmayer Gallery
of Old Masters

Stross-
Mayerov

Bumerang

N

Bradt

Zagreb
County

KOVAĆIĆEVA

Modern
Gallery

5

6

Mažuranić

0   200m
0   200yds

KATAN ĆIĆEVA

GAJEVA

TRENKOVA

PETRINJSKA

1   7

ŽERJAVIĆEVA

DONJI
GRAD

Zagreb Puppet
Theatre

Art Pavilion

10

7

36

Marulićev

49

Plitvice Lakes
NP office

Tomislava

ŠENOINA

11

A   B   C   D

year round (that's if you make a reservation well in advance, otherwise you can expect some of the more exclusive hotels to charge a fairly breathtaking €250-plus). There are some excellent **boutique hotels** – the President (page 93) is one of the updater's favourite places to stay anywhere in Croatia – plus some truly lovely **self-catering** apartments which give you a whole different take on your stay in the Croatian capital (page 94), and a new breed of stylish, shiny-clean and affordable **hostels**. **Private rooms** remain in comparatively short supply (and are generally twice the price of anywhere else in the country, with the exception of Dubrovnik), although there's an ever-increasing number of places opening, with many listed on AirBnB (*www.airbnb.co.uk*). There is also a campsite, but for staying in and seeing Zagreb, this is not an option we can honestly recommend.

Of course, the nicest places fill up fast at any time of year, so it's recommended that you reserve well ahead of time, and get confirmation that your booking's in place.

HOTELS Zagreb's hotels are classified by the standard international star system; however, as with anywhere, the quality implied by this rating can occasionally be a little bit hit and miss, so I've done my best to let you know what places are really like.

Hotels are detailed below in four categories – exclusive, upmarket, mid-range and budget – and are listed within each section in alphabetical order by price code. Note that with the exception of the Esplanade's undisputed historical opulence, five stars doesn't necessarily get you anything better or more luxurious than some of the better four-stars, such as the excellent DoubleTree by Hilton. None of Zagreb's hotels can really be counted as 'budget' choices, however four of the cheapest are listed below – and in terms of quality, there's not much between them and some of the mid-range places. For slightly lower prices still, check out some of the apartments and hostels sections below. It's also worth pointing out that if you book several months ahead online, you can find doubles even at places like the Esplanade for well under €150. The budget-conscious should also check out the hostel listings (pages 95–6), since many of the newer ones offer doubles as well as dorm beds.

Exclusive

🏠 **Esplanade** [84 D6] (209 rooms) Mihanovićeva 1; ☏ 456 6666, 456 6600; www. esplanade.hr. Built in 1925 as a swanky stopover for Orient Express passengers en route to Istanbul, the Esplanade (formerly the Regent Esplanade) has now been restored to its former glory. The public areas reek of 1920s European opulence, the rooms are ultra-stylish & spacious, & the staff combine 5-star professionalism with unfailing friendliness. Check-in is a sit-down affair with complimentary fizz while the formalities are completed. There are even discounts at w/ends. Check out the fabulous Emerald Ballroom & the set of clocks inside the main entrance that tell the time in New York, Buenos Aires, London, Zagreb, Moscow, Tokyo & Sydney. B/fast is simply wonderful – but then so it should be, at over 200kn a head. €€€€€–€€€€

🏠 **Westin Zagreb** [84 B6] Krsnjavoga 1; ☏ 489 2000; www.westin.com. Formerly known

as the Opera (the National Theatre is just up the road), the hotel might be a bit of an architectural monstrosity, but inside it's all tasteful opulence & impeccable service. Rooms are spacious & comfortable, with a special emphasis on luxurious bed & bath facilities (though personally I still think the bathrooms at the Esplanade are nicer). For fitness fans there's a gym & an indoor pool, & the b/fast is terrific – unlimited *pršut*, *paški sir*, smoked salmon & the like, & dishes cooked to order. B/fast is an additional 140kn pp & secure parking an extra 60kn a day; but the hotel does offer 20% discount on room rates at w/ends. €€€€€–€€€€

Upmarket

✳🏠 **DoubleTree by Hilton** [77 E6] (152 rooms) Grada Vukovarska 269a; ☏ 600 1900; e zagreb.info@hilton.com; http://doubletree3. hilton.com. Outstanding new hotel around 600m southeast of the bus station, with spacious rooms boasting floor-to-ceiling windows (go for the corner rooms for the best views), spotless bathrooms with separate bathtubs & walk-in showers, & impeccably friendly staff. Very good restaurant (OXBO Urban Bar & Grill; €€€€), delicious b/fasts, bar, fitness centre, indoor pool & sauna. Easily within the same league as the better-known Esplanade & Westin. Highly recommended. €€€€€–€€€€

🏠 **Dubrovnik** [91 C4] (237 rooms) Gajeva 1; ☏ 486 3555; www.hotel-dubrovnik.hr. If the exterior is a tribute to 1970s socialist architecture, 50 of the Dubrovnik's rooms have recently been refurbished – & the location, overlooking Jelačić Square, is unbeatable if you want to be right in the thick of things. Rooms are comfortable & have AC, & those overlooking the square – & it's one of the best views of the square you'll find anywhere – are also noise-proofed against the coming & going of Zagreb's trams. €€€€€–€€€€

🏠 **Sheraton Zagreb** [85 F6] (300 rooms) Kneza Borne 2; ☏ 455 3535; www.hotel-sheratonzagreb.com. Located 2 blocks up & 3 blocks east of the station, the Sheraton is a glass-fronted city block that offers as much luxury & all the facilities anyone's going to need, including a gym & an indoor pool – though you have to ask yourself which humorist was responsible for putting the fitness centre on the smokers' floor. €€€€€–€€€€

🏠 **9** [85 H7] (20 rooms) Marina Držića 9; ☏ 562 5040; www.hotel9.hr. Stylish new boutique hotel just across the road from the bus station, with floors & rooms themed in white, silver(ish) or gold. €€€€

🏠 **AS** [76 D4] Zelengaj 2; ☏ 460 9111; www. hotel-as.hr. Excellent hotel with clean, spacious rooms & good service hidden out amid the greenery of Zelengaj, north of Britanski Square. €€€€

🏠 **Best Western Premier Astoria** [91 D7] (102 rooms) Petrinjska 71; ☏ 480 8900; www. bestwestern.com. Handy location in the town centre, with comfortable rooms. The hotel also boasts a fairly upmarket Croatian restaurant, the Ragusa. €€€€

🏠 **International** [76 D6] (207 rooms) Miramarska 24; ☏ 610 8800/8400; www.hotel-international.hr. This modern 4-star business hotel is a 10min walk south of the railway & features elegantly appointed rooms. €€€€

🏠 **Jaegerhorn** [91 B4] (13 rooms) Ilica 14; ☏ 483 3877; www.hotel-jagerhorn.hr. Perfectly located, but tucked away from the hustle & bustle of Ilica itself, at the end of a narrow shopping arcade, this family-run hotel has simple, pleasant rooms & was refurbished in 2011. There's also a decent restaurant & leafy, tranquil garden terrace with a waterfall, backing on to the steep park that leads up to the old town. Popular, so reserve well in advance. €€€€

🏠 **Palace Hotel** [91 C6] (125 rooms) Strossmayerov 10; ☏ 489 9600; www.palace.hr. The Palace was built in 1891 & has been a hotel since 1907. While it retains much of its old-fashioned Secession-era charm, its rooms have all been modernised, though some remain surprisingly boxy. €€€€

✳ 🏠 **President** [76 C4] (7 rooms) Pantovčak 52; ☏ 488 1480; www.president-zagreb.com. Extremely nice, stylish boutique hotel, only a short distance up Pantovčak from Britanski Square. One of the best places to stay in Zagreb. Highly recommended. €€€€

🏠 **Arcotel Allegra** [85 F6] (150 rooms) Branimirova 29, Branimir Centar; ☏ 469 6000; www.arcotel.at/allegra. Very modern, very chic, with spacious, minimalist rooms. Part of an Austrian chain, the Arcotel has earned a reputation for gay-friendliness in a town that's still a bit uneasy about same-sex couples. If you plan to partake of the copious b/fast buffet, count an extra €14.50pp; there's a cheaper breakfast (€5) on offer in the bar; vegan options available. €€€€–€€€

Mid-range

🏠 **Jadran** [85 F3] (49 rooms) Vlaška 50; ☏ 455 3777; www.hoteljadran.com.hr. Extremely well located on Vlaška, just a few mins east of Trg Jelačića & round the corner from the cathedral, the ageing Jadran was completely renovated in 2013. The staff are friendly & the prices reasonable for a place this central. €€€€–€€€

🏠 **Vila Tina** [77 E4] (24 rooms) Bukovačka Cesta 213; ☏ 244 5204; www.hotelvilatina.hr; take tram #1, #9 or #17 to Svetice (the stop before Borongaj, the terminus), & then bus #203, & look for the small stone lions flanking the hotel's gate on the left-hand side of Bukovačka, heading up the hill. A modern Italianate villa set in the pleasant hills near Maksimir Park, this is a stylish option. A small outdoor swimming pool is complemented by a jacuzzi, solarium & sauna, & there's also a nice restaurant. €€€€–€€€

⌂ **Central** [85 E6] (76 rooms) Branimirova 3; ☎484 1122; www.hotel-central.hr. An affordable 3-star hotel, the recently renovated Central is extremely well located just across from the railway station, & has straightforward AC. If the building's façade is rather characterless, the friendly, helpful staff will do their best to make you feel at home. €€€

⌂ **Meridijan 16** [77 E5] (25 rooms) Vukovarska 241; ☎606 5200; www.meridijan16.com. Located bang on the 16th meridian, just 500m south of the main bus station, this hotel's rooms are all tastefully furnished & have AC. The situation, on most of Zagreb's main tram routes, makes getting in & out of town a breeze (#2 & #6 run direct to the bus & train stations, #6 & #13 direct to Jelačić Square). €€€

⌂ **Panorama** [76 D5] (228 rooms, 51 apts) Trg Krešimira Ćosića 9; ☎365 8299; www.panorama-zagreb.com. Formerly Four Points by Sheraton. Smart, business-oriented hotel about 3km southwest of the city centre, near Dom Sportova. Popular for wedding receptions. €€€

⌂ **Rebro** [77 E4] (60 rooms) Kišpatićeva 12; ☎888 6900; e info@hotelrebro.com; www.hotelrebro.com. Near Maksimir Park. Pet friendly. €€€

Budget

⌂ **Sliško** [77 E5] (49 rooms) Supilova 13; ☎618 4777; e hotel@slisko.hr; www.slisko.hr. A clean, well-run establishment located just 300m southeast of the main bus station in a quiet street with a couple of useful grocery stores nearby. Bright, airy rooms in pastel tones, & its own bar & café/restaurant. Very good value. €€€

⌂ **Fala** [76 D6] (15 rooms) Trnjanske Ledine II 18; ☎611 1062; www.hotelfala.hr. Another pleasant affordable choice, spotless, newly furnished – if a bit spartan. Just south of Slavonska avenija – take bus # 219, 220, 221 or 268 from the main train or bus stations & head a couple of stops south towards Novi Zagreb. €€€–€€

⌂ **Ilica** [84 A4] (23 rooms, 1 apt) Ilica 102; ☎377 7522; www.hotel-ilica.hr. Set in a courtyard just 2 tram stops (or 10–15min walk) west of Jelačić Square (& 100m west of Britanski Square). Rooms are a bargain (at least, for central Zagreb) & get booked up very fast indeed. €€€–€€

⌂ **Maksimir** [77 E5] (12 rooms) Maksimirska 57a; ☎666 6160; www.hotel-maksimir.hr. Brand new, clean & well-priced little hotel just a few stops out towards Maksimir (tram #11 or #12 from Jelačić Square). Very good value. €€

APARTMENTS, PRIVATE ROOMS & B&BS For a big city, Zagreb (unlike most places on the coast and islands) has a surprisingly limited supply of private rooms, so count yourself lucky if you manage to secure one of the few rooms in the city centre – otherwise you'll find yourself out in the suburbs, using public transport to get into town. However, a number of stylish new apartments have been popping up in recent years, many of them centrally located and in most cases exceptionally good value, providing a very welcome boost to the range of accommodation available in the Croatian capital.

The Zagreb County Tourist Office also maintains a list of private accommodation options on its website (*www.zagreb-touristinfo.hr*) – you can find them by clicking on the 'Accommodation' option on the home page.

Evistas also handles private room bookings [85 E6] (*Šenoina 28;* ☎ *483 9554; www.evistas.hr;* ⏰ *09.00–20.00 Mon–Fri, 09.30–17.00 Sat*), a block north of Branimirova (the main road running east–west in front of the train station). Private room rates are usually quoted per person per night for a minimum of two nights; add 20% to the standard per-night rate if you're only planning an overnight stay. As rooms go quickly, try to arrive early.

⌂ **InZagreb** (10 apts) Various locations; ☎091 6523 201; e info@inzagreb.com; www.inzagreb.com. Beautifully decorated apartments in various locations. €€€

⌂ **Lobagola** [76 C5] (6 rooms) Bosanska 3; ☎580 1990, 091 4311 070; e 4guests@lobagola.com; www.lobagola.com. Small, cycle-friendly B&B, 10min walk west of Britanski trg. Tastefully decorated dbl, trpl & quad rooms, all with private bathrooms, AC, Wi-Fi, use of garage, & b/fast. €€€

⌂ **Zigzag** [91 D5] (11 apts, 4 dbls, 1 sgl) Petrinjska 9; ☎ 889 5433; e info@zigzag.hr; www. zigzag.hr. Stylish, centrally located apartments. €€€

⌂ **Studio Kairos B&B** [85 G3] (4 rooms) Vlaška 92; ☎ 091 4640 690; e info@studio-kairos. com; www.studio-kairos.com. Can be booked as individual rooms or whole house (sleeping up to 10). Bike rental available. €€€–€€

❋ ⌂ **Zagreb Point Apartments** (9 apts) ☎ 099 5622 485; e zagrebapartment@gmail. com; www.zagreb-apartment.net. Excellent, spacious apts, all conveniently located around or near the city centre, spotlessly clean, stylishly decorated & run as efficiently as any upmarket hotel. Prices range from €50

to €130 depending on the apt & sleep up to 4 or even 5. Good value, arguably better than any other accommodation Zagreb has on offer. €€€–€€

⌂ **Camera Felice** [76 D5] (2 rooms) Trg Vladka Mačeka 2; ☎ 091 9000 342, 098 282 040; e info@camera-felice.com; http://camera-felice. com. Nicely decorated en-suite rooms in a decent location, 10min walk west of the National Theatre, at the far end of Gjure Deželića. AC, Wi-Fi. €€

⌂ **Apartment Katarina** [77 E6] (1 apt) Vranovina 26; m 099 8119 882; e info@ apartmanka.com; www.apartmanka.com. Large, nicely decorated spacious apt in a convenient location, 5min walk east of the Lisinski Theatre. Very good value, with rates dropping even further for stays of more than 5 nights. €€–€

YOUTH HOSTELS AND STUDENT ACCOMMODATION Zagreb has two official hostels that are part of the Croatian Youth Hostel Association (HFHS), one in the centre of town, and the other in the suburb of Remetinec, southwest of the city, across the river from the Jarun Lake. Several private hostels have now opened, offering doubles as well as dorms and representing excellent value. There's also an excellent private hostel in the suburb of Ravnice, east of the city centre and easily reachable on the tram.

In summer, it's also sometimes possible to get a bed in the university student dorms (ask at the Tourist Office on Jelačić Square), though prices aren't always as low as you might expect. A handful of other budget possibilities is posted on the Zagreb Tourist Office website (*www.zagreb-touristinfo.hr*); click on the Accommodation section and follow the link 'For students and youth'.

⌂ **Taban** [91 C1] (16 rooms) Tkalčićeva 82; ☎ 553 3527; e reception@tabanzagreb.com; www. tabanzagreb.com. Opened in 2012 at the far end of Zagreb's ultimate café/bar street, with its own nice, laid-back café spilling out on to the pavement. Friendly staff & clean rooms, available as singles, doubles (more like a boutique hotel than a hostel) & 5- to 6-bed dorms, priced 100kn per person in dorms to 420kn for a deluxe double. Excursions & bike rental available. €€€–€

⌂ **Chillout Hostel** [91 B4] (89 beds) Tomićeva 5a; ☎ 484 9605; e info@chillout-hostel- zagreb.com; www.chillout-hostel-zagreb.com. Opened in 2012, just off Ilica near the bottom of the funicular, with friendly staff & clean rooms, including two doubles & various sized dorms, the latter priced 120–140kn per person in season. €€–€

⌂ **Youth Hostel** [91 D7] (210 beds) Petrinjska 77; ☎ 484 1261; e zagreb@hfhs.hr; www.hfhs.hr. Centrally located near the train station & recently renovated, but despite having over 200 beds it's almost invariably full, & (at least in the past) had a reputation for being a bit rough, especially if you're travelling alone. €€–€

⌂ **Brit Hostel** [84 A4] (72 rooms) Fra Andrije Kačića Miošića 3b; ☎ 484 7516; e info@brithostel- zagreb.com; www.brithostel-zagreb.com. Another new hostel, this one near Britanski trg. 6- to 12-bed dorms as well as dbls, 93kn–173kn in season. €

⌂ **Swanky Mint Hostel** [84 B3] (57 beds) Ilica 50; ☎ 01 4004 248; www.swanky-hostel.com. Popular new place on the corner of Ilica & Frankopanska in renovated old textile factory, with accommodation ranging from 4-bed studio apts & dbls to 4-, 6-, 8- & 9-bed dorms. Has its own bar. €€€–€

🏠 **Ravnice Youth Hostel** [77 F5] (30 beds) Ravnice 38d; ☎ 233 2325; e ravnice-youth-hostel@zg.hinet.hr; www.ravnice-youth-hostel.hr; tram #4, #7, #11 or #12 (direction Dubrava or Dubec) to the Ravnice stop, walk south for about 3mins, & look for the large hostel sign on the building itself. This bright, friendly family-run place is located past the Dinamo Stadium & Maksimir Park, on the right-hand side, by the tennis courts (follow the wonderful smell emanating from the Kraš Chocolate Factory). Spotless rooms, including dbls & sgls as well as 3- to 8-bed dorms, from €12 to €14 (dorms) & €34 (dbls) in season. **€**

CAMPING At the time of writing, Zagreb really wasn't set up for campers at all, and you're pretty much limited to the campsites at Motel Plitvice [76 A7] (☎ 653 0444; e recepcija@motel-plitvice.hr; www.motel-plitvice.hr; **€**), which is rather dismally situated on the Plitvice road, southwest of the city, near the motorway junction – and the rooms will set you back more than budget and even some mid-range choices in Zagreb itself. A bridge over the highway brings you to the service station, where you can at least take advantage of the shops and self-service restaurants.

✖ WHERE TO EAT AND DRINK

Food and drink are easy to find in Zagreb, with restaurants, bars and cafés for all tastes – and budgets – and a wonderful seven-day-a-week open market in Dolac, just north of Jelačić Square (page 104).

As you'd expect in a fast-moving city, there are plenty of places where you can get a bite on the hoof, fast food coming in traditional (sausages etc) or contemporary (burgers and the like) formats, and the city having quite a few sandwich bars, both local and US-style, as well as plentiful ice-cream shops.

You can also go for Zagreb's big speciality (and it is big), *štrukli*, which is something of a death by cream, doughy-pasta and cottage-cheese experience. It's somewhere between a giant cream-soaked ravioli and a cheese-stuffed dumpling. The dish technically comes from outside Zagreb, but the locals consume it here by the plate-load (boiled or baked; sweet or savoury; as a starter, main or dessert), and argue fiercely over where the best štrukli can be found (at the Esplanade hotel, in the author's opinion, or at Ivica i Marica in the updater's).

Zagreb also has its very own chocolate factory, Kraš, beyond Maksimir Park, which smells absolutely mouth-watering from anywhere in the vicinity (notably the Ravnice Youth Hostel), and churns out a good wide range of tasty sweetmeats.

RESTAURANTS At places marked as inexpensive in the listings on pages 97–101, expect to pay around 200kn for two, including wine; mid-range places will set you back 250–500kn for a couple; while at expensive restaurants two can easily pay 600kn and up – though there's nothing to stop you having a soup, a salad and a glass of wine at a ritzy place and coming away with change from 300kn for two. There's a recently initiated annual 'restaurant week' (so far, February/March, and actually lasting two weeks) in Zagreb, which sees participating restaurants offer discounts on meals.

Most restaurants catering to tourists stay open from around 11.00 to 23.00, though some (especially top-end establishments) will close for a period during the afternoon. Reservations are not normally expected (or accepted) except at the very upper end; where they are recommended, I've included the phone number with the listing.

I've listed restaurants here in four groupings for convenience: the upper town (everything from Gradec to Kaptol and along Tkalčićeva); Jelačić Square and the area west, south and east of it; the rest of the lower town (as far as the railway station); and restaurants a bit further afield (not including Mount Medvednica, which is covered separately in the Surrounds section).

Upper town

✗ Gašpar [91 C1] Nova Ves 4; ✆466 6999; ◷ noon–midnight Mon–Sat, noon–17.00 Sun. Shares a kitchen with its neighbour Baltazar (see below), but specialises in seafood. A good choice of freshly prepared dishes, served in a polished-wood setting styled to resemble the interior of an ocean cruiser. Reservations recommended. €€€€

✗ Pod Gričkim Topom [91 B3] Zakmardijeve Stube 5; ✆483 3607; www.restoran-pod-grickim-topom.hr; ◷ 11.00–midnight Mon–Sat. Tucked away from the crowds just under Strossmayerovo Šetalište on the edge of Gornji Grad, with a fine view out over the lower town from the garden terrace, this friendly, professional place serves up well-cooked Croatian favourites in a homey setting. It's located at the top of the steps leading down to Ilica, or easily reachable on the path up from the bottom of Radićeva, or from the Lotrščak Tower. €€€€

✗ Takenoko [84 D1] Nova Ves 17 (in the Kaptol Centar); ✆486 0530; www.takenoko.hr; ◷ noon–01.00 Mon–Sat, noon–18.00 Sun. On the Tkalčićeva side of the Kaptol Centar, this very chic Japanese restaurant is a welcome addition to Zagreb's rather Eurocentric restaurant scene, serving traditional sushi & sashimi along with more adventurous Japanese fusion cooking. Reservations recommended. There's another branch at Radnička cesta 37b (✆638 9398; ◷ 11.00–23.00 Mon–Sat). €€€€

✗ Agava [91 C3] Tkalčićeva 39; ✆482 9826; www.restaurant-agava.hr; ◷ 09.00–23.00 daily. The situation & setting – spread over several small terraces cascading down on to bustling Tkalčićeva – is just about unbeatable, & the food isn't bad either. Informal atmosphere, large range of salads, & an extensive choice of well-cooked pasta dishes (though they curiously only had one sort of pasta, fusilli, in stock, on the day I ate there). €€€€–€€€

✗ Baltazar [91 C1] Nova Ves 4; ✆466 6999; ◷ noon–midnight Mon–Sat, noon–17.00 Sun. A traditional, upper-end restaurant just up from the cathedral, popular with business people & large groups, with an extensive menu featuring mainly meat dishes (for fish from the same kitchen, see

Gašpar). Chef Tomislav Špiček carried off Croatia's coveted Chef of the Year award in 2003 & 2004. Reservations recommended. €€€€–€€€

✳✗ Ivica i Marica [91 C2] Tkalčićeva 70; ✆481 7321, 482 8999; www.ivicaimarica.com; ◷ 11.00–22.00 daily. Taking its name from the Croatian for 'Hansel & Gretel' – look out for the gingerbread motifs – this excellent restaurant takes its food seriously. The emphasis is on organic, locally grown fresh produce, there's a good wine list, & manageable portion sizes mean you might even find room to indulge in one of the sumptuous desserts. If you're in the mood for something local, try the top-notch baked štrukli – one of the finest in town, & certainly the only serious rival in Zagreb to Le Bistro at the Esplanade (page 99). Reservations recommended. €€€€–€€€

✗ Kaptolska Klet [91 C3] Kaptol 5; ✆487 6502; www.kaptolska-klet.eu; ◷ 11.00–midnight daily. Right opposite the cathedral, with a large, rustic internal courtyard, this large restaurant is popular with tour groups & invariably busy. Service can be slow & rather offhand, but the food – traditional country-style Croatian cooking – is good for the price. €€€

✳✗ Kerempuh [91 C3] Kaptol 3; ✆481 9000; ◷ 06.00–23.00 Mon–Sat, 07.00–16.00 Sun. Right on the corner of the Dolac market square is my favourite restaurant in all of Zagreb. Run by the ever-cheerful Nikica Vuksan, it's only open at lunchtime & at least half the tables seem to be permanently reserved by an eclectic bunch of retired university professors, former footballers & journalists. The menu is made fresh daily, & varies according to whatever's best in the market that morning. Chic, stylish interior, brisk, friendly service, & the view out over the market square from the newly extended terrace is wonderful. Reservations recommended. €€€

✗ Trilogija [91 B3] Kamenita 5; ✆485 1394; www.trilogija.com; ◷ 11.00–23.00 Mon–Thu, 11.00–01.00 Fri–Sat. Light snacks, imaginative tapas & an enormous wine list, near the Stone Gate. €€€

✗ Capuciner [91 C3] Kaptol 6; ✆481 0487; www.capuciner.hr; ◷ 08.00–midnight daily. Next door to Kaptolska Klet, this place is popular

3

with independent travellers in spite of (or perhaps because of) its simple, unpretentious décor. Efficient service, cheap prices & great pizza & pasta dishes with a pleasant side terrace. It does pizza deliveries too (same phone number). €€€–€€

✕ **Katedralis** [91 C3] Tome Bakača 9; 481 4938; www.katedralis.eu; ⏰ 07.00–23.00 daily. A conveniently located place in a pleasant setting facing the cathedral. You'll find most of the local staples at good prices, along with a tourist menu offering 4 courses for 90kn. €€€–€€

✳✕ **Pivnica Mali Medo** [91 C2] Tkalčićeva 36; www.pivnica-medvedgrad.hr. Of the various pivnicas in Zagreb, Mali Medo ('Little Bear') wins hands down in terms of location, on Tkalčićeva. Solid pub fare complimented by excellent locally brewed beers (from Pivnica Medvedgrad) – try the Crna kraljica ('black queen', a dark stout) or Grička vještica (a strong ruby ale). Recommended. €€€–€€

✕ **Nokturno** [91 C3] Skalinska 4; 481 3394; www.restoran.nokturno.hr; ⏰ 08.00–midnight Sun–Thu, 09.00–01.00 Fri–Sat. The ever-popular Nokturno, on the steep street running down from Kaptol to Tkalčićeva, serves up good pizzas & a wide range of pasta dishes in a simple, cheerful setting. There's a lively terrace, which is usually packed. Good value. €€

On & off Jelačić Square

✕ **Boban** [91 C5] Gajeva 3; 481 1549; www.boban.hr; ⏰ 11.00–23.00 Mon–Thu, 11.00–midnight Fri–Sat, noon–23.00 Sun. This enduringly popular & well-located establishment (just down from Jelačić Square) is owned by former football superstar Zvonimir Boban, who played for the Croatian national team & AC Milan. Underneath the café you'll find a busy Italian-themed restaurant in a brick-vaulted cellar, with excellent pasta dishes. Under the same ownership, a new restaurant, **Il Secondo**, has now opened at Avenijia Dubrovnik 12 (*www.ilsecondo.hr*). €€€

✕ **Jaegerhorn** [91 B4] Ilica 14; www.hotel-jagerhorn.hr. Part of the Jaegerhorn Pansion, the restaurant is located at the end of a narrow arcade off Ilica, with a lovely summer terrace (though the fountain really is noisy) & a large indoor seating area for colder weather. Traditional Croatian fare. €€€

✳✕ **Korčula** [91 B5] Teslina 17; 487 2159; ⏰ 11.00–23.00 Mon–Sat. Excellent, long-established & unpretentious traditional seafood restaurant, serving some of the best octopus *ispod peka* you're likely to taste anywhere. Highly recommended. €€€

✕ **Piccolo Mondo** [91 C4] Gajeva 1 (in the Hotel Dubrovnik); 486 5555; www.hotel-dubrovnik.hr; ⏰ 07.00–23.00 daily. Don't be fooled by the rather middle-of-the-road décor; this place does some of the best al dente pasta in Croatia, along with pizzas & good international-style fish & meat dishes. Service is efficient & friendly, & the location (right on Jelačić Square) couldn't be more central. €€€

✕ **Stari Fijaker** [91 A3] Mesnička 6; 483 3829; www.starifijaker.hr; ⏰ 11.00–23.00 Mon–Sat, 11.00–22.00 Sun. The name means 'old coach', & the emphasis is very much on old-fashioned country cooking from the Zagorje region north of Zagreb. The menu can be a little earthy for some – specialities include blood sausage, offal, *sarma* (stuffed cabbage leaves), turkey & *grah* (hearty bean stew), accompanied by an extensive selection of local & international beers. €€€

✕ **Purger** [91 D5] Petrinjska 33; 481 0713; www.purger.hr; ⏰ 07.00–23.00 Mon–Sat. A wholesome Croatian place on the street running southeast out of Jelačić Square, named after the local word for 'citizen' (a variant on burgher). It's modestly priced, popular with local politicians, & has a terrace at the back in summer. €€€–€€

✕ **Vallis Aurea** [91 B4] Tomićeva 4; 483 1305; www.vallis-aurea.com; ⏰ 11.00–23.00 Mon–Sat. A wonderful, rustic, down-to-earth place on the short pedestrian street off Ilica that leads up to the funicular, specialising in Slavonian & traditional Croatian dishes, served simply & in generous portions. Menu changes daily. Has a miniature terrace in summer on the street. €€€–€€

✳✕ **Pivnica Medvedgrad** [84 B4] Ilica 46; www.pivnica-medvedgrad.hr; ⏰ 10.00–midnight Mon–Sat, noon–midnight Sun. One of Zagreb's best pivnicas, serving Croatia's best beer (page 61), with a lovely beer garden out the back & some suitably tasty food to accompany those fine ales (try the *trganci*, small pieces of pasta ribbon smothered with sour cream & laced with bacon & sausage – ultimate comfort food; otherwise, the meat platter for 2 goes a long, long way). An essential stop for the updater on any visit to Zagreb. €€€–€

✕ **Lav** [89 D4] Vlaška 23; ⏰ 11.00–23.00 daily. A basic place (the name means 'lion') just east of

Jelačić Square with vaulted interior & a wee terrace tucked into an alleyway, serving decent pizzas from a wood-fired oven. €€

✖ **Lari i Penati** [91 D7] Petrinjska 42a; ☏465 5776; www.laripenati.hr; ⏰ 09.00–23.00 Mon–Fri, noon–17.00 Sat. Very good value soups & other light bites in a rather groovy little place with saucepans stuck to the walls. €€–€

✖ **Mimice** [91 D4] Jurišićeva 21; ⏰ 08.00–21.00 Mon–Fri, 08.00–17.00 Sat. No-frills whatsoever local seafood eatery with barstool type seats – fried squid or sardines served with French fries, a wedge of bread & a tumbler (that is, not a wine glass) of red wine. €€–€

✖ **Vegehop** [85 G3] Vlaška 79; ☏464 9400; www.vegehop.hr; ⏰ 11.00–19.00 Mon–Fri, noon–18.00 Sat/Sun. Stylish & very good value little vegetarian option, down an alley a couple of tram stops along Vlaška. Also does takeaways. €€–€

Lower town

✖ **Fontana** [85 F6] Kneza Borne 2 (at the Sheraton); ☏459 9158; www.hotel-sheratonzagreb.com; ⏰ 06.30–23.00 daily. With swanky surroundings, a renowned buffet, & a fairly traditional à-la-carte menu, this restaurant is mainly favoured by the hotel's own business travellers & upmarket package tour groups. €€€€€–€€€€

✖ **Gallo** [91 B6] Hebrangova 34; ☏481 4014; www.gallo.hr; ⏰ noon–midnight daily. Located one block west of Preradovićeva in the atrium of the Castellum Centre, Gallo is one of Zagreb's most upmarket eateries (though it has been suggested that it's been resting on its laurels in the past). The décor & menu have a Mediterranean flavour, with lots of terracotta, wrought iron, Tuscan tones & a pleasant garden terrace complementing the seafood specialities. Reservations recommended. €€€€€–€€€€

✖ **Zinfandel's** [84 D6] Mihanovićeva 1 (in the Esplanade hotel); ☏456 6666; www.esplanade. hr; ⏰ 06.00–23.00 Mon–Sat, 06.30–23.00 Sun. Chef Ana Grgić heads up the Esplanade's flagship restaurant, offering Mediterranean-inspired fare with an Asian twist. Named after the celebrated wine grape believed to have originated on the Adriatic coast, the restaurant's emphasis on using the very best Croatian produce means prices reflect quality. Modern, sumptuous interior, or eat out

on the lovely Oleander Terrace in warm weather. Reservations recommended. €€€€€–€€€€

✖ **Radicchio** [85 F6] Branimirova 29 (Branimir Centar); ☏469 6040; www.restaurantradicchio. com; ⏰ 06.00–22.30 daily. Part of the Arcotel Allegra hotel complex, this is modern, Mediterranean-inspired cuisine at its Croatian best. Good value for lunch, when it does a fixed-price menu inc wine. €€€€€–€€€

✖ **Art Paviljon** [91 D7] Trg Kralja Tomislava 22; ☏481 3066; ⏰ noon–midnight Mon–Sat. In an old glass & wrought-iron exhibition pavilion set in pleasant parkland opposite the station, the Paviljon is one of Zagreb's oldest upper-end restaurants. The spacious dining room & outdoor terrace attract diners with a decent expense account – which you'll certainly need if you're going for the vintage champagnes. Happily, those with more modest tastes can still get a first-rate plate of pasta here or a dish of štrukli without breaking the bank. Reservations recommended. €€€€

✖ **Atlanta Bocca Marai** [84 C7] Miramarska 22; ☏617 0207; www.bocca-marai.hr; ⏰ 10.00–midnight Mon–Sat, 10.00–18.00 Sun. Upscale place south of the railway line (formerly on Tkalčićeva) offering a wide choice of pasta, fish & seafood, steak & traditional Croatian dishes. Reservations recommended. €€€€

✖ **Kaptol** [84 A6] Krsnjavoga 1; ☏489 2000; www.hotelwestinzagreb.com; ⏰ 06.30–23.00 Mon–Fri, 07.00–23.00 Sat–Sun. The Westin Zagreb's large, airy restaurant is surprisingly good value (steady on the extensive & expensive wine list, however), mixing international dishes with good Croatian staples. €€€€

✖ **Le Bistro** [84 B6] Mihanovićeva 1 (in the Esplanade); ☏456 6666/611; www.esplanade.hr; ⏰ 09.00–23.00 daily. Lovely French-style glass-roofed balcony & outdoor terrace, with pretty good value lunch options, excellent homemade pastries, & the very best štrukli in town. Reservations recommended. €€€€

✖ **Asia** [91 D7] Šenoina 1; www.asia.hr; ⏰ 11.30–23.30 daily. With a location overlooking Tomislav Square, Asia is one of the very few places serving upmarket Asian food. Good range of traditional Chinese dishes, though if you're used to takeaway prices back home, you'll find it on the expensive side. There's another branch at Nova Ves 88 (☏466 7826), north of the centre towards Mirogoj Cemetery. €€€€€–€€€

✗ Mašklin i Lata [91 B6] Hebrangova 11a; ☎ 481 8273; ⏰ noon–23.00 Mon–Sat. Located in the basement underneath the Old Pharmacy Pub (page 103), this small family-run restaurant serves up Šibenik-style food with an emphasis – as you'd expect – on fish dishes. €€€€–€€€

✗ Opium [85 F6] Branimirova 29 (Branimir Centar); ☎ 461 5679; ⏰ 08.00–midnight Mon–Thu, 08.00–01.00 Fri–Sat, 11.00–midnight Sun. A stylish place serving upmarket southeast Asian & Japanese cuisine. Reservations recommended. €€€€–€€€

✗ Palace [91 C6] Strossmayerov Trg 10; ☎ 489 9600; www.palace.hr; ⏰ 11.00–23.00 daily. A favourite venue for the city's better-heeled residents during the socialist era, the Palace's dining room retains a good deal of its old-world charm, even if the food lacks sparkle for a place of this calibre. Reservations recommended. €€€€–€€€

✗ Sorriso [85 E5] Boškovićeva 11; ☎ 487 6392; ⏰ 10.00–midnight Mon–Sat. A very stylish Mediterranean-inspired place, half a floor below street level in an old brick cellar, midway between Jelačić Square & the Sheraton Hotel. Modern Italian & French cuisine, beautifully presented, make this a popular choice for a special night out. Set menus for 200kn. Reservations recommended. €€€€–€€€

✗ Hrvatski Kulturni Klub [84 B5] Trg Maršala Tita 10; ⏰ 11.00–23.00 daily. Tucked away in the basement of the Arts & Crafts Museum with a lovely terrace at the back, this traditional restaurant is popular with intellectuals & arty types, & serves up solid Croatian fare. Reservations recommended. €€€

✳✗ Sofra [77 E5] Radnička cesta 50; ☎ 411 1621; www.sofra.hr; ⏰ 09.00–midnight Mon–Sat, noon–18.00 Sun. Excellent Bosnian restaurant a short walk from the Museum of Contemporary Art – come here for Zagreb's best *ćevapi*, or a good range of less well known traditional Bosnian dishes. Recommended, but you may need to check your bill. €€€

✳✗ Zrno [84 A5] Medulićeva 20; ☎ 484 7540; www.zrnobiobistro.hr; ⏰ noon–21.30 Mon–Sat. A stylish new place serving some of the best vegetarian, vegan & macrobiotic food you'll find anywhere in Croatia, in a pleasant relaxed atmosphere. Highly recommended. €€€

✗ Maslina [76 D6] Stupnička 14; ☎ 619 1225; www.maslina.hr; ⏰ 10.00–midnight daily. Turns out some of the capital's best pizzas. Roughly halfway between Bundek & Jarun. €€

✗ Pivnica Tomislav [91 C7] Trg Kralja Tomsilava 18 (almost opposite the Paviljon); ⏰ 07.00–23.00 Mon–Fri, 07.00–21.00 Sat, 09.00–21.00 Sun. Hearty fixed-price lunch menus as well as an à-la-carte range of simple, home-cooked dishes. Very popular with locals, there's a small street-side café, with the main restaurant halfway underground indoors. €€–€

Further afield

✗ Dubravkin Put [91 B1] Dubravkin Put 2; ☎ 483 4975; http://dubravkin-put.com; ⏰ 11.00–midnight Mon–Sat. Northwest of the old town, tucked into the woods, this very fashionable restaurant serves up excellent fish, shellfish & meat dishes – all specialities of the Dubrovnik area. Reservations are essential, & prices are on the steep side. €€€€

✗ Kod Pavela [76 D3] Gračanska Cesta 46; ☎ 467 5036; ⏰ noon–23.00 Tue–Sat, noon–22.00 Sun; tram #8 or #14 to the terminus, then walk up the hill, signed Sljeme, for 10mins; the restaurant is on the right. Out of the way, but sumptuous Istrian cuisine in a charming garden setting, accompanied by a great selection of the region's best wines & liqueurs, makes the journey worthwhile. Black & white truffles, homemade pasta & gnocchi, fresh sea fish, & gorgeous Italian-inspired desserts make this a great choice for a special lunch or evening out. It's much-frequented by Zagreb's well-heeled set, so be sure to book ahead. €€€€

✗ Mex Cantina [76 D6] Savska 154; ☎ 619 2156; www.mex-cantina.hr; ⏰ noon–midnight daily; tram #13, #14 or #17 down Savska. As Zagreb's most authentic Mexican diner, the slightly out-of-town location is worth the journey if you're in the mood for spicy home-cooked Tex-Mex treats in a cosy cantina-style atmosphere. Its popularity with students makes it worth booking ahead on busy nights. €€€

✳✗ Okrugljak [76 D3] Mlinovi 28; ☎ 467 4112; www.okrugljak.hr; ⏰ 11.00–midnight daily. Head out to Šestine (bus #102 from Kaptol) for this excellent & longstanding favourite, which has been going for around a century & specialises in meat & grills & local dishes. Huge portions. Highly recommended. Reservations a good idea. €€€

✗ Zlatni Medo [76 D6] Savska 56 (on the cnr of Vukovarska); ☎ 617 7119; www.pivnica.hr; ⏰ 10.00–midnight daily; tram #13, #14 or #17. On Savska about 10 mins south of the Westin Zagreb, this cavernous, noisy boutique brewery serves up its own range of beers & vast, wholesome platefuls of local food. In addition to the fabulous *weiss* beer, try the *zlatno* (lager), *trenk* (brown) or *ban* (dark) varieties, along with homemade food including various types of sausage, *grah*, steaks & other dishes. Prices are reasonable and serving sizes are huge, making it exceptionally good value for money. €€€–€€

CAFES, BARS AND PUBS
With great summer weather and lots of visitors, there's no shortage of cafés, bars and pubs in Zagreb. Most restaurants with terraces will also be happy to serve you drinks between meals.

Café society is firmly centred in the area around **Jelačić Square** – the pedestrianised streets and squares to the southwest become one vast terrace in summer, and the ambience is wonderful, with frequent more or less impromptu live music in the area.

On Sunday mornings, it plays host to one of the most unusual spectacles in the world, when the Croatian political elite – from the president down – comes out to sit at the café terraces and chew the fat. Blasé locals have been known to criticise this overt populism, but it's a refreshing change from the aloof remoteness of most of the world's leaders.

Saturdays are even busier, with the weekly *špica*, a Zagreb tradition that is a bit like a sit-down version of Italy's *passeggiata*. It basically involves dolling yourself up to the nines and meeting friends for a leisurely coffee/brunch at a favourite watering hole – for preference, one of the high-profile ones off to the southwest of Jelačić Square. The aim is to see and be seen, while catching up on the week's news and gossip in a relaxed, unhurried atmosphere. Former President Mesić used Charlie's, one of his favourite cafés opposite the Hotel Dubrovnik, as the stump from which he launched his election – and subsequent re-election – campaigns.

North of the main square, **Tkalčićeva**, a long, winding, pedestrianised street, is very much the humming heart of Zagreb nightlife. The charming old-style houses along here are now almost all cafés, bars and cheap restaurants – there's a great relaxed vibe just about any time of the day or night, and it's absolutely the place to kick off an evening out.

Cafés and bars tend to open early, 07.00 or 08.00 (more usually an hour later on Sundays), and stay open until 23.00 or midnight, with many bars staying open until 01.00 or 02.00 in particular on Friday and Saturday.

We've grouped cafés, bars and pubs – like restaurants on the previous pages – into four sections for convenience: the upper town (everything from Gradec to Kaptol and along Tkalčićeva); Jelačić Square and the area nearby to the west, south and east; the rest of the lower town (as far as the railway station); and places further afield (not including Mount Medvednica, which is covered separately, see page 133).

Upper town
Caffe Palainovka [91 C1] Ilirski Trg; ⏰ 08.00–midnight Mon–Thu, 08.00–01.00 Fri–Sat, 09.00–23.00 Sun. In a picturesque part of the old town, right next to the Priest's Tower, this old-fashioned café boasts a lovely garden terrace & a 19th-century-inspired interior decorated with old photographs & even a penny-farthing bicycle.

Žabica [91 B2] Opatička 5; ⏰ 08.00–23.00 Mon–Sat. A traditional, refined, genuinely old haunt up in the old town, with lots of authentic detail & fabulous hot chocolate.
Cica [91 C3] Tkalčićeva 18; ⏰ 08.00–midnight Mon–Sat. Groovy place decorated with bohemian bric-a-brac & specialising in exotically flavoured artisan rakijas. Honey & rose, blueberry, fig & pear

took my fancy. If the bar staff are to be believed (I had had a few), the bar's name means 'tits'.

♀ Čvenk [91 B3] Radićeva 23; ◷ 08.00–23.00 Mon–Thu, 08.00–midnight Fri–Sat, 17.00–23.00 Sun. Popular with locals for its long opening hours, keen bar prices & appealing brick-vaulted interior. Has a leaning towards grungy rock music.

♀ Giardino [91 C2] Tkalčićeva 37; ◷ 08.00–midnight daily. Comfy wicker sofas on the pavement for summer, & a postmodern interior for winter, marred only slightly by the presence of a large-screen TV.

♀ Gulliver [91 C3] Tržnica Dolac. One of several down-to-earth cafés along the mezzanine level on the steps leading up from Jelačić Square to Dolac market, & catering largely to traders & local customers. Large terrace, cheap beer.

♀ Jackie Brown [84 D1] Nova Ves 17 (in the Kaptol Centar, but downstairs, actually on Tkalčićeva); ◷ 08.00–01.00 daily. A trendy lounge bar with a retro-70s feel, attracting an affluent, older set.

♀ Khala [84 D1] Nova Ves 17; www.khala.hr. Also located in the Kaptol Centar at the very top of Tkalčićeva, another groovy lounge bar, but this time with a Persian/Central Asian vibe. Serves up appetising nibbles & upmarket wines by the glass.

♀ Lav [91 D4] Opatička 2. Nice location on a corner just above the Stone Gate, with a decent range of teas.

✳♀ Pivnica Mali Medo [91 C2] Tkalčićeva 36; www.pivnica-medvedgrad.hr. Excellent locally brewed beers (from Pivnica Medvedgrad) & decent pub food on Tkalčićeva.

♀ Oliver Twist [91 C2] Tkalčićeva 60. Snuggled into a cutting about halfway along Tkalčićeva, the large green Tuborg umbrellas & vast terrace make it hard to miss. Or indeed pass up, with friendly service, a welcoming wood & brass interior for colder weather, & an extensive menu of foreign beers.

♀ Strossmayer Bar [91 B3] Strossmayerovo Šetalište bb. Perched at the top of the steep climb up to the old town from Radićeva, serving keenly priced drinks on a quiet, shady terrace overlooking the Zagreb rooftops (also accessible by walking along from the bottom of the Lotrščak Tower, or down from the corner of St Catherine's Square). If you're game, you can venture indoors & shoot pool in a cavernous hall.

♀ Tolkien's House [91 C2] Opatovina 49; ◷ till late. Hobbits will feel right at home in this homage

to *Lord of the Rings* & all things Middle Earth up in a quiet part of the old town. Nice terrace.

On & off Jelačić Square

⬛ Ban Caffe [91 C4] Jelačić Square. Like Mala Kavana next door, what you're paying for here is the location right on the main square. It's a great place to unwind after a tough morning's shopping in nearby Dolac market. Gradska Kavana, at the end of the square, is marginally less expensive &, if anything, swankier.

⬛ Dubrovnik Hotel Café [91 C4] Gajeva 1 (next to Charlie's); ◷ 07.00–23.00 daily. With an ample terrace & an excellent location bordering on Jelačić Square, this place is a little pricey, but wonderfully convenient if you've been trawling around the city's shops.

⬛ Eli's Caffe [84 A4] Ilica 63; www.eliscaffe. com; ◷ 08.00–19.00 Mon–Fri, 08.00–16.00 Sat, 09.00–14.00 Sun. Small café with upmarket clientele near Britanski trg, owned by specialist coffee roaster Nik Orosi.

⬛ Gradska Kavana [91 D4] Jelačić Square; ◷ 08.30–23.00 Mon–Sat, 09.00–22.00 Sun. With an outdoor terrace & huge Art-Deco-inspired interior on 3 levels, at times reputedly the favourite Sunday morning coffee spot for the president & the political elite. The usual selection of cakes, coffee, soft drinks, wine & beer, at prices marginally more modest than at the Ban Caffe & Mala Kavana along the square. There's an adjoining restaurant serving traditional dishes at moderate prices.

⬛ Juice&Juice [91 A5] Masarykova 26; www. juiceandjuice.com.hr; ◷ 08.00–20.00 Mon–Sat. Small juice bar, also does soups.

⬛ K&K (Knjiga & Kava) [91 D4] Jurišićeva 5; ◷ 08.00–23.00 Mon–Sat. Cosy café on two levels just east of Jelačić Square, with an old-world, bookish feel & walls crammed with vintage photos of Zagreb (the name means 'books & coffee'). Ensconce yourself at one of the marble tables, or on the small outdoor terrace if the smoky atmosphere gets too much, & settle into a traditional *sachertorte* accompanied by coffee, beer or a glass of wine, all without blowing the budget. Owner Miličić is a popular local writer & a close friend of the great & the good.

⬛ Kraljevac Caffe [84 A4] Britanski Trg 9; ◷ 07.00–23.00 daily. This café, 2 tram stops west of Jelačić Square, comes into its own on Sun, when the lively antiques market at Britanski Square gets into full swing. Take time out from perusing the bric-a-brac & haggling with the stall owners to enjoy a coffee, beer or a *spricer*.

☕♀ **Mala Kavana** [91 C4] ⏰ 08.00–22.00 daily. On the north side of Jelačić Square, next door to the Ban Caffe (page 102), the central location has made the Mala Kavana a long-standing favourite. Serves light snacks, cakes, ice-cream sundaes & the usual selection of drinks, with prices at the upper end.

☕ **Maraschino** [91 B4] Margaretska 1. Trendy place just off Ilica, a very popular hang-out that takes its name from Zadar's world-famous cherry liqueur, known to locals as *maraska*. Good hot chocolate – its own version, infused with the aforementioned liqueur, is a special treat – & a selection of cocktails & Croatian wines.

☕♀ **Pif** [91 B5] Preradovićeva 4; ⏰ 07.00– midnight Mon–Sat, 09.00–midnight Sun. Nice little café just off the Flower Square, with tables spilling outside in the summer. The updater's favourite haunt when living in Zagreb.

☕ **Škola** [91 B4] Bogovićeva 7 (3rd flr). A renovated school that's now as trendy bar, with prices & snooty staff to match. A slick pure-white interior houses chic drinking & eating areas ranged over two levels. Very busy on Fri/Sat after 21.00, but otherwise a quiet haven for an afternoon drink.

✳♀ **La Bodega Pub** [91 B4] Bogovićeva 5; ⏰ 08.00–midnight Sun–Tue, 08.00–02.00 Wed– Sat. Excellent new wine bar with an extensive list of Croatian wines on offer, impeccable coffee as well as freshly squeezed juices & snacks. Recommended.

♀ **Bulldog Pub** [91 B4] Bogovićeva 6. Extremely popular place in this café-filled, pedestrianised street off the Flower Square.

♀ **Charlie's** [91 C4] Gajeva 4; ⏰ 07.00–23.00 Mon–Sat, 09.00–23.00 Sun. A popular Zagreb institution & one of the president's favourite watering holes. Founded by former Dinamo Zagreb player Mirko 'Charlie' Braun (who died in 2004), & easy to recognise by the black wicker chairs.

♀ **Hole in One** [85 E3] Vlaška 42; www. holeinone.hr; ⏰ 08.00–midnight Mon–Sat. Polished dark wood & brass railings make for a homely pub-like atmosphere, though prices are also scarily reminiscent of London. The smoky little pizzeria next door is part of the same establishment; for reasons unexplained, the day

I was there it claimed to have no house wine, & wanted 180kn for a very ordinary-looking bottle of white – which I was easily able to resist.

Lower town

♀ **Hemingway** [91 A5] Trg Maršala Tita 1 (opposite the Croatian National Theatre); www. hemingway.hr. Spacious terrace, large cushioned benches & trendy but uncomfortable oriental glass & wicker stools. The interior is a spartan all-white affair with large photos of Papa. Extensive (& expensive) selection of cocktails, foreign beers & wines. Young, affluent crowd, but service can be on the surly side – & heaven only knows what the old man himself would have made of it.

♀ **Jo's Bar** [85 F6] Branimirova 29 (Branimir Centar, at the Arcotel Allegra); www.joesbar-zagreb.com. Modern & gay-friendly; it also does light food, & sometimes has live jazz.

♀ **Kazališka Kavana** [91 A5] Trg Maršala Tita 1. Next door to Hemingway (see above), but with an altogether less affected, friendlier atmosphere, cheaper prices, & the same great view of the National Theatre across the road; the location of choice for pre-theatre drinks.

♀ **Old Pharmacy Pub** [91 C6] Hebrangova 11. On the south side of the street just east of Preradovićeva, this charming venue is a firm favourite with locals, who like to relax on the banquettes & sofas & partake of a coffee, beer or glass of wine in an authentic, turn-of-the-century atmosphere. One of the original 'theme' pubs in Zagreb.

♀ **Sedmica** [84 A4] Kačićeva 7a; http://caffebar-sedmica.com; ⏰ 08.00–midnight Mon–Sat, 17.00–midnight Sun. Fashionable, unpretentious place that remains popular with Zagreb's boho crowd (it's not far from the National Theatre). Marble bar tables flanked by tall bar stools, a retro, grungy look & a back room that's practically a semi-terrace.

Further afield

♀ **Dublin Pub** [77 E5] Maksimirska 75; tram #4, #11 or #12 towards the zoo & the Dinamo Stadium. With walls clad in photos of old Dublin, décor featuring the humble potato, & comfy brown leather sofas, this is as Irish an atmosphere as you're going to find in the heart of Croatia.

♀ **Godot** [84 A7] Savska 23; www.cafe-godot. com. Authentic pub feel & cheap *travarica* just south of the railway line. The youngish crowd reflects the bar's location in the student district.

♀ Hemingway Bar [84 B3] Tuškanec 21/23 (behind the Kino Tuškanec cinema); www. hemingway.hr. Zagreb's original Hemingway's, west of the old town, has evolved from a swanky cocktail bar to an upmarket eatery/nightclub, mainly used for hosting functions. Smart, with prices to match.

♀ Movie Pub [76 D6] Savska 141; www. the-movie-pub.com.; tram #13, #14 or #17. Enormously popular place out of the city centre, with seating for 350 & an authentic pub feel – though a little too faux-British (& pricey) for my taste. If the crowd inside gets noisy, there's also a small but pleasant outdoor terrace.

♀ SPUNK [76 D6] Hrvatske Bratske Zajednice bb. On the main road south to the Sava & Novi Zagreb, on the right-hand side, between Vukovarska & Slavonska, & part of the giant University Library complex. This small, modern bar is a favourite with students, not least because of its cheap beer & regular live music. Also makes for a handy freshener on your way out to the Močvara Club (page 107).

♀ Velvet [84 B3] Dežmanova 9; www.velvet. hr; ⏰ 08.00–22.00 Mon–Fri, 08.00–15.00 Sat, 08.00–14.00 Sun. Smart & supremely fashionable café/art gallery tucked away just off Ilica, heading towards the base of Tuškanec, with a lovely terrace.

ICE CREAM Zagreb's first ice cream is believed to have been served up on 2 May 1847 by local restaurateur Mato Pallain in the coffee shop he'd opened on the city's North Promenade a decade earlier. Since then, it has firmly entrenched itself as a national staple whose enormous popularity is attested to by the large numbers of ice-cream parlours – *slastičarnica* – dotting the city. The most famous, and popular, are Vincek and Millenium.

Croatians favour Italian-style gelati, though the local version tends to be somewhat heavier. Note that, as in Italy, the cost of your cone or cup depends on the number of flavours you choose – and you can expect a wealth of these to be available, some with English translations, some not.

☕ Centar [91 D4] On Jurišićeva, on the right-hand side heading away from Jelačić Square towards Palmotićeva. The author's absolute number one favourite in Zagreb.

☕ Mak na Kolac [85 G4] Ulica popa Dukljanina 1 (just off the northeast corner of Trg žrtava fašisma); www.maknakonac. com; ⏰ 09.00–21.00 Mon–Sat. Ice cream & mouthwatering cakes, including some gluten &/or dairy free.

☕ Millennium [91 B4] Bogovićeva 7. Excellent ice cream. Heavier & creamier than Centar's more Italian-style fare. Zagreb's most extensive & exotic choice of flavours. Nice outdoor seating in this pedestrianised street.

☕ Oranž [91 B4] Ilica 7. Popular new place with good ice cream & fabulous cakes, as well as

salads & other lite bites, & not to mention a good wine bar next door.

☕ Orient [77 E5] Maksimirska 34 (close to the tram stop). Run by 2 sisters who serve up the usual classic favourites along with more imaginative options. The homemade cakes are also much prized by sweet-toothed locals.

☕ Trakošćan [91 B4] Bogovićeva 7. Next door to Millennium, & longer established & less flashy than its newer rival. Has a very loyal old-school following.

☕ Vincek [91 B4] Ilica 18 (& various other locations around the city); www.vincek.com.hr. A Zagreb institution offering excellent quality & a wide variety of flavours. Also makes an outrageous all-cream torta & a slew of other cakes.

MARKETS, SUPERMARKETS AND BAKERIES Seven mornings a week, **Dolac market** [91 C3] does its wonderful, bustling thing, with all kinds of fresh produce available, from seasonal fruit and vegetables on the upper level to meat, cheese and dairy goods, fresh pasta and delicatessen items in the basement, and the catch of the day in a separate fish section upstairs.

Locals still come here daily to sell their own vegetables and other produce, and most people in Zagreb are loyal to their preferred *kumica* (literally 'godmother') – usually an older woman who serves as their trusted source for the best home-grown produce. A bronze statue of a kumica has been placed in honour of the tradition at the top of the stairs up from Jelačić Square.

The action generally kicks off at about 07.00 – earlier for the fish market, where you'll be jostling for the choicest items with buyers from Zagreb's best restaurants – and winds up before 14.00, when the big clean-up begins, ready for the next day's trading. At the foot of the steps leading up to the market there's also a daily flower market, dominated, again, by local women selling their own cuttings.

If you're near the bus station, it's worth knowing that there's also a smaller daily market at the eastern end of Branimira, just north of the railway line. And if you're west of the city centre, there's also a daily market on Britanski Square, two tram stops along Ilica from Jelačić Square; on Sundays, bric-a-brac replaces the fruit and veg – see page 108 for details. East of the city centre, there's a big market on Kvaternikov trg.

There are also plenty of **supermarkets** large and small in Zagreb, where you can stock up on essentials. The local Konzum chain is the most widespread, with branches throughout the city (including a reasonably large one on the corner of Ilica and Britanski trg [84 A4], and another in the underpass beneath the main railway station [84 D7]), but there are also quite a few independent shops as well. Prices are generally competitive, and there's usually a good selection of local produce as well as wholesale food. You can ask for sandwiches to be made up to order at the deli-counter in most supermarkets – just point at the type of bread you want filled, say '*sendvič*' and indicate your choice of filling(s); you're just charged for the ingredients by weight.

Bakeries (*pekarnica*) are also widespread and sell a good variety of breads and sometimes also offer ready-made sandwiches (*sendviči*) with cheese (sir), ham (šunka), tuna, egg (*jaja*) and occasionally more exotic fillings, as well as various pies, sausage rolls and the like. This is also where to go for *štrudl* (strudel) and other pastries, as well as *bučnica* (cheese- and courgette-filled pastry), *burek* (you've a better chance of finding this in the morning) and other savoury treats.

Finally, if you find yourself craving American-style snacks, there's a **doughnut shop** two blocks east of Jelačić Square opposite the main post office [89 D4], and a Subway sandwich outlet on Gajeva, right by the Hotel Dubrovnik, where you can sate your appetite with a foot-long sandwich or US-style muffins and cookies.

ENTERTAINMENT AND NIGHTLIFE

As the capital, Zagreb gets more than its fair share of cultural happenings, ranging from excellent ballet, opera and theatre (notably at the national theatre), to an entire summer schedule chock-full of local and international performances – everything from classical to jazz to rock and beyond. In summer, you'll often find free street concerts taking place in and around the city, in addition to more organised happenings, and the capital is also endowed with a good number of clubs and venues large enough to attract big-name stars. It's worth checking the Zagreb Tourist Information Centre website (*www.zagreb-touristinfo.hr*), the monthly 'Events and Performances' guide, and street hoardings, for details of events as they come up.

FESTIVALS As in Dubrovnik, there's also a major **summer festival**, which runs for two weeks from the end of July. This features some of Croatia's best folk

3

performances, and remains one of your best opportunities to see genuine folk dancing with the traditional costumes being worn.

Zagreb also hosts several other festivals, one of the biggest being **Animafest** (*www.animafest.hr*), the world festival of animated films, which has a week of short films and full-length features (usually in June). **Cest is d'Best** (*www.cestisdbest. com*) is a wonderfully entertaining week-long festival of international street theatre, also taking place in June. Odd-numbered years also see modern music celebrated at the **Music Biennial**.

MUSIC, OPERA, BALLET AND THEATRE

Lisinski Concert Hall [85 E7] (*Just south of the railway station, off Vukovarska; Trg Stjepana Radića 4; box office* ✎ *612 1166; info* ✎ *612 1111; www.lisinski. hr*) There's a regular programme of concerts at the Lisinski Concert Hall by the Zagreb Philharmonic Orchestra, visiting artists, and the city's many other classical ensembles. The venue offers a rich and varied programme featuring classical, jazz, contemporary world music and even popular rock acts, and you can choose, book and pay for your seats online in English. Collect your tickets from the box office 60 minutes before the performance begins.

Croatian National Theatre [91 A6] (*Trg Maršala Tita 15; box office* ✎ *488 8415; info* ✎ *488 8418; www.hnk.hr*) For opera, ballet and theatre the Croatian National Theatre dominates, with an impressive year-round programme of new productions and revivals, featuring plenty of popular favourites mixed with more eclectic pieces. Unless you're fluent in Croatian, the theatre programme is hard work. Instead, head along to the opera or ballet, where you'll see and hear top local and visiting performers for just a fraction of the price you'd pay in the larger European capitals. The theatre has a useful online booking facility (in Croatian and English), which shows seat availability and pricing.

Live gigs Keep your eyes peeled for posters around town advertising upcoming events, which mostly take place at one of the venues listed under Nightlife (below) or, for the biggest names, at sports stadiums and open-air festivals. Big names aside, Croatia has a thriving local music scene, of which Zagreb is the natural hub. There's plenty of talent about, and if you're relaxed about the fact that you won't usually understand the lyrics (though some artists do perform in English), it won't be long before you find yourself carried away by local bands' energy and enthusiasm.

NIGHTLIFE Zagreb has plenty of late evening lounge bars and cafés, and in summer popular haunts like Tkalčićeva stay humming until the early hours. There's also a fair sprinkling of dance clubs, generally open to around 04.00. In summer, the mainstream dance music scene – like much of the city's population – moves out to the Adriatic coast, and things stay pretty quiet in the capital until September. The inverse is true of live music, which consistently draws crowds large enough to ensure Zagreb remains a fixture on major European tours. The summer months welcome plenty of visiting bands, who play open-air festivals as well as the various live venues around town.

☆ **Aquarius** [76 C7] Aleja Matije Ljubeka; www.aquarius.hr; tram #17 to Horvati. Situated lakeside at Jarun, Zagreb's longest-established dance club is still the most popular, with dance floors thumping to commercial hip-hop, R&B & some of Europe's best celebrity DJs. The club has a massively popular offshoot in summer on the island of Pag, at Zrče beach.

☆ **Best** [76 C6] Jarunski Cesta 5; www.thebest.hr; tram #14 or #17 to Savski Most. Huge, glitzy venue specialising in commercial techno, disco, house & hip-hop, along with special theme nights featuring soul, trance & the like.

☆ **Boogaloo** [76 D6] Vukovarska 68; tram #13 to Miramarska. A vast place accommodating 1,000+, located in the OTV Dom building, a venue with a long history of breaking new ground in the Zagreb music scene. Features DJs & live bands.

☆ **Brazil** [76 D6] Veslačka; tram #14 or #17 to Veslačka, then head to the riverbank. This dilapidated barge on the Sava stays open very late, making it a popular end-of-evening stopover for those on their way back from other venues like Močvara (see below). Reggae & world music, mostly.

☆ **Gallery** [76 C6] Aleja Matije Ljubeka; http:// gallery.hr; tram #17 to Horvati. Another of Jarun Lake's popular nightspots, Gallery is the capital's most exclusive dance venue, with a very strict dress code (yep, no trainers) & a wealthy young crowd. The focus in the chic interior is on the latest celebrity DJs. One of the few clubs to accept credit cards – & you'll quickly see why, if they deign to let you in.

☆ **KSET** [76 D6] Unska 3; ☎ 612 9758; www. kset.org. A small venue that's actually part of the University of Electrotechnical Science, KSET has a long tradition of pioneering new bands & hosting stylistically diverse genres, from punk & underground to avant-garde jazz. Friendly atmosphere, & prices way cheaper than at the glitzier clubs.

☆ **Močvara ('Swamp')** [76 D6] Trnjanski nasip; ☎ 615 9667; www.mochvara.hr; tram #13 to Lisinski, then walk south towards the river; the club's down behind the Sava dyke. Set up in an old factory, this legendary venue is popular with an alternative crowd interested in punk, thrash,

grunge & indie sounds, & puts on all manner of gigs & special events, including big names like Thurston Moore (of Sonic Youth fame). Occasional DJ nights, & cheap drinks. If you're aiming to get home by taxi, you need to head across to the restaurant nearby, just 100m north of the venue.

☆ **Route 66** [76 D6] Paromlinska 47; ☎ 611 8737. Behind the University Library complex (see SPUNK, below), on a parallel road heading down to the river. Classic rock & blues dive with a grungy feel & cheap beer, & popular with musicians. Also features country & western cover bands & demos from local new contenders.

☆ **Saloon** [84 B3] Tuškanac 1; www.saloon.hr. Smart, minimalist venue playing a mainstream disco sound; popular with the young & affluent.

☆ **Sax!** [85 E4] Palmotićeva 22; ☎ 487 2836; www.sax-zg.hr. A block or so east of Jelačić Square, & owned by the Croatian Musicians' Union. Informal venue hosting good jazz sessions & album promotions Tue–Sat.

☆ **Shamballa** [84 A7] Savska 30; www. shamballa.hr. Enormous new café/club on Savska, near the Westin.

☆ **SPUNK** [76 D6] Hrvatske bratske zajednice; ☎ 615 1528; tram #13 to Lisinski & then walk south towards the river; the bar's on the right, & part of the University Library complex. While technically a bar, this exceedingly popular student venue is also one of Zagreb's top spots for garage & underground music – & has some of the cheapest beer in town.

☆ **Tvornica** [85 H5] Šubićeva 2; ☎ 457 8389; www.tvornicakulture.com; tram #1 or #17 to Šubićeva station. A large (1,500+) live venue hosting names like David Byrne, Faithless, Madradeus & John Cale; also does big club nights.

GAY AND LESBIAN After decades of being very firmly in the closet, Zagreb's burgeoning gay scene is beginning to come out with confidence, with a couple of good venues, its own annual Gay Pride march, and the Queer Zagreb festival. All too predictably, old Croatia's Catholic/macho culture means male gays are still better served than lesbians both for venues and cultural acceptance.

The city's Gay Pride march (*www.zagreb-pride.net*) takes place in June. While the event still seems to need vigorous policing, it's gradually gaining acceptance as part of the city's mainstream festival calendar. Queer Zagreb (*www.queerzagreb. org*), a cultural festival focusing on art, theory and activism, with an extensive film programme, takes place in April, and is the largest event of its kind in eastern and central Europe. The **Bumerang** sauna [89 A6] (*Mažuranićev Trg 2;* ☎ *485 4754; www.bumerang.hr;* ⊕ *summer 16.00–23.00 daily, winter 14.00–23.00 daily*) is located between Trg Maršala Tita and the Botanical Gardens.

See the Zagreb listings on www.croatia-gay.com for more information.

SHOPPING CENTRES AND CINEMAS If you want to go to a good old-fashioned cinema rather than a multiplex in a shopping mall, head for **Europa** on the Flower Square (Cvjetni Trg).

Avenue Mall [77 E7] Avenija Dubrovnik 16; www.avenuemall.hr. Zagreb's newest shopping mall, with some 130 shops including Zara, Marks & Spencer, Esprit, Calvin Klein, Tommy Hilfiger, Next & Mango, as well as cafés & restaurants & a cinema complex. In Novi Zagreb, south of the River Sava.

Branimir Centar [85 F6] Branimirova 29; www.branimircentar.hr. Just east of the railway station. Offers a good mix of fashion, beauty, bars, restaurants, the 13-screen Cinestar cinema multiplex & the Wettpunkt 24hr casino.

Importanne Centar [84 D6] Starčevićev Trg; http://importannecentar.hr. Located underground between the railway station & the Esplanade hotel. Considerably more downmarket, but has a good selection of shops including fashion & jewellery, photo processing, shoes, stationery & so on. There's also a good number of takeaway sandwich & hot fast-food stalls, a biggish supermarket, a couple of newsagents & a branch of DM (for toiletries, etc).

Importanne Galleria [85 F4] Iblerov Trg (on Vlaška, between Draškovićeva & Smičiklasova); http://importannegalleria.hr. Just east of the Jadran hotel, this modern complex covers everything from electronics, music, photo-processing, jewellery, clothes & the inevitable shoe emporia, to pets, eyeglasses, perfume, toys & children's wear. There's a fast-food hall downstairs, along with a good supermarket & a large DM outlet.

Kaptol Centar [84 D1] Nova Ves 17; www.centarkaptol.hr (just up from Kaptol, & connecting the top of Tkalčićeva with Nova Ves). One of Zagreb's newer (& most glamorous) shopping temples, housing big-name brands like Armani Jeans, Burberry & Tommy Hilfiger, along with Marks & Spencer (clothing only). The centre also boasts the Broadway 5 cinema multiplex & a few plush bars & restaurants.

Secondhand goods For secondhand bargain hunters, there's an excellent Sunday crafts and bric-a-brac market at Britanski Square, two tram stops west along Ilica from Jelačić Square. There's everything here from bayonets to wagon wheels, old china, music scores, clothing and wooden farming implements. If prices seem high at first, remember that bargaining is virtually obligatory, so expect to be able to knock 20–40% – depending on your negotiating skills – off. Loads of fun, though you might have a job getting that 19th-century scythe through customs.

Bookshops The two best English bookshops in Zagreb are **Profil megastore** [91 B5] (*Bogovićeva 7; www.profil.hr*) and **Algoritam** [91 C4] (*Gajeva 1; www. algoritam.hr*).

SPORTS

Fans in Zagreb will need to know that the stadium of city's main **football** stadium, home to Zagreb's football team, Dinamo Zagreb, is out opposite Maximir (Stadion Maximir). Dinamo Zagreb are one of the country's top teams, in endless rivalry with Hajduk Split – and many consider the Croatian War of Independence to have, well, 'kicked off' during an infamous game against Red Star Belgrade in May 1990, when fighting broke out between the rival fans, who invaded the pitch and clashed with police. A few Dinamo players remained on the pitch during all this, including Dinamo's captain Zvonimir Boban, who famously kicked a policeman for attacking a Dinamo fan – 'the kick that started the war', as it is often known. If you want to go and see Dinamo Zagreb play, check out their schedule at www.gnkdinamo.hr/EN.

If you fancy going **bowling**, Bowling Centar Klub 300 (*www.bowling.hr*) is at Savska Opatovina 16, near the One West shopping centre.

BANKS AND POST OFFICES Zagreb has dozens of different banks, and ATMs abound – locally based Zagrebačka Banka has more than 150 dotted around the city, including around a dozen on Ilica alone, accepting MasterCard, Maestro, Visa, Visa Electron and Diners.

There are two vast main post offices – one right next to the train station, and the other a block east of Jelačić Square on Jurišićeva.

If you're based south of the railway line or arriving or departing by bus, there's also a convenient post office at the main bus station (*Autobusni Kolodvor, Marina Držića 4;* ⏰ *08.00–19.30 Mon–Fri, 07.30–14.00 Sat*).

✉ **24-hour post office** [85 E6] Branimirova 4; ⏰ 24/7. Send letters weighing less than 5g from lines 9–11, packages less than 3kg from the parcel area on the east side of the building, & heavier items from the HPT office 50m further east of the main entrance. Local & international phone calls can be made from the first floor – get a phonecard from reception, & pay for the time used after you've made your call.

✉ **Central Post Office** [91 D4] Jurišićeva 13; ⏰ 07.00–20.00 Mon–Fri, 07.30–13.00 Sat

PHONE AND INTERNET
Mobile phones The main mobile operators have a big local presence:

T-Mobile Shops dotted throughout the city, the most convenient of which is the one next to the church at Preradovićeva 3 [91 B4] (⏰ *09.00–20.00 Mon–Fri, 09.00–15.00 Sat*), near the corner with Bogovićeva.

VIP Centar [91 C4] Gajeva 2b; ⏰ 08.00–20.00 Mon–Fri, 08.00–15.00 Sat. Located right opposite the Dubrovnik Hotel, near the corner with Jelačić Square.

Internet cafés Many cafés (and most hotels) have free Wi-Fi. If you're travelling with your laptop, you'll also be able to take advantage of the city's growing number of Wi-Fi hotspots with a fast wireless connection, courtesy of T-Com or VIP. Payment can be made via pre-paid voucher or online via credit card. There are also several conveniently located internet cafés, with hourly fees coming in at anything from 20 to 40kn. There's a list of internet cafés at www.zagreb-touristinfo.hr.

🖵 **Juice&Juice** [91 A5] Masarykova 26; www. juiceandjuice.com.hr; ⏰ 08.00–20.00 Mon–Sat. Also does a wide range of smoothies & juices. See page 102.
🖵 **Sublink** [91 B5] Teslina 12; www.sublink. hr; ⏰ 09.00–22.00 Mon–Sat, 15.00–22.00 Sun.

Excellent, fast, friendly & convenient. Hidden away at the back of a courtyard, this was Croatia's first internet café, opened in 1996.
🖵 **VIP** [91 B5] Preradovićeva 5; www. viprestoran.com; ⏰ 09.00–23.00 Mon–Thu, 09.00–midnight Fri–Sat, 09.00–23.00 Sun

HOSPITAL AND PHARMACIES Zagreb's main hospital [85 F5] (*opća bolnica;* ☎ *469 7000; for emergencies, call* ☎ *194*) is located at Draškovićeva 19, on the corner with Boškovićeva near the Sheraton Hotel, and as you'd expect the accident and emergency service works 24/7.

There are dozens of pharmacies (*ljekarne*) spread around Zagreb. Opening hours are usually from 07.00 to 20.00 Monday to Friday, 07.00 to 14.00 Saturday, but the first three of those listed on page 110 operate 24/7. See the website of Gradska Ljekarna Zagreb (*www.gljz.hr*) for locations and opening times (click on 'Ljekarne' and then 'Lokacije ljekarni na karti').

✚ **Gradska Ljekarna Zagreb** [91 C4] Trg Jelačića 3; ☎ 481 6198; [76 C5] Ilica 301; ☎ 375 0321; [76 D6] Ozaljska 1; ☎ 309 7586; [84 A4]

Ilica 79; ☎ 377 1651; [91 B5] Masarykova 2; ☎ 487 2850

WHAT TO SEE AND DO

To see all of Zagreb's sights would take several intense weeks, with an astonishing 60-plus varieties of museum and gallery open to the public, not counting monuments, public sculptures or even churches. If you want to see the top-rated attractions, you'll need to allow three or four days – partly because opening hours don't always mesh as well as they might.

There's a lot to see, but don't be too obsessive. Not everything needs a visit (or is open), and in the end the main sight is the city itself, along with the wealth of café terraces, bars and restaurants that make Zagreb such an agreeable place. A trip up to the top of Sljeme followed by an alfresco dinner might turn out to be much more rewarding than religiously ticking off some of the more arcane subjects in the following pages.

Outdoor attractions such as the zoo or Mount Medvednica, and more out-of-the-way sights, such as the monastery church in Remete, are covered in the next section, Surrounds. In this section, within each subsection, the sights are listed – very roughly speaking – in order of merit.

A WALKING TOUR OF THE CITY The route suggested here is a figure of eight, starting and ending on the city's central square, Jelačić Square, covering the old, upper town first and the lower town second. It would make for a leisurely two- to four-hour tour, depending on how much you choose to visit on the way.

Jelačić Square and the Lotrščak Tower

The main attraction in Jelačić Square [91 C4] is the terrific **equestrian statue** of Ban Josip Jelačić himself. As the viceroy of Croatia in the middle of the 19th century, Jelačić was a natural reformer, and did a great deal to advance the causes of Croatian statehood. After he died, the heroic statue (by the Austrian sculptor, Fernkorn) was erected in 1866, with Jelačić's drawn sword facing Budapest as a sign of defiance – by this time Croatia was already losing what little independence it had.

After World War II, the statue was torn down because it was considered unpatriotic within Tito's Yugoslavia, and the square was renamed Trg Republike. For more than 40 years, Jelačić languished in pieces, in a cellar. However, when the statue was restored to its former glory, on Croatian independence in 1991, it was put up facing the other way – towards Belgrade rather than Budapest – and today the drawn sword points uncompromisingly towards Knin, the short-lived capital of the erstwhile Republika Srpska Krajina (RSK). (For more Croatian history, see pages 12–21.) Old photographs – such as those on the ground floor corridor of the Hotel Dubrovnik, connecting the restaurant to reception – show the statue on the other side of the square, facing north.

Head west out of the square on Ilica, Zagreb's longest street. After 250m you'll come to Tomislava, a short dead-end street which leads up to the diminutive **funicular** [91 B4] (page 87), the easiest route up to the upper town (Gornji Grad, also known as Gradec).

The funicular leads straight up to **Strossmayerovo Šetalište**, a lovely west–east promenade giving magnificent views south out over the city, and the **Lotrščak Tower** [91 B3], one of the few vestiges of the original 13th-century city fortifications.

Don't be fooled into thinking there's nothing to do to keep young children interested once away from the fun, sea and sun of the Croatian coast – there's plenty for them to see and do inland and Zagreb is no exception. Here are some of the top attractions for anyone in Zagreb with kids.

ZAGREB ZOO (See page 132) Zagreb has a good zoo; it's a great chance for kids to see lynx, wolves, bears and other animals which inhabit Croatia's national parks and mountains, albeit in small numbers, as well as species from all over the world.

ZAGREB PUPPET THEATRE [91 C7] (*www.zkl.hr*) Good range of puppet shows (in Croatian), which in the past has included the likes of Julia Donaldson's *The Smartest Giant in Town*.

TREŠNJA CHILDREN'S THEATRE [76 C6] (*www.kazaliste-tresnja.hr*) Good children's theatre, outside the city centre (take tram #12 towards Ljubljanica) with performances in Croatian.

MAKSIMIR (See page 132) Zagreb's most famous park, with plenty of green grass and woodland for children to run around in.

SLJEME The large, wooded mountain on the north side of town is great for hiking in spring, summer and autumn (note that there are ticks present in early summer, see page 39), and for skiing in winter. There's an educational trail starting on Kraljičin zdenac, and also the old fort at Medvedgrad (which has a small medieval festival in the summer).

ICE SKATING During the winter months there's a small ice-skating rink on the main square (though kids will need to have their own skates).

MUSEUMS (See pages 117–30) Zagreb is awash with museums and galleries, some of which (such as the Technical Museum and Zagreb City Museum) have plenty to interest kids.

FESTIVALS (See page 105) Zagreb has plenty of these. Kids (and grown-ups) will love Cest is d'Best, a festival of international street theatre held in June.

PLAYGROUNDS Some handy playground locations in central Zagreb (there are well over 400 playgrounds in Zagreb as a whole) include: the small park at the top of Opatinova, just east of Tkalčićeva, beside the Kaptol Centar [84 D1]; and on Tuškanac (but this was getting decidedly run down in 2015). The best by far, however, is out of the centre in Bundek [79 E6].

DAY TRIPS Lonjsko Polje (pages 177–9), with its huge population of storks, is an easy day trip from Zagreb, even by public transport, as are the rolling hills and hiking trails of Samoborsko Gorje (pages 161–4).

Zagreb WHAT TO SEE AND DO

3

The climb up to the tower's tiny rooftop terrace (⊕ *May–Oct 11.00–19.00 Tue–Sun; 10kn*) gives even finer panoramic views.

For centuries a bell was rung from the tower every evening to announce the closing of the city's four gates (only one survives – see pages 113–14), but now it's the midday cannon which is the main attraction. The tradition started on New Year's Eve 1877, and has continued every day since. They're on the fourth cannon now (the other three are in the City Museum), with the current version being an American 76mm model from World War II; a gift from the Yugoslav army for the 1987 University Games in Zagreb.

If you climb the tower shortly before noon you can see the cannon being fired by Alem Tutundžić, who stepped into the shoes of Stjepan Možar, the latter having done the job for some 35 years and becoming something of a Zagreb institution in the process, before finally going into retirement a few years ago. For the first 20 years, Možar didn't take a single day off. He famously wore three separate watches to make sure he got the timing right – though he was pretty confident that, after firing the cannon for over a third of a century, he could do it no problem using his finely tuned internal clock.

To St Mark's Square From the tower, head east along the promenade, and then up at the end, via the lovely café terrace here, on to **St Catherine's Square** (Katarina Trg). The northern side of the square is taken up with the Kulmer Palace, formerly the Museum of Contemporary Art (which is now in Novi Zagreb), while on the southern side you'll find the Dverce Mansion and the Jesuit College, the 1607 Gymnasium, which is still a grammar school today.

The Jesuits were also responsible for the square's main attraction, and Zagreb's finest Baroque church, **St Catherine's** [91 B3]. Built between 1620 and 1632, it features some highly superior 18th-century stucco work and an amazing *trompe l'oeil* altarpiece (those aren't real pillars), an extraordinary work from 1762, by the Slovene painter Kristof Andrej Jelovšek.

Before leaving the square, check out what's on at the **Klovićevi Dvori** gallery [91 B3] (page 130), a lovely space that now houses part of the Marton Collection (page 160). Opposite, there's a small but dramatic sculpture of a fisherman wrestling with a vicious-looking snake, by Simeon Roksandić. Trivia fans will be pleased to know that there's a much larger version of the same statue in Belgrade's main park, up above the confluence of the Sava and Danube rivers.

The street running north from the corner of St Catherine's Square is Ćirilometodska, which leads along to St Mark's Square, Zagreb's political heart. On the way up the street you'll find the excellent **Museum of Broken Relationships** [91 B3] (page 119) on your right, and the Greek Orthodox **Church of Sts Cyril and Methodius** (Sv Ćirila i Metoda) [91 B3] on your left, the latter boxed rather uncomfortably between two small townhouses. Cyril and Method were the men responsible for the Glagolitic script (the best example of which is in the cathedral, page 117), and ultimately, the Cyrillic alphabet. To see inside – typical orthodox layout with an iconostasis separating the clergy from the congregation, and not much in the way of furniture – you normally need to ask at the Greek Catholic seminary next door.

Adjacent on the other side again is the **Croatian Museum of Naïve Art** [91 B3] (pages 128–30), which is well worth a visit, while at the end of the street, as you come on to **St Mark's Square** (Markov Trg), is the **Zagreb City Hall** [91 B3], which was originally built as a theatre in 1835 by a man called Stanković who had won a huge lottery the year before. It was used for various historic parliament meetings in the 19th century, and is today a place for ceremonial gatherings – and weddings, upstairs in the registry office. On the opposite (right-hand) corner you'll notice a sculpted stone head depicting the unfortunate Matija Gubec, doomed leader of a 16th-century peasant uprising. Gubec was supposedly dramatically put to death right in front of the church here by the Austro-Hungarians, who held a mock coronation for him with a crown of red-hot iron.

Today the square is dominated by swanky German cars and lots of police – which is hardly surprising, as it's the seat of the Croatian government. On the left-hand side of the square is the original **Ban's Palace** [91 B2] (Jelačić himself lived and died here), which was the target of a Serb rocket attack on Zagreb in 1991 – Tuđman, Mesić and the Croatian prime minister were all inside when it happened, so it's lucky there were no casualties (see page 79 for more historical detail). On the other side of the square is the **Croatian Parliament** [91 B2], the Sabor.

Between the two stands **St Mark's Church** [91 B2], its distinctive roof (which finally emerged from scaffolding in 2009) gaudily tiled in the fashion of seaside resorts with clock flowerbeds. The left-hand coat of arms is that of the Kingdom of Croatia (the chequerboard you still see on the national team's football shirts today), Slavonia (a *kuna* running between two rivers, the Sava and the Drava) and Dalmatia (three lions); on the right-hand side is the city of Zagreb's.

The original church here was built in the 13th century, with 14th- and 15th-century additions. Most of the church of this era has long since disappeared, though the southern portal, with 15 beautifully carved statues by the Parler family, from Prague, dates from 1420; if they ever finish restoring it, it's well worth a look.

Most of the rest of the church is a late 19th-century Gothic reconstruction. Like so much of post-1880 earthquake Zagreb, it's by Hermann Bollé, though the bell tower is an 1841 original. The interior was refurbished in the late 1930s by the painter Kljaković and the sculptor Meštrović; the former's frescoes are closer to socialist realism than Gothic masterpieces, but the latter's crucifix is suitably imposing and dramatic.

From the top of Gradec to the Stone Gate
Head out of the far left corner of the square and up Mletačka, where you'll find the excellent **Meštrović Atelier** [91 B2] (page 126) on the right-hand side, housed in the famous sculptor's house and studio. At the top of the street it's worth taking a detour down to the left, where you'll find the charmingly old-fashioned **Natural History Museum** [91 A2] (pages 125–6), and the elegant dead-end street of Visoka. Heading back up Demetrova, check out the classic façade of the Jelačić Mansion at number 7, home to the famous Ban's brother, and the Balbi Mansion at number 11, with the old town's last original wooden well in the courtyard.

At the top of Demetrova turn left and then round the corner to the right, where you'll find the **Priest's Tower** (Popov Toranj) [91 B1], which was originally the only defence allowed to be used by neighbouring Kaptol, which had no defences of its own. It's now part of the tremendous **Museum of the City of Zagreb** [91 B1] (page 120), which has its entrance on Opatička.

Continue down Opatička and then turn left into Kamenita, which leads to the Stone Gate. Before you get there, note two curiosities. On the left is a section of heavy black chain, which is supposed to have come from Nelson's ship, HMS *Victory*, though nobody seems to have the faintest idea how or why. On the other side of the street is a pharmacy, which has been in business since 1355, apparently, when it was opened by one of Dante's family – making it the second oldest in Europe, after Dubrovnik's.

The **Stone Gate** (Porta Lapidea) [91 B3] is the only one of the four original 13th-century city gates, which were closed at nightfall and reopened at dawn the following day, to protect the old settlement of Gradec from outsiders, and notably from their neighbours in Kaptol.

The gate owes its present appearance to a fire that ravaged the town in 1731. Among the ashes in a first-floor flat were found a perfectly preserved icon of the Virgin Mary (provenance unknown), so in 1760 a church was built into the fabric of the gate, and the icon given pride of place (the gold gem-studded crowns were added in 1931, to celebrate the bicentennial of the miracle).

A protective iron grille was added in 1778, presumably to keep grubby fingers away from the miraculous icon, and – in spite of curiously persistent calls for the gate's demolition over the centuries – it's still a major place of pilgrimage today. The walls are cluttered with votive plaques thanking the Virgin for her intercession in answering prayers, and a multitude of candles sends flickering shadows over the faces of the faithful in the semi-darkness. It's an atmospheric place, whatever your religious beliefs (or lack thereof).

Head through the Stone Gate and down the ramp, where you'll find a fine statue of St George and the (curiously catfish-faced, in this version) Dragon, with St George looking remarkably contrite. The road leads out on to Radićeva (originally called Duga Ulica, meaning 'long street' – and if you're heading uphill with a lot of shopping it certainly is), which continues downhill until it meets **Krvavi Most** (Blood Bridge) [91 C3], named for the bloody feuds between Gradec and Kaptol long ago (page 78).

To Kaptol Krvavi Most connects the bottom of Radićeva with the bottom of Tkalčićeva, which is more or less one continuous café. It was originally a creek (hence the bridge), but it was diverted and the street paved over in 1899, as the stench from the tanneries upstream had become intolerable. Take a detour up the street – even if it's only for a coffee or a beer – and check out the statue on the left-hand side of Marija Zagorka, Croatia's first female journalist and something of a proto-feminist (she died in 1957) as well as a popular novelist.

Returning to the bottom of Tkalčićeva, take the steps up to **St Mary's Church** (Sv Marija) [91 C3], the last remnant of the Cistercian abbey that was pulled down to make room for **Dolac** [91 C3], the main market square. Although the foundations of St Mary's are 13th century or so, the current model is mostly 18th century, including a fine fresco behind the altar by Jelovšek, the man also responsible for the great frescoes in St Catherine's (page 112).

Heading across Dolac brings you to the unmistakable twin spires of the **cathedral** [91 D3] (page 117). On the square in front of the cathedral stands a gilt Madonna, surrounded by four angels, by Fernkorn, the Austrian sculptor also responsible for the statue of Jelačić on his horse in the main square. The cathedral is flanked by the vast 18th-century Archbishop's Palace, and the canons' distinctive houses; all that's now left of the great fortress that once dominated Kaptol. After visiting the cathedral, it's a short drop back down to Jelačić Square.

The lower town After the winding streets and old houses of the upper town comes the planned munificence of the lower town (Donji Grad), which was made possible by the draining of the swamp below Kaptol and Gradec and the building of the railway embankment in the second half of the 19th century.

Head south out of Jelačić Square on Praška to the first of the three great, green leafy park-squares, which eventually bring you down to the railway station. The squares – Zrinjevac, Strossmayerov and Tomislava – are lined with sober, imposing buildings, and closed off at the southern end with the formal elegance of the railway station. They form the eastern wing of Lenuci's 'Green Horseshoe', which was designed by Milan Lenuci after the catastrophic 1880 earthquake, and is completed by the Botanical Gardens at the bottom, and the western arm heading up through three more leafy spacious squares culminating in the national theatre.

Zrinjevac, Strossmayerov and Tomislava The first attraction you come to on Zrinjevac, on the northern side of the square, is a rather charming 19th-century meteorological station, where you can check out the weather for your walk. Over on the right-hand side, if you're looking south, is the huge **Archaeological Museum** [91 C5] (pages 120–1), which is well worth a visit, if you have the time – and there's a very pleasant courtyard café behind it, if you're ready for a break.

Further down towards the station, on the same side of the road as the Archaeological Museum, on the corner, is Zagreb's excellent and nicely refurbished **Modern Gallery** [91 C6] (pages 126–8).

Centre stage in the square itself is the **Croatian Academy of Arts and Sciences** building, which you should pop into even if you don't want to visit the **Strossmayer Gallery of Old Masters** [91 D6] (page 128), upstairs. The reason to check it out is that in the foyer are two particularly important bits of Croatian art/history: the first is the 11th-century Baška Tablet, which was found on the island of Krk, and records the gratitude of the local monastery to the king for his donation of a block of land. Originally part of a rood screen, the tablet was once coloured blue, yellow and green, and you can still see vestiges of paint in the upper left-hand corner. The Baška Tablet in Baška itself, since you're asking, is a good copy; this is the original.

Also in the atrium of the Academy is the magnificent Sarcophagus of St Simeon, supported by four angels. Although this time it's the one here that's the copy (the original is in Zadar), the benefit is that here you can see all the way round and admire the fabulous 15th-century gold-plated silverwork by Francesco da Milano. Check out the central panel on the front, which is directly inspired by one of Giotto's frescoes in the Scrovegni Chapel in Padua, and the panel to the left, which depicts the burial scene (even if it looks more like the poor chap's actually being chopped up). Round at the back, note the excellent medieval scene of a woman fainting melodramatically at the sight of the dead body.

Behind the Academy, looking pensively down towards the station, is Bishop Strossmayer himself, as portrayed by Ivan Meštrović ('What time is the last train to Đakovo, Ivan?' he muses, consulting an imaginary timetable).

At the top of the next square, Tomislava, is the charming **Art Pavilion** [91 D7] (*Umjetnički Paviljon; www.umjetnicki-paviljon.hr;* ☉ *11.00–20.00 Tue–Thu & Sat/Sun, 11.00–21.00 Fri; 50kn*), which was beautifully restored recently, and has high profile exhibitions of artists such as Rodin and Miró. It also does service as a good restaurant, Art Paviljon (page 99). It's actually a pre-fabricated iron-framed structure, which was the brainchild of Vlaho Bukovac (page 378), who had it built for the Millennium Exhibition in Budapest in 1896, and then shipped it back to Zagreb afterwards (which, when you consider its size, is probably why it's not very far from the train station, even now). Indeed, the only thing separating it from the railway is enough of an expanse of lawn to set off the grand equestrian statue of **King Tomislav** [84 D6], who was crowned in AD925 as medieval Croatia's first king.

From here, turn right, and head west from the station past the Esplanade hotel to the **Botanical Gardens** (Botanički vrt) [84 C6], which have been providing an oasis of calm to generations of visitors since being opened to the public in 1894. It's a low-key affair, and the glasshouses are for botany enthusiasts only, but it's a pleasant place for a break.

Nominated as Archbishop of Zagreb in 1937, Alojzije Stepinac courted controversy during World War II by not being quick enough to denounce the Ustaše fascists or the Independent State of Croatia (NDH) – though he subsequently not only criticised the regime but also helped Jews escape from it, and spoke out in favour of persecuted minorities, much to the ire of the NDH, and later the Germans.

He was no friend of Tito's communists, either, refusing to separate the Croatian Catholic Church from Rome and after the war he was arrested. After a disgraceful show trial in 1948, he was condemned to 16 years' hard labour. He served five years of the sentence, in total isolation, and was then released, only to spend the rest of his life under house arrest in Krašić (page 163).

In spite of being forbidden from pursuing his religious duties by the state, Stepinac was made a cardinal by the Pope in 1953, though he never went to Rome to receive the crimson, as he was certain he'd never be allowed home to his beloved Croatia. He died in 1960 (quite possibly of poisoning), and in 1998 was beatified by the Pope.

Marulića, Mažuranića and Maršala Tita Running north from here are the other three big squares that complete the horseshoe, Marulića, Mažuranića and Maršala Tita. The first big building you'll see here is the **Croatian State Archives** [84 B6] (page 124), which seems sober and formal enough until you notice the giant owls perched on the roof. In the square beyond, there's a statue of Marko Marulić, the father of Croatian literature, who was from Split.

On the west side of the next square north, you'll find the undeservedly under-visited **Ethnographic Museum** [84 B5] (pages 122–4), where you can admire a comprehensive collection of Croatia's myriad national costumes. Round the corner, a block further west, and unmissable on Roosevelt Square, is the palatial neoclassical building (formerly a school) which houses the extraordinary **Mimara Museum** [84 B5] (pages 117–19), which is probably the one museum to visit in Zagreb even if you see no other.

Up from here, you come on to Maršala Tita, which is pretty much the last place in Zagreb to publicly acknowledge the man who created – and sowed the seeds of destruction of – modern Yugoslavia. On the left-hand side is the **Arts and Crafts Museum** [84 B5] (page 125), in yet another huge, late-19th-century building (by Hermann Bollé). In the greenery, as you come out of the museum, look out for another Fernkorn sculpture, this time of St George slaying the dragon.

Across the square is the **Croatian National Theatre** [91 A6], which was designed by the Viennese architects Ferdinand Fellner and Hermann Helmer, who made something of a career of theatre design, being responsible for over 40 across central Europe, from Switzerland to the Ukraine. An opportunity to see one of the frequent performances here (opera, ballet, theatre) shouldn't be missed (page 106).

In front of the theatre is Meštrović's sculpture, the *Well of Life* (*Zdenac Života*), dating from 1905, and one of the clearest indicators that his early work was influenced by Rodin, whom he'd met and studied with – in this case the source of inspiration is clearly *The Burghers of Calais*, though the *Well of Life* itself couldn't be mistaken for a Rodin. Across the road, in front of the university's elegant Faculty of Law, is another Meštrović masterpiece, the *History of the Croats*, a simple composition of a single, seated woman, serene but stern, holding a stone tablet.

From the theatre, a few hundred metres up Masarykova brings you to the beginning of the pedestrian zone heading up into Cvjetni Trg, the old flower market, and a wealth of places to sit and have a drink along Bogovićeva. At the top of the square is the **Serbian Orthodox Cathedral** (actually the **Church of the Holy Transfiguration**) [91 B4], with a rather drab 19th-century exterior hiding quite an imposing iconostasis and a dramatic deep-blue fresco across the apse depicting an unusually benign-looking Jesus with outspread arms. It's a particularly atmospheric place when there's a service on, with lots of smoke and incense on the go.

At the end of Bogovićeva you'll see the 1970s plate-glass windows of the Hotel Dubrovnik, which brings you right back out on to Jelačić Square.

The cathedral [91 D3] The unmistakable twin spires of Zagreb's cathedral can be seen from all over town, which makes it a pity that they've been undergoing restoration for as long as I can remember – though one spire miraculously emerged from scaffolding in 2012. Up close you can see just why the façade has needed restoring: the sculpture is astonishingly worn and damaged after a mere century of existence; cheap sandstone is to blame.

The cathedral was built from the 13th to the 15th centuries on the site of an earlier Romanesque church, but what you see today is mostly the work of the Viennese architect Hermann Bollé, following the 1880 earthquake, including the neo-Gothic façade, and the 104m and 105m spires (don't ask). Inside, the cathedral's a light, spacious building, with an uncluttered feel to it. A touch of drama is added by the enormous 1941 Glagolitic Memorial, commemorating the 1,300th anniversary of the first contacts with the Holy See, during the reign of Pope John IV (AD640–642). It takes up most of the wall behind you as you come into the cathedral, and it really is a strange script, even to eyes used to Cyrillic.

(Just in case your Glagolitic's got a bit rusty, the inscription reads: 'Glory to God in the highest! In memory of the 1,300th anniversary of the conversion of the Croatian people, who promised an eternal allegiance to Peter the Rock, having received from him the promised protection in every trial. Placed by The Society of the Brotherhood of the Croatian Dragon – conserving the relics of our ancestors and commending the Croatian homeland to the Mother of God – 641–1941.')

There isn't a great deal in the cathedral that pre-dates the earthquake, though the inlaid choir stalls are early 16th-century, and several of the altars and the pulpit are Baroque, from the beginning of the 18th century. There are also a few faded medieval fresco fragments in the sacristy, which date from the 13th century, along with an interesting triptych featuring the *Crucifixion of Golgotha* by Albrecht Dürer.

The biggest draws, however, are the monument and tomb of Alojzije Stepinac (box, page 116); the monument is a great casket, with a life-size effigy of the cardinal, behind the altar, while his tomb is over on the north wall, with a touching Meštrović sculpture. Until 1991, and Croatia's independence, you'd have been unwise to spend much time near either; these days you'll only be one of many people paying your respects.

On your way out of the cathedral, check out the enormous organ, made by Walcker of Ludwigsburg, which was first installed in 1855, and expanded and renewed in 1912, 1939 and 1987. It's reckoned to be among the ten most valuable in the world.

MUSEUMS

Mimara Museum [84 B5] (*Muzej Mimara; Rooseveltov trg 5; \ 482 8100; www. mimara.hr;* ◷ *Jul–Sep 10.00–19.00 Tue–Fri, 10.00–17.00 Sat, 10.00–14.00 Sun, Oct–*

Jun 10.00–17.00 Tue, Wed, Fri & Sat, 10.00–19.00 Thu, 10.00–14.00 Sun; 40kn) One of Zagreb's most interesting and intriguing museums is the Mimara. Housed in a palatial neoclassical building (formerly a school) on Roosevelt Square, it covers everything from Egyptian glassware to old masters, and medieval sculpture to French Impressionists. Altogether there are more than 1,500 items on display, so allow plenty of time.

The entire collection was given to the state in 1985 by Ante Topić Mimara (1898–1987) and his wife Wiltrud. But how on earth did the ebullient, bon vivant Mimara manage to accumulate such a wealth of treasures? One answer may be his having lived in Berlin between the wars; a period of exceptionally ripe pickings for canny art collectors. Nonetheless, it's never been clear how Mimara came by either his money or the great majority of his artefacts, and many may well be … well, not quite the real thing. (Authenticity, of course, is especially troublesome to establish when the provenance is unknown.) Mimara himself was said not to be that bothered; he cared more about an object's beauty than it being 'genuine'.

The collection is broadly chronological in arrangement, but unless you have a particular speciality you want to start with, it's most easily handled from the top floor down, giving you time to appreciate the most famous and obvious works before succumbing to museum-fatigue.

Second floor: Western art

At the top of the stairs on the second floor pop into the donor's room, where you'll find a bronze death mask of Mimara himself, looking positively beatific after a full and hedonistic existence.

Turn right out of here and head round the floor anticlockwise for a chronological tour through Western art, starting with icons in rooms 29 and 30 and sticking with solid religious themes through to room 35. The big draw here is Raphael's *St Luke the Evangelist*, which is almost certainly not by Raphael, though very much of the period/style.

Other attractions in the same room – which is the heart of the old masters' collection – include a disputed Rembrandt of a noble lady with a neck ruff the size of a wheel of brie, and van den Eekhout's *Ruth and Boaz*, which is very fine and almost certainly the real McCoy. Still staying in room 35, check out Rubens's vast *Virgin with the Innocents*, which brims over with more fleshy pink infant bottoms per square metre than was surely strictly necessary (or indeed tasteful), and an unusual Hoppner portrait of Wellington and his family, all oddly disassociated from one another, as if they'd been Photoshopped in later.

Moving on, there's a fleshy *Venus* in room 36 by Jordaens, notable mainly for the poor cupid doing his level best to hold up the goddess's extra chins, but it's the last room (#40) which is most popular, with a disputed double-sided Renoir in the middle, and a couple of lovely Manet still lifes, with succulent oysters, and shiny, organic-looking apples.

First floor: archaeology, sculpture, arts and crafts

Downstairs, on the first floor, start in room 13 (under the donor's room), which has some excellent and rare archaeological artefacts, including a fine lion's head which was probably the central boss of a shield and dates back to the 7th century BC, and a Persian pin and disc from the same period, with a lion/goddess in the centre, and pomegranates for fertility around the outside (picked up by Mimara in a market in Tehran in the 1930s, apparently).

Among Greek theatrical masks, Roman artefacts and Mesopotamian figures you'll also see a Hellenistic sculpture of an *ephebe* (young boy), claiming to be from the 3rd century BC, though the curator is pretty sure it's actually 16th-century German – not just because the hair and the base seem odd for the period, but because the statue has a distinctly slack Renaissance bum.

Rooms 14 to 28 cover a huge range of European sculpture and arts and crafts from the early Christian era right through to the beginning of the 20th century. There are hundreds of things to see, but look out for fishy lamps (room 14), an intricate English hunting horn carved from a walrus tusk (room 17), and a wooden monk carrying a cross and looking decidedly unsteady on his feet (room 19).

In room 20, there's an excellent wasp-waisted ballet dancer of a St George (Jacques de Baerze, 14th century), and a feisty 15th-century Flemish Archangel Gabriel, apparently in the act of saying 'up yours!'. Both the archangel and his attendant angels have been modelled on the likes of Felicity Kendal and Zoë Wanamaker.

Moving on, check out a two-foot wooden *Hercules* from 16th-century Florence (room 23), clearly inspired by the Farnese version of the same, and a stunning enamel jewellery box (room 24), dating from 1540 and possibly by Pierre Raymond. Finally, room 26 has some extraordinary ivory, including a Polish ivory-carved pyx (for consecrated communion bread) and a scabbard, both commemorating King Jan III Sobieski's 1683 defeat over the Turks in Vienna. When Poland approached Mimara to acquire them, he's playfully said to have agreed, but only in exchange for one of their better Rembrandts.

Ground floor: glass, carpets and Far Eastern art If your appetite's still unsated, head downstairs to the ground floor, where there's enough glass – ancient Egyptian, Roman, Islamic, Venetian, European – in rooms 1–5 to leave you utterly glassy-eyed, not to mention oriental carpets in room 6, and an extensive collection of Far Eastern art in rooms 7–12. Among the bronze, ceramics, jade, and porcelain, the most unusual artefact is an amazing pair of 19th-century 'goblets' in room 10, made from whole carved rhinoceros horns standing on intricately sculpted wooden bases depicting Taoist landscapes. You probably wouldn't want them at home.

Museum of Broken Relationships [91 B3] (*Muzej prekinutih veza; Ćirilometodska 2;* ✆ *485 1021; http://brokenships.com;* ☉ *Jun–Sep 09.00–22.30 daily, Oct–May 09.00–21.00 daily; 25kn*) When the Museum of Broken Relationships opened in Zagreb in 2010, it instantly became the most talked about museum in the capital (or indeed the whole of Croatia), attracting more international attention than perhaps any other. The following year, at the European Museum Awards, it won the Kenneth Hudson Award for the Most Innovative Museum in Europe. Physical fragments of people's past, failed relationships are displayed alongside the story of that relationship's demise, written by one of the former couple. At turns fascinating, hilarious and deeply touching, this is unlike any other museum you are ever likely to visit. Highly recommended.

Lauba [78 C5] (*Baruna Filipovića 23a;* ✆ *630 2115; http://www.lauba.hr;* ☉ *14.00– 22.00 Mon–Fri, 11.00–22.00 Sat; 25kn*) Opened in 2011, out towards Črnomerec, Lauba is one of most exciting gallery spaces in the Croatian capital – a restored Austro-Hungarian cavalry barracks (later a textile factory), built exactly 100 years earlier. Very contemporary Croatian artworks, with continually changing exhibits from the Filip Trade Collection, a private collection which contains over 500 works by Croatian artists from 1950 to the present day.

Museum of the City of Zagreb [91 B1] (*Muzej Grada Zagreba; Opatička 20;* \ *485 1361; www.mgz.hr;* ⊕ *10.00–18.00 Tue–Fri, 11.00–19.00 Sat, 10.00–14.00 Sun; 30kn*) It might seem unlikely, but the City Museum is one of Zagreb's most appealing. It was founded in 1907 and originally housed – bizarrely – in the Stone Gate (pages 113–14), before being transferred in 1925 to the Art Pavilion (page 115), and finally finding a permanent home in 1947 in a former convent at the top of the old town, abutting on to the Priest's Tower (page 113). It's a wonderful museum, with good English-language labelling (sadly still something of a rarity in Croatia) and imaginative displays, and well worth a visit; happily, only a small fraction of the total of 75,000 items in the collection are on display.

The visit starts with an excellent archaeological dig within the museum itself, and moves engagingly through Zagreb's history, giving you a real flavour of life at different periods, from Neolithic times right up to the damaged furniture from the 1991 rocket attack on the Ban's Palace.

There are some fine bits of sculpture from the portal of the original pre-earthquake cathedral, as well as pennants, charters, Golden Bulls and coats of arms, and a genuinely unpleasant 17th-century cast-iron 'mask of shame', used to punish miscreant market traders.

Perhaps most interesting of all, however, are the reconstructions of various shops from the past and the working rooms of several Croatian notables, along with my personal favourite, a fabulous room with a coloured map of the city inlaid into the floor, with scale models of the main buildings on small pedestals.

There are good temporary exhibitions too – on Zagreb during the First World War, Zagreb as a location in international cinema, etc.

Archaeological Museum [91 C5] (*Arheološki Muzej; Trg Nikole Šubića Zrinskog 19;* \ *487 3100; www.amz.hr;* ⊕ *10.00–18.00 Tue, Wed, Fri & Sat, 10.00–20.00 Thu, 10.00–13.00 Sun; 20kn, free museum tours 15.00 Sat*) The Archaeological Museum, on the west side of Zrinjevac, is a truly monumental collection ranging from prehistoric times through to the early medieval period.

Most of the four million or so objects here were collected in the 19th century, but thanks to major revamps since 1999, and the very best in modern display techniques, the museum is a light and airy place, and well worth a visit if you have even a glancing interest in archaeology, Egyptology, classical studies or numismatics. Clearly numbered explanations in Croatian and English go a long way to help.

Start at the top floor, where you'll find the recently renovated prehistoric and Egyptian displays. The prehistoric collection is excellent, with highlights including a headless Bronze Age figurine from Dalj (near Osijek) decorated with geometric patterns, and large collections of Bronze Age and Iron Age pots, axe-heads, jewellery, and cloak pins, etc, all well displayed. Also noteworthy is the lapodium collection; the lapods were an ethnic group from the Plitvice Lakes area, and cultural finds on display here (mostly from gravesites) are characterised by unusual headdresses and the lavish use of chunky amber jewellery.

The star attraction, though, is the so-called Vučedol Dove (which should really be the Vučedol Partridge). The three-footed Copper-Age vessel dates back to the fourth millennium BC, and is one of the best artefacts from the period ever found. It's decorated with the grooved geometrical patterns typical of objects from this era and area (along the Danube, near Vukovar), with the white paste filling the grooves being made from seashells. The partridge became a major symbol for Croatian peace and unity, and a memorial for Vukovar, after the 1990s war, so you'll see it everywhere – including on the 20kn note.

The Egyptian collection is also outstanding, with several hundred artefacts, including painted coffins and treasures from tombs, mainly from the Ptolemaic period (1070BC to AD30). In its own separate room is the real prize of the collection, the Zagreb Mummy, who was the wife of a tailor at the court of the Pharaoh, and still looks frighteningly deathlike today.

The mummy was acquired by Zagreb in 1859, and when unwrapped, it was discovered that the linen bandages were actually an Etruscan manuscript. At around 1,200 words, the 'Linen Book of Zagreb' is the longest text ever found in that obscure, still undeciphered, language. It appears to be an Etruscan liturgical calendar; if you have any clearer notions, or indeed a translation, I'm sure the museum curators would be delighted to hear from you.

Head downstairs to the newly renovated Greek, Roman and medieval displays. Among an impressive collection of Greek vases and Roman artefacts of all kinds, check out one of the more unusual and tranquil works from antiquity, the 2nd-century AD *Head of a Girl* from Solin.

You may also be able to admire the astonishing *Apoxyomenos* statue, which was found by a Belgian diver off the coast of Lošinj in 1998. The larger than life-size figure of a young Greek athlete is believed to be a Hellenic copy of a classical piece, and was painstakingly restored over many years before finally going on display in 2006. It has subsequently been part of several travelling exhibitions, including Zadar's Museum of Ancient Glass in 2010. Finally, numismatists will hardly be able to contain themselves in their rush to see the museum's stunning coin collection; one of the world's most comprehensive, with over quarter of a million pieces.

When you've had enough – or even if you just fancy a break during the visit – scope out the café in the courtyard behind the museum, where you can sit outside among ancient sculpture (fragments from the 1st to 4th centuries AD) and enjoy a pleasant drink.

Technical Museum [84 A7] (*Tehnički Muzej; Savska cesta 18;* \ *484 4050; http:// tehnicki-muzej.hr;* ☺ *09.00–17.00 Tue–Fri, 09.00–13.00 Sat/Sun; 15kn*) Zagreb's Technical Museum is a bit out of the way, but well worth the detour – and trams #13, #14 and #17 take you straight there.

If you're in town with kids of almost any age, then it's a must; as a grown-up kid myself, it ranks among my favourite diversions in the city. The museum is housed in an industrial-looking barn on the right-hand side of Savska, at #18, not far past the railway bridge.

The collection starts with fire engines, including Zagreb's first, a horse-drawn number that was bought for the city by a public-spirited lottery winner. It goes on to cover various machines, ancient and modern, which are used to transform energy, from watermills to great steam engines to a whole collection of aircraft engines.

The main central hall houses a wide range of goodies, from a pint-sized 1935 Fiat tank to an Italian submarine abandoned during World War II near the island of Lošinj, to various old cars, including a 1926 Renault NN and a Mercedes sportster from the same period, with a frightening top speed of 170km/h. Even more terrifying is a motor sleigh from 1931, which was powered by a giant propeller on the back and has no visible means of stopping.

Also on display is Dubrovnik's last tram – after derailing and killing two people, it was permanently taken out of service (as anyone who's battled with Dubrovnik's traffic today will still lament); a replica of an old horse-drawn Zagreb tram; and the delightful *Samoborček*, the mini steam train that made the short run over to Samobor from 1930–1960, so the locals could indulge in their weekend *kremšnite* (page 158).

To one side there are scale models of ships (everything from a 5th-century BC Greek trireme to a 17th-century Venetian galley to modern warships), while hanging from the ceiling are various flying machines, from biplanes to a US Thunderbolt to the tatty-looking helicopter that was pressed back into service during the war of the 1990s.

Two other displays on the ground floor are of particular note. The first deals with early aviation, and in particular the pioneer Otto Lilienthal, who made 2,000 successful glider flights in planes of his own design, but died after falling 17m and breaking his spine on his 2,001st flight. His last words were '*Opfer müssen gebracht werden!*' ('Sacrifices must be made!'). The photos make you realise just how unsuited humans are for winged flight.

There's also a good display on the dirigibles pioneered by Croatian aviator David Schwarz – called Schwarzoplans, naturally. They were commissioned by the German army and tested in 1897 in Berlin, but although successful, one also crashed; Schwarz died of a heart attack soon after, reportedly brought on by the news that the invention had actually been accepted. Schwarz's widow sold the plans to a certain Count Ferdinand von Zeppelin, who of course went on to build his eponymous airships, including the extraordinary *Hindenburg*.

Upstairs there's a rather dry exhibition on the 'basics of agriculture', but the effort is amply rewarded by a fantastic bee exhibit at the far end, consisting of three working beehives with glass sides and tubes giving the industrious workers access to the great outdoors, allowing you to see what the bees are really getting up to. It's an excellent display.

Also upstairs is an optical planetarium, which gives you anatomically correct views of the star-filled night sky at any time of year, and from the poles to the equator. It costs an extra 10kn to get in, and is usually only open during the hour before the museum closes.

Back downstairs, there are two more major highlights, both only visitable by guided tour. The first, underneath the museum, is a mine, with some 300m of tunnels, showing what working conditions in mines at different periods were (and indeed are) like – tours usually go at 15.00 daily, 11.00 at weekends, or you can try to hitch on to the back of a group visit. It's a truly excellent experience.

And finally, there's an amazing reconstruction of some of Nikola Tesla's working experiments, including both 3MW and 12MW sparks around a Faraday Cage (lightning is around 20MW, for comparison), along with an interactive exhibition, which has been fully revamped in honour of the 150th anniversary of the inventor's birth in Croatia. Tours happen at 15.30 on weekdays, 11.30 at weekends.

Tesla was an extraordinary man, pretty much defining the way we use electricity even today, and also inventing the radio ahead of Marconi – though this wasn't recognised until after Tesla's death, impoverished and forgotten, in 1943. Tesla demonstrated a radio-controlled boat in Manhattan, almost 50 years earlier, in 1897, though such things didn't become commonplace until the 1960s, and at the time of his death he was working on a teleforce weapon, or death-ray (intended of course as a peace-ray).

Ethnographic Museum [85 B5] (*Etnografski Muzej; Trg Mažuranića 14;* ＼*482 6220; www.emz.hr;* ☉ *10.00–18.00 Tue–Thu, 10.00–13.00 Fri–Sun; 15kn*) The Ethnographic Museum is occasionally invaded by noisy school groups, but usually curiously deserted – which is unfair, as it's a tremendous insight into the way life was lived by most Croatian people until relatively recent times.

The collection is housed in a Jugendstil building which was originally designed at the turn of the 20th century to be a museum of trade and commerce (check out the allegorical figures around the dome). After World War I, it took on its new function as the Ethnographic Museum, focusing on everyday village life, special festive items, and national costumes – and unless you're in Zagreb on the right dates in July (pages 105–6), this will be the absolute best chance you get to see the huge variety from across the country.

The current exhibition dates back to 1972, and is definitely showing its age. Happily, full renovations are planned, though at the time of writing (2015) financial restrictions still prevented these from being completed.

The permanent collection upstairs starts with a simple village house interior. Note the photograph of a large village clan of over 30 people; the abolition of the feudal system by Jelačić (page 16) in 1848 saw most clans disintegrate, but some persisted through until the 1930s.

Opposite the house interior there's a display of decorative women's headwear from northern Croatia, which tells you a lot about hair-related superstition. Young girls' hair is allowed to be seen, but married women's woven bonnets cover it all up, and bridal bonnets are often highly reflective to ward off the evil eye. The superstition reigned that a woman's strength and goodness lay in her hair, and so this should be reserved for the family; as a result, any hair lost had to be burnt, to prevent witches from getting hold of it. In some of the more remote villages of Croatia, these beliefs still persist today. Even in Zagreb, you'll find people being superstitious about chimney sweeps (you see them in the streets) and nuns, with one for good luck, two for bad, three for good, etc. It can't be a coincidence that nuns and sweeps usually work in pairs.

Looking at the fabrics and costumes, you'll see lots of red, black and white. Red was believed to ward off evil spirits, and was often used during childbirth to divide the room, to separate the women from the rest of the household. Red dresses also symbolise youth and vitality. Black, of course, is usually associated with death – to wrap the body for burial or cover the burial chest. But until around a century ago, white was the traditional colour for mourning across most of Europe, and still is in Croatia, Hungary, and even parts of Spain today. White was the simplest fabric, so the total absence of decoration and colour signifies a lack of interest in personal appearance in the wake of tragedy.

In the main display rooms you'll also see rustic furniture, communal ovens, baking implements, and valuable bridal chests, usually made from wood from the island of Rab. The wood was sold off so enthusiastically to the Italians and French – it was a favourite for cognac casks – that the island eventually became denuded and entirely barren on the east side, and remains so today.

Also noteworthy are hand-operated corn mills, which were once the 'morning music' heard in every village; primitive wooden carnival masks used to chase away the evil winter spirits (local carnivals continue today, and there's a huge one in Rijeka); small wax votives (of limbs in need of repair, or sick animals); and the ubiquitous red-iced gingerbread hearts (*licitarsko srce*) decorated with mirrors, traditionally given by young men to their brides-to-be: 'look who I have in my heart'.

Among the costumes themselves, look out for the grass capes used by shepherds to keep the rain off, and the shaggy (positively hippy) costumes and rugs from the Lika region, which come from vertical looms which can't be used to make linen.

Richer garments reflect wealthier parts of the country, and notably the Slavonian costumes, with silver and gold thread, complex embroidery, and an abundance of fabric, as well as necklaces with coins sewn in to them for unmarried daughters, symbolically representing their dowry.

Downstairs, don't miss the unusual – and quite entertaining – foreign ethnographic collection, with artefacts and costumes from India, Bengal, the

Pacific islands, Australia, Africa, Easter Island, Japan, Brazil and Latin America. Most of the material here came from the expeditions led at the turn of the 20th century by Mirko and Stjepan Seljan, an exotic pair of explorer brothers from Karlovac.

And last but not least, see what's happening on the rest of the ground floor; the temporary exhibitions here are generally first-rate.

Croatian State Archives [84 B6] (*Hrvatski Državni Arhiv; Trg Marka Marulića 21;* \ *480 1999; 480 1981; www.arhiv.hr;* ☉ *08.00–16.00 Mon–Fri; guided tours in English, German & Croatian noon, 13.00, 14.00 Mon–Fri & 2nd Sat each month, by special arrangement; 20kn*) The Croatian State Archives are housed in Zagreb's finest Jugendstil building, down near the Botanical Gardens. If you have the time, it's well worth taking a tour, as the inside is as grand as the exterior.

At first sight, the edifice seems as sober and formal as you'd expect from something that was originally built as a monumental university library in 1913, but wait until you see the four sets of giant green owls supporting globes on the roof – they're fabulous! Before you go inside, also check out the four sets of reliefs above the main entrance, which are allegories of the four collegiate sciences – from left to right as you're looking at them, Medicine, Theology, Philosophy (Socrates confronting the very naked truth indeed) and Law.

The magnificent building is the work of local boy Rudolf Lubynski, who used the knowledge he gained studying architecture in Karlsruhe to create Zagreb's first concrete building. He also took charge of the sumptuous interior decoration, which includes geometric marble inlay floors, Bohemian crystal glass panelling, Slavonian oak wainscoting, and light fittings from Murano, all set off by tasteful touches of gold leaf decoration.

Inside the main hall, notice the mosaic depictions of some of Croatia's most important sites, including Đakovo, Dubrovnik, Senj and of course Zagreb. There are plenty of other owls around too, symbolising illumination and knowledge.

The tour takes in the lovely Professors' Reading Room, which features comfortable reading desks and fine Art Nouveau lamps, as well as several large allegorical paintings by Ivan Tišov, depicting the natural sciences, the liberal arts and the scholastic arts. Above the entrance hangs Robert Auer's image of Athene Palladia holding a figure of Athene Nike, a pictorial embodiment of the maxim 'through knowledge to victory'.

The other main attraction inside is the aptly named and genuinely enormous Large Reading Room, which is still in use today. Two vast chandeliers (imported from Prague and weighing in at over a tonne apiece) complement the elegant beaded reading lamps and the lovely stained glass in the ceiling.

On the north wall (above the entrance doors) are three imposing paintings by Mirko Rački, depicting Science in Antiquity to the left (note Homer), Science in the Middle Ages to the right (featuring Dante), and Science in the Modern Age in the middle. The huge canvas opposite is the *Evolution of Croatian Culture* by Vlaho Bukovac (page 378), and features 27 Croatian luminaries – with a little knowledge and a sharp eye you can spot the playwright Ivan Gundulić, Bishop Strossmayer and Ljudevit Gaj, while that person on the right-hand side peeking out from behind the figure in a green cape may well be Lubynski himself.

Back outside, dizzy from all the accumulated knowledge and wisdom – not to mention the owls – see if the small graffito telling you what it's really all about ('Sex and Money and Guns') has been cleaned off yet. It's on one of the small pillars holding up the chain fence, to the left as you leave – or it was on my last visit, anyway.

Arts and Crafts Museum [84 B5] (*Muzej za Umjetnost i Obrt; Trg maršala Tita 10;* ✆ *488 2111; www.muo.hr;* ⊕ *10.00–19.00 Tue–Sat, 10.00–14.00 Sun; 30kn*) Zagreb also has an outstanding Arts and Crafts Museum, housed in yet another huge, late 19th-century building (Bollé, again), just across the square from the National Theatre. The only real disappointment is the almost complete lack of English-language captions and legends.

The great pastel edifice was purpose-built for the museum, and was designed to house a 'collection of samples for masters, crafts and artists' – a remit it certainly manages to fulfil to this day, covering pretty much everything from the 14th to the 20th centuries, and displaying around 3,000 objects from its total collection of over 150,000 artefacts.

What you find most appealing will depend on your own specialist areas of interest: you can choose from furniture; textiles and clothing; ceramics; glass; Gothic and Baroque sculpture; European miniatures from the 17th to 19th centuries; ivory; silverware; musical instruments; religious art and liturgical objects; a magnificent collection of 400 clocks and some 200 pocket and wristwatches; and pretty much all the Secession and Biedermeier you can eat.

If that's not enough to knock the stuffing out of you, there are also sections on printing, graphic and industrial design, and photography – with both old photographic equipment and photographs on display, including early daguerreotypes, documentary photographs from World War I, and pictures from dashing mountaineering expeditions of the 1920s. Finally, there's an interesting collection of European art, with the focus primarily on the 17th century. Rembrandt's student Ferdinand Bol is represented here, along with Charles Le Brun, the painter who (with Poussin) pretty much determined the course of 17th-century French painting.

The museum has a nice, classy shop, where you can buy good reproductions as well as modern ceramics and textiles, and downstairs (with its own courtyard at the back) is the Hrvatski Kulturni Klub – nothing whatsoever to do with a Croatian Boy George, but instead a rather good café and restaurant (page 100).

Natural History Museum [91 A2] (*Hrvatski Prirodoslovni Muzej; Demetrova 1;* ✆ *485 1700; http://hpm.web.link2.hr;* ⊕ *10.00–17.00 Tue, Wed & Fri, 10.00–20.00 Thu, 10.00–19.00 Sat, 10.00–13.00 Sun; 20kn*) If you fancy a trip back in time, then Zagreb's Natural History Museum is just the ticket.

Situated up in the old town in a palatial but rather run-down building, the collection comprises around two million specimens, most of them in anachronistic wooden glass-fronted cabinets.

Get past the surly socialist-era ticket sellers, and you can lose yourself in room after room of rocks and fossils, moon dust and meteorites, and bones, skeletons and specimens you'd rather not think about in formaldehyde-filled glass jars.

The top floor is the main attraction, especially if you're travelling with kids. Here you'll find seriously old-fashioned displays of stuffed and preserved animals from throughout Europe, including a large shark in a suitably aquamarine environment, and a long corridor of specimen jars leading through to mammals, birds, insects and some very fine butterflies.

For serious naturalists, the museum also houses a library of some 40,000 volumes that you can consult; the oldest is a natural history encyclopaedia in Latin dating from 1638.

Before you leave, make sure you step into the museum's courtyard, where you can check out the excellent mineralogical map of Croatia, made from a bit of stone from each part of the country, and a geological column stretching from 350 million BC to about 10,000 years ago. One side shows rocks from Mediterranean Croatia; the other stone from the continental interior, including various fossils representative of different eras.

Finally, don't be surprised if you see anthropologists of world renown snooping around the museum, as it's also the repository of the extraordinary Krapina Man find, the world's largest collection of Neanderthal fossils from a single site. This isn't open to the public, but a dedicated museum on the subject has been developed at Krapina itself (see page 152, and the box on page 127).

Croatia Historical Museum [91 A3] (*Hrvatski Povijesni Muzej; Matoševa 9;* ✆ *485 1900; www.hismus.hr;* ⏱ *10.00–18.00 Mon–Fri, 10.00–13.00 Sat & Sun; 10kn*) If you're kicking your heels or it's a rainy day, pop into the Croatia Historical Museum, which has temporary exhibitions focusing on – yep – Croatia's history. The museum is one block west of St Mark's Square in the old town.

There's no permanent exhibition, which is a pity, as there are all sorts of important goodies in stock, from Jelačić's 1848 flag to armour, weapons, stone sculpture, painting, clocks, maps and photographs. The temporary exhibitions are usually good, but the amount of information you'll get in English varies.

Museum of Illusions [84 B3] (*Muzej Iluzija; Ilica 72;* ✆ *799 9609; http:// muzejiluzija.com;* ⏱ *09.00–22.00 daily; 40kn*) Zagreb's newest museum, opened in 2015 and located towards Britanski trg, is packed full of bizarre and disorienting optical illusions, including one of the largest hologram exhibits in Europe.

GALLERIES
Meštrović Atelier [91 B2] (*Fondacija Ivana Meštrovića; Mletačka 8;* ✆ *485 1123; http://www.mestrovic.hr/muzeji/atelijer-mestrovic/atelijer-mestrovic.html;* ⏱ *10.00– 18.00 Tue–Fri, 10.00–14.00 Sat & Sun; 30kn*) Arguably the most interesting, and certainly the most accessible, of Zagreb's galleries is the Meštrović Atelier. Ivan Meštrović was Croatia's most famous sculptor, and he lived at this house in the upper town between the two world wars, before emigrating to the United States.

Inside, you'll find an excellent collection of the sculptor's work, in a much more intimate setting than the vast Meštrović Gallery in Split. The house itself is lovely, with the collection spread across three floors and the artist's studio, and demonstrating the diversity of his work. There's more than a nod to Rodin, who Meštrović befriended in Paris before World War I, but the sculpture goes a good deal deeper than that, and also owes a debt to Slavic culture, Christian iconography and the work of Michelangelo.

The collection is a fine introduction to some of the large Meštrović works dotted around Zagreb – Bishop Strossmayer behind the Strossmayer Gallery, Marulić in front of the State Archives, the *Well of Life* in front of the National Theatre, the *History of the Croats* next to the Faculty of Law, or the great *Crucifixion* in St Mark's Church.

Modern Gallery [91 C6] (*Moderna Galerija; Andrije Hebranga 1;* ✆ *604 1040; www.moderna-galerija.hr;* ⏱ *10.00–19.00 Tue–Fri, 11.00–14.00 Sat/Sun; 40kn*) The Modern Gallery on Strossmayerov houses 'Two centuries of Croatian Visual Arts'. In spite of one of the steepest entry fees in Zagreb, and the works being mainly by artists most of us haven't heard of, this is nonetheless one of the best galleries in Zagreb.

It's been expensively and beautifully restored, and the rooms are bright, light and airy, running chronologically from around 1800 onwards. For me personally, the show is stolen by Vlaho Bukovac (see box, page 378), and the gallery holds some great works by him – but don't let that stop you enjoying the rest of what's on show here.

The first room you come into sets you up a treat, with a symbolic feast from the 'School of Zagreb' painters, dominated by a vast bacchanalia from Celestin Mato Medović. That leads you into something of a vacuum in the next couple of rooms, but it's worth sparing a moment for Fernkorn's models of the statues of St George and the Dragon, and Ban Jelačić, the full-scale versions of which you'll have seen in the city. There are also four very strange portraits by Vjekoslav Karas, which fall uncomfortably between the naïve and the expressive, and were painted before the young artist drowned himself in Karlovac in 1858 (page 171).

The next room's more cheerful altogether, with some wonderful Bukovac works, and a couple of excellent hyper-realistic sculptures by Robert Frageš Mihanović; his St Dominic is particularly good.

In the next long room check out the transition from Jugendstil to Symbolism, and a fine picture of water lilies by Croatia's first important female painter, Slava Raškaj; a deaf mute, she died before the age of 30 in an institution. In the same room, there's a fine diptych in a Jugendstil frame by one of Croatia's most influential painters, Emanuel Vidović – it's entitled *Mali Svjet* (Small World), with the house he was born in on the left, and the graveyard where he will be buried on the right.

The main oval room, which comes next, showcases the arrival of German Expressionism, and sees Vidović retreat into his dream world of *The City of the Dead*. Also check out the photographically framed seascapes by Menci Clement Crnčić, and some dramatic portraits by the short-lived Josip Račić (he died when he was just 23), including the *Lady in White*.

Moving on, there are two excellent self-portraits by Miroslav Kraljević, who made it to the ripe old age of 28 before dying of consumption; a great painting of a woman with a gun by Croatia's second great female painter, Nasta Rojc; a fabulous 1923 self-portrait by Milivoj Uzelac – Schiele-influenced and Expressionism at its cruellest; and a 1927 Picasso-feel self-portrait by Ivo Režek.

Head up the stairs and check out the works by the socially committed architect Drago Ibler in the first room – distinguished by the brick wall backgrounds denoting lack of choice. There are also some fantastic photographs in the same

KRAPINA MAN

Krapina Man was discovered in August 1899 by Dragutin Gorjanović-Kramberger – or to be more accurate, a fossilised human molar was found, pointing to the existence of a Neanderthal settlement in the area some 130,000 years ago. Thanks to Gorjanović-Kramberger's enormous diligence, scholarship and plain hard work, the collection grew in size to become the world's largest and most important set of Neanderthal fossils from a single site, comprising 900 pieces from 70 to 80 individuals.

The current curator, Jakov Radovčić, has dedicated a great part of his life to the collection, and is the author of a fascinating biography of the finder (page 430).

His great personal achievement – after decades of lobbying – is the new, state-of-the-art interactive museum at Krapina (page 152).

room of 1930s workers by Tošo Dabac, and a couple of very late works by Vidović of Split and Trogir cathedrals.

After World War II you get everything from beauty to landscapes to social realism and – post 1951 – geometrical abstractionism. Look out for works by the husband and wife team Frano Šimunović and Ksenija Kantoci: abstract landscapes of fields and dry stone walls from the Dalmatian hinterland from the former, and abstract sculptures from the same landscapes, usually of peasant women, from the latter.

The exhibition ends with art that was banned during the Yugoslav era, including an excellent conceptual work featuring doctored hyperinflation banknotes and worthless coins being scooped up by a ladle.

Strossmayer Gallery of Old Masters [91 D6] (*Strossmayerova Galerija; Zrinski trg 11;* \ *4895 117; http://info.hazu.hr;* ⊕ *10.00–13.00 & 17.00–19.00 Tue, 10.00–13.00 Wed–Sun; 10kn*) In the square across the street from the Modern Gallery you'll find the Croatian Academy of Arts and Sciences (page 115), the top floor of which is given over to the excellent Strossmayer Gallery of Old Masters.

Josip Juraj Strossmayer was the fervently pro-Croat bishop of Đakovo, in eastern Slavonia, and was the founder of the Academy. He was also a serious art collector, and what you get here is his private collection of some 256 works from 1884, supplemented by various donations over the years from the likes of Augustinčić (page 147) and Mimara (page 117).

The gallery is at the top of the stairs, and spans religious works from the Renaissance right through to 19th-century France. The lack of English-language captions is a pity, but not a show-stopper. Heading clockwise, chronologically around the gallery, the first room is noteworthy for a fine 15th-century work by Fra Angelico depicting St Francis and St Peter, and a *Madonna and Child* by Cosimo Rosselli, featuring dreary-looking angels – even by the standards of the day.

The next room houses Strossmayer's own favourite works, and notably another *Madonna and Child*, this time by a follower of Raphael. Rooms three and four make the small stylistic leap from the Ferrara school to the Venetian school – a bit less detail in the works, but still camp as Christmas. Look out for a dramatic *Resurrection* from Carpaccio, with Jesus positively leaping out of his grave and stepping on the sleeping soldiers on his way out, an inspiringly simple *Ecco Homo* by Filippo Mazzola, and a suggestive *San Sebastian* by Andrea del Sarto.

In the next three rooms, check out Ribera's dramatic *Jerome* (clearly inspired by Caravaggio), a wonderful *Mary Magdalene* by El Greco (centuries ahead of his time as usual), and a great treatment of *Salome*, by Elisabetta Sirani, who managed to churn out more than 170 oils by the time of her death, aged just 27, in 1665.

Rooms 8, 9 and 10 take you through Croatian, Flemish and French works for the most part, with the likes of Breughel, Poussin, Delacroix and Courbet on show – and a fantastically stodgy portrait of famous beauty and salon-hostess Juliette Récamier by Antoine-Jean Gros.

As you leave, look out for Carpeaux's bust of Eugène-Emmanuel-Ernest d'Halwyn, Marquis de Piennes, who was France's ambassador to Zagreb under Napoleon III – and known here as plain old Etienne. Piennes bequeathed his private art collection to the Strossmayer Gallery on his death in 1911.

Croatian Museum of Naïve Art [91 B3] (*Muzej Naivne Umjetnosti; Sv Ćirila i Metoda 3;* \ *485 1911; www.hmnu.org;* ⊕ *10.00–18.00 Tue–Fri, 10.00–13.00 Sat &*

Sun; 20kn) This is one of Zagreb's most interesting galleries, up in the old town, just south of St Mark's Square.

The gallery was opened in 1952, as the Peasant Art Gallery, making it the oldest museum of naïve art in the world. From 1956 it was called the Gallery of Primitive Art, and in 1994 took its present name. There are around 80 works on show, from a total collection of over 1,600, covering naïve artists who had no professional training and little or no education – but all went on to make a living from their work.

Croatian naïve art developed from the 1930s in Hlebine, near the Hungarian border, with the first important artist being Ivan Generalić, who showed in Paris to great critical and commercial acclaim in 1953. Characteristic of Generalić and his followers was the technique of painting highly stylised rural scenes on glass, which was then reversed for framing. Apart from being valuable in its own right, the movement was particularly important for giving us a record of the terrible hardships of peasant life until quite recent times.

A common motif is the rooster, a symbol of rebirth (as it is in the work of Federico García Lorca); look out for the Godzilla-sized version on the barn roof in one of the paintings in the first room, which is dedicated to Generalić's work, or the particularly colourful cockerel in *The Death of Virius*, a homage to another painter from Hlebine who died during World War II – note the dead trees and concentration camp, with life going on far behind the barbed wire. Finally, check out the striking self-portrait from 1975, with its uniform background and Generalić looking down in contemplation.

In complete contrast is follower Ivan Večenaj's *Evangelists on Calvary*, with blood pouring down the cross, the evangelists present in their animal form (ox, lion, eagle), people strung up in the trees, inscribed parchments everywhere, and a blood-red sky; the stuff of nightmares. If you don't like it, you probably won't much enjoy his portrait of an inbred peasant woman with her cat, either.

More palatable – to this author, anyway – are the winter landscapes by Mijo Kovačić. Reminiscent somewhat of Brueghel, particularly good examples are 1962's *Singeing a Pig* (using burning straw to remove the pig's hair and bristles), 1967's *Swineherd*, and 1974's *Frozen in the Snow*, depicting dead partisans in a super-realistic snowdrift.

Moving into the third room, check out the large, accomplished work by Genarlić's son Josip, *Guiana '78*, which deals with the mass suicide of Jim Jones and his 900 followers that year, and marks the start of a general trend towards the depiction of more modern life, rather than simply peasant culture.

Two other artists are particularly worth singling out: Emerik Feješ and Ivan Rabuzin. You can spot a Feješ a mile off, as the scenes are mostly geometric multi-coloured churches, including Vienna and Milan cathedrals, St Mark's in Venice, and Sainte-Chapelle in Paris.

Rabuzin's work is also highly distinctive, and he's arguably the most accessible of all the naïve artists, as he leaves people out of the picture (literally; he believed that the presence of people was a 'blot' on the beauty of the world). His bright, optimistic pastel landscapes feature repetitive geometric forms in the trees and flowers – and I even once saw a reproduction in a French hotel.

Finally, check out the work of naïve sculptor Petar Smajić, and particularly his charming *Adam and Eve*, which is Henry Moore-like in its simplicity.

If you're really serious about naïve art, then it's well worth making the trip up to Hlebine, a couple of hours northeast of Zagreb, where you can visit both a state gallery and the private collection of Generalić father and son. The virgin landscape of the early paintings may no longer exist, but the old way of life persists. Around

Easter and during other festive periods, giant Easter eggs, painted in naïve style, are often placed in squares and other locations in central Zagreb.

Museum of Contemporary Art [77 E7] (*Muzej Suvremene Umjetnosti; Av Dubrovnik 17;* \ *605 2700; www.msu.hr;* ⊕ *11.00–18.00 Tue–Fri & Sun, 11.00–20.00 Sat; 30kn*) For a long while, the Museum of Contemporary Art was housed in the Kulmer Palace, on the other side of St Catherine's Church, but the space was much too small for comfort. As a result, a large new museum building was built on Avenija Dubrovnik in Novi Zagreb, finally giving the collection the space it deserves, which opened in December 2009.

Galerija Klovićevi Dvori [91 B3] (*Jezuitski trg 4; http://gkd.hr;* ⊕ *11.00–19.00 Tue–Sun; free*) A nice gallery in the Upper Town with some interesting exhibitions including, in the past, the Organ Vida international photography festival and Italian Baroque painting. Also houses part of the Marten Collection.

Gliptoteka [76 D4] (*Medvedgradska 2;* \ *468 6050; http://gliptoteka.mdc.hr;* ⊕ *11.00–19.00 Tue–Fri, 10.00–14.00 Sat/Sun; 10kn*) An important permanent collection of plaster casts and copies of artworks from Antiquity to the present, with some fascinating contemporary temporary exhibitions. Part of the Croatian Academy of Arts and Sciences.

OTHER NOTEWORTHY BUILDINGS
The Stock Exchange [85 F4] Zagreb's most dramatic Neoclassical building is the former stock exchange, now home to the Croatian National Bank (Hrvatska narodna banka). It was designed by the architect Viktor Kovačić, though he didn't live to see its completion; it was finished off in 1927 by his associate Hugo Erlich.

The front of the building is a striking white marble porch, supported by Ionic columns, which dominates the square it's on. If you get a chance to peek inside, do (it's not all that likely, but there's no harm in trying). A tremendous staircase leads up from the entrance hall to the foyer of the original trading floor, a great circular room topped by a huge cupola with a round opening to let in the light.

The Croatian Artists' Centre [85 F5] (*Dom Hrvatskih Likovnih Umjetnika; Trg žrtava fašizma 16; www.hdlu.hr;* ⊕ *11.00–19.00 Wed–Fri, 10.00–18.00 Sat/ Sun; 20kn*) All roads in the eastern part of the lower town seem to home in on Zagreb's only large circular building, the white marble Croatian Artists Centre. Supported by a colonnade of fine white marble pillars, the building was designed by Ivan Meštrović (page 126) to house temporary art exhibitions, a function it still performs to this day (though it's also seen service as a mosque and a socialist museum in the meantime). It's worth popping in, even if the current exhibition's not something you're mad about, just to see the great space, diffusely lit from above by its glass ceiling.

The Golden Hall [91 B2] (*Zlatna dvorana; Opatička 10*) In the old town (easy to find because of the big wrought-iron gates) is the mansion housing the Croatian History Institute (*Hrvatski institut za povijest; www.isp.hr*). And inside that, there's an extraordinary Baroque room called the Golden Hall, which is used mainly for swanky functions. If you ever get the chance to see inside, it's well worth it, with abundant gilding that gives it its name, and major paintings celebrating great Croatian moments in history. Best of the lot is the dramatic depiction by Vlaho

Bukovac (see page 378) of Emperor Franz Josef arriving in Zagreb, with the back of what's now the Mimara Museum (it was then a school) clearly visible behind the assembled welcome reception.

St Blaise's Church [84 A4] (Sv Blaž) Situated a few blocks west of the National Theatre, St Blaise's Church is mainly famous for its reinforced concrete dome. The church was the brainchild of local architect Viktor Kovačić, and was built according to his designs between 1912 and 1915. Sceptics were certain that the 18m-wide dome would collapse the moment the supporting pillars were removed, so Kovačić sat out the night underneath it to confound his critics, and the dome still looks pretty solid today. The church is pretty plain inside, and usually closed (except during services), but you can get into the porch and have a peek through the bars if you're keen.

AROUND ZAGREB

If you just worked your way through everything in the previous sections, you'll clearly be after a breath of fresh air and some outdoor attractions. Happily, Zagreb has plenty to offer here too, from one of the best cemeteries anywhere, Mirogoj, to the huge city park, Maksimir, where you'll also find a great zoo, to a hike or bike ride (or, when it's been reopened, cable car ride) on the easily accessible Sljeme, the peak of Mount Medvednica. Zagreb even has its own beaches, at Jarun Lake and Bundek – and if that's still not enough, there's also the charming monastery church of Remete to visit in the northern suburbs.

MIROGOJ CEMETERY [77 E4] You don't have to be in the least bit morbid to enjoy a trip up to Mirogoj Cemetery, one of the best burial grounds I've ever visited. Just hop on bus #106, which runs up from Kaptol, above the cathedral, and get off ten minutes later when you see the semi-circular entrance gate to the cemetery, dominated by the dome of the main chapel.

Mirogoj was opened in 1876 as the city's monumental municipal cemetery, and the main feature is a series of divine, greening cupola-ed arcades running either way along the inside of the walls. They're the work of Hermann Bollé, and in their own way every bit as impressive as the cathedral.

The cemetery is not just non-denominational but a positive Pantheon, housing Jews and Muslims, Orthodox Christians and Catholics, communist partisans and the German dead from World War II. There are literally thousands of touching memorials to individuals, families, and different historical tragedies, with sculpture from pretty much every notable Croatian artist.

The largest and most impressive memorial of all is right at the top of the main avenue, where Croatia's first president, Franjo Tuđman, is honoured by a vast expanse of black marble. It's big, but it's not as poignant as the memorial to Stjepan Radić, who was shot in Belgrade's parliament in 1928 (page 16), which you'll find to the right of the entrance as you come in, under the arcades. Just before Radić is the memorial to the poet Petar Preradović, which features a wonderfully sculpted mourner laying a single flower on the bier, while four cupolas beyond, check out the lovely monument to Emanuel Prister (whoever he was), with a tremendous depiction of a woman closed in upon herself with grief.

Once you've paid your respects, you can return to the city on the bus, or simply walk down the hill – it takes around half an hour, heading down Mirogojska (head straight out of the cemetery, not left down Hermana Bolléa) until you reach the tram stop at the bottom of the hill, and then make your way across at the lights to the top end of Medvedgradska, which runs down the hill until it becomes Tkalčićeva (it's one street across from the top of Nova Ves, which then becomes Kaptol).

MAKSIMIR PARK AND THE ZOO [77 F4] A few kilometres east of the city centre is the sprawling Maksimir Park, easily reached on tram #4, #7, #11 or #12 (get off at the Bukovačka stop, heading towards Dubrava or Dubec), which also plays host to Zagreb's wonderful zoo. It's right across the street from the Dinamo Stadium, home to Zagreb's 'Bad Blue Boys', the local – and enormously popular – football team.

Maksimir itself is a real oasis of calm, feeling far away from the noisy city streets. Measuring around 2km by 1.5km, it was landscaped in the manner of a 19th-century English park, and features lakes, woods, hidden paths, meadows, and even the occasional folly to divert you. It's a great place for a stroll or a picnic.

Zagreb's **zoo** (*www.zgzoo.com;* ⊕ *May–Aug 09.00–20.00 daily, Apr/Sep 09.00–19.00 daily, Mar/Oct 09.00–18.00 daily, Feb 09.00–17.00 daily, Nov–Jan 09.00–16.00 daily; last admission 90mins before closing in the summer, 60mins before closing in the winter; 30kn*) is spread along the southern edge of Maksimir Park, and is absolutely first-rate, putting far bigger cities like London and Paris to shame. From its founding in 1925, when it boasted just three young foxes and a pair of owls, it's grown – and indeed matured – to become one of the nicest zoos I know.

Many of the 2,000 or so animals here, from nearly 300 species, live in modern, airy, outdoor enclosures, rather than cages, and there are some real treats in store for visitors, from a fearsome pack of wolves, to the most charming red panda I've ever seen, to a pygmy hippo (called 'Hypo' after the local mortgage lender), to a comic pool of savvy seals and sea lions. There are excellently themed didactic exhibitions covering different regions of the world, with the emphasis on ecosystems rather than simply the fauna to be found there.

Two particular exhibits make the zoo stand out even further. The first is a house that shows off domestic fauna in its actual setting, from mice in the cupboards to cockroaches under the floorboards to birds nesting in the roof. The second is even more adventurous, comprising two cages marked 'Homo Sapiens', complete with full species data, such as height, weight, longevity and average number of young. You can go inside, of course, to see what it's like behind the bars, but the trick is: you get to choose whether you want the cage furnished with plastic and non-renewable materials, and junk food on the table, or the cage done out with wooden and cane furniture, and a bowl of fresh fruit.

MOUNT MEDVEDNICA For a real breath of fresh air, look no further than Mount Medvednica, the mountain that provides Zagreb's permanent backdrop and an excellent local resource. As a well-managed nature park, there's lots to see and do up here, from pleasant not-too-strenuous walking to cycling, to just taking in the views and the cooler air above the city. The biodiversity here is wonderful, with 1,200 plant species on Medvednica, compared to 1,600 in the whole of Great Britain.

If that's not enough to tempt you, there's also Medvedgrad Fortress (a splendid medieval castle), a bat cave to explore, and a small reconstructed mine to visit, as well as places you can stay and eat. In winter you can even ski down the back of the mountain and pretend you're local hero and four-time Olympic winner Janica Kostelić.

Getting there (and skiing) Getting up the mountain isn't difficult at all, and can be comfortably managed in a half-day trip, using public transport. Take tram #8 or

#14 to the Mihaljevac terminus, followed by tram #15 to the end of the line at Dolje. From here it's a pleasant ten-minute walk through a short tunnel and up a forest path to the cable-car station (Žičara Sljeme), and a 23-minute ride (hourly, on the hour) up to the 1,035m peak of Sljeme, the highest point on Mount Medvednica. If it's windy, the cable car doesn't operate, and they usefully post a notice at the Mihaljevac terminus saying so (Žičara ne vozi). At present (2015) the cable car is still closed for a major upgrade (for the possible destruction of forest this upgrade may entail, see www.zelena-akcija.hr).

By road (assuming you have your own wheels), head north from the city and follow signs to Sljeme, turning right at the Mihaljevac tram and bus terminus, and then left a couple of kilometres further on, at Bliznec. The road, which winds up the mountain, along the top, and down again a few kilometres west, is a one-way system (after you've passed the nature park's office on the first left-hand hairpin), so when you come down the mountain it's actually into the suburb of Šestine – more or less due north of Britanski Square, on Ilica.

If you're planning on skiing, you can rent kit at the top of the mountain – but be warned that since the Kostelić phenomenon kicked in, Zagreb's gone skiing mad, and it can get pretty busy. Best fun of all is the Snow Queen, a twice-weekly night-slalom that takes place throughout the season (from the end of November to the beginning of April).

 Where to stay and eat There are several places to stay on Medvednica, and you're unlikely to go hungry as there are a number of cafés and restaurants at the top of the mountain (as well as the two near Medvedgrad).

Pansion Zvonimir (Zvonimirov dom) [76 C1] (30 rooms) 458 0397; www. en.zvonimirov-dom.com. Pleasant rooms in a largish chalet overlooking the Hunjka meadow, about 4km east of Sljeme, on the old road heading down off the back of the mountain. €€€

Tomislav Dom [76 C1] (42 rooms) 456 0400; www.sljeme.hr. This is just a few minutes up from the top of the cable car, with chalet-like dbls. It's a bit expensive for something this far out of town, although there are discounts for longer stays. €€€

Dom Grafičar [76 C2] 455 5844. An excellent place to stop for hearty, reasonably priced food near the summit of Sljeme. €€

Puntijarka [76 D1] 458 0384. This is our personal favourite, situated in the Ivan Pačkovski mountain lodge. It's out of the way a bit, about 3km east of Sljeme, but serves up lashings of mountain food at unbeatable prices. Fill up on a delicious bowl of *grah* (heavy, meaty bean soup) for just 15kn, or turkey with *mlinci* (thin homemade doughy pasta) for 40kn. Be warned: portion sizes are almost as big as the mountain itself. €€

Other practicalities You can get heaps of information from the cheerful, friendly and helpful staff at the **nature park** [76 D2] (*Park Prirode Medvednica;* 458 6317; *www.pp-medvednica.hr*), whose office is situated on the main road into the park, above Bliznec – you can hardly miss it, as there's a fabulous bear trimmed from a large bush on the corner. Just below the park office, criss-crossing the stream, is an excellent **nature trail**, which – in a world first for the blind – has all the legends in Braille as well as access for the handicapped. From the far end of this, a longer, steeper trail continues up to Tomislav Dom on the top of Sljeme.

What to see and do
Medvedgrad Fortress [76 C3] From the top of the cable car, it's a little under an hour on foot to the 13th-century Medvedgrad Fortress. This was abandoned in the late 16th century and fell into ruin, but was expensively restored in the 1990s,

3

as a patriotic gesture by Franjo Tuđman – it's become something of a nationalist symbol, and as such is mildly controversial: could the money have been better spent on something else, the locals ask, not unreasonably. Whatever the politics, it's an atmospheric place in a great location, all the same, on a bluff with lovely views out over the city, and a fine restaurant in the vaults. Try to catch the medieval festival if you're up here in October.

If you're coming by car, Medvedgrad is a bit non-intuitive to find, as it has its own access road. If you're coming down the mountain, pass the Šestinski Lagvić restaurant, then turn right at the attractive, gaudily roofed Šestine Church, towards Talane, and then right again at the next junction, which is signed for Medvedgrad; the road takes you straight up to the castle.

The **Šestinski Lagvić** restaurant itself is an excellent place to eat, but quite pricey. For something a little more reasonable, there's the **Kraljičin Zdenac** restaurant further up the hill (ie: before you get to Šestinski Lagvić, if you're driving). If you fancy a stroll, it's a lovely shady walk up to Kraljičin Zdenac along the Kraljevic stream, avoiding the road.

If you're driving (or cycling) down the hill, look out for the huge, newly restored mansion to the right, after you come out of the woods and before you get to Šestine church; it's called **Kulmerovi Dvori** [76 C3], and now belongs to the Todorić family, the owners of the successful Konzum supermarket chain.

Veternica Cave [76 B3] (*Špilja Veternica; www.pp-medvednica.hr*) On the
southwestern corner of Medvednica is the Veternica Cave complex (named after the eddies of wind at the entrance which led to its discovery), over 7km of which have been explored. On Sundays from May to August you can visit the first well-lit 400m of the cave as part of an excellent guided tour (*call the Nature Park office on ☏ 458 6317 for more detailed information; 25kn*), which covers the cave's geological and natural history, as well as its former use as (probably) a Neanderthal shrine of some kind; over 100 bear skulls were found in the cave, but the original entrance is too small for bears.

You'll see a date on one wall in an inner cave. This was daubed here by a daring young blood called Fabrici, who came inside in the dark in 1934; unfortunately his mates didn't believe he'd actually done it, so he had to climb the cathedral tower instead to prove his worth – happily without unfortunate consequences.

Serious speleologists can go much deeper into the complex (by arrangement with the Nature Park authorities), and squirm their way on hands and knees up the Stairs of Calvary, past the Stinky Lake and through Ramses' Passage (ooh-err).

Outside the summer season, the cave is closed to the public, as it's the natural hibernation place for 14 of Croatia's species of bat, as well as all sorts of other unusual wildlife, including the peculiar *Chthonius jalzici*, a mock scorpion endemic to Veternica that was only classified in 1988.

The easiest route to Veternica is the 20-minute hike downhill from the Glavica mountain hut, itself a three-hour hike from Grafičar hut. The other route to the cave is by taking tram #2, #6 or #11 to the Črnomerec terminus, and then bus #124 to the end of the line, after which it's a kilometre or so uphill to the cave entrance – allow 45 minutes up and 30 minutes back.

The Zrinski Mine [76 C2] (*Rudnik Zrinski; www.pp-medvednica.hr*) More
historical nuggets (though no silver ones, these days) can be gleaned from the Zrinski Mine (also called Rudarski Vrt, especially on maps – meaning 'miners' garden'), which has been excellently and evocatively reconstructed to give you a feel for miners' life in the 16th century.

What that feel is, mostly, is of just how hard a miner's life was (and in many places still is). If mining was your chosen (or designated) career up here, you could expect to start work at age 12, and die of lead poisoning by the time you were 30. In the brief years between, you worked the mine, doing a 12-hour shift, six days a week, plus the hour and a half commute each way from the bottom of the mountain (ironically where you'll now find Zagreb's ritziest real estate). Each day, you would dig out, with the other 15 miners on your watch, around a tonne of rock, which might yield a little silver and a bit more lead.

The mine was abandoned for over 400 years, but has now been restored (by the Nature Park) to show something of its history and workings. Most important of all is the presence in mines everywhere of St Barbara, the patron saint of miners. Why St Barbara should be their protector is a bit of a mystery, as the unfortunate Barbara is best known for having her head cut off by her father, and her father then being killed by lightning by God (so why didn't He throw the lightning bolt before Barbara's untimely decapitation, you have to ask?).

The tour is enlivened by talking wooden statues of Zagorje mining types (whose accents are apparently especially hard for Dalmatians to understand), the first of which is the mine manager – you can tell by the silver buttons on his coat. With low ceilings and narrow corridors, along with drippy-water sound effects, it's an atmospheric experience and especially worthwhile if you're here with kids.

The mine is open on weekends and public holidays (when it's not snow-covered) between April and October (but only Sundays and holidays in July and August), from 11.00 to 17.00, and also by arrangement (with the park office, see page 133) for groups; entry is 20kn. The mine is located about 25 minutes' walk west of the top of the cable car, on the main road, just below the Grafičar hut. If you're walking up from Medvedgrad, allow around 40 minutes.

Walking and cycling Medvednica is ideal for both walking and cycling, and there are good maps available for both pursuits – either direct from the park office or at the main tourist office on Jelačić Square. The walking is on the whole rather less demanding than the cycling (walkers can use the cable car to cut out a good deal of the legwork), which requires you to get up the mountain in the first place. The cycling map – available for the time being in Croatian only – details 15 rides of varying difficulty, and helpfully gives not just distances and routes, but profiles too, as well as the total climb you're in for. For more information on walking on Medvednica see Rudolf Abraham's book *Walking in Croatia* (page 429).

JARUN LAKE [76 C6/7] About 5km southwest of the city centre, Jarun Lake is an artificial playground tucked into a bend of the River Sava. It was built for the 1987 World University Games, and comprises a great big lake, with a handful of islands, long pebbled swimming (and sunning) beaches, cycle paths, jogging tracks and places you can rent bikes, pedalos, deckchairs, canoes and even sculls.

As the lake warms up quickly and stays that way throughout the summer months, with average water temperatures of around 24°C, it can get pretty busy with swimmers and strollers on summer weekends. And as you'd expect, there are plenty of bars and cafés as well as snack- and ice cream-type establishments to keep you going. Jarun is also home to a couple of Zagreb's most important nightspots, **Aquarius** (page 106) and **Gallery** (page 107).

You can get to Jarun Lake easily enough, either directly on the #113 bus from behind the main railway station (Jarun is the last stop), or almost all the way on tram #5 or #17 to the Jarun stop, which is just a few minutes' walk north from the lake.

BUNDEK [77 E6] Bundek, just across the River Sava on the way to Novi Zagreb, and opposite the racecourse and fairgrounds, is a pleasant park where you'll find lovely flowerbeds and a glistening lake spanned by an elegant bridge at its narrowest point, as well as numerous cycle paths, pebble beaches and lots of lawn space for sitting around on – and the best kids' playground in Zagreb. It's all very pleasant, and very popular at weekends.

REMETE [76 E3] If you're looking for a bit of an excursion, then the monastery **Church of St Mary** (Sv Marija) in the northern suburb of Remete is a nice place to visit – but don't go unless you've really covered a lot of ground already, or are particularly passionate about Mary, as it's a little over 5km from the city centre and not that easy to get to without your own transport (take bus #203 or #226).

The church is famous primarily for the wooden sculpted Virgin Mary, which the faithful still come to admire, particularly on the Feast of the Assumption (15 August), though it's also a popular place to get married, or – if you're sufficiently famous – buried. Before you go inside, check out the excellent reliefs outside the front door, with the saint on the left apparently holding a dodo, and the one on the right standing on a wild boar.

Inside, apart from the Holy Virgin herself, the big deal is the wealth of amateurish but powerful frescoes depicting her intervention in a huge range of domestic dramas. On the right-hand side, on the upper wall near the door, there's an endearing gentleman who looks as if he's definitely had one *travarica* too many.

4

Inland Croatia

Inland Croatia is in complete contrast to the dramatic karstic landscapes of the coast and the holiday resorts on the islands. With the exception of the famous Plitvice Lakes, Croatia's most popular national park, the area is still largely unvisited – and unjustly so.

North of Zagreb is the delightful **Zagorje** region, with hundreds of churches and dozens of castles and country houses set among wooded hills, while the country's northern provincial capital, **Varaždin**, is a Baroque masterpiece. Southwest of the capital are the low mountains, remote villages and excellent vineyards of the **Žumberak**, bracketed by the lovely little town of Samobor on one side and the purpose-built Renaissance fortress town of **Karlovac** on the other.

South of Karlovac are the **Plitvice Lakes**, while to the southeast are the marshes and wetlands loved by birdlife – practically anywhere south and east of Zagreb you'll see nesting storks, but most notably in the **Lonjsko Polje**.

Further east of here you're into Slavonia, where hunting castles and deep forests contrast with the big Pannonian plains. The fine provincial town of Požega is the obvious access point to the **Papuk Nature Park**, where you'll find burbling streams and shady woods to walk in, while Slavonski Brod and Đakovo offer some of the region's most interesting folk events.

Here, you're in the heart of Slavonia, bordered by the three great rivers, the Sava, the Drava and the Danube. The region's busy capital, **Osijek**, is the gateway to the huge wetlands of **Kopački Rit**, one of Europe's most important bird sanctuaries, and the breeding ground for some of the world's most vicious mosquitoes. Make sure you wear repellent, even in the daytime, and use one of those protective wall-

CYCLING IN ZAGREB COUNTY

Cyclists should jump at the opportunity of taking advantage of an excellent series of maps entitled *Biking Routes of Zagreb County* published by the Zagreb County tourist board (page 89). These describe a series of routes to the north and west of the capital following low-traffic-density roads across beautiful rolling countryside, and range from the easy to the moderately strenuous. Altitude and distance profiles let you know exactly what you're in for and full details are provided of everything you could possibly need along the way, from restaurants and accommodation options to bike repair shops. It's a wonderful initiative – but go for knobbly tyres, as quite a few of the trails go off the tarmac and on to gravel to avoid the traffic. There's another good map of bicycle trails covering the Žumberak Nature Park (pages 161–4), which you can pick up in Samobor (page 158).

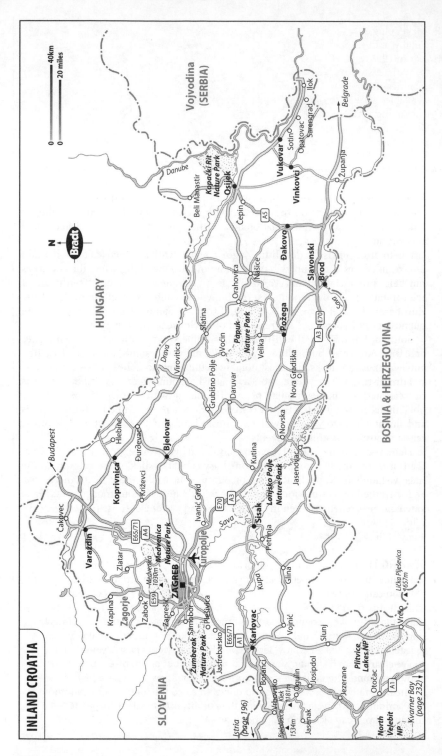

INLAND CROATIA

0 ———— 40km
0 ———— 20 miles

N Bradt

SLOVENIA

HUNGARY

Vojvodina
(SERBIA)

BOSNIA & HERZEGOVINA

Budapest →

Danube

Beli Manastir

Kopački Rit
Nature Park

Osijek

Čepin

A5

Vukovar

Sotin

Opatovac

Ilok

Sarengrad

Belgrade →

Vinkovci

Županja

Đakovo

Slavonski
Brod

Sava

E70

A3

Orahovica

Našice

Slatina

Papuk
Nature Park

Požega

Velika

Vočin

Virovitica

Drava

Grubišno Polje

Daruvar

Nova Gradiška

Novska

Hlebine

Đurđevac

Bjelovar

Koprivnica

Križevci

Čakovec

Varaždin

Zlatar

Krapina

Zagorje

Zabok

E65/71

A4

Medvenica
1030m

Medvenica
Nature Park

E59

ZAGREB

Turopolje

Ivanić Grad

E70

A3

Sava

Sisak

Petrinja

Lonjsko Polje
Nature Park

Jasenovac

Kutina

Zaprešić

Samobor

Plešivica

Žumberak
Nature Park

Jastrebarsko

E65/71

A1

Karlovac

Vojnić

Glina

Kupa

Slunj

Bosanci

Ogulin

Josipdol

Jezerane

Vrbovsko

Klek
1181m

Bjelolasica
1534m

Jasenak

Istria
(page 196) →

North
Velebit
NP

Plitvice
Lakes NP

Otočac

A1

Vrelo

Lička Plješevica
1657m

Kvarner Bay
(page 232) →

138

socket plug-ins at night – you can buy them anywhere round here, not surprisingly. Finally, at the eastern end of Slavonia is **Vukovar**, which suffered terribly during the war in 1991, but is now gradually finding its feet once again.

With few tourists, once you're inland you'll find a general lack of accommodation facilities in some areas, though there are more and more agro-tourism offerings available, as well as several hotels in converted country houses. It's well worth contacting the Zagreb County tourist office (*Preradovićeva 42, Zagreb;* \ *01 487 3665;* e *info@tzzz.hr; www.tzzz.hr*) ahead of time for the latest information.

Further east, there are really only a handful of places to stay (they're listed in the text), with the whole of Slavonia boasting fewer than half the number of hotels you can find in Poreč alone.

Phone codes vary across the region – they're included within each listing.

VARAŽDIN

Tucked into the northernmost corner of Croatia, about 80km north of Zagreb and just 45km from the Hungarian border, Varaždin is a provincial capital and a Baroque delight. It has great architecture, a fine castle, a wonderful pedestrianised city centre, and enough to see and do without it being anything like hard work. The city is the most cycle-friendly in Croatia (over 20,000 bicycles for a population of just 50,000), and one of the most wealthy – the elegant buildings and spacious streets are the result of centuries of prosperous agriculture and trade, and very little damage from recent wars.

HISTORY Known as Garestin in Roman times, little of importance happened here until Varaždin was recognised by Hungary in AD1181, and then developed first as an administrative and later as a defensive centre – from the 15th century on, the city was on the front line against the Ottoman Empire.

With the Turkish threat under control by the early 17th century, Varaždin became an affluent and influential city, and in 1756 even became the capital of Croatia. It wasn't to last – after a catastrophic fire in 1776, the Ban (the local governor) moved to Zagreb. Varaždin was still a prosperous city, however, and its wealthy merchants didn't miss the opportunity of rebuilding their houses and palaces according to the latest fashion of the day.

Today, the Baroque centre of town has been beautifully restored, and it deserves to win its bid (submitted in 2005) to be included on UNESCO's World Heritage list. With everything comfortably within walking distance in the centre, and plaques on many of the buildings in Croatian, English and German, it's also an easy place to visit.

GETTING THERE AND AROUND Varaždin is easy to reach, with **buses** running at least once an hour from Zagreb, and **trains** making the journey a dozen times a day – so you can easily visit as a day trip from the capital. Buses take around 1½ hours, while trains rarely achieve the distance in under 2½, though the notoriously slow train ride is a much more picturesque way of making the journey. Varaždin is also a stop on the major international bus and train routes north to Austria and Hungary. By **car**, it's not much more than half an hour on the motorway from Zagreb, once you've cleared the city. Parking is metered in the city centre, and you can pay in cash or by sending an SMS from your mobile phone.

The bus station is 5 minutes southwest of the town centre, while the train station is 10 minutes away to the east. Most of the old town is pedestrianised, with the curving shopping street Gundulića leading up to the main square Trg Kralja Tomislava. A block northwest, on Padovca, you'll find a friendly and helpful **tourist**

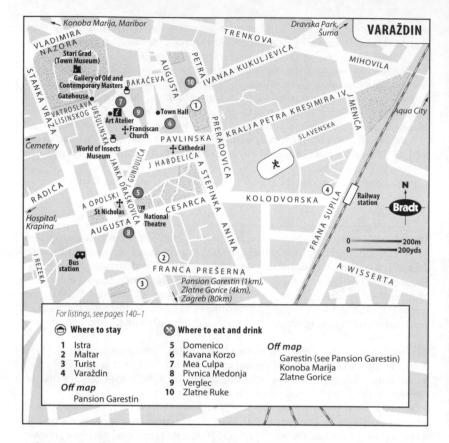

Konoba Marija, Maribor

VARAŽDIN

Dravska Park, Šuma

TRENKOVA

VLADIMIRA NAZORA

Stari Grad (Town Museum)

Gallery of Old and Contemporary Masters

Gatehouse

AUGUSTA

PETRA

IVANAA KUKULJEVIĆA

MIHOVILA

BAKAČEVA

10

Aqua City

STANKA VRAZA

VATROSLAVA LISINSKOG

URŠULINSKA

7

9

Town Hall

1

PRERADOVIĆA

KRALJA PETRA KREŠIMIRA IV

SLAVENSKA

J. MENIČA

Art Atelier

6

Franciscan Church

PAVLINSKA

Cemetery

World of Insects Museum

Cathedral

RADIĆA

JANKA GUNDULIĆA

J HABDELIĆA

A STEPINKA

Hospital, Krapina

A OPOLSKI

St Nicholas

5

DRAŠKOVIĆA

CESARCA

KOLODVORSKA

4

FRANA SUPILA

Railway station

Bradt

N

National Theatre

AUGUSTA

8

ANINA

0   200m
0   200yds

I REZEKA

Bus station

2

FRANCA PREŠERNA

A WISSERTA

3

Pansion Garestin (1km),
Zlatne Gorice (4km),
Zagreb (80km)

For listings, see pages 140–1

Where to stay

1 Istra
2 Maltar
3 Turist
4 Varaždin

Off map
Pansion Garestin

Where to eat and drink

5 Domenico
6 Kavana Korzo
7 Mea Culpa
8 Pivnica Medonja
9 Verglec
10 Zlatne Ruke

Off map
Garestin (see Pansion Garestin)
Konoba Marija
Zlatne Gorice

information office (*Ivana Padovca 3; ☎ 042 210 987; www.tourism-varazdin.hr*). It has a good, expanded city map for a small fee as well as plenty of free materials, and several brochures can be downloaded from its website.

WHERE TO STAY *Map, above*

Varaždin's only real shortcoming is a general lack of upmarket accommodation. There have been plans for boutique hotels for years, but nothing's materialised yet, so for the time being you'll have to make do with one of the town's existing hotels, which are mostly within 5 or 10 minutes' walk of the bus station, on the southern side of town. All cater primarily to business people passing through, so reserve ahead if you're coming midweek, particularly at the Maltar and Turist.

Varaždin also has a limited supply of **private rooms**, though you'd be unlucky not to find one in town or the surrounding countryside. The best place to look for these is on the city and county tourist board websites (*www.tourism-varazdin.hr/en/ accommodation or www.turizam-vzz.hr*) – expect to pay at least €35 for a room all year round, and for once there's no surcharge for short stays. You can also try **Rooms Novosel** (*Zagredačka 291; ☎ 042 241 716; www.rooms-novosel-varazdin.hr; €€*).

Istra (11 rooms) Ivana Kukuljevića 6; ☎042 659 659; www.istra-hotel.hr. The most expensive place in town. €€€€

Turist (109 rooms) Aleja kralja Zvonimira 1; ☎042 395 395; www.hotel-turist.hr. Much bigger & slightly swankier than Maltar. €€€€

🏠 **Maltar** (25 rooms) Franca Prešerna 1; ☎042 311 100; www.maltar.hr. Well appointed, with very friendly staff & en-suite dbls. €€€

🏠 **Varaždin** (27 rooms) Kolodvorska 19; ☎042 290 720; www.hotelvarazdin.com. Opened in 2007, a stone's throw from the bus station. A lovely option if you don't mind being slightly further (though still only 500m) from the town centre. €€€

🏠 **Pansion Garestin** (13 rooms) Zagrebačka 34; ☎042 214 314; www.gastrocom-ugostiteljstvo. com. The rooms are on the small side, but this is a good place to stay, above the restaurant of the same name (one of the best in town). Great value, & an easy 20-min walk into town. Consider HB/FB, only an extra 50/100kn pp. €€

✗ WHERE TO EAT AND DRINK *Map, page 140*

As a prosperous town, Varaždin has no shortage of places to eat and drink, and some of the restaurants and bars have terraces in pleasant courtyards hidden away behind the Baroque façades, or overlooking the park.

✗ **Konoba Marija** Kralja Tomislava 27, Hrašćica; ☎042 711 722; www.konoba-marija.com; ⏰ 09.00–23.00 Mon–Sat, 09.00–16.00 Sun. Octopus ispod peka & other Dalmatian dishes. Just northwest of town on the road to Maribor. €€€

✗ **Zlatne Gorice** Banjščina 104, Gornji Kneginec; ☎042 666 054; www.zlatne-gorice.com. Situated out of town, about 4km south of Varaždin, on the main road to Varaždinske Toplice (Varaždin's spa complex), in the locality called Turčin – it's on the left, right at the top of the hill. Upmarket restaurant, owned by the same people who run Zlatne Ruke (see above). €€€

✗ **Zlatne Ruke** Ivana Kukuljevića 13; ☎042 320 650; ⏰ 10.00–23.00 daily. Reckoned to be the best table in town, under the same ownership as Zlatne Gorice (see below) et al. Vaulted stone basement & a covered terrace, with traditional local dishes including venison tartare & goulash. €€€

✗ **Garestin** Zagrebačka 34; ☎042 214 314; www. gastrocom-ugostiteljstvo.com; ⏰ 08.00–23.00

daily. Local favourite around 1km south of the town centre; also has rooms (see above). €€€–€€

✗ **Verglec** Ul Silvija Strahimira Kranjčevića 12; ☎042 211 131; http://verglec.com; ⏰ 08.00–23.00 daily. Nice-looking place under the same ownership as the Garestin. €€€–€€

✗ **Domenico** Trg Slobode 7; ⏰ 08.00–23.00 Sun–Thu, 08.00–midnight Fri/Sat. One of Varaždin's most popular pizzerias, on Trg Slobode – though there are reports of the quality deteriorating recently. €€

🍺 **Kavana Korzo** ⏰ 07.30–23.00 daily. Right on the main square, the place to hang out with a coffee & be seen.

🍷 **Mea Culpa** Padovčeva 1; http://meaculpa. com.hr; ⏰ 06.30–23.30 Mon–Thu, 06.30–04.00 Fri/Sat, 07.30–23.00 Sun. Popular lounge & cocktail bar situated next door to the tourist office.

🍷 **Pivnica Medonja** Kapucinski trg 2; ⏰ 08.00–23.00 daily. Best place in town to try local beers. Near the bus station.

WHAT TO SEE AND DO The main sight in Varaždin is the harmonious old town, which you'll likely be approaching from the south, as this is where the hotels and bus station are. Across the bottom of town is a lovely park, with the **National Theatre** on the southwest corner – if you have the chance to look inside, or see a performance here, you'll find it a sumptuous red velvet and gilded treat.

In the park itself, look out for the statue of Vatroslav Jagić, the Slavic languages expert who was born here in 1838. His statue's a bit of an embarrassment for local clothes manufacturer Varteks (Varaždinska Tekstilna), as his coat buttons are on the wrong side for a gentleman's garment.

Moving up into town, stop at the **Church of St Nicholas** (Sv Nikole) on Trg Slobode (Freedom Square). Nicholas is usually the patron of seafaring cities, but got chosen here because of Varaždin's dependence on the Drava River for trade. The church is also dedicated to St Florian, with his red flag – he's the patron saint of firemen – as a reminder of the 1776 fire. Up on the tower there's a stone bear; the legend is that the bear turned to stone on returning to the site of the church to find her cubs gone.

Turn up into Gundulića, which is known locally as Dučanska, as this is the place to shop (*dućan* = shop). Note the casement windows at the corner of Habdelića, which were designed so that wealthy ladies could snoop on what was going on below. At the top of the street, take a detour left to the 17th-century **Franciscan Church**, which was built on the foundations of something much earlier – its tower, at 54m, is the tallest thing in Varaždin.

Outside the church, anyone who's been to Split will recognise the pint-sized version of Ivan Meštrović's most distinctive statue, *Grgur Ninski* – strangely undramatic in its reduced form. As in Split, the erstwhile bishop's big toe has been worn golden by people hoping their wishes will come true.

Almost next door in the Herzer Palace, and an absolute must for entomologists, is Varaždin's wonderful **World of Insects Museum** (*Franjevački trg 6; www.gmv.hr; ⊕ 09.00–17.00 Tue–Fri, 09.00–13.00 Sat/Sun; 25kn or 55kn with entry to the fortress/ Town Museum & Gallery of Old & Contemporary Masters*), featuring a thousand species of bugs and more than 4,000 exhibits. It was the work of Franjo Košćec, who spent decades collecting the specimens here, and was personally responsible for the museum's creation in 1954. It's one of the best collections of its kind, demonstrating not only Croatia's endemic species, but also the life cycle and habitats of various insects, in a modern, stylish setting – and there's even a charming re-creation of Košćec's study. If you're interested, or have kids, the interactive '*Kukci*' CD-Rom for sale here is simply excellent.

Heading back the way you came brings you to Varaždin's 17th-century **cathedral**, on the right, with a plain Baroque façade giving away few secrets about the riotous over-the-top altarpiece inside. Multi-coloured pillars frame dramatic saints in late-medieval garb, overlooked by gesticulating angels and overflown by abundant putti. It's absolutely marvellous – but you wouldn't want one at home. The doors, dating from 2002, celebrate Varaždin becoming a diocese, with its own bishop.

On the corner of the main square opposite the cathedral stands the Drašković Palace, which was the Ban's residence during Varaždin's (very) brief stint as Croatia's capital in the 18th century. The main square itself – **Trg Kralja Tomislava** – is dominated by the town hall, dating from 1523, with an unlikely spire rising from its centre. Look out for the mermaid sign hanging outside the Bonbonnière Kraš sweet shop on one side of the square – the sign originally denoted a shop selling exotic goods sourced from abroad (the original sign is in the town museum, if you want to see it). You'll also notice the Ritz and Jacomini buildings side by side in the main square; the family plots are also side by side in the cemetery (page 143). Finally, while you're here, scope out the arcades that lead off the square and the surrounding streets, and hide enticing boutiques, cafés and restaurants.

Heading north from the main square brings you round on to Trg Milijenka Stančića, which faces on to the drawbridge and gatehouse that lead across to the castle and town museum. On the square itself, in the gaudily fronted Sermage Palace, is the **Gallery of Old and Contemporary Masters** (*Galerija starih i novih majstora; Trg Miljenka Stančića 3; www.gmv.hr; ⊕ 09.00–17.00 Tue–Fri, 09.00–13.00 Sat/Sun; 25kn or 55kn with entry to the fortress/Town Museum & World of Insects Museum*), which mostly comprises old masters by artists you won't have heard of – but it's none the less interesting for that.

From here head through the gate into the park housing Varaždin's trademark whitewashed fortress, the **Stari Grad**. Set among defensive earthworks that have pleasantly metamorphosed into lovely gardens, the fortress was originally built in the 14th century, before becoming a major defence against the Turks in the 15th century and evolving into its present shape during the 16th century.

The fortress now houses the **Town Museum** (*Gradski Muzej; Strossmayerovo šetalište 7;* \ *042 658 754; www.gmv.hr;* ⊕ *09.00–17.00 Tue–Fri, 09.00–13.00 Sat/Sun; 25kn, or 55kn with entry to World of Insects Museum & Gallery of Old & Contemporary Masters*), which was established in 1925, and is one of the best municipal collections outside Zagreb. Even if you're not especially into the paintings, weaponry and furnishings on display here, the entry fee is amply repaid by the chance to wander round the rooms and the two three-tiered courtyards – and there are some old and droll hunting targets on display, including one featuring the faces of the hunters' wives. Of particular interest are a series of rooms each furnished in a different period style, from the 17th century through to Biedermeier, with original paintings, furniture and furnishings. Finally, don't miss the chapel and sacristy built into the tower on the first floor – and drop me a line if you have the faintest idea how they got that massive piece of furniture in there.

From the fortress it's a 10-minute stroll west to the town's wonderful **cemetery**, which has much more in common with a well-tended garden than a traditional resting place, with the plants and shrubs dominating the graves. It's the life-work of Herman Haller, who ran the cemetery from 1905 until 1946, with the intention of creating a 'park of the living' rather than a 'place of the dead'. You'll find all sorts of wonderful memorials here, among the avenues and promenades, including 376 red rose bushes commemorating the town's fallen in World War 1. One of the most interesting graves of all is that of the mountaineer Lucijan Zlatko, which features a piece of rock from every peak he climbed. It seems terribly ironic that as a climber he lived to the age of 93, while his wife Vera succumbed when she was only 48.

If you're still looking for something to do in town, you can also visit the **Art Atelier** of eccentric and bohemian local sculptor, painter and performance artist Darwin Butković, which is next door to the tourist office, in a space converted from the old Franciscan granary – the tourist office will introduce you to him, if you're interested.

If all the sightseeing's left you hot and bothered, and you have your own transport, head a few kilometres east out of town to **Aqua City**, where you'll find a lake to swim in, a shingle beach to sun yourself on, and a restaurant. Without wheels you can still get the shore-side experience by walking 20 minutes northeast of the old town to the **Dravska Park Šuma**, where you'll find jogging paths along the banks of the great, still River Drava.

Varaždin festivals Varaždin is the perfect venue for many festivals during the year, with the two largest being the **Špancirfest** at the end of August and the **Festival of Baroque Music** in late September. There are also weekly festivals every Saturday from April to October, which feature workshops around the old town highlighting traditional metiers and arts and crafts, along with music and theatre for children.

The Špancirfest (*www.spancirfest.com*), one of Croatia's biggest annual festivals, runs for ten days from the last Friday in August and features music from all over the world, as well as comedy performances and street theatre, and draws around 150,000 people a year.

A month later, the Festival of Baroque Music features a host of first-rate concerts which take place in the city's churches and old buildings; it's well worth trying to get tickets (ask at the tourist office) if you're going to be in town.

ČAKOVEC AND THE MEĐIMURJE

North of Varaždin is Croatia's smallest but most densely populated county, the Međimurje. Sandwiched between the Mura and Drava rivers, the area has always been seen as something of an island, both geographically and culturally – it was known as Insula Dravanam by the Romans – while benefiting from its position at the trade crossroads between east and west, and north and south. The region only joined Croatia in 1919, after centuries of Austro-Hungarian control, when it proved it was 98% Croatian-speaking.

You're most likely to arrive over the Ban Josip Jelačić bridge, which was used by the Ban himself in 1848 to cross the Drava and boot out the Hungarians (temporarily), and today carries both the road and the railway from Varaždin to Čakovec and on to Budapest. The other access to the region is the motorway from Zagreb to Hungary, which passes just east of both Varaždin and Čakovec.

ČAKOVEC Situated just 13km northeast of Varaždin, Čakovec is the northernmost town in Croatia, and though there's not a whole lot to do or see, it's worth a visit even if only to take in the Museum of the Međimurje. Several buses and trains a day come up from Varaždin, usually heading on to Hungary. The bus station is just north of the town centre, while the train station is just south.

The town's history is dominated by the influential and colourful Zrinski dynasty, who were in charge here from 1546–1691, and whose main role was to use the Međimurje as a buffer zone against the Turks – they manned 23 forts along the Mura River. After the Hungarians made peace with the Turks in 1664, Petar Zrinski and his cousin Fran Krsto Frankopan led an ill-advised campaign against the monarchy; once they realised this had failed, they went to Vienna to apologise, but were imprisoned for a year instead, before finally being executed on 29 April 1671. Their bones were returned to Croatia in 1919, and reburied in Zagreb Cathedral.

🏠 **Where to stay, eat and drink** If you want to stay or eat in town, there are a few options:

🏠 **Hotel Aurora** (10 rooms) Franje Punčeca 2; ✆040 310 700; http://roomsaurora.freshcreator. com. 5mins north of the castle, on the road to Lendava, in Slovenia, with a handful of clean, comfortable dbl rooms upstairs from the Allegro Restaurant. €€€€

🏠 **Hotel Park** (60 rooms) Zrinsko Frankopanska bb; ✆040 311 255; www.hotel-park.info. Just west of the castle, on the Varaždin road, a boxy socialist-era place with rooms that are nicer than the building might suggest, with a strange Modernist hunting mural in the bar. €€€

🏠 **Pansion Mamica** (8 rooms) Čakovečka 47; ✆040 373 433; http://mamica.com.hr. Simple, clean rooms at restaurant of the same name. €€€

🏠 **Vinska Kuča Obitelji Turk** Vučetinec 107b, Sv Juraj na Brijegu; ✆040 855 154; m 098 241 926; http://seoskiturizam-turk.hr. In Vučetinec, 10km northwest of Čakovec, this is run by the former manager of a Yugoslav band. There are several good-value rooms available & great local food to go with its own very palatable wine – though English is very much a second (or third) language. €

✗ **Katarina** Matice hrvatske 6; ⏱ 10.00–23.00 daily; http://restoran-katarina.com. This is definitely one of the best in town, situated underground in the modern shopping centre on the west side of town, towards the castle (and owned by the same people as Zlatne Ruke in Varaždin). The restaurant is in the suitably atmospheric brick cellar of the original building on the site here, & features the famous letter from Petar to Katarina Zrinski, as well as a fine range of soups, salads & pasta dishes – & more expensive fare for those who want it. Definitely worth trying is the local *Turoš* cheese, a spicy, salty, paprika-flavoured tower quite unlike anything else I've ever tasted. €€€

✳ ✗ **Mala Hiža** Balogovec 1, Mačkovec; ✆040 341 101; http://mala-hiza.hr; ⏱ 09.00–23.00 daily. This is well worth the short trip outside of town, about 4km north on the road to Slovenia. It's rated as one of the best restaurants in Croatia, & serves regional & local dishes with an emphasis on seasonal produce. They have some beautiful private rooms, too. €€€

What to see and do The Zrinski Castle, west of the town centre, looks a bit shabby these days, but it does house the eclectic **Museum of the Međimurje** (*Muzej Međimurja; Trg Republike 5; www.muzej-medjimurja.hr;* ☉ *10.00–15.00 Mon–Fri, 10.00–13.00 Sat/Sun; 15kn*), a collection ranging from Neolithic finds to an excellent, if small, Roman collection (with labels in English), to period furniture, to arts and crafts, and silverware and glass – all from the Međimurje. The most poignant exhibit is Petar Zrinski's letter to his wife Katarina, written the day before his execution in Vienna. Also check out the reconstructed old-time pharmacy, a 19th-century telescope, and the small art gallery, as well as the interesting ethnographic collection on the first floor, which goes through the seasons of the year, starting with the February carnival and the strange Poklad masks used to chase away the evil spirits of winter.

Heading back into town you'll cross the castle's old moat, which was drained in the 1980s (to extirpate the town's once-serious mosquito problem), and a lovely park, which brings you into the pedestrianised town centre. The first thing you'll notice here is the wonderful Secessionist **Trade Union Hall**, which was built in 1904 and still looks moderately bonkers today, with its frivolous decorative brickwork quite unsuited to the serious business of organised labour.

Across the street is the friendly **tourist office** (*Kralja Tomislava 1;* ℡ *040 313 319; www.tourism-cakovec.hr*), which will help you out with local information and give you details of the Međimurje Wine Road, as well as accommodation options in the region. Round the corner from the Trade Union Hall is the town's smartest café, the **Gradska Kavana**, which has a nice terrace – though there's no shortage of alternatives if you can't find a table – with a newly renovated concert hall and art gallery opposite. Further down the same street, towards the market, on the left-hand side, there's a small memorial to the Jewish community, which was strong in Čakovec until World War II, when all the Jews were rounded up and deported to Auschwitz, and the synagogue here was destroyed.

If you have the energy, it's also worth going to have a look at the extraordinary **Feštetić Castle** in the village of Pribislavec, about 3km east of Čakovec. It's an extraordinary neo-Gothic pile with a marvellous tower on one end dating from 1870. You can't go inside, unfortunately, as it's now the village school.

THE MEĐIMURJE The practically unvisited Međimurje region is now working hard to attract visitors, notably to the attractive Međimurje Wine Road, which comprises more than 25 vineyards set among the lovely rolling hills which lead up to the Slovenian border to the north and west of the county.

What to see and do Wine's been a big deal here for a while – back to Roman times, in fact – but recent years have seen a dramatic increase in quantity, variety and most importantly quality. If you have the time, it's well worth picking up information from the tourist office in Čakovec and taking a tour – many properties offer tastings, and some also have restaurants and/or rooms, which adds to the atmosphere. See the 'wine cellars' page of the useful Međimurje County **tourist office** website (*Josip Ban Jelačića 22;* ℡ *040 390 191; www.tzm.hr*) for details.

Some of the best wine in the region can be found at **Vino Lovrec** (*Sveti Urban 133, Štrigova;* ℡ *040 830 171;* e *info@vino-lovrec.hr; www.vino-lovrec.hr*) in Sveti Urban, near Štrigova (northwest from Čakovec near the Slovenian border), and they speak English, so give them a call if you fancy a tasting. If you happen to be at this end of the county, it's worth stopping to have a look at the enormous twin-spired **Church of St Jerome** in Štrigova itself, which was built to celebrate the birth of the saint here (although he was actually born, it's thought, in Stridon, in what's now Bosnia

145

Trains and buses regularly ply the route up from Zagreb through Varaždin and Čakovec to Budapest, and the formalities are minimal as visitors from the EU and most English-speaking countries don't need a visa for a tourist visit of up to three months.

The motorway north from Zagreb goes as far as the border at Goričan, which claims to be Croatia's busiest border crossing. There's a decent restaurant, the Zelengaj, on the river here, with a floating terrace and lots of good Međimurje staples on the menu.

If you're planning to go across the border, grab a copy of the excellent *Hungary: The Bradt Travel Guide* or *Budapest: The Bradt City Guide*.

& Herzegovina). If the church is open – which it often isn't – check out the fabulous frescoes inside by Ivan Ranger, the best of the local fresco masters. Contact the Štrigova **tourist office** for more details (✆ *040 851 325; http://strigova.info*).

If you're heading north from Čakovec then you probably shouldn't miss **Mala Hiža** restaurant (page 144) in Mačkovec, specialising in local dishes and rated as one of Croatia's best restaurants.

If you've overdone it on the wine tasting and fancy a spa to recover, then head up to the northern part of Međimurje, near the Slovenian border, where the **Sveti Martin Baths** (*Grkaveščak bb;* ✆ *040 371 111; www.spa-sport.hr*) offer indoor and outdoor pools, as well as saunas, massages and the rest. It's a well-developed resort, and very popular in summer. Just east of here, towards the river, you can visit a reconstructed **watermill** on the Mura, at Žabnik – back in the 1920s there were 90 mills like this along the river, but the last original one closed down in the 1980s.

The Eastern, 'lower' Međimurje is flat as a pancake and dominated by fields of maize and sunflowers. The main centre here is the small industrial town of **Prelog**, which is famous locally as being home to an international speedway centre, if that's your thing. If you're here, however, it's well worth trying to get inside **St Jacob's Church** (Sv Jakov), whose plain pale grey exterior hides a magnificent Baroque altar, stretching all the way across the end of the church.

Between Prelog and Goričan is the village of **Donji Kraljevec**, which is famous for being the birthplace of the scientist and philosopher **Rudolf Steiner**. Until recently, the house he was born in (at Ludbreška 13) was being used as a stable, but it can now be visited by appointment – contact the Međimurje County tourist office (page 145) for details.

THE ZAGORJE

The northwestern corner of Croatia, known as the Zagorje, is one of the most beautiful parts of the country, with scores of castles, country houses and hilltop churches looking down across rolling wooded hills and vineyards. It's largely neglected by foreigners on their way to the beach, but it's no secret to locals, who come out here at weekends to relax.

Many of the old houses – and especially the little buildings adjoining the vineyards (*klets*) – have been converted into weekenders for people escaping Zagreb, but come here on the right Tuesday in February and you'll find the local winemakers' wives getting plastered in klets on every vineyard, which seems to me to be a splendid tradition.

Many of the castles (the French word châteaux is more appropriate, really) are in ill-repair, empty and abandoned, and could do with fixing up, and of those which have been restored, many are in private hands and can't be visited – with a few notable exceptions (see www.dvorci.hr). As Croatia becomes more prosperous, however, more of this wonderful heritage is being restored and opened to the public, and some places are in the process of being transformed into upmarket hotels. There's also talk of building a tunnel through Mount Medvednica to make the region easier to get to from Zagreb, but – in this author's humble opinion – it seems easy enough to access already on the motorway round the western end of the mountain.

It is difficult to get the most out of the Zagorje without your own wheels, however; even though many of the sights can be reached on public transport, it may take you all day to see a place worth only an hour of your time. Consider renting a car for a couple of days – but be prepared for some of the roads being narrow and winding.

There aren't that many places to stay, with most of the area's hotels being attached to the various spas in the region, but agro-tourism is on the rise, and there are a number of other options listed within this section (and notably Dvorac Bežanec, Vuglec Breg and Dvorac Gjalski, which are all excellent).

Zagorje eating is almost always a treat, whether you stick to the simple standards or try the local dishes, such as štrukli (page 96), which is usually at its finest here. Intended for decoration rather than eating are the *licitarsko srce*, iced gingerbread hearts. As gifts they're keenly priced; as snacks they're expensive (and tooth threatening).

The following attractions are ordered here in an itinerary heading very roughly clockwise from Zagreb towards Varaždin and back again, with those to the east of the main road to Hungary appearing at the end of the section. Covering the whole lot would make for a fairly hectic two- or more-relaxed three-day tour.

ZABOK AND KLANJEC Heading northwest out of Zagreb, it's around 20km to **Zabok**, which is nothing special, but as you come off the motorway you'll see a newly restored mansion up on the hill which is now the nice **Dvorac Gjalski** hotel (*Gredice Zaboče 7;* ☎ *049 201 100; www.dvorac-gjalski.hr;* €€€). It makes a lovely stopover, even though the views to the back of Mount Medvednica are blighted somewhat by the light industrial landscape in between – fortunately there's a lovely terrace behind the hotel, and a fine restaurant within. The rooms are impeccable, too, and very good value indeed.

From here, it's under 20km northwest to the small town of **Klanjec**, nestled right up against the Slovenian border. If you're on public transport, buses make the journey two or three times a day and there's also a train – change at Savski Marof. The main reason to stop here is to visit the **Antun Augustinčić Gallery** (*Trg A Mihanovića 10;* ☎ *049 550 343; http://mdc.hr/augustincic/eng/home.html;* ⊕ *Apr–Sep 09.00–17.00 daily, Oct–Mar 09.00–15.00 Tue–Sun; 20kn*), which maintains a comprehensive collection of the sculptor's work from the 1920s right through to the 1970s.

You may not think you've heard of Augustinčić, but if you've ever seen the monumental horse and rider outside the UN building in New York, or the pick-wielding miner outside the International Labour Organization (ILO) in Geneva, then you'll recognise his work (there's a large mural of the horse and rider being loaded on to a ship opposite the Jadrolinija building in Rijeka).

Augustinčić was born in Klanjec in 1900, and studied sculpture under Croatia's most famous sculptor, Ivan Meštrović, and in Paris, where he exhibited in the annual salon from 1925. By winning various prestigious public commissions –

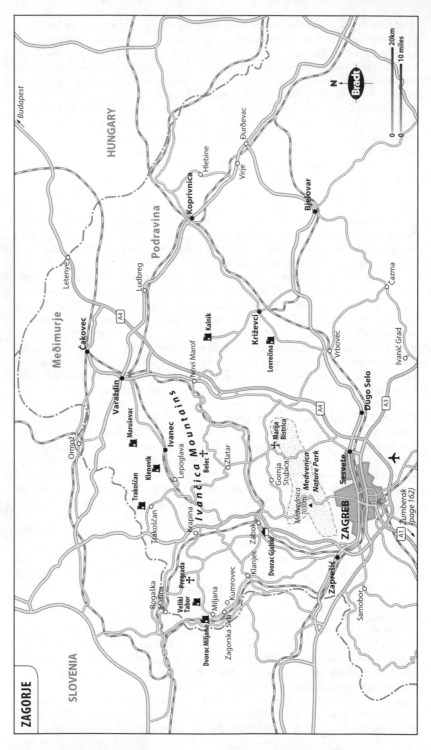

ZAGORJE

SLOVENIA

HUNGARY

Budapest

Međimurje

Podravina

Ivančica Mountains

Medvednica Nature Park

ZAGREB

Letenye

Ormož

Ormoz

Čakovec

Varaždin

Ludbreg

Koprivnica

Hlebine

Virje

Đurđevac

Bjelovar

Čazma

Ivanić Grad

Vrbovec

Dugo Selo

Novi Marof

Kalnik

Križevci

Lovrečina

Trakošćan

Trakošćan

Maruševec

Klenovik

Ivanec

Lepoglava

Belec

Zlatar

Gornja Stubica

Marija Bistrica

Medvednica 1030m

Sesvete

Krapina

Zabok

Dvorac Gjalski

Klanjec

Kumrovec

Zagorska Sela

Miljana

Veliki Tabor

Pregrada

Dvorac Miljana

Rogaška Slatina

Zaprešić

Samobor

Žumberak (page 162)

A1

A3

A4

A4

Bradt

N

0   10 miles

0   20km

148

including those mentioned above – he became Yugoslavia's official state sculptor. In 1970 he donated a wide range of works to his native town, and the museum here was opened in 1976.

The gallery comprises three rooms and a small sculpture garden. The public monuments – including a life-size copy of the UN sculpture, *Peace* – are far and away the most impressive, though if you catch the ILO miner on the right angle it does look exactly like a cricketer hitting a ball for six. Augustinčić and his wife are buried in the garden, watched over by the touching sculpture *The Carrying of the Wounded* – it's only a pity that Augustinčić's *Boy*, an unpleasantly realistic copy of the Manneken Pis in Brussels, wasn't suppressed by the taste police.

On the way out of town there's a monument to Antun Mihanović, the 19th-century polymath who wrote the lyrics to the Croatian national anthem here, clearly inspired by the ravine along the Sutla River.

KUMROVEC Continuing north, another 10km up the road brings you to the ethnographic museum-village of Kumrovec – which you can get to on public transport as for Klanjec (page 147). The **Old Village Museum** (*Muzej 'Staro Selo'; Kumrovec bb;* \ *049 225 830; http://www.mdc.hr/kumrovec/hr/index.html;* ⊕ *Apr–Sep 09.00–19.00 daily, Oct–Mar 09.00–16.00 daily; 20kn*) is a 15-minute walk from the train station.

For half a century the Kumrovec name was synonymous with Josip Broz Tito (see box opposite), as he was born here, but these days that angle's very much downplayed – except on his birthday, 25 May, when rival pro-Tito groups congregate here and get amusingly huffy with one another. Generally, however, although the authorities haven't quite gone as far as removing the marshal's life-sized statue (another work by Augustinčić) from outside his mum and dad's front door, you don't see much mention of Tito anywhere else in Croatia. Which is a pity; whatever your feelings about the man, he was an important player in 20th-century history.

Today the museum part of the village consists of more than 30 houses, each displaying a different feature of life as it would have been lived at the end of the 19th century, when Tito was a boy. Mannequins in period costume, the full range of authentic furnishings, tools and implements, and excellent labelling in English make this easily the best of Croatia's many ethnographic museums.

In different houses you can imagine what it must have been like (hard work, mostly) to be a wheelwright, a baker, a blacksmith, a linen manufacturer, a toy-maker, a potter or a gingerbread maker. One house is given over to a wedding feast, with a shy bride-to-be in her bedroom, doubtless deafened by the jolly music-making going on at the banquet across the hall.

The Broz family house is a low-key testament to Tito's fairly humble origins. The main room is given over to a small collection of Tito memorabilia – a few documents, one of his wartime uniforms, and a handful of photos of Tito with other statesmen from Churchill to Nixon. Without exception, the whole lot look as if they've been amusingly doctored to include Tito after the fact. In 1956, Nasser and Nehru shake hands, but Tito appears to have been pasted in behind; by 1963, it's John and Jackie Kennedy in the frame, with Tito scissored-in on the left-hand side.

The chickens wandering around and the hay drying on the attractive Slovenian-style lattice frames should alert you to the fact that not all the houses are part of the museum – before you wander unannounced into someone else's authentically rustic living room (as I did), check for the tell-tale trainers or gumboots outside.

Within the museum complex there's a nice place to eat, the **Zagorska Klet** (€€), where you'll find a wholesome range of local food at reasonable prices (try the turkey with *mlinci*, an authentic Christmas dish from northern Croatia). You can then pick up a *licitar* heart in the gift shop. If you want to stay in Kumrovec, **Stara Vura** is a small pansion and restaurant owned by the same family as Zagorska Klet (*Josipa Broza Tita 13;* ☎ *049 553 137;* €).

Heading up the Slovenian border from Kumrovec, the countryside becomes ever more beautiful, with Austro-Hungarian spires crowning hilltop churches – stop briefly for the photo-op at Zagorskje Sela, where from **St Catherine's Church** (Sv Katarina) you get lovely views across the valley into Slovenia.

Not much further up the road from here, as you come into Miljana, is the turn-off to Desinić, which is the road for Veliki Tabor. The lovely Renaissance manor house here, **Dvorac Miljana**, is probably the very finest of the restored châteaux of the Zagorje – but is not currently open for public viewing (though it's worth contacting the local tourist office in case this changes).

Don't miss the turn-off to **Veliki Tabor** and **Desinić** – you'll find yourself in Slovenia before you know it, either through the heavily manned border post, or on a mountainous road leading across an unmanned bridge to the spa town of

JOSIP BROZ TITO

Josip Broz was born in Kumrovec in 1892, to a Slovene mother and a Croat father. Drafted into the Austro-Hungarian army in 1914 to fight in World War I, he was captured the following year, but escaped early enough to join the Red Army in 1917. In 1920, he returned to Croatia, where he devoted his time to communism and unionism while employed as a metalworker.

With the Communist Party banned in 1928, Broz was frequently in trouble (and jail) but quickly worked his way up through the ranks. On joining the Central Committee in 1934, he took the name Tito. By 1939 he was Secretary-General of Yugoslavia's Communist Party, and when Yugoslavia capitulated in 1941 he was in a good position to rally resistance – not just to the Germans and the Italians, but also to the NDH (page 17), and indeed to anyone who wasn't a communist, including other factions of the resistance.

Charismatic, ruthless and utterly determined – though not the military genius he liked to think he was – Tito persuaded the Allies to switch their aid from the Četniks to the Partisans in 1943, and ended the war as the de facto dictator of the new Yugoslavia. His enemies – including large numbers of Croatian reservists and civilians – were brutally purged (notably at Bleiburg).

In 1948, Tito became the first communist leader to break ranks with Stalin, and was the founder of the non-aligned movement, which included India and Egypt. He continued to embrace communism, though a considerably softer version than that espoused by the USSR and the Eastern Bloc – Yugoslavs, notably, were allowed to own private property, and were free to travel, live and work abroad. But neither Tito himself nor the Communist Party ever brooked the slightest dissent, and prison was a real possibility for anyone who tried.

As Marshal and President for life, Tito made a point of trying to hold the country together, and was quick to quash nationalistic sentiment from the divergent republics – notably the Croatian Spring in 1971 – in spite of being half Croatian and half Slovene himself. Nonetheless, he put in place the legislation that would inevitably lead to the break up of Yugoslavia after his death, in particular by guaranteeing the republics' right to secede. Since his death in 1980, the entire country has broken up into its constituent pieces.

Atomske Toplice. If that's your route into Slovenia, you can forget about trying to argue your way back into Croatia anywhere near here – head all the way back to the Kumrovec border post instead.

VELIKI TABOR, PREGRADA AND DVORAC BEŽANEC

Veliki Tabor (*Košnički Hum 1;* \ *049 374 970; www.velikitabor.com;* ⊕ *Apr–Sep 09.00–17.00 Tue–Fri, 09.00–19.00 Sat/Sun; Mar/Oct 09.00–16.00 Tue–Fri, 09.00–17.00 Sat/Sun; Nov–Feb 09.00–16.00 Tue–Sun; 20kn*) A few kilometres up the road from Miljana, on a 333m hill, is Veliki Tabor, arguably the most picturesque authentic castle in Croatia. Originally dating from the 12th century, the distinctive defensive round towers were added in the 16th century. From the road there's a lovely view – as indeed there is from the excellent and authentically rustic **Grešna Gorica** restaurant, clearly signed off the main road, a few hundred metres beyond the steep track leading up to the castle.

Following several years of ongoing renovation, the castle was finally reopened to the public in January 2012, so the lovely five-sided, three-tiered courtyard can now be visited again.

Like all good medieval castles, Veliki Tabor has its own romantic fable attached to it. In this case the local landowner's son wouldn't renounce the peasant girl of his desires, and was imprisoned in the castle until his death. The girl, for her part in the sorry story, was bricked up into the castle walls – they say the skull in the chapel here is hers. Count yourself lucky if you live in a time or country where you can choose who you marry. There are also several events held at the castle, including archery and puppet workshops.

Getting there and away There are over half a dozen buses from Zagreb to Desinić, from where it's a 3km walk to Veliki Tabor. Contact the tourist information office in Desinić if you're unsure of the way (*Trg Sv Jurja 7;* \ *049 343 146; www.desinic.hr*).

Pregrada Eight kilometres east of Veliki Tabor is the village of Pregrada, where the local parish church is so big it's known locally as the Zagorje Cathedral. It's 38m long and 19m wide, and its two 45m towers dominate the village. Inside, check out the monumental organ (avoiding 'monumental organ' jokes of course), by Focht, which used to belong to Zagreb Cathedral until they sold it to Pregrada for 600 forints in 1854. Frankly, it's much better value than the 600 forints the church then spent eight years later on the vast altarpiece of *The Adoration*, which looks like it can only have been bought by the square metre – or indeed the rather druggy modern stained glass in some of the church's windows.

Dvorac Bežanec Another 4km east leads to Dvorac Bežanec (*Valentinovo 55;* \ *049 376 800; www.hotel-dvorac-bezanec.hr;* €€€€–€€€), which is in a great setting and has been converted into a swanky hotel and conference centre. Originally built in the 17th century, the château was remodelled in 1830 in the classicist style, and it can be a wonderfully luxurious place to stay, with nice suites – be fussy about your room, however, as some of the standard doubles could really use a lick of paint, and there's no excuse in a place this nice for thin towels or plastic shower curtains. Call ahead if you want to take advantage of the horse riding or ballooning opportunities; they can also arrange transfers from Zagreb, if you want to get out of the city, for around €100 return, per carload. The hotel's restaurant – which serves up meals in the courtyard or out on the terrace in fine weather – is absolutely first-rate.

KRAPINA AND KRAPINSKE TOPLICE A further 12km east brings you to Krapina, which is on the main road running north from Zagreb to Maribor (in Slovenia) and Graz (in Austria). It's a busy, commercial little town, but the main reason for visiting is that in 1899 the site of an important Neanderthal settlement dating back 130,000 years was unearthed here, on the Hušnjakovo hill above town.

Krapina Man was discovered by Dragutin Gorjanović-Kramberger, who went on to collect the world's largest and most important set of Neanderthal fossils from a single site, comprising 900 pieces from 70 to 80 individuals. The original bones are under lock and key in the Natural History Museum in Zagreb (pages 125–6), but there is also an outstanding, brand-new museum here in Krapina, the **Krapina Neanderthal Museum** (*Muzej Krapinskih Neandertalaca; Šetalište Vilibalda Sluge bb;* `049 371 491; www.mkn.mhz.hr;` ⊕ *Jul/Aug 09.00–19.00 Sat/Sun, 09.00–18.00 Tue–Fri, Apr–Jun & Sep 09.00–19.00 Tue–Sun, Mar/Oct 09.00–18.00 Tue–Sun, Nov–Feb 09.00–17.00 Sat/Sun, 09.00–16.00 Tue–Fri; 50kn/25kn adult/child, family ticket 100kn*), which traces the story of human evolution. The design of the museum (the work of architect Željko Kovačić and paleontologist Jakov Radovčić) is worth a visit in itself.

You can also walk up to the actual site, where you'll find life-sized (and quite life-like) statues of the Neanderthals brandishing clubs. One of them looks alarmingly like the exchange student we had one year at our school.

Krapina is relatively easy to reach by public transport, with weekday buses running every hour or so from Zagreb, and taking an hour. At weekends you're probably better off taking the train – change at Zabok.

🏠 **Where to stay and eat** If you want to stay in town, contact the **tourist office** (*Magistratska 11;* `049 371 330; http://tzg-krapina.hr`), which should be able to find you a private room in the area.

There are also a couple of places to stay in **Krapinske Toplice**, the spa town 14km southwest of Krapina – contact the Krapina–Zagorje County tourist office (*D.G. Krambergera 1, Krapina;* `049 233 653; www.tzkzz.hr`) for more information.

For somewhere much nicer, and in a fabulous location up in the hills between Krapina and Krapinske Toplice, you can't beat **Vuglec Breg** (*Škarićevo 151;* `049 345 015;` e *info@vuglec-breg.hr; www.vuglec-breg.hr;* €€€), in the locality known as Škarićevo. A handful of old village houses have been beautifully restored and converted into accommodation with all mod cons, and there's a restaurant and vineyard attached, with excellent local wines (especially the whites).

TRAKOŠĆAN (`042 796 281; www.trakoscan.hr;` ⊕ *Apr–Oct 09.00–18.00 daily, Nov–Mar 09.00–16.00 daily; 30kn*) Northeast from Krapina is the Zagorje's most-visited attraction, Trakošćan. Billed as a 13th-century castle, you don't have to read much of the small print – or use much architectural intelligence – to work out that what you're seeing here isn't medieval at all but mid-19th-century neo-Romantic all over. That doesn't make it any less worth visiting – although it's all a bit shabby and run down, it's still extraordinary inside and out, with a complete collection of the original (19th-century) furniture and fittings.

The castle was given to the powerful Drašković family in 1584, probably as a belated thank-you for its role in putting down the peasants' uprising a decade earlier (see page 155). After the first century or so, the family didn't do much with Trakošćan, preferring to live at the better-appointed Klenovik (see page 153). But with the Romantic revival in full swing, they then spent a fortune – and more than 20 years – building the castle you see today, and damming and flooding the valley below to give themselves a decent lake.

Access is up a lovely spiralling path and through mock-defensive gates, overlooked by imaginatively crenellated walls and ramparts. Inside it's all heavy neo-Gothic. On the ground floor you'll find the Knights' Room, with lots of clumsy-looking armour and the usual hideous array of pikes and swords. There's also a curious fireplace, with wooden dragons supporting the mantelpiece. At the other end of the building there's a Hunting Hall that verges dangerously close to self-parody.

Upstairs there's room after room of heavy furniture and heavier furnishings, hideous to most modern sensibilities, but a real insight into the mid-19th-century mindset of the ruling classes. You'll also see ten generations of smug Drašković portraits, by the famous local painter Nepozanti Slikar, and presumably his eponymous descendants – since they date from 1680 to at least 1823. (No, I'm kidding – *'nepozanti slikar'* just means 'anonymous painter'.)

Far from anonymous, as far as the paintings here go, are those by Julijana Drašković (née Erdödy, 1847–1901). Much of her surviving work is here in the castle and – although most of it doesn't stand extended 21st-century scrutiny – there are several truly excellent impressionistic portraits.

Other things to look out for, among the absurdly chunky Baroque furniture, are an unusual three-seater neo-Gothic sofa (inspired no doubt by church architecture), superb stoves in every room (usually fed from behind, to avoid the unpleasantness of intrusive servants), and what must have been a boy's room on the top floor, with wallpaper consisting of tapestries depicting massive armies of tin soldiers on parade.

You can clear your head outside by a promenade around the lake – the whole circuit takes a leisurely hour and a half.

Practicalities You can't get to Trakošćan directly from Zagreb on public transport, but there are buses roughly every hour from Varaždin, taking less than an hour. Once you're here there's a perfectly acceptable accommodation option, the 126-room **Hotel Trakošćan** (*Trakošćan bb;* \ *042 440 800; www.hotel-trakoscan.hr;* €€€), right across from the castle, which has a sauna and gym too. The dining room tends to cater to large tour buses and noisy school groups, but you can escape on to the terrace easily enough, and enjoy the view across to the castle.

LEPOGLAVA, KLENOVIK AND MARUŠEVAC CASTLE From Trakošćan it's about 10km southeast to **Lepoglava,** (in)famous mainly for being the site of Croatia's largest prison. There's hardly a big name in 20th-century Croatian politics who didn't do time here, from Tito himself between the wars, to Archbishop Stepinac after World War II, to Franjo Tuđman, who was banged up here during the 1980s for disagreeing with Serbia's take on history – he suffered four heart attacks in jail here before being released.

The prison's still there, but it was moved away from the town centre to a new location in 2001. The main reason for coming here – the town's pleasant enough, but nothing special – is the fine whitewashed Austro-Hungarian church, with saints in niches on the outside. Inside, the church has a curious right-curving nave, colourful frescoes and a big Baroque altar – which you can see even if the church is closed, as there's a grille inside the portico you can peer through.

Northeast 10km from Lepoglava is Croatia's biggest castle, **Klenovik,** which claims to have 90 rooms and 365 windows. Built in the 17th century, it was for a brief time the seat of the Croatian parliament, and is now a sanatorium, dealing mainly with respiratory complaints. You can only visit today if you're a patient.

Halfway between Klenovik and Varaždin is the mysterious and hard-to-find **Maruševec Castle** (*www.dvorac-marusevec.hr*). Originally dating from the 16th

4

century, today's version is a 19th-century neo-Gothic pile, home to a theology school of the Adventist Church.

BELEC Barely 10km southeast of Lepoglava as the crow flies, but on the other side of the 1,100m Ivančićica mountains (you have to skirt round through Zlatar, and then head 8km north), is the village of Belec, and more importantly the **Church of St Mary of the Snow** (Sv Marija Snejžne). Simple enough on the outside, it's profligate Baroque gone mad once you get inside.

There's hardly an unadorned surface in sight. Putti proliferate off every balcony, mantelpiece and archway, extravagantly gestured saints camp it up like drama queens, and the accumulated wealth of gilt, carving and paintwork is completely overwhelming. Restrained simplicity it ain't – it has to be seen to be believed. Although it's usually only open on Sunday mornings, the woman who lives opposite the gate has a key, and will let you see inside. Expect to make a small donation to the restoration fund.

MARIJA BISTRICA Heading south 10km from Zlatar brings you into Marija Bistrica, a pleasant little town dedicated to looking after the more than 600,000 pilgrims who come here every year, making it Croatia's premier pilgrimage site. The reason? A late 15th- or early 16th-century Black Madonna, which already had a huge following, even before a fire in 1880 destroyed almost everything except the statue itself.

With pilgrims on the increase for centuries, the congregation has frequently outgrown the church, and the church has equally frequently had to be expanded. The current incarnation was completed in 1883 by Hermann Bollé, the man behind lots of buildings in Zagreb, including the cathedral – though here he's been more imaginative (or perhaps less constrained).

From the outside, the **Pilgrimage Church of St Mary** is halfway between a castle and a cathedral. An elegant piazza leads through a gate into a half-cloister, lined with thousands of marble plaques of gratitude from pilgrims whose wishes have been granted over the years, and topped with paintings of specific miracles attributable to the Black Madonna.

Inside, the church is a quiet, awed place, with a continuously shifting congregation of the hopeful (mostly older women) saying their prayers, but also seizing the opportunity to photograph and film the famous Madonna behind the altar.

Behind the church, there's an enormous open-air auditorium, which was built for the Pope's visit in 1998 (when he came here to beatify Cardinal Stepinac – page 116), and a Way of the Cross, leading up Calvary Hill. The church and town look lovely from the top, even if you haven't climbed up here on your knees.

Marija Bistrica is also a good place to buy decorated gingerbread hearts – the gingerbread craft of northern Croatia is inscribed on the UNESCO List of Intangible Cultural Heritage.

You may want to steer clear of the town, however – unless of course you're a pilgrim too – on 15 August, when thousands upon thousands of people come to celebrate the Assumption of the Virgin Mary (Velika Gospa).

Practicalities There are buses every hour or so from Zagreb to Marija Bistrica on most days, but fewer on Sundays. The helpful **tourist office** (*Zagrebačka bb;* ⟍ *049 468 380; www.tz-marija-bistrica.hr*) can point you at private rooms nearby, though it's good to have your own wheels, as some of them are some way out into the country.

Marija Bistrica's also a good place to eat, with pizzerias and grills aplenty. The following two places are especially good:

✳ ✘ **Restaurant Bistricza** Zagrebačka bb; ☎ 049 326 600; www.hotelkaj.hr. In town, this 66-room 4-star Hotel Kaj (€€€€) has an outstandingly good restaurant, with impeccable service, & serving excellent local specialties & some very, very good wines (including from the hotel owner's vineyards on Hvar). Highly recommended. €€€€–€€€

✳ ✘ **Vinarija Mičak** Hum Bistrički 69a; ☎ 049 469 198; m 098 829 378; www.vinarija-micak. hr. This local vineyard has 4 apts, an excellent restaurant & some fantastic wines – on the updater's last visit, the cabernet sauvignon (which had just won a gold medal in France) was phenomenal. The vineyard is just under 1km from the town centre. Highly recommended. €€€

GORNJA STUBICA From Marija Bistrica it's 11km west to Gornja Stubica, home to the radically named **Museum of Peasant Uprisings** (*Muzej Seljačkih Buna; Samci 64;* ☎ *049 587 889; www.mdc.hr/msb;* ⊕ *Apr–Sep 09.00–19.00 daily, Oct–Mar 09.00–19.00 daily; 20kn*), housed in the local Oršić Palace. Back in the 16th century, peasants were treated appallingly, overloaded with dues to foreign overlords, expected to fight their battles for them, and driven to the brink of starvation by people who mostly lived idle lives in opulent palaces. By 1573, in this area, it was all too much, and the peasants revolted. The uprising was quickly and ruthlessly put down by the bishop of Zagreb, a Drašković, who spread word that the ringleader, Matija Gubec, had been made king of the peasants. Within weeks he was horribly executed in St Mark's Square, in Zagreb, by being 'crowned' peasant king with a band of red-hot iron.

There's a dramatic communist-era statue of Gubec on the hill above the town, framed by a huge bronze frieze depicting revolting peasants – it's the work of local boy Antun Augustinčić (page 147). The museum is well-enough signed if you're coming from Donja Stubica or Gornja Stubica, but if you're coming from Marija Bistrica, the sharp turn up to the monument and museum is easy to miss – if you've crossed over the Oršić River or the railway, or got as far as the Grof Bistro, then you've gone too far.

The museum, over the hill behind the monument, is actually a bit of a misnomer, telling you more about the luxurious lifestyle of the oppressors than the beaten-down existence of the oppressed – though maybe that's the point: this is what you're meant to revolt against. (To be fair, however, there are lots of explanatory panels, in Croatian only, which may do the trick.)

The first thing you can visit is the family chapel, dating from 1756, which has a stunningly convincing *trompe l'oeil* altarpiece and fake dome. The chapel and the room next door house some richly embroidered ecclesiastical garments, originally used at Marija Bistrica at the end of the 19th century. Look out for the distinctive hammer and pliers motif, along with a brightly stitched chicken, sheep, ladder and cross, paintbrush, and wicker basket.

The rest of the museum is upstairs. Above the chapel, out of sight of the peasants below, an Oršić countess sits reading her prayer book in haughty isolation. A roomful of furniture and trinkets only confirms the distance between rich and poor, though you can't help admiring the pocket sundial dating from 1755. 'What time is it, your honour?' 'I'm afraid I can't tell you – it's raining.'

From here there's a bridge through to the rest of the collection, with a group of ragged-looking peasants on one side, and a couple of well-shod militia on the other. You can see the peasants wouldn't have stood a chance.

Practicalities You can get here by **train** from Zagreb half a dozen times a day – change at Zabok on the Varaždin line, and then take the branch line to Gornja Stubica. In the courtyard of the palace there's a small **restaurant** with an even smaller menu, but the terrace is a nice place to sit. Otherwise, if you have your own wheels, head uphill to **Rody**, signed 250m north off the road between the town and the museum – you get a great view south to the back of Medvednica from the terrace, and the food and wine are good value.

VRBOVEC Situated just 45km east of Zagreb, the small town of Vrbovec is way off the tourist radar screen. While the town's nothing special in itself, it does make a great base for exploring the practically unvisited local area, and it has an incredible-value place to stay. Given that it's only 40 minutes by rail into Zagreb, with trains running more than once an hour, and with frequent buses too, Vrbovec is also a possible base for seeing the capital – hotel rooms here are far cheaper than even private rooms in the city.

Four kilometres north of Vrbovec, on the road to Križevci, there's the charming 16th-century **Lovrečina Castle**, with distinctive round towers at either end. Today, Lovrečina is run as a Cenacolo rehabilitation centre, mainly for former drug users.

Where to stay and eat The train station is a 10-minute walk north from the town centre, while the bus station is on the southwestern corner of town, just downhill from the church. From the bus station it's a 5-minute walk along Zagrebačka (the main road from Zagreb to Bjelovar) to the excellent and very good value **Motel Marina** (*Matija Gupca 26;* ☎ *01 279 1502; www.motel-marina.com;* €), which has great rooms with all facilities (phone, satellite TV, minibar, air conditioning). If that weren't enough, there's a nice terrace, and the food is excellent – local produce and local recipes dominate the menu.

Another accommodation option is the 40-room **Hotel Bunčić** (*Zagrebačka 4;* ☎ *01 278 1133; www.buncic.hr;* €€), which also has its own restaurant.

KRIŽEVCI Just 20km northeast of Vrbovec, and roughly equidistant from Zagreb and Varaždin, is the thriving town of Križevci. It's only an hour or so from the capital by rail, on trains that run about once an hour, but it's far enough off the beaten track to be tourist-free. The town, which has been firmly on the map since the middle of the 13th century, has more than its fair share of churches and old buildings, as well as a fine city museum.

The most obvious sight is the **Greek Catholic Cathedral**. Many of the locals here, as well as the majority of the people in the Žumberak, southwest of Zagreb, were originally Orthodox Slavs. In the face of Turkish expansion they were protected by the Austro-Hungarians, as long as they agreed to recognise the Pope – hence Greek Catholics. The church was rebuilt by the ubiquitous Hermann Bollé in his trademark neo-Gothic style, while the iconostasis inside is marvellous, half an acre of gold leaf surrounding colourful icons of the saints and keeping the congregation separate from the priests behind.

Also worth visiting is the **Church of the Holy Cross** (Sv Križa), which started life in the 13th and 14th centuries but has been much remodelled and restored since. Inside there's a dramatic painting of the so-called *Bloody Diet of Križevci* which took place in 1397, when the Hungarian King Sigismund successfully tricked and murdered the cream of Croatia's nobility here.

Back in the centre of town, the 17th-century **Church of St Anne** (Sv Anne) is also interesting – the niches outside feature painted saints in the absence of statuary, while inside it's simple Romanesque, with a few fresco fragments on the right-hand wall.

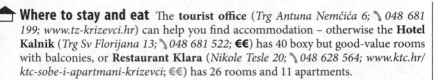

Where to stay and eat The **tourist office** (*Trg Antuna Nemčića 6;* \ *048 681 199; www.tz-krizevci.hr*) can help you find accommodation – otherwise the **Hotel Kalnik** (*Trg Sv Florijana 13;* \ *048 681 522;* €€) has 40 boxy but good-value rooms with balconies, or **Restaurant Klara** (*Nikole Tesle 20;* \ *048 628 564; www.ktc.hr/ ktc-sobe-i-apartmani-krizevci;* €€) has 26 rooms and 11 apartments.

KALNIK FORTRESS Heading out of Križevci towards Varaždin, there's a turn-off after about 10km leading up towards Kalnik, 9km off the main road. The road climbs up steeply to stop right underneath a fabulous ruined ridge-top fortress. Originally built in the 13th century, it must once have been magnificent, although it's been abandoned since the 17th century.

It's been restored enough to make it safe, and stop further deterioration, and it's well worth scrambling up to the highest point – there are handrails on the dodgy sections. You're only 500m above sea-level here, but you can see for miles – to Medvednica in the southwest, and on a very clear day all the way to Papuk, over 100km away.

If you're travelling through **Bjelovar** there's an excellent local producer of fruit wines and liqueurs, **OPG Škudar** (*www.vocno-vino.com*) – their bottles of cherry wine and walnut liqueur make great gifts to take home.

Just below the fortress there's a lodge run by the mountaineering association, the renovated **Planinarski Dom Kalnik** (\ *048 857 091; www.pdkalnik.hr; restaurant* ⊙ *08.00–23.00 Tue–Sun;* €€€–€€), which has a great terrace, fine food (including lamb cooked ispod peka) and a few rooms upstairs (*33 beds in dbls, a tpl & a dorm;* €), and information on walks in the area.

THE PODRAVINA AND HLEBINE Further northeast of Zagreb, running up to the Drava River and the Hungarian border, is the **Podravina**, a rich agricultural basin marked by fields of sunflowers and maize. There's not much to bring tourists here, to be honest, though if you're in the region you may be interested in visiting the village of Hlebine, where Croatian naïve art took off in the 1930s and is still going strong today.

The main centre in the region is the busy town of **Koprivnica**, which is on major rail and road routes. The town is nice enough, though there's nothing special to see or do here. It does make a good place for a layover, however, as there are a couple of useful and affordable places to stay. The nicer of the two is the 14-room **Bijela Kuća** (*Kolodvorska 12;* \ *048 240 320; www.hotel-podravina.hr;* €€€), which is close to both the bus and train stations, a 10-minute walk from the town centre. Bigger, boxier and right in the town centre is its sister hotel, the **Podravina** (*Hrvatske državnosti 9;* \ *048 621 025; www.hotel-podravina.hr;* €€€). Both places have reasonable (and fairly priced) restaurants.

From Koprivnica it's about 15km to **Hlebine**, and you should expect to use your own transport or take a taxi, as buses are rare. Ever since a local artist fortuitously discovered the works of the self-taught Ivan Generalić in the local shop, in 1930, Hlebine has been a centre of naïve art, and today there are more than 100 painters and sculptors in the area, continuing the tradition. The **Hlebine Gallery** (\ *048 836 075; www.koprivnicatourism.com;* ⊙ *10.00–16.00 Tue–Fri, 10.00–14.00 Sat/Sun; 10kn*) features a rotating collection of works from the village, but you can always be sure of catching some of the original and most striking pictures by Ivan Generalić. Also in Hlebine, but you need to arrange a visit ahead of time (*call the tourist office, Trg Bana Josipa Jelačića 7, on* \ *048 621 433; www.koprivnicatourism.com*), is the Generalić Gallery, which features work by Ivan's son, Josip, who worked here until his death in December 2004, and his grandson Goran, who continues in the family tradition. If you're interested in naïve art, it's also well worth visiting the excellent

Museum of Naïve Art in Zagreb (pages 128–30), and checking out the Generalić website, at www.generalic.com.

SAMOBOR

Less than 20km from downtown Zagreb, and just 5 minutes from the Slovenian border, Samobor is an attractive little town, with a compact heart set on an elegant, elongated square. A shallow, trout-filled stream is spanned by narrow bridges, and it's a lovely place to sit and soak up the atmosphere while you're tucking into Samobor's culinary specialities.

With buses from Zagreb every half hour (hourly on Sundays), it's easy to reach, and even makes a realistic alternative to staying in the capital itself. The friendly **tourist office** (*Trg kralja Tomislava 5;* \ *01 336 0044; www.tz-samobor.hr*), located right on the main square, will set you up with good local information, and maps of the surrounding area, including the lovely Žumberak region, to which Samobor is the natural gateway.

 WHERE TO STAY *Map, page 159*
There are two good hotel options, the first of which is among my favourites in all Croatia, as well as some nice pansions and a good new hostel.

Hotel Livadić (21 rooms) Trg Kralja Tomislava 1; \ 01 336 5850; www.hotel-livadic.hr. On the main square, with a lovely flower-bedecked central courtyard & utterly charming rooms, with old furniture & good-sized bathrooms, at an absolute snip compared to anything in Zagreb. The real treat is a handful of gorgeous, beautifully renovated suites at the top of the building. Room #34 has its bed on a mezzanine, & a sitting room downstairs, while room #35 is spacious & airy & gives on to the courtyard below. **€€€–€€**

Hostel Samobor (82 beds) Obrtnička 34; \ 01 337 4107; www.hostel-samobor.hr. Beds in 2-, 4-, 6- & 10-bed dorms for €17pp. Bike rental available. **€**

Hotel Lavica (22 rooms) Ferde Livadica 5; \ 01 336 8000; www.lavica-hotel.hr. Just across the river from the Livadić, & next door to the town museum, the Lavica has clean, simple rooms at a bargain price, each named after a Croatian intellectual. Its brick-vaulted restaurant – like pretty much everywhere in Samobor – serves up solid local specialities, too. **€**

Pansion Gogo (5 rooms) Slani Dol; \ 01 338 4096; www.izletiste-gogo.hr. Very good value homely accommodation & meals, just 7km outside Samobor in the village of Slani Dol. **€**

Pansion Gołubić (2 rooms) Obrtnička 12; \ 01 336 0937. Simple, welcoming accommodation in the town centre. **€**

✗ **WHERE TO EAT AND DRINK** *Map, page 159*
Samobor – as a long-standing day-out for Zagreb's workers – is very big on edible treats, and notably its famous *Samoborske kremšnite* – a mountain of cream filling, sandwiched between two slices of flaky pastry. The recipe published by the tourist board makes it sound all too simple: 'Dress lightly. Throw a sweater over your shoulder. Take a vehicle. Go to main square of Samobor. Take a seat. Order and enjoy.'

The two best places to buy kremšnite – we did several tests – are U Prolazu and Gradska Slastičarnica, both on the main square; the latter slightly sweeter, but with lighter pastry than the former. But personally, in the cake department, my money's on the *rudarska greblica*, which is big on walnuts and not quite so creamy. As its name implies, it comes from the village of Rude, just up the valley.

Samobor is also big on sausages, with a **Salami Festival** in April, and produces excellent local *muštarda*, a type of mustard (*senf*), to go with them. If you're going

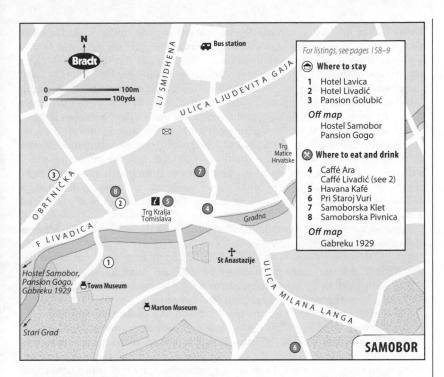

For listings, see pages 158–9

Where to stay
1 Hotel Lavica
2 Hotel Livadić
3 Pansion Golubić

Off map
Hostel Samobor
Pansion Gogo

Where to eat and drink
4 Caffé Ara
Caffé Livadić (see 2)
5 Havana Kafé
6 Pri Staroj Vuri
7 Samoborska Klet
8 Samoborska Pivnica

Off map
Gabreku 1929

SAMOBOR

the whole hog (insert sausage joke here), also make sure you try the local aperitif, *bermet*, which is red wine flavoured with herbs and spices; it's not to all tastes, but the locals love it.

For sit-down eating and drinking, Samobor is particularly blessed, though – perhaps because it's still focused on visitors from Zagreb, rather than international tourism – there's nothing especially upmarket.

✗ **Gabreku 1929** Starogradska 46; ☏ 01 336 0702; www.gabrek.hr; ⊕ noon–midnight daily. Highly rated restaurant around 500m west of town, on the main road heading towards the fortress, with grills, trout & local dishes. €€€

✗ **Pri Staroj Vuri** Giznik 2; ☏ 01 336 0548; www.pristarojvuri.com; ⊕ noon–23.00 Mon–Sat, 11.00–18.00 Sun. Nice little restaurant on Giznik, a short walk south of the main square, serving hearty traditional dishes. €€€

✗ **Samoborska Klet** Trg kralja Tomislava 7; ☏ 01 32 6536; www.samoborska-klet.hr; ⊕ 08.00–midnight. Excellent place, set off the north side of the main square down a short alley, in a shady courtyard adjoining a capacious, simple interior, & offering a regular selection of sensibly priced soups, grilled meats, calamari & side salads, with a 10% discount for cash payment. €€€

✗ **Samoborska Pivnica** Šmidhenova 3; ☏ 01 337 9924; www.samoborskapivnica.com; ⊕ 09.00–23.00 daily. You can't go wrong here, even if the terrace is actually part of the car park behind the Hotel Livadić. Serves up all the local specialities, & a particularly generous portion of štrukli (page 96). €€€

☕ **Caffé Ara** Trg kralja Tomislava 9; ⊕ 08.00–23.00 daily. At the end of the main square, on the north side of the river bridge, a cool place to hang out & sip a cocktail.

☕ **Caffé Livadić** Trg kralja Tomislava 1; www.hotel-livadic.hr; ⊕ 08.00–23.00 daily. Standout café on the main square, part of the excellent Hotel Livadić, with a lovely courtyard.

🍸 **Havana Kafé** Trg kralja Tomislava 3; ⊕ 08.00–23.00 daily. Groovy hang-out on the main square, with the usual range of cocktails & drinks, but watch out for the squashy seats.

Inland Croatia SAMOBOR

4

WHAT TO SEE AND DO If you can tempt yourself away from the cakes, the most obvious thing to see is Samobor's **Town Museum** (*Gradski Muzej; Livadićeva 7;* ❧ *01 336 1014; www.samoborskimuzej.hr;* ⊕ *09.00–15.00 Tue–Thu, 09.00–19.00 Fri, 10.00–14.00 Sat, 10.00–17.00 Sun; 10kn*), spread out over both floors of local composer Ferdo Livadić's solid town house. Downstairs there are two interesting 1/100 scale models, both by local model-maker Marijan Majdak; one of the castle above the town, as it was in 1776, and the other of the whole of Samobor in 1764 – with the only two things you'll recognise being the church and the Livadić house itself. Also check out the Samobor Chicken (a possible rival to the Vučedol Dove in Zagreb, see page 120), a small local collection of Roman coins, and a well-intentioned palaeontological historical tower, from plastic dinosaurs right up the present day. Upstairs, highlights include an 1877 penny-farthing, a 1920 Puch motorbike, and – if my notes are to be believed – an 1830 portrait of Scooby Doo.

Samobor's other main museum is, if anything, even more eclectic. The **Marton Museum** (*Muzej Marton; Jurjevska 7;* ❧ *01 332 6426; www.muzej-marton.hr;* ⊕ *10.00–13.00 Sat/Sun; 20kn*) is housed in a fine building from 1841, just above the church, and comprises a private collection of furniture, paintings, glass and china, skilfully put together by local businessman Veljko Marton. Part of the collection was moved to new premises in Zagreb in 2011 (page 130).

Up to the west of the town is Samobor's 13th-century castle, **Stari Grad**, and the 25-minute walk up to inspect the ruins will do much to get you in shape for the next culinary delight. Follow the path along the stream, then veer left when you see the tennis courts off to the right, and zigzag your way fairly steeply uphill to the overgrown, agreeable ruins of the fortress. Coming back, take the wider, flatter path that leads through the woods to the little Church of St Anne, where you can turn left past a wooden gazebo on to the road which brings you back into Samobor, or uphill through the woods to another chapel, higher up.

More ambitious hiking – but not much more ambitious – is available in the **Samoborsko Gorje** mountains further to the west of town. Increasingly popular at weekends (it's some of the nearest hiking to Zagreb, and not too demanding), you'll find the well-marked trails almost empty out of season, especially if you're here midweek – get a map from the tourist office.

The tourist office also has an excellent **cycle route** marked out, and a free map with English instructions on it. The circuit's only 24km long, but the first nine of these are all steeply uphill, gaining 450m – unless you're pretty fit, you may want to do the route in reverse, which makes the climb at a gentler gradient. You can rent bikes from Hostel Samobor (page 158).

As if the salami festival wasn't enough, Samobor also hosts a huge pre-Lent **carnival**. It's one of the most popular in Croatia, attracting hundreds of thousands of visitors, which makes it enormous fun – but no joke at all if you're looking for a room.

Finally, Samobor is a great place to pick up **souvenirs**. On Stražnička, the street heading north out of the main square (to the left of the Hotel Livadić) you can find bead necklaces, *bermet* (dessert wine), and other curiosities at the first shop, and paintings, metalwork and wood next door. At the top of the same street is the Filipec family shop, which is reckoned to be the best place locally for muštarda, while on the next street east (to the right of the hotel), you'll find Samoborska Delicije, the most upmarket shop in town, which does nice *licitar* hearts, homemade pâtés, local olive oil, wine and rakija, beautifully presented in attractive packaging and gift boxes.

ŽUMBERAK

Southwest of Zagreb, and tucked up against the Slovenian border, is the Žumberak region, a sparsely populated expanse of dense forests, steep hills, and sleepy villages, which is a designated nature park (*www.pp-zumberak-samoborsko-gorje.hr*). There isn't that much to do in the way of specific sightseeing and you can't get to many places using public transport – indeed, lots of the smaller hamlets and villages don't even have metalled roads to them – but if you do have your own wheels it makes for a lovely region to explore at leisure (especially if you're cycling – there are four marked cycling trails in the park, check the website). See www.park-zumberak.hr/destinacije_en.html for an idea of what there is to see in the area, or contact the information centre in Slani dol (3327 660).

The northern part of the Žumberak is mountainous and forested, while further to the south are the beautiful steep vineyards of the Plešivica region (page 164). The obvious gateway to the region is the pretty town of Samobor, though you can also access it from Karlovac or Jastrebarsko.

There's not much to do or see in the Žumberak itself – beyond enjoying the fine scenery and splendid vistas, and perhaps hiking or biking through the hills – but if you have wheels then there's a good circuit you can do anticlockwise through the region, starting at Samobor, heading round to Karlovac and coming back via Jastrebarsko and the Plešivica vineyards. You need to allow at least two days to see everything, or skip various parts of the itinerary – it's a minimum 200km circuit, with quite long sections on gravel roads. (The circuit works just as well starting in Karlovac, if that's where you're based.)

Start by heading due north to Bregana, but turn left before you get whisked into Slovenia. The road then follows the river (the Slovenian border) for about 10km, until you reach **Divlje Vode**, which becomes something of a minor recreation area at weekends. The restaurant here serves excellent local trout.

ŽUMBERAČKO EKO SELO Shortly after Divlje Vode, the road forks – take the left-hand fork, heading up to Žumberačko Eko Selo. After a short while the tarmac runs out, and you're on about 8km of gravel all the way up to the camp, a collection of wooden buildings centred on a biggish restaurant in a valley with a pretty stream running through it (it's just off to the right of the main gravel road, when you get as high up as you're going to go).

You can stay up here, in one of the wooden huts (€25 a head) – call Željko Milovanović (m *095 549 2645*) or Damir Foršner (m *098 163 3903*) ahead of time for more detailed information. You can also book yourself in for horse riding – there's a stable, which only adds to the thoroughly American-cowboy atmosphere; a Stetson wouldn't be entirely out of place. Even if you don't stay, do consider eating here – not only is the restaurant first-rate, it's also the last place for a long time ahead.

There's no question that the easiest way onwards is to head back the way you came, but if you're feeling adventurous then press on – at a number of points the network of gravel roads rejoins the tarred road which winds its way around the northern and western sides of the Žumberak. A good sense of direction and the best maps available will help, but are unlikely to prevent you from getting lost up here. Essentially you want to keep heading west and/or south, and don't be afraid to ask smallholders the way to towns on the main road – Kostanjevac, Pribić and Krašić are all good names to ask for.

Up here life goes on the way it has for centuries, with tiny villages far from the rest of the world, and almost all the work in the small fields still being done by hand.

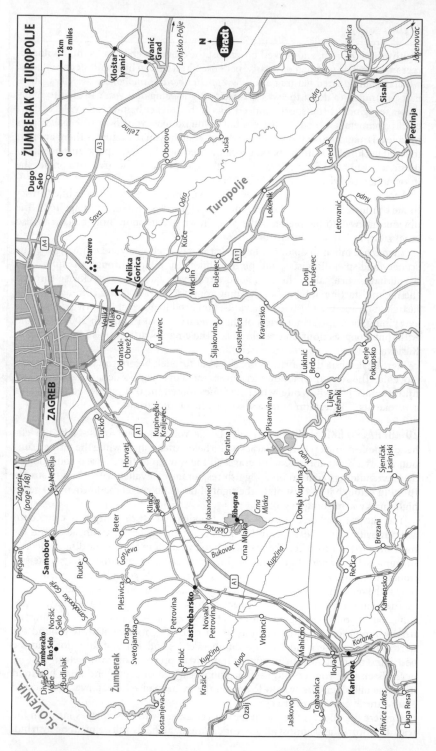

ŽUMBERAK & TUROPOLJE

There's an interesting educational trail up in the northwestern corner of the nature park called the **Trail of the Princes** (Staza Kneževa), which takes in prehistoric tumuli, an early Roman cemetery and ancient rock formations, and takes around two hours. The access point is on the main road winding its way west along the Slovenian border (if you'd turned right at the fork after Divlje Vode, rather than left), just before the village of Budinjak – look out for the 'Eko Centar' here (*www.pp-zumberak-samoborsko-gorje.hr*).

On your way down towards Pribić and Krašić, it's worth briefly stopping at **Medven Draga**, where you'll find a couple of excellent old watermills. You used to be able to stay at the manor here, but it doesn't look now as if it's still a going concern – if you're interested, contact the Zagreb County tourist office in Zagreb ahead of time (page 89).

PRIBIĆ The next place you come to after Medven Draga is Pribić – it's easy to overshoot, so look out for a Byzantine-looking church on the right-hand side of the main road, and park here.

You'd certainly never know it now, but Pribić was once an important Greek Catholic centre. Today all there's left to see is the outside of the church and the doomed 'castle' next door, which is gradually losing its battle with the encroaching vegetation.

The church itself sits on a tiny islet, reached over a diminutive bridge. The mosaics on the front are still lovely, kneeling angels flanking a Madonna and child among stylised lilies. Over the doorway is a fine carved coat of arms. Look more closely and you'll also see some fine sardonic architectural flourishes, in the form of nightmare gargoyles and a couple of carved eagles – which actually look more like cheesed-off parrots.

KRAŠIĆ From Pribić it's a short, straight run down to Krašić, the home town of Cardinal Stepinac (page 116), and the place where he was kept under house arrest during the final years of his life, after being released from Lepoglava. In front of the church there's a statue of the cardinal, while behind it, in the parish priest's house, his two-room flat has been preserved the way he left it. To visit, ring the bell and wait for a nun to let you in. There isn't much to see – the bed he died in, his writing desk, and quite a few photos of the Cardinal (looking worryingly like Vladimir Putin in some shots) – but it's a poignant place all the same. It would be churlish not to make a donation as you leave.

The church itself was rebuilt in 1913, and first impressions of the exterior are misleading – look out for the Jugendstil touches, with stern female friezes built into the walls. Inside, there's not a whole lot to comment on, though the vaulting is attractive, and the altar is positively understated – by Zagorje Baroque standards, anyway.

Unfortunately there's nowhere to stay in Krašić, and – in spite of plenty of cafés and a couple of shops – nothing much to eat, either.

OZALJ From Krašić it's a 10km dog-leg west to Ozalj (another turning that's easy to miss – the main road to Karlovac, which you don't want, goes southeast), where you'll find the best of the region's castles.

In a perfect situation, high up above the River Kupa, the medieval settlement here was owned by the Frankopans from 1398, and taken over by the Zrinskis in 1550 – the impressive entrance tower was commissioned by Juraj Zrinski in 1599. During the 18th century, the medieval village was converted into a defensive castle, with the only access being across the drawbridge – the stone bridge you walk across today was built in 1821. It's being restored, but is already a wonder, and has everything you'd want in a castle – towers, solid bastions, ramparts, and great views down to the river.

There's not much else to see in Ozalj, but down in the town, by the bridge across the Kupa, have a look at the neo-Gothic building by the water – it's actually a hydro-electric plant, built in 1908 and still operational today.

From Ozalj it's only about 15km to Karlovac (page 168), which is a great place to stop and spend the night. And from Karlovac, it's 20km northeast to the one-street town of Jastrebarsko (page 165), which is the access point for the Plešivica Wine Road, as well as the fish lakes and bird reserve at Crna Mlaka.

JASTREBARSKO AND THE TUROPOLJE

Halfway between Zagreb and Karlovac, the town of Jastrebarsko gives access to the Plešivica vineyards to the north, while to the south there's a special ornithological reserve, at Crna Mlaka. Further east you'll find the Turopolje, a region characterised by old villages and wooden houses and churches, bordered by the Vukomeričke Gorice hills to the west, the meandering Sava to the east, and bracketed by Zagreb to the northwest and Sisak to the southeast.

Exploring the region is harder without your own transport, although you can get to Jastrebarsko easily enough. Velika Mlaka and Velika Gorica in the Turopolje are both on Zagreb bus route #268, and local buses serve a handful of villages, albeit very infrequently. Cycling is a great way to explore the area – contact the Zagreb County Tourist Board for information on bike hire (*www.tzzz.hr*).

For a map of the area, see page 162.

PLEŠIVICA WINE ROAD The 25km road from Jastrebarsko to Samobor is among the most beautiful in Croatia, winding its way up into the hills and then down a long, pretty valley through the village of Rude to complete the circuit of the Žumberak.

The route up brings you through the lovely Plešivica wine-growing region, and it's well worth stopping in at one of the dozen or so vineyards for a tasting if you have time – and if you can persuade your designated driver it's a good thing, or indeed stay over (see listings below). Make a special effort to sample the local speciality, Portugizac Plešivica, a claret-like red, though personally I'm much keener on the crisp white Rajnski Rizling, which is also made here. The Samobor or Karlovac tourist offices should be able to furnish you with a copy of the useful Plešivička Vinska Cesta (Plešivica Wine Road) leaflet, which helps with navigation (though you also need a good road map as well – the best one by far is the map issued by the Jastrebarsko tourist board, if you can find it).

The Plešivica countryside is delightful. Apart from the vineyards, there are lots of fruit trees in the steep fields, and in summer every village has hay drying picturesquely on the charming Slovenian-style latticed hayricks – designed surely with aesthetics rather than practicality in mind. Wagons and trailers full of brightly coloured beehives are strategically placed to allow the bees access to the best of the local nectar, and romantic hilltop churches crest every horizon.

🏠 **Where to stay and eat** As well as those listed, see www.tzgj.hr/en for a list of other places to stay or eat along the wine road.

🏠 **Krešimir Režek** Plešivica 39; ☏ 01 629 4836; m 091 5646 240; www.rezek.hr. Down below

Ivančić, this winery not only does tastings but has a handful of nice rooms, with the same wonderful views you get from the restaurant. Krešimir himself is very friendly & helpful, but doesn't have much in the way of English; fortunately his excellent Rajnski Rizling does a great job of breaking down the language barrier. €€

🏠 **Vinska Kuća Jana** Prodin Dol; 📞01 628 7372; m 098 281 583; ⏱ 08.00–22.00 daily. If the setting isn't as picturesque as the other places listed, the welcome is just as warm, & you can stay in one of the 9 refurbished rooms upstairs. Wine tasting happens all year round, by appointment, while the restaurant specialises in grilled meat & freshly caught trout. It's a bit hard to find: from Prodin Dol go 2.1km south on a gravel track marked 'Klet Jana', then turn hard right at the sign 'Vinsko Kuća Jana' & continue up a few hundred metres. If you're coming from the south, look for a sign that says 'Klet Jana' to the right, then follow the gravel road uphill for 1.7km to the junction & turn left at the same sign. €€

🍴 **Restoran Ivančić** Plešivica 45; 📞01 629 3303; www.restoran-ivancic.hr; ⏱ 09.00–23.00

Tue–Sun, noon–20.00 Mon. Housed in a large green building that's easy to spot from below, & with a view to die for from the terrace, this local favourite has been serving up its own homemade specialities like *pršut*, dried sausage & cheese since 1999. Famous for its goulash, meat stews & hearty soups, it's also vegetarian-friendly, with cheeses, vegetable dishes, gourmet omelettes & the like. Extremely popular at w/ends – booking strongly recommended. €€

🍴 **Velimir Korak** Plešivica 34; 📞01 629 3088; m 098 410 345; www.vino-korak.hr; ⏱ noon–21.00 Fri, 09.00–21.00 Sat. Above Režek, near the church, this place also has a stunning view out over the neighbouring vineyards, & is one of the nicest places of all to try wines or the locally made rakija, including a fabulous *oskoruša* liqueur, made from the fruit of its service tree (*sorbus domestica*). A tasting area is set out in the garden under the shade of the lime trees, & there's also a family-run restaurant serving up tasty local specialities for groups, but only if you book in advance. €€

JASTREBARSKO Jastrebarsko itself is a bit of a commercial one-street town, spread out along the main road from Zagreb to Karlovac. It's worth checking in at the **tourist office** (*Strossmayerov trg 4;* 📞 *01 627 2940; www.tzgj.hr*), across the street from the bus station, for easily the best map of the area and details of the local vineyards, as well as the particulars of a growing number of agro-tourism offerings.

If you're stuck in town there's a moderately interesting **Town Museum** (*Gradski Muzej; Vladka Mačeka 1;* 📞*01 628 3991;* ⏱ *10.00–14.00 Mon/Tue/Fri, 14.00–18.00 Wed/Thu; 15kn*), and there's a pleasant **park** (walk west down Zrinsko Frankopanska, and across the stream) around the decaying fortress-like Erdödy Castle, built in the 16th century and apparently unmaintained ever since – though there are plans to renovate it someday.

🏠 **Where to stay and eat** There are a few private rooms in town (check with the tourist office, or see its website) and the **Pastuh Pivnica** (*Franje Tuđmana 31;* 📞*01 6283 642; www.pastuhpub.hr;* €€) has a few rooms. However, agro-tourism is really the way to go here, and there are two very nice options just outside town.

🏠 **Ciban Family Guesthouse** (6 dbls) Obiteljsko gospodarstvo Ciban; Pavlovčani 12c; m 098 365 986. This beautifully restored wooden home is set among lovely rolling vineyards, with nice rooms & delicious food, including local specialities such as roast duck with *mlinci* – & of course its own wine. To get there, head

north from town towards Zdihovo & turn right. €€€

🏠 **Kolarić** (16 rooms) Hrastje Plešivičko 24; m 098 9827 245, 098 227 678; www.kolaric-vina. hr. This vineyard just north of town on the road to Ivančići has nice rooms as well as a restaurant & wine tasting. €€€

CRNA MLAKA Southeast, across the motorway, is Crna Mlaka (literally Black Marsh). The area was originally conceived as a vast fish farm by the Austro-Hungarians at the end of the 19th century, complete with a narrow-gauge railway running up to join the main line to Zagreb, and a mansion, endearingly named Ribograd ('fish city'). The railway's long disused, and Ribograd's falling apart, but Crna Mlaka lives on as a **bird sanctuary** and it's now home to all sorts of rare and endangered species, including herons in abundance, and highly secretive black storks, who, unlike their white compatriots, prefer to stay in the woods, well away from people. There's talk of the lakes being drained to make way for a golf course, but there's no sign of one yet. It's on private land so you'll need to ask permission to visit – contact the tourist office in Jastrebarsko (❋ *01 627 2940*).

To reach Crna Mlaka, turn left immediately after paying the toll off the motorway (or right immediately before reaching it, if you're coming from Jastrebarsko), and drive 7km down gravel tracks (turn left after 5km, at the sign saying 'IHOR Crna Mlaka'), keeping your eyes peeled for herons. If you're lucky, the restaurant, specialising unsurprisingly in freshwater fish, will be open (it seems unable to make up its mind whether or not it's actually a going concern), but even if it's not, it's great to explore the unmarked gravel tracks which make for pleasant, undisturbed walking around the huge ponds.

THE TUROPOLJE The region southeast of Zagreb along the west bank of the Sava is known as the Turopolje, and is worth passing through on your way to Lonjsko Polje (page 177). Once Zagreb's suburbs have petered out, you'll find old villages and timber churches, and wooden staircases leading up the outside of houses to the upper quarters. If you're planning on exploring the region in any detail – and it's well worth doing so – get maps and information ahead of time from the friendly and helpful Zagreb County tourist office in Zagreb (page 89 for details).

In **Velika Gorica**, the de facto capital of the region, it's well worth stopping in at the excellent **Museum of the Turopolje** (*Muzej Turopolje; Trg kralja Tomislava 1;* ❋*01 622 1325; www.muzej-turopolja.hr;* ⊕ *09.00–17.30 Tue–Fri, 10.00–13.00 Sat/Sun; 10kn*). The museum is situated in a nice pastel building on the main street – because of Velika Gorica's one-way system, this is actually the road back towards Zagreb – and contains a small art gallery downstairs and the main museum upstairs. The collection is the usual hotchpotch of everything from ethnographic exhibits to artefacts and images that are historically important to the region. Check out the mammoth tusks and molar, and a small room of naïve art, and in particular the bitter 1977 work by Dragutin Tombetaš, entitled *Gastarbeiter in Öl* (immigrant workers in a sardine can).

If you're into Roman excavations, then you may want to head 9km northeast of Velika Gorica, almost as far as the Sava River, to **Šćitarevo**, which was the former 4th-century Roman town of **Andautonia**. The excavations are quite extensive, but you need to know your stuff to get the most out of the site. For details on accommodation and the wooden churches of Turopolje (page 167) contact the helpful Velika Gorica **tourist office** (*Kurilovečka 2;* ❋ *01 622 1666; www.tzvg.hr*).

🏠 **Where to stay and eat** If you want to stay in Velika Gorica, there are a handful of options, as well as one in Sisak:

🏠 **Hotel Pleso** (27 rooms) Mikulčićeva 7a; ❋01 625 3600; www.hotel-pleso.hr. Formerly known as the Garni. The rooms are perhaps a bit functional for the price, but the swimming pool & sauna compensate. €€€€
🏠 **Hotel Panonija** (42 rooms) Sisak; ❋044 515 600; www.hotel-panonija.hr. Three blocks

back from the river & 5mins south of the bus & train stations, this has spacious dbls. Make sure you ask for a renovated room, however, as the hotel served as refugee accommodation during the homeland war. €€€
🏠 **Pleška Rooms & Buffet** (4 rooms) Pleška 46; ❋01 626 5277; www.pleska.hr. Small

guesthouse & buffet with simple rooms, sgl, dbl & trpls; much better value than the Hotel Pleso. On the north side of town, towards the airport. €€

🏠 **Prenoćiške Ikar** (4 rooms) Klarići 46; ☎01 622 3302. Another popular place, out of town near the airport. €€

🏠 **Rooms Pleso** (4 rooms) V Nazor 8; ☎01 626 5048; www.rooms-pleso.com. Simple, good-value rooms just 5mins' walk to the airport. €€

✗ **Turopolje** Trg Kralja Krešimira IV 29; ⏰ 08.00–23.00 daily. Good-value local favourite on a corner near the bus station, with welcoming smiles & vast portions. €€

What to see and do The Turopolje is most famous for its old **wooden churches**, of which more than a dozen remain – though some of them are spectacularly hard to find – some dating from the 17th century. If you see only one, make it **St Barbara's**, which is incongruous among the suburban houses of **Velika Mlaka**, off to the left, just before you get to Pleso Airport. The all-wooden church was originally built in 1642, and the decorative work inside covers every available surface. Most interesting of all is the double altarpiece, which folds out to reveal further religious scenes behind. If the church is closed – which it is, usually – ask for Ljubica Lacković, who has a key (and will expect you to make a donation), or contact the Velika Gorica tourist office.

Another wooden church that is easy to see is the **Chapel of the Wounded Jesus**, which you'll have noticed if you arrived by plane, as it's right by Pleso Airport. Less accessible altogether, and not really worth the detour unless restoration work has advanced substantially, is the **Chapel of St John the Baptist**, in **Buševec**, 8km southeast of Velika Gorica, on the road to Sisak. If you're in the area, however, it is worth turning off the main road to the village of **Mraclin**, which still has quite a few original Turopolje wooden houses, and retains much more of a 19th-century than 21st-century feel.

Further south, and lost in the hills above the River Kupa, are several more wooden churches worth a look. The first, in a wonderful hilltop location, is the **Chapel of Sts Peter and Paul**, at **Cerje Pokupsko**, about 15km southwest of Buševec. The church looks like it could be centuries old, but the date on the front says 1932. It's also worth stopping to see the late-19th-century **Chapel of St Anthony of Padova** at **Gustelnica** – a comparatively tall, narrow building, which differs in style from most of the other Turopolje churches since it was not built by local craftsmen, and hiding a beautifully painted interior. The next, the little **Chapel of St George**, at **Lijevi Štefanki**, is one of the oldest churches, which was built at another location in 1677 and then moved here in 1704 – it's quite hard to find, however: turn left down a track about 5km west of Cerje Pokupsko, on a sharp right-hand bend, on the road to Donja Kupčina. The key is held at the farmhouse next door, and it's well worth making the effort as the interior is beautifully painted. Finally, if you've come this far, the **Chapel of St John the Baptist**, at **Lukinić Brdo**, has been well renovated (following damage in the homeland war) and makes a great spot for a picnic, with a table – just below the cemetery containing generation after generation of the same family names – offering fine views out over rolling forested hills.

At the western extremity of the region – on the road to Karlovac, and close to Crna Mlaka (pages 165–6), is the small, pretty town of **Donja Kupčina**. It's a favourite nesting spot for storks (see also Lonjsko Polje, below), and there's a small open-air **Ethnographic Museum** (*Etnografski Muzej; www.pisarovina.hr/muzej;* ⏰ *09.00–13.00 Tue–Fri, 10.00–14.00 Sat; 10kn*), which gives you a good insight into how village life was lived here until relatively recent times. To visit officially, you need to contact the assistant restorer, Zoran Petričić (☎ *01 629 1111*) or the

4

Pisarovina tourist office (✆01 629 1197), and make an appointment – though on the day we were there you could wander round happily enough on your own.

The southeastern end of the Turopolje – marked by the first bridge across the Sava since Zagreb – is dominated by the industrial town of **Sisak**, the northern gateway to the Lonjsko Polje (pages 177–9). It's quick and easy to get to from Zagreb by bus and train (around an hour either way, slightly longer on the train). The solid **medieval castle** on the river doesn't entirely compensate for the huge oil refinery here, or the complete absence of road directions. There's a nice riverside walk, watched over a sculpture of the seated figure of poet A G Matoš, a copy of the one in Zagreb's Upper Town. If you fancy staying here, there's the no-nonsense five-storey **Hotel Panonija** (page 166), and the **tourist office** (*Rimska bb;* ✆*044 522 655; www.sisakturist.com*) has information on private rooms.

KARLOVAC

Most people never see more of Karlovac than the big town suburbs and housing blocks on the outskirts as they speed past on the motorway, but dig a little deeper and you'll find a wonderful provincial old town and somewhere great to stay.

Karlovac (originally Carlstadt) was created from nothing, by the Austro-Hungarians, as a defence against the Turks, with the foundations being laid on 13 July 1579. A Renaissance six-pointed star defined the limits of the town, and its moats were kept well supplied with water by the citadel's location, between the Kupa and Korana rivers.

As the Turkish threat receded, Karlovac grew in size and importance – notwithstanding a catastrophic fire in 1692 that razed it to the ground – and became a wealthy and influential provincial capital. Baroque houses and palaces sprang up, and the town walls were pulled down. The shape of the old town is still clearly defined, however, with the moats and earthworks now forming a near-continuous circuit of lovely parks and gardens around the former citadel, or Zvijezda (star).

Karlovac's great claim to fame is its local brewery, one of Croatia's first, which produces the excellent, and deservedly popular beer, Karlovačko Pivo, which you'll see all over the country.

GETTING THERE AND AROUND Getting to Karlovac is easy – it's under an hour from Zagreb, and both buses and trains run pretty much every half hour. There are also good onward connections to Rijeka and Zadar.

The **bus** station is less than 10 minutes southwest of the old town – head up the main north–south axis, Prilaz Vjećeslava Holjevca, and then turn right along Kralja Tomislava, which takes you all the way in. The **train** station is on the other side of the River Kupa, a kilometre north, also on Prilaz Vjećeslava Holjevca. Just east of the main bridge is the central district where you'll find the Hotel Carlstadt and the **tourist office** (*Petra Zrinskog 3;* ✆*047 615 115; www.karlovac-touristinfo.hr*), with the old town just behind it, away from the Kupa, to the southeast. The tourist office has good maps and can help you find a private room, at around €30 for doubles. It also has an excellent set of maps aimed at cyclists who want to pedal round Karlovac county, and is a keen participant in the 'Bike & Bed' initiative (page 52).

 WHERE TO STAY *Map, page 169*
Karlovac has a handful of good places to stay, our favourites of which are the Korana-Srakovčić and the newly opened Hostel Na Putu. There's also a nice campsite, 15km south of town – see page 172 for details:

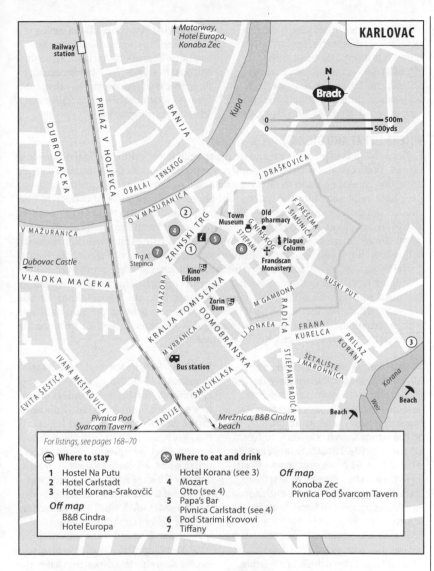

KARLOVAC

↑ Motorway,
Hotel Europa,
Konaba Zec

Railway
station

N

Bradt

0 _____ 500m
0 _____ 500yds

PRILAZ V HOLJEVCA

BANIJA

DUBROVAČKA

Kupa

J DRAŠKOVIĆA

OBALA I TRNSKOG

O V MAŽURANIĆA

V MAŽURANIĆA

ZRINSKI TRG

Town
Museum

Old
pharmacy

F PRESEMA

I ŠIMUNIĆA

GNINSKOG

STJEPANA

Plague
Column

Franciscan
Monastery

2

4

i

5

1

6

7

Trg A
Stepinca

Dubovac Castle

VLADKA MAČEKA

Kino
Edison

V NAZORA

KRALJA TOMISLAVA

DOMOBRANSKA

Zorin
Dom

M GAMBONA

RADIĆA

RUSKI PUT

FRANA
KURELCA

PRILAZ
KORANI

3

M VRBANIĆA

LJ JONKEA

ŠETALIŠTE
J MAROHNIĆA

Korana

IVANA MEŠTROVIĆA

EVITA ŠESTIĆA

Bus station

SMIČIKLASA

STJEPANA RADIĆA

Weir

Beach

Beach

TADIJE

Pivnica Pod
Švarcom Tavern

Mrežnica, B&B Cindra,
beach

Beach

For listings, see pages 168–70

🛏 **Where to stay**

1 Hostel Na Putu
2 Hotel Carlstadt
3 Hotel Korana-Srakovčić

Off map
  B&B Cindra
  Hotel Europa

✕ **Where to eat and drink**

  Hotel Korana (see 3)
4 Mozart
  Otto (see 4)
5 Papa's Bar
  Pivnica Carlstadt (see 4)
6 Pod Starimi Krovovi
7 Tiffany

Off map
  Konoba Zec
  Pivnica Pod Švarcom Tavern

Inland Croatia   KARLOVAC

4

🏠 **Hotel Europa** (33 rooms) Banija 161;
📞047 609 666; www.hotel-europa.com.hr.
Situated out by the motorway junction, this is a
convenient stopover if you have your own car &
you're taking a break on your way to or from the
coast, but it's not well located if you're relying on
public transport & planning on walking round
town. It's also a bit pricey for what it is. €€€€

🏠 **Hotel Korana-Srakovčić** (15 dbls, 3 suites)
Perivoj Josipa Vrbanića 8; 📞047 609 090; e info@
hotelkorana.hr; www.hotelkorana.hr. An excellent
4-star establishment in a gracious building on the

banks of the River Korana, situated in a lovely park,
about 10mins' walk southeast from the Korzo. The
rooms are tastefully furnished; the more expensive
ones have balconies, & there's a wonderful suite.
There's a nice dining room & a delightful terrace
overlooking the river, & an excellent restaurant
(page 170). The hotel also does bike hire. €€€€

🏠 **Hotel Carlstadt** (9 sgls, 25 dbls, 3 tpls, 3
suites) Vraniczanyeva 1; 📞047 611 111; www.
carlstadt.hr. Situated handily right across the
street from the tourist office, 1st-rate dbls come
with full facilities & include a substantial buffet

169

b/fast. It's exceptionally good value, & with such easy transport connections to Zagreb it's a viable alternative to staying in the capital. €€€

🏠 **B&B Cindra** (2 rooms) Rakavac 50; m 095 8855 962; http://bnbcindra.wix.com/home. Small, family-run B&B, 10mins walk south of the old town centre on the banks of the Korana. AC €10 extra. €€€

🏠 **Hostel Na Putu** (20 beds) Petra Zrinskog 17; ☏ 047 296 235; www.hostelnaputu.com. New hostel in the old town – the first in Karlovac – with beds going for €15 in 5-, 7- & 8-bed dorms during the summer, slightly less in winter. AC, lockers, communal kitchen, free Wi-Fi & secure cycle parking. Ask about local rafting tours. €

✖ WHERE TO EAT AND DRINK *Map, page 169*

Karlovac has lots of places to eat and drink, though fewer within the 'star' than you'd expect. That's because when the old town was bombed out in the homeland war, all the action moved up on to the Korzo, and much of it remains there, though things have now crept back into the quieter old town. The three cafés next door to one another opposite the tourist office – **Pivnica Carlstadt**, **Mozart** and **Otto** – tend to be the busiest places, which is a bit of a shame as they're on the main road through town, though there is also a lovely fountain with a pair of mermaids attractively sitting in it. But if you head into the old town, there are plenty of cafés/bars.

Karlovac also has an annual **beer festival**, which takes place on the last Friday of August (and goes well into Saturday, as you'd expect). This used to happen in the main square, with the central fountain converted into a beer pump for the occasion, which was lots of fun, but the festival is now held on the Korana River, with international folklore performances and – of course – lots of drinking. If you're in the area, it's definitely not to be missed.

✖ **Hotel Korana** Perivoj Josipa Vrbanića 8; ☏ 047 609 090; ⏰ 08.00–midnight daily. The smartest place to eat in town in the hotel of the same name. Serves up specialities such as quail – though there's plenty for vegetarians too. €€€

✖ **Pod Starimi Krovovi** Radićeva 8–10; ☏ 047 615 420; ⏰ 09.00–22.00 daily. Has a nice location in the old town, & a largish, quiet terrace – though the service was a bit sniffy when we were there. The food's good value, as it's actually a training establishment for cooks, etc (hopefully not for waiters). €€€

✖ **Konoba Zec** Bogovićeva 2; ⏰ 07.00–midnight daily. Grills, goulash, pizza from a wood-fired oven & other dishes in a rustic setting. €€€–€€

✖ **Pivnica Pod Švarcom Tavern** Senjska 63; ⏰ 07.00–23.00 daily. Specialising in grilled meat & steaks (& beer, of course). Has a children's play area. €€€–€€

✖ **Tiffany** Dr Vladko Macek 6/1; ☏ 047 614 666; ⏰ summer 07.00–23.00 daily, winter 07.00–22.00 daily. The author's absolute favourite in town (which curiously doesn't do breakfast) is this busy, cheap & cheerful pizzeria with a wood-fired oven that's now expanded its menu to include grills & barbecue dishes. The *mala* pizza is a good size, the *velika* is what it says (large) & the monster really is a meal for 6. Don't be put off by the surroundings – it's located down a slot to the left-hand side of the supermarket, which is itself down the street to the left of the Hotel Carlstadt. €€€–€€

♀ **Papa's Bar** Šetalište Dr Franje Tuđmana 1; ⏰ 07.00–midnight Mon–Sat, 08.00–midnight Sun. The nicest place for a drink in town is this shameless copy of Hemingway (in Zagreb, Dubrovnik and elsewhere) without the pretension. Formerly the Gradska Kavana, it's in a perfect location with a big terrace & nice teak furniture overlooking the park. It's not cheap, but it's groovy, cheerful, & well worth paying for.

WHAT TO SEE AND DO The old town is centred on the big main square, Trg Bana Jelačića, which is still rather forlorn and abandoned following the damage sustained in the 1991 war. There's talk of one of the big buildings here being turned into a hotel, which would liven the place up – even a café terrace would help – but for the time being it's still only talk.

Check out the **Plague Column** on the west side of the square, dating from 1691, and then move smartly on to the **Franciscan Monastery and Holy Trinity Church** (Franjevački samostan i Sveto Trojstvo), on the corner. Here you'll find fine Baroque altars and a series of dramatic, neck-cricking, 18th-century frescoes across the ceiling – why they were painted alternately upside down and the right way up is anyone's guess.

Heading north out of the square towards the Kupa River you'll see an old **pharmacy**, called Crnom Orla (the black eagle), which is worth stopping in at as it retains most of its original 1726 fittings. The street leads through to the elegant Trg Strossmayer, where you'll find some vestigial ruins from Karlovac's first-ever church, as well as the **Town Museum** (*Gradski Muzej; Strossmayerov trg 7;* \ *047 615 980; www.gmk.hr;* ⊕ *08.00–16.00 Tue/Thu/Fri, 08.00–19.00 Wed, 10.00–noon Sat/Sun; 10kn*), housed in a former Frankopan summer residence.

The museum is a fascinating collection of everything from fossils to Roman fragments to local art to peasant costumes to civic souvenirs – it's just a pity that the captions are in Croatian only, which can make it a bit hard to follow. In the middle of the collection there's a scale model of how Karlovac used to look, and there are some old pictures of other castles in the Žumberak region. There are also some great photographs of people hauling grain barges along the river, along with the harnesses they used to do it – when the railway came along, Karlovac lost one of its main sources of wealth.

You'll notice a couple of works by the local artist Vjekoslav Karas (1821–58). Recognised for his ready talent with a brush, Karas was sent to Florence in 1838 to study, and spent a decade in Italy perfecting his craft before returning home to his native Karlovac. Unfortunately many of his paintings have been lost, and – given that he rarely signed his work, and experimented with many different styles – there's a big problem of attribution. Some of the works are way ahead of their time, wonderfully insightful portraits that are practically Modernist, while others are embarrassingly amateurish, perhaps reflecting Karas's poor state of mental health. After a failed suicide attempt in Đakovo, where he was the guest of Bishop Strossmayer (a keen art collector), Karas successfully drowned himself in the Korana River at Karlovac, aged just 37. If you're interested in seeing more of his work, there's a whole gallery in an annexe in the new town. Staff at the museum will be happy to point you in the right direction, and may even accompany you there.

The last room of the museum features an excellent collection of peasant costumes and crafts, from pottery and weaving to embroidery and basket-work.

Continuing towards the Korzo and the Korana River, it's well worth taking a turn around the parks that were formerly the **walls and moats** of the old citadel – allow a half hour or so for the full circuit.

Heading anticlockwise, the first thing you'll see is a small pink *glorietta*, primarily dedicated to Croatia's fallen in World War I, and the vast neoclassical façade of the Karlovac bank. Heading west, you'll see a large, graffiti-strewn, concrete plinth, which – until its destruction by the locals in the homeland war – was the base of a huge anti-fascist monument. A little further on you'll see **Kino Edison** (*Šetalište dr. Franje Tuđmana 13;* 🅵 *Kino Edison*), which was Croatia's first cinema. It's still operational, and used as a concert venue as well as for the occasional film showing.

Beyond the cinema is Karlovac's theatre, the endearing **Zorin Dom**, which was opened in 1892, and has a small version of the Ivan Meštrović masterpiece, the *History of the Croats* (page 126).

If you have time, it's also well worth visiting **Dubovac Castle** (\ *City Museum; 047 615 980;* ⊕ *Apr–Sep 16.00–20.00 Tue–Fri, 10.00–18.00 Sat, 16.00–19.00 Sun; if* *visiting Oct–Mar, call the City Museum at least a day in advance; 10kn*), up on the hill 2km west of town (it's a short drive or a half-hour walk). The castle dates from 1339 (or possibly even earlier), and was a Frankopan and then Zrinski stronghold right through to the beginning of the 19th century, when it was taken over by the French, who added crenellations to make it look more appealingly medieval (there's a picture in the town museum of what this looked like). Fortunately, it recovered its genuinely medieval look in the 20th century, and you get a great view out over the town from the top of the tower – check out the excellent relief map, which shows all the different castles and rivers in the area. And if you're here in May, don't miss out on the annual medieval fair that takes place.

Finally, if you're hot and bothered – and it certainly can be baking here – head down to the Korana River to the wonderful **beach**, just 10 minutes from the old town centre; you can bathe in the weir here, which is excellent, or head out to less busy beaches on the Mrežnica River, 3km south of town.

SOUTH OF KARLOVAC

Southwest of Karlovac, on the road to Ogulin and Senj, you pass through **Duga Resa**, which isn't much to write home about, but there is a nice campsite, signed **Autokamp Slapić** (*047 854 754 Apr–Oct;**047 854 700 Oct–Apr; www.campslapic. hr;* €) south of town, just across the River Mrežnica (on an old wooden bridge) from Belavići train station. There's canoeing and safe swimming here, and it's an idyllic spot for families.

Another few kilometres down the main road brings you to **Zvečaj**, which wouldn't necessarily merit a mention here, were it not for the **Zeleni Kut** restaurant (*047 866 100; www.zeleni-kut-puskaric.hr;* ⊕ *09.00–23.00 daily;* €€), which also has a few rooms upstairs as part of the 'Bike & Bed' scheme (€€). On a lovely terrace overlooking the river, the restaurant serves up heaps of freshwater fish, including *pastrva* (trout), *som* (catfish), *smuđ* (zander) and *štuka* (pike), at around 150kn/kg. It can also organise rafting and canoeing trips for you. (For information on Ogulin, Klek and Bjelolasica, further southwest in this direction, turn to page 242.)

Heading south rather than southwest of Karlovac, towards the Plitvice Lakes, brings you (after about 50km, and 20km short of the lakes) to the former Austro-Hungarian garrison town of **Slunj**. Badly damaged during the war of the 1990s, the town's churches at least have now been fully restored, along with the main reason for coming here, the **Rastoke Mills**.

Built to take advantage of the waterfalls where the Slunjčica River drops into the Korana, some of the watermills are now back in working order and a stroll around them is a delight. If you want to swim make sure you choose the Korana, not the Slunjčica – the former warms up to a balmy 28°C in summer, while the latter never rises above a chilly 14°C. If it's 'first-class trouts' you're fishing for, however, then the Slunjčica is your man.

If you want to stay in the area, there's the **Mirjana Rastoke Hotel** (*Donji Nikšić 101;**047 787 205; www.mirjana-rastoke.com;* €€), which also arranges excursions, a few kilometres back along the road towards Karlovac.

PLITVICE LAKES NATIONAL PARK

Croatia's best-known and most-visited natural attraction – and a UNESCO World Heritage Site since 1979 – is the Plitvice Lakes National Park (*053 751 015; www. np-plitvicka-jezera.hr;* ⊕ *all year 07.00–20.00 daily*). Covering a total of nearly

300km², the prize here is 16 lakes, falling from one to the next in a series of gushing waterfalls. The lakes are set in deep forests still populated by bears, wolves and wild boar, and are all the more unusual for being found in the middle of a typically dry karst region, where surface water is extremely rare.

The national park has been very carefully exploited, and although it can get busy – 600,000 people come annually, averaging around 4,000 people a day in the summer months – the crowds are rarely intolerable. Traffic is encouraged round one-way systems to avoid congestion, and the routes are often carried along attractive wooden walkways serving the dual purpose of avoiding erosion and allowing people to walk over, under, across and alongside the waterfalls, and around the lakes.

The whole park ranges in altitude from 380m to 1,280m, but the lakes are all situated between 502m and 637m, with the largest single waterfall (Veliki Slap) being nearly 70m tall. The combination of running water and altitude makes the park wonderfully refreshing almost all through the summer, although it can be cold and gloomy – not to mention frozen solid – in winter (but you'll have the place largely to yourself, and the waterfalls turn into curtains of icicles). April and October are the best times to visit – the former with the water flow increased by melting snows, and the latter with the deciduous woods enriched with fabulous autumn colours.

Plitvice was occupied by the Serbs from 1991 to 1995, and the staff and management became refugees. On their return, they found the park mercifully undamaged ecologically, although the park offices and the hotels were totally unusable. Since then, the hotels and other facilities have been entirely rebuilt, and the park today is better than ever.

GETTING THERE AND AWAY Plitvice is situated a little over halfway down the main road from Zagreb to Zadar. Regular buses run from both, and also up from Split. The park has two entrances, wittily called Ulaz 1 and Ulaz 2.

In theory Ulaz 1 (the northern entrance) serves the lower lakes, while Ulaz 2 (the southern entrance) is the access point for the upper ones, but for most people Ulaz 2 is the more useful. It's here that you'll find most of the infrastructure, including the three hotels, the tourist office with access to private accommodation, a post office, a shop and a self-service restaurant – and it's in fact within easy reach of both the upper and lower lakes.

If you don't have your own transport, then leaving the park may be more difficult than arriving. Regular buses pass through on their way to Zadar, Zagreb and Split, but if these are full, or the driver doesn't like the cut of your jib, they have a habit of cruising right on past. There isn't much you can do to improve this situation, but earlier buses do seem to be better than ones later in the day.

At the tourist office you can buy a map and obtain multi-lingual information on the park. Beside the office there's a small and slightly overpriced supermarket, and nearby there's an open-air grill bar (with trick bitumen on the seats when I was last here, just waiting to stain your clothes). If you have your own car, there's more than adequate parking at both entrances.

ENTRANCE FEES Entry to the national park now costs a whopping 180kn in July/August falling to 110kn in April to June and just 55kn in winter, though the money is well spent, going towards the park's upkeep and protection. If you're here for more than one day, make sure you get a two-day ticket (280kn/180kn/90kn). Children under 7 go free. On the ticket is a wonderful series of hieroglyphs explaining the

PLITVICE LAKES NATIONAL PARK

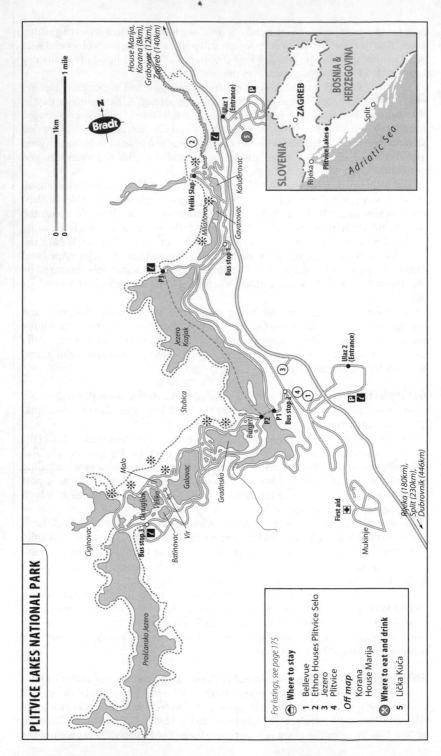

BOSNIA & HERZEGOVINA

SLOVENIA

ZAGREB

Rijeka

Plitvice Lakes

Split

Adriatic Sea

House Marija, Korana (8km), Graboyac (12km), Zagreb (140km)

Ulaz 1 (Entrance)

Kaluđerovac

Veliki Slap

Milǰanovac

Gavanovac

Bus stop 1

P3

Jezero Kozjak

Stubica

Bus stop 2

P2 P1

Burget

Ulaz 2 (Entrance)

Malo

Galovac

Gradinsko

Rijeka (180km), Split (230km), Dubrovnik (446km)

First aid

Mukinje

Ciginovac

Okrugljak

Veliki

Vir

Batinovac

Bus stop 3

Prošćansko Jezero

1km

1 mile

Bradt

For listings, see page 175

Where to stay
1 Bellevue
2 Ethno Houses Plitvice Selo
3 Jezero
4 Plitvice

Off map
Korana
House Marija

Where to eat and drink
5 Lička Kuća

park rules, most of which go without saying: don't pick flowers, make fires, engrave trees, steal nests or break stalactites. Some of the others aren't so obvious: don't leave the paths, sleep rough, go paddling in the lakes or dance wildly around to the sound of your boom-box. Ticket sales close about four hours before the park closes.

🏠 WHERE TO STAY *Map, page 174*

There are three **hotels** in the park, the **Bellevue** (€€€), the **Plitvice** (€€€€) and the **Jezero** (€€€€) (*central reservations for all three, as well as tourist information & private rooms on* ✆ *053 751 015*), with prices rising slightly and quality rising significantly as you move up the scale. Expect to pay €78 for the cheapest double at the Bellevue off season, or €120 for the cheapest double at the Jezero in the middle of summer. Book way, way ahead, if you want to stay here, as even off season all three tend to draw the conference crowd. If you have your own wheels there's also the Grabovac (*same contact details as above;* €€€) 12km up the road towards Zagreb, which has doubles in season for €70.

Alternatively you can stay at **Ethno Houses Plitvice Selo** (*Plitvica Selo 66/1;* ✆ *091 123 4175; http://ethnoplitvice.com;* €€€€) in Plitvica village, on the north side of the lakes – though prices for a double are slightly more than a room at Hotel Jezero.

Private rooms are widely available, but often far away, which can be a problem if you don't have your own transport. Prices – expect to pay €35–70 for a double – depend much more on location than quality, which is universally fine. The room the author stayed in was at the upper end of the range but only a couple of kilometres from Ulaz 2; cheaper rooms can be anything up to 15km away. **House Marija** (*2 rooms, 1 apt; Selište Drežničko 8;* m *098 1821 576; www.house-marija.com;* €€€) is one of the closer places, in the village of Selište Drežničko. There's a list of private rooms on the national park website.

Camping is a problem if you don't have your own wheels – the nearest campsite is **Korana** (✆ *053 751 888*), 8km north of Ulaz 1, which charges €23 for two adults with a tent and car, and €44 for a bungalow including breakfast. Another campsite, the Borje, is on the road heading south (✆ *053 751 790*).

✕ WHERE TO EAT AND DRINK *Map, page 174*

For eating, your options are fairly limited. There's a good-value self-service restaurant at Ulaz 2, though it's not always open in the evening. The capacious and excellent **Lička Kuća** restaurant (*Ulaz 1;* ⊕ *11.00–23.00 daily;* €€€) reopened in 2015 after a fire a couple of years ago – it serves some fine local specialities (the lamb here is first rate). Otherwise the hotels all have restaurants but they may be full with their own residents. If you do get in at the Jezero's restaurant, downstairs from reception – the tagliatelle with truffles is truly excellent. Otherwise you can pick up picnic food at the mini-market at Ulaz 2.

WHAT TO SEE AND DO The lakes were created and are maintained by their unusual vegetation – the mosses, algae and other freshwater plants absorb the calcium in the water and then deposit it as calciferous mud. This can be seen clearly as a white coating on submerged tree trunks and roots in the smaller lakes. The water flow causes this calciferous mud to be carried to the lips of the lakes, and deposited there, eventually solidifying as travertine (*tufa*), with the long-term effect that the whole lake system is gradually gaining altitude.

In the short term, the effect is that lots of people are keen to come and see Plitvice, and life has been organised so that this is as easy as possible – to the extent that there's a panoramic train ride, a couple of boats on one of the largest lakes, and a series of itineraries from 1 to 10 hours long that take in the most scenic parts of the park.

After the initial impression of being almost too looked after has worn off, it tends to be replaced by something akin to euphoria – the lakes really are beautiful, after all, and you'd have to be very determined not to be impressed by that much moving water. You can even begin to see why people who live in these conditions start believing in water gods.

Each of the lakes seems to be a different colour, ranging from turquoise to emerald through every blue and green you could imagine. In places the lakes seem as still and reflective as a cathedral, elsewhere they run away fast, frothing through steep gullies and shooting out from fissures in the rock. The magical noise of falling water drowns out even the shrillest of small children. On the less frequented paths it's easy to imagine the bears and wolves, as you walk across a deeply shaded bed of leaves, crunching underfoot.

In a perfect world you'd have at least two full days (ie: three nights) to explore the whole park, but you can get a good impression of it all in a single day. Even if you're on an excursion, up from the coast or down from Zagreb, and you have only a couple of hours here, you won't regret it. Either way, try to start as early as possible, to avoid the worst of the crowds.

Apart from the marked itineraries, which lead you round the best-known sights, there are many other **paths** open to the public in the national park, though access to them is quietly discouraged by the park management, as there have been incidents of people despoiling nature off the beaten track. If you are wandering away from the marked trails, be ecologically friendly and stay on the paths.

If you're doing any serious walking – or even if you're just interested – the park publishes an excellent 1:50,000 scale map of the area, including all the footpaths, with a 1:25,000 scale bird's-eye view of the lakes themselves on the reverse, along with all sorts of useful information about the lakes' relative altitudes etc. With the aid of this you can easily find a couple of days' walking in the area, none of which is too strenuous.

It's inadvisable, however, to be in the wilds after nightfall – the bears and wolves avoid the main paths and the crowds, but they do patrol at night. The wolves are normally only seen in winter, but a hungry bear, or one that thinks you're too close to its cubs, may be inquisitive.

There have been no incidents in recent years involving tourists, but it was here, on 16 April 1988 (a few days before my first-ever visit to the lakes), that a national park warden was killed by a bear. The poor animal was apparently confused by a storm, and anxious to protect its cub, when it was surprised by the unfortunate warden. Being a Serb, he could probably be counted as the first victim in the Serbo-Croat war, which actually took off here in Plitvice, when the Serbs took over the management offices in March 1991.

Fortunately, the warden is the only recorded human fatality from a Croatian bear in more than 50 years, but local people remain understandably cautious, and discourage the idea of camping out in the woods (which is illegal, anyway). Walk in the daytime and stay on the paths marked on the maps and you'll be quite safe. There are absolutely no wild animals round here that would attack in the daytime unless seriously provoked.

If you're in Plitvice on the last Sunday of May there's a **folk wedding** held by Veliki Slap. This was once no doubt a highly traditional affair, but now has the air of being staged for the tourists. Nonetheless, even the most cynical visitor should be impressed by the traditional dress, the falling water all but drowning out the songs, and the folk dancing and festivities held afterwards.

Downstream from Sisak, the River Sava meanders slowly through the great marshy swamplands of the Lonjsko Polje. Prone to frequent flooding (the Sava can rise by up to 10m) and full of fish, the area is hugely popular with migrating birds, and especially with storks. The reedy shores of the oxbow lakes make for excellent nesting grounds for wading birds such as white egrets, grey herons and spoonbills.

Spotted Turopolje pigs root through the flooded oak forests (or at least they once did – most of the pigs you see now are not purebreds, which are increasingly rare), while dark, chunky Posavina horses – protected, and seen only in this region – graze in the summer pastures. Rustic villages preserve traditional oak houses, with barns on the ground floor and external wooden stairs leading to the living accommodation upstairs. It's a rare chance to see a landscape that was once common across central Europe, and is on the tentative list of UNESCO World Heritage Sites.

On top of many of the houses in the area, and sometimes on platforms on telegraph poles, you'll see big, tatty storks' nests, and (if you're here between April and August) plenty of big, tatty storks, too. They're most endearing. The storks arrive here in spring, and lay three to five eggs per couple, with both parents sharing the month-long incubation duty. The chicks then spend around two months in the nest, and if you're here in May or June you'll see lots of activity going on, with the young growing fast and permanently hungry, and one of the parents always on the move, looking for food.

During August and September, the storks ship out, using the eastern migration path through Turkey and the Middle East, and then along the Nile to central Africa, with some even ending up in South Africa every year.

Lonjsko Polje (*www.pp-lonjsko-polje.hr*) was declared a nature park in 1990, but you wouldn't necessarily know it – apart from the uninformative sign at the park's border. There's an information centre in the main stork village, Čigoć, at number 26 (\ *044 715 115*). It's officially open daily from 08.00 to 16.00, but if you find it closed then call Davor Anzil on his mobile (m *098 222 085*). There's also another office in Krapje at number 16 (\ *044 672 080*).

Most visitors will be content enough to drive along the pretty 70km road, now largely tarred, which runs through the park from Sisak to Jasenovac. There's a bus from Sisak (departs Sisak 10.30, 14.50, 16.50, 19.50 Mon–Fri & 14.50 Sat), meaning that if you leave reasonably early you can easily come on a day trip from Zagreb – though staying for a day or two is more rewarding. The villages along here are among the prettiest in the region, and all have storks in greater or fewer numbers, along with yards full of ducks, chickens, bantams and the occasional turkey. Many of the older traditional wooden houses are collapsing in on themselves, but a good number have been restored as weekenders, and some are open as guesthouses. They're really quite beautiful, and the route makes a lovely cycle ride.

From Sisak it's 30km to Čigoć, via the single-street villages of Topolovac, Prelošćica, Lukavec Posavski and Gušće. After Čigoć it's another 40km on to Jasenovac, passing through Kratečko, Možilovčica, Suvoj, Lonja, Trebež, Puska, Krapje and Drenov Bok on the way. There are a handful of places where you can sleep or eat (page 179).

More serious birdwatchers should contact the park office in advance, as there are several special ornithological reserves, protecting some 236 species of bird.

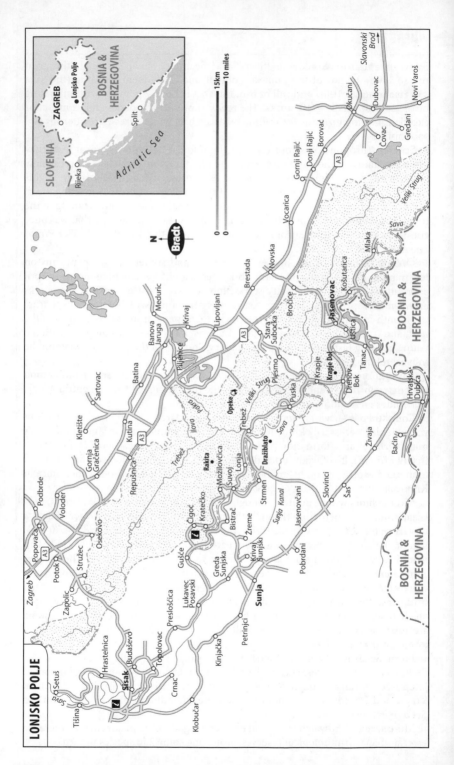

LONJSKO POLJE

SLOVENIA

ZAGREB
● Lonjsko Polje

BOSNIA &
HERZEGOVINA

Rijeka

Split

Adriatic Sea

15km

10 miles

0

0

N

Bradt

WHERE TO STAY AND EAT There are some lovely village homes and farmsteads in the area, serving delicious homecooked food. For a list of more places to stay and eat, see the nature park's website.

 Etno Selo Stara Lonja (3 rooms, 1 apt) Lonja; ☎044 710 619; m 091 505 5543; www. etnoselo-staralonja.com. Accommodation in traditional village houses, food & local organised trips in Lonja. €€€–€€

 Iza na Trem (1 room, 2 apts) Čigoć 57; ☎044 715 167; m 099 503 2171; http://iza-na-

trem.hr. Nice, friendly, family-run B&B in Čigoć, with lovely rooms & apts. Very good value – €16/€19pp in a room/apt, €19/€21pp with b/fast, €26/€29 HB. €€

 Tradicije Čigoć (6 rooms) Čigoć 7a; ☎044 715 124; www.tradicije-cigoc.hr. In Čigoć itself, with a restaurant, & accommodation. €€

WHAT TO SEE AND DO If you're in the area (or driving along the *autocesta* east of Zagreb) it's well worth stopping at the 18th-century church of **Our Lady of the Snows**, in the otherwise unremarkable town of **Kutina** – though there is an adequate hotel, the eponymous **Kutina** (☎ *044 692 400; www.hoteli-daim.hr;* €€–€€€). The plain, simple exterior of the church hides a plain, simple interior. No, of course it doesn't. Inside, it's wildly over-decorated, with stucco, putti, plaster saints, carved pilasters, gilt, medallions, *trompe l'oeil*, the whole bit. The main altar, entirely filling the sanctuary, is almost impossible to look at.

JASENOVAC

Where the Sava joins the Bosnian border, you'll find what must be the saddest town in Croatia. Famous only for having been the site of Croatia's worst concentration camp during World War II, Jasenovac was then fought over by both sides in the 1990s war.

Today the town is still half-abandoned and has a moderately desperate air. Many of the bombed-out buildings have yet to be properly repaired, and it looks as if Jasenovac must be way down on someone's agenda of places to fix up. With the Hotel Sava still in ruins, there's nowhere to stay (not, frankly, that you'd want to) and nothing to do. You could eat at **Kod Ribiča** (☎ *044 672 066; www.kod-ribica.com;* ⊕ *08.00–22.00 Mon–Sat, 11.00–18.00 Sun;* €€€) however, which seems to attract Bosnians from across the border and does plenty of local freshwater fish dishes, including a pretty mean fish stew, *fiš paprikaš*. It also has 11 rooms available (€€€).

The main – let's be honest, the only – reason to visit Jasenovac is to see the site of the **former concentration camp**. To many visitors it seems as if Croatia would rather forget the camp altogether. In the museum (☎ *044 672 319; www. jusp-jasenovac.hr;* ⊕ *Mar–Nov 09.00–17.00 Tue–Fri, 10.00–16.00 Sat/Sun; Dec– Feb 09.00–16.00 Mon–Fri; free*), you can see a small collection of photographs and uniforms, but little else. The main memorial is a dramatic concrete sculpture in the shape of an enormous flower. The path to it is made of old railway sleepers, and on the way you'll find a brass map showing where the huts once stood. There's also a poignant train and cattle wagons (a gift from the Slovenian railway company), like the ones which would have brought prisoners here in the 1940s.

POŽEGA

Set in pretty countryside 175km east of Zagreb (35km from the Nova Gradiska exit off the *autocesta*), the town of Požega makes a great overnight stop if you're heading east, and is within striking distance of the Papuk Nature Park. Under Turkish occupation from 1537 to 1691, it became thoroughly Baroque during the 18th century and still has an attractive old town, centred on the elongated triangular main square, Trg Svetog Trojstva.

GETTING THERE AND AWAY Požega is on a branch line of the rail network, with eight trains a day coming up from the junction with the main line to Slavonski Brod (change at Nova Kapela-Batrina), and is also well served by buses to Zagreb and elsewhere. The bus and train stations are both northeast of the centre of town – head straight down Stjepan Radića to the main square.

 WHERE TO STAY AND EAT There are a number of small pansions in Požega. For eating and drinking you'll find heaps of cheap and cheerful places in the pedestrianised streets just north of the main square.

Grgin Dol This hotel is remembered by the author for its astoundingly greasy yet tasty cooked breakfast. €€€

Villa Maria (8 dbl, 1 apt) Dr Franje Tuđmana 14; 034 271 271; m 091 205 9016; www.villa-maria.hr. Centrally located, family-run place with a nice terrace. €€€

Vila Stanišić (23 rooms) Dr Franje Tuđmana 10; 034 312 168; http://vila-stanisic.hr. This is the nicest & best located of the pansions, with clean rooms & its own restaurant. To get here, head north up the main pedestrian street, which turns into Kamenita Vrata, then turn right & it's on the right, just after the first intersection. €€

WHAT TO SEE AND DO On the south side of the square there are two **churches**, separated by the huge pale-grey wedding-cake frontage of the Franciscan monastery, while the north side is made up of a lovely row of ochre-yellow arcaded houses. In the centre of the square is the restored Baroque **Plague Column** from the middle of the 18th century, which apparently cost – according to the inscription – the princely sum of 300 forints and 2,000 eggs.

A block away to the east is the **Church of St Teresa** (Sv Terezija), which became the town's cathedral in 1997 on the creation of the diocese. It has a beautiful, freshly restored front, all pale yellow with decorative mustard-icing swirls. The lower Baroque capitals are topped with winged angels, while those higher up are crowned with formalised stone vases, the whole leading up to an elegant clock tower. Inside there's a big Baroque altarpiece and choir, and dark paintings everywhere.

Opposite the church entrance, in the small park, there's a fine, soldierly statue of Fra Luka Ibrišimović Sokol, who apparently single-handedly smote the Turks here in 1689, although he was nearly 70 at the time.

Finally, head north to where the road intersects with **Kamenita Vrata** (literally Stone Gates), and you'll find a new brick-built spiral memorial to the (mostly young) men who lost their lives here during the war of the early 1990s. Each of the 102 victims has a plaque at eye-level, and it's heart-rending to read their names and dates.

Like most towns in Slavonia, Požega livens things up with plenty of **festivals**. Starting the spring off with a bang – literally – is the annual show of cannons and mortars on 12 March, St Gregory's Day, which also features mortar fire in Požega's vineyards, to symbolise the routing of the Turks. In May you can choose between the National Dog Show or the unusual festival of Croatian one-minute films held here, and a month later there are contests to see who can cook up the best fish stews and spicy *kulen* sausages. In September, the town hosts the Golden Strings of Slavonia music festival, which brings in crowds from miles around. Contact the **tourist office** (*Antuna Kanižlića 3;* 034 274 900; *www.pozega-tz.hr*) for more details.

PAPUK NATURE PARK

The Papuk Nature Park (*www.pp-papuk.hr; 25/20kn adult/child*) covers the hills about 15km north of Požega, and rises from the plain up to nearly 1,000m. There's nothing especially dramatic or spectacular about it, but the walking up here is lovely, through deep deciduous woods and along clear, burbling brooks.

The park was only designated in 1999, so there's not much in the way of infrastructure in place yet, though there are two small **park offices**, one in Velika (*Stjepana Radića 46;* ✆ *034 313 030*), 12km north of Požega, and the other over the hill, on the northwestern side of the park, in Voćin (✆ *033 565 296*). Whichever one you call first, you're likely to be asked to speak to the other, but they're friendly and helpful when you finally get through.

The park acts as a watershed for numerous refreshing streams that flow down to the Drava to the north and the Sava to the south, and has lots of well-marked trails through the beech and oak woods. None of the hiking is especially challenging, and the fairly dense forest cover means that spectacular views are few and far between, but it's nonetheless one of the pleasantest places in Slavonia. The flora is exceptional (with around 1,500 species) and there's a 33m waterfall hidden deep in the woods. Geological curiosities include rock columns that were thrown up millions of years ago during volcanic disturbances, and there are even three ruined castles you can clamber up to – the **ruins of Ružica** grad are about 20 minutes up a marked trail from the town of Orahovica, and there's another **old fort** above Velika.

As you come up through Velika from Požega, the road forks right and leads up to **thermal baths,** which are extremely popular on hot summer weekends with the locals. Above here, on the last stretch of tarred road, there are some lovely picnic and barbecue spots in the meadows along the river, and even a couple of small grill restaurants. It's a charming place, though there's no obvious public transport that would get you here.

SLAVONSKI BROD

Heading east into Slavonia, especially on public transport, you're likely to pass through Slavonski Brod, as it's a major transport hub. There's no particular reason to break your journey here, however, unless you've come specifically for the Brodsko Kolo, in June, which is arguably Slavonia's (and the updater would argue Croatia's) best folk festival. On the other hand, if you have a couple of hours between buses or trains, there are things to see. There are plenty of buses to Zagreb (2½ hours) as well as services elsewhere in Slavonia; the train from Zagreb takes between 3 and 4 hours. Until 1891, Slavonski Brod was a military town, but during the 20th century it became an important staging post for trade and industry, both on the Sava, and across the river into Bosnia & Herzegovina. Today, there's still not a great deal of traffic across the bridge to Bosanski Brod (called Srpski Brod by the mainly Serbian population on that side of the Sava), and the remaining shell-scarred Austro-Hungarian buildings on the Croatian side continue to bear witness to the shelling from the Bosnian Serb side during the homeland war.

From the bus or train stations, head south down Vukovarska towards the river, 15 minutes away on foot. On the left you'll pass the large grassy park which was the essence of the town for centuries – there's not a whole lot of the **ruined fortress** (*trvd-ava*) left now, however, but you can get an idea of the size and scale of the place from the earthworks and the crumbling, overgrown brick walls.

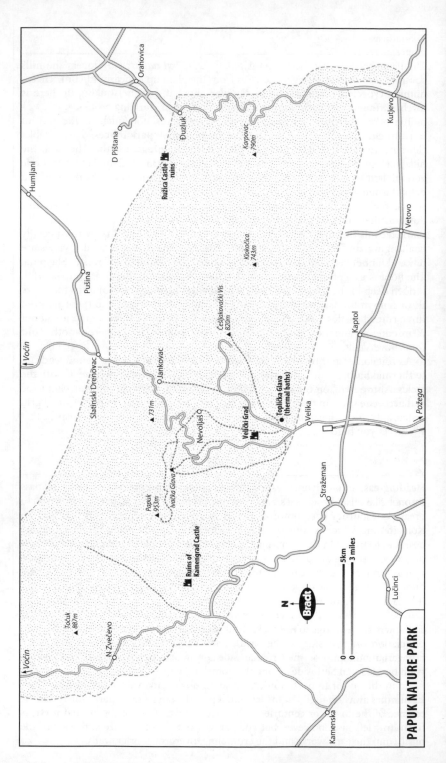

Orahovica

Humljani

D Pištana

Đuzluk

Ružica Castle
ruins

Karpovac
790m ▲

Kutjevo

Vetovo

Pušina

Klokočica
743m ▲

Kaptol

Vočin

Slatinski Drenovac

Jankovac

731m ▲

Češljakovački Vis
820m ▲

Nevoljaš

Velički Grad

Topličica Glava
(thermal baths)
●

Velika

Papuk
953m ▲

Ivačka Glava ▲

Stražeman

Požega

Ruins of
Kamengrad Castle

Točuk
887m ▲

N Zvečevo

Lučinci

Vočin

N

Bradt

5km
3 miles

0
0

PAPUK NATURE PARK

Kamenska

Southeast of the fortress, on the other side of Vukovarska is the pedestrianised main square, Trg Mažuranić, which gives on to the river. Here you'll find a number of shops, banks and café terraces but not a whole lot else. Along the river from the main square is Slavonski Brod's only other main attraction, the 18th-century **Franciscan Monastery**, which was the religious and cultural heart of the town when it was a garrison. The church is nothing special, but the Baroque cloisters are lovely, with the monks' cells overlooking the garden in the middle, an oasis of tranquillity.

During June, the town hosts the **Brodsko Kolo**, Croatia's oldest folk dance festival (it's been running for over 50 years), which features three days/evenings of folk dancing by folk dance ensembles from all over Croatia as well as from Bosnia and Serbia, with traditional music and spectacular costumes. It's a hugely prestigious event for the region, and definitely not something just put on for tourists, unlike so many of the folk festivals elsewhere in Croatia, particularly on the coast. There are also horse-drawn cart and carriage contests, and plenty of eating and drinking. For more information see the website of Folklorni ansambl Broda (*www.fa-broda.hr*), the award-winning local ensemble who effectively host the event. The tourist office also has details.

 WHERE TO STAY AND EAT The **tourist information office** (*Trg Pobjede 28/1;* ☎ 035 447 721; *www.tzgsb.hr*) will be able to help you with accommodation if you want to stay over. There are a handful of hotels in the centre. There are also a number of rooms and apartments – for some of the better ones contact **Apartmani na Savi** (☎ 035 411 160; m 091 597 2072; *www.apartmani-na-savi.com.hr*), with doubles for €27. For cafés, you'll have plenty to choose from around the pedestrianised Trg Ivana Brlić Mažuranić – named after Croatia's much-loved author of fairy tales and childen's stories, born in Ogulin (page 243), who lived much of her adult life here in Slavonski Brod.

🏠 **Art** (27 rooms) Nikole Zrinskog 44; ☎ 035 638 950; www.art-hotel.hr. Has its own spa & wellness centre. €€€€

🏠 **Central** (16 rooms) Ulica Petra Krešimira IV 45; ☎ 035 492 030; www.hotelcentralsb.hr. Opened in 2008, is the best choice. €€€€

🏠 **Savus** (15 rooms) ☎ 035 405 888; www. savus-hotel.com. A more expensive alternative to the Central. €€€€

🏠 **Hotel Eko Garten** (18 rooms) Vinogorska 69; ☎ 035 465 072; www.garten.hr. Good option if you don't mind being out of town, with doubles for €59. Around 4km north of the town centre on the other side of the main highway. €€

✕ **Krčma Eden** Josipa Jurja Strossmayera 1; www.krcma-eden.com; ⏲ 09.00–23.00 Mon– Thu, 09.00–midnight Sat/Sun. €€€

✕ **Restoran Pizzeria Uno** Nikole Zrinskog 7; ⏲ 09.00–23.00 daily. Decent pizzeria, just along the road from the Art Hotel. €€

ĐAKOVO

The town of Đakovo lies 50km northeast of Slavonski Brod and 35km south of Osijek. With an inspired, twin-spired cathedral and excellent local food and drink, it makes a near-perfect Slavonian stopover – assuming, of course, you don't crash your car here, like the author did (before, not after, the gourmet lunch).

GETTING THERE AND AWAY Đakovo is well connected with other towns in the region by bus and train. The bus station is two blocks east of the cathedral, while the train station is 20 minutes northeast of the centre – walk down Kralja Tomislava until you reach the pedestrian zone. Buses come in every half hour or so from

Osijek and Slavonski Brod, while trains run to both towns six times a day (for Slavonski Brod change at Strizivojna Vrpolje). The helpful **tourist office** (*Kralja Tomislava 3;* \ *031 812 319; http://tzdjakovo.eu*) is opposite All Saints Church, on Kralja Tomislava.

🏠 WHERE TO STAY AND EAT

🏠 **Croatia-Turist** (8 rooms) Preradovića 25; \031 813 391; www.croatiaturist.hr. The only hotel in town itself, a 2min walk south of the cathedral, on the road out towards Slavonski Brod. It's a great place, with rooms above a fabulous restaurant of many separate dining areas, which makes its own spicy sausage (*kulen*). €€€

🏠 **Hotel Đakovo** (25 rooms) Nikole Tesle 52; \031 840 570; www.hotel-djakovo.hr. A good-value little place on the edge of town, on the road leading out to Osijek. €€€

🏠 **Pansion Komfort** (23 rooms) S Radića 17; \031 821 634; www.laguna-ugostiteljstvo.hr. This no-frills pansion is just around the corner from the pedestrianised street Pape Ivana Pavla II. €

WHAT TO SEE AND DO Whichever way you come into town, the fantastic red-brick neo-Romanesque **Cathedral of St Peter** (Sv Petra) stands out for miles. Commissioned by Bishop Strossmayer – Đakovo was his see – it was built between 1866 and 1882, and features a wealth of attractive minimalist detail among the brickwork. The 84m twin towers are topped with small spires, while from the centre of the church rises a fine 54m cupola.

Inside, it's a glorious, spacious building, with fluted columns, Romanesque arches, and high ceilings. The upper sides of the nave feature almost Pre-Raphaelite biblical frescoes – the first scene on the left shows Adam and Eve, with Adam stolen shamelessly from the roof of the Sistine Chapel, and Eve a passable copy of Botticelli's *Venus*. The ceilings, with gold stars on a deep blue background, wouldn't look out of place in a Tuscan cathedral, while the walls of the apses and sanctuary are decorated with startlingly realistic *trompe l'œil* curtains. The whole is quite delightful.

Underground there's a large crypt, with Strossmayer's tomb, but it's rarely open. If you're a Strossmayer completist, you'll also want to visit the **Strossmayer Museum** (*Spomen-muzej biskupa Josipa Jurja Strossmayera;* ⊕ *08.00–18.00 Mon–Fri, 08.00–13.00 Sat; 20kn*), across the street from the cathedral, on the corner of the pedestrian zone, where you'll find the bishop's letters and other personal items, but it really is for fanatics only.

At the far end of the pedestrian street – full of cafés, bars and ice-cream parlours spilling out on to the pavement – is **All Saints Church** (Svih Sveti), which was the town's main mosque (Đakovo was occupied by the Turks from 1536 to 1678) until the plain Baroque façade was slapped on in the 19th century.

Đakovo's main annual event is the **Đakovački Vezovi** (meaning 'Đakovo embroidery') at the beginning of July, which features lots of traditional costumes (and embroidery), folk singing and dancing, and parades of the traditional wedding wagons, which are a whole lot of fun. Concerts are put on in the cathedral, while at the racecourse you'll also get the chance to see competitive trap-and-wagon driving, with elegant pure-bred Lippizaners strutting their stuff – Lippizaner horses have been bred in and around Đakovo since 1506. Book well in advance if you want to be there. Another important event is the annual procession of the **Ljelje**, young and unmarried women, in the nearby village of Gorjani on Whitsun.

If you want to see **Lippizaners**, there's a stable on the edge of town, 15 minutes due east down Matije Gupica from the cathedral. Ask politely and you may be allowed in to see the horses, or watch them at their morning training sessions.

Osijek is the biggest town in Slavonia, and it's a major administrative, economic and cultural centre. Spread along the southern shore of the River Drava, it's a city of wide streets, rumbling trams and attractive parks and gardens, with two city centres, the 18th-century Austro-Hungarian military fortress town of Tvrđa, to the east, and the 19th-century commercial centre of Gornji Grad, upstream to the west. Until 1786, when they were joined together (along with the residential town of Donji Grad, downstream from Tvrđa), they were entirely separate towns.

HISTORY The Romans had a settlement called Mursa here in the 1st century AD, and by 331 it was sufficiently important for the Emperor Hadrian to raise its status to that of a colony. Destroyed by rampaging Goths and Huns in the 7th century, its next settlers were Croats, who built a thriving town near the current site in the Middle Ages, until it was destroyed by incoming Turks. The major Turkish town built here was then destroyed in its own turn, when Osijek was finally captured by the Austro-Hungarians in 1687.

From 1712 to 1721, the Austro-Hungarians built a brand-new military-urban complex, Tvrđa, on the site of the Turkish town, as a reflection of its strategic importance in the military border zone. What you see here today has escaped more or less intact, though the Tvrđa town walls were pulled down in the 1920s.

In 1779, the building of a new bridge across the Drava connected Osijek not just to Bilje, but to the rest of Europe, and paved the way for the rapid expansion of Gornji Grad and Donji Grad, upstream and downstream from Tvrđa. In 1786 the three towns were joined together, and in 1884 the first tram started operating between them. During the late 19th and early 20th century, Gornji Grad became the administrative and business heart of Osijek, and indeed still is today.

From the middle of 1991 until early 1992, Osijek was bombarded, but never captured, and though restoration has been quick and effective, there are still a few scars to be seen, with shrapnel-pocked buildings in evidence around the town.

GETTING THERE AND AROUND As the biggest regional centre east of Zagreb, Osijek is a major transport hub, and it's easy to get here and easy to get around. Ten **buses** a day make the 4-hour journey from Zagreb, for example, while three a day head up to Pécs (Pečuh in Croatian) in southern Hungary. Every half hour or so there's also a departure for Bizovac, half an hour away, as well as for Slavonski Brod, 2 hours down the road. Five **trains** a day head across Slavonia to Zagreb (4–5 hours), while there are departures roughly every 2 hours for Bizovac, only 25 minutes away.

The new bus and old train stations are 15 minutes' walk southeast of Gornji Grad and 20 minutes southwest of Tvrđa – tram #2 does a loop from the stations up to Gornji Grad, while tram #1 runs between Gornji Grad and Tvrđa. You can also walk between the two centres in 20 minutes or so along Kapucinska and the pretty Europska Avenija, or along the riverside.

The **tourist office** (*Zupanijska 2;* \ *031 203 755; www.tzosijek.hr*), opposite the theatre and almost next door to the cathedral, in a grand administrative building, has maps and useful information on the town and region.

WHERE TO STAY *Map, page 187*

Osijek (140 rooms) Šamačka 4; \ 031 230 333; www.hotelosijek.hr. Of Osijek's hotels, the smartest option is the eponymous Osijek, a tower-block right on the waterfront, which has been impressively upgraded to a 4-star hotel with stylish, spacious dbl rooms, the best of which have a lovely view of the river – the same view can be enjoyed from the 14th-floor wellness centre. There's also much less noise from the cathedral bells than in many other places. Service here really is first rate, & the breakfast simply outstanding. €€€€

🏠 **Waldinger** (16 rooms) Zupanijska ulica 8; ✆031 250 450; www.waldinger.hr. Plush boutique 4-star just a short distance from the cathedral & the main square, in a beautifully renovated building dating from 1904. €€€€

🏠 **Central** (32 rooms) Trg Ante Starčevića 6; ✆031 283 399; www.hotel-central-os.hr. Right on the main square near the cathedral, the Central is a good option. The renovated 3-star hotel retains

some of its original 1899 charm & is good value – though being on a busy street, it can be a bit noisy. €€€

🏠 **Silver** (16 rooms) Divaltova 84; ✆031 582 535; www.hotel-silver.hr. Nice 3-star, slightly out from the city centre. €€€

🏠 **Guesthouse Maksimilian** (8 rooms) Franje Kuhača 12; ✆031 497 567; www.maksimilian. hr. Good-value place, housed in an 18th-century building right in the heart of Tvrđa. €€

🏠 **Hostel Tufna** Franje Kuhača 10; ✆031 215 020; www.tufna.com.hr. Located right in the centre of Tvrđa, with bargain beds for only 107kn. Also a popular nightclub. €

✗ WHERE TO EAT AND DRINK *Map, page 187*

Osijek's a treat for eating out, being good value for money and offering plenty of restaurants and pizzerias. Local specialities tend to be spicy, in sharp contrast with places on the coast, and reflecting Osijek's proximity to paprika-mad Hungary. There's an excellent hot fish stew, made of carp, catfish and pike, fittingly called *fiš paprikaš*, while almost everywhere serves up its own variations on *kulen*, a spicy smoked sausage. The best place to sink an Osječko Pivo, proudly brewed in Osijek since 1697, is right in the centre of Tvrđa, where a string of bar and café terraces face the old Military Command across the square.

✗ **Alas** Reisnerova 12a; www.restoranalasosijek. com; ⊕ 10.00–23.00 Mon–Sat, 11.00–16.00 Sun. A great place for fish dishes, near the railway station. The name means 'fisherman' in the local dialect. €€€

✗ **Baranjska kuća** Kolodvorska 99, Karanac; ✆031 720 180; m 098 652 900; www.baranjska-kuca.com; ⊕ 11.00–22.00 Mon–Thu, 11.00–01.00 Fri/Sat, 11.00–17.00 Sun. Superb traditional restaurant in the village of Karanac, around 30km north of Osijek, serving local specialties such as fiš paprikaš & *čobanac* (a thick stew) at long wooden tables, with live music on Fri/Sat evenings. It also has 5 private rooms available. €€€

✗ **Kod Ruže** Franje Kuhača 25; ✆031 206 066; ⊕ 09.00–23.00 Mon–Wed, 09.00–midnight Thu–Sat, 10.00–16.00 Sun. Another favourite in Tvrđa, with folksy décor, live music & dishes such as wild boar or venison *perkelt* with homemade gnocchi, as well as slightly cheaper eats such as *ćevapčići* on the 'Balkan Express' menu. €€€

✗ **Rustika** Ulica Pavla Pejačevića 32; ✆031 369 400; www.rustika.hr; ⊕ 10.00–23.00 daily. Good-value grill & pizzeria. It also has 4 nice apartments available. €€€–€€

✗ **Slavonska Kuća** Kamila Firinger 26; ✆031 369 955; www.slavonskakuca.com; ⊕ 09.00–23.00 Mon–Sat. Low key local favourite in Tvrđa. The homemade *kulen* and fine *fiš* more than compensate for the somewhat folksy décor. €€

☕ **Mala Kavana** Županjska 2. This really is *the* place to go for a coffee on the main square, near the cathedral.

☕ **San Francisco Coffee House** Stjepana Radića 12; http://sfch.com.hr; ⊕ 08.00–23.00 daily. All variations on coffee, as well as beer & other drinks in swish, comfy leather chairs.

♀ **Amsterdam** Stjepana Radića 18; ⊕ 07.30–23.00 daily. Busy underground bar & student hangout.

WHAT TO SEE AND DO The main sight in Gornji Grad is the neo-Gothic red-brick **cathedral**. It's actually not a cathedral, rather the parish Church of Saints Peter and Paul, but being vast, and sporting Croatia's second tallest spire (90m), the cathedral tag is hardly surprising. Built at the end of the 19th century, in the style of the great German cathedrals, complete with flying buttresses, the church has a fine,

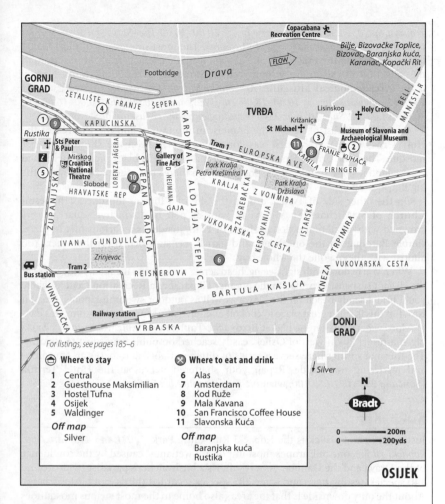

For listings, see pages 185–6

Where to stay

1 Central
2 Guesthouse Maksimilian
3 Hostel Tufna
4 Osijek
5 Waldinger

Off map
   Silver

Where to eat and drink

6   Alas
7   Amsterdam
8   Kod Ruže
9   Mala Kavana
10 San Francisco Coffee House
11 Slavonska Kuća

Off map
   Baranjska kuća
   Rustika

OSIJEK

spacious interior featuring lovely vaulting and plain, simple frescoes on the ceilings and along the nave.

Across and down the street you'll see the freshly restored **Croatian National Theatre**, spoiled somewhat by the garish McDonald's outlet. Inside, it's a beautiful example of classic late-19th-century opulence – the theatre, not McDonald's.

Heading towards Tvrđa, it's worth stopping in at the **Gallery of Fine Arts** (*Galerija Likovnih Umjetnosti; Europska Avenija 9;* ☏ *031 251 280; www.gluo.hr;* ⊕ *10.00–18.00 Tue/Wed/Fri, 10.00–20.00 Thu, 17.00–21.00 Sat, 10.00–13.00 Sun; 15kn*) on Europska Avenija, housed in a luxurious neoclassical villa. The gallery is one of Croatia's best, and you shouldn't be put off by not recognising many of the names on show – the paintings are on the whole excellent. As you head further east on Europska Avenija check out the Jugendstil (German Art Nouveau) houses along here.

Everything in Tvrđa is on or close to the harmonious main square, Trg Svetog Trojstva, which has a distinctive Baroque **Plague Column** at its centre, dating from 1729. The entire north side of the square is taken up with the vast **Austro-Hungarian Military Command**, while the Magistrate building, on the eastern side, now houses the sprawling **Museum of Slavonia** (*Muzej Slavonije; Trg Svetog*

Trojstva 6; ☏ *031 250 730; www.mso.hr;* ⊕ *10.00–18.00 Tue–Sat; 15kn 10kn or 25kn including entry into Archaeological Museum).* The most interesting of the 130,000 bits and pieces in the museum's care are the Roman artefacts from Mursa, though the collection also spans everything from the Stone Age to the 20th century. Nearby is the **Archaeological Museum** *(Arheološki Muzej; Trg Svetog Trojstva 2;* ☏ *031 232 132; www.mso.hr;* ⊕ *10.00–18.00 Tue/Wed, noon–20.00 Thu, 10.00–16.00 Fri, 10.00–14.00 Sat/Sun; 10kn or 25kn including entry into Museum of Slavonia etc).*

A block northeast of here is the Franciscan monastery and the **Church of the Holy Cross** (Sv Križa), which was completed in 1732, on the site of a former mosque. The dark, ornate Baroque interior, and women in black praying in hushed voices, lend it some spooky atmosphere, though there's not much to see beyond the big Baroque altar.

On the other side of Tvrđa, also on the site of a former mosque, is the Jesuit **Church of St Michael** (Sv Mihovila), with its pair of distinctive square towers crowned with small onion domes. Built in 1748, inside it's a curious mix of plain, simple Baroque on the one hand, and garish, ornate Rococo on the other. You almost wish they'd gone the whole hog.

When you're done with sightseeing, head across the river on the main bridge or over the elegant suspension bridge to the popular **Copacabana Recreation Centre**, where you'll find a sandy beach on the Drava as well as outdoor swimming pools. Brazil it isn't, but this is still a great place to cool off and have some fun on a hot summer's day.

More watery fun can be had at **Bizovačke Toplice** *(www.bizovacke-toplice.hr)*, a big spa resort 20km west of Osijek, easily reached on public transport to Bizovac. The thermal springs here serve a series of different pools, and there's an enormous and terrifying water-slide. Repair your shattered nerves at the **Hotel Termia** *(Sunčana 39;* ☏ *031 685 100; www.bizovacke-toplice.hr;* €€€*).*

KOPAČKI RIT

Just northeast of Osijek is the Kopački Rit Nature Park (☏ *031 445 445; http://pp-kopacki-rit.hr)*, one of Europe's most important wetlands, caused by the confluence of the Drava and the Danube. As a result, it's a birdwatcher's paradise, with around 140 species nesting here, and some 285 species recorded (birds, not birdwatchers). About the only downside is that the area's also home to the most vicious mosquitoes I've ever encountered, biting even in broad daylight, and through everything but the thickest clothing. Take effective repellent.

Among the nesting species are geese, grey, white and purple herons, egrets, coots, kingfishers, woodpeckers and storks. There's also the endangered ferruginous duck, several pairs of rare black storks, and a number of white-tailed sea eagles, as well as a cormorant colony. During the spring and autumn migrations, the park is used as a layover by hundreds of thousands of birds, so that's the best time to come, but in summer it's still a wonderful place, even for the most lackadaisical of ornithologists.

For most of the 1990s, the park was closed, being either under Serbian or UN control (it runs along the border with the Serbian province of Vojvodina), and it's been a tough job to clear most of the mines from the area – indeed, some areas are still contaminated by landmines and other ordnance, though de-mining work continues. Stick to marked paths and take any warnings seriously.

Most people visit the park on a bus tour (ask at any travel agent in Slavonia or in Zagreb), which takes in the main sights. You can also drive round the park yourself, though the best way of seeing it is from the water, as part of a tour which includes a boat trip to the Special Ornithological Reserve and a visit to Tikveš Dvorec.

Tickets are 80kn. Standard entry tickets, including access to walking routes and Tikveš Dvorec without boat tour, cost 20kn.

There are also various special ornithological tours in small boats, lasting several hours with prices starting at around 100kn per person per hour – book well in advance through the park office. It's one of the best places in Europe for birdwatching, and you can expect to see up to 90 species here in a single day.

It's also possible to adopt a species of bird here – contact the park office or see its website for details (page 188).

To reach the park, take the Beli Manastir road out of Osijek until you reach Bilje, just 7km out of town (buses run about once an hour). Turn right, passing Prince Eugene of Savoy's splendid hunting lodge (dating from 1707), and continue to the entrance to the park at Kopačevo, 3km further on, where there's an information centre and souvenir shop, and the departure point for the boat tours.

The road into the park goes between the two main lakes, Sakadaško and Kopačko, and then heads up through a reedy area of canals and cultivated fields – a great place to see herons – and home to an excellent konoba at Kozjak.

The road then heads up into the woods around Tikveš, which conceal one of Tito's most-prized hunting lodges, **Tikveš Dvorac** – he and his pals would come up here for a spot of privacy to blast away at the local game. On the road to the castle there's a sentry box, which would presumably have been used to keep away the hoi polloi, though it's now, like the lodge itself, in a sorry state of repair. There are plans to use the lodge to good effect, however, as a study centre for research scientists, and there are a couple of cafés where you can stop for a drink in the shade. A visit to Tikveš Dvorec is included in the tours on offer at the park entrance.

The **Bilje tourist office** (*Kralja Zvonimira 10;* ☎ *031 751 480; www.tzo-bilje.hr*) can put you in touch with local people with private rooms, if you'd like to stay in the area.

VINKOVCI

In spite of the graffiti announcing Vinkovci as 'Punk City', the reality is somewhat more prosaic, though the town was a centre of stubborn Croatian resistance during the 1990s war. Situated 40km south of Osijek, 35km east of Đakovo and a little under 20km short of Vukovar, the town is Croatia's second-biggest railway junction and a staging post for buses, so it's quite possible you may be breaking your journey here. It takes around 1½ hours from Osijek by bus, and 4½ hours from Zagreb.

Both the bus and train stations are a 15-minute walk just north of the harmonious Baroque town centre, which still sits within the limits of the (mostly long-gone) Roman walls of the Aurelia Cibalae colony which was once here. Vinkovci was the birthplace of two Roman emperors (Valens and Valentinian) and the composer of the music of Croatia's national anthem, Josip Runjanin, but today it's best known for the Vinkovačke Jeseni, the annual autumn folk festival which brings in big crowds from across Slavonia and features a boozy and excellent Plum Brandy Fair.

 WHERE TO STAY AND EAT If you want to stay over, there are several hotels downtown. The **tourist office** (*Trg bana Josipa Šokčevića 3;* ☎ *032 334 653; www.tz-vinkovci.hr*) also has a list of other pansions in the area, and can give you more details on the festival.

Villa Lenije (22 dbls) Genschera 3; ☎ 032 340 140; www.hotelvillalenije.com. 4-star wing attached to an old villa. €€€€

Hotel Admiral (60 rooms) Bana Jelačića 6; ☎ 032 332 221; www.hotel-admiral.hr. First opened in 1938 but renovated in recent years. Central location & good value. €€

🏠 **Hotel Kunjevci** (30 rooms) Kunjevci bb; 🕾032 352 999; www.hotel-kunjevci.hr. Rooms & apts on the main road (an River Bosut) south of Vinkovci. (**Hostel Plus**, in the town centre, is under the same ownership as Hotel Kunjevci, but has cheaper beds in basic, hostel-style rooms €.) €€

🏠 **Hotel Slavonija** (108 rooms) Kralja Zvonimira 120; 🕾032 342 555; www.

hotel-slavonija.eu. Right in the city centre & towering over the river, with rather functional accommodation. €€

✖ **Srijem Bana** Josipa Jelačića 23; 🕾032 339 208; http://restoran-srijem.hr; ⏲ 07.30–22.00 Mon–Sat. Popular restaurant serving freshwater fish & other Slavonian dishes. €€€–€€

VUKOVAR

When I first came back to Vukovar after the Homeland War, in 2002, the reality, after approaching through bucolic fields of maize and sunflowers, was a terrible shock. Gone was the fine Baroque centre and the general air of prosperity delivered by the local shoe and tyre factory at Borovo, which I remembered from the 1980s. In its place was a shambles. The Borovo factory was totally destroyed, and most of the town centre was bombed out, a mess of devastated houses and ruined buildings.

Vukovar suffered more than any other town in Croatia during the war (see box, page 192), and if there's still reconstruction to be done, it's happily now looking incomparably better than the way it was at the end of 1991, when the town finally fell, after the horrifying siege and concomitant massacre, or even at the beginning of 1998, when the UN handed Vukovar back to Croatia. The Franciscan Monastery has been beautifully restored, along with the big school behind it. Shops and banks are open again, while a few apartment blocks – and the Dunav and Lav hotels – have been rebuilt and refurbished, and there's a film festival in August (*www.vukovarfilmfestival.com*). There's a genuine feeling of optimism, of triumph over adversity, which is hopefully more than simple guidebook-writer naïvety – after all, schooling was segregated following the war, for example, with separate entrances for Croats and Serbs; and although the children all follow the same curriculum, different languages and alphabets are used for teaching. However, the New School Project and Nansen Dialogue Centre (*www. ndcosijek.hr*) conducted research on the effectiveness of this segregation (which a large percentage of parents were unhappy with), and have in recent years implemented a voluntary alternative system of schooling without segregation, which has been adopted by several schools across eastern Slavonia. In 2014, work began on establishing the non-segregated New Vukovar School, which is due to open in 2016.

Vukovar's history goes back a long, long way – as you'll know if you've ever seen the partridge-shaped vessel, popular all over the country, known as the Vučedol Dove. The Vučedol site, after a gap of several years, has now been excavated, and a new museum has opened here – the Museum of Vučedol Culture (see page 192). It dates back nearly 5,000 years, and was found just downriver from Vukovar in 1938. The Vučedol site, after a ten-year gap, is now at last being excavated again, with plans to open it up as a proper heritage site for visitors (there's already a Vučedol Restaurant there, which is a good sign).

Vukovar lies along the southern bank of the River Danube (Dunav), with the little River Vuka flowing lethargically through town to join it. The main street, running parallel to the Danube, changes its name from Strossmayerov west of the Vuka, to Franjo Tuđman across the bridge, where you'll find the old town centre.

GETTING THERE AND AROUND The train station is 2km north along the river, a 25-minute walk upstream towards Borovo. The bus station is closer to town, a block south of Strossmayerov, next to a big daily market, and is served by buses roughly every hour from Osijek, 36km away. On Strossmayerov itself you'll find the **tourist office** (*Strossmayera 15;* ☎ *032 442 889; www.turizamvukovar.hr*), next door to Vukovar's most obvious travel agent, Panturist Plus (☎ *032 441 790*).

🏠 **WHERE TO STAY AND EAT** At the time of writing, Vukovar has one excellent 4-star hotel (the Lav), and a handful of small pansions/B&Bs, as well as some private rooms. The old Hotel Dunav, a curious grain-store of a building, is currently undergoing renovation but is due to reopen for business in 2016.

✳ 🏠 **Hotel Lav** (38 rooms, 4 suites) J J Strossmayera 18; ☎ 032 445 100; www.hotel-lav.hr. Vukovar's citizens are justifiably proud of this recently restored & reopened hotel on the river, which symbolises lasting peace as much as somewhere to stay. Smart, spotless, spanking-new 4-star dbls & impeccable service are the order of the day. There's also a fine, modern, & quite upmarket restaurant, serving up Slavonian specialities, & an extensive wine list (including around 100 from Slavonia). Highly recommended. €€€€

🏠 **Sobe and Restaurant Nada** (8 rooms) Matic Hrvatske 3; ☎ 032 430 315; 🆕 Restoran i Sobe NADA Vukovar. Opened in 2013, 3 dbls & 5 sgls above restaurant of same name. €€€

🏠 **Pansion Vila Vanda** (13 rooms) Dalmatinska 3; 📱 097 6262 852; www.konoba-megaron.hr. Opened in 2013. Smart rooms in a central location, above (& under same ownership as) Konoba Megaron. €€€–€€

🏠 **Vila Rose** (5 rooms) Josipa Rukavine 2b; 📱 091 520 4036. Smart, good-value rooms in a central location, just south of the old Hotel Dunav. Opened in 2013. €€

✳ ✗ **Vrške** Parobrodska 3; ☎ 032 441 788; www.restoran-vrske.hr; ⊕ 08.00–23.00 daily. Great restaurant with a terrace on the Danube, serving up excellent freshwater fish dishes. We can recommend the Riba Vrške – grilled carp (*šaran*), fried perch (*smuđ*) & deep fried battered catfish (*som*), served with vegetables, which is excellent value at 60kn. Highly recommended. €€€

WHAT TO SEE AND DO The 18th-century **Eltz Palace**, badly damaged during the Homeland War but now beautifully restored and finally reopened, is west of here, also on Strossmayerov, heading out of town. If it seems familiar, flip over a 20kn note, where you'll also find a picture of the Vučedol Dove. The palace collections were all destroyed or looted during the war, but efforts to recover some of the works from museums in Serbia have proved successful, and it now houses the **Vukovar City Museum** (*Gradski Muzej; Županijska 2;* ☎ *032 638 475;* ⊕ *10.00–18.00 Tue–Fri, 10.00–13.00 Sat/Sun; 25kn*). The former house of **Lavoslav Ružička** (*Županijska 2;* ☎ *032 441 270*) is where Croatia's first Nobel Prize winner was born in 1887.

The bridge across to the old town leads on to one corner of Trg Republike, where you'll find the new town hall, the ruins of the elegant **Workers' Party Building** (home to the second congress of the Communist Party of Yugoslavia in 1920, and formerly the Grand Hotel built during the late 1890s, but for the time being an empty shell) and the Hotel Dunav. Behind the hotel, on the riverbank, there's a touching **memorial**, with stylised gravestones set like falling dominoes, under a couple of poplars, with the broad sweep of the endless Danube behind, and a large white **memorial cross** stands at the confluence of the Vuka and the Danube, the work of Pula-born sculptor Šime Vidulin. The Glagolitic text reads 'He who dies justly, shall live forever.'

The main street through town (Franjo Tuđman), whose arcaded houses and shops still wear very visible scars above quiet cafés and ice-cream shops, was once Vukovar's Baroque heart. Turn left, uphill, at the brewery (storks nest picturesquely here, on the main chimney), to reach the **Franciscan Monastery**, now restored. The brilliant exterior hides a still partially ruined interior, with bare brickwork where

Vukovar's position, right on Croatia's border (that's Serbian Vojvodina you see across the Danube), and its ethnic mix (in the 1991 census, 37% of locals considered themselves as Serbs, while 44% said they were Croats) was at the heart of the disaster in 1991. With Croatian independence on the agenda, barricades were thrown up in Vukovar's Serbian suburbs after a build-up of Serb paramilitaries and provocations instigated from Belgrade. As tensions grew, Croatian policemen were murdered and the Yugoslav army, the JNA, moved in, supposedly to separate the two sides.

By the autumn, Vukovar was surrounded by hundreds of tanks and thousands of soldiers – both regular Yugoslav army forces and Serb irregulars, as well as opportunists. When ground attacks failed, the town was pounded mercilessly by artillery and bombing raids. The residents took shelter in their cellars, living on meagre rations. In the streets above, resistance was fierce, but eventually doomed in the face of the numerically superior and far more heavily armed Serbs.

On 18 November 1991, Vukovar, now completely destroyed, finally fell. With nowhere to run – the ruins of the town were surrounded by enemy forces – the remaining population sought shelter in the hospital. The following day, ahead of the planned Red Cross evacuation, the Serbs cleared the hospital themselves, transporting the male survivors off to nearby Ovčara, where they were all killed.

The world – with its attention diverted by the far more photogenic siege of Dubrovnik's beautiful and well-known old town – paid little heed.

Wherever Croats fell into Serb hands, families were separated, and the men were taken away in trucks. Approximately 2,300 soldiers and civilians died in the defence of Vukovar, and another 2,600 people simply disappeared. Many have been found in the mass graves around the town, but others may be buried anonymously in Serbia, unmarked victims of the worst atrocity of the 1990s war in Croatia.

once were pastel plaster and Baroque frescoes. There are good photos showing what the monastery used to look like, and just how badly ruined it got in 1991.

Also newly opened is the **Museum of Vučedol Culture** (*Muzej Vučedolske Kulture; Trojstvo bb;* ☏ *032 373 930;* ☉ *10.00–18.00 Tue–Sun; 30kn*), one of the most highly anticipated museum projects in Croatia in recent years, 5km outside Vukovar.

If you've come all the way to Vukovar you should definitely make the effort to get out to the **Vukovar War Cemetery**, one of the most heartbreaking places in the whole of Croatia. This was built on the site of Europe's largest mass grave since World War II, and 938 plain white crosses have been symbolically placed here to commemorate the dead, as well as a large memorial with an eternal flame burning at its centre. There are also the black and grey marble tombs of Vukovar's defenders, strewn with flowers, along with the grim sight of unmarked empty graves ready to receive the bodies of the known missing, should they ever be found. It's a terribly moving place, and there's rarely a time when you can come here and not find tearful family members mourning their dead. The images of the all-too-young victims tell their own story. Be aware that there may still be landmines in the surrounding woods, so don't stray beyond the cemetery itself.

The cemetery is situated about 3.5km out of town on the road to Ilok, and the easiest way to get there is on the regular Ilok bus. If you're walking (it takes about

45 minutes), head along Stjepan Radić out of town. The street is named after the Croatian firebrand who was shot in the Belgrade parliament in 1928; under Serb occupation in the 1990s the name was changed to that of his assassin, Puniša Račić, but now it's been changed back. The street first leads 1km to the war-ravaged **water tower**, which has been left unrestored as a permanent memorial to the conflict.

EAST TO ILOK

East of Vukovar, past the war cemetery, Croatia narrows along the Danube's southern bank, into Vojvodina, and ends in a point at the town of Ilok, 35km later.

If you're coming this way under your own steam, the first place to stop is at the **Ovčara Memorial**, where you can pay your respects to the 200 doctors, nurses and patients taken from Vukovar's hospital on 19 November 1991 who were found buried in a mass grave here. The grave was found in 1997 after an anonymous tip-off, and 200 small bushes mark the spot, along with memorial plaques and a lone dark obelisk, the work of Zagreb sculptor Slavomir Drinković. Standing here it's truly awful to think of the tragic end of so many people in such calm, quiet countryside, where today all you can hear is birds singing and crickets chirping. The grave is just past the small farming village of Ovčara – take the right-hand turning (marked with a dove for peace) almost exactly 2.5km after the Vukovar War Cemetery. Follow the road for 5km to Ovčara, then turn left at the end of the road (marked with another dove), and turn left again after 200m or so. A **Memorial Centre** was opened here in 2006 in an old hangar, used as a transit port for prisoners bound for Serbian concentration camps.

If you're on public transport (ie: the Vukovar to Ilok bus), the first town you come to is **Sotin**, which is not much more than a single street with rebuilt houses, after which you'll pass through **Opatovac**, which has nice vineyards and a shrapnel-pocked church tower. About 10km further on is **Šarengrad**, which was obviously once quite charming. There are two pretty churches and a fish-rich lake, though the signs of war are still omnipresent.

A final 7km brings you to **Ilok**, Croatia's easternmost town. While the Osijek tourist office's description of the town as 'Dubrovnik on the Danube' is a triumph of optimism over reality, it's still well worth coming here to see the fortified old town, up on the hill above the Danube.

The old town is set within tall, narrow-bricked walls, which were originally built in medieval times but were then beefed up by the Turks, who ran Ilok from 1566 to 1697. At the centre of the old town is the imposing **Odescalchi Castle**, given as a gift by Emperor Leopold to Pope Innocent XI Odescalchi and his family as a reward for their help in liberating Ilok from the Turks. The aristocratic Italian Odescalchi family rebuilt much of the existing castle in Baroque style, installed huge wine cellars, and their descendants were here until 1945. The castle now houses the **Museum of the City of Ilok** (*Gradski Muzej; Šetalište oca Mladena Barbarića 5; www.mgi.hr;* ⊕ *09.00–15.00 Tue–Thu, 09.00–18.00 Fri, 11.00–18.00 Sat; 20kn*) which reopened to visitors in this location in 2010.

The church to one side of the museum is dedicated to **St Ivan Kapistran**, the so-called 'Defender of Belgrade', who died in Ilok in 1456, though the building is mostly much more recent, having been remodelled in 1906 by the busy Hermann Bollé (see Zagreb, etc).

There's an unusual statue of St Francis, right in the middle of the nave, and a couple of 15th- and 16th-century tombs to look at before you get to the dark, sagging altarpiece (senselessly destroyed and left to rot by Serbs), depicting St Ivan – though without restoration it won't be doing so for much longer.

The Romans were here, nearly 2,000 years ago, and it was they who planted the first **vineyards**. After being wiped out during the recent war and ensuing occupation, Ilok's vineyards reopened for business in 1997, and fine white wines are once again being produced. Look out for Chardonnay, Graševina, Traminac, White Pinot and Riesling, and head for the **tourist office** (*Trg Nikole Iločkog 2;* ☎ *032 590 020; www.turizamilok.hr*) for information on local wine tours. Wine tastings can also be arranged in the old wine cellars of the castle (*Šetalište Barbarića 4;* ☎ *032 590 088; www.ilocki-podrumi.hr*).

⌂ WHERE TO STAY AND EAT

⌂ **Hotel Dunav** (9 sgls, 5 dbls, 2 apts) Julija Benešića 62; ☎ 032 596 500; www.hoteldunavilok. com. In a peaceful setting on the Danube, with its own restaurant. €€€

⌂ **Pansion Comfort Masarini** (6 dbls) Stjepana Radića 4; ☎ 032 590 050; m 098 1646 855; www.masarini.hr. Good-value pansion, centrally located. €€

⌂ **Srijemska kuća** (2 dbls, 1 trpl) Gupca 89; m 098 718 612, 098 845 414; www.srijemska-kuca.com.hr. Small B&B under 10mins' walk south of the town centre, with its own restaurant. €€

⌂ **Cinema Old Town Hostel** (30 beds) Julija Benešića 42; ☎ 032 591 159; www.cinema.com. hr. Hostel in converted cinema, with 4-, 6- & 8-bed rooms (priced from 100kn in dorms to 400kn for 2 people in one of the smaller rooms), & its own café/bar & pizzeria. €€–€

✗ **Kapetanova kuća** (2 rooms) Dunavska 6, Šarengrad; m 099 4414 672, 098 942598. Traditional farm out near Šarengrad, on the banks of the Danube, serving all sorts of fish specialties. It also rents out boats, & offers horseriding . Bookings required. €€€

5

Istria

Telephone code for Istria 052 (except Opatija 051)

Of Croatia's busy coast, Istria, the northwestern peninsula, is by far the most visited, with holiday accommodation for over a quarter of a million people. What's remarkable, however, is how the region has managed to keep tourist development away from the pretty Venetian old towns along the west coast, or the medieval villages of the hilly, wooded interior. You'll even find picturesque coves and hidden rocky beaches that feel off the beaten track. Roman ruins and Byzantine mosaics are complemented by clear unpolluted waters and a gentle climate, helping to explain why millions of people keep coming back here, year after year. Even if some of the large socialist-era hotel complexes and mega campsites aren't necessarily for you, Istria has a great deal to offer.

On the west coast, you'll find Byzantine mosaics in **Poreč** and the wonderful Venetian town of **Rovinj**, while on the east lies **Opatija**, the swanky resort of choice for turn-of-the-20th-century Austro-Hungarians. **Pazin**, inland, is the administrative centre, whereas **Pula**, on the southern tip, with its extraordinary Roman amphitheatre, is the economic heart of the region. Off the west coast stand the **Brijuni Islands**, now a pretty national park, while the **Učka Mountains** in the northeast rising above Opatija provide a welcome relief from the crowds, even at the season's peak.

WARNING

Croatia's coastal resorts and towns are very busy indeed from late June until early September and you might find that hotels, private rooms and campsites are fully booked if you arrive on spec; and even if not, the owners of private rooms and campsites are often simply unwilling to take guests who aren't staying for a minimum of three nights. In high season stays of fewer than three nights in private accommodation usually carry a surcharge. If you want to secure centrally located accommodation, or have a specific hotel in mind, then it pays to book well ahead. If you find yourself struggling to find somewhere to stay then base yourself in Pula, where it's usually easier to find a vacant room, and make day trips out. Another option, if you have your own transport, is to take advantage of the increasing number of farms and villages in the interior offering agro-tourism (bed and breakfast) accommodation – there are now many of these places, and more are coming on board all the time. There is plenty of information (including a brochure, *Holidays in Green Istria*) available from the websites of the Istrian tourist board (www.istra.hr, go to 'Planning Your Travel and Stay' and select 'Brochures') and the Central Istrian tourist board (*www.central-istria.com*).

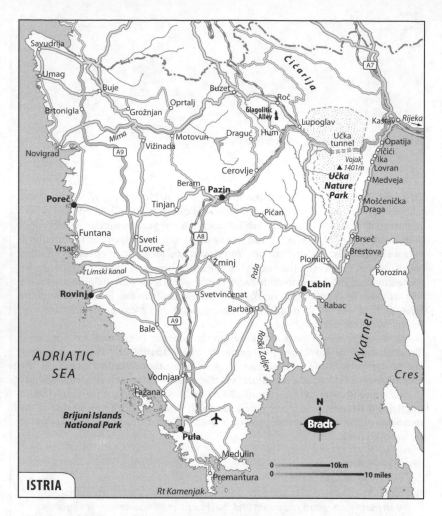

Early and late season are great times to visit, with the weather often being good and the towns empty of tourists. April/May and September/October are especially good – in winter the peninsula gets a fair amount of rain, and though Pula and Rovinj are open all year round, resort towns like Poreč, Novigrad and Rabac pretty much close down altogether.

Istria had five sets of rulers during the 20th century, going from Austro-Hungarian to Italian to German to Yugoslav to Croatian in the space of 70-odd years – prompting anecdotes from tour guides across the region about families with four nationalities in the space of three generations. It makes for an unusually tolerant part of the country, and particularly on the west coast you'll still find many people bilingual in Croatian and Italian.

THE WEST COAST TO POREČ

Working anticlockwise round Istria, the first main settlements are **Umag** and **Novigrad**. These were both once Roman towns, on their own mini-peninsulas, but have long been given over unashamedly to the holiday business, with little to show for their historic past. The lack of industry anywhere near here, the clear waters, and the pleasant enough coastal hotels and campsites draw regular crowds. Umag is currently booming and is the host venue for the annual ATP tennis tournament, while Novigrad is emerging as a serious yachting destination with massive investment in a new marina. Big name hotels such as Kempinski are also currently moving into this part of Istria.

Just north of the twin resorts is **Savudrija**, home to a lighthouse with a charming story. Locals insist that it was built by a lovestruck noble in an attempt to win over his unrequited love. Tragically she died before it was finished, but it remains as an eternal tribute to her. Today it's a quiet spot where you can enjoy the sea views or swim off the rocks, with an adjacent campsite (Pineta) for those who want to stay the night. It's also possible to stay at the lighthouse (*www.lighthouses-croatia.com*), which is a wonderful treat.

Poreč (Parenzo) itself is the undisputed capital of Croatian tourism. Its resident population may be just under 8,000, but it hosts over 400,000 visitors annually (and over 2.5 million tourist nights) spending upwards of 4.5 million nights in the huge resorts spread along the 50km stretch of coast running south from the Mirna River to the Limski Kanal (Lim Fjord). The unashamed devotion to holidaying here means you can find just about anything to divert you (in season), from plain old-fashioned sunbathing and swimming to walking, cycling, riding, water-skiing, diving, jet-skiing, ballooning or paragliding, not to mention tennis, volleyball and the rest. The tourist infrastructure is excellent, with walking and cycling trails (up to 50km circuits), and maps available from the **tourist office** (*at the entrance to the old town, just up from Trg Slobode, at Zagrebačka 9;* \ *451 293; www.to-porec.com*), as well as over 100 restaurants and more than 25,000 beds in the vicinity. Lonely, you won't be.

At the centre of all this is the pretty town itself (more of a village, really), tightly fitting on to a peninsula measuring just 440m long and 200m wide. Here, you'll find stone-paved streets, fine medieval buildings, traces of the Roman colony and arguably the world's best-preserved early Christian cathedral complex, featuring those famous mosaics – enough, in any case, to warrant Poreč being on UNESCO's list of World Heritage Sites.

HISTORY Inhabited for over 6,000 years by the Histrian tribes who gave their name to the Istrian peninsula, Poreč was finally subdued by the Romans in the 2nd century BC and – with the new name of Julia Parentium – was upgraded to the status of colony during the 2nd century AD. There's a small walled garden near the peninsula's tip with lots of Roman bits and pieces from this era, as well as more in the town's museum, but the main thing you'll notice is the street layout – and even the street names, Decumanus and Cardo Maximus – which are still Roman rather than medieval.

ON TO SLOVENIA

Visitors to Istria may well be tempted to nip over the border into Slovenia. This even smaller ex-Yugoslav republic has lots to recommend it, and you'll see excursions offered from Istrian resorts to the famous cave complex of Postojna, along with camera-pleasing Predjama Castle, as well as to the youthful capital, Ljubljana, which mixes abundant cafés, bars and restaurants with numerous museums and galleries. For more information see *Istria: The Bradt Travel Guide* (page 429).

Early Christians worshipped in secret here, and Poreč's first bishop, Maurus, was martyred in the 4th century – the town still puts on a good show for his feast day, 21 November, should you still be around that far out of season.

By the 6th century, with Byzantium in charge (from 539 to 751), Bishop Euphrasius reckoned it was time for a major rebuilding programme, tearing down the existing church and putting up a complex consisting of a basilica, an atrium, a baptistery and – naturally – a bishop's palace.

After the usual takeover by Goths and the like, Venice was in power here for more than 500 years (1267–1797), though in charge of not very much, with the plague scything down the local population to just 100 by the 17th century. Venice repopulated the town from southern Dalmatia, before collapsing and leaving the way free for the Austro-Hungarians. With the first guidebook to the area available in 1845 and the first public beach opened in 1895, Poreč was well on the way to its true destiny as a holiday haven.

GETTING THERE AND AWAY Poreč is easily reached by **bus** – it's just under an hour away from Pula or Koper (in Slovenia), both 55km distant, with frequent services from Rijeka (2 hours) and Zagreb (4½ hours, around a dozen times a day). The nearest **train** stations are Pazin (connecting with Ljubljana via Lupoglav) or Koper, while the nearest **airport** is at Pula (page 213). In summer there are also **ferries** from Pula, Rovinj, Trieste and Venice.

If you're coming in by **car**, Poreč is well signposted – just follow signs to the main resort of Plava Laguna and you won't go far wrong. For **car hire**, the best local outfit is Ventura (*Trg J Rakovca 2; ✆ 434 700; www.vetura-rentacar.com*).

GETTING AROUND In summer, there's a 'tourist train' that plies its way up and down the coast south of Poreč to the main resort areas of Plava Laguna and Zelena Laguna (blue lagoon; green lagoon), with a local boat covering the same turf from the seaward side. Out of season, you'll have to rely on the bus to Vrsar or your own transport. If you're just coming in to see the old town, it's all perfectly manageable on foot from the bus station, at the eastern end of the peninsula, next to the small harbour. The bus station has left-luggage facilities.

WHERE TO STAY With some 25,000 beds in the vicinity – 5,000 of them in private rooms – accommodation ought to be a doddle in Poreč. Ought to be, but if you're here in season, without a booking, you could well find yourself on the bus back out to Pula in search of shelter. There are more than 20 agencies in the area, the most popular of which is Di-Tours (✆ *432 100; www.di-tours.com; at several locations*), handling private rooms, which go for around €40 for a double in summer, but more like €25 out of season. From June to September, you'll find agencies open until 22.00 daily, but outside these months most close after lunch and don't open on Sundays – though you can find plenty of others listed at www.to-porec.com.

Hotels and apartments The nicest hotels in the town itself are the Riviera and the Villa Parentino, both housed in semi-grand, 19th-century buildings right on the waterfront. Out of town, there's a huge range of three- and two-star complexes, all run either by Valamar (*www.valamar.com*) or by Laguna Poreč (*www.lagunaporec.com*), which between them control almost the entire Poreč economy. The enormous two-star **Delfin** hotel [200 E4] (*793 rooms; Zelena Laguna; ✆ 414 000, 410 102; www.lagunaporec.com; €€€*) in Zelena Laguna is good value for money.

🏠 **Grand Hotel Palazzo** [200 A2] (70 rooms) Obala Maršala Tita 24; ☎ 858 800; www.hotel-palazzo.hr. Originally the Hotel Riviera, built in 1910 by the enterprising Mr Klein, who already owned swanky hotels at the time in Opatija. Failing to get planning permission from a competition-concerned Poreč council, he was sold a piece of sea instead, & reclaimed the land on which he then built his hotel. The Riviera was 'restored' in 1953, then finally given a more recent full 4-star makeover (including a new name). €€€€€

🏠 **Hotel Riviera and Villa Parentino** [200 B2] Obala Maršala Tita 15–18 (105 rooms, 8 suites) ☎ 400 800, 465 120; www.valamar.com; ⊕ Apr–Nov. Renovated 4-star with outdoor pool & spa spread over 2 properties right on the waterfront. Now 'adults only', so great for couples. €€€€€

🏠 **Isabella Villas** [200 A4] (108 apts) Sv Nikola; ☎ 465 120, 406 000; www.valamar.com. Upscale apartments on the island of Sv Nikola, part of the huge new Valamar Isabella Island Resort which opened on the island in 2015. €€€€€

🏠 **Gargamelo Pension** [200 F1] (20 rooms) Dalmatinska 10; 📱 095 5180 261; http://gargamelo.info. Small family-run pansion around 2.5km from the town centre, with its own restaurant. €€€€

🏠 **Kaštel** [200 F1] (4 rooms) Kaštelir 28, Kaštelir; ☎ 455 310, www.kastel-kastelir.hr. Small family-run pansion/restaurant in the village of Kaštelir, around 7km north of town. €€€€

🏠 **Hotel Poreč** [200 E4] (54 rooms) Rade Končara 1; ☎ 451 811; www.hotelporec.com. Standard-issue comfort in a building overlooking the bus station. €€€€

🏠 **Jadran** [200 A2] (22 rooms) Obala Maršala Tita 24; ☎ 465 120, 465 000; www.valamar.com; ⊕ May–Sep. Solid 2-star in a semi-grand, 19th-century building right on the waterfront. €€€€–€€€

🏠 **Hostel Papalinna** [200 D2] (22 rooms) Vladimira Nazora 9; ☎ 465 000; www.hostelpapalinna.com. New hostel, opened in 2014, with 4- & 8-bed dorms, all with en suite, smack in the middle of the old town. Actually owned by Valamar. €€€

🏠 **Sobe Daniela** [200 G3] (4 rooms) Veleniki 15a; ☎ 460 519; www.konobadaniela.com. Excellent-value rooms, above a homely konoba (see below). 4km from the town centre. €€€

🏠 **Ty Istra** [200 G3] (sleeps 10+) Dračevac; ☎ 052 433 624; e info@solis-porec.com; www.tyistra.com; see ad, page 420. Beautifully renovated stone farmhouse & 2 studio apts, just 10mins' drive from Poreč. Private pool, fully equipped kitchen, garden; small kitchenette in studios. Owned by co-author of Bradt's *Istria* guide. From €800 (Oct–May) to €1,800 (Jul/Aug) p/w for whole house & 1 of the studios (other configurations possible). €€€–€€

Camping There are seven main campsites in the vicinity, but four – Solaris and Ulika (to the north) and Istra and Koversada (to the south) – are reserved for naturists. If you prefer to keep your kit on, then try Zelena Laguna or Bijela Uvala (*both* ☎ 410 102; www.lagunaporec.com), both in Zelena Laguna, or Lanternacamp (*to the north, reserve ahead;* ☎ 465 010; www.camping-adriatic.com).

🍴 **WHERE TO EAT AND DRINK** With around 100 restaurants and over 20 pizzerias – not to mention countless snack bars and ice-cream parlours – the Poreč area must have one of the highest eatery-densities on the planet relative to its resident population, although practically all are closed out of season. In town itself the emphasis is more firmly on cafés and bars, but you'll have no trouble finding pizza, pasta, or Istrian specialities like *pršut*, *maneštra* (bean soup) and a dizzying array of fish dishes. Lobster (*jastog*) is expensive but popular, especially in pasta (*sa rezancima*). In spring and early summer make an effort to try the fine local wild asparagus, dark and slightly bitter, but delicious.

🍴 **Istra** [200 D4] Bože Milanovića 30; ☎ 434 636; ⊕ noon–midnight daily. Up by the bus station, this is the right place to splash out on top-of-the-range seafood and other local specialities. €€€€

🍴 **Konoba Daniela** [200 G3] Veleniki 15a; ☎ 460 519; www.konobadaniela.com; ⊕ 11.00–23.00 daily. Highly rated & extremely popular family-run konoba around 4km inland from the town centre. It also has rooms (see above). €€€

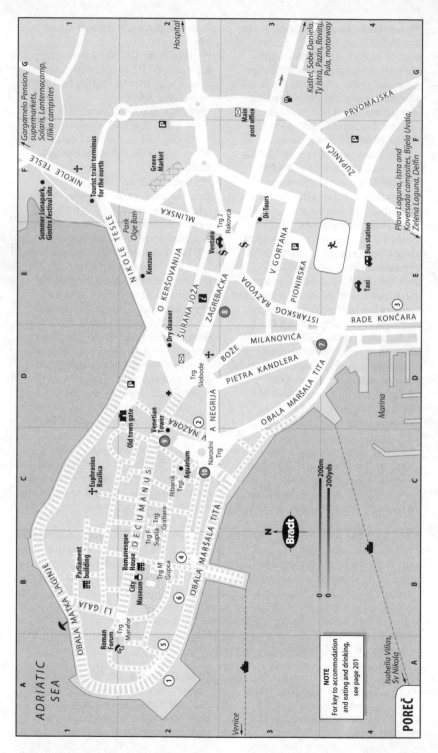

200

ADRIATIC SEA

POREČ

Venice

Isabella Villas,
Sv Nikola

NOTE
For key to accommodation
and eating and drinking, see page 201

Gargamelo Pension,
supermarkets,
Solaris, Lanternacamp,
Ulika campsites

Summer Lunapark,
Giostra festival site

Tourist train terminus
for the north

Hospital

Main
post office

Green
Market

Park
Olge Ban

Konzum

Dry cleaner

Venturia

Trg J
Rakovca

Di-Tours

Euphrasius
Basilica

Old town gate

Venetian
Tower

Parliament
building

Romanesque
House

City
Museum

Trg M
Gupca

Trg F
Supila

Trg
Grabara

Ribarsk
Trg.

Aquarium

Narodni
Trg

Trg
Slobode

Roman
Forum

Trg
Marafor

Taxi

Bus station

RADE KONČARA

PIETRA KANDLERA

MILANOVIĆA

BOŽE

OBALA MARSALA TITA

Marina

N

Bradt

200m
200yds

0

0

Kaštel, Sobe Daniela,
Ty Istra, Pazin, Rovinj,
Pula, motorway

Plava Laguna, Istra and
Koversada campsites, Bijela Uvala,
Zelena Laguna, Delfin

PRVOMAJSKA

ŽUPANICA

ISTARSKOG RAZVODA

PIONIRSKA

V GORTANA

ZAGREBAČKA

ŠURANA JOŽA

O KERŠOVANIJA

NIKOLE TESLE

NIKOLE TESLE

MLINSKA

A NEGRIJA

V NAZORA

DECUMANUS

OBALA MATKA LAGINJE

LJ GAJA

OBALA MARSALA TITA

✕ Peterokutna Kula [200 C2] Decumanus 1; ☎ 451 378; www.kula-porec.com.hr; ⏲ 11.00–23.00 daily. Serves a range of Istrian dishes in a 15th-century tower. €€€

✕ Nono [200 E3] Zagrebačka 4; ☎ 453 088; http://nono.com.hr; ⏲ 11.00–23.00 daily. Pizzeria just down from the tourist office, reputed to have the best pizzas in town – & it's certainly popular, even off-season. €€

⌨ Torre Rotonda [200 C2] Narodni trg 3a; www.torrerotonda.com; ⏲ 11.00–23.00 daily. Café & cocktail bar at the top of another 15th-century tower.

WHAT TO SEE AND DO Poreč's main draw is the **Euphrasius Basilica** [200 C1] and its remarkable series of 6th-century Byzantine mosaics (⏲ *Jul/Aug: 09.00–21.00 Mon–Sat; Apr–Jun & Sep/Oct: 09.00–18.00 Mon–Sat; Nov–Mar: 09.00–16.00 Mon–Sat; 40kn*). Access is via the largely reconstructed (albeit with very old materials) atrium, and is free, though it's worth paying to see the small museum in the Bishop's Palace behind the basilica. This houses lots of stone and mosaic fragments, including some from Maurus's so-called 'oratory' – probably in fact what was his own house, given the clandestine nature of 4th-century Christianity. Note the mosaic fish, the early Christians' secret symbol. You might also want to splash out on climbing the **campanile**, which was added to the complex in 1522 (access through the baptistery) for great views out over the town.

But, like everyone else, you'll end up in the basilica itself, stunned by the mosaics in the main apse. The very plainness of the rest of the church sets these off fantastically. Dating from the second half of the 6th century, they show Byzantine art at its best, following on in the tradition started 100 years earlier in Ravenna, and roughly contemporaneous with the mosaics in Aya Sofya in Istanbul – indeed, craftsmen from Constantinople worked on the wall furnishings here too.

Dominated by the Virgin and Child, you'll see Euphrasius himself on the left-hand side with a handy-sized model of the basilica. To the left of the main windows is the Annunciation, while on the right a nosy servant gets a rare peek at the Visitation. Over the arch are the first 12 women saints, with Agnus Dei (the Lamb of God) as the centrepiece, while across the top are Christ and the Apostles. Complemented by coloured stones and fabulous mother-of-pearl – whole scallop and oyster shells have been used – the ensemble is still almost unnaturally vibrant some 1,500 years on.

The stone altar canopy, modelled on the one in St Mark's in Venice, wasn't added until 1277, but blends in surprisingly well with the whole.

On your way out, you can see where excavations have revealed part of the mosaic floor of one of the earlier churches on the site.

The rest of the town is mainly remarkable for its narrow stone streets, pretty squares and occasional

5

201

architectural one-offs, like the **Venetian Tower** [200 C2] at the top end of Decumanus and the so-called **Romanesque House** [200 B2] further down, with its distinctive 13th-century wooden balcony. Down at the bottom of Decumanus is Trg Marafor, once the Roman Forum. In the low-walled garden behind this you'll find a collection of Roman ruins, mainly coming from a couple of temples that once stood here.

Finally, there's the **City Museum** (*Gradski Muzej, www.muzejporec.hr, closed for renovation in 2015*) [200 B2], housed in the early 18th-century Sinčić Palace on the main drag, with Greek and Roman artefacts and some monumental canvases.

Poreč's increasingly popular **Giostra** festival takes place on the first weekend of September, with jousting on horseback on the beach, and other events (*http://giostra.info*).

AROUND POREČ Heading south from Poreč you soon come to **Vrsar**, famous mostly as the access point for Europe's largest naturist resort, at **Koversada** (see below). Koversada sits on the northwest corner of the **Limski Kanal** (Lim Channel), a 10km-long flooded valley ideal for cultivating oysters and mussels. There are two ways to get there, either by road or by taking an excursion boat from Poreč, Vrsar or Rovinj. It used to be a secret place, used by pirates and buccaneers as a hideout between raids on Venetian shipping, but these days, with foodies and tour buses flocking here for the shellfish, there's quite a bustle to it all.

Whether or not Francis Drake's treasure is hidden hereabouts is highly debatable, but it doesn't stop treasure-hunters coming each year to look; what you should be looking for, however, are the dolphins that sometimes come into the channel to play. For the best view of the channel, continue on the road to Vrsar, stopping off at the viewing tower, which opens up a whole swathe of the emerald water and surrounding forest.

🏠 **Where to stay and eat**

🏠 **Koversada** 🗣800 200; www.campingrovinjvrsar.com for the campsite; 🗣800 250 for apartments & villas; www.maistra.com. Established in 1960 & catering for the best part of 1,000 people indoors & more than 7,000 campers outside, it's fully booked all season long. Reserve well ahead. €41.50 for 2 adults & standard pitch in high season. €€

✖ **Trošt Obala** Maršala Tita 1a, Vrsar; 🗣052 445 197; www.restoran-trost.hr; ⏰ 10.00–midnight daily. Excellent & highly regarded restaurant on the waterfront in Vrsar, with a nice terrace. €€€€

✖ **Fjord** Limski Kanal; 🗣448 222; ⏰ 11.00–22.00 daily. This place has the best view, but the food isn't always as good as Viking's. All part of the experience, however, is watching the local fishermen landing & sorting the catch of the day by the waterfront. €€€

✖ **Viking Restaurant** Limski Kanal; ⏰ 11.00–16.30 & 18.30–23.00 daily. Of the flurry of eateries, Viking has perhaps the best food, with a wide variety of fish & meat dishes accompanying the range of crustaceans. €€€

ROVINJ

Dominated by its outsize church and campanile, Rovinj (Rovigno) is one of the most attractive places in Croatia, with the steep cobbled streets of the walled old town giving way to sunny Venetian quayside cafés and restaurants. Serious tourist development is encroaching on this photogenic, once-upon-a-time island city, but it still manages to accommodate increasing numbers of visitors with ease – mostly away from the old town, along the coast or on one of the nearby islands.

It's also the most Italian place in Croatia, with the people, street signs and menus all being bilingual. A centuries-old fishing tradition is alive and well, though on the wide quaysides you're as likely to witness spontaneous concerts or vibrant café life as fishermen bringing in the catch or mending their nets.

While you're there, check out the curiously flat-bottomed, square-stemmed boats unique to Rovinj – the *batana* probably only survived into the 21st century with UNESCO help, and contrast sharply with the bonanza of visiting super yachts.

HISTORY The island of Rovinj – it wasn't joined to the coast until 1763 – was known in Roman times and was fortified and inhabited through the decline of the Roman Empire and into the Middle Ages. The frequent subject of barbarian attacks, Rovinj's people developed a densely packed, organic urban architecture on the island, and as the population increased and the space ran out, families found themselves living literally on top of one another. Each insisted nonetheless on its own fireplace and chimney, giving Rovinj's old walled town the distinctively jumbled look it has today.

Most of the buildings date from the 13th century on, when the Venetians secured control, retaining it right up to the collapse of the republic at the end of the 18th century. (Quarries near Rovinj furnished the marble you can see today in the lovely church of Santa Maria della Salute, in Venice.)

During the scourge of the bubonic plague, Rovinj remained miraculously unscathed. While Poreč, to the north, and Pula, to the south, saw their populations plunge in the mid-17th century to just 100 and 300 inhabitants respectively, Rovinj could boast 10,000 healthy souls – not far off today's 13,000.

With the isthmus paved over, Rovinj spread across to the mainland from the end of the 18th century, while the introduction of Croatia's first tobacco factory in 1872 brought prosperity – even today the factory makes most of Croatia's cigarettes.

GETTING THERE AND AWAY Rovinj is less than 40km from Pula, and can be reached by bus or car in not much over half an hour from Pula's train station, airport or city-centre bus station – buses run a dozen times a day between the two. If you're coming from the north or east by car you'll see Rovinj clearly signed off the main road. From mid-April to early October the Venezia Line ferry from Venice also stops at Rovinj (*www.venezialines.com*).

GETTING AROUND The **bus station** (with left-luggage facilities) is halfway between the old town and the marina, a 5-minute walk from the main town quay, home to the highly informative if not always especially friendly **tourist office** (*Pino Budicin 12; \ 811 566; www.tzgrovinj.hr*). Once you're there, everything's easily (and only) reachable on foot. If you're coming in by **car**, you'll almost certainly end up on the northern side of the old town, where you'll find the only large car park, with spectacular views of the ancient walls, crowned by the Venetian campanile. For **car hire**, a good bet is Stop (m *099 2102 582; www.stop-rentacar.com*), and if you want to **rent a bike**, head for Planet (\ *840 494; www.planetrovinj.com; 100kn/day*), which can also arrange private accommodation.

🏠 **WHERE TO STAY** *Map, page 205*

Popular with well-heeled Croatians, Rovinj has something of a shortage of accommodation in season, and you may find it easier to stay in Pula and make a day trip of it. If you do get seduced by the idea of staying here – and who wouldn't be? – start by checking out the following options. As well as in the old town itself, there are many other hotels in the south on the Zlatni rt/Punta Corrente cape, a 15–20-minute walk from town, or on Katarina or Andrea islands, a short boat-ride away.

Istria ROVINJ

5

Rovinj also has plenty of **private rooms**, though many are outside the old town. Rooms can be booked through any of the more than 20 travel agents in town (*try contacting Dik & Co;* ✆ *818 181; www.dik-rovinj.com; or see the tourist office website www.tzgrovinj.hr*), and go for about €60–70 for a double in season, though that's sometimes based on a six-night stay, in which case expect to stump up a supplement for a one- or two-night stay.

For camping, you can't do better than the pleasantly pine-shaded **Porton Biondi** (*Aleja Porton Biondi 1;* ✆ *813 557; www.portonbiondi.hr;* €), a 15-minute walk north of the old town with its own beach and fabulous views back to Rovinj.

Old town

🏠 **Adriatic** (18 rooms) Pino Budicin; ✆ 815 088, 800 250; www.maistra.hr. The small & swanky Adriatic is the oldest hotel in Rovinj, & occupies an ideal spot right on the old quay. It re-opened in 2015 after extensive refurbishment by the same architects responsible for the Lone, its rooms individually decorated with original art works. €€€€€

🏠 **Villa Valdibora** (9 rooms) S Chiurcio 8; ✆ 845 040; www.valdibora.com. Beautifully restored old townhouse right in the town centre, with dbls & studio apartments. €€€€€

🏠 **Casa Garzotto** (4 rooms) Garzotto 8; ✆ 811 884; www.casa-garzotto.com. Nice boutique hotel in the centre of town, a renovated house decorated in period style. €€€€

🏠 **Villa Tuttorotto** (7 rooms) Dvor Massatto 4; ✆ 815 181; www.istriahotelrovinj.com. Very stylish boutique hotel set in a beautifully restored 16th-century Venetian *palazzo*, with lovely rooms. €€€€

🏠 **Pansion Romano** (1 dbl, 1 apt) Vukovarska 2a; ✆ 817 275; www.romano.hr. Very good-value pansion, on the southeast edge of town. €€

Further afield

🏠 **Hotel Lone** (248 rooms) Luje Adamovica 31; ✆ 800 250; www.lonehotel.com. Exceptionally swish 5-star designer hotel, opened in 2011, where even the staff are outfitted by Croatian designer label I-GLE. €€€€€

🏠 **Monte Mulini** (113 rooms) A Smareglia; ✆ 800 250; www.maistra.hr. Luxuriously renovated 5-star. €€€€€

🏠 **Eden** (325 rooms) L Adamovića; ✆ 800 250; www.maistra.hr. The Eden is a large 4-star complex. €€€€

🏠 **Istra** (376 rooms) Sv Andreja (also confusingly known as Crveni); ✆ 800 250; www. maistra.hr. A little further away, the Istra offers 4-star accommodation on an island. €€€€

🏠 **Park** (202 rooms) I M Ronjgova 11; ✆ 800 250; www.maistra.hr. Another large refurbished hotel, the nicest rooms have lovely views back across the water to the old town. €€€€

🏠 **Katarina** (120 rooms) Sv Katarina; ✆ 800 250; www.maistra.hr. If you want to be on an island then try the 3-star Katarina. €€€€

✖ WHERE TO EAT AND DRINK *Map, page 205*

Restaurants in Rovinj mainly cater to well-off tourists – often locals – who come here for the excellent fish. Don't expect bargains on the quayside, but consider splashing out while you're here, as the quality is exceptional.

✖ **Al Gastaldo** Iza Kasarne 14; ✆ 814 109; ⏰ 11.00–15.00 & 18.00–01.00 daily. Abundant soft furnishings, old paintings & hundreds of bottles of wine stored in racks combine to create a cosy interior, with a few tables in the narrow street outside the closest thing the Al Gastaldo has to a summer terrace. The food is much better than in the overpriced photo-menu restaurants on the waterfront a block away, but there are reports of poor service. No credit cards. €€€€

✖ **Monte** Montalbano 75; ✆ 830 203; www. monte.hr; ⏰ mid-Apr–mid-Oct 18.30–23.30

Mon–Fri, noon–14.00 & 18.30–23.30 Sat/Sun. Up near the cathedral, Monte is considered by many to be Rovinj's top dining spot. €€€€

✖ **Puntulina** Sv Križa 38; ✆ 813 186; ⏰ Apr–Oct noon–15.00 & 18.00–22.00 Thu–Tue (daily in Jul–Aug). Good food & tables overlooking the sea. €€€€

✖ **Aqua2** Obala Alda Rismonda 20; ✆ 817 328; 🇫 Aqua 2; ⏰ 09.00–midnight daily. Very popular place by the waterfront on the harbour. €€€

✖ **Blu** Val de Lesso 9; ✆ 811 265; ⏰ 10.00–01.00 daily. Tables on a lovely little terrace by the sea,

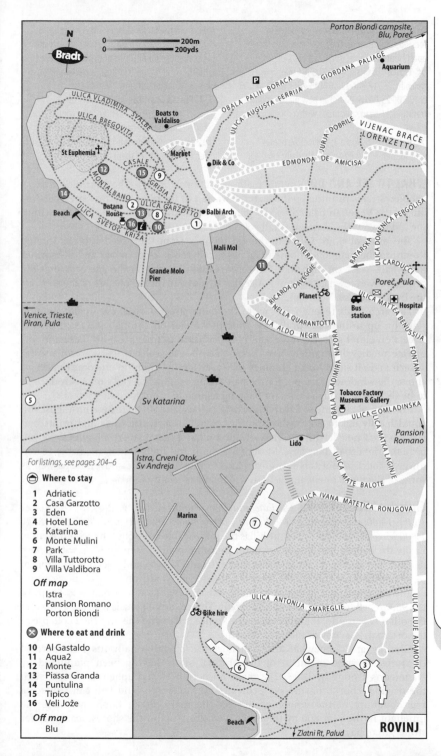

ROVINJ

For listings, see pages 204–6

Where to stay

1 Adriatic
2 Casa Garzotto
3 Eden
4 Hotel Lone
5 Katarina
6 Monte Mulini
7 Park
8 Villa Tuttorotto
9 Villa Valdibora

Off map
   Istra
   Pansion Romano
   Porton Biondi

Where to eat and drink

10 Al Gastaldo
11 Aqua2
12 Monte
13 Piassa Granda
14 Puntulina
15 Tipico
16 Veli Jože

Off map
   Blu

& dishes such as Novigrad scallops coated in toasted sesame seeds. They also have some lovely apartments available. Northeast of town. €€€

✖ **Tipico** Ul Grisia; m 091 3494 006; www. tipico.hr; ⊕ 17.30–22.30 Mon–Thu, noon–15.00 & 17.30–23.00 Fri–Sun. Hip new place serving traditional Istrian specialties with a modern twist. €€€

✖ **Veli Jože** Sv Križa 1; ☎ 816 337; http:// velijoze.net; ⊕ 10.00–midnight daily. Up the steps from the Stella di Mare is this cheerful, cluttered konoba oozing atmosphere & specialising in excellent seafood & Istrian cuisine. Try dishes with the local *tartufi* (truffles), especially if you're here in spring or autumn. €€€

🛋 **Piassa Granda** Veli trg 1; m 098 824 322; ⊕ summer 10.00–01.00 daily, winter 10.00–23.00 daily. Super wine bar/café on this busy square, with around 150 different wines on offer, the majority of them Istrian.

WHAT TO SEE AND DO Rovinj's main attraction is itself – the charming narrow cobbled streets running up through the warren of the old town, the paved car-free quays, the Venetian palazzi and medieval houses, and the 30-odd churches within the old town walls, some so small you'd never know they were there.

The most obvious access to the old town is from the paved isthmus joining Rovinj to the mainland, home to an elegant Baroque clock tower and the former town hall. Walk through the 17th-century **Balbi Arch** (on the site of one of the original seven town gates) and notice the Turk's head on the outside of the arch; on the inside there's a Venetian.

The arch leads through and up to the main street, Grisia, eventually running right on up to the cathedral. Take time to wander off through the maze of tiny streets on either side, however, and you can begin to imagine how dense and un-private medieval life might have been. Each house still has its own stone water cistern and oil store, and a chimney for every family. High up on some buildings, above the windows, look out for the pairs of protruding carved stones – rods used to be threaded through these, for hanging fishing nets out to dry.

Rovinj is also home to a thriving artists' colony, and if you're here in August you could hardly fail to notice the paintings, watercolours, drawings and prints that festoon the whole length of Grisia – tradition has it that if you're a Rovinj artist you have the right to display here. Most of the shops and stalls are unashamedly geared towards tourists, but this is a great place to pick up artistic souvenirs, as well as some of the more interesting Istrian wines and speciality foods.

Church of St Euphemia (*Sv Eufemija; Petro Stankovica;* ⊕ *visitors 10.00–14.00 & 15.00–18.00; mass 08.00, 09.00 (Italian), 10.30, noon, 18.00, 19.00 Sun; 07.30, 18.00, 19.00 Mon–Sat*) At the top of the hill is the improbably large church of St Euphemia. Easily the biggest building in town, on a ground plan of 50m by 30m, with a nave nearly 18m tall, the present structure dates from 1725–36 and is a good example of Venetian Baroque, though the front is a 19th-century add-on.

The enormous campanile from 1680 – Istria's biggest, at over 62m – is a copy of the 98.6m bell tower in St Mark's Square in Venice. Rovinj locals insist of course it's the other way round: that the version in Venice, following the July 1902 collapse of the original, is a copy of the one in Rovinj.

Gloomy and somewhat airless inside, the church retains its fair share of treasures, in spite of much of the original silver having been plundered by Napoleon's troops in 1806. The main attraction is St Euphemia herself; with the original church on the site dedicated to St George (and you can still see a fine sculpture of the dragon-basher on the main altar), Euphemia stole the limelight in the year 800 by improbably washing up on the shores nearby in her stone sarcophagus.

Euphemia was one of a group of early Christians arrested in Chalcedon, near Constantinople, in AD304, and is said to have suffered terrible tortures under Diocletian for failing to recant. Miraculously surviving death by fire, a pit of poisonous snakes and being broken on the wheel, it's likely she was still only a teenager when she was fatally thrown to the lions.

Christians managed to recover her body, which was placed in a church built in her honour. The iconoclasts threw her remains into the sea in the late 8th century, but sailors recovered them and took her to the Greek island of Lemnos. By 796, she was back in Constantinople, mysteriously disappearing in early 800, only to turn up in Rovinj. Hardly surprising, therefore, that the people here gave her co-patroness status, with St George, and built church after church to house her sarcophagus.

The sarcophagus itself is behind the altar in the right-hand aisle of the church, though there's confusion about whether it's 3rd or 6th century, and it was in any case altered in later centuries. Inside are the saint's relics, wrapped in gold cloth. On the altar is a 16th-century gold-plated stone statue of Euphemia, while by the south door is a 14th-century marble relief of her, incorporating bits of earlier sculpture. Most impressive of all is the 4.7m copper statue of the saint adorning the campanile. Cast in 1758, following the destruction by lightning of an earlier wooden statue (which must have been a dramatic moment), Euphemia also does practical duty as a weather vane, just like the original angel on the Campanile di San Marco used to.

On 16 September – the anniversary of her martyrdom – Rovinj celebrates Euphemia's arrival in the town with processions and the performance of miracle plays in the square in front of the church. It's said that in the year 2000 festivities, on the 1,200th anniversary of her arrival, a cloud formed in the shape of the saint.

Beaches and nature reserves Rovinj itself just has a tiny rocky beach past the end of the main quay, but if you go beyond the marina on to the Zlatni rt/Punta Corrente peninsula – a protected park/forest covering around 70ha of land – you'll find footpaths leading to any number of bathing spots. The park itself is charming, featuring cypresses, pines, firs and lovely cedar trees, including the unusual Himalayan cedar.

The 19 islands and rocky outcrops off Rovinj also make up a dedicated nature reserve with an unusual biodiversity – on Katerina alone, there are supposedly 456 varieties of flora. Katerina and Andrea (Crveni) islands also have lovely rocky

THE BITINADA AND THE *ARIA DA NUOTO*

Peculiar to Rovinj are two especially interesting types of folk song, the *bitinada* and the *aria da nuoto*.

The bitinada developed, it's said, from music-loving fishermen's inability to play instruments and mend nets at the same time, and depends on an 'orchestra' of human voices. A lead tenor acts as the conductor, singing a phrase that is then echoed by the other 'instruments' in a waltzing rhythm. So convincing is this vocal trickery that there's a popular story told about Mussolini, having commanded a bitinada performance in Italy during World War II, insisting on going backstage to find out where the real musicians were hiding.

The aria da nuoto (night aria), for its part, echoes the fragments of song that would be passed from boat to boat after dark, with fishermen joining in with new harmonies as the song developed. You can hear both bitinada and arie da nuoto performed during Rovinj's summer-long festival.

beaches and the clearest water imaginable. Boats motor out from Rovinj harbour every half hour or so in summer.

Back onshore, 10km south of Rovinj is the **Palud ornithological reserve** (*www. natura-histrica.hr/ENGLISH/palud_en.html; 50kn*). Palud (from the Latin *palud*, meaning 'marsh') now provides shelter to a variety of both migratory and non-migratory bird species, as well as turtles, eels and mullet, though it was once supposedly a Roman fish farm. Off the coast from here are the Dvije Sestrice (two sisters) islands, a major seagull nesting site.

Finally, if you're into **diving**, you're unlikely to find the remains of Cissa, the legendary city that supposedly sank near Rovinj during earthquakes in 754 and 801, but excursions from the town will help you swim down to the wreck of the *Baron Gautsch*. The ship was the Austro-Hungarians' pride and joy until – after hitting one of its own side's mines in 1914 – it sank, about 10km off Rovinj, with the loss of 284 lives.

Rovinj's old **Tobacco Factory**, built in the 19th century, now houses a big convention centre, and there's a small tobacco museum there too.

BRIJUNI ISLANDS

Just northwest of Pula lie the pretty Brijuni (Brioni) Islands, formerly a holiday retreat for Austro-Hungarians, then the private residence of Marshal Tito for 30 years before becoming a national park in 1983 and opening to visitors in 1984 (*www.brijuni.hr*). Not worth an extensive detour, they're nonetheless well worth a visit if you're in Istria, and can comfortably be managed in a day trip from Pula, Rovinj or Poreč.

Visits remain carefully controlled – the Brijuni is still a state residence as well as a national park – and you can only visit parts of two of the islands, Veliki Brijun and Mali Brijun, on an organised tour or by staying at one of the two hotels or half-dozen villas on the main island. Diving, off-limits for years, is now allowed if you're with a recognised professional operator – check with the national park office (page 210).

HISTORY The Romans made wine and olive oil here, and left behind the remains of a swanky country estate on Veriga bay; Byzantium built an important fortress; and Benedictine monks and Venetian overlords left their mark. But it wasn't until 1893 – when Paul Kupelweiser, an Austrian steel magnate, purchased the islands with a view to starting up a health resort – that Brijuni started featuring on the tour map.

Kupelweiser pursued his dream relentlessly by ridding the islands of malaria (kind of important, that, in a sanatorium), clearing the land, building hotels, villas and heated pools, and providing all the luxury accoutrements demanded by the aristocracy. In the years before World War I, they came in droves. On one day in September 1910 no fewer than 11 archdukes and duchesses were logged, while 31 March 1911 saw 16 princes and princesses and 15 counts and countesses in residence. Franz Ferdinand was here before being shot in Sarajevo, kicking off World War I; so was Kaiser Wilhelm, Thomas Mann, James Joyce, George Bernard Shaw, Richard Strauss and the ubiquitous Marconi, always on hand with a radio experiment to be performed in Europe's best holiday destinations.

On Kupelweiser's death in 1919, his son Karl took over the business, adding a casino and an 18-hole golf course, but ending up bankrupt and suicidal, killing himself here in 1930. The Italians took over, but nothing of much note happened until the islands caught Tito's eye in 1947. From 1949 onwards, for six months of

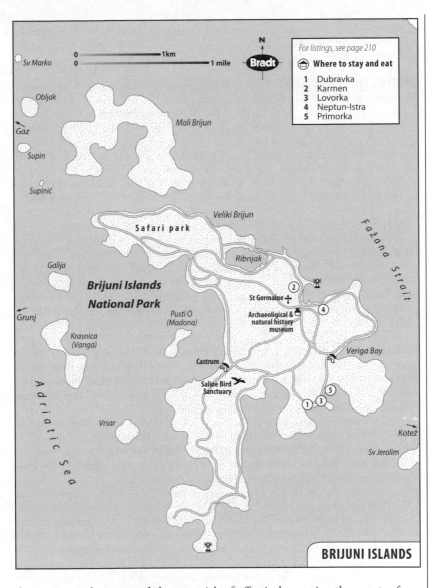

For listings, see page 210

Where to stay and eat
1 Dubravka
2 Karmen
3 Lovorka
4 Neptun-Istra
5 Primorka

Sv Marko

Obljak

Gaz

Supin

Supinić

Mali Brijun

Safari park

Veliki Brijun

Fažana Strait

Ribnjak

Galija

Brijuni Islands
National Park

Grunj

Krasnica
(Vanga)

Pusti O
(Madona)

St Germaine ✝

Archaeoligical &
natural history
museum

2

4

Veriga Bay

Castrum

Saline Bird
Sanctuary

5

1 3

Adriatic Sea

Vrsar

Kotež

Sv Jerolim

0 1km
0 1 mile

N

Bradt

BRIJUNI ISLANDS

the year or so, he managed the rare trick of effectively running the country from his holiday house, something only the Roman Emperor Tiberius on Capri had previously achieved.

Tito had sub-tropical plants brought in and created a private game reserve on the northwestern end of Veliki Brijun from the animals he was given by fellow heads of state. Their descendants are still here, along with one or two of the originals – notably the elephant, Lanka, a gift from Indira Gandhi (the other elephant, Sony, died in 2010). He also welcomed nearly 100 heads of state, including Queen Elizabeth II, Ho Chi Minh and the Ethiopian Emperor Haile Selassie, as well as dozens of celebrities, among them Josephine Baker, Sophia Loren, Elizabeth Taylor and Richard Burton.

After Croatia's independence, President Tuđman continued Tito's tradition by summering here, but his successors Presidents Mesić and Josipović have spent a good deal less time on the islands than their predecessor(s).

GETTING THERE AND AWAY The Brijuni Islands are 20 minutes offshore from the small port of Fažana, 8km northwest of Pula, easily reached on Pula city bus #21. Excursion tickets are available from the Brijuni National Park office on the front in Fažana (525 883; e izleti@brijuni.hr; www.brijuni.hr), and cost 210kn in summer and 125kn in winter. Up to 12 tours a day set off in summer, with just four trips in winter; it's worth reserving ahead at any time of year. The national park office will organise your transfer to the island if you're staying over.

Almost any hotel from Poreč to Rovinj to Pula will also be able to put you on an excursion, with the trip (including the bus to Fažana, and – sometimes – lunch) coming in at around 250–300kn.

In Pula you'll find excursions offered to the islands by private operators for around 250kn a head, but be careful what you're buying, as some of the trips take you round the islands but not on to them, while others are effectively ferries to Mali Brijun for a picnic and a swim. Nice though these trips are, be sure that's what you wanted to do.

Note On the way over to Veliki Brijun keep your eyes peeled for dolphins – small schools are sometimes seen making their way from the Limski Kanal towards the island of Lošinj.

WHERE TO STAY AND EAT Eighty years ago there were five swanky hotels to choose from – not to mention the casino, a horseriding centre, and two polo fields. These days you can either stay at the three-star **Neptun-Istra (€€€€€)**, right next to where the boats come in – and the place most of Tito's guests were lodged – or the two-star **Karmen (€€€€)** on the other side of the bay.

Doubles go for around €176 at the Neptun-Istra during August but drop right back to €79 from November to April, while rooms at the Karmen are about 25% cheaper. Prices include breakfast and unlimited use of the ferries to and from the mainland, and while they're steep for what you get, they do offer you the only chance to see the islands outside of a formal excursion.

A choice alternative, if you're in a group, is one of the lovely three- or four-star villas (**€€€**), on the southern end of Veliki Brijun, of which there are half a dozen, sleeping four to eight people. The four-star establishments – **Primorka**, **Lovorka** and **Dubravka**, which are situated right on the beach – come in at around €135 per person per night for bed and breakfast in peak season (€120 in low season).

If you're booked in for accommodation on the island and have driven to Fažana, then you can leave your car in secure parking there for €15 a day. As for food, unless you brought a picnic with you – a sound idea – you'll almost certainly be eating at one of the hotels (a €13 supplement for dinner); apart from a summer grill (the Plaža) it's all there is.

All accommodation is booked directly through the park office in Fažana (525 807; www.brijuni.hr).

WHAT TO SEE AND DO The standard excursion consists of a 3-hour miniature-train ride with an English-speaking guide, which takes in the main sights and culminates with an hour or so to explore the museum/exhibitions.

The first thing you'll notice is the herds of deer – there are at least 800 out in the open here, along with mouflon, pheasants and peacocks roaming free. The keener-eyed will also notice the remarkable number of species of flora – at least 600 local and 30 imported.

The northwestern end of the island is fenced-off as a dedicated **safari park**, featuring zebra, dromedaries, llamas, antelopes, zebu, sheep and an elephant. The idea of foreign fauna here isn't new – Kupelweiser had the bright idea as far back as 1911 of using the Brijuni Islands to acclimatise tropical animals on their way to European zoos.

You'll also be taken to see the rather tatty ruins of the 1st-century BC **Roman country estate** at Veriga Bay, which must have been extraordinary at the time but is hard to imagine now. More impressive is the ruined Byzantine fortress on the other side of the island, the heart of the settlement of **Castrum**, which was inhabited from the 2nd century BC until the early 14th century, when the plague arrived.

The rest of the west coast features the three **residential villas** of Tito's time, the White Villa, Jadranka and Brijunka. Tito himself had his quarters, along with his exquisite tropical gardens, on the offshore island of Vanga (also called Krasnica), charging between the two and around the other islands by speedboat. The White Villa was used for formal receptions, while Jadranka was where visiting royalty overnighted.

There's no doubt you'll also be shown the **Old Lady**, an olive tree more than 1,600 years old – carbon-dating says so. In a botanical triumph, and as a vindication of the programme to revitalise the island's olive production, the Old Lady produced enough olives to make oil for the first time in more than 100 years at the end of 2001.

Back at the starting point, the **archaeological museum** (*Arheološki Muzej;* ☉ *summer 09.00–19.00 daily, winter 09.00–15.00 daily*), housed in a small 14th-century Venetian castle, merits a short visit, while the **Church of St Germaine**, next door, has an interesting collection of copies of Istrian frescoes and Glagolitic inscriptions.

The **natural history museum** next door is a rather poignant collection of stuffed animals which either died here or on the way here from foreign climes. Upstairs there are two collections, the fascinating photos which make up *Josip Broz Tito on Brijuni*, and a collection entitled *From the memory of an old Austrian*, dedicated to Paul Kupelweiser.

If you want to see more than is on the tour, you'll probably have to stay over, and hire a guide from the hotel – in-depth freelancing is strongly discouraged. It's a pity, but understandable, given Brijuni's triple function as state residence, national park and tourist destination.

TRAVELLING POSITIVELY: HELP BRIJUNI'S ELEPHANT!

For lack of funds, the Brijuni National Park can't provide ideal living conditions for its one surviving elephant, and is calling for your help. Although in good health, the elephant doesn't have enough room, and its 480m² living area badly needs to be enlarged, both for the sake of the animal and for the sake of its keepers and visitors. Extra funds are also needed for healthcare and food costs.

So why not become a Brijuni benefactor? Contact the national park office if you want to make a contribution. Your help will be greatly appreciated – indeed since the first edition of this guide was published in 2003, dozens of benefactors have answered the appeal.

Birdwatchers will most likely want to check out the marshy lakes near the Saline Bay (in the south, not marked on all maps), which have now been fenced off as a tentative **ornithological reservation**. Here you'll find excellent nesting grounds for marsh birds including ducks, coots, grebes, quail and noisy pratincoles, as well as warblers, nightingales and other songbirds, while the pine trees provide shelter for goshawks, buzzards and sparrowhawks. Late summer sees the arrival of egrets, storks, herons and bitterns. Contact the national park directly (page 210).

PULA

Strategically situated at Istria's tip, and benefiting from a kind climate and a large, sheltered harbour, Pula (Pola) has been continuously inhabited for the past 3,000 years. What you'll find today, however, is a whole clutch of superb Roman ruins (including one of the world's best-preserved amphitheatres) set in a cheerful, cosmopolitan, street-café city of 65,000 people. Pula lives on the fence, caught halfway between its shipyard, docks and busy commercial port, and the beaches, coves and tourist developments strung out along the indented peninsula a couple of kilometres south of the centre.

Bombarded by both sides during World War II – a rare distinction – the city was quickly restored, and during the Yugoslav era became popular as a holiday destination. The recent war didn't come anywhere near here, but drove away the tourists all the same – though they've now returned in force. Pula's role as a yachting centre, together with the increasing availability of budget flights and the annual Pula Film Festival (see box, page 218) mean that visitor numbers are likely to rise further still.

HISTORY Mentioned in ancient Greek despatches in connection with Jason and the Argonauts, archaeological findings show that Pula (myths notwithstanding) had already been established as a settlement long before the Histri fortified it in the 1st century BC. Once the Romans had successfully overpowered the Histri, Pula grew rapidly in status and became a colony. Under the first Roman emperor, Augustus, it became an important regional centre, and temples, theatres, a forum and an amphitheatre were built.

At its most prosperous, in the time of Septimius Severus (AD193–211), Pula was an important Roman war harbour, and was by then – according to my 1911 *Encyclopaedia Britannica* – home to a population of 35,000 to 50,000 inhabitants. Mysteriously, contemporary sources never mention a figure of more than 5,000 to 10,000.

After the decline of Rome, Pula's fortunes were subjected to the usual roller-coaster ride of Goths, Ostrogoths, Byzantium and Venice, and the combination of invasion and plague saw the city shrink to 1,000 inhabitants in the 16th century. By 1631 the population was down to just 300 – hardly surprising therefore that the Venetians considered having the amphitheatre removed from Pula and put up in Venice instead.

Over the centuries Pula was visited by the likes of Dante, Michelangelo, Palladio and Lord Byron, spreading the Pula influence into Italian, French and British architecture – Inigo Jones is said to have used the Sergius Arch (page 219) as the inspiration for many a loving detail on an English country house.

By 1842, Pula's population had inched up to 1,126, but change was right around the corner. With the collapse of Venice, 50 years earlier, the Austro-Hungarian Empire was seeking major outlets to the Mediterranean, and in 1853 they settled on Pula, rebuilding the town, installing a garrison, starting a shipyard and making it their naval HQ for the empire. By the end of the century Pula's population had exploded to over 45,000.

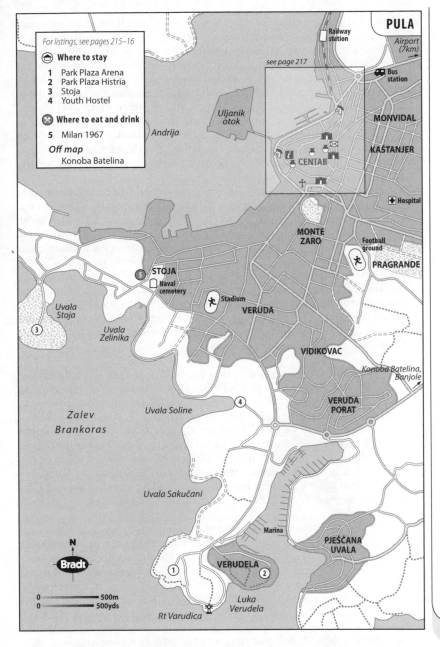

see page 217

PULA

For listings, see pages 215–16

Where to stay
1 Park Plaza Arena
2 Park Plaza Histria
3 Stoja
4 Youth Hostel

Where to eat and drink
5 Milan 1967

Off map
Konoba Batelina

Railway station

Airport (7km)

Bus station

Andrija

Uljanik otok

MONVIDAL

KAŠTANJER

CENTAR

Hospital

MONTE ZARO

Football ground

PRAGRANDE

STOJA

Naval cemetery

Stadium

VERUDA

VIDIKOVAC

Konoba Batelina, Banjole

Uvala Stoja

Uvala Zelinika

VERUDA PORAT

Zalev Brankoras

Uvala Soline

Uvala Sakučani

Marina

PJEŠČANA UVALA

N

Bradt

0   500m
0   500yds

VERUDELA

Luka Verudela

Rt Varudica

Badly bombed during World War II, Pula came under Allied administration until 1947, when it passed to Yugoslavia. Today it's the headquarters of the Croatian Navy as well as one of Croatia's three main shipyards, alongside Rijeka and Split.

GETTING THERE AND AWAY Pula **airport** is 7km northeast of the city, and a reasonably regular airport shuttle bus (30kn) will bring you into town in around 15 minutes or so (*http://prodaja.fils.hr/pindex.php*). Otherwise if you're taking a taxi, call the airport information desk to book (☎ *060 308 308*) or try Taxi Pula (m *098 440 844; www.taxipula.com; 100–140kn into town*) or Taxi Hodak (m *098 9396 618; www.taxi-hodak.com*) – unfortunately Taxi Cammeo, which was by far the cheapest option, stopped operating in Pula recently. If you're on an Istrian package tour of any kind, then you'll probably be transferred straight from the airport to your hotel. An alternative is to fly to Venice and connect with the **car ferry**, which takes around 6 hours to make the crossing. From July until the end of August, Venezia Lines (*www.venezialines.com*) makes this journey three times a week – see its website for a timetable. Alternatively Trieste Lines (*www.triestelines.it*) sails between Trieste and Pula from June to September, three days a week (if you're looking for the timetable on its website, it's under 'rates').

If you're coming in by **train**, you'll find the station on the waterfront, 10 minutes north of the old town – just head towards the amphitheatre past the Hotel Riviera. There are left-luggage facilities here, but the hours are much shorter than those at the bus station, only being open Monday to Saturday. Up to eight trains a day connect Pula with Pazin (*1hr*) and during the summer there's a fast service to Ljubljana and Maribor.

If you're travelling round by **bus**, then you'll find the new station a couple of blocks north of the amphitheatre, though most buses do a loop into town via the old bus station as well. Left-luggage facilities are open here 05.00–23.00 seven days a week. A dozen or so buses a day head up to each of Rovinj (40 minutes) and Zagreb (5½ hours), while eight or more go daily to Poreč (1½ hours), two to Split (11 hours) and one to Dubrovnik (15 hours).

GETTING AROUND Driving round Pula is pretty easy, though in high summer parking in the centre of town can be a problem – not, however, the insurmountable one you'll find in Opatija. If you want to hire a **car**, Vetura (*www.vetura-rentacar. com*) has offices at the airport (☎ *550 900*) and at Verudela (*Verudela 11;* ☎ *210 294*). The centre of town is all walkable – and mostly pedestrianised – but you might find yourself on bus #21 if you're going up to Fažana to catch a boat to the Brijuni Islands, #2 if you're hostelling, #1 if you're heading towards Stoja, and #2a or #3a for Verudela, where the beaches, the hostel and most of the hotels can be found. See www.pulapromet.hr for a bus route map. Bus tickets go for 11kn in town and 15kn or more for longer journeys (eg: Fažana) on the bus.

WHERE TO STAY *Map, page 217, unless otherwise stated*
Pula has relatively few **hotels** in town, but many more on the Verudela peninsula, handy for the beaches. Small family-run hotels are opening up all the time, with the encouragement of the tourist board, so check out the **tourist information office** (*Fourm 3;* ☎ *219 917; www.pulainfo.hr;* ⊕ *Jun–Aug 08.00–22.00 Mon–Fri, 09.00–22.00 Sat/Sun, Sep–May 08.00–21.00 Mon–Fri, 09.00–21.00 Sat/Sun*), which can also give you maps and useful information. The revamped Park Plaza Histria and another dozen hotels can also be booked directly through Arenaturist, which manages most of them, during office hours (☎ *529 400; www.arenaturist.hr*).

The hotels at Verudela are a 15-minute bus ride (#2a or #3a) to the south; Stoja, with some of the best beaches, is to the west (#1 bus), within striking distance of the town itself.

Pula has its fair share of **private rooms**, which cost €40–60 for a double, but the locations often leave something to be desired. Book through any of the 20-odd travel agents in town, and expect to pay a 50% surcharge for a one-night stay in summer.

There's also a good list of private accommodation on the tourist office website (*www. pulainfo.hr*). The excellent **Apartments Arena** (*Flavijevska 2;* ☏ *506 217;* m *098 486 109; www.pula-apartments.com;* €€€–€€) is right next to the amphitheatre.

If you're on a budget, Pula also has a some good **hostels**, and is also great for **camping**, with an easy-to-reach campground at **Stoja** (☏ *387 144;* e *acstoja@ arenaturist.hr; www.arenacamps.com*) – just take the #1 bus to the last stop, about 3km out of town. The Stoja has fairly basic facilities, but an absolutely unbeatable location and some of the best swimming near Pula.

🏠 **Hotel Amfiteatar** (16 dbls, 2 sgls) Amfiteatarska 6; ☏375 600; www.hotelamfiteatar. com. Recently opened boutique hotel near the arena, with smart rooms & its own restaurant. €€€€

🏠 **Park Plaza Arena** [map, page 213] (175 rooms) Verudela bb; ☏375 000; www.arenaturist. hr. Formerly the Hotel Park, the Arena opened in 2015 under the Park Plaza brand following a complete makeover. €€€€

🏠 **Park Plaza Histria** [map, page 213] (233 rooms) Verudela bb; ☏590 000; www.arenaturist. hr. Nicest of all the hotels at Verudela is this palatial 4-star, renovated & rebranded under the Park Plaza chain, which has practically an entire promontory to itself, & views out to sea, back to the marina & all conceivable facilities – including nice private balconies, big indoor & outdoor pools, & its own beach. Dbls include a vast buffet b/fast, & HB is excellent value at only a few euros more. Take the #2a bus to the last stop, & walk 200m. €€€€

🏠 **Scaletta** (12 rooms) Flavijevska 26; ☏541 599; www.hotel-scaletta.com. In the middle of town, almost next door to the amphitheatre. The rooms are all delightful, & the food here is also excellent (page 216), so consider HB – if you can get a room. €€€€

🏠 **Galija** (20 rooms) Epulonova 3; ☏383 802; www.hotelgalija.hr. Just around the corner from

the Omir, also with its own restaurant, & also much better value than the Riviera. €€€

🏠 **Omir** (19 rooms) Serglia Dobrića 6; ☏213 944; www.hotel-omir.com. The 2-star Omir, just to the east of the old town & close to both the Sergius Arch & the market square, is simple but much better value than the Riviera. Has its own restaurant & long-serving pizzeria. €€€

🏠 **Riviera** (67 rooms) Splitska 1; ☏211 166; www.arenaturist.hr. Most striking from the outside is this pre-World War I hotel just down from the train station, a fantastic Austro-Hungarian edifice that would look more at home in Zagreb than Istria. Once very much luxury class, the hotel is now on its uppers – 1-star, & quite appealing for that, though you're paying a lot for the privilege of former elegance (& lack of AC). €€€

🏠 **Hostel Pipištrelo** (30 beds) Flaciusova 6; ☏393 568; m 091 2230 769; www.pipistrelo. com. Lovely hostel right on the Riva. 4-bed dorms with shared bathroom €18.15 in season, dbls with private bathroom €24pp in season. €€–€

🏠 **Youth Hostel** [map, page 213] (216 beds) Zaljev Valsaline 4; ☏391 133; www.hfhs.hr. Pula's Youth Hostel is basic & simple but in an incredible location, with its own beach & a diving club next door. B&B costs from €12.70pp/night. Catch bus #2 or #3 from town. €

❌ **WHERE TO EAT AND DRINK** *Map, page 217, unless otherwise stated*
The best restaurants in Pula are reckoned by many to be south of the town: Milan 1967 in Stoja and Konoba Batelina in the village of Banjole.

In town the emphasis is as much on café life as restaurants, and every district has huge terraces spreading out on to the pavements, packed in summer and surprisingly well attended in spring and autumn. With most of the old town traffic-free, you can take a leaf out of the Puležani's book and take the time to linger over a coffee or an aperitif.

✳❌ **Konoba Batelina** [map, page 213] Čimulje 25, Banjole; ☏573 767; ⏱ 17.00–23.00

Mon–Sat. Outstanding seafood restaurant in the village of Banjole, already extremely popular even before it was included in a list of Europe's top 101 eateries a few years ago, so reservations are definitely advised. €€€€

✕ **Milan 1967** [map, page 213] Stoja 4; ☎300 200; www.milan1967.hr; ⏰ 11.00–midnight daily, closed Sun during winter. Highly rated seafood restaurant near the naval cemetery, at the base of the Stoja Peninsula. €€€€

✕ **Scaletta** Flavijenska 26; ☎541 599; ⏰ summer 10.30–23.00 daily, winter 10.30–23.00 Mon–Sat. If you're near the amphitheatre you might eat at the Scaletta hotel's very good restaurant – not inexpensive but well worth the splash. €€€€

✕ **Kantina** Flanatička 16; ☎214 054; www.kantina-pula.com; ⏰ 08.00–23.00 daily. Great food right next to Pula's open market. €€€

✕ **Jupiter** Castropola 42; ☎214 333; ⏰ 10.00–23.00 Mon–Fri, noon–23.00 Sat, 13.00–23.00 Sun. Great for pizzas, squid & other dishes, with friendly service & generous portions. Much, much better than the overpriced places on Sergijevica & the Forum. €€

💻 **Caffe Diana** Forum 4; ⏰ 07.00–22.00 daily. One of several cafés on & around the forum.

💻 **Caffe Milan** Narodni Trg bb; ⏰ 10.00–23.00 Mon–Fri, 07.00–21.00, 07.00–14.00 Sat/Sun. Alongside the lovely Secessionist cast-iron market building, famous not just for its coffees but also for the underfloor heating on the terrace. It would have suited James Joyce a treat. Inside the market you'll find fresh meat & fish every day, while on the shady square behind there's a vast range of produce on sale, protected from the flies by the chestnut trees – the perfect place to cruise for picnic food.

💻 **Galerija Cvajner** Forum 2; ⏰ 08.00–22.00 daily. Down at the bottom of the town in the Forum you'll find the Galerija Cvajner, a café-cum-art gallery run by the former director of the film festival. It has a lovely terrace (right next door to the tourist office) while inside are great 16th-century ceilings & the remains of old frescoes, uncovered by chance during restoration.

🍷 **Uliks** Trg Portarata 1; ⏰ 07.00–22.00 daily. Up at the other end of the old town, all the way up Sergijevaca, you'll find Uliks, in the building in which James Joyce used to teach (see box, below).

JAMES JOYCE AND PULA

After eloping to Europe in October 1904 with Nora Barnacle, a 20-year-old chambermaid, the 22-year-old James Joyce finally managed to find part-time work teaching English at the Berlitz School in Pula that November.

Moving in with Nora to an unheated apartment in Villa Giulia, just round the corner from the school (in the large yellow building right beside the Sergius Arch – there's a plaque), Jim and Nora spent the winter in Pula half-freezing to death, and spent as much time as they could at the warmer Caffe Miramare delle Specce, down on the waterfront (it's now a furniture shop). In letters to his brother he described Pula as 'Siberia by the sea', but it's clear that Joyce grew to love the city, and he would often be seen on long walks around town and up the coast as far as the fishing village of Fažana.

In February 1905, he was taken to the island of Veliki Brijun for his 23rd birthday by his Berlitz colleagues, and on this trip he broke the news that his first child was on the way. The couple, deciding to settle in Pula, moved to a more comfortable apartment at 1 Medulinska (next door to the university's faculty of philosophy), but following a confusing incident – was Joyce suspected of spying for the Italians or the British? – they packed their bags and hurriedly moved to Trieste, where their son Giorgio was born that July.

Today you'll find little in the way of Joyce memorabilia in town – the Uliks bar, on the ground floor of the apartment building housing the language school, does celebrate the author of *Ulysses* in a modest way with a life-size seated statue of the great artist waiting to be served at one of the terrace tables.

above Sea kayaking around the sea caves on Lokrum (T/D) pages 375–6

right Windsurfing is a popular activity off the Pelješac peninsula (RA) pages 393–4

below There are plenty of opportunities for cyclists on the Učka massif (LT/CTB) page 231

above Risnjak National Park in Gorski Kotar is home to wild populations of wolf, brown bear and lynx (RA) pages 240–2

left The Northern Velebit National Park has excellent hiking routes and spectacular limestone scenery, as well as a diverse range of plants and wildlife (RA) pages 244–6

below The stunning Plitvice Lakes National Park comprises 16 lakes interconnected by waterfalls (RA) pages 172–6

above   Eurasian lynx (*Lynx lynx*) at the zoo in Maksimir Park, Zagreb (RA) page 132

above right   Lonjsko Polje is home to one of Europe's largest concentrations of storks (SA/S) pages 177–9

right   Croatia has several species of butterfly — pictured here, a high brown fritillary (RA) page 6

below   Lokrum hosts an enormous variety of vegetation and numerous species of bird, including peacocks (GD) page 376

left On Assumption Day a statue of the Virgin Mary is carried in a solemn procession from a shrine in Pag's old town to the town centre (RA) page 294

below Folk music is popular across Croatia, with festivals taking place throughout the summer. Here, musicians in the Istrian village of Buzet during the Subotina festival (RA) pages 225–6

above   The Rijeka Carnival attracts 10,000 participants and over 100,000 spectators every year, featuring parades and into-the-night festivities. Pictured, the Zvončari (RA) page 239

below left Stall selling sheep's cheese from the island of Krk, near Zagreb's main square (RA)

below right Fish on sale at Rijeka's market (RA) page 237

bottom right Open seven mornings a week, Zagreb's Dolac market sells everything from fine cheese to traditional Croatian craft, such as these wooden toys (RA) page 104

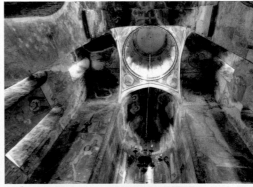

above left Veli Losinj is the smaller of the island's two main settlements (P/D) page 254

above right The leaf-veined network of narrow streets in Korçula town were designed to keep the place cool in summer yet sheltered in winter (RA) pages 394–402

below It may be one of the Adriatic's worst-kept secrets, but the island of Hvar has plenty of beaches and an elegant Venetian capital overlooked by a 16th-century fortress, making it well worth a visit (AS/S) page 332

right The beautiful monastery on St Mary's Island, a short boat ride from Mljet (OZ/S) page 388

below Just a 10-minute boat ride from the bustle of Dubrovnik, the sub-tropical island of Lokrum is home to a ruined Benedictine monastery (N/S) pages 375–6

bottom The iconic Zlatni Rat beach, on Brač, is a 600m spit of fine shingle that changes shape according to the sea currents and seasonal winds (SS/S) page 325

©Zagreb Electric Company

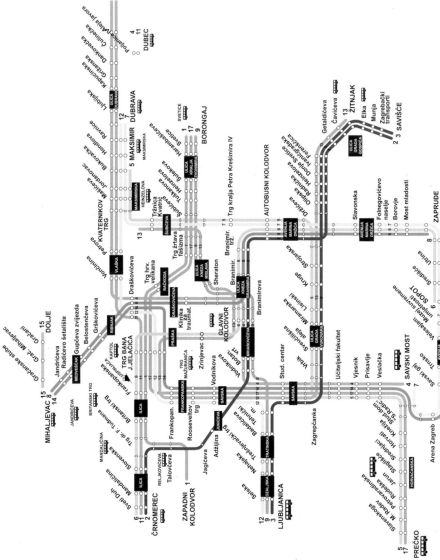

ZAGREB
Tram services

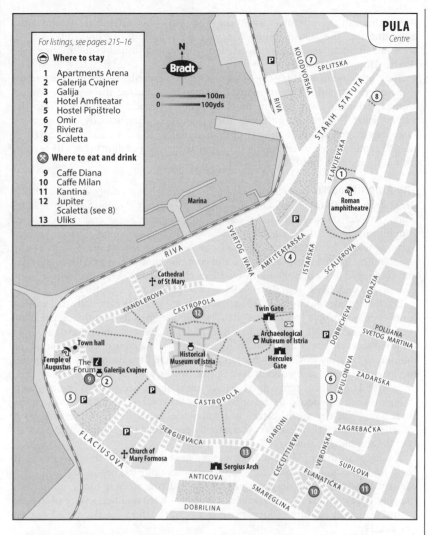

For listings, see pages 215–16

🛏 **Where to stay**
1 Apartments Arena
2 Galerija Cvajner
3 Galija
4 Hotel Amfiteatar
5 Hostel Pipištrelo
6 Omir
7 Riviera
8 Scaletta

❌ **Where to eat and drink**
9 Caffe Diana
10 Caffe Milan
11 Kantina
12 Jupiter
   Scaletta (see 8)
13 Uliks

PULA
Centre

0 ————— 100m
0 ————— 100yds

WHAT TO SEE AND DO The best way to see Pula is on foot and the best place to start is in the Forum, the large paved square just back from the front, on the southwestern corner of town. Stop in at the tourist office and pick up a free map.

The first thing you'll have seen as you came into the square won't have been tourist information but the **Temple of Augustus**. Built in 2BC, according to most modern sources, the temple is one of the best complete Roman monuments outside Italy, rivalling the Maison Carrée in Nîmes. After suffering a direct hit during World War II, it was pieced lovingly back together in 1947, and you wouldn't know the difference.

Originally this was one of three temples on the Forum, and you can still clearly see the shape and placing of the Temple of Diana, one of the other two (the third has gone without trace), by walking round to the back of the 13th-century **town hall** next door. While you're there don't miss the sculpted Renaissance siren/mermaid on the northernmost corner, warding off evil.

Walking up Kandlerova will take you past the cathedral towards the amphitheatre. The houses along the way are reflective of Pula's mixed past, with Renaissance blending into Venetian Gothic, and Romanesque mixing into Austro-Hungarian solidity.

The **Cathedral of St Mary** (Sv Marija) itself would doubtless get more attention if it weren't surrounded by so many Roman ruins – indeed the separate (rather chunky) campanile was built in the 17th century entirely from stones from the amphitheatre. Pop into the cathedral for a peek at the altar, actually a 3rd-century sarcophagus, and some fragments of floor mosaics. The cathedral was started in the 5th century as a conversion job on a Roman temple, but didn't reach its present form until the 16th and 17th centuries.

The Amphitheatre (*www.ami-pula.hr;* ⊕ *Apr 08.00–20.00 daily, May/Sep 08.00–21.00 daily, Jun 08.00–21.30 daily, Jul/Aug, 08.00–midnight daily, Oct 09.00–19.00 daily, Oct–Mar 09.00–17.00 daily; 40kn*) You can't miss Pula's enormous Roman Amphitheatre – it's the sixth biggest in the world (after Rome, Capua, Verona, Syracuse and Arles, since you ask), and has the most complete outer walls of any still standing. Started under Augustus, and continued under Flavian, it was enlarged and completed to its present 130m-by-105m ellipse under Vespasian (whose lover Antonia, it's said, came from Pula) in the second half of the 1st century AD.

Erected outside the city walls, the triple-storeyed building originally had seating for over 20,000 people (odd, given the total population at its completion is widely reckoned to be considerably less than this) and had 20 entrances and exits to allow for rapid access to the seats. Most of the seating has long gone of course – used for building as far away as Venice – but once there would have been stone benches up to the second storey and wooden seating (for women and commoners) above that. Seats were a tight 38cm across and season-ticket holders had engraved nameplates.

Four towers gave access to the upper rows – the southwestern tower housed the royal box, while the northwestern one today features a plaque to the Pula-born Venetian Senator Gabriele Emo, who happily persuaded the Senate in 1583 not to take the amphitheatre away.

The arena in the middle would originally have been filled with sand (arena is Latin for sand) and was used for bloody combats until the beginning of the 5th century. Watching a film-screening or taking in a concert here today, it's hard to imagine the awfulness of real gladiator combats – lions and bears were used here against gladiators (mostly luckless prisoners of war), who were also pitted against one another.

After Rome collapsed the arena was used as a marketplace and for medieval jousting tournaments, but the seating was mostly quarried; today's concerts and screenings seat just 5,000–6,000, and even the biggest gigs – your Stings, your Three

Tenors – can't pack in many more than 10,000 fans. If you're here in summer, don't miss out on the opera or film festivals.

Back into town Walking back towards the town turn half-left into Carrarina and have a look at the **Twin Gate** (Porta Gemina), from the 2nd century AD. This was once part of the aqueduct providing water to the town and one of its 12 gates, and was one of the few monuments built with private money. It's now the entrance to the exhaustive **Archaeological Museum of Istria** (*Arheološki Muzej Istre;* \ *351 300; www.ami-pula.hr*), closed for renovation at the time of writing in 2015. The upper road to the right of the museum leads up to the tatty, 17th-century Venetian **fortress**, housing the **Historical Museum of Istria** (*Prati Povijesni i pomorski muzej Istre; www.ppmi.hr;* ⊕ *summer 08.00–21.00 daily, winter 09.00–17.00 daily; 20kn*) – only worth seeing if you've done everything else, though the views out over the town and particularly of the amphitheatre are excellent from up here.

Back down at the Twin Gate keep the wall on your right and follow Carrarina down past the **Hercules Gate** (Porta Eroole). This is Pula's oldest monument, dating from the middle of the 1st century BC; it's now the entrance to the centre for the Italian minority. The gate's unusual oblique angle is a reminder that the road originally leading out wasn't at right angles to the wall.

Turning into the shady Giardini, follow the walls down to the **Sergius Arch** (also known as Porta Aurea). This was completed in 27BC as a memorial to three soldiers from the same family, Sergius Lepidus, Gaius Lucius Sergius and Gnaeus Sergius. The arch was originally backed by a gate, so only the inside is decorated – check out the winged victories, imagery which was later co-opted wholesale by Christianity when portraying angels.

The Sergius Arch leads – not surprisingly – into Sergijevaca, the old town's main pedestrian street, running back down to the Forum. Halfway down, cut left to the small, 6th-century Byzantine **Church of Mary Formosa** (Sv Marije Formoze), once part of a larger basilica, built to a similar plan to the one in Poreč (page 201). The best mosaics from inside are now in the Archaeological Museum. Just down from here is an impressive 3rd-century mosaic floor, discovered by accident in 1959. Among some fine decorative geometrical work the main panel depicts the Punishment of Dirce – Dirce is the woman in the middle, about to be trampled by the bull, in yet another rendition of the story made famous by the Farnese Bull in Naples. Dirce was the classic cruel stepmother, who treated her husband Lycus's daughter Antiope as a slave. Unfortunately for her, Antiope had already borne two children by Zeus, and once they grew up – after the traditional hillside abandonment – the boys returned to kill Dirce by binding her to a mad bull. Not a great way to go.

Out of town Out of town, the main attractions are the Brijuni Islands (page 208), which are well worth a visit, and the 30km of beaches, coves and bays to the south of the city. The nearest of these are just a 20- to 25-minute walk away from the town centre, or a short bus ride (on #1, #2 or #2a).

Further south, right on Istria's point, are the resorts of **Medulin** and **Premantura**. Each has long stretches of beach with fairly shallow waters, making them popular with families. The **Kažela** camp (*Kapovica 350;* \ *577 277;* e *ackazela@arenaturist. hr; www.arenacamps.com*), on Medulin's sandy beach, has a large (separate) section for naturists. On the other side of the bay, the peninsula's spectacular southernmost spur, Rt Kamenjak, is a dedicated nature park (for more information see *Istria: The Bradt Travel Guide*).

THE EAST COAST TO LABIN AND RABAC

From Pula to the resort of Rabac, the Istrian coast is at its least developed and least visited. The new main road barrels up through the centre of Istria to Pazin before cutting through the Učka tunnel to Rijeka, while the old main road stays 5–10km inland from the undeveloped east coast, only returning to the sea after Labin.

There's little or no public transport, and few places to stay, but if you have your own wheels (and some persistence) you can find deserted coves and beaches here at the end of winding footpaths, even though the steep cliffs often make the coast literally inaccessible. It's a great area to explore on day trips from the coastal resorts, or *en route* to Opatija.

If you're on the bus from Pula to Opatija in the last week of August, it's definitely worth stopping in the village of **Barban**, where the annual Tilting at the Ring (*Trka na prstenac*) festival takes place. The dangerous habit of trying to spear a ring suspended on a rope with a lance from a fast-moving horse used to be commonplace, apparently; today it survives only here and in Sinj (page 315).

Labin, a charming medieval hilltop town, used to be the centre of a thriving mining industry. You won't see much sign of that now, since the mines closed after subsidence in the 1970s. Today it's a lovely place to visit, with steep and narrow streets, a sprinkling of churches and a handful of Baroque and Renaissance palazzi. The **town museum** (*Gradski Muzej; I svbinja 6;* \ *852 477;* e *narodni.muzej.labin@put.t-com. hr; www.uciliste-labin.hr/sec_muzej.htm;* ☼ *summer 10.00–13.00 & 17.00–19.00 Mon–Fri, 10.00–13.00 Sat; winter 07.00–15.00 Mon–Fri*) features an excellent mining exhibition, complete with a suitably claustrophobic tunnel you can go into, as well as various archaeological bits and pieces from the area. Ask at the museum if Matija Vlačić's birthplace is open – if so you'll find an interesting collection of manuscripts and books by (and about) this 16th-century protestant firebrand, contemporary and colleague of Martin Luther. On the way you can walk up to the fortress (*Fortica*) for a fine view out over Rabac and across the water towards the island of Cres.

Rabac, down on the coast, was once a fishing village but is now unashamedly a tourist resort, with nothing much other than apartments and hotels, though it does have a nice (if busy) pebbly beach.

GETTING THERE AND AWAY Pula–Opatija buses stop in Labin's lower town, a steep 15-minute hike below the old town, and you change here if you're going on to Rabac – buses take 10 minutes and run half-hourly down to the resort. Alternatively if you've made it up into Labin's old town you can then walk down to Rabac – it takes about three-quarters of an hour, all downhill, on the old mule path.

WHERE TO STAY AND EAT There aren't any hotels in Labin, though there are a few private rooms – check at whichever tourist agency is open, or at the **tourist office** (*Aldo Negri 20;* \ *855 560; www.rabac-labin.com*). There are also a couple of lovely farmsteads just outside town – try **Villa Calussovo** in the village of Ripenda (\ *851 188; www.villa-calussovo.com;* €€€€–€€€). Rabac, on the other hand, has a dozen or so, though none are open all year round. Try the four-star **Bellevue** (\ *465 120; www.valamar.com;* €€€€), the two-star **Mediteran** (\ *465 120; www.valamar.com;* €€€), the good value, family-run **Nostromo** (\ *872 601; www.nostromo.hr;* €€€) or the 12-room boutique **Adoral** (\ *535 840; www.adoral-hotel.com;* €€€€€–€€€€). Two of the nicest places to eat in Labin are **Due Fratelli** (*Montozi 6;* \ *853 577; www.due-fratelli.com;* ☼ *noon–23.00 Mon–Sat, noon–17.00 Sun;* €€€) and **Velo Café** (*Titov trg 10;* \ *852 745; www.velokafe.com;* ☼ *11.00–23.00 daily;* €€€).

Head just a few kilometres inland in Istria and the scenery and atmosphere changes completely. The rustic interior, dubbed the 'New Tuscany' by many a travel writer, is characterised by rolling agricultural land, pretty medieval hilltop villages, and a thinner spread of people – in spite of efforts to resettle some villages with artists and the like, the inland population still hasn't fully recovered from the exodus of the Italian population following World War II, and the advent of mass tourism in the 1960s which drew young people away to coastal jobs. The emerging trend for today is agro-tourism, with the region perfectly suited to it, sharing central Italy's advantages of great food, fine wine, avenues of cypresses and charming villages. Indeed, there's a certain irony about the many Italian gastronomes flocking here to enjoy great-value, high-quality Istrian cuisine, and notably the prized white truffle. The region is also being opened up through a series of signposted wine routes.

The lack of public transport makes some villages hard to get to without your own wheels. Nonetheless, be prepared throughout the season to encounter coachloads of tourists being ferried up on day trips from the coast – especially in Motovun. If you're on a coastal package holiday yourself, however, the Istrian interior makes for an excursion you shouldn't miss.

Istria is famous throughout Croatia and beyond for its truffles (*tartufi*), and you'll find truffle dishes here which are affordable – at least when compared with the prices for those in France and Italy. The world's largest-ever white truffle was found in Istria in November 1999, near Buje, putting the town and its finder, Giancarlo Zigante, into the *Guinness Book of Records*. The monster truffle weighed in at 1.31kg, and measured 19.5cm by 12.4cm by 13.5cm (though it was finally surpassed by a white truffle from Alba, weighing 1.59kg, which was sold in November 2006 for €125,000, making it considerably more expensive, per gram, than gold). Zigante himself has mushroomed (ahem) since, and now owns a string of shops in Pula, Buzet, Grožnjan, Livade, Motovun and Umag, specialising in truffle sales (*www. zigantetartufi.com*). Another Istrian speciality is *biska*, or *biskovačka*, a fairly lethal but (at its best) wonderful mistletoe-flavoured spirit.

GETTING THERE AND AROUND In terms of access, public transport is centred on the administrative capital of Istria, Pazin, with buses from all over the region connecting here with trains on the Ljubljana to Pula line. Buses run up to Buzet – and occasionally Motovun – but you'll find your own transport easier for Oprtalj, Grožnjan, Hum or Roč, though the first two are within a few kilometres' walk of bus routes and the last two within a few kilometres of the train line. The local tourist office (*www.central-istria.com*) has also done a superb job of opening up local cycle routes in recent years – in particular the **Parenzana**, a 123km cycling route following the course of a former narrow gauge railway (*www.parenzana.com*). Look out for the Istra Bike leaflets (*www.istria-bike.com*), and there are several cycling routes in *Istria: The Bradt Guide* (page 429).

🏠 **WHERE TO STAY** If you have your own transport then agro-tourism is definitely the way to go – see www.istra.hr. Accommodation options for individual towns are listed under the relevant sections. In smaller villages it's also worth asking at local bars or cafés whether anyone has a room they're willing to let out.

PAZIN If you're visiting the Istrian interior by public transport you're certain to come through Pazin, and there are worse places to stop. Its status as Istria's capital dates back to the end of World War II, when Yugoslavia was keen to moderate the Italian influence – one in the eye for the much larger and more logical Pula. Pazin has its own attractions, but the main source of interest in the area is the extraordinary 15th-century frescoes at St Mary's Church near Beram (see below).

From the bus and train station walk down towards the town and castle, stopping off at the helpful **tourist office**, which can not only provide you with a map, but also has a list of walks and cycle trails in the area.

Where to stay and eat Pazin itself has only one hotel, but there's also a sprinkling of private rooms that are nicer and better value – ask at the **tourist office** (*Franina i Jurine 14;* ☎ *622 460; www.central-istria.com*).

Hotel Lovac (27 rooms) Šime Kurelića 4; ☎ 624 324; e tisadoo@inet.hr. 2-star option, with spartan but clean rooms & a nice terrace restaurant. €€

✳✘ Konoba Vinja Stacija Pataj 73a; ☎ 623 006; ⊕ 11.00–23.00 daily. This is hands down the best place to eat around Pazin, about 3km outside town. €€€

✘ Pod Lipom Trg pod Lipom 2a; www. podlipom.com.hr; ⊕ 07.00–22.00 Thu–Tue, 07.00–15.00 Wed. Great little bistro, the best place to eat in town itself. €€€

What to see and do The main attraction in Pazin itself is **Pazin Castle**, a 16th-century pile built on 10th-century remains, right down at the bottom of the town. Inside the monumental building you'll find the **Ethnographic Museum of Istria** (*Etnografski Muzej Istre;* ☎ *622 220; www.emi.hr;* ⊕ *10.00–18.00 daily; entry 25kn*), featuring Istrian costumes and handicrafts, along with a curious collection of church bells from Istrian churches through the ages. The castle itself overhangs the dramatic gorge into which the river Pazinčica disappears, supposedly the inspiration for Dante's entrance to hell (plausible: we know Dante was in Pula) as well as a major scene in Jules Verne's 1885 novel *Mathias Sandorf*; the title character disappears underground here, only to reappear six hours later in the Limski Kanal, near Rovinj, a good 40km away.

If you're a **Jules Verne** fan you should definitely contact Davor Šišiović at the Jules Verne Club in Pazin (☎ *622 460; www.ice.hr/davors/ejvclub.htm*), who can tell you all about Pazin and the novelist. For information on the annual Jules Verne Days in June, contact the tourist office.

Pazin's other main attraction is **Pazinska jama** (*Pazin Abyss; www.pazinska-jama.com; entry 30kn*), a gorge and sinkhole where the river disappears, which has a nice, well-marked footpath. There's also the **Parish Church of St Nicholas** (Sv Nikolaj), which has a magnificent free-standing campanile next to it. Inside the church there are some wonderful, if badly faded, 15th-century frescoes – notable are the creation cycle and a battle scene, with baddie angels toughing it out with the good guys.

BERAM The old village of Beram is 1km off the main road to Poreč, about 5km west of Pazin. Just under 1km west of the village, at the end of a pretty road running into the woods, is the **Church of St Mary** (Sv Marija). The keyholder is Sonja Šestan (*Beram 38;* ☎ *622 903*) – call beforehand, or ask at the tourist information office in Pazin (see above). It's a good idea to give something in return for their time and trouble – 20kn or so wouldn't be unreasonable.

The little church itself wouldn't be anything to write home about were it not for the Gothic frescoes inside. Dating from 1474 and painted by Master Vincent of Kastav (see the inscription over the south door) and his assistants, they're a triumph of late-Gothic art. That they survived the centuries relatively intact is no doubt due to their having been plastered over; they were only rediscovered in 1913.

In all there are some 46 panels, most depicting scenes from the lives of Jesus and Mary, but what really catch the eye are the 8m-long *Adoration of the Magi* on the north wall, and the *Dance of Death* (more of a walk, really) over the old main door. Medieval pageantry and Istrian scenery dominate the first, while in the second you'll see all classes heading for the same inevitable fate: death. First come the Pope, a cardinal and a bishop, followed by a king and queen, an innkeeper, a child and a cripple. Bringing up the rear are a knight, and a greedy merchant pointing at his worldly goods. Accompanied by fiendishly lifelike skeletons with musical instruments – and one with the obligatory scythe – the frescoes are a chilling reminder of life's impermanence.

PIĆAN If you're driving round the area, it's also worth stopping at the hilltop village of Pićan, about 10km east of Pazin. There's almost nothing to the place, these days, beyond a fine stone gate into town and a monumental 17th-century church – with an even more monumental campanile beside it – but the views across the Istrian countryside are wonderful.

MOTOVUN Motovun, 15km northwest of Pazin, is the classic medieval hilltop town, and you can see it from miles around. Like many gems of the interior, it can get overwhelmed by visitors – usually on a day trip up from the coast – although even then there's certainly enough charm left to merit a visit. In the last week of July Motovun hosts an increasingly popular international **film festival** (*www.motovunfilmfestival.com*).

Where to stay and eat In addition to Motovun's excellent hotel, you can contact the **tourist office** in the main square (*Trg Andrea Antico 1;* ☏ *681 726; www.tz-motovun.hr*) for details of private accommodation.

✻ ⌂ **Hotel Kaštel** (29 rooms) Trg Andrea Antico 7; ☏ 681 607; e info@hotel-kastel-motovun.hr; www.hotel-kastel-motovun.hr. Set in a lovely 18th-century palace, with spacious high-ceilinged refurbished rooms, its own spa centre & a wonderful terrace restaurant, it's an idyllic place to stay (& eat) – one of the best in central Istria. It's an awfully steep hike up with heavy bags, but the hotel can send someone down to pick you up with prior notice. Highly recommended. €€€€
✗ **Restaurant Zigante** Livade 7, Livade; ☏ 664 302; www.restaurantzigante.com; ⊕ noon–22.00 daily. In the village of Livade, just north of Motovun, this is the place to try if you want to splash out. This fine-dining establishment at the

heart of the Zigante empire is regarded by many gastronomes as one of Croatia's best restaurants, & after dining on sheep's cheese infused with black truffle, king scallops & black truffles with a croissant shell & tagliatelle with fresh white truffle, it would be hard to disagree. The opulent interior & immaculately turned-out waiters hint at the high prices to come. €€€€€
✗ **Konoba Mondo** Barbacan 1; ☏ 681 791; ⊕ noon–15.00 & 18.00–midnight daily. A nice little place well known for its truffle dishes. €€€
✗ **Pod Voltum** Šetališta V Nazora; ⊕ summer noon–22.00 daily, winter noon–22.00 Thu–Sun. A good, down-to-earth place serving Istrian specialities. €€€

What to see and do The **town walls** have been restored and offer a lovely promenade – all of 10 minutes' walk – with wonderful views out over the surrounding countryside. Otherwise, the town itself is pretty much limited to a single street, cobbled and traffic free in its upper reaches, running up from the valley floor. It works its way up through two ancient city gates, the first of which houses a lapidarium of sorts – Roman fragments on the right and Venetian lions on the left. Note the unusual 1755 face-on attempt at portraying the iconic sculpture – it looks more primitive than its 15th-century counterparts.

Between the two gates there's a lovely sloping terrace, where an ice cream goes down a treat, and an unusual triangular loggia, before the street turns sharply up into the second gate, housing a cheerful restaurant. Through the second gate is the heart of the **old town**, consisting of the ramparts, a main square under which a cistern used to hold the whole town's water supply, the 18th-century church, and the Hotel Kaštel, with its lovely shady terrace out front and gardens at the back (page 223). The **Church of St Stephen** (Sv Stjepan) was designed by Palladio in 1614. Outside it's halfway between Renaissance and Baroque; inside it's plain and airy, with a flat-ceilinged aisle and naves, and some fine portraits of saints high up. Incongruously, the day I was there the church was filled with the strains of a local singing group rehearsing Roberta Flack's *Killing Me Softly*. Next door is the sturdy, crenellated campanile, which looks a good deal older than it is (18th century).

Motovun is famous both for the Malvasija (white) and Teran (red) wines produced locally, as well as the delicious but breathtakingly expensive truffles hidden in the nearby woods. Try both, if you can afford to.

OPRTALJ Six kilometres north of Motovun, up a windy road, is Oprtalj, an almost deserted hilltop village which gives you a good idea of what Motovun and Grožnjan would have been like had the restorers not moved in. It's a charming place, in a run-down sort of way, with a population of barely 100, and though tourist infrastructure is in its infancy, you can eat various Istrian specialties at the homely **Konoba Oprtalj** (*Matka Laginje 17;* m *092 2990 516; www.konobaoprtalj.com;* ⊕ *11.00–22.00 daily but worth calling to check before making a trip up here specially;* €€) with a menu focusing on locally sourced, seasonal ingredients. For private accommodation contact the **tourist office** (*Matka Laginje 21;* ☏ *644 077; www.oprtalj.hr*).

GROŽNJAN Halfway between Motovun and Buje, a few kilometres north of the main road, on a spectacular bluff, is yet another hilltop village, Grožnjan. Adopted by artists from the late 1960s on, it's also home to *Jeunesses Musicales Croatia* in the summer, when the strains of classical music echo around the old cobbled streets. It is an increasingly lively place to be during the summer and autumn, with a myriad of art galleries and craft workshops, offering everything from ceramics and installations through to avant-garde art and tourist-orientated oil paintings of the village.

You can easily idle away a day here visiting the various small-scale venues, checking out the Venetian-era loggia, relaxing in a café – try **Kaya Energy Bar** (*Vincenta iz Kastava 2;* ⊕ *Apr–Dec 09.00–23.00 daily*) – or savouring a lunch of fresh pasta with truffle sauce, before reluctantly leaving one of inland Istria's most attractive towns behind. Mid-September brings the four-day **Extempore** festival to the town in a celebration of white truffles, red wine and music, while the excellent summer **jazz festival** (*www.jazzisbackbp.com*) was voted Europe's best boutique jazz festival in 2008.

🏠 **Where to stay and eat** There are a few places offering private accommodation in Grožnjan. Try one of the nice **apartments** run by the Armani Dešković Mirosav family (☏ *776 113; www.villa-olea.com*), which go for €40–50, or contact the **tourist office** on U Gorjana (☏ *776 131; www.tz-groznjan.hr*) for more options.

For meals try either **Konoba Bastia** (*I Svibnja 1;* ⊕ *summer 08.00–midnight daily, winter 10.00–22.00;* €€€) which serves good Istrian fare on a shady terrace, or the homely **Konoba Pintur** (*Gorjana 9;* \ *776 397;* ⊕ *Mar–Sep 08.00–22.00 Tue–Sun;* €€€) where you can eat on a tree-shaded terrace in the centre of town and enjoy Istrian staples like pršut, cheese and excellent pasta with truffle sauce and risotto. There are also four rooms (€€€).

BUJE The pleasant Italianate town of Buje is famous for producing the world's largest truffle (page 221). The best accommodation in the area is the award-winning boutique **San Rocco** (*Srednja ulica 2, Brtonigla;* \ *725 000; www.san-rocco.hr;* €€€€€). Alternatively, the **tourist office** has a list of private accommodation in the town itself (*Istarske 2;* \ *773 353; www.coloursofistria.com*).

VIŽINADA The sleepy hill town of Vižinada, south of Grožnjan, is worth a stop off if you want to discover somewhere where you'll feel like you're the only tourist in town. Park your car by the café on the main road and then walk down the hill to the old centre. The Venetian lion proudly overlooks the old Venetian well, with its Latin and Italian inscriptions, and the newer water pump is strictly in Italian only, but the town's Italian population has been posted missing since World War II. The imposing church and bell tower await restoration patiently, while the real estate agency back up the hill hints at Vižinada's future. Not too far from Vižinada you'll find **Franc Arman Vineyards** (*Narduči 5;* \ *446 226;* m *091 446 2266; www.francarman.hr*), where you can buy wine or arrange a tasting of some award-winning wines. Don't miss trying the excellent, oak-aged Malvazija Classic.

BUZET Backed by the Ćićarija Mountains to the northeast, the town of Buzet (self-billed as the 'City of Truffles') is less touched by tourism than Motovun, and makes a great base for walking, cycling and – of course – eating.

The medieval town on the hill is excellent, in a slightly run-down sort of way, with two well-preserved 16th-century gates, a maze of narrow streets and a couple of marble-paved squares. At the top of the hill, the pale-yellow church has an unusual onion-domed altar canopy inside and some 19th-century paintings – look out for St Mark, on the left-hand side, with St Mark's Basilica, in Venice, as a backdrop.

Below the old town, in the more modern Fontana, you'll find the bus station and the eponymous hotel. Make sure you try a truffle-based dish while you're in Buzet (most commonly with pasta or an omelette) as well as the local beer, even if some visitors do find it unpalatably sweet. Come here on the first Saturday in September to share in the giant truffle-infused omelette that is cooked to celebrate the start of the truffle season.

 Where to stay and eat There are a couple of hotels, or alternatively contact the **tourist office**, next door to the Vela Vrata, about private accommodation (*Šetalište Vladimira Gortana 9;* \ *662 343; www.tz-buzet.hr*).

Istarske Toplice (236 rooms) Sv Stjepana 60, Livade; \ 603 410; www.istarske-toplice.hr. In Istarske Toplice ('Istrian Hot Springs'), 10km southwest of Buzet, there's the eponymous Istarske Toplice. It's part of a 100-year-old thermal health resort, which explains why there's a large hotel in a canyon in the middle of nowhere. Check in here to enjoy the sulphurous waters, a mineral-mud wrap & a variety of massage treatments. €€€€

✳ **Hotel Vela Vrata** (12 rooms) Šetalište Vladimira Gortana 7; \ 494 750; www.velavrata. net. The best place to stay in Buzet, this is an outstanding boutique hotel in the old town, which also does great food. €€€€

Fontana (54 rooms) Trg Fontana 1; \ 662 615; www.hotelfontanabuzet.com. Big place below the old town. €€€

✕ Restaurant Konoba Marino Kremenje 96/B, Momyan; ☏779 047; www.konoba-marino-kremenje.hr; ⏰ noon–22.00 daily. 4km southwest of Buzet. Gastronomes visit Marino to dine on dishes made with black & white truffles. You can try the aromatic fungi with scrambled eggs, served as an accompaniment to homemade pasta or with tender fillets of beef. The seasonal menu also features wild asparagus & mushrooms. €€€

☀✕ Stara Oštarija Petra Flega 5; ☏694 003; ⏰ noon–17.00 Mon, Wed–Fri, noon–22.00 Sat/Sun. A great place to eat in town, with excellent game, trout & truffle-based dishes in a lovely dining area with a spectacular view. €€€

✕ Vrh Vrh 2; ☏667 123; www.vrh.com.hr/restoran.html; ⏰ 13.00–22.00 daily. Just out of town, here a shady terrace, the welcoming multi-lingual waitress & the delicate meat, ham, mushroom & truffle-infused Istrian *fuži* combine to make dining one of the highlights of an inland Istrian tour. The restaurant is well known locally & its owners produce their own wine alongside a range of fiery grappa that finds its way on to many menus in Zagreb. The truffle-flavoured grappa is worth trying for the novelty value alone. €€€

ROČ AND THE GLAGOLITIC ALLEY
When you're boozed-up and truffled-out, head for the tiny 'villages' of Roč and Hum, and the so-called 'Glagolitic Alley' which connects them. Roč is 8km east of Buzet, Hum a further 7km south of Roč. Hum claims to be the smallest town on earth (with all the basic trappings of a town).

Buses from Buzet to Rijeka will drop you at the turn-off, a 10-minute walk uphill to Roč, while if you get off the train at the Roč stop you'll find yourself around 2km out of town. Hum is harder to reach, since it is not on any bus route.

It's hard to believe it now, but **Roč** was an important centre of Glagolitic literature from the 13th century on, and the tiny town, with its low 15th-century walls, is the repository of many treasures of Glagolitic literature from the 16th and 17th centuries. These days there's not a whole lot to see, and the chances are you'll be in and out in half an hour.

Within the main gate there's an interesting collection of Roman stone fragments, and inside, to the right, by the pint-sized concrete playing field, there's a solitary Venetian cannon. On the day I was here, it was Roč and not Hum that was humming, but it turned out just to be a swarm of bees. Within the walls you'll also notice various bits of modern sculpture, all donated by the 'Friends of Roč', and it's worth glancing inside the Church of St Anthony – nice vaulting inside the apse and odd sedan chair-like confessionals. Once a year, in May, Roč really does swing, during the 'Triestina', the annual international knees-up for the harmonica-playing fraternity.

Keen hang-gliders and those with their own transport may want to follow the road past Roč towards **Gornja Nugla**. Carefully follow the signs towards Gornja Nugla, then after reaching the village head right for Slum and continue on the sealed road until you reach a crossroads with two hand-written signs for the southern take-off and the northern take-off. Follow the unsealed road (southern take-off) that branches to the left. After a few minutes you'll arrive at a local hang-gliding mecca – worth a trip for the wonderful views over Buzet and the distant hill towns, even if the hang-gliders aren't in evidence.

The 7km road south to Hum is known as '**Glagolitic Alley**' (*Aleja Glagoljaša*), and if you have the time it makes for a pleasant-enough walk – or a very nice bike ride; contact Gral-Putovanja in Buzet about bike hire (*Trg Fontana 7/1;* ☏*662 959; http://gral-putovanja.eu*) – a comfortable 3-hour return trip to Hum and back from Roč. The memorial consists of 11 monuments along the roadside, which were put up in 1977 to celebrate the Glagolitic priests who were among the first people to raise Croatian national consciousness in the 18th and 19th centuries.

The concrete sculptures are variations on representations of letters of the Glagolitic alphabet and other references to its history, which was kept alive in Istria and the islands of the Kvarner Bay long after it had disappeared elsewhere. Invented by St Cyril and St Methodius in the 9th century, the alphabet was adapted by St Clement into the Cyrillic seen today in much of the Balkans and across Russia.

HUM The road ends at Hum, which has all the features you'd expect in a medieval town, though very little in the way of people. An imposing entrance gate (complete with Glagolitic knockers), fortified walls, cobbled alleys, dilapidated stone houses and a small church make up the village. It's in the process of being restored – steeplejacks in harnesses were pulling tufts of grass from between the cracks in the church tower when I was in town – and several of the houses are being done up, but it's still a very, very small place. Commerce exists in the form of a small museum (actually a souvenir shop), and a renowned konoba, which serves up excellent Istrian dishes, including pršut, and pasta with truffles.

Be warned, however: it may be hard to get to, but Hum can switch from being deserted to being positively overcrowded in the seconds it takes for a tour bus to disgorge its passengers. Trips come up here from the coast, lured by that 'smallest town' tag.

✗ Where to eat and drink Hum's only restaurant is **Konoba Hum** (☎ 660 005; www.hum.hr/humskakonoba; ⊕ 15 May–15 Oct 11.00–22.00 daily, 15 Mar–15 May & 15 Oct–15 Nov 11.00–22.00 Tue–Sun, 15 Nov–15 Mar 11.00–22.00 Sat/Sun; €€), which has a lovely terrace. If a tour bus arrives, it will be packed, so it's worth phoning ahead to reserve a table.

TO OPATIJA AND UČKA Telephone code 051 (+385 51 from abroad)

Istria's northeastern corner has been popular with visitors for over a century, though it's now more nouveau riche than Habsburg chic. If you're here in the middle of August with your own car, expect to have trouble finding anywhere to park, but remember you can get away from it all by climbing up into the Učka mountains behind Opatija.

THE COAST TO OPATIJA Soon after you've left Labin, the road rejoins the steep coast, and you pass the medieval – and abandoned – village of **Plomin**, before turning north on the winding route to the Opatija Riviera, which is technically part of the Kvarner Gulf. If you happen to be driving past Plomin there's a great restaurant on the main road here called Dorina (page 228). The first part of the coast here is undeveloped – it's too steep to build on – though you'll see plenty of summer traffic heading down to Brestova, departure-point for ferries to Cres. At the height of the season drivers sometimes have to queue for hours to get on board.

From **Brseč** you can take a higher, less busy, parallel road along the coast for 8km or so, offering terrific vertiginous views – keep your eyes on the road and your hands on the wheel if you're driving. Brseč itself is well worth a wander around with some appealing little churches, cute cobbled lanes and stone archways leading you around this hillside town. If you have one too many (ie: one, as the blood alcohol limit is 0.05% for drivers) in the local konoba (page 228), you can stay the night in one of the village's many private rooms. If you're driving to Opatija, just beyond Brseč you'll find a couple of lovely coves blessed with white shingle sand: follow the steps down through the undergrowth to enjoy a spot of sunbathing or a dip in the Adriatic. The roads meet up again in **Mošćenička Draga**, the first resort in the Opatija Riviera, with the tiny village dwarfed by the four-star **Hotel Marina**.

Things get more serious 4km later when you reach the pebbles of **Medveja**, the last long concrete-free beach before the far side of Rijeka.

Next up is the Opatija Riviera's prettiest resort, **Lovran**, featuring lots of late Habsburg-era villas and a well-preserved nugget of an old town. Lovran is just 5km south of Opatija and practically merges with it – you can walk along the pedestrianised front between the two in about an hour. It makes an ideal base for walking in the Učka massif (page 231), and the tourist office has a good walking map.

The name Lovran derives from the laurel tree, and you'll see plenty of these in the resort – along with cypresses, palm trees and lovely flowers. You'll also notice the town's obsession with chestnuts, not just as far as trees are concerned, but also in terms of the food. In October, over a two-week period, the Maranuda (chestnut festival) is an excuse to binge on every conceivable chestnut-related goodie. North of Lovran, the small towns and little bays (but biggish resorts) of **Ika** and **Ičići** lead seamlessly on to Opatija.

⌂ **Where to stay and eat** There's plenty of private accommodation available, through any of the tourist agencies on the main road, though you may have trouble finding a room if you don't book well ahead. Get the latest list from the Lovran **tourist office** (*Trg Slobode 1;* ☎ *291 740; www.tz-lovran.hr*).

⌂ **Excelsior** Šetalište Maršala Tita 15, Lovran; ☎710 444; www.remisens.com. Next door to the Lovran, but larger & swankier. €€€€

⌂ **Hotel Marina** Aljea Slatina 2, Mošćenička Draga; ☎710 444. Big waterfront 4-star. €€€€

⌂ **Lovran** Šetalište Maršala Tita 19/2, Lovran; ☎291 222; e office@hotel-lovran.hr; www.hotel-lovran.hr. Just 1 block from the sea & few mins' walk from the old town. Has sea-views & a small spa. €€€€–€€€

✖ **Dorina** Plomin 54; ☎863 023; ⏱ 11.00–23.00 daily. Serves up hearty Istrian staples at very reasonable rates – it's understandably popular

with locals. The asparagus soup is unrivalled, & the *maneštra* (thick bean soup) is excellent. For main courses try the *fuži* (pasta) with truffles or the amazing *njoki* (gnocchi) which – in a triumph of excess – is served with both squid & truffles together. If that's not enough to convince you, the bargain house white will. €€€

✖ **Konoba Batelan** Brseč 4; ⏱ 10.00–23.00 daily. Local as well as Italian dishes. €€€

✖ **Delfino** 26 divizije 4; ☎293 293; www.delfino.hr; ⏱ 11.00–23.00 daily. Hugely popular pizzeria. €€

OPATIJA Opatija (originally Abbazia, after the former Benedictine abbey) is astonishingly popular, and has been for over a century. Rooms in the nicest hotels are booked a year or more ahead, and don't even think about trying to find street parking in August.

'Vienna on Sea' is justifiably proud of its Habsburg villas and palaces, its exotic palms and manicured gardens and its 12km-long pedestrianised front, stretching from Lovran in the south to Volosko in the north, but the fashionable winter resort of Opatija never quite made the post-World War II leap from winter to summer tourism. The beaches here are concrete, and netted in (my trusty 1966 *Gateway Guide* explains: 'the visitor should stay within the barriers and never swim far out from the shore since there are sometimes sharks' – in fact shark sightings, let alone attacks, are extremely rare in the Croatian Adriatic); the summer crowds can intimidate; and beyond the late 19th-century swank, there's really nothing to see. It's still a great place to come in winter, however, when the town slips quietly back into a nostalgic reverie, and afternoon cakes are picked at with silver forks by retired Austrians.

Until the arrival of the wealthy Rijeka trader Iginio Scarpa in 1844, Opatija was the proverbial sleepy fishing village. Scarpa built the **Villa Angiolina** (named after his wife) and created its exotic gardens as a summer retreat, and the high and mighty were soon paying visits.

Given a clean bill of health by doctors to the wealthy – like so many nice places to stay – Opatija soon became a spa town, and *the* place to take a 'cure' (and be seen) in winter. It was helped on its way by the arrival of the railway in Rijeka in 1873 – by 1884 the Kvarner hotel was up and running, and demand was so high that the Imperial was opened only a year later, with the Palace-Bellevue hot on its heels.

Anyone who was anyone in the Austro-Hungarian sphere of influence came here, and it was hugely popular with the aristocracy. Anton Chekhov, Gustav Mahler and Sigmund Freud gave their patronage, while Vladimir Nabokov spent his childhood holidays here (probably up in the hills collecting butterflies).

If you're planning on staying in Opatija in summer it's a good idea to try to book a year in advance – though you may be lucky with private rooms through one of the many tourist agencies in town. It may also be worth writing or calling ahead to the friendly and helpful **tourist board** (*Vladimira Nazora 3;* ☎ *271 710; www.opatija-tourism.hr*), where you can also get plenty of other information about Opatija and its surroundings.

Getting there and away There are plenty of intercity buses to and from Opatija, including Rijeka, Pula and Zagreb, and you can also get there by local bus from Rijeka.

Where to stay and eat If you have the time to plan, and the budget, Opatija is one place where it's really worth splashing out, as the opulent 19th-century hotels are remarkably good value in their class. Opatija is also home, as you'd expect, to several of Istria's big five-star hotels: the Ambassador, the Milenij and the Mozart. The first two have indoor and outdoor pools; the third offers remarkably good-value Viennese-style elegance.

🏠 **Ambassador** (180 rooms) Feliksa Peršića 1; ☎710 444; www.remisens.com. Big, swanky & modern, with sea views. €€€€€

🏠 **Imperial** (126 rooms) Šetalište Maršala Tita 124/3; ☎710 444; www.remisens.com. Classic hotel with tastefully elegant lobby & bars. €€€€

🏠 **Milenij** (125 rooms) Šetalište Maršala Tita 109; ☎278 016, 202 000; www.milenijhoteli.hr. Elegant hotel spanning 3 fin-de-siècle villas, with rooms decorated in classic or modern style. €€€€

🏠 **Mozart** (30 rooms) Šetalište Maršala Tita 138; ☎718 260; www.hotel-mozart.hr. Much smaller in scale than some of the others in Opatija, with very smart dbls with sea view. €€€€

🏠 **Villa Amalia** (87 rooms) Pave Tomašića 1–4; ☎710 444; www.remisens.com. Another classic hotel with an astounding 1913 Crystal Ballroom, & a lovely seaside terrace. €€€€

🏠 **Continental** (53 rooms) Šetalište Maršala Tita 85; ☎278 000, 278 007; www.milenijhoteli. hr. Elegant hotel, housed in a villa dating back to 1898. There's a nice brick-vaulted champagne bar, & the cakes served in the café here are

legendary – you shouldn't leave Opatija without trying the *sacher torta*. Finally, at the 'Choco World' (🕐 *08.00–18.00 Sun–Thu, 08.00–20.00 Fri/Sat*) downstairs, you can see the hotel's skilled chocolatier at work, & buy delicious handmade chocolates in the small shop. €€€€–€€€

🏠 **Palace Bellevue** (210 rooms) Šetalište Maršala Tita 144–148; ☎710 444; www.remisens. com. Worth staying at to check out the fabulous reception rooms alone. €€€

🍴 **Gostiona Istranka** B Milanovića 2; ☎271 835; http://istranka.net; 🕐 10.00–23.00 daily. Good value family-run restaurant serving seafood, grills, pasta, venison goulash & more, with an emphasis, as the name implies, on Istrian specialties. €€€

🍴 **Pizzeria Roko** Šetalište Maršala Tita 114; 🕐 11.00–23.00 daily. Opatija's most popular pizzeria. €€€

🍴 **Ružmarin** Veprinački put 2; ☎712 673; 🕐 10.00–01.00 daily. Good value & very popular restaurant serving seafood, grills, pizza & pasta. €€€

✳✘ Kavana Continental Šetalište Maršala Tita 85; www.milenijhoteli.hr; ⊕ 07.00–23.00   Sun–Thu, 07.00–midnight Fri/Sat. *The* place in Opatija to indulge in cakes. €€€–€€

What to see and do

The best place to start a tour of Opatija is the beautifully restored **Villa Angelina**, standing amid lovely manicured gardens. Built in 1844, this was the summer house of Iginio Scarpa, the wealthy businessman largely responsible for launching Opatija into the limelight as a fashionable tourist destination par excellence. It now houses the fascinating **Museum of Tourism** (*Muzej Turizma; www.hrmt.hr;* ⊕ *summer 10.00–20.00 daily, winter 10.00–18.00 daily; 15kn*). Almost opposite across the park, there's a rather good, extended **mural** by Anja Ferenčić with portraits of some of Opatija's many famous visitors over the years, including Gustav Mahler, Albert Einstein and American born dancer Isadore Duncan. Nearby **St James' Church** dates from the 15th/16th century, although much of what you see now is 19th-century renovation.

One of the nicest things to do in Opatija is follow the **waterfront promenade** (*lungomare*), which you can follow all the way to Volosko, or in the other direction to Lovran. Near the start of the promenade, you'll find the *Maiden with Seagull* sculpture, one of the most familiar symbols of Opatija.

VOLOSKO If you're in Opatija, make the effort to walk along the shore to Volosko, still a fishing village even though it's barely half an hour on foot from the summer throngs. It's Mediterranean to Opatija's Habsburg, and though it's no secret, it is a pretty place to go for lunch on the shores of the Adriatic looking out towards the islands of the Kvarner Gulf. In recent years it has evolved into something of a gastronomic destination with Le Mandrač, which many Croats rate as the best restaurant in the entire country, Plavi Podrum and other restaurants of note. There's also an argument for staying here rather than in Opatija itself, and Villa Kapetanović, a short walk uphill from the village, can be counted one of the nicest places to stay anywhere in Croatia, with a restaurant which is a destination in its own right.

⌂ Where to stay, eat and drink

⌂ Hotel Navis (44 rooms) Ivana Matetića Ronjgova 10; ☏444 600; www.hotel-navis.hr. Opened in 2015 by the owners of Villa Kapetanović, this supremely stylish design hotel is located right on the waterfront on the edge of Volosko. All rooms have sea views, & the hotel has its own restaurant & spa. €€€€

✳ **⌂ Villa Kapetanović** (24 rooms, 3 suites) Nova cesta 12A; ☏741 355; www.villa-kapetanovic.hr. Truly outstanding boutique hotel, perched a few hundred metres above the Optaija-Rijeka road, just a 10-min walk from the waterfront in Volosko. Rooms are spacious & stylish – go for the sea-facing ones, the balconies of which have unbeatable views of the Kvarner Gulf & islands. Friendly & welcoming, with a spa & outdoor pool, & the terrace restaurant is superb (see below). There's a shuttle service to pick up/drop off guests in Opatija. Highly recommended. €€€€

✳✘ **Laurus** Nova cesta 12A; ☏741 355; m 091 2210 971; www.villa-kapetanovic. hr; ⊕ 11.30–23.00 daily. Opened in 2003, the restaurant at Villa Kapetanović (see above) has built up a reputation for outstanding cuisine, with an emphasis on fresh, seasonal local ingredients. Consider the 4- or 7-course tasting menu, with mouthwatering carpaccio, seafood, truffles & pasta dishes, as well as delicious home-baked bread, & excellent wines. Highly recommended. €€€€

✳✘ **Le Mandrač** Frana Supila 10; ☏051 701 357; www.lemandrac.com; ⊕ noon–23.00 daily. Opened in 2004, this stylish eatery, which fuses Istrian & Asian influences, has consistently been rated as one of Croatia's top restaurants – many would put it at the top of that list – & is well worth the splurge, set in a floor-to-ceiling glass conservatory overlooking the Adriatic. For lunch try the 4-course mini-degustation menu; for dinner splash out on the 'exploring menu', a 9-course culinary extravaganza that might well be the best meal you ever have in Croatia. Recommended. €€€€

✘ **Plavi Podrum** Frana Supila 12; 📞701 223; www.plavipodrum.com; ⏱ noon–midnight daily. As-good-as-it-gets seafood restaurant overlooking Volosko's bijou harbour. It does the standards such as grilled squid & white fish extremely well, alongside plenty of innovative dishes & a degustation menu. Book early in season if you want a table on the popular terrace. €€€€

✘ **Valle Losca** Andrije Štangera 2; m 095 580 3757; ⏱ noon–23.00 daily. Much more low-key than the big names down on the waterfront, but still very popular, this is a little konoba-style place serving Istrian specialties. €€€€

✘ **Pizzeria Moho** Obala Frana Supila 8; m 099 2562 289; ⏱ 11.00–23.00 daily. Great little pizzeria on the waterfront. €€€

♀ **Hemingway** Zert 2; 📞718 802; www.hemingway.hr; ⏱ 11.00–01.00 daily. Opatija's own branch of this ultra-trendy chain of bars.

UČKA Rising up above the Opatija Riviera – and giving it its mild winter/cool summer climate, while cutting it off from the rest of Istria – is the Učka massif, culminating in the 1,401m summit of Vojak, the highest point on Veli Učka (Monte Maggiore). On a clear evening they say you can see the lights of Venice from here; what's sure is that you get a great view of the Kvarner Bay and the island of Cres.

With your own transport you can drive right to the top of the mountain on a tarred road (leading up to the TV transmitter), though parking is limited; walking is a far better way of exploring. Good maps are available from the tourist offices in Rijeka, Opatija and Lovran, with well-marked trails and the chance to really get away from it all.

The most obvious ascent starts off from a junction at a saddle on the old Rijeka–Pazin road (not the main road, which heads through the Učka tunnel) – this can also be reached from Opatija, or via a dizzying series of hairpins from Ičići. The #34 bus from Opatija heads up to the saddle, but operates on Sundays only, once in each direction. Alternatively, you can hike up.

At the saddle where the road branches off to the summit, you'll find a mountaineering hut, **Poklon dom** (📞 299 610; www.pdopatija.hr; usually ⏱ weekends in the summer but it's always worth calling to check; €€), and a restaurant, **Pansion Učka** (📞 516 899; www.pansion-ucka.com; €€), which also has rooms available. On the far (inland) side of the saddle is **Dopolovaro Restaurant** (Učka 9; 📞 299 641; www.dopolovoro.hr; ⏱ noon–23.00 daily; €€€), with lots of game and truffles on the menu. Just beyond this (if you're coming up from Opatija) you'll find the road on the left that leads up to the summit almost exactly 6km up the road. On foot it's a pleasant hike up, starting from the saddle itself and following a clear hiking trail between the hairpins, with great views on the way and even better ones from the top – turn left at the TV and radio mast, and follow the path up to the trig point, on top of a small tower. Avoid sliding down the hang-glider take-off ramp on the way up – unless of course you've brought your hang-glider with you.

Real hikers will of course want to climb the Učka massif from sea level. To do this the obvious base is Lovran, though there is a path up from Medveja. The Lovran path starts steep and stays that way – it's a fairly tough 4 hours up to the summit (3 hours coming down), so make sure you have plenty of water and food with you (and from Medveja count on an extra hour each way). Most of the walk up is through lovely oak and then beech woods, before you emerge on the grassy shoulder of the mountain itself. By the time you get this far you're less than half an hour from the summit and the TV antenna. See Rudolf Abraham's book *Walking in Croatia* (page 429) for further details.

If you're in Lovran and keen to walk you should also consider the paths leading to the abandoned village of Sučići, high above Mošćenička Draga, as well as other paths that keep you far from the madding crowds.

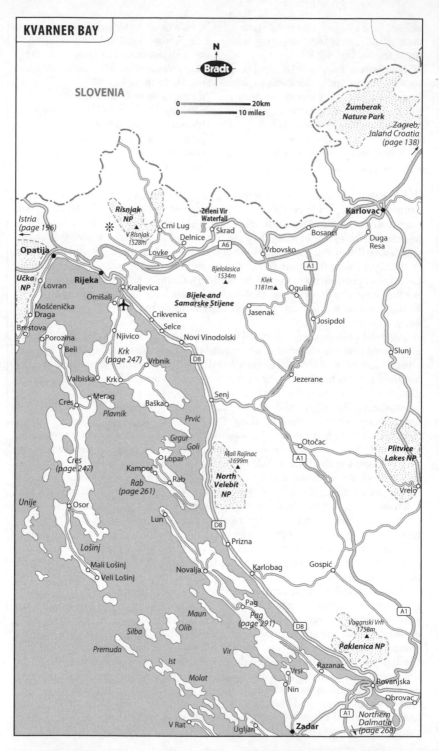

KVARNER BAY

SLOVENIA

N

0 _____ 20km
0 _____ 10 miles

Žumberak
Nature Park

Zagreb,
Inland Croatia
(page 138)

Risnjak
NP

Zeleni Vir
Waterfall

Crni Lug

Karlovac

Istria
(page 196)

V Risnjak
1528m

Skrad

Bosana

Delnice

Duga
Resa

Opatija

Lovke

A6

Vrbovsko

Učka
NP

Lovran

Rijeka

Bjelolasica
1534m

Klek
1181m

A1

Kraljevica

Ogulin

Omišalj

Bijele and
Samarske Stijene

Jasenak

Josipdol

Moščenička
Draga

Crikvenica

Brestova

Porozina

Selce

Beli

Njivico

Novi Vinodolski

Krk
(page 247)

Vrbnik

D8

Slunj

Valbiska

Krk

Jezerane

Cres

Merag

Baška

Senj

Plavnik

Prvić

Grgur

Goli

Mali Rajinac
1699m

Otočac

Plitvice
Lakes NP

Cres
(page 247)

Lopar

A1

Kampor

Rab

North
Velebit
NP

Vrelo

Unije

Rab
(page 261)

Osor

Lun

D8

Lošinj

Prizna

Mali Lošinj

Novalja

Karlobag

Gospić

Veli Lošinj

A1

Maun

Pag

Silba

Olib

Pag
(page 291)

D8

Vaganski Vrh
1758m

Premuda

Vir

Paklenica NP

Ist

Molat

Vrsi

Razanac

Nin

Rovanjska

Obrovac

V Rat

Ugljan

Zadar

A1

Northern
Dalmatia
(page 268)

6

Kvarner Bay and Islands

The Kvarner Bay, with Rijeka at its head and Croatia's largest islands in the middle, has been popular as a holiday destination for over a century. **Rijeka** itself is a lively port and shipyard, and while it's not somewhere you'd spend your holidays, there's nonetheless plenty to see. Offshore is **Cres**, home to wonderful griffon vultures, and **Lošinj**, one of Croatia's busiest and trendiest islands (at least for a fortnight in August). East of Cres and south of Rijeka lies the somewhat lower-key **Krk**, Croatia's largest island, while the island of **Rab** sits to the south, blessed by sandy beaches and one of Croatia's prettiest medieval towns.

According to legend the four islands of the Kvarner Bay (Kvarner = Quattro = four) are the limbs of Medea's brother. She enticed the poor lad on board Jason's ship as he fled away with the Golden Fleece, and Jason chopped him up and cast his limbs overboard to slow down the pursuers.

The coast from Rijeka southwards is backed by the steepest part of the **Velebit massif** and occupied by a string of resort towns and villages centred on Kraljevica, Crikvenica, Selce and Novi Vinodolski, all of which are popular vacation spots in summer with Croatians escaping from the capital, as well as increasingly with independent visitors in search of the low key rather than the high life.

Inland from Rijeka is the wonderfully protected and unspoiled **Gorski Kotar** region, centred on **Risnjak National Park**, while further south is the enormous Velebit massif, with **North Velebit National Park** home to a good proportion of Croatia's remaining brown bear population, and also providing some of the finest hiking in Croatia.

Phone codes vary throughout the region – they're included within each listing.

RIJEKA

Rijeka, Croatia's busiest and most industrial port, with a population of over 128,000 (and over 100,000 more living in the surrounding metropolitan area), isn't really a holiday destination at all – the assumption is that you'll head straight over to Opatija, 14km west (page 228), or out on to the islands of the Kvarner Bay. It nonetheless has plenty of sights worth seeing, including the excellent Trsat Castle on its hill, and a number of fine Austro-Hungarian palaces and Secessionist buildings down in the town itself.

A massive investment programme to tart up the waterfront is one sign that Rijeka is on the up, and the sense of returning civic pride is evident in the street sculptures and the recent success of the local football team, whose stadium must have one of the best views in Europe, overlooking the Adriatic and the Opatija Riviera.

Rijeka probably won't be your favourite Croatian city, but if you are passing through – and you may well be, as this is the main transit hub for the entire region – then it

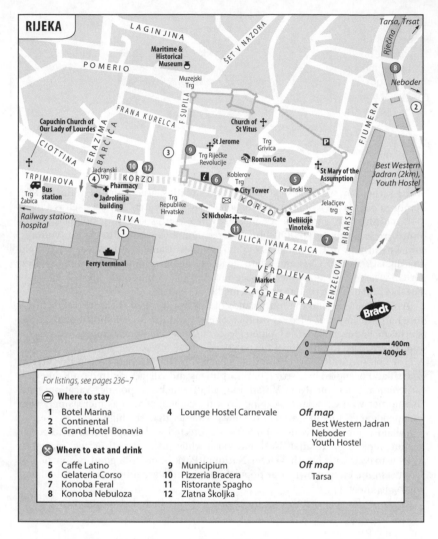

RIJEKA

LAGINJINA

Maritime & Historical Museum

POMERIO

Muzejski Trg

ŠET V NAZORA

Tarsa, Trsat

Riječina

Neboder **8**

2

FRANA KURELCA

Capuchin Church of Our Lady of Lourdes

ERAZMA BARČIĆA

CIOTTINA

F SUPILA

Church of St Vitus

St Jerome
Trg Riječke Revolucije
Trg Grivica
Roman Gate
St Mary of the Assumption

FIUMERA

Best Western Jadran (2km), Youth Hostel

TRPIMIROVA

Jadranski trg
KORZO **4**
10 12
Pharmacy

Koblerov Trg
6
City Tower
5
Pavlinski trg

KORZO

Jelačicev trg

Best Western Jadran

Trg Žabica
Bus station
Jadrolinija building

Trg Republike Hrvatske

St Nicholas

RIBARSKA

Railway station, hospital

RIVA

1

11
Deliiicije Vinoteka
7

ULICA IVANA ZAJCA

Ferry terminal

VERDIJEVA
Market
ZAGREBAČKA

WENZELOVA

N

Bradt

0 ————— 400m
0 ————— 400yds

For listings, see pages 236–7

🛏 **Where to stay**

1	Botel Marina	4	Lounge Hostel Carnevale
2	Continental		
3	Grand Hotel Bonavia		

Off map
Best Western Jadran
Neboder
Youth Hostel

✖ **Where to eat and drink**

5	Caffe Latino	9	Municipium
6	Gelateria Corso	10	Pizzeria Bracera
7	Konoba Feral	11	Ristorante Spagho
8	Konoba Nebuloza	12	Zlatna Školjka

Off map
Tarsa

is worth at least one night of your time. There's little to beat a relaxing beer or coffee on the central thoroughfare, the stately Korzo, with its lavish Austro-Hungarian buildings. And the carnival here is the biggest and best in Croatia (page 239).

HISTORY Like most of the region, the area round Rijeka was home to Liburnian Illyrians until the Romans arrived, and built a port here, on the site of what's now the old town – everything south of the Korzo is on land reclaimed from the sea. Slavs moved in when Rome collapsed, but it wasn't until the 13th century that Rijeka started to grow in importance, though from then until 1947 it was two distinct settlements – Rijeka on the west bank of the river and Trsat (and later Sušak) on the east bank.

Unlike pretty much everywhere else on the Croatian coast, Rijeka never fell under the control of Venice, becoming a key Habsburg possession instead, though it was briefly under Frankopan control. From the early 18th century onwards,

Rijeka became a major centre for shipbuilding, and today it's still Croatia's most important shipyard.

During the 19th century, tension increased between Vienna and Budapest, with Hungary insisting it should have its own access to the Adriatic, Austria already having both Trieste and Pula. Rijeka therefore came under the direct control of Hungary, and a railway was built from Budapest via Zagreb to the port (the station, like Zagreb's, is the work of Ferenc Pfaff), dramatically increasing its importance. Under the Hungarians, Rijeka grew wealthy, with its own sugar factory, refinery and paper factory.

In 1915, as a way of persuading the Italians into World War I on the Allied side, Britain promised pretty much the entire post-war Dalmatian coast to Italy. Once the war was won, the Allies reneged on the deal, and the coast fell to the Kingdom of the Serbs, Croats and Slovenes instead – though Italy did get Zadar and some islands as compensation.

This wasn't enough, however, to stop Gabriele D'Annunzio (see box, below) from marching into Rijeka in September 1919, using the pro-Italian census (which cleverly excluded Sušak) as an excuse. D'Annunzio then ruled Rijeka for nearly 18 months – in spite of not even having the Italian government's support. Italy finally pushed D'Annunzio out in early 1921, and for three years Rijeka was a free city. But that wasn't stopping Mussolini, who annexed it in 1924.

Rijeka – then called Fiume (both names just mean 'river') – was a divided city once more. The west side was Italian, and fell into decline, while the east side, Sušak, rapidly gained in prosperity as one of Yugoslavia's main shipyards, even though the ships themselves actually had to sail from Rijeka's harbour.

GABRIELE D'ANNUNZIO

By 1919, Gabriele D'Annunzio was one of the most fêted men in Italy. Already hugely famous before World War I for his poetry and novels, he signed up for military service, in his fifties, and became a war hero – he even lost an eye in a flying accident.

He was the perfect stooge, then, to lead an officer-backed group of 'volunteers' (discreetly assisted by soldiers whose superiors turned a blind eye) into Rijeka in September 1919, claiming the city for Italy. His troops were the first to wear black shirts, kicking off a hideously popular trend in fascist fashion that would last a whole generation.

But Rome wasn't interested in Rijeka, as it was busy negotiating instead at the Paris Peace Conference for Zadar and some Dalmatian islands. So D'Annunzio, cool as a cucumber, set himself up as *Il Commandante*, at the head of the independent state of Rijeka. For nearly 18 months he got away with it, declaiming manifestos from his balcony every morning.

It couldn't last, of course. At the end of 1920, Italy shelled the town and D'Annunzio gave it up in January 1921. As a successful role model for Mussolini, he was later rewarded by Il Duce with a place in the Italian senate, and was up for even greater honours when he died suddenly in 1938.

Rebecca West, author of the extraordinary *Black Lamb and Grey Falcon* (page 430), was no fan. 'D'Annunzio marched his volunteers into Fiume, in an adventure which, in mindlessness, violence and futility, exactly matched his deplorable literary works', she wrote, by way of an epitaph to the whole sorry affair.

After World War II, Rijeka was returned to Yugoslavia, along with the rest of Dalmatian Italy, and in 1991 the city became part of the new state of Croatia – though it still has a large Italian-speaking population.

GETTING THERE AND AROUND If you're using public transport, you'll sometimes feel there's no way of not getting to Rijeka. **Trains** come in from Zagreb four or five times a day (*3hrs 40mins*), while there are **ferries** and ships constantly on their way in and out of the harbour. The main Jadrolinija coastal line between Rijeka and Dubrovnik unfortunately stopped running in 2015 – although it may start again in the future – but there are catamaran services to Rab and Novalja from here, as well as to Cres and Mali Lošinj (see the individual sections in this chapter).

Rijeka Airport is out on the island of Krk (connected by a big bridge to the mainland), and caters mainly for charter flights bringing in package tours to Opatija and the islands of the Kvarner Bay – budget airline routes between Rijeka and the UK tend to come and go. There are flights from Zagreb, too, which are met by the Croatia Airlines bus; by the time you've allowed for transfers and check-in time, it's a pretty expensive way of saving a couple of hours on the bus or train, though if you're coming from outside Croatia the onward leg may already be included in your fare.

A vast array of **buses** run frequently to Rijeka from just about everywhere, coming from Pula (*2hrs*) and Zagreb (*3hrs, some faster*) roughly every half hour, from Krk (*1½hrs*), Zadar (*4½hrs*) and Split (*9hrs*) about once an hour, and from a wealth of other destinations besides.

You probably won't need to use local buses much, though it's worth knowing that bus #32 runs from the train station to Opatija twice an hour, and if you want to avoid the walk up to Trsat you can catch bus #2 or #8 from Fiumera.

The train station, bus station and ferry terminal are in a line running west–east along less than a kilometre's length of the harbour.

TOURIST INFORMATION The **tourist information office** (*Korzo 14;* ☎ *051 335 882; www.visitrijeka.eu*) has good maps and brochures, and can be found halfway along the Korzo.

WHERE TO STAY *Map, page 234*

Rijeka's accommodation – or comparative lack of it – speaks volumes about the city knowing it's a staging post rather than a destination in its own right. There's no campsite, there are no agencies handling private rooms, and there are only a handful of hotels in the middle of town – though there are several new hostels.

🏠 **Grand Hotel Bonavia** (121 rooms) Dolac 4; ☎ 051 357 100; www.bonavia.hr. The lavish 4-star Grand Hotel Bonavia is well located just a block north of the main west–east thoroughfare, Korzo, & is easily the poshest place to stay in the city. It's a modernised old building, & a few of the rooms on the top floors have balconies overlooking the port – rooms 712, 713 & 714 are especially spacious. None of this comes cheap, of course, but the hotel does have all the luxuries you'd expect for the price. It even has that rarest thing of all in downtown Rijeka, its own parking spaces (if you're driving here, you need to get into the one-way system that brings you out on Jadranska Trg, then head up the hill & round behind the back of the hotel). The hotel is also home to a restaurant worth staying in for. €€€€–€€€€€

🏠 **Best Western Jadran** (69 rooms) Šetalište XIII Divizije 46; ☎ 051 216 600; www.jadran-hoteli. hr. Just 2km along the coast (you can get there on the #1 city bus), & upgraded from 2 to 4 stars, with lovely views out over the island of Cres. €€€€

🏠 **Continental** (69 rooms) Šetalište Andrije Kačića – Miošića 1; ☎ 051 372 008; www.jadran-hoteli.hr. The only other option right in town is the nice (& recently renovated) Continental, now 3-star, which is in a Parisian-looking building just across the river, below the Trsat hill. There's a lovely terrace out front in the shade of giant trees. €€€

🏠 **Neboder** (54 rooms) Strossmayerova 1; ☎051 373 538; www.jadran-hoteli.hr. Just down the road from the Continental, this is the place to head if you're after a reasonably priced option & the latter is full. It's a rather charmless block of a place, though it was renovated in 2008 & most of the rooms have balconies – & those on the upper floor have stunning views of the city. €€€

🏠 **Botel Marina** (35 rooms) Adamićev gat; ☎051 410 162; www.botel-marina.com.

Accommodation aboard a 1936 Danish passenger ship, renovated & converted into a floating hotel/hostel in 2013, & permanently moored in Rijeka. Sgl, dbl, trpl, quad & dorm beds. B/fast inc. €€€–€

🏠 **Lounge Hostel Carnevale** (8 rooms) Jadranski trg 1; www.hostelcarnevale.com. Newly opened hostel with a central location on Jadranski trg, at one end of the Korzo. Dbls, quads & 6-bed dorms. €€

🏠 **Youth Hostel** (61 beds) Šetalište XIII Divizije 23; ☎051 406 420; www.hfhs.hr. Also on the way out of town (& reachable on the #1 bus) is Rijeka's excellent youth hostel, located in a 19th-century villa – it's only around 15mins away on foot. €

✖ WHERE TO EAT AND DRINK Map, page 234

For a town of its size, Rijeka has surprisingly few restaurants – again a product of the relatively few tourists around to keep business booming. Locals wanting to splash out tend to head over to Opatija, but you can find something to eat easily enough in the streets on either side of the Korzo – and some of the places are excellent. There's also a booming café culture, with terraces spilling out on to practically every pavement in the old town, especially along the lifeblood Korzo and the waterfront Riva.

✖ **Municipium** Trg Riječke Rezolucije 5; ☎051 213 000; ⏰ 11.00–23.00 Mon–Sat. Smart, old-school place, where business deals are cemented over good, solid, Croatian fare. €€€€

✳✖ **Zlatna Školjka** (the Golden Shell) Kručina 12a; ☎051 213 782; www.zlatna-skoljka.hr; ⏰ 11.00–23.00 daily. The author's personal favourite, right off the Korzo, with stiff tablecloths, cheerful, semi-formal service & excellent seafood in a cellar-like setting. €€€€

✳✖ **Konoba Feral** Matije Gupca 5b; ☎051 212 274; www.konoba-feral.com; ⏰ 08.00–midnight Mon–Sat, noon–18.00 Sun. One of the best local places in Rijeka to eat seafood, unpretentious with delicious food & friendly service. Recommended. €€€

✖ **Konoba Nebuloza** Titov trg 2b; ☎051 374 501; www.konobanebuloza.com; ⏰ 11.00–midnight Mon–Fri, noon–midnight Sat. Highly rated local favourite, located on the Rječina just a short distance from the Hotel Continental. €€€

✖ **Pizzeria Bracera** Kružna 12; ☎051 213 782; www.pizzeria-bracera.com.hr; ⏰ 11.00–23.00 daily. Opposite Zlatna Skoljka, this is definitely the best place in town to go for a pizza. €€€

✳✖ **Ristorante Spagho** I Zajca 24; ☎051 311 122; ⏰ noon–23.00 Mon–Sat, noon–21.00 Sun. Impeccable pasta, risotto & other dishes, as well as pizza, friendly service & a good wine list. Recommended. €€€

✖ **Tarsa** Josip Kulfaneka 10; ☎051 452 089; ⏰ noon–midnight daily. Highly rated locally, this place up near Trsat Castle is an excellent place to try *tartufi* (truffles) if you're not heading into Istria. €€€

☕ **Caffe Latino** Pavlinski trg 4a; ⏰ 06.30–22.00 Mon–Fri, 07.00–14.00 Sun. Latino serves excellent coffee on a square between the Korzo & Ante Starčevica.

☕ **Gelateria Corso** Korzo 20; ⏰ 07.00–23.00 Mon–Sat, 08.00–22.00 Sun. The best & most popular ice cream joint in town. Savour it like a local as you stroll along the Korzo.

SHOPPING Rijeka has a wonderful **market** (*Velika tržnica*), centred around three large Art Deco buildings between the harbour and the National Theatre. For wine, head for Deliiicije Vinoteka just off the Korzo (*Ante Starčevića 7a*).

OTHER PRACTICALITIES The main **post office** is located on the Korzo (*Korzo 13;* ⏰ *07.00–20.00 Mon–Fri, 07.00–14.00 Sat*). Rijeka's **hospital** is near the railway station (*Krešimirova 42*).

WHAT TO SEE AND DO Most of Rijeka was destroyed by a huge earthquake in 1750, and was rebuilt in the monumental Habsburg style, particularly in the reclaimed area south of the Korzo, where you can still be impressed by the sheer grandeur of buildings like the **Jadran** (home of Jadrolinija, the ferry company), or the **Royal Navy Palace**.

Up on the Korzo, one of the few pre-1750 survivors was the **City Tower**, although it was embellished post-earthquake with the Baroque trimmings and the distinctive clock and cupola you see today – not to mention the pompously bewigged reliefs of the Austro-Hungarian Emperors Charles VI and Leopold I over the archway. North of here, through the gate, is a warren of streets and squares marking the site of the original walled city. The town's oldest monument, a plain **Roman Gate** (probably the entrance to a barracks, rather than anything more significant), is up here, on the way to the 17th-century **Church of St Vitus** (Sv Vida).

Built on the site of an existing church by the Jesuits, St Vitus is an unusual circular building with a cupola supported by massive marble pillars. The 13th-century crucifix inside (from the original church) supposedly had a rock thrown at it in 1296 by a man called Petar Lončarić. He was swallowed up by the ground, but the body of Christ bled convincingly, and the blood was stored in a vial, starting up a useful counter-cult to Our Lady of Trsat (see below).

Heading west from here it's a few blocks to the splendid **Maritime and Historical Museum** (*Pomorski i povijesni muzej Hrvatskog primorja Rijeka; Mujejski trg 1;* ☏ *051 213 578; http://ppmhp.hr;* ⏰ *09.00–16.00 Mon, 09.00–20.00 Tue–Sat, 16.00–20.00 Sun; 15kn*), housed in the former Governor's Palace, home briefly to D'Annunzio during his occupation of the city. The exhibits are interesting enough, but it's the palatial rooms and décor that really make the visit worthwhile.

The other church worth seeing down in the town is the **Capuchin Church of Our Lady of Lourdes** (Gospe Lurdske), conveniently located right by the bus station. The neo-Gothic striped façade stands at the top of a fancy double staircase

---

MORETTO

You won't go far these days without seeing a Moretto (also called Mori, Morči, Morčeki and Morčići, depending on where you're from – and who you ask), as it's become the symbol of Rijeka.

The androgynous turbaned black figure is most commonly seen adorning earrings, but also features on other jewellery, and is prominent during Rijeka's carnival.

Various stories are told of the Moretto's origin – rich women over-fond of black slaves, Turkish invaders slaughtered in answer to local prayers, and others – but it seems the truth is more prosaic, reflecting a 17th- and 18th-century love affair with the Orient. The Moretto first appeared in Venice, and then in Rijeka during the 19th century, in a more modest and affordable form.

A single Moretto earring was frequently worn by men (especially sailors) as a sign of their provenance, though after World War II its production pretty much died out, only being revived with the establishment of an independent Croatia in 1991.

that wouldn't look out of place in front of one of the palazzi on Lake Como, in Italy. Started in 1904, the lower part was completed by 1908, but the upper part wasn't finished until 1929, in spite of the cash-strapped Capuchins taking advantage of the credulous local people by employing a charlatan calling himself St Johanca, who would raise money by sweating blood on demand (until his arrest for fraud in 1913).

Trsat Up on the hill above Rijeka is the leafy suburb of Trsat, originally the site of an Illyrian hill-fort, and a strategic defence point for people from the Frankopans. Up here is the **Church of Our Lady of Trsat** (Gospe Trsatske), supposedly the site where the Virgin Mary's house stopped and stayed from 10 May 1291 to 10 December 1294, on its way from Nazareth to its present resting place in Loreto, Italy. Fortunately, the loss of the Holy home was compensated for by the gift of a miraculous icon of the Virgin by Pope Urban V in 1367, which the Frankopans built the church to house, as well as the monastery next door. The icon embedded into the gaudy altarpiece here is actually a copy; the original is in the monastery treasury, which is hardly ever open. The copy was originally made for a church in Opatija in the early 20th century, so that people there could see it without having to cross to Rijeka, which was Italian-occupied at the time.

It still draws the pilgrims in good numbers, as you can see from the clutter of offerings in the **Chapel of Votive Gifts**, across the cloisters, and serious pilgrims will climb here from Rijeka on their knees, all the way up the 500-odd stairs leading from the town below. Less serious pilgrims will jump on a #2 bus.

The other big attraction in Trsat is the **castle**, which has been here forever, though in its present form only since Frankopan times. It was bought in 1826 by an Austrian army officer of Irish descent, Count Laval Nugent de Westmeath, and was restored to include the family mausoleum, where the sarcophagi were not just above ground, but upright, too, ready to face their makers. Among the people originally buried here was George Bernard Shaw's aunt, Jane Shaw, though nobody seems to have the foggiest idea why. On the front of the mausoleum there's an inscription reading 'Mir Yunaka', which means 'Peace to the Heroes' – given the area's turbulent history, it's something of an irony. The castle and mausoleum now serve as a low-key **museum** (⊕ *summer 09.00–02.00, winter 09.00–23.00; free*), though the whereabouts of the sarcophagi is a mystery; they were still here when Rebecca West came through in 1937, but they're certainly not there now. In their place are maps, drawings and photos showing Rijeka through the ages.

The view from the fort across the sea, and down to the shipyards, is great, and can be enjoyed over a cool drink on the terrace.

The Rijeka Carnival The pre-Lent carnival is easily Croatia's biggest (second only in Europe to the one in Venice, in fact) and Rijeka's most exciting annual event, attracting more than 10,000 active participants and 100,000 spectators. What's most extraordinary about the carnival is its adoption as an instant tradition – it was only revived in 1982, and has grown out of all proportion to expectations, attracting nationwide TV coverage as well as visitors from all over Croatia.

The main event of the week-long carnival is the huge international carnival parade on the Sunday before Lent, and you should look out especially for the *zvončari* – men wearing sheepskins, masks and enormous cattle bells, who hark back to a centuries-old tradition of driving out the evil spirits from villagers' houses at this time of year – and indeed still do so in the Kastav area just inland from Rijeka.

The mountainous area inland from Rijeka is one of the best remaining examples of forested karst, and is home to a wide diversity of flora and fauna. There's a small national park, Risnjak, and there are many other natural attractions, and mountains to hike up, but although the area's reasonably well known to Croatians it's practically unvisited by foreigners. This is starting to change as hotel developers and tourist agencies realise just how attractive this part of the country is and that not every foreign visitor wants to do the coast to death on every visit. Check out www.gorskikotar.hr and www.np-risnjak.hr if you're planning to explore this green oasis.

Buses and trains run through Gorski Kotar – it's crossed by the main road and railway from Karlovac to Rijeka, and there are local buses, though it's admittedly easier to explore round here if you have your own transport. Accommodation is also more scarce across the region than on the coast (although this is also beginning to change). However, there is an extensive network of hiking trails and mountain huts, enough to keep you busy for days, and there's also plenty of scope for cycling (see http://gorskikotarbike.com for routes and GPS logs).

RISNJAK NATIONAL PARK (*www.np-risnjak.hr; 45kn/25kn, or 100kn for a family ticket, valid for 2 days*) Only 15km inland from Rijeka as the crow flies, Risnjak National Park is a wonderful place to come in late spring and summer, with great walking, lovely flowers, spectacular scenery, and a relatively easy peak to scale. The weather can be extreme here, however, with the park affected by four different types of climate – harsh alpine, Dinaric mountain, mild Adriatic and continental Pannonian. In autumn it tends towards the very wet indeed, and in winter there's a good deal of snow – at the Risnjak mountain hut, at 1,418m, there's snow on the ground for an average of 157 days a year, and it can be up to 4m deep – though this can be a beautiful time to hike in the area, for those suitably equipped. For further information on hiking in Gorski Kotar, see Rudolf Abraham's book *Walking in Croatia* (page 429).

The local flora includes the protected edelweiss, black vanilla orchids, mountain yarrows, alpine clematis, saxifrage and yellow wood violets, among many others, while the fauna includes wild cats, roe deer, red deer, chamois, wild boar, brown bears and a small population of wolves. After nearly a century away, the lynx has not reappeared, and is behind the park's name (*ris* meaning lynx).

Crni Lug The main entrance to the park is through the village of Crni Lug, a narrow and winding 12km west of **Delnice**, itself on the main road and railway line from Karlovac to Rijeka. Buses run twice a day to the village from Delnice, though not at especially convenient times of day – if you're stuck in Delnice itself you could do worse than the **Scorpion Pizzeria** (€€–€) which serves up good-value fare.

Just over 1km beyond Crni Lug you'll find the **national park office** (*Bijela Vodica 48;* ☎ *051 836 133*), where you can pick up maps and a good guide, as well as an excellent little leaflet detailing the Leska Nature Trail, which is well worth a couple of hours of anyone's time. The office is also home to a cheerful restaurant (the trout was good on our visit), and there are five double rooms available (€€€–€€), though you should book well ahead if you want to stay in summer, as the lodge is popular with locals.

From the park office, at around 700m, it's a well-marked 9km walk (count on a little over 3 hours up) to the main peak, **Veliki Risnjak** – at 1,528m, it's the second

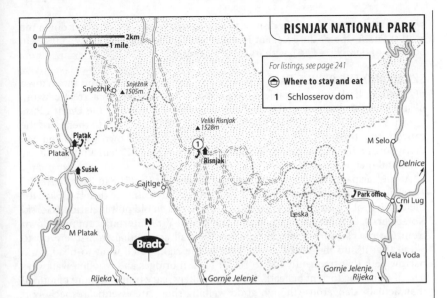

For listings, see page 241

RISNJAK NATIONAL PARK

For listings, see page 241

🏠 **Where to stay and eat**
1   Schlosserov dom

highest mountain in Gorski Kotar, being trumped by a mere 6m by Bjelolasica, which is at the heart of the main skiing centre in the area, 25km southeast of here.

Under the peak of Risnjak is a mountain hut, called Schlosserov dom (⊕ *May–Oct excl Tue; check opening times/availability of beds at the national park office beforehand, or contact* m *099 4282 072;* €€) but you'll need to bring your own sleeping bag. From the hut it's a rocky 20-minute scramble to the top, with some great views out across Gorski Kotar to the sea. The best are on clear days in the depths of winter, but if you're climbing at that time of year you need to be a seriously proficient mountaineer, and equipped with an ice-axe and crampons. If you're a winter visitor, it's worth knowing there's an unstaffed winter room in the hut, which sleeps six, but make sure you've cleared this with the park office in Crni Lug first.

Gorje Jelenje A considerably shorter route to the summit of Veliki Risnjak, also well signed, starts from the village of Gornje Jelenje, 16km southwest of Crni Lug (21km west of Delnice). Drive up to the head of the gravel road, at around 1,200m, and count on under an hour and a half from here on foot. The summit can also be reached in 3 hours or so from the small ski station at **Platak**, to the west of the park – this is also the best place to start the climb up the 1,505m summit of **Snježnik**, which can easily be combined with Veliki Risnjak.

Lokvarka Cave (*Špilja Lokvarka;* ☏ *051 831 250;* m *099 8451 931; http://lokvarka. hr;* ⊕ *09.00–17.00 Wed–Sat, 10.00–16.00 Sun, last entrance 1hr before closing; Mon/ Tue by appointment; 40kn*) If you're into the underground rather than the mountain peaks, then you'll love the Lokvarka Cave, just outside **Lokve**, 6km west of Delnice, on the main road to Rijeka – it's over 1km long, and has truly excellent stalagmites and stalactites. It's open weekdays from June to September, with guided visits every hour if there are at least six people; outside these times ask at the Lokve **tourist office** (*Rudolfa Strohala 118;* ☏ *051 831 250; www.tz-lokve.hr*) for more details. The tourist office also has access to a handful of attractive, private rooms in the pretty village. If you're here in spring, don't miss out on the **Frog Fiesta**, which features various froggy frolics and folk music – after all this froggy fun, however, you may

6

want to miss out on the main dish of the day: frogs' legs. A little further down the road at **Fužine** there's the excellent **Hotel Bitoraj** (*20 rooms; Sveti križ 1;* ☏ *051 830 005; www.bitoraj.hr;* €€€€), with its own restaurant.

SKRAD AND THE DEVIL'S PASS

About 12km east of Delnice is the small town of Skrad, in itself unremarkable enough. But below the town is a great canyon, nearly 2km long but sometimes as little as 2m wide, known as the **Devil's Pass** (Vražji Prolaz). There's a path, which takes under an hour, down to the top of the canyon from the train station in Skrad, or if you have your own wheels you can drive down a hair-raising 6km to the valley floor (signed Zeleni Vir) to the car park, and then walk up.

At the car park there's a restaurant, the **Zeleni Vir** (☏ *051 810 214;* ⏰ *09.00–19.00 daily in summer;* €€€–€€), and you can also buy entrance tickets (15kn) for the Vražji Prolaz and Zeleni Vir walks. To the left is an old power station (Gorski Kotar's first), beyond which you'll find the **Zeleni Vir Waterfall**, dropping down from the river's source, with the Zeleni Vir trail continuing from there up to Skrad. But it's up the Vražji Prolaz trail to the right you'll want to head, on a narrow path that frequently has to resort to iron bridges and wooden walkways over the gushing torrent beneath. It's a moderately scary trail, but more of a thrill than actually dangerous (though good walking shoes are essential, especially if it's been raining).

It takes around half an hour to walk up through the canyon, after which you'll see a sign to the left to **Muževa Hišica**, a deep cave which was used as a refuge in times of war – you'll need a torch if you want to explore the tunnel, which leads to a biggish chamber containing a good selection of stalactites and stalagmites, and the occasional bat.

Back on the main trail, the path cuts up through the woods to Skrad, some 400m above – count on an hour to reach the station.

Practicalities

There are several **trains** a day that stop in Skrad on the way from Zagreb to Rijeka and up to 20 buses a day. Skrad's **tourist office** (*Goranska bb;* ☏ *051 810 316; www.tz-skrad.hr*) has access to a number of private rooms. **Bistro Viktoria** (*Josipa Blaževića Blaža 1;* ☏ *051 810 173;* €€) is a large but friendly place near the tourist office, serving decent local game and other dishes.

OGULIN, KLEK AND BJELOLASICA

The train line from Karlovac to Rijeka takes a loop southwards away from the main road, before rejoining it near Delnice. On the loop, there's a stop at the small town of Ogulin, which is the access point by public transport to the easily accessible peak of **Klek** (you can also walk there from Ogulin), and the skiing, hiking and biking at **Bjelolasica**. Ogulin is also easy enough to reach by bus from either Rijeka or Karlovac.

For information on points further north and east, heading up to Karlovac, and across to the Plitvice Lakes, turn back to page 172.

Ogulin

There's not a great deal to do or see in Ogulin, but if you're here you can pick up useful information about the town and the gorgeous mountainous region which surrounds it from the **tourist office** (*Kardinala A Stepinca 1;* ☏ *047 532 278; www.tz-grada-ogulina.hr*). At the other end of town – all of 300m north – are Ogulin's main attractions, the solid twin-towered 16th-century fortress, which dates back to Frankopan times, the House of Fairy Tales and the spectacular gorge from which the Dobra River emerges.

The fortress houses the **Town Museum** (*Gradski Muzej;* ⊕ *08.00–14.00 Mon–Fri, 08.00–noon Sat; 15kn*), a modest collection of ethnographic and archaeological bits and pieces spread over a couple of floors. The most interesting highlight is the prison cell on the top floor, which housed no less celebrated an inmate than Tito, twice, in the 1920s and 1930s. On the same floor, there's a separate mountaineering section (the local mountain peak, Klek, is prominent enough that it is the emblem of the Croatian Mountaineering Association).

Next door to the Town Museum is the excellent **House of Fairy Tales** (*Ivana Kuća Bajke;* ☏ *047 525 398; www.ivaninakucabajke.hr;* ⊕ *11.00–18.00 Tue–Sun; entry 25kn*), a modern interactive museum on the life and works of Ivana Brlić Mažuranić, Croatia's most famous fairy-tale author, who was born in Ogulin. Kids will love it here, as the museum organises various workshops, but it's interesting for grown-ups too. The town also puts on an annual **fairy-tale festival** in June.

Outside, you can hardly miss the gorge, which is known as **Đula's Abyss**, after the love-struck princess who is said to have thrown herself to her death here. If you go across to the other side, and look carefully – and the lighting is just so – the more imaginative among you will be able to make out the mournful craggy face of her lover, Milan, looking down into the gorge; you can see his face in profile, with the eyes, nose and a chunky moustache. Maybe.

🏠 ***Where to stay and eat*** There is a new four-star hotel, the 21-room **Hotel Frankopan** (*Ivana Gorana Kovačića 1;* ☏ *047 525 509; www.hotel-frankopan.hr;* €€€€), right next to the castle.

Klek
West of Ogulin is the dramatic peak of Klek, which isn't the highest mountain in the area (it's a fraction under 1,200m), but is one of the most accessible. It can even be walked from Ogulin in 3 hours or so each way, though if you have a car or can get to Dom Lovački, 12km out of Ogulin (take the main road west, past the castle, for 2km, then turn left and head up 10km further), at the locality known as Bjelsko, first, then you'll save yourself a good deal of time. From here it's only about a 45-minute walk up through the woods to the Klek mountain hut (which usually serves snacks on summer weekends) and a further half hour to the summit, up a rather vertiginous rocky path above the trees. The panoramic view from the summit is excellent.

The tourist office in Ogulin has information on local cycle routes, photo safaris (with the chance to see to wild boar and deer) and rafting trips on the Dobra. Finally, Klek has long been associated with witches, so look out for the annual **Witches Festival** here, or the **Witches Challenge** cycle race, which charges up the mountain.

Bjelolasica
The ski centre on Bjelolasica went into bankruptcy in 2015, so is closed at the time of writing.

BIJELE AND SAMARSKE STIJENE
Further south, and slightly more difficult to reach unless you have your own wheels (though there are clearly marked hiking trails from Bjelolasica, and you can also walk up from the village of Jasenac on the road between Ogulin and Plitvice Lakes National Park), is the protected nature reserve of Bijele and Samarske Stijene, which has a wealth of dramatic karstic formations and cliffs rising out of the unspoiled woods. It's a reasonably popular place with local hikers and climbers – some of the cliffs are up to 50m high – but otherwise beautifully untouched by the hand of man, and a great place to find peace, quiet and edelweiss. For more information about hiking in this area and nearby Bjelolasica, see Rudolf Abraham's book *Walking in Croatia* (page 429).

(*www.np-sjeverni-velebit.hr*; *45kn/25kn adult/child, valid for 3 days*) The vast Velebit range – covering 2,000km² and stretching over 100km from Senj to Zadar – contains two national parks, Paklenica, to the south (pages 277–84), and North Velebit, between Senj and Karlobag, to the north. Of the two, North Velebit is the more remote, and far and away the least visited – it only achieved national park status in 1999, and development of any tourist infrastructure is still in its relative infancy. You can reach the Zavižan and Alan mountain huts by minor roads, and there are marked hiking trails to both these and other points from the coast.

Even though the current national park is itself very recent, conservation history in North Velebit goes back a long way – Štirovača park here was one of the country's first, along with Plitvice, back in 1929, and since 1978 it has been part of the UNESCO MAB (Man and Biosphere) programme. There's an inevitable conflict of interest along the park's borders with the highly lucrative local logging industry – most of the jobs in the area are logging-related – but the 1999 legislation promises to keep North Velebit well protected.

Being cool, high up, well forested and very sparsely inhabited, the park is an ideal habitat for brown bears, and there are now reckoned to be around 500 in the area, though they're just as unlikely to be seen here as anywhere else, bears being notoriously people-shy. The park is also home to wild boar, lynx, wild cats, red and roe deer and several species of eagle, along with many other animals – including, deep in one of the caves, *Croatobranhus mestrovi*, a previously unknown (and to this author's eyes, especially revolting) species of leech.

The park also features some of the country's most diverse flora, with a wide range of rare and protected plant species. The **Velebitski Botanički Vrt** botanical gardens – the remotest I've ever visited – were established back in 1967, at 1,480m, to highlight the flora unique to the region. You'll find them on the open hillside about a 15-minute walk from the Zavižan hut.

Deep within the park there's an even more strictly protected nature reserve, **Hajdučki Kukovi**, which you'll need special permission (and a very good reason) to visit. Within this reserve is one of the world's fifteen deepest caves, **Lukina Jama**, which was only discovered in 1993. Over the next two years the cave, whose entrance is at 1,436m above sea level, was explored down to a depth of 1,392m, just 44m above the sea (and it's down here that the new leech was found). In the same area is **Patkov Gušt**, one of the deepest vertical shafts in the world, dropping a giddying 553m. It's for the most serious of speleologists only. Just to the west of this is the breathtaking limestone scenery of **Rožanski Kukovi**, and passing through this, Premužićeva staza, arguably Croatia's finest hiking trail (see box, page 246).

North Velebit has two **park offices** (✆ 053 665 380), with a small branch on the coast, in Senj, and the main office up in the hills, in Krasno, on the minor road from Sveti Juraj (10km south of Senj) to Otočac. Watch out for giant logging vehicles.

There are several access points to the park itself, with the main entrance being off the road from Sveti Juraj to Krasno. There's a well-signed turning off to the right, just after the village of Oltari, 15km uphill from Sveti Juraj. You can also enter the park from the southern end, heading steeply uphill from Jablanac towards Veliki Alan, though you'll need a 4×4 to get beyond this. Buy your entrance ticket (45kn for a one- to three-day visit) as you come into the park or at Zavižan Dom.

WHERE TO STAY AND EAT Within the park there are three mountain lodges where hikers can overnight, the best equipped of which is **Zavižan Dom** (✆ 053 614 209;

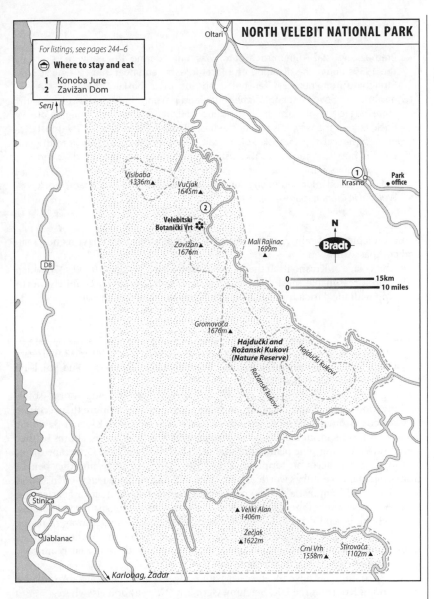

For listings, see pages 244–6

NORTH VELEBIT NATIONAL PARK

Oltari

For listings, see pages 244–6

🍴 **Where to stay and eat**
1 Konoba Jure
2 Zavižan Dom

Senj

Visibaba
1336m ▲

Vučjak
1645m ▲

**Velebitski
Botanički Vrt** ❀

Zavižan ▲
1676m

Mali Rajinac
1699m ▲

Krasno

1

Park
• office

N

Bradt

0 ——— 15km
0 ——— 10 miles

D8

Gromovoča
1676m ▲

**Hajdučki and
Rožanski Kukovi
(Nature Reserve)**

Hajdučki kukovi

Rožanski kukovi

Stinica

Jablanac

▲ Veliki Alan
1406m

Zečjak
▲ 1622m

Crni Vrh
1558m ▲

Štirovača
1102m ▲

Karlobag, Zadar

Kvarner Bay and Islands   NORTH VELEBIT NATIONAL PARK

€€–€), situated at 1,594m, not far from the botanical gardens. The lodge is also an important weather station, managed by Ante Vukusić and his family, who live up here – with an ongoing stream of local hikers to keep them company, not to mention some fiery homemade spirit from the local mountain herbs (including mint and rosemary) and lovely herbal tea.

Zavižan Dom makes an excellent base for hikes through the park, from the 10-minute scramble to the nearby peak of Vučjak, at 1,645m (fabulous views down to the island of Rab), to the 6-hour walk over to the Alan Lodge, at the other end of the park. The trails are mostly well marked, but given the rapid changes in weather here (visibility can drop to nothing in a matter of moments,

6

PREMUŽIĆEVA STAZA

Premužićeva staza (Premužić's path) was built during the early years of the 1930s under the direction of a local forestry engineer, Ante Premužić. Stretching from near Zavižan hut in the north to Baške Oštarije (in the mountains above Karlobag) in the south, and passing through the amazing limestone crags of Rožanski kukovi and below the weird rock fingers of Bačić kuk on the way, it is one of the best hiking trails in Croatia. The most impressive section, Rožanski kukovi, can be visited as a day trip from the Zavižan hut; to continue to Baške Oštarije you'll need to allow four days and be fully equipped.

For detailed information on hiking on Velebit, see Rudolf Abraham's book *Walking in Croatia* (page 429).

and there's plenty of rain), make sure you're well equipped and have a good map and compass with you.

In the village of Krasno itself there's the **Konoba Jure** (\ *053 851 100*; €€), which serves up a reasonable meal and has some accommodation. It's definitely worth checking with the park administration first if you want to stay or visit.

CRES AND LOŠINJ

Until the 11m-wide channel was dug between them, between 2,000 and 3,000 years ago, Cres (try saying something halfway between tsress and trress and you'll be fine) and Lošinj were a single island.

Geographically, they're the spindly, submerged, 80km-long north–south prolongation of the Učka mountain range, with nowhere being more than a couple of kilometres from the sea. Forming the western boundary of the Kvarner Bay, their deciduous forests in the north give way to dense scrub and barren shores further south, though newer pine plantations on Lošinj have softened the landscape there.

Today tourism accounts for practically all the islands' revenue, and they benefit from more than a century's worth of hospitality and tourist infrastructure. In season you may find Lošinj just a tad too popular for comfort – it attracts a quarter of a million visitors a year (about half as many as Dubrovnik) – but spring and autumn are lovely here. And even in high summer it's easy enough to get away from the crowds by hiking or mountain-biking across the islands on one of the numerous trails and paths. Once you're away from the paved roads, there are far more rock beaches and pebbly coves than people looking for them.

Access to both has never been easier with budget flights into Rijeka Airport on the island of Krk from the UK, Belgium, Germany, Norway and elsewhere.

HISTORY Inhabited since the Stone Age, Cres and Lošinj were home to important Iron and Bronze Age hilltop settlements, before being settled by the Liburnians, an Illyrian tribe, around 3,500 years ago. The islands were conquered by the Romans during the 1st century BC, passing to Byzantium on the collapse of the empire, and gradually settled by Slavs from the 7th century on.

Venice took control from 1000 to 1797, with a 50-year break at the end of the 14th century, during which the Croat-Hungarian kings were in charge. Austro-Hungarians stepped in from 1797, after which the islands passed to Italy in 1918, Germany in 1943, and Yugoslavia in 1945, before finally becoming Croatian in 1991.

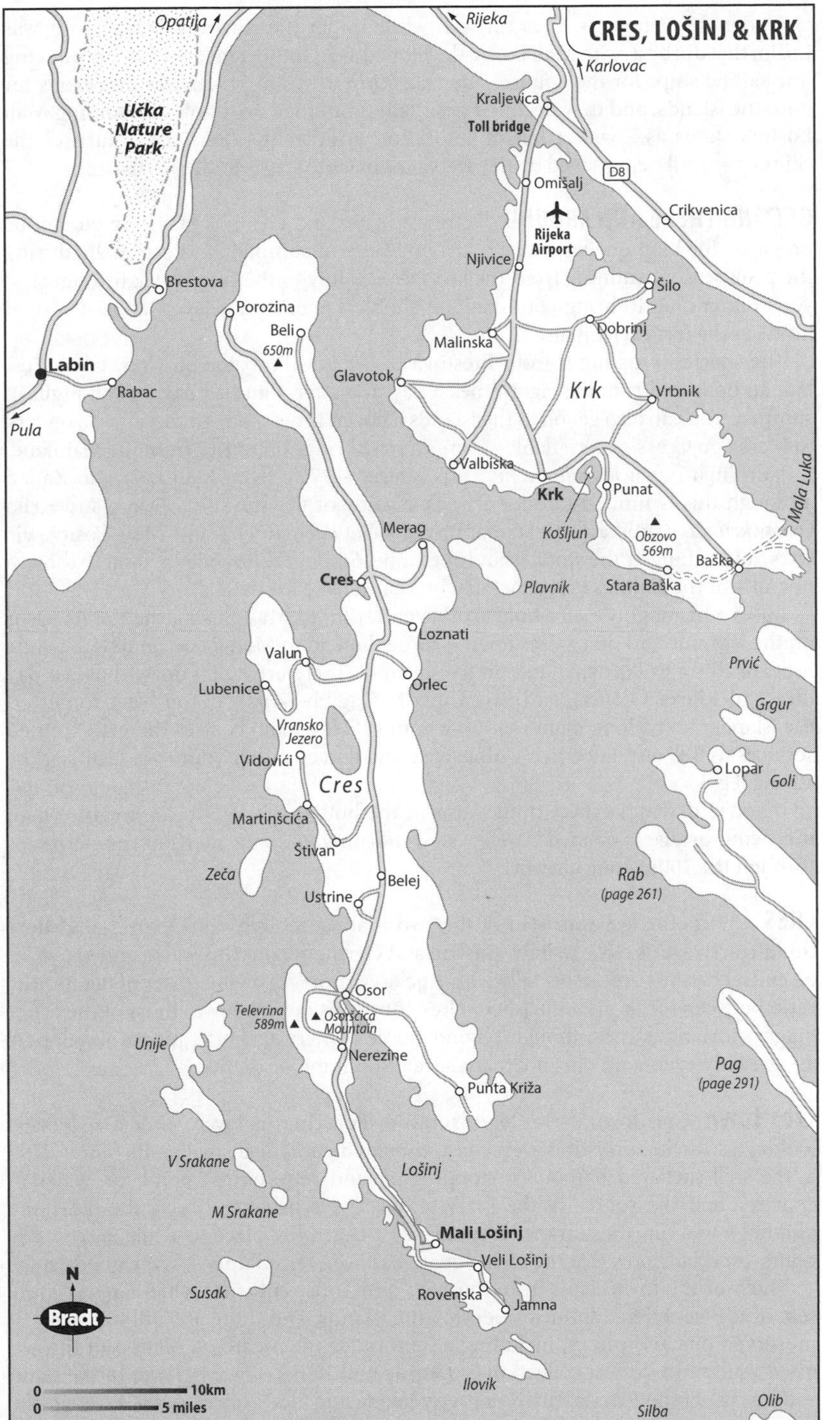
CRES, LOŠINJ & KRK
Opatija
Rijeka
Karlovac
Kraljevica
Toll bridge
D8
Učka Nature Park
Omišalj
Crikvenica
Rijeka Airport
Njivice
Brestova
Šilo
Porozina
Beli
650m
Malinska
Dobrinj
Labin
Rabac
Glavotok
Krk
Vrbnik
Pula
Valbiska
Krk
Punat
Mala Luka
Košljun
Obzovo 569m
Merag
Baška
Stara Baška
Cres
Plavnik
Loznati
Valun
Prvić
Orlec
Lubenice
Grgur
Vransko Jezero
Vidovići
Lopar
Goli
Cres
Martinšcića
Štivan
Zeča
Rab (page 261)
Belej
Ustrine
Osor
Televrina 589m
Osorščica Mountain
Unije
Nerezine
Pag (page 291)
Punta Križa
V Srakane
Lošinj
M Srakane
Mali Lošinj
Veli Lošinj
N
Bradt
Susak
Rovenska
Jamna
Ilovik
0
10km
0
5 miles
Silba
Olib

Under the Venetians, Cres thrived, while under the Austro-Hungarians it was Lošinj that did best, with Mali Lošinj developed as an important dockyard, producing fine sailing ships for the empire. The transition to steam power was disastrous for both the islands, and they declined gradually from then on – notwithstanding Mali Lošinj's status as a winter health resort for wealthy Austrians at the turn of the century – until being saved by the arrival of mass tourism in the 1970s.

GETTING THERE AND AROUND Getting to Cres and Lošinj is easy enough, but be prepared for long queues if you're driving here in summer, and especially during the peak season, running from the last week of July to the third week in August. If you're intending to bring your car, you should factor in a delay of at least several hours at the ferry terminal.

The shortest crossing is from Brestova in Istria to Porozina on Cres, taking just half an hour and running eight times a day in winter – and all day and all night in summer. You can also get on to the islands a dozen times a day from Valbiska on Krk to Merag on Cres's eastern flank – there's a road bridge on to Krk from the mainland.

Jadrolinija (*www.jadrolinija.hr*) runs a ferry service from Mali Lošinj to Zadar, although this is limited to once a week outside of the summer season, and Krilo (*www.krilo.hr*) runs a fast catamaran daily between Rijeka and Mali Lošinj, via Cres, and calling at the small islands of Unije, Sisak and Ilovnik on some – though not all – of the sailings (see timetable on the website for details).

Buses run roughly every hour from Veli Lošinj to Mali Lošinj, then up to Osor on the isthmus and on to Cres town – some then go to Merag and on to Krk, while most head up to Porozina and on to Brestova. There are half a dozen buses a day direct to Rijeka (*3½hrs*), and two a day to Zagreb (*7hrs*). If you want to get off the islands' 80km-long main road that connects the main centres there are limited services to Beli and Lubenice – otherwise you'll need either your own transport or strong legs.

If you're driving, expect traffic jams at the bottleneck at Osor, especially when the swing-bridge is opened (twice a day, morning and late afternoon) to let boats through the 100m-long channel.

CRES Cres is the less-touristed of the two islands, though don't expect anywhere this attractive, this close to Italy, Austria and Germany, and this warm and sunny, to be entirely visitor-free, especially with Rijeka Airport's growing roster of flights. The ratio between locals and tourists in Cres compares favourably to most of the other bigger Adriatic islands, though second-home owners and big tourism developers are greedily eyeing up one of Croatia's least spoilt major islands.

Cres town Cres town itself (26km south of Porozina) is lovely, almost as Italian-looking as Rovinj, on Istria's west coast, though a good deal smaller. Its *raison d'être* is the well-sheltered harbour, a stopping-off and refreshment point for Venetian convoys, and the source of the island's long-ago prosperity. Today the old stone buildings soak up the summer sun and it's a charming place to while away a few hours, especially now that the main square has been tarted up in a sympathetic style.

Much of the town dates from the 15th and 16th centuries, when Cres was the seat of the Venetian administration for the islands, and there are still lots of well-preserved bits and pieces, including a handful of town gates, a section of the old town walls, and quite a collection of Gothic and Renaissance palazzi. In the main square, Trg Frane Petrića, there's a pretty loggia and clock tower, while through the town gate from here you'll find the sober façade of the 15th-century **Church of St**

Mary (Sv Marija) and its fortified campanile. The church is only usually opened for services – if it is open, however, pop inside to see the fine Gothic (15th-century) wooden carved *pieta*, and a rather sad-looking griffon on the pulpit.

Where to stay Accommodation in the town itself is limited to private rooms, which you can book through the **tourist office** (*Cons 10;* \571 535; *www.tzg-cres. hr*), right where the bus stops. Expect to pay €40–60 for doubles in high season, plus a 30% surcharge for stays of under four nights.

Kimen (221 rooms) Melin I/16; \051 573 305; www.hotel-kimen.com. 1km west of Cres, this is the only hotel near town. It's pretty big but it's set in nice grounds a couple of hundred metres back from the pebble beach. The main building was recently renovated, transforming itself into a 3-star establishment, while the 2 smaller buildings nearby were not, & retain their 'old school' 2-star character. €€€€–€€€

Kovačine Autocamp Melin I/20; \051 573 150; www.camp-kovacine.com. Another km west from Kimen, along a pleasant seaside path, on the Kovačine headland, & set among pinewoods & olive trees, the Kovačine Autocamp is a small town in itself, with accommodation for up to 2,000 people (including a naturist section), 4 restaurants & bars, a supermarket, a small marina & its own beaches, & offering courses in windsurfing & scuba diving. If you don't have your own tent or camper van then you can book one of the 177 mobile homes, which sleep 2 or 4–6 people for €92/€145. €

Where to eat and drink Cres boasts an impressive array of local produce – look out for the excellent local lamb, great seafood, the award-winning local olive oil and *udič*, the EU directive-defying mutton version of pršut. You won't see the latter on many menus but ask the locals for tips and where to try it if you dare.

Belona Šetalište 23 Travnja; \051 571 203; ⊕ summer 09.00–midnight daily, winter 09.00–22.00 daily. It may not have the Adriatic views, but the fact that it's so popular with the locals says enough. A solid range of seafood & meat dishes with more marauding cats than fellow tourists in the shoulder seasons. €€€

Bistro Melin Melin II/22; \051 571 481; ⊕ 11.00–23.00 daily. Seafood bistro in the Melin district, 10mins' walk west from the centre of Cres. €€€

Bukaleta Loznati; m 099 481 120; www. mali-losinj.com/bukaleta.htm; ⊕ noon–midnight daily. Cres lamb is right up there in quality with its more famous sibling further down the Adriatic in Pag. Worth the 10-min taxi ride out of town to enjoy lamb in various permutations. €€€

Riva Creskih Kapetana 13; \051 571 107; ⊕ 11.00–23.00 daily. Sit on the terrace overlooking the harbour feasting on langoustines (scampi) & white fish, which you can see being cooked in the open kitchen. Rated highly for its seafood, but – like many places with prime waterfront location – low for service. €€€

✷ **Al Buon Gusto** Sv Sidar 14; \051 571 878; ⊕ 11.00–14.00 & 17.30–midnight daily. Great little spaghetteria/trattoria in the backstreets of the old town, which easily outdoes the more flashy places on waterfront, in terms of food, atmosphere & service. Recommended. €€€–€€

Beli and the griffon vulture

Up on Cres's rocky northeastern tip, separated from the dramatic main road along the island's spine by its highest peak (650m), is the old hilltop village of Beli, overlooking the western corner of Krk, and sitting high up above a pretty pebble beach. There are buses to Beli from Cres, running twice daily (once very early in the morning, once in the afternoon – see www.island-losinj.com/transport/bus for timetables). If you're walking, it's a good hour and a half from the bus stop at the junction on the main road halfway between Cres and Porozina.

Apart from the peace and tranquillity here, the main reason for a visit to Beli is the wonderful Eurasian griffon vulture, one of the largest flying birds, which was saved from the jaws of extinction here by the efforts of the Eco-Centre Caput Insulae Beli (ECCIB) – a non-profit, non-governmental organisation established in 1993, which closed in 2013.

The vultures themselves are truly magnificent, with a wingspan reaching 2.8m, a body weight of up to 15kg and a life expectancy of up to 60 years. They can be super-fast, reaching speeds of up to 120km/h, but usually cruise at 40–50km/h in search of a carcass. Given the relative rarity of dead animals, the vultures cruise in formation, with no more than one per kilometre, to cover the maximum ground area, signalling a find by circling.

The birds live only on carrion, which was once provided by the abundance of sheep ranging free here – diseased animals would be cleared up by the vultures, keeping the shepherds happy by saving the rest of the flock from contamination. Today, with depopulation, there are fewer shepherds, fewer sheep and fewer vultures.

The vultures are also endangered by tourism, particularly by motorboats coming too close to the cliffs and scaring fledgling into flights that can't be sustained, leading to youngsters drowning. With only one egg per couple per year (during the two-month incubation period both parents alternate in keeping it warm and protected), and a five-year delay before sexual maturity, you can see why they're scarce. Fortunately they're now legally protected, and the fine for killing or disturbing the vultures, or stealing their eggs or chicks, is an off-putting 40,000kn.

From just 24 nesting couples in the mid 1980s, the population has now increased to a still precarious 70-odd couples nesting annually, thanks mostly to the work of the ECCIB.

Where to stay and eat

✷ 🏠 **Pansion Tramontana** (6 rooms) Beli 2; ✆ 051 840 519; m 099 216 5011; www.beli-tramontana.com. This is the best accommodation option in Beli, run by the friendly & welcoming Nina & Robi Malatestinić. The pansion serves good food using locally sourced ingredients as much as possible, & they bake their own bread. Robi also runs dive courses, & other activities including griffon watching, hiking & cycling are also offered. Highly recommended. The Pansion Tramontana (Tramontana is the name of this northern part of Cres) also marks the start of a series of hiking trails exploring the culture, flora & fauna of the area around Beli. There's a small leaflet & rough map available from the tourist office in Cres, but the paths themselves are in many cases quite overgrown and can be quite difficult to follow. €€€

🏕 **Camp Brajdi** ✆ 051 840 532; m 091 560 1332. This pleasant campsite is down in the olive groves towards the shore, & has a restaurant & a small shop. €

South of Cres town

The hilly main road from Cres town winds 35km south to the village of Osor, on the isthmus. On the way south you'll see the 5km-long and 1.5km-wide Vransko Jezero, the only lake on the Kvarner islands, and the only water supply for the whole of Cres and Lošinj – hence the ban on swimming here.

Valun Before the lake, there's a turn-off to the exquisite village and bay of Valun. There's a bus service to Valun from Cres (*20mins*) running daily (twice on Friday) except Tuesdays and Sundays (timetable at www.island-losinj.com/transport/bus). If you're cycling, be prepared for a steep ride back uphill!

Access to the village – even for car drivers – is down a flight of steps leading to the harbour, where you'll find a handful of stone houses and the pretty little church holding Valun's only cultural treasure, the **Valun Tablet**. Housed in the sacristy, this 11th-century engraving was originally a tombstone, and it's one of the oldest pieces of Glagolitic stone-carving in Croatia – with a helpful Latin translation for the Glagolitically challenged.

Accommodation in Valun is limited to a few private rooms, which are listed on the Cres tourist office website – book ahead, as although there's a tourist office here in July and August, that's when the rooms are already full of holidaying Italians. Otherwise there's the **Zdovice campsite** (☏ *051 571 161;* €), but you should book well ahead to be sure of a space.

Lubenice Beyond the turnoff to Valun, the road leads up to the partly abandoned – and spectacularly situated – clifftop village of Lubenice, served by the same bus route as Valun. The village sits on a bluff at nearly 400m above sea level, and makes for a popular summer evening excursion venue – the views are fantastic – and in season the half-dozen local residents do brisk trade selling their own wine and honey and keeping the bar and restaurant going. For the rest of the year it's a deserted and windblown place.

Below the town (far, far below) there's a wonderful bay and beach – the 1 hour hike back up puts most people off, however, meaning that it's far from crowded.

Martinšćica Back on the main road south, the first turn-off after Vransko Jezero leads 8km or so west to the little holiday village of Martinšćica, set on a pretty shingle bay with an attractive half-kilometre beach. At one end there's the large **Slatina campsite** (☏ *051 574 127; www.camp-slatina.com;* €), which also has a few apartments. There's also **Hotel Zlatni Lav** (☏*051 574 020; www.hotel-zlatni-lav.com;* €€€€). Only some of the buses between Mali Lošinj and Cres (and going on to Rijeka and Zagreb) stop at Martinšćica, otherwise it's a 9km walk from the turnoff on the main road (timetable at *www.island-losinj.com/transport/bus*).

Osor Located on the isthmus, Osor was the capital of Cres and Lošinj until the end of the 15th century, when a combination of plague, epidemic, pirates and Venetians shifted the capital up to Cres town, 35km north. Which is why the tiny village of today (population less than 100) still has a town hall and loggia, a 15th-century cathedral, a bishop's palace and the extant remnants of old stone walls.

It's a lovely stop, in the process of reinventing itself as a museum-village, and for once it's an easy enough place to get to, being on the regular Cres–Mali Lošinj bus route. The cathedral is shut more often than not, but if it's open it's worth popping in to admire the sizeable altarpiece and the somewhat over-the-top chapel to the left – both a good deal more sightly than the ghastly modern Stations of the Cross adorning the side walls.

Behind the cathedral, in the town square, you'll find a dozen sculptures by the likes of Meštrović and Kršnić, a couple of cafés, and the small town museum (☉ *weekday mornings*). Housed in the old town hall, the museum has an interesting collection of 1st- and 2nd-century Roman artefacts from all over the empire, a testimony to Osor's former importance as a maritime trading port.

If you want to stay, there are a few private rooms and apartments – try **Apartments Mikulec** (*Osor 37;* 📱 *091 5159 383; www.apartmanimikulec.com;* €€) – as well as a couple of good campsites, **Preko Mosta** (☏ *051 237 350; www.jazon.hr;* €) and **Bijar** (☏ *051 237 147; www.camp-bijar.com;* €), both close to the town and to the beaches. In summer Osor puts on excellent classical concerts – check the Cres town or (better) Mali Lošinj tourist offices for details (*http://visitlosinj.hr*).

Southeast of Osor – off the public transport map altogether – are Cres's best beaches, spread around a crenulated coast, south and east of the village of **Punta Križa**, that's deserted save for the **Baldarin** (☏ *051 235 680; www.camp-baldarin.com*)

naturist campsite. The beaches are no secret, but you should be able to find yourself a quiet spot, away from an incipient off-roading recreational-vehicle community.

LOŠINJ Smaller than Cres, but more populous (and more popular) is the island of Lošinj. That has its advantages and disadvantages – the extra tourists mean there are better facilities on hand, while the smaller size makes the island far more manageable on foot. Walking maps are available from the tourist offices in Mali and Veli Lošinj, and the moment you head uphill you'll find you have plenty of space to yourself. Mali Lošinj in the first couple of weeks in August, however, can be seriously busy – seething wouldn't be an exaggeration. The waters around Lošinj are busy too, with playful dolphins that are best visited on organised boat trips from Veli Lošinj, where there's also a dedicated dolphin research centre.

Nerezine The first settlement you come to, 4km south of Osor, is Nerezine, a cheerily dispersed village and harbour with a large, well-situated campsite, **Rapoča** (‑ *051 237 145; www.losinia.hr*), in the woods by the beach along the north shore. There are also private rooms available – contact Lošinjska Plovidba (‑ *051 231 077; www.losinia.hr*), or ask at the Marina travel agency (*Obala Nerezinskih Pomoraca;* ‑ *051 237 038; www.marina-nerezine.hr*).

Nerezine lies at the foot of Osorščica Mountain, which culminates in the peak of Televrin (589m), a steep hike up, but one of the best pay-offs in the country, with fabulous views in all directions when you get there – the length of Lošinj and its offshore islands to the south, and Istria to the northwest. Just below the peak is the tiny **Chapel of St Nicholas** (Sv Nikola), still a place of pilgrimage for the Nerezine locals. A hike up Televrin from Nerezine, descending to Osor on the other side, takes about 4½ hours (see Rudolf Abraham's *The Islands of Croatia,* page 429).

Mali Lošinj Mali Lošinj made its reputation in the 19th century as a dockyard, producing great sailing ships for the Austro-Hungarian Empire. When steam came in, the dockyards went out, but tourism of a sort started here around the same time, with the town gaining favour (like Opatija) with well-heeled Austrians as a fine place for a winter rest cure. Many of the elegant villas they built can still be seen above the Čikat Bay and peninsula, home today to the main resort hotels.

The annual influx of visitors – mainly Italian and German – hasn't done much to spoil the old town, spreading along both sides of the v-shaped harbour and meeting in a triangular piazza that leads off into the small but pretty clutter of narrow streets making up the old quarter. The landscaped waterfront with its swaying palms and cacti is the place to head for a relaxing stroll with an ice cream in hand.

There's remarkably little in terms of sights, but the **art collections** of the **Lošinj Museum** (*www.muzej.losinj.hr;* ⊕ *28 Mar–14 Jun & 16 Sep–1 Nov 10.00–13.00 & 18.00–20.00 Tue–Fri, 10.00–13.00 Sat; 15 Jun–15 Sep 10.00–13.00 & 19.00–22.00 Tue–Sun; 2 Nov–2 Jan 10.00–13.00 & 17.00–19.00 Tue–Fri, 10.00–13.00 Sat; 10kn*), housed a block back from the Riva (waterfront) in the Fritzy Palace, are well worth a visit. The gallery comprises two separate private collections, with old masters collected by Guiseppe Piperata on the one hand and more contemporary works collected by Andro Vid Mihičić on the other. Otherwise it's a question of drifting around and soaking up the old town atmosphere before returning to the endless quayside cafés for a well-deserved aperitif.

The main **tourist office** (*Riva Lošinjskih Kapetana 29;* ‑ *051 231 884; www. tz-malilosinj.hr*), halfway along the Riva between the ferry terminal and the main square, has excellent documentation, and you should definitely pick up the

Promenades and Footpaths map which gives you the walking times between most of the major points on the southern part of the island – an indispensable guide if you're to get away from the crowds in season.

Hotel accommodation is plentiful, but you'd do well to book way ahead in high summer. If you're staying out at Čikat or Sunčana uvala, there's a regular shuttle bus running from the bus station (timetable at http://visitlosinj.hr) – you can buy a ticket (*10kn one-way*) on the bus, but it's best (when coming into town from your hotel for the day) to buy an all-day ticket (*20kn*), covering multiple journeys, which is only available at hotels. If you fancy walking, it's an easy 25-minute stroll out to Sunčana uvala. From the piazza, walk left then right up an alley, following the signs to DM pharmacy. Go straight past DM then up a flight of steps to the main road, cross the main road and follow the walled path alongside the road then downhill on the right to Sunčana uvala.

Where to stay There is accommodation in town and – even better – across the headland at Čikat and Sunčana uvala. Private rooms are also in good supply and you shouldn't have any trouble in finding one – ask at any of the dozen or so agencies in town and expect to pay around €50–60 for a double, with a 30% surcharge for three-day stays or less. One place well worth trying is the **Ivanka** (*Bočac 19;* 051 231 934; €€), just behind the western quayside, right in town, which is a cheerful restaurant with a handful of nice rooms upstairs.

Alhambra (36 dbls, 15 suites) Čikat; 051 661 101; www.losinj-hotels.com. Reopening in 2015 after a substantial makeover, the Alhambra is now one of the most luxurious boutique hotels on the island. €€€€€

Apoksiomen (25 rooms) Riva Lošinjskih Kapetana 1; 051 520 820; www.apoksiomen. com. Boutique 4-star hotel right on the waterfront with its own quayside café. Light & airy rooms feature rattan furniture, Wi-Fi & satellite TV, & the helpful staff go that extra mile for you. €€€€

Aurora (393 rooms) Sunčana bb; 051 667 200; www.losinj-hotels.com. The best place to stay at Sunčana uvala, & one of the nicest hotels on the island – smart, clean rooms (go for the ones with a sea-facing view & enjoy the sunset on your balcony), right by a lovely spot for swimming & sunbathing on level rock terraces (the water here is much cleaner than by the pebble beach of Sunčana uvala itself). The food is excellent & it's well worth paying a few euros more for HB. Highly recommended. €€€€

Bellevue (226 rooms) Čikat; 051 679 000; www.losinj-hotels.com. Vast modern place, now renovated into a luxury 5-star. €€€€

Vespera (404 rooms) Sunčana bb; 051 667 300; www.losinj-hotels.com. Next door to & sharing the same outdoor swimming pools as the Aurora, this is a great choice for families, & is now part of the Kinderhotels brand. Oodles of activities to keep kids happy even when they're not throwing themselves in the pool or the sea. As with the Aurora, go for HB. Recommended. €€€€

Villa Margarita (6 dbls, 4 apts) Bočac 64; 051 233 837; www.vud.hr. Small, central hotel in a restored 19th-century villa, with own restaurant – but up for sale at the time of writing in 2015, so that might be set to change. €€€€

Čikat 051 232 125. Campsite is a half-hour walk across the headland, & it's enormous, but well located, right on a good beach. €€

Where to eat and drink

Artatore Artatore 132; 051 232 932; www. restaurant-artatore.hr; 11.00–23.00 daily. Highly regarded, family-run seafood restaurant out at Artatore, 8km from Mali Lošinj heading towards Nerezine. €€€€

Baracuda Priko 31; 051 233 309; 10.00–23.00 daily. The claim 'we offer you only fresh fish, so we appreciate on understanding if some kind of fish missing momentary' may not win any grammar awards, but the fresh seafood on offer here deserves all the acclaim it gets. Book a seat on the coveted leafy outside terrace. Daily specials tempt from the handwritten board but you can't go wrong with one of Croatia's best fish platters for 2, a snip at under 300kn for squid, langoustine, 2 whole sea bass, shark steaks & a tuna kebab. €€€

✗ Konoba Dišpe Sv Martin 10; m 091 569 1955; ⊕ 11.00–14.00 & 17.00–23.00 daily. Good low-key konoba near the town centre. €€€
✗ Konoba Hajduk Brace Vidulica 11; ⊕ 11.00–14.00 &17.00–23.00 daily. Small local place near the town centre with a nice terrace. €€€

Veli Lošinj

In spite of the name (*veli* means large; *mali* means small), Veli Lošinj has under 1,000 residents to Mali Lošinj's 7,000, and although it also has much fewer visitors, there's much less space here, too, so this picture postcard town can get almost as crowded in summer as its larger cousin.

Veli Lošinj is the terminus for the regular bus up to Cres. It's also only about 45 minutes on foot from Mali Lošinj, with the last two-thirds of the route along the coastal path, coming in past the Punta hotel complex. Bring your swimming gear if you fancy a dip in one of the coves *en route*.

The tiny harbour is dominated by the fortified, barn-like **Church of St Anthony** (Sv Antuna), built in the 17th century on the ruins of a smaller 15th-century church, and testifying to the former wealth and grandeur of the town. Inside it's stately Baroque, and has a fine collection of paintings from the Titian and Tiepolo schools, though you're only likely to see these during the half hour before or after a service, as the church is usually closed at other times.

Behind the church, stand-offishly distant, is a 15th-century Venetian campanile. Also 15th-century Venetian is the crenellated tower built to protect the town from pirates and now restored to house the municipal museum – a minor triumph of form over content.

Where to stay and eat Everything you need is on or near the harbour front, including a couple of agencies that will find you a private room for anything from €40 for a double or €50 for an apartment, with a hefty 50% surcharge for one-night stays. Try the helpful VAL agency (*Vladimira Nazora 29;* ☏ *051 236 604; www.val-losinj.hr*), which also rents bikes – an excellent way of exploring the island – or Palma (*Vladimira Nazora 22;* ☏ *051 236 179; www.losinj.com*).

Vitality Hotel Punta (181 sgls & dbls, 53 family rooms) Veli Lošinj bb; ☏ 051 661 111; www.losinj-hotels.com. Up on the northwestern corner of the Veli Lošinj bay, this is something of a sprawling affair but the location is beautiful & there are indoor & outdoor pools & many sports facilities. €€€€
Pansion Villa Saturn (9 rooms) Obala Maršala Tita bb; ☏ 051 236 604; www.pansion-saturn.com. Good, bargain-priced place, renovated in 2005 – right on the front, next door to St Anthony's. Simple but nice rooms, though with the terrace below it's not as quiet as it might be. €€€
Youth Hostel (50 beds) Kaciol 4; ☏ 051 236 234; www.hfhs.hr. Veli Lošinj also has a fine youth hostel with its own small park – book as far ahead as you possibly can, as it's usually full. €
✗ Boca Vera Vladimira Gortana 4; ⊕ 11.00–23.00 daily. Popular place for pasta & pizza, also serving other dishes. €€€

Southern Lošinj and islands

A 20-minute walk south of Veli Lošinj along the shore or a 5-minute hike across the village brings you to the little bay and pretty fishing 'suburb' of **Rovenska**, home to one of Lošinj's best restaurants, **Bora Bar** (*Rovenska 3;* ☏ *051 867 544; www.borabar.net;* ⊕ *10.00–midnight daily (kitchen closes 22.00 in August);* €€€). Italian chef Sasso has been serving excellent and imaginative dishes with an emphasis on fresh local produce since 2006. Truffles and seafood both feature strongly on the menu, and there are some delicious pasta dishes.

Another restaurant here is the cheerful **Sirius** (✆ *051 236 399;* ⊕ *summer 09.00–01.00 daily;* €€€) serving up the catch of the day, super-fresh, and local dishes such as stuffed squid with olives and polenta. Ask here about private rooms if you want to stay in the village. If Sirius is full, try the **Mol** (✆ *051 236 008;* ⊕ *summer 09.00–midnight daily;* €€€) next door, which has excellent daily specials.

The attractive coastal path continues for another 75 minutes south past the villages of **Javorna** and **Kriška**, terminating in **Jamna** – there's also a wealth of hiking up to and along the spine of the island, with paths leading down to various settlements, coves and beaches on the pretty west coast. Take plenty to drink, however, as there's not much shade and no water at all.

When you're done with the main island, there are day trips to the offshore ones from Mali Lošinj – you can arrange these through any of the travel agencies, or just negotiate on the harbour front with one of the taxi-boats. There's also a Jadrolinija ferry – the aging passenger ship, *Premuda* – that makes the circuit of the main offshore islands (Unije, Susak, Ilovnik) twice daily (*www.jadrolinija.hr*), and the fast catamaran service between Pula and Zadar calls at the islands as well (*http://lnp.hr*). If you take the early morning (and it is very early) sailing of the *Premuda* out to one of the islands, it's quite feasible to visit as a day trip, returning in the afternoon on the ferry or catamaran.

Most popular is **Susak**, the sandy island off to the west of Lošinj, which is famous for its excellent wines and colourful local costume, featuring orange and yellow pleated dresses and bright-red tights – you're more likely to see this on a local postcard than a local person, however, as most of the population has long since emigrated.

Unije, the westernmost of the islands in the Kvarner Bay, is also lovely. With only one settlement and fewer visitors than most places it makes for a lovely haven to spend a day or so if it's total quiet you're after. It also has a couple of very well-sheltered moorings if you're sailing.

Finally, to the south of Lošinj there's a handful of islands, the biggest of which is **Ilovik**, famous for its flowers and eucalyptus trees, a testimony to the unusual amount of water here.

There are some private rooms available on all three islands – book these through one of the agencies in Mali Lošinj. There are no cars on either Unije or Susak.

KRK

Croatia's biggest island (410km² to Cres's 405km²) has been connected to the mainland by a 1.4km toll bridge since 1980, and it's been one of the most popular holiday spots on the Adriatic ever since – at the height of the season you should definitely try to book ahead to be sure of a room, when it seems like the bridge is directly connected to Vienna and Munich.

Krk – impossible to pronounce correctly without being Croatian (somewhere between Sean Connery saying 'kirk' and a dog coughing) – is home to industry as well as tourism, with a petrochemical plant near Omišalj, and Rijeka's airport also being on the island. People living in the north commute to Rijeka for work, while in summer Krk is busy and popular with holidaymakers, primarily from Austria and Germany.

The island's infrastructure and local transport are good, making a visit here an easy one, and Krk was fortunate in barely being affected by the war at the beginning of the 1990s – tourism continues to boom and is expected to grow further as the airport sees more budget flights from northern Europe.

The northeastern side of the island is mostly barren, while the main centres and most of the trees are in the softer and milder southern half. Running down the northwestern shore are a string of fully developed package resorts, including **Omišalj, Njivice** and **Malinska**.

At the south of the island is **Baška,** with its hugely popular beach, a great arc of fine shingle rather than sand. The area around Baška also has one of the best networks of hiking trails of any of the islands.

If you're on Krk at the end of July you'll be within easy earshot of the popular **Krk Folk Festival**, which is big on the local bagpipes.

HISTORY People have lived on Krk since time immemorial, but the island was first known to have been settled by the Liburnian Illyrians, who were usurped in due course by the Romans. When Rome fell, Byzantium stepped in, to be followed by Venice, and then Croatia–Hungary.

During the 11th century, Krk became the most important centre of Glagolitic culture in Croatia, and much of the country's valuable Glagolitic heritage comes from the island – the script was used here continuously until the beginning of the 19th century and the arrival of the Austro-Hungarians.

In 1358 Venice granted custody of the island to the Dukes of Krk, who ruled semi-autonomously until 1480. They owed their ascendancy, according to Rebecca West (in *Black Lamb and Grey Falcon*): 'not to virtue nor to superior culture, but to unusual steadfastness in seeing that it was always the other man who was beheaded or tossed from the window or smothered'.

From 1430 onwards, the dukes successfully re-branded themselves (with the Pope's benediction) as '**Frankopans**', allying themselves to the Frangepan nobility of Roman times. Their new coat of arms gave a nod both to Venice and the Frangepans (which derives, as New Testament scholars will have guessed, from *frangere panem,* the breaking of the bread), and therefore featured lions with loaves.

The return of Krk to Venice in 1480 wasn't good news for the island. The Venetians tore down the oak forests to build their galleys, and then pressed the islanders into service as oarsmen. In spite of a succession of rulers – from the Austro-Hungarians to the French (briefly) to Yugoslavia itself – little else of great note affected Krk until the arrival of mass tourism in the 1970s.

GETTING THERE AND AROUND Being popular, close to Rijeka and connected to the mainland by a road bridge, Krk is pretty well served by public transport. Several **buses** a day make the 2-hour journey from Rijeka to Baška, stopping on the way at Omišalj, Malinska, Krk and Punat (timetables at www.autotrans.hr). Only a couple of buses a day, however, make the 10km journey across the island from Krk town to Vrbnik.

Around nine buses also go direct from Zagreb to Baška, 4 hours away and stopping at Krk, etc, with one of these starting in Varaždin, and another running to Osijek (timetables at www.autotrans.hr). Direct buses from Lošinj and Cres arrive via the Merag–Valbiska ferry several times a day and pass through Malinska on their way to Rijeka and Zagreb (timetables at www.island-losinj.com/transport/bus).

By **car**, the vast majority of people arrive over the bridge, though there's also the ferry connection ten times a day from Merag on the island of Cres, and another ferry from Lopar, on Rab, to Valbiska (*www.jadrolinija.hr*).

Rijeka Airport is served by Ryanair and other budget airlines flying in direct from destinations in northern Europe; there are also flights to Zagreb with Croatia Airlines, and the airport is also used for charter flights bringing in package tours to Krk, Cres, Lošinj and Opatija.

KRK TOWN The island's capital is a bit of a suburban (and growing) sprawl, but at its core is a well-preserved old town, with cobbled streets and alleys. The Romans walled the town and built extensive baths here, but the remnants you'll see today are mostly 15th-century Frankopan and onwards.

Krk's most striking sight is arguably the onion-dome on top of the campanile, itself topped by a trumpet-blowing angel. The campanile dates from 1515, though the cupola and angel weren't added until 1765, and the angel you see today (not that you'd know) is a 1975 plastic replica, the original copper-plated wooden version having deteriorated beyond salvation. This campanile is shared by two churches across a covered alley from one another, the cathedral and the Church of St Quirinus. Worth a visit is the **church museum**, if only for the remarkable silver altarpiece of the Madonna, a gift to the last Duke of Krk in 1477.

The Romanesque **cathedral** is usually only open around the time of church services, but it's worth the wait, and you can often peer in from the vestibule anyway. Built on the site of an early basilica founded on the site of the Roman baths, today's cathedral dates from the 12th century on. While much of what you see inside is 15th and 16th century, there are some interesting mosaic fragments, and the columns are mostly Roman – the last capital on the left, by the choir, sports an unusual early Christian Eucharist motif of two birds eating a fish. There are some good 15th- and 16th-century paintings, including the altarpiece, by Pordenone, while the fine 15th-century Gothic chapel on the left-hand side was the Frankopan place of worship, and features their various coats of arms on the ceiling.

St Quirinus, next door, is another fine example of clean, spare Romanesque architecture, also dating mostly from the 12th century. It claims to be the only two-storey church on the eastern Adriatic coast, and it was in the crypt here, dedicated to St Margaret, that condemned men said their final mass before execution in Frankopan days.

Otherwise, there's not a whole lot to see, though the remnants of the medieval walls and the old alleys and streets are suitably atmospheric – as indeed are the summer concerts put on in the old Venetian fortress marking the corner of the old town.

Getting there and around Buses arrive at the southern end of town; it's a short walk past the bustling harbour to the old town. The **tourist office** (*Vela Placa 1/1;* `051 221 414; www.tz-krk.hr`) is just inside the main gate, on the left, but was out of maps on the day I came through – fortunately that's not a problem as the old town is tiny, and it's easy to find your way around.

Where to stay and eat Most of the town's hotel accommodation is a 15-minute walk east of town, though there's one place, the Marina, right on the waterfront, and the Placa, in the old town. There's also a list of agencies and accommodation on the tourist office website: try **Aurea**, on the northern edge of town (*Vršanska 26/L;* `051 221 777; www.aurea-krk.com`), or **AdriaSun** on the waterfront (*Šetalište Sv Bernardina bb;* `051 880 333; www.adriasun.hr`), and expect to pay around €40 for a double in summer. A list of campsites can also be found on the tourist office website – there's the **Ježevac,** the **Škrila,** and the **Krk,** all of which are now firmly 'textile'. The newest of these is Camping Krk which is an eco- and family-friendly makeover of the former naturist Politin (*Narodnog Preporoda 80;* `051 221 351; www.camping-adriatic.com/camping-krk-politin`).

Marina (6 rooms, 4 suites) Obala Hrvatske
Mornarice 8; `051 221 128; www.hotelmarina.hr`.

Straightforward rooms in an unbeatable location.
€€€€€

🏠 **Bor** (20 rooms) Šetalište Dražica 5; ☎051 220 200; www.hotelbor.hr. Just 600m east along the shore from the marina is the Bor, which offers plain but spacious rooms a stone's throw from the beach. €€€€

🏠 **Boutique Hotel Placa** (5 rooms) Ribarska 5; ☎051 587 429; www.hotel-placa.com. Beautifully renovated stone house on the site of a former Roman spa, complete with Roman mosaic, with wooden floors & beams & rattan furniture right in the centre of the old town. €€€€

🏠 **Dražica/Villa Lovorka/Tamaris** (137 rooms, 73 rooms & 26 rooms) Ružmarinska 6; ☎051 655 755; www.hotelikrk.hr. All 3-star, forming a large resort close to the sea. €€€€

🏠 **Koralj** (173 rooms) Vlade Tomašića bb; ☎051 655 400, 052 465 130; www.valamar.com. Best value of the out-of-town package places is the 3-star Koralj, which is on a narrow beach in the woods & has modern dbls & for a lot less than you'll pay at the equally 3-starred Dražica/Lovorka/Tamaris. €€€

🏠 **Hostel Krk** Dinka Vitezića 32; ☎051 220 212; www.hostel-krk.hr. Krk also has a youth hostel housed in what was originally the island's very first hotel. There's a surcharge for stays of under 3 days; it works out the same or more expensive than private rooms – but the setting is lovely, right in the old town. €€

✗ **Galija** Frankopanska 38; ⏱ 11.00–23.00 daily. Krk's most popular restaurant, with a good range of seafood, grills, pizza & pasta. €€€

✗ **Konoba Nono Krčkih** Iseljenika 8; ☎051 222 221; www.nono-krk.com; ⏱ 11.00–midnight daily. Popular little seafood konoba. €€€

AROUND KRK TOWN Krk town is a good base for excursions around the island, both onshore and off. On the quay – or through any of the travel agents – you'll find boats offering the traditional fish picnic, combined with the chance to swim at one of the southern beaches, as well as trips out to the islands between Krk and Rab. There are also a couple of glass-bottomed boats that go out on excellent two-hour trips, giving you a fine view of the marine life.

Vrbnik If you have your own transport, can work out the twice-daily buses, or fancy the walk, then the old stone hilltop village of Vrbnik, 10km across Krk on the empty east coast of the island, is a lovely place to visit. The **tourist office** (*Placa Vrbničkog Statuta 4;* ☎ *051 857 479; www.vrbnik.hr*) can help with finding you a private room if you want to stay, or there's the 12-room **Argentum** (*Supec 68;* ☎*051 857 370; www.hotel-argentum.net;* €€€€), which has simple doubles.

The town was famous in the old days for having been one of the havens of the Glagolitic script, but today its reputation is sealed with a cork – you'll have trouble getting away from Vrbnik without trying the excellent local white wine, Žlahtina, best sampled at one of the several wine cellars. When you're done with wandering and wining, Vrbnik also has a beach below the town.

Punat and Košljun Eight kilometres southeast of Krk town, facing west into a big sheltered bay, is the former shipbuilding and fishing village of **Punat**. It still makes a handsome living from the sea, but it's now the yachting trade that keeps the village afloat, with one of the bigger marinas in Croatia attracting a busy passing trade in summer. The main attraction, however, is the island of **Košljun**, out in the bay, and its famous 16th-century Franciscan monastery. You can reach the island by taxi-boat from Punat, itself on a regular bus route from Krk town. Unless you're planning on staying in Punat, however, it's more convenient (if more expensive) to take a boat directly from Krk town.

In the airy church on Košljun there are some superb religious paintings from the 16th and 17th centuries, while the monastery also has one of Croatia's finest libraries, home to countless rare volumes, manuscripts, parchments and old maps. As if that weren't enough, the industrious monks have also put together an interesting ethnographic museum, a natural history collection and an assortment of numismatic rarities.

With your head spinning from the surfeit of information absorbed, the perfect cure is a walk around the pretty island before catching the return boat.

Practicalities I wouldn't especially recommend staying in Punat, but if you want to, the **tourist office** (*Pod Topol 2;* \ *051 854 860; www.tzpunat.hr*) can point you at agencies handling private rooms, and also has maps and brochures available. There's plenty of hotel accommodation in the complex south of town, near where the bus stops, including the 219-room **Hotel Park** (\ *051 655 800; www.hoteli-punat.hr;* €€€€), though it may – like everywhere on Krk – be fully booked in summer. There's also the **Hotel Kanajt** (\ *051 654 340; www.kanajt.hr;* €€€€), which has 20 simple doubles and one single near the marina, and the 83-room **Omorika** (*Frankopanska bb;* \ *051 654 500; www.omorika-punat.com;* €€€€).

BAŠKA In a wide bay on the southeastern end of the island is Baška, Krk's most popular resort, with some 200,000 tourist nights annually. The reason for its popularity is obvious enough – Baška (population around 1,000) sits at the eastern end of what is certainly one of Croatia's best beaches, a 1,800m stretch of shingle and pebbles in a wide sweep under the mountains.

Getting there and around Baška is easily reached on the bus from Zagreb, Rijeka and Krk town (timetables at www.autotrans.hr; 45mins from Krk), and with its popularity with tourists there are also any number of taxi-boats around, which will take you to less busy beaches and hidden coves both on Krk and on the neighbouring islands to the south.

Where to stay and eat Private rooms can be booked through Primaturist (*Kralja Zvonimira 98;* \ *051 856 132; www.primaturist.hr*), with doubles going from €35–45, with a surcharge for three days or less (if you can find anyone willing to let you have one) – in summer you should book well ahead. This is even truer if you want hotel accommodation.

Atrium Residence (18 dbls, 46 apts) Emila Geistlicha 39; \ 051 656 890; www.hotelibaska. hr. Hoteli Baška's most upmarket offering, halfway along the beach promenade. €€€€€

Villa Adria (28 apts) Emila Geistlicha 39; \ 051 656 890; www.hotelibaska.hr. Upmarket apartments right on the waterfront. €€€€€

Corinthia (430 rooms) Emilia Geistlicha 34; \ 051 656 800; www.hotelibaska.hr Massive place on the promenade. €€€€

Forza (6 rooms) Kralja Zvonimira 98; m 099 305 7530; www.hotelforza.hr. Small, family-run hotel, opened in 2015 above the popular restaurant of the same name, offering rooms in a nicely renovated old property. €€€€

Tamaris (15 rooms) Emila Geistlicha bb; \ 051 864 200; www.baska-tamaris.com. One of the nicest places to stay in Baška is this little place towards the far (western) end of the beach. €€€€

Lantino Emila Geistlicha 30; \ 051 856 484; http://lantino.eu; ⊕ 09.00–23.00 daily. Popular restaurant – hardly surprisingly, given its location, right on the beach. €€€€

Bistro Forza Kralja Zvonimira 98; \ 051 856 611; www.hotelforza.hr; ⊕ 08.00–midnight. Popular bistro offering meat & seafood dishes, as well as salads, pasta & pizza. €€€

Bistro Francesca Kralja Zvonimira (aka Zvonimirova) 56; www.bistrofrancesca.com; ⊕ 11.00–23.00 daily. Nice, intimate, family-run place in the old town, with a lovely vine-covered courtyard. From 2015, also offers rooms. €€€

Konoba Garofulin Palada 60a; ⓕ Garofulin Konoba; ⊕ 08.00–02.00 daily. Small, popular bar/café in the old town serving cold snacks as well as sangria, cocktails & other drinks.

What to see and do The little village dates from the 16th century, and the colourful fishermen's houses and narrow alleys off the small harbour are still very attractive, even among the summer crowds. While you won't escape these along the seafront promenade, stretching for a total length of 4km, it's easy enough to get away from it all into the hills behind town, and the **tourist office** (*Kralja Zvonimira 114;* \ *051 856 817; www.tz-baska.hr*) has a great map detailing 19 different marked walks in the vicinity, from 2 to 10km long and taking anything from 30 minutes to several hours – making the area around Baška one of the best for hiking of any of the islands. Several of these hikes are described in detail in Rudolf Abraham's *The Islands of Croatia* (page 429). As always, make sure you have decent footwear and plenty of water.

The 4-hour walk over to the twin bays and beaches of **Mala Luka** and **Vela Luka** to the east, passing the naturist campsite and beach at **Bunculuka** (\ *051 656 111; www.hotelibaska.hr;* €€€€) on the way, is moderately strenuous but well worth the effort (you can usually get a taxi-boat back), as are the trails to Obzova, the highest point on the island, to the west. *Mrgari* are a particularly interesting feature of the landscape, ancient, dry-stone walled enclosures for sorting sheep.

A kilometre or so north of Baška is the **Church of St Lucy** (Sv Lucije), in **Jurandvor**, the site of one of Croatia's most important Glagolitic finds, the Baška Tablet, discovered in the floor of the church in 1851 by a local priest. It took over 20 years to decipher the script, which mentions King Zvonimir and dates from around 1100. The original is now in Zagreb (in the atrium of the building that houses the Strossmayer Gallery), but there's a good copy here – and rather less good, smaller, souvenir copies on sale all over town. Walk #6 makes a pleasant 1-hour stroll, from Baška to the church at Jurandvor; it's around 20 minutes back along the road, or you can wait for a bus.

RAB

Cruising along the old coast road from Rijeka to Zadar you'd have no idea at all that Rab was worth visiting – it's a barren, denuded place, with no settlements and no sign of life.

Go round to the southwestern side of the island, however, and it suddenly becomes clear why Rab hosts around 250,000 visitors a year, staying more than 1.5 million tourist nights. It's a green and pleasant land, with sandy beaches, hidden coves, and a wonderfully preserved medieval old town.

HISTORY Like Cres and Krk, Rab was first settled by Liburnian Illyrians, before the arrival of the Romans, who established an important base here. The Byzantines and Croat-Hungarians followed, before Venice finally imposed itself on the island definitively at the beginning of the 15th century. The rich architectural heritage of the old town of Rab belies the Venetian plunder of the island's timber, resulting in that denuded northeastern coast, or the republic's limiting of essential supplies of salt (fish preservative), generally keeping the population both poor and subdued for the best part of 400 years.

The late 19th century ushered in new hope for the island as a tourist resort. The Austrians and Czechs were the first to invest in hotels – the Praha opened in 1909, a year after the Grand. They were also the first to encourage naturist holidays, heralding in a long tradition on the island – a tradition embraced in August 1936 by Edward VIII, King of England, and his girlfriend Wallis Simpson, it's said (though to an English sensibility it seems implausible that the king would be getting his kit off in public).

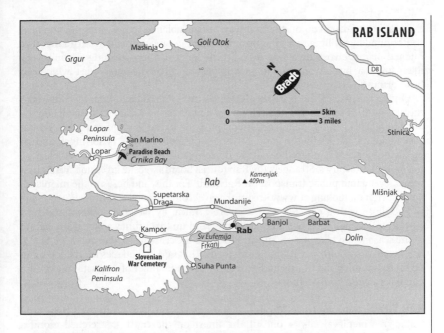

During World War II, Rab was occupied by the Italians and then by the Germans, before becoming Yugoslav in 1945. When Tito split with Stalin in 1948 he turned the barren island of **Goli** (Goli Otok), between Rab and the mainland, into an internment camp for Stalinists, and just mentioning it was enough to get you a one-way ticket to the horrors of the local gulag – it wasn't until after Tito's death that the Goli camp's very existence was made public.

Life on Goli Otok was appalling. Apart from the sheer brutality and cruelty, typical tasks for the prisoners would include breaking rocks and hauling them across the island, where they could be used to spell out a giant 'Tito' or other party slogans, only to have to dismantle them and return the rocks to the quarry.

Today, both it and its neighbour, **Grgur** (which used to be a women's prison), have less traumatic potential as offshore day trips.

GETTING THERE AND AROUND Rab ought to be a perfect stop for island-hoppers on their way from Krk to Pag or vice versa, but the idiosyncrasies of local transport make it difficult. The **ferry** from Valbiska on Krk, to Lopar at Rab's northern end, does run four times daily during summer – but there's only one daily catamaran between Novalja (on Pag), Rab and Rijeka (*www.jadrolinija.hr*), and one small boat between Rab and Lun, near the tip of Pag, once a day in each direction, plus two extra sailings on Tuesday, Thursday and Friday during summer (*www.rapska-plovidba.hr*).

If you can't make these timings work for you, there's the twice-daily direct **bus** from Rijeka, which takes around 3 hours, crossing on the ferry from Jablanac to Mišnjak (roughly every hour during the summer, down to around 13 sailings off season, *www.rapska-plovidba.hr*) on Rab's southern end before heading into Rab town. In summer, try to book ahead, as the bus fills up quickly. There are also direct buses to and from Zagreb in summer (*4½hrs*) – again, book ahead if you can.

Onward travel south by bus is problematic – you have to go back to Senj on the Rijeka-bound bus and then retrace your steps on the next bus to Zadar (getting the first bus to drop you on the highway, above Jablanac, and waiting for the next southbound bus willing to stop is unreliable and not recommended). And if you've hitched or made your own way over on the ferry as a foot passenger, you'll very likely find that buses won't stop to pick up passengers on the other side – which can be enormously frustrating.

On the island itself there are regular buses from Rab town to Lopar, as well as to the other tourist settlements, though there's no local service at all to Mišnjak and the ferry to Jablanac on the mainland. If you miss the Rijeka bus you can get to Barbat easily enough, but it's then a good 1½ hours on foot to the ferry terminal, and an uphill 2km once you get to the mainland, from Jablanac up to the highway plied by the main coastal buses. Strangely the Rab tourist board's website gives no information whatsoever about public transport on Rab itself. For this, and buses to the mainland, you're better off looking at www.kristofor-travel.com/en/public-transport/29/9.

For those with a **car**, ferries run from Stinica, by Jablanac (100km south of Rijeka) to Mišnjak 13 times daily in winter and up to 23 times a day at the height of the season, and take just 15 minutes to make the crossing (*www.rapska-plovidba. hr*). From Mišnjak it's just 10km to Rab town. That said, the queues for the ferry can be pretty intimidating in July and especially in the first half of August – make sure you have a good book to hand.

RAB TOWN Rab, the town, capital of Rab, the island, is a lovely well-preserved traffic-free medieval city – one of the finest on the coast – stretched along a peninsula, with the town's harbour to one side and the long inlet of St Euphemia Bay on the other. It's crowned by a distinctive line of four strikingly beautiful campanili, and is best seen at least once from the sea.

The town has an unusually rich stock of ancient churches, a reminder that there were once many more people living on the island than there are today – in winter, anyway. In high summer you'll find you're not alone admiring Rab's medieval heart, but set an early alarm, walk the streets in the soft morning light, and you'll get quite a different impression of the town, soulful and quiet, settled into its long, long past.

⌂ **Where to stay** *Map, page 263*
As well as the hotels listed, there are plenty of private rooms also available, though very few in the old town itself, and you may find everything already taken if you haven't booked ahead in high season. Use any of the several travel agencies to secure a room, and expect to pay €40–50 for a double in summer, along with the usual 30% surcharge for short stays. Try Kristofor (*Mali Palit 70;* ☎ *051 725 543; www.kristofor-travel.com*) near the bus station, or Eros (*J de Marisa 22;* ☎ *051 724 688/788; www. rab-novalja.com*) by the northern end of the old town. Note that you'll be charged a supplement for stays of three days or fewer at any hotel in town in summer.

The nearest campsite, **Padova III** (*Banjol 496;* ☎ *051 724 355, 667 788; www. rab-camping.com;* €), is 2km away to the south, past the eponymously named hotel.

⌂ **Arbiana** (28 rooms) Obala kralja Krešimira IV; ☎ 051 775 900; www.arbianahotel.com. Set in a lovely old villa in the old town, & renovated to a very high standard in 2006. Most rooms have balcony & sea view. €€€€€

⌂ **Imperial** (134 rooms) Plait bb; ☎ 051 724 522, 667 788; www.imperialrab.com. One of the nicest hotels in town, in fine shape after nearly

a century in business. It's in the woods adjoining the Komrčar Park, close to the bus station & the harbour, & a short walk from the old town. €€€€

⌂ **Istra** (100 rooms) Markantuna de Dominisa bb; ☎ 051 724 134; www.hotel-istra.hr. Right on the corner of the harbour. €€€€

⌂ **Padova** (175 rooms) Banjol 322; ☎ 051 724 544, 667 788; www.imperialrab.com. If you're after

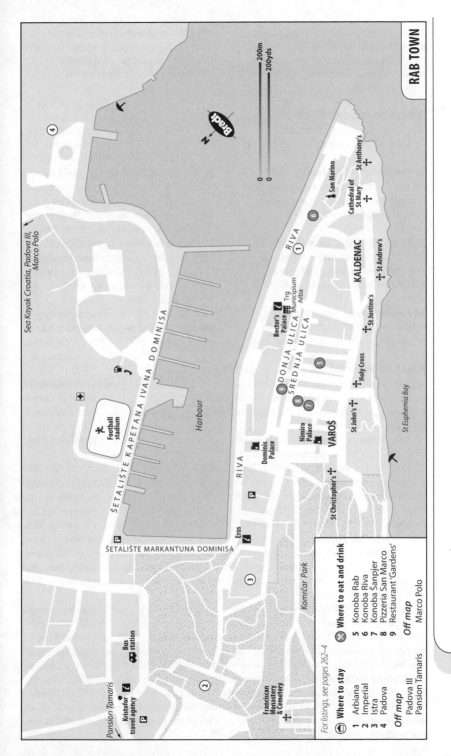

RAB TOWN

Brač

200m
200yds
0
0

Sea Kayak Croatia, Padova III,
Marco Polo

ŠETALIŠTE KAPETANA IVANA DOMINISA

Harbour

Football
stadium

ŠETALIŠTE MARKANTUNA DOMINISA

Pansion Tamaris

Bus
station

Kristofor
travel agency

Eros

Komrčar Park

RIVA

St Christopher's

Dominis
Palace

Nimira
Palace

St John's

Holy Cross

VAROŠ

St Euphemia Bay

9 DONJA ULICA
8 SREDNJA ULICA
7
5

St Justine's

St Andrew's

KALDENAC

Rector's
Palace

Trg
Municipium
Arba

RIVA

1

6

San Marino

Cathedral of
St Mary

St Anthony's

Franciscan
Monastery
& Cemetery

For listings, see pages 262–4

Where to stay
1 Arbiana
2 Imperial
3 Istra
4 Padova
Off map
Padova III
Pansion Tamaris

Where to eat and drink
5 Konoba Rab
6 Konoba Riva
7 Konoba Šanpjer
8 Pizzeria San Marco
9 Restaurant 'Gardens'
Off map
Marco Polo

a beach, a decent pool & a bit of tourist luxury, then head around the harbour & 1km south of town to this big, modern affair, with good-sized dbls with balconies & HB thrown in for not very much extra. €€€€

🏠 **Pansion Tamaris** (14 rooms) Palit 285; ✆051 724 925; www.tamaris-rab.com. Good-value little family-run place just north of Komrčar Park, with its own restaurant. €€€€–€€€

✖ Where to eat and drink *Map, page 263*

With its traffic-free streets and open squares, Rab's a good place to eat and drink, with lots of restaurants and even more cafés and bars.

✖ **Konoba Rab** Kneza Branimira 3; ✆051 725 666; ⏰ 10.00–23.00 daily. Slightly more upmarket than the Riva, it's set inside heavy medieval walls, & serves up excellent squid. €€€€

✖ **Konoba Riva** Ulica biskupa Draga 3; ✆051 725 887; www.konoba-riva.hr; ⏰ 10.00–23.00 daily. Spilling out of its courtyard on to the Riva itself, the author had wonderful mackerel here. €€€

✖ **Konoba Šanpjer** Šetalište Kralja Petra Krešimira IV; ⏰ 10.00–23.00 daily. Another popular spot for seafood in the old town. €€€

✖ **Marco Polo** Banjol 486; ✆051 725 846; 📱 098 9814 900; www.marcopolo-rab.com; ⏰ 11.30–22.30 daily. If you feel like heading out of town to Banjol, you'll find this highly rated restaurant, which also offers apartments. €€€

✖ **Pizzeria San Marco** Rapske Brigade 6; ✆051 724 820; www.pizzeria-sanmarco-rab.com; ⏰11.00–23.00 daily. Serves decent pizza, with tables spilling out on to a narrow side street. €€€

✖ **Restaurant 'Gardens'** Donja ulica 7a; ⏰ 11.30–14.30 & 17.30–midnight daily. Good-value grills, seafood, pasta & other dishes, & a nice terrace. €€€

What to see and do Three roughly parallel streets – Gornja, Srednja, Donja (upper, middle, lower) – run the length of old town, connecting the older **Kaldenac**, at the tip of the peninsula, with **Varoš**, the newer (15th- to 17th-century) part of town, where it widens out. The popular Riva running along the harbour-side makes for a fourth thoroughfare.

As you wander round, prepare to be churched-out – but bear in mind that most of them will only be open just before and after religious services.

The most important church in town is the **Cathedral of St Mary** (Sv Marija), a superb Romanesque building consecrated by the Pope himself in 1177, though much altered and rebuilt in the early 16th century – the fine *pietà* above the door dates from 1514. (Observant readers will point out at this stage that it's not technically a cathedral, since Rab lost its bishopric in 1828 – but let's not quibble with the locals.) Inside, harmonious whitewashed Romanesque arches support the triple nave, with each capital subtly different. Dark carved choir stalls, dating from 1445, lead to an elegant grey altar canopy (*baldacchino*) from the 11th century. It all goes back much further, even, than this – under the altar floor they're still excavating Roman mosaics.

Behind the cathedral (church, if you must), at the tip of the peninsula, is the small **Church of St Anthony** (Sv Antonije) and a Franciscan convent. Beneath this, in the gardens below, you'll find a statue of **San Marino**, which was inaugurated here on 9 May 2004, to coincide with the annual crossbow contest (see box, page 265) – San Marino, the founder of the eponymous republic in Italy, was a Rab native.

Heading back along the upper road, the first thing you come to, opposite the cathedral, is the town's tallest **campanile**, an elegant 26m structure from around 1200, topped off with a balustrade with a mini octagonal 15th-century spire rising from within it. You can climb up for fine views of the town and harbour, and across the water to the uninhabited island of **Dolin**.

In a line running northwest from here are the town's other three campanili, interspersed with the churches of **St Andrew, St Justine**, the **Holy Cross, St John** and **St Christopher**, dating from the 11th to 16th centuries (except St Justine's bell tower, a 17th-century impostor). St Justine's Church now houses the **Museum of Sacred Art** (Muzej Sakralne Umjetnosti), where you can admire St Christopher's skull in its reliquary, which was used in 1358 to break a siege here (allegedly – see box, below). All that's really left of St John's Church is the last of the town's campanili, which you can climb up – though it's fairly vertiginous – for wonderful views. St Christopher's, a little further along, houses a fairly sparse **lapidarium**, but more importantly gives access to one of the few remaining parts of Rab's **medieval walls**, where you can take the famous pictures of all four campanili in a row.

Below the row of churches and campanili there are even more churches and any number of palazzi, most notably the impressive 15th-century **Dominis Palace** at the northern end of town, and the **Nimira Palace** not far away. The former has a splendid carved portal, with chubby putti pulling aside curtains to reveal the family crest. Indeed, all over town you should keep an eye out for medieval details, Latin inscriptions, Venetian lions and Gothic windows. In the main square (Trg Municipium Arba) you'll find the **Rector's Palace**, with its 15th-century loggia, which was originally the public court. Leading off this is one of the old city gates, crowned with a 14th-century clock on a 13th-century tower.

When you're ready for a breather (or a picnic) head north to the **Komrčar Park**. The 19th-century landscaped woodland was the work of Pravdoje Belia, who spent years defying the local sheep farmers in his efforts to create a public park – and was rewarded by a small statue in the park itself. It's all agreeably in a slightly run-down state, but the fine mature trees provide welcome shade. At the far end of the park there's a ruined Franciscan monastery and a quiet cemetery.

Paths lead down through the park to the shoreline of **St Euphemia Bay**, and there are places to swim here – though most people prefer to take a taxi-boat across

MEDIEVAL PAGEANTRY AND THE ART OF THE CROSSBOW

Living in a place like Rab you'd be mad not to dress up in medieval clothes from time to time, so that's what the locals do for the medieval crossbow contests on 9 May and again on 25 June, 27 July and 15 August – and sometimes on other feast days and national holidays too. Amid much pageantry, fanfares of trumpets and formal processions, the tournament itself is taken very seriously – it's one of only two such tournaments remaining in the world (the other in San Marino) using the medieval crossbow, an enormous, heavy weapon which requires a stand to rest on during firing. The tournament takes place on trg Sv Kristofora – and you need to stay behind the crossbows, they're absolutely lethal.

The tradition dates back to 9 May 1358, when Rab was liberated from a nasty Italo-Norman siege through the intervention of the enterprising bishop of the day, who saw off the besieging army by waving the relics of St Christopher from the city walls. The day has been celebrated ever since, and not only could exiles return for the festivities but husbands also had official permission to beat their wives. Today the wife-beating is mercifully outlawed, but the party does go on for three days, with folk processions, much eating and drinking, and the crossbow contest itself on the final day.

to the **Frkanj Peninsula**, which has lots of coves and inlets, and the famous naturist beaches on the far side (the scene of King Edward VIII's supposed skinny-dipping). The main **tourist office** (*Trg Municipium Arba 8;* \ *051 724 064; www.rab-visit. com*) is handily on the main square, and it has an information-rich map, with the town on one side and the whole island on the other. If you want to hire bikes and head out to Kalifron or further afield, the best place in town is Eros (*J de Marisa 22;* \ *724 688/788; www.rab-novalja.com*), a friendly and helpful agency on the waterfront at the northern end of the old town. It also does sea kayak and boat excursions. Another place to contact if you fancy a spot of sea kayaking while in Rab is Sea Kayak Croatia (*Banjol 341;* m *091 464 1565, 099 282 8628; www.seakayak.hr*).

AROUND RAB The rest of Rab is hedonistically given over pretty much wholeheartedly to holidays, with well-organised resorts catering mostly for sun-seeking Austrians, Czechs and Germans. There are lots of excellent beaches, and excursions available both to Rab town and to the neighbouring islands.

Southern Rab A few kilometres south of Rab town, facing on to the empty island of Dolin, is the rambling village of **Barbat**, which has a few beaches and quite a large number of private rooms and private moorings. With plenty of buses to Rab Town it's a good accommodation alternative in high season. Contact the **Der Barbat** (*Banjol 778;* \ *051 721 500; www.der.hr*) travel agency for reservations.

Western Rab Immediately to the west of the Frkanj Peninsula and Rab town is the tourist complex of **Suha Punta**. It's unashamedly package country, but in a very pretty setting, with plenty of rock beaches, pine woods, and sheltered coves in the vicinity – part of the huge, forested **Kalifron Peninsula**, criss-crossed by hiking trails and forest tracks, and absolutely perfect for cycling. One of the shorter hiking trails in this area, following a route laid out by forestry engineer Ante Premužić (page 246), is described in a leaflet available from the tourist office in Rab. You can walk or cycle over to the less-crowded sandy beaches at **Kampor**, and it's within easy reach of Rab Town. The place to stay in Suha Punta is the renovated 134-room **Carolina** (*Kampor 82;* \ *051 724 133, 667 788; www.imperialrab.com;* €€€€), with doubles overlooking the beach. The 196-room **Eva** (*Kampor 78;* \ *051 724 233, 667 788; www.imperialrab.com;* €€€€) is cheaper but less well situated.

Around 5km northwest of Rab and 1km short of Kampor, on the left-hand side, is the **Slovenian War Cemetery**, on the site of the 1942–43 concentration camp. It's a sobering place, with rows of graves set out as a memorial to the 1,443 victims of fascism who lost their lives in this quiet spot, where today all you'll hear is the wind in the cypresses and distant dogs barking.

Across the headland from Kampor is **Supertaska Draga**, home to a good marina, as well as quite a few private moorings and private rooms – contact the Rab (page 262) or Lopar (*Lopar 284;* \ *051 775 508; www.lopar.com*) **tourist offices** or **agencies** for more information.

Northern Rab Rab's northern tip is the **Lopar Peninsula**, which not only has the ferry terminal hooking up with Valbiska, on Krk, but also (across the headland, on Crnika Bay, and centred on the settlement of San Marino) the famous **Paradise Beach**, 1.5km-worth of sand and sea. The small **Hotel Epario** (*Lopar 456a;* \ *051 777 500; www.epario.net;* €€€€) is a good bet. Otherwise there's the enormous **San Marino** (*Lopar 608;* \ *051 775 144, 667 788; www.imperialrab.com;* €€€€) complex, consisting of five hotels with nice doubles, tucked into the woods behind the beach, or the San Marino campsite. Smaller places include the **Pansion Bellevue** (*Lopar 574;* ☎ *051 775 613; www.bellevue-lopar.com;* €€€€) and **Pansion Dragica** (*Lopar 562;* ☎ *051 775 420; www.dragica-lopar.com;* €€€€). Private rooms are listed on the tourist board website, and with agencies such as Sahara Tours (*Lopar bb;* ☎ *051 775 633; www.sahara-lopar.com*).

There are at least 20 shallow sandy beaches on the peninsula (including the lovely, primarily naturist **Sahara**, designated FKK), within pretty easy walking distance of Lopar or San Marino, making the area extremely popular with families. It's not too hard to get away from the crowds, however, by using the excellent network of marked paths and trails, leading up on to the plateau overlooking Paradise Beach, and down to the more remote beaches. There are also some lovely hikes on this side of the island – see Rudolf Abraham's *The Islands of Croatia* (page 429).

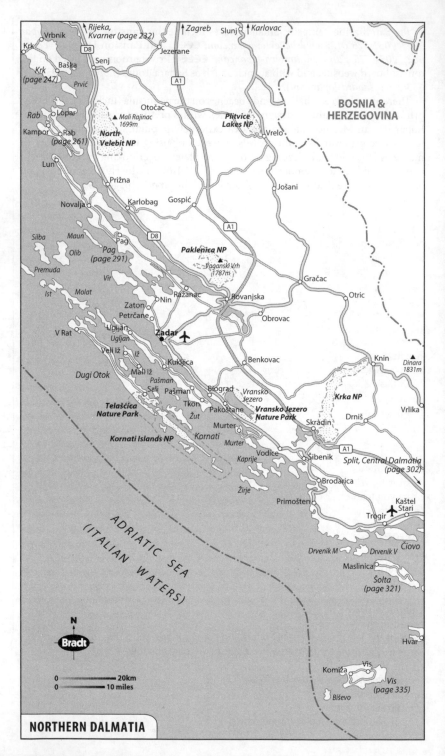

Rijeka, Kvarner *(page 232)* ↑Zagreb Slunj ↑*Karlovac*

Vrbnik

Krk

D8

Krk Baška Senj

(page 247) Prvić

Jezerane

A1

Otočac

▲ *Mali Rajinac*
1699m

Plitvice
Lakes NP

Rab Lopar

Kampor Rab

(page 261)

North
Velebit NP

Vrelo

BOSNIA &
HERZEGOVINA

Lun

Prižna

Jošani

Novalja Karlobag Gospić

A1

Silba *Maun*

Olib

Pag D8

Premuda

Vir

Pag
(page 291)

Paklenica NP

~ *Vaganski Vrh*
1787m

Gračac

Otric

Ist *Molat*

Zaton

Petrčane

Nin Ražanac

Rovanjska

Obrovac

V Rat

Ugljan

Ugljan

Zadar ✈

Veli Iž Iž

Dugi Otok *Mali Iž*

Pašman

Sali Pašman

Tkon

Kukljica

Biograd

Benkovac

Knin

▲ *Dinara*
1831m

Vransko
Jezero

Krka NP

Vrlika

Telašćica
Nature Park

Žut

Pakoštane

Vransko Jezero
Nature Park

Skradin

Drniš

Kornati Islands NP *Kornati*

Murter

Murter

Vodice

Kaprije

Šibenik

A1

Split, Central Dalmatia
(page 302)

Brodarica

Žirje

Primošten

Kaštel
Stari

Trogir ✈

ADRIATIC SEA
(ITALIAN WATERS)

Drvenik M Drvenik V Čiovo

Maslinica

Šolta
(page 321)

N

Bradt

Hvar

0 ————————— 20km
0 ————————— 10 miles

Komiža Vis

Vis
(page 335)

Biševo

NORTHERN DALMATIA

7

Northern Dalmatia

Northern Dalmatia is a region of extreme contrasts – you'd never dream, swimming at the foot of the Krka waterfalls, that the most barren islands of the Kornati archipelago were only a few kilometres offshore. Just as you'd never guess, confronted by a wall of heat on dry and dusty **Pag**, that the island of **Pašman** offered such sweet shelter on its wooded southern bays.

Zadar, the region's economic and transport capital, offers a wealth of things to see in a cultured old town, while Šibenik's Renaissance cathedral is one of the highlights not just of Dalmatia but of the whole of Croatia. The region is home, too, to three near-perfect national parks and a dedicated nature park: **Paklenica**, where you can hike serious summits and still go swimming in the same day; **Krka**, where you can visit a 14th-century monastery on an island between waterfalls; **Kornati**, where 89 islands, islets and reefs offer the true desert-island experience; and **Vransko Jezero**, privileged home to 100,000 wading birds. Add in the islands of **Ugljan** (Zadar's quiet holiday retreat) and **Dugi Otok** (a sailor's heaven), and you could spend all your holidays here.

Phone codes vary across the region – they're included with each listing.

ZADAR

Zadar, with a population of around 100,000, is the economic and transport centre for northern Dalmatia. While its suburbs sprawl along the coast and inland, at its heart you'll find an unpretentious, partially walled old town on a narrow peninsula, full of fine churches and excellent museums.

HISTORY Zadar was first settled by Liburnian Illyrians the best part of 3,000 years ago, but from as early as the 3rd century BC onwards the Romans had their eye on it, finally making a *Municipium* of it in 59BC and giving Jadera colony status 11 years later.

On the partition of the empire, Zadar became the capital of Byzantine Dalmatia, and had a period of some prosperity until the rise of Venice. Locals today are still proud of the fight Zadar put up against the Venetians, but in spite of four revolts in the 12th century and further uprisings over the next 200 years, Zadar went the same way as the rest of Dalmatia, ceding to Venice in 1409.

The Venetians' endless feuds with the Turks did nothing special for Zadar, though they did leave the city with a fine set of 16th-century defensive walls. Austria picked up the reins on the fall of Venice, with a brief French interlude, and allowed Italian immigrants to take care of the city – something that continued after World War I, with Zadar not joining the nascent Kingdom of the Serbs, Croats and Slovenes, but becoming Italian (Zara) instead. Indeed, some older people still speak Italian,

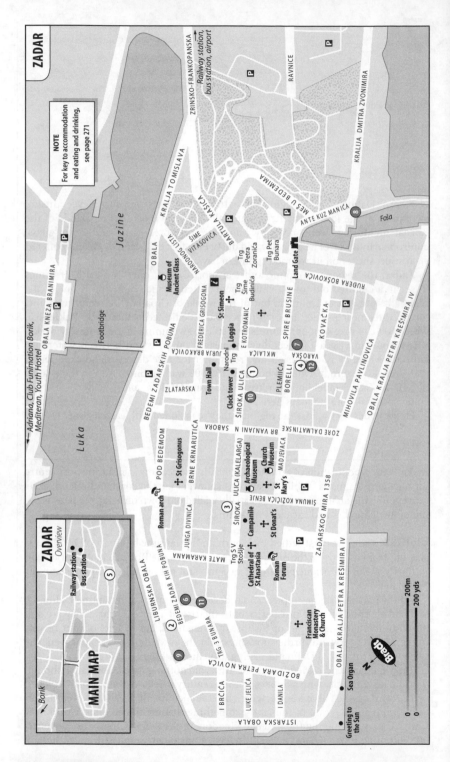

ZADAR

NOTE
For key to accommodation and eating and drinking, see page 271

Jazine

Footbridge

Adriana, Club Funimation Borik,
Mediteran, Youth Hostel

Luka

OBALA KNEZA BRANIMIRA

OBALA

KRALJA TOMISLAVA

Museum of Ancient Glass

NARODNOG LISTA

ŠIME VITASOVICA

BARTULA KAŠICA

Railway station,
bus station, airport
ZRINSKO-FRANKOPANSKA

RAVNICE

KRALJA DMITRA ZVONIMIRA

ANTE KUZMANICA

Foša

MEŠ U BEDEMIMA

Land Gate

RUĐERA BOŠKOVICA

KOVAČKA

VAROŠKA

SPIRE BRUSINE

PLEMIĆA BORELLI

Trg Petra Zoranica

Trg Pet Bunara

Trg Sime Budinića

St Simeon

Loggia

E KOTROMANIĆ

Narodni Trg

MIKLAIČA

ZORE DALMATINSKE

MIHOVILA PAVLINOVICA

OBALA KRALJA PETRA KREŠIMIRA IV

Clock tower

Town Hall

SIROKA ULICA

JURJA BRAKOVIĆA

FREDERICA GRISOGONA

PUBUNA

ZLATARSKA

BEDEMI ZADARSKIH

POD BEDEMOM

BRNE KRNARUTICA

ULICA (KALELARGA)

SABORA

BR VANJANI N

Archaeological Museum

Church Museum

St Mary's

MADIJEVACA

ŠIMUNA KOŽIČICA BENJE

ZADARSKOG MIRA 1358

St Grisogonus

Roman arch

SIROKA

St Donat's

Campanile

JURGA DIVINICA

Trg S V Stošije

Cathedral of St Anastasia

Roman Forum

MATE KARAMANA

LIBURNSKA OBALA

BEDEM ZADAR KIH POBUNA

TRG 3 BUNARA

BOŽIDARA PETRA NOVIĆA

Franciscan Monastery & Church

OBALA KRALJA PETRA KREŠIMIRA IV

I BRĆICA

LUKE JELICA

I DANILA

ISTARSKA OBALA

Sea Organ

Greeting to the Sun

200m
200yds

N

Bradt

ZADAR
Overview

Railway station
Bus station

MAIN MAP

Borik

0
0

270

though you'll find the younger generation more switched on to German or English as a first foreign language.

When Italy capitulated in 1943, Germany took over Zadar, and the Allies practically bombed it into oblivion, a fate many feared might happen again during the winter of 1991, when the Serbs laid siege to the city. People went hungry and thirsty during the siege, but the old town remained intact, something that can't be said for the inland suburbs, some of which still show the scars of warfare more than a decade after it ended. What the UN termed 'low-level warfare' continued as late as 1995.

GETTING THERE AND AROUND Zadar is a transport hub, with regular **bus** arrivals and departures (hourly, for the most part) to and from Zagreb (*3½hrs*), Rijeka (*4–5hrs*), Split (*3½hrs*) and Dubrovnik (*6–7hrs*), as well as several weekly runs to and from places like Frankfurt and Munich. If you want to save yourself a trip to the bus station, you can also buy long-distance bus tickets at Croatia Express (☏ *023 250 502*), on Široka, right in the middle of the old town.

Trains come in from Zagreb twice a day, but it's a long, long journey which, quite rightly, no one bothers with, as the route takes a dog-leg via Knin (where you have to change), and works out around three times as long as the bus.

Zadar airport (*www.zadar-airport.hr*) is about 10km away to the southeast, with daily Zagreb flights with Croatia Airlines (*40mins*), and Ryanair also flies direct to Zadar from the UK. There's a **shuttle bus** running into town from the airport (*www.zadar-airport.hr/; 25kn*), or if you want to take a **taxi** you can book online with **Taxi Jadera** (*www.taxi-jadera.com; 130kn*), a good, reliable and low-priced new operator, with fares *much* lower than Zadar's main taxi outfit, Lulić.

There are lots of **ferries** out to the islands of the Zadar archipelago (notably Ugljan and Dugi Otok), as well as regular excursions to the Kornati archipelago – see the relevant sections later in this chapter for details. There is a daily ferry up to Lošinj (*www.jadrolinija.hr*), and another which goes to Ancona in Italy. Finally, there's a catamaran running up to the island of Silba (*www.miatours.hr*) in summer, and there's a fast catamaran that runs four days a week up to Pula via Mali Lošinj (*www.lnp.hr*).

Zadar's bus and train stations are 1km southeast of the old town and port, while most of the hotels and beaches – and the town's marina – are 3km northwest of it, at Borik. There's a bus about three times an hour from the bus station up to Borik, via the harbour. Local ferries and catamarans (to Ugljan, Dugi Otok, etc) depart from Liburska obala, the waterfront by the old town; longer routes (eg: Mali Lošinj) depart from Gaženica, a short bus ride out of town (buses depart from beside the Jadrolinija office on Liburska obala).

ZADAR
For listings, see pages 272–3

🛏 **Where to stay**
1 Art Hotel Kalelarga
2 Bastion
3 Boutique Hostel Forum
4 Đina
5 Kolovare

Off map
Adriana
Club Funimation Borik
Mediteran
Youth Hostel

✖ **Where to eat and drink**
6 Arsenal
7 Dva Ribara
8 Foša
   The Garden (see 5)
9 Kornat
10 La Bodega
11 Pizzeria Tri Bunara
12 Providenca

🏠 **WHERE TO STAY** *Map, page 270*
The bulk of Zadar's hotels are out towards Borik, which has a campsite (*www.campingborik.com*; €) and a clutch of

7

mostly package-oriented hotels (take bus #8). There's also accommodation a bit further along the coast at Zaton, Petrčane and Nin, all of which are on a regular bus service to Zadar (page 275). However, a few places have opened up in the old town itself in recent years, including the lovely Bastion and the excellent Boutique Hostel Forum.

The **tourist office** (*Ilije Smiljanića 5;* \ *023 212 222; www.zadar.travel*), on the southeastern corner of the old town, has good maps and other documentation, and friendly staff. Private rooms, of which comparatively few are in or really close to town, are handled by travel agencies, including Jadera Tours (*Poljana Pape Aleksandra III 5/1;* \ *023 250 350; www.jaderatours.hr*), off Široka ulica. You'll be lucky to get away with paying under €50 for a double, plus the usual 30% surcharge for short stays. Most agencies can of course also organise excursions for you, of which there are any number from Zadar, including trips up to the Plitvice Lakes, down to the Krka River and waterfalls, or out to the Kornati archipelago.

Zadar centre

🏠 **Art Hotel Kalelarga** (10 dbls) Majke Margarite 3; \ 023 233 000; e info@arthotel-kalelarga.com; www.arthotel-kalelarga.com. Boutique 4-star in the centre of the old town. €€€€€

✳🏠 **Bastion** (28 rooms) Bedemi Zadarskih Pobuna 13; \ 023 494 950; www.hotel-bastion. hr. Top-notch boutique 4-star in the centre of town, incorporating part of the remains of the medieval fortifications – plush, efficient, with a truly wonderful spa & lovely rooms. Highly recommended. €€€€€€

🏠 **Kolovare** (191 rooms) Bože Peričića 14; \ 023 203 200; www.hotel-kolovare.com. The Kolovare is large, modern & has a small pool & its own beach, & is located about halfway between the old town & the bus station. Some rooms have views across to Ugljan. €€€€€–€€€€

🏠 **Central Apartments** (11 apts) Several locations; m 091 243 6880; www.centralapartments.hr. Good selection of nice apartments in central Zadar. €€€

🏠 **Đina** (3 dbls, 1 apt) Varoška 2; \ 314 774; m 091 324 75 55; e dario.longin@zd.t-com.hr. Nice rooms above a well-known café/gallery (Gina) in the Varoš neighbourhood of the old town. €€€

✳🏠 **Zadar Apartments** (8 apts) Several locations; m 091 535 4557; http://apartmentszadar.eu. Spacious, stylish apartments in a number of locations including one in the old

town, sleeping between 2 & 7 people. Highly recommended. €€€

✳🏠 **Boutique Hostel Forum** (111 beds) Široka ulica 20; \ 023 250 705; e info@hostelforumzadar.com; http://en.hostelforumzadar.com. Excellent modern hostel in the centre of the old town (quads, twins & dbls), with good b/fast. Friendly, efficient, good value & supremely stylish – the rooms really are more 'boutique' than 'hostel' – & hands down the best location in Zadar, overlooking the Forum. Highly recommended. €€€–€€

Borik

🏠 **Adriana** (48 rooms) Majstora Radovana 7; \ 023 555 600; www.falkensteiner.com. Falkensteiner's top-end offering in the area, with its own spa. €€€€€

🏠 **Club Funimation Borik** (306 rooms) Majstora Radovana 7; \ 023 206 100, 023 555 600; www.falkensteiner.com. Large, smart, family-friendly 4-star, with oodles of swimming pools & plenty to keep kids entertained. Well worth getting HB. €€€€€

🏠 **Mediteran** (30 rooms) Matije Gupca 19; \ 023 337 500; www.hotelmediteran-zd.hr. One of the better hotels in Borik, with nice dbls with balconies & sea views. €€€€

🏠 **Youth Hostel** (308 beds) Obala Kneza Trpimira 76; \ 023 331 145; www.hfhs.hr. Located between the marina & Borik beach. €€–€

✗ WHERE TO EAT AND DRINK *Map, page 270*

The city boasts lively cafés and bars, with terraces spilling out on to the pavements, as well as a handful of good restaurants. This is the place to try Zadar's most famous speciality, Maraskino, the cherry liqueur that has been produced here since the 1820s. It was long Austrian royalty's most popular tipple, and if it's a touch *démodé* now, that shouldn't stop you trying it. Once. Široka ulica – more commonly known as Kalelarga – is lined with a whole string of ice-cream shops (particularly as you get closer to the Forum), serving some stupendously good flavours.

✖ **Kornat** Liburnska 6; ☎023 254 501; www.restaurant-kornat.com; ⊕ noon–midnight. As close to fine dining as Zadar gets, & worth a splurge, serving up Croatian fish & meat mains infused with a Mediterranean twist. €€€€

✳ ✖ **Foša** Kralja Dmitra Zvonimira 2; ☎023 314 421; www.fosa.hr; ⊕ noon–midnight. Dine on fresh seafood on the terrace of the restaurant at the eponymous gate. The grilled squid & Swiss chard (*blitva*) are highly recommended. €€€€–€€€

✖ **Dva Ribara** Blaža Jurjeva 1; ☎023 213 445; www.2ribara.com/zadar; ⊕ noon–23.00 daily. Very good place serving grills, seafood & other dishes. €€€

✳ ✖ **Pizzeria Tri Bunara** Trg tri bunari bb; ⊕ 07.00–23.00 Mon–Sat, 08.00–23.00 Sun. Good-value, unpretentious pizzeria behind Hotel Bastion. Much better pizzas (& service) than Pizzeria Šime out at Borik. Recommended. €€

✖ **Providenca** Varoška 6; ⊕ 07.00–01.00 daily. On the corner of Stomorica. Good for salads, though portion size seems to have shrunk over the past couple of years. €€

🍺 **Arsenal** Trg tri bunara 1; ☎023 253 833; www.arsenalzadar.com; ⊕ 07.00–03.00 daily. Café-bar-gallery-restaurant-concert venue in a renovated 18th-century warehouse.

🍷 **The Garden** Liburnska 6; ☎023 364 739; www.watchthegardengrow.eu; ⊕ May–Sep 10.00–01.00 daily. This British-owned (by UB40 drummer Jimmy Brown) bar-cum-lounge-cum-club is the trendiest place in Northern Dalmatia; to Zadar what Carpe Diem is to Hvar.

🍷 **La Bodega** Široka ulica; ⊕ 08.00–midnight daily. Coffee, freshly squeezed juices & other drinks, including an extensive wine list, pršut & cheese, with tables outside on this pedestrianised street at the heart of the old town.

WHAT TO SEE AND DO All of Zadar's sights are in the old town, within a few hundred metres of each other. They're ordered in the text from the northwestern corner, working back towards the southeast. To get to the start, either walk along the tree-lined, sea-facing promenade (a nice place for a picnic) or walk around the remains of the town walls facing the harbour – these are mostly 16th-century Venetian, though you'll see Roman fragments, particularly near the footbridge across the harbour.

The **Franciscan Monastery and Church** (*Franjevački Samastan i Crkva*; ⊕ 09.00–18.00; 15kn) dates back to the 13th century, but it's been much remodelled since and you wouldn't know it wasn't entirely 18th-century Baroque these days. The choir stalls inside are late 14th century, however, and the treasury – rarely open – houses some important works, including a big 12th-century crucifix. The monastery's fine cloisters are mid-16th-century Renaissance.

From here, it's a stone's throw (if they haven't finished tidying up the piles of Roman rubble) to the site of the **Roman Forum**. Originally 90m by 45m, the forum would have made a decent-sized football pitch. Until the 19th century, criminals were tied to the pillar here, and … well, pilloried, I suppose.

Many of the original bits of Roman stonework ended up in the solid church that dominates what's left of the forum today. The Church of the Holy Trinity was started in the 9th century by Bishop Donat, and has been known as **St Donat's** (Sv Donata) ever since. It's a 27m-high structure, built on a circular ground-plan, and its tall interior is now used for secular concerts rather than religious worship. Look out for everything from upside-down capitals to gravestones to altars to whole pillars within the structure of the walls – all Roman. Parts of the floor, too, are the original Roman flagstones. You can walk upstairs to the gallery, looking down into the church, but don't lean on the handrails, as they're not very sturdy and it's a long way down.

Round the corner from St Donat's is the triple-naved Romanesque **Cathedral of St Anastasia** (Sv Stošije) dating from the 12th and 13th centuries. Badly bombed during World War II, it was painstakingly rebuilt afterwards. The façade features an attractive series of blind arches and two rosette windows. Inside there are some 13th-century frescoes, a 14th-century altar canopy (sheltering an altar containing bits of 9th-century stonework), some 15th-century choir stalls and the marble sarcophagus commissioned by Donat in the 9th century to house the mortal remains of St Anastasia herself.

Behind the cathedral, the bottom half of the lovely **campanile** dates from the 15th century, though it wasn't completed until the 1890s, to a design by the British architect (and sometime writer of ghost stories) Sir Thomas Graham Jackson. Given the centuries-old rivalry between the bishops of Zadar and Rab, and Rab having lost its bishopric in 1828, it can only have been professional irony that made Jackson model his campanile on Rab's most famous bell tower. Or perhaps simply he was very good at copying things – his most famous work in England is the Bridge of Sighs, in Oxford. He did get away – for a while – with one amusing prank, however, which was to make the bell tower play 'God Save the Queen'.

Across the forum is **St Mary's Church** (Sv Marija) – the squat, 16th-century Renaissance front hides a church originally consecrated in the 11th century, along with a few more bits of the Roman forum. Behind it stands yet another Rab-like campanile, though this one's original, dating back to the early 12th century.

Next to this is Zadar's excellent **Church Museum** (*Crkva Muzej*; ⊕ *summer 10.00–13.00 & 18.00–20.00 Mon–Sat, 10.00–13.00 Sun, winter 10.00–12.30 & 17.00–18.30 Mon–Sat, 10.00–12.30 Sun; 30kn*), which houses a wonderful collection of reliquaries, paintings and sculpture, presented in a dazzling permanent exhibition, 'The Gold and Silver of Zadar'. Nearby, in a modern building, there's the **Archaeological Museum** (*Arheološki muzej; Trg opatice Čike 1;* ☎ *023 250 542; http://amzd.hr;* ⊕ *Jul/Aug 09.00–22.00 daily, Jun & Sep 09.00–21.00 daily, Apr/May/ Oct 09.00–15.00 Mon–Sat, Nov–Mar 09.00–14.00 Mon–Fri, 09.00–15.00 Sat; 30kn*), a fine collection from Liburnian times on, including some of the finest medieval sculpture in Croatia. Some of the labels are only in Croatian, however.

Continue from the Forum to the waterfront (Obala Kralja Petra Krešimira IV) and turn right, which will bring you to Zadar's two large outdoor art installations, the **Sea Organ** (Morske orgulje) and **Greeting to the Sun** (Pozdrav suncu). The latter is *the* place to watch the sun set over the islands. The steps down to the water by the *Sea Organ* are a popular spot for swimming.

Heading towards the harbour, the 12th-century Romanesque **Church of St Grisogonus** (also called Chrysogonus – Krševan in Croatian) is all that's left of one of Croatia's oldest monasteries, founded in 908. The outside, with its rows of blind arches and a pretty Tuscan-inspired colonnade on the back of the church, is more endearing than the rather shabby 13th- and 14th-century frescoes inside.

The town gate leading on to the harbour, down from St Grisogonus, contains all that's left of a **Roman triumphal arch** from Trajan's time. Back inside the walls, head towards Narodni Trg, the heart of business life in medieval times, now overlooked by an impressive clock tower. The **town hall** features fine reliefs of Šibenik Cathedral and Diocletian's Palace in Split, while the 16th-century **loggia** across the square, with unusually tall pillars, does service these days as a gallery.

Heading towards the city gate leading to the footbridge over the harbour, turn right up a flight of steps to reach Zadar's excellent **Museum of Ancient Glass** (*Muzej Antičkog Stakla; Poljana Zemaljskog odbora 1;* ☎ *023 363 831; www.mas-zadar.hr;* ⊕ *09.00–21.00 daily; 30kn*). Opened in 2009, it has a magnificent collection of glassware from the 1st century BC to the 5th century AD from the surrounding area, well displayed and labelled, and is one of the best museums in Croatia.

A block east from Narodni trg is the **Church of St Simeon** (Sv Šimeon). The Baroque building itself can't compete with Zadar's other churches, but **St Simeon's Sarcophagus**, inside, certainly can. Commissioned in 1377, and delivered in 1380, it's an impressively chunky burnished silver and gold coffin, with dramatic reliefs on the front and a life-sized portrait of the saint on the lid, complete with swept-back hair and bushy eyebrows. For more detail, come on the saint's feast day, 8 October, and you'll find even more silverwork and some fine reliquaries on the inside, when the sarcophagus is opened up for its annual inspection. (If you don't see it here, there's a very good copy in Zagreb, in the atrium of the building that houses the Strossmayer Gallery.)

Trg Pet Bunara ('the square of five wells'), nearby, was the town's main water supply for centuries – the Romans of course had proper running water, but from medieval times until the arrival of the businesslike Austrians, the underground cistern here was as good as plumbing got.

From here the easiest way out is through the **Land Gate** (Kopnena vrata). On the outside of this there's a big relief of a no-nonsense Venetian lion – the open Bible tells you that Venice was at peace at the time. The miniature harbour nearby is all that's left of the defensive moat that once protected the city.

The enormous annual dance music festival, **The Garden Festival** (*www. thegardenfestival.eu*), takes place at Petrčane, near Zadar, in July.

NIN, ZATON AND PETRČANE When you've run out of things to do in Zadar, an excursion can be made up to the gorgeous little town of **Nin**, north along the coast from Zadar beyond Petrčane and Zaton.

Nin was an important settlement already in Roman times, and even more so as a religious centre in the Middle Ages – witness Meštrović's enormous statue of **Gregorius of Nin**, in Nin and Split (and the far smaller version of the same, in Varaždin).

These days (and for most of the past thousand years, if truth be told), Nin's a quiet town, on its own little island, connected to the mainland by a pair of bridges. There's not a whole lot to see and do, but the tiny **Church of the Holy Cross** (Sv Križa) is Croatia's oldest (from around AD800), and you can absorb some more history at the local **Archaeological Museum** (*Muzej Ninskih Starina;* 023 264 160; ⊕ *1 Jun–15 Jul 09.00–21.00 daily, 15 Jul–15 Aug 09.00–22.00 daily, 15 Aug–1 Sep 09.00–21.00 Mon-Sat, Sep–May 09.00–14.00 Mon–Sat; 20kn*). When you're done, there are a couple of sandy beaches at nearby **Sabunike** (though you have to wade out a long way before getting knee deep!), with views across to the Velebit massif nearby.

On the road out from Zadar to Nin, you'll pass the once not-so-busy town of **Petrčane** – these days the site of the enormously popular **Garden Festival** (*www. thegardenfestival.eu*) during the summer, and of slick new family-oriented resorts out at Punta Skala – and **Zaton**, where there's also an excellent resort, and one of northern Dalmatia's best beaches. Though comparatively little known to visitors from the UK, the area around Zaton is one of Croatia's most upmarket stretches of coastline.

There's a regular bus service to Nin/Zaton from Zadar's main bus station, running every hour or so (timetables at www.liburnija-zadar.hr).

Where to stay and eat

Iadere Hotel and Spa (210 rooms) Punta Skala, Petrčane; 023 555 600; www.falkensteiner. com. Falkensteiner's top-end offering at Punta Skala. Slick & stylish with excellent spa facilities. €€€€€

🏠 **Falkensteiner Family Hotel Diadora** (250 rooms) Punta Skala, Petrčane; ☎ 023 555 600; www.falkensteiner.com. Upmarket family-oriented hotel with plenty of activities for kids. €€€€

※🏠 **Zaton Holiday Resort** (600 apts) Zaton; ☎ 023 205 588; www.zaton.hr. Beautiful apartments by Zaton's great swath of sandy beach, surrounded by shady pine trees. Restaurants, supermarket. Great for kids, with outdoor pools & playgrounds. The 4-star apts with AC are the ones to go for. Highly recommended. €€€€

✖ **Pansion MarcoPolo** (8 apts) Petrčane ulica VI 2; m 091 567 1426; www.marco-polo-pansion. hr. Popular family-run pansion with its own restaurant, 100m from the sea. €€€

RAŽANAC Continuing north from Nin, on the far side of the road leading to Pag, is the small fishing village of Ražanac, which has a long stretch of nice sand-and-pebble beach. It has a couple of small shops, a market, ATM, restaurants and cafés, and a few apartments – try **Apartmani Mimi** (m *095 897 2554;* e *ivapotocnjak@ hotmail.com;* €€€), located right on the beach just a few minutes' walk from the village; or **Miro Apartmani** (*http://miroapartmani.com;* €€€). There are around half a dozen bus services to Ražanac from Zadar on weekdays, only a couple at weekends (timetables at www.liburnija-zadar.hr).

SOUTH TO VRANSKO JEZERO South of Zadar are a string of unpretentious resort towns leading to the island of **Murter**, connected to the mainland by a bridge, and the best jumping-off point for the Kornati archipelago (page 299).

On the way, just past **Biograd** (where you can catch the ferry to Pašman, see page 297), is Croatia's largest natural lake, Vransko Jezero – turn left as you approach Pakoštane, 5km south of Biograd, and then right after just under 2km.

Already an ornithological reserve since 1983, **Vransko Jezero** (*www.pp-vransko-jezero.hr; 20kn/10kn adult/child*) was declared as a nature park in 1999 in a bid to reinforce the protection of its unique habitat and birdlife, and was declared a RAMSAR site (Wetland of International Importance) in 2012. The lake is nearly 14km long and between 1.5 and 3.5km wide, and has a surface area of over 30km², but it's never more than 4m deep. A channel that was dug at the end of the 18th century, in an attempt to drain the lake, now provides it with an occasional top-up of saltwater at high tide, and it's also partly connected with the sea by underground fissures in the limestone.

A total of 111 bird species have been recorded here, while 41 species over-winter in the park and 49 nest here – including a small colony of rare purple herons. You can also expect to see marsh harriers, ducks, terns and white egrets, and 100,000 coots, which over-winter here.

There are cycle trails around the lake (though some sections are apt to be fairly rough, so a decent mountain bike is advised), and bird hides are in place in the ornithological reserve at the northern end of the lake. You can hire bikes and kayaks through the nature park office. Otherwise so far there's comparatively little in the way of infrastructure for the visitor, though that certainly doesn't make the place any less worth visiting.

There's a road running behind the hills on the lake's northeastern shore that goes from the village of Vrana to the settlement of **Banjevci**. If you turn up the gravel road to the right here, it leads steeply up a Križni Put (Way of the Cross) to a small chapel on top of the hills, built as a memorial to the people who were thrown into a deep sinkhole here by the partisans at the end of World War II. There's a café (very welcome in the summer, when it gets seriously hot up here) and souvenir shop, and a good path beyond leading up to Kamenjak, a rocky hilltop with unrivalled views out west over the lake and the Kornati archipelago.

For more information, contact the park office (*Kralja P Svačića 2, Biograd;* ✆ *023 383 181;* ⊙ *08.00–16.00 daily*) directly.

PAKLENICA NATIONAL PARK

(*www.np-paklenica.hr; May–Sep 50kn, Oct–Apr 40kn; a 3-day climbing pass is 100kn/80kn, inc entrance ticket, or 150kn/120kn for 5 days*) Situated halfway between Karlobag and Zadar – an hour from either, by bus – is Paklenica National Park, a pair of wonderful limestone gorges running up from the sea, deep into the Velebit massif. Popular with Croatian walkers and climbers, it's also one of my favourite places in the whole country, offering everything from a gentle stroll to a seriously strenuous trek, and pitches for rock climbers of every level.

The park was opened in 1949, and is unusually interesting for both climatic and physical reasons. Situated under the highest peak of the Velebit massif (Vaganski Vrh, 1,757m), the area experiences three distinct climates – coastal, continental and sub-alpine. The rock is Velebit Karst (page 244), and walking is possible from sea level up to the top of the massif.

Most of the lower reaches are heavily forested with deciduous trees, while higher up mountain pastures support sub-alpine flowers and herbs. One of the most attractive features of the park, however, is the more than 80 species of butterfly found here, making it a lepidopterist's paradise.

There are also lots of beetles and several reptiles (you'll see snakes slithering off the path as you approach) and amphibians, and an extraordinary 209 species of bird to watch out for. Sadly, this no longer includes the griffon vulture (page 249) – the last pair were poisoned. But in the remoter parts of the park you can still scope for peregrine falcons and sparrowhawks, and you're almost certain to see red-backed shrikes.

On the other hand, you're equally certain not to come in contact with the bears that live in the furthest reaches of the park – they're extremely discreet.

GETTING THERE AND AWAY All buses from Rijeka to Zadar make three Paklenica-related stops. From north to south, the first stop is at Starigrad Paklenica, the second is at the Hotel Alan (the closest stop to the main entrance to the park), and the last is at Seline (closest to the southern gorge, Mala Paklenica). If you're coming from Zagreb then change buses in Zadar.

Although there are lots of buses up and down the coast, leaving in the middle of summer can be harder than arriving, as it depends on the passing buses not being full already. Early mornings are generally better than other times of day, but it's not a guaranteed recipe for success.

🏠 **WHERE TO STAY** *Map, page 278*
The stretch of coast along here is one of the easiest places in Croatia for accommodation, though not one of the most luxurious.

You can't **camp** within the park itself, but there is a staffed mountain hut and several unstaffed mountain shelters along the massif. The main campsite is across the road from the entrance to the park, next to the Hotel Alan, and is actually attached to the hotel (page 279). Other smaller campsites are along the road north and south of town.

There are any number of **private rooms** in the area, including some on the trail up into the park. No official agency handles these, so your best bet is to wander up and down the road and ask at the numerous places with *sobe* signs – expect to pay

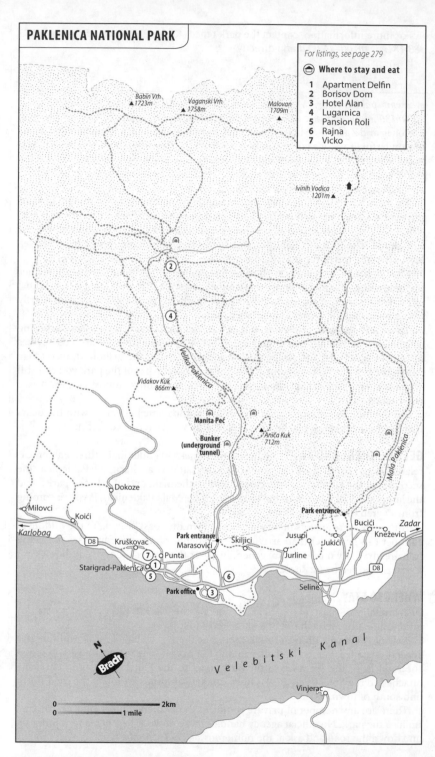

PAKLENICA NATIONAL PARK

For listings, see page 279

Where to stay and eat

1 Apartment Delfin
2 Borisov Dom
3 Hotel Alan
4 Lugarnica
5 Pansion Roli
6 Rajna
7 Vicko

Babin Vrh
▲1723m

Vaganski Vrh
▲1758m

Malovan
1709m
▲

Ivinih Vodica
1201m ▲

②

④

Velika Paklenica

Vidakov Kuk
866m ▲

Manita Peć

Aniča Kuk
712m ▲

**Bunker
(underground
tunnel)**

Mala Paklenica

Dokoze

Milovci

Koići

Park entrance

Bucići

Zadar

Karlobag

D8

Kruškovac

⑦ Punta

Starigrad-Paklenica

①

⑤

Park entrance
Marasovići

Škiljici

Jusupi

Jukići

Kneževici

Jurline

D8

⑥

Seline

Park office ● ③

V e l e b i t s k i   K a n a l

N

Bradt

0 ────── 2km
0 ────── 1 mile

Vinjerac

270

€35–50 for a double. The nicest ones, some with lovely balconies and sea views, are in the villages of Seline and Starigrad, but these are only practical if you have your own wheels. If you're really stuck, the **tourist office** (*Trg Tome Marasovića 1;* ☎ *369 255; www.rivijera-paklenica.hr*) in Starigrad itself, while not having a private-room mandate, will usually help you out. There are also three hotels and a number of smaller pansions.

🏠 **Hotel Alan** (138 rooms, 24 apts) Dr Franje Tuđmana 14; ☎ 023 209 050; www.hotel-alan.hr. Out on the main coast road is this 1970s high-rise hotel, now revamped & part of the Blue Sun chain & with a great location on the beach & good views. Also has a campsite (€). €€€€

🏠 **Vicko** (23 rooms) Jose Dokoze 20; ☎ 023 369 304; www.hotel-vicko.hr. Small, cheerful & family run, with nice rooms in the main hotel & lovely sea-view rooms. Also has a 4-star annexe, **Villa Vicko**, just across the street (16 rooms, 2 apts). In addition, the hotel has a good restaurant. €€€€–€€€

🏠 **Apartment Delfin** (9 rooms/apts) Stipana Bušljete 4; ☎ 023 369 211; www. apartman-delfin.com. Apts & rooms just 100m from the centre of Starigrad-Paklenica & 10m from the beach. €€€

🏠 **Pansion Roli** (14 rooms) Stipana Bušljete 1; ☎ 023 633 455; http://pansionroli.weebly.com. If it's the seaside you're after, you can't do better than the Pansion Roli, in Starigrad itself & right on the waterfront, where the fishing boats tie up. It serves fabulous mussels & other seafood. €€€

🏠 **Rajna** (10 rooms) Dr Franje Tuđmana 105; ☎ 023 359 121; m 098 272 878; www.hotel-rajna. com. Good-value, family-run place right by the entrance to the park, with its own restaurant. They also have renovated stone guesthouses at Varoš (*3 interconnected houses sleeping up to a total of 12, €210–€310/night*), and within the national park itself at the hamlet of Marasovići (*sleeps 4, €75–€85/night*). €€

🗡 **Borisov Dom** (50 dorm beds) ☎ 023 301 636; m 095 358 2111 (Dalibor Bračić), 095 813 1841 (Ines Pajić); ⊕ Jun–Sep daily, Oct–May weekends. The biggest & best equipped of the mountain huts, this is the place to stay if you want to base yourself in the valley & make day trips from there. Book yourself in ahead of time, & make sure you have a sleeping bag. Managed by PD Paklenica hiking club in Zadar. €

✖ WHERE TO EAT AND DRINK *Map, page 278*
There are a whole clutch of places where you can eat out, including both the **Vicko** and **Rajna**, along with informal grills and seafood places along the main road and on the shore, and at least one pizzeria. Inside the park, the **Lugarnica** hut, on the way to Borisov Dom, does great sausages, *grah* (bean stew) and other food (⊕ *May–Oct 10.30–16.30 daily*; €€).

OTHER PRACTICALITIES Everything you need is within easy reach of the park entrance, including a supermarket with good long opening hours and all the makings of a decent picnic, a couple of kiosks, and the park office (page 277) itself. Here you'll be given a standard free map which comes with the entrance ticket, and you can buy detailed maps (essential if you're doing much walking) – the best are the national park map and the SMAND map (you'll want sheet #19 for the national park) – as well as more detailed climbing and hiking guides. This is also the place to arrange accommodation at the mountain hut, or to check the opening/visiting times of Manita Peć or the Bunkers (see page 280).

For swimming, there are beaches either side of the Hotel Alan.

THE NATIONAL PARK The national park's geomorphology consists primarily of a horizontal plateau running between the Velebit massif and the sea. Two gorge valleys, Velika and Mala (large and small) Paklenica, with cliffs over 400m high in places, cut through this to the sea, and there are also several networks of subterranean caves. The most famous of these is Manita Peć, which has been explored for nearly 200m of its depth into the mountain and contains two enormous halls.

Because of its triple climate the weather is unusually variable. It's the only place I've ever walked where I've been drenched by rain, then sunburned and finally hailed on, before going for an afternoon swim in the sea. Prepare for all weathers, especially in May and early June, when there's still snow on the north-facing slopes above 1,500m. In high summer the inner parts of the park can be fearsomely hot, but even when the sun's shining on the coast, localised storms can see you hailed on.

There are two official routes into the park, up the two canyons. The main entrance is up a clearly marked road 300m south of Hotel Alan. A brisk kilometre up here brings you to the park office, where you buy your ticket, and maps, after which it's a further 2km to the end of the road and the car park. You'll come across the entrance here to what used to be one of Paklenica's greatest secrets, the enormous **bunker complex** built for Tito in the 1950s as a crisis headquarters in times of war. For decades nobody was allowed to even mention its existence, but you can now visit parts of the huge complex, and it's a fascinating glimpse into the paranoia of power. The bunkers are open somewhat irregularly; contact the park administration for more details.

The other entrance to the park is up Mala Paklenica, 4km south, just after and opposite the Church of St Mark. Turn inland and it's nearly 2km to the clearly visible canyon entrance, where you can park.

Anića Kuk This is easily the most-climbed peak in the national park. There are something like 25 routes up the sheer west and north faces, and these are all serious climbs that shouldn't be attempted without ropes and proper climbing equipment and experience. There's also a good walking route to the 712m summit, which makes for a fine six-hour return trip from Hotel Alan (4½ hours if you have a car).

Anića Kuk is not high, but it's an isolated, exposed peak, and it's the nearest major summit to the sea. The side facing into the gorge is a near-vertical drop of over 400m; don't stray too close to the edge.

The walking route follows Velika Paklenica upstream from the car park, on a well-made erosion-avoiding paved road, until you reach a sharp uphill left-hand bend, hard on the river, after half an hour. Cross the river here at the sign, and follow the faded red and white markers towards the base of the cliff, and then up to the left below the cliff in a wide sweep up through woods and scrub, before emerging on to naked karst, where a path continues to the summit.

It's a bit of a scramble, and can be hard on the hands, but another half an hour brings you to the airy, vertiginous summit, which is easily worth it for the fabulous views out across to the barren island of Pag.

Manita Peć (2hrs) This trail takes in the cave at Manita Peć. The walk is sometimes steep but never difficult, taking around two hours from Hotel Alan, with beautiful views out over the gorge. Manita Peć itself can only be visited with a guide, and is usually open three times a week in summer, on Monday, Wednesday and Saturday mornings – check at the park office before you head up here, to avoid disappointment.

From the car park head up the gorge for around 30 minutes until the path levels out (turning from paved to grit). After a short while there's the sign to Anića Kuk to the right, and indicators to Lugarnica (30 minutes) and Planinarski Dom (Borisov Dom, 50 minutes). It's not far from here to the path heading off to the right, which eventually leads to Mala Paklenica (page 282), after which you soon reach the sign saying it's 40 minutes to Manita Peć, and that's about how long you should allow to cover the long zigzags heading uphill to the left, to the cave at 550m.

The cave itself – like most caves – is nothing special outside, but inside it's marvellous. A tunnel-like entrance leads through to two huge chambers, some 40m long and 40–65m wide, with a height of over 30m. The atmospheric artificial lighting shows off the stalactites and stalagmites, and the weird dripstone pillars. Nature's a wonderful thing.

Blinking outside in the daylight, there's an unmarked (and very hard to find) path up to Vidakov Kuk which heads off to the left (with your back to the cave). However, despite Vidakov Kuk having splendid views, following the trail up from Manita Peć is really *not* advised. For a start, it's poorly marked, rough and largely overgrown. Secondly, the section where it climbs steeply uphill a few minutes beyond Manita Peć has been used as an open toilet by less considerate visitors. Bear in mind that you'd need to scramble up through this section, using your hands and probably slipping on the loose rock and scree a few times, and any interest in climbing Vidakov Kuk from this side should sensibly evaporate. Truly, there's no shortage of nicer walks in the national park!

STAYING ON THE RIGHT TRACK

Within the park, the trails marked on the map in red are marked in reality with red and white flashes on rocks and trees, and it's very rare that you can't easily see from one mark to the next. Some of the least-used paths may have faded markings, but others will impress you with their fresh brightness. There are also lots of paths used by local people that aren't guided on the ground; these are marked with dotted lines on the map. On the steeper paths you may well appreciate the use of a stick or walking-poles, especially if it's been raining, as some of the trails can be pretty slippery.

A word of warning: it's highly inadvisable to leave the marked paths – high up in the park there are still minefields, while lower down you'll have to cross naked karst. And believe me, wild karst is awful stuff to cross – you'll find it extremely wearing, both mentally and on your clothes and hands. The shallowest slopes will confront you with jagged rocks, and even 2m climbs or drops are difficult.

The first time I came here, a marked path up Anića Kuk took me three hours, including a 700m climb. The same descent, across just 4km of shallow karst, took nearly seven hours. I was never in danger of being lost, since everything was clearly visible, but the rocks were nearly impossible to cross, and my fingers were worn to all but the last layer of skin by the end. For a week I couldn't even hold a cup of coffee.

Assistance in case of an emergency depends in the first instance on members of your party, or other walkers and climbers – there is a mountain rescue service (*www.gss.hr; in case of emergency in the mountains call* ☏ *112*), but they need to be alerted. It's a good idea therefore to let people know where you're headed before you set out.

Good, detailed local maps (published by the National Park Office and by SMAND; www.smand.hr) are available through the park office or some of the larger bookshops in Zagreb and other cities. Rudolf Abraham's book *Walking in Croatia* (page 429) has details of hiking in Paklenica and other mountain areas in the country.

Velika Golić (*10hrs*) Some of the more spectacular views in Paklenica can be had from the long ridge of Velika Golić, and an excellent 10-hour walk (8½ if you have a car) takes in this ridge and returns via Borisov Dom.

The walk starts exactly as if you were going to Manita Peć (page 280), but heads straight on when the path branches up and left to the cave. After half an hour you'll come to a water trough and a sign saying 'Borisov Dom 30 minutes'. The main path branches up to the left here, and 10 minutes further on you need to take the path branching steeply uphill, away from the river. Follow this up its zigzags for about 40 minutes, after which you'll come to a straighter section, with markings on the dry stone wall leading to the farm at Ramići (not the only place named Ramići in the immediate vicinity, unfortunately).

The main marked trail leading through the farm leads up to Vidakov Kuk – the path you want, to Velika Golić, is a hard right-hand turn, almost behind you as you arrive at the farm. From here, after skirting between a series of dry stone walls, the path rises steadily, and you're soon a long way above the farm. The ground becomes rougher as the path skirts the 903m summit of Čelinka and crosses a rocky wood before surfacing on an open pasture. This leads directly to the corner of the ridge, level with the top of Čelinka. It takes about 2 hours from the river to this point, from which there are fine views down on to the refuge below, across to the peak of Anića Kuk and over to the sea.

The ridge is an extraordinary formation, consisting of a series of parallel broken limestone ridges at an angle of about 40 degrees. The valley side is nearly a sheer drop, but the side from which you've approached is relatively shallow, as is the line of the ridge itself, which takes the best part of 2km to rise from 900m to 1,285m. There are endless false crests to this, but the summit is superb, with spectacular panoramic views making the four- to five-hour ascent well worthwhile. Make sure you have appropriate clothing, however – this is where I was once caught in a late-May hailstorm.

The best way down is to continue along the ridge, scaling a secondary summit of 1,160m, before the path curves back on itself to bring you down to Borisov Dom. This takes around 2 hours, after which it's an easy 1½ hours back to the car park.

Mala and Velika Paklenica (*10hrs*) This is a terrific circular walk, including both gorges and some very fine views. It runs from Hotel Alan to Seline, up Mala Paklenica, across the broad ridge between the two canyons and then down Velika Paklenica. It can be done in reverse, but with Mala Paklenica being the tougher walk, you're better off tackling it while you're fresh, and preferably before it gets too hot.

If you take your time, and aren't in a hurry, the walk takes around ten hours, including the hour between the two villages, which you can't avoid unless someone gives you a lift, as you end up where you started. It's a pretty long, tough day out, so be prepared, but it's well worth the effort.

At the entrance to the Mala Paklenica gorge, the dirt road peters out and you're on the trail upstream. It's very rustic and empty compared to Velika Paklenica, and less well marked at first, but the route is clear enough, starting on the left-hand side of the gully before crossing over to the other side. Unless there's been exceptional rain, the gully is dry from May to September.

As you enter the canyon proper the walls steepen and the path becomes clearer and better marked. At the first big boulders on the valley floor the path climbs to the right, crossing the first of three assisted sections, with steel cables and well-secured pitons to help you up.

The next two hours are hard, ascending sharply, but the way the rock's been sculpted by flowing water, the small flowers and trees growing tenaciously from pockets in the cliffs, and the fine views should cheer you up. After a while you'll notice puddles on the valley floor, which gradually become a rivulet and eventually turn into a bubbling, refreshing stream. The path criss-crosses this on well-marked boulders.

When the gorge forks, take the left-hand one, following the stream. Twenty minutes later the path definitively leaves the stream, but only after a couple of false alarms, and then heads steeply uphill, zigzagging until you're at 650m. At the top there's a dry stone wall clearly marked Sv Jakov, though there's no obvious church. This junction is easy to pinpoint on the map.

Take the left-hand of the two paths, marked Starigrad. The path is a bit indistinct here, running across pastures, but there are markers. If you lose these, head west-northwest until you join the marked path coming in from your right. At this point the trail starts down a rocky gully. It divides fairly often, but the correct path is always well marked, eventually coming out at a small farm.

Leave the farm on the leftmost track, and then fork immediately right on the marked path. From here it's easy to find your way to the valley floor – even if there aren't signs, you can follow the donkey droppings, as you're now on the farm's access road. The path comes out suddenly and unexpectedly to the top edge of Velika Paklenica, and it's an ideal picnic spot – it's almost all downhill from here, and the views are great.

The path down is a steep, knee-testing zigzag – you might be grateful of walking-poles here – until you reach the valley floor, after which it's an easy walk back to the entrance of Velika Paklenica.

Other walks The walks described above are only a fraction of what you can do in the area, particularly given that none of them even take you up on to the spectacular Velebit ridge.

You can also wander happily around at lower altitudes to the west of the park, discovering the abandoned and near-abandoned villages in the hills. One of these, **Bristovac Tomići** (the locals leave off the Bristovac), is the start of a good walk up to Vidakov Kuk, and provides a poignant look at a world where electricity supplies, running water and central heating never quite caught on.

The more ambitious, however, will want to scale the region's highest peak, **Vaganski Vrh**, just 73m lower than Croatia's highest point, Dinara. Bear in mind, however, that the ridge hasn't entirely been de-mined, so discuss your route with the park staff before heading off, and stay on the marked trails.

While an ascent of Vaganski Vrh is possible to complete within a day from the park's entrance, the 14-hour minimum round trip isn't for the faint-hearted, and you need to set off very early in the morning indeed, and be extremely well equipped – friends who've done it reckoned that two litres of water per person was nothing like enough.

Better by far is to stay overnight at Borisov Dom or one of the other mountain huts, and start the 5–6-hour climb to the summit from there. On a clear day they say you can see Italy on one side and a good 100km into Bosnia on the other, but those days do tend to come in winter, when a combination of snow and a vicious bura are likely to dissuade you from making the ascent at all.

Best of all is a three-day circuit covering the **Velebit ridge** – again, discuss your route in detail with the park staff before heading out, and remember there are still mines in the ground. On the first day head up Mala Paklenica, going straight on instead of left at Sv Jakov (see above), and then right instead of straight on at the junction for Borisov Dom. The route then skirts left of the 999m summit of

Martinovo Mirilo, eventually reaching the Ivine Vodice hut at 1,200m, where you can stay the night (check it's open, of course, before you start out).

Day two then starts with the climb up to the ridge, and the chance to reach the summits of Malovan (1,709m, around four hours from the refuge) and Vaganski Vrh (1,758m), among others, before coming down at Borisov Dom for the second night out. Bear in mind that it's a lot further on to Babin Vrh (1,723m) than you might think – count on 14 hours just from the Ivine Vodice hut – and that you don't want to get caught out at this altitude at any time of year.

ŠIBENIK

Šibenik is something of an odd-man-out on the Dalmatian coast, firstly because it has no classical history – it was founded by the Croats and doesn't show up until the 11th century – and secondly because it's not really a tourist town. Indeed, until the 1990s, and the war with Serbia, it was a light industrial hub with a moderately busy port, and nothing much in the way of either beaches or visitors.

It's well worth stopping here, however, not just for the cathedral – the most important piece of Renaissance architecture in Croatia (and classified by UNESCO as a World Heritage Site in 2000) – but also for its charming medieval old town, and its position as a springboard for trips into the Krka National Park and to the Kornati archipelago (see pages 288 and 299).

By the end of the war in 1995, Šibenik's industrial base was in ruins, and during the second half of the 1990s the town found it hard to recover, with high unemployment and consequently very little money around for spending. The past decade seems to have brought with it new optimism, however, and in summer it's hard to find a seat at any of the seafront cafés on a Sunday morning. Recovery isn't complete, but Šibenik's well on the mend.

HISTORY After first being mentioned in 1066, Šibenik was tossed back and forth between Venetians, Hungarians, Byzantines, Croats and Bosnians, before knuckling definitively under Venice (1412–1797) and the Austro-Hungarian Empire (1797–1918). Italy was very briefly in control (only until 1920) before the city became Yugoslav, and finally, in 1991, Croatian.

The Venetians built the defensive walls (best preserved on the north side of town) running all the way up to the three fortresses at the top of the hill, and it was also under Venice that St Jacob's Cathedral was built, in fits and starts, over more than a century.

GETTING THERE AND AROUND Šibenik is easy to reach. A **catamaran** sails between Šibenik and the islands of Kaprije and Žirje, twice daily in summer, less frequently October–December and March–May (*http://lnp.hr*), docking at the southern end of the old town. The **bus** station is 200m further south, in the new town – there are regular buses up and down the coast, including every hour or so to Zadar (*90mins*) and Split (*90mins*). The train station (only serving local routes inland) is a further 300m to the southeast. Both the bus and train stations have left-luggage facilities.

The old town is entirely pedestrianised, which is excellent, so once you've arrived you'll be on foot – it's all perfectly manageable, though the narrow streets running up to the St Anne Fortress are pretty steep.

The friendly **tourist office** (*Fausta Vrančića 18;* \ *022 212 075; www.sibenik-tourism.hr*), with town plans, etc, is bang in the middle of the old town, just off the main artery of Zagrebačka, across from St John's (Sv Ivan) Church. For those

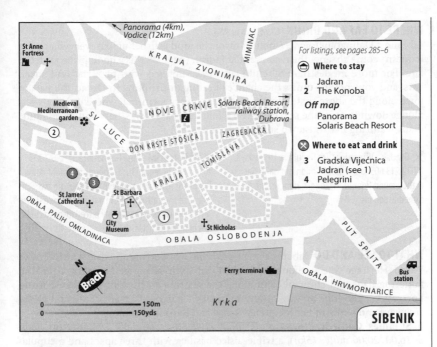

For listings, see pages 285–6

Where to stay

1   Jadran
2   The Konoba

Off map
      Panorama
      Solaris Beach Resort

Where to eat and drink

3   Gradska Vijećnica
      Jadran (see 1)
4   Pelegrini

ŠIBENIK

exploring the surrounding area, head for the **Šibenik County Tourist Office** (*Nikole Ružića bb;* ☎ *022 219 072; www.sibenikregion.com*).

WHERE TO STAY *Map, above*

With accommodation in fairly short supply in Šibenik (there are very few private rooms in the old town and only one hotel) you may find it easier to make a day trip from Zadar, Trogir or Split – or indeed go for one of the slew of private rooms in shamelessly touristy **Vodice**, just 12km up the coast, which is enormously popular with Croatians and eastern Europeans. That said, it's worth persevering – with few visitors spending the night here, you'll find Šibenik evenings pleasant at any time of year.

Most private rooms are out of town, along the coast, though with regular buses this needn't be a problem. If you arrive in summer you'll likely be met off the ferry or bus by women offering rooms – check the location before you agree.

Solaris Beach Resort (5 hotels & 2 apt villas) ☎ 022 361 001; www.solarishotelsresort. com. Slick, modern resort outside town, on the waterfront facing the island of Zlarin. Hotels range from the large, upscale Ivan to the family-oriented and very child-friendly Andrija. Spa, pools, beach, campsite, restaurants, clubs & bars. €€€€

The Konoba (1 dbl, 2 apts) Andrije Kacica 8; m 091 601 9789; www.bbdalmatia.com. Lovely Dutch-run B&B in the old town, offering 3 choices of accommodation in 2 beautifully renovated stone houses – a studio (sleeping up to 3) and 2 apartments (sleeping 3 & 4). €€€

Jadran (57 rooms) Obala Dr Franje Tuđmana 52; ☎ 022 242 000/9; www.rivijera.hr. The old town's only hotel is rather boxy & unexciting, & in need of a good makeover – but it's clean, reasonably modern & well equipped, & it's right on the harbour. €€€€

Panorama (20 rooms) Šibenski most 1; ☎ 022 213 398; www.hotel-panorama.hr. The best alternative to staying in Šibenik itself is the smart, modern Panorama – 4km northwest of town, perched above the gorge of the River Krka by the Šibenik Bridge, with great views. You can get here on the local bus to Zaton, or intercity buses will drop you off (though they're unlikely to pick you up). €€€€

✕ WHERE TO EAT AND DRINK Map, page 285

Like most Dalmatian towns, Šibenik's favourite food is fish, but like everywhere else it doesn't come cheap – the restaurant at **Jadran** (page 285) is a good place for fresh fare. For more modest fare Šibenik's also well supplied with pizzerias and snack bars, and you shouldn't miss the chance of eating or drinking in **Dolac**, the part of town along the shore that is furthest from the ferry terminal, where the city walls plunge down to meet the sea. Here you'll find dozens of cafés, bars and restaurants, many featuring live music on summer evenings.

✕ **Gradska Vijećnica** Trg Republike Hrvatske 3; ✆022 213 605; open 09.00–midnight daily. Set in the ground floor of the loggia, right on the cathedral square. €€€

✻✕ **Pelegrini** Jurja Dalmatinca 1; ✆022 213 701; www.pelegrini.hr; ☺ noon–midnight daily. The nicest restaurant in town, overlooking the façade of the cathedral from a flight of stone steps. Serves delicious & reasonably priced dishes as well as a good wine list. €€€

WHAT TO SEE AND DO Šibenik's must-see is the wonderful cathedral – a UNESCO World Heritage Site – though the old town itself is perfectly lovely, from the fluttering flags and cheerful cafés along the seafront to the ruins of the **St Anne Fortress** on the hill, by way of any number of narrow flagged streets, medieval archways and a mix of Gothic, Renaissance and Baroque buildings.

    St James' Cathedral (*Sv Jakov;* ☺ *summer 08.30–20.00 daily, winter 08.30–noon & 16.00–20.00 daily; 15kn*), a triple-aisled basilica with three apses and a cupola, was started in 1431 but not completed until 1536, and reflects the transition from Venetian Gothic to Tuscan Renaissance. What makes it unique, however, is the extraordinary barrel-vaulting, consisting of stones chiselled to fit together snugly using carpentry techniques, and leading to the cathedral's exterior being almost identical to its interior – something you won't see in any other church. It's difficult to get a good look at the roof from outside, as the town crowds up to the cathedral, but postcards – or a hike up to the St Anne Fortress – will give you a good idea. A result of the design is also that the façade is the only one in Europe able to reflect the true shape of the triple-aisled church behind it – all the others are effectively stage-scenery, stuck on for effect.

    The cathedral is largely the work of Juraj Dalmatinac (George the Dalmatian), a sculptor who was born in Zadar, but rose to fame in Venice (perhaps under the tutelage of Donatello). He was chief architect here, on and off, from the early 1440s until his death in 1473. The extraordinary frieze on the outside of the cathedral of 74 individual heads running round the apses (a fabulous glimpse of 15th-century life), along with the stunning baptistery inside the big echoing church, are his finest works. In front of the cathedral you'll find a Meštrović statue of him.

    The north side of the cathedral makes up one side of the elegant Trg Republika Hrvatske; the other is occupied by a fine loggia, built between 1533 and 1542. Originally the town hall, the version you see today is mostly a post-war reconstruction, following the 1943 bombing of the town – though it's no less lovely for that.

    Otherwise the rest of the old town is really its own attraction, though there are several other churches worth visiting (notably **St Nicholas** and **St Barbara**), as well as a small **City Museum** (*Gradski Muzej; www.muzej-sibenik.hr;* ☺ *10.00–18.00 Mon–Sat; 30kn*). Up at the top of the town, the St Anne Fortress isn't much to look at, but has great views out over the town and across the bay. Walking up to the fortress takes you past the pretty **medieval Mediterranean garden** (⊕ *summer 08.00–23.00 daily, winter 09.00–16.00 daily; 15kn*) of the monastery of St Lawrence, well worth popping into.

About 7km from Šibenik, near the village of Dubrava, there is a **falconry centre** (*Sokolarski Center Dubrava; Škugori bb, Dubrava;* m *091 506 7610;* e *sokolarski. centar@gmail.com; www.sokolarskicentar.com;* ⊕ *09.00–19.00 daily; 45kn*). As well as informative 45-minute presentations on birds of prey, the centre runs environmental education programmes and one- and five-day falconry courses, and has a small hospital where sick or injured birds are cared for and rehabilitated. Larger groups are asked to call in advance.

PRIMOŠTEN A little over 25km south of Šibenik the coast road passes Primošten, the old town of which occupies a photogenic, teardrop-shaped peninsula covered in stone houses with a church-spire protruding above them. The 'peninsula' was originally an island connected to the mainland by a wooden bridge (hence its name, from *pri mostu*, meaning 'at the bridge'), though the bridge was later replaced by an embankment. Adjacent to this is a second, slightly larger peninsula, mainly covered with pine forest and separated from the old town by a nice beach. The **tourist office** (✆ *022 571 111; www.tz-primosten.hr*), at the entrance to the old town, has details of private accommodation.

🏠 **Where to stay and eat** Kamenar (*Rudina Biskupa Arnerića 5;* ✆ *022 570 889;* m *098 336 246;* e *tomislav.jurin@si.t-com.hr; www.restaurant-kamenar.com;* €€), near the entrance to the old town, has seven clean, pine-furnished rooms above the restaurant of the same name. There's one large hotel here, the 324-room **Zora** (✆ *022 581 111; www.hotelzora-adriatiq.com;* ⊕ *Mar–Nov;* €€€€) on the forested peninsula just north of the old town. **Koboba Toni** (*Podakraje 26; www.konoba-toni.com;* ⊕ *summer 08.00–midnight daily;* €€€) is a nice tavern in the old town with apartments above. The restaurant at the Kamenar is slightly more upmarket.

NORTH TO KNIN From Šibenik the road runs north along the eastern border of Krka National Park (see page 287), to **Knin**, some 60km distant. You're also likely to come through Knin on any other road from central or southern Dalmatia to Zagreb, which is why the town had such significance in the conflict of the 1990s, as the capital of the Serbian RSK (Republika Srpska Krajina) – it effectively cut off southern Croatia from the rest of the country.

Driving up past the unremarkable town of **Drniš**, towards Knin, and on towards Gračac and Zagreb, the scars of the war are still very much in evidence. Several properties in the area remain devastated, windowless and roofless, and while some of the older Serbs who'd lived here for generations have clearly returned, there are few if any young people around. Houses that weren't destroyed by shells were gutted by fire, and the torched wrecks of cars still stand in their driveways. The farming villages of **Kaldrina** and **Kosovo** in particular are a dreadful reminder of the awfulness of war.

Knin, the short-lived capital of the Serb enclave of Krajina, is an uninspiring place and its population is nothing like what it was 15 years ago. If you stop in Knin (and it's easy, with so many onward buses, and trains to Zagreb and Split), then make the effort to climb up the hill to the terrific **medieval fortress** which dominates the town. It's the way fortresses are meant to be, with great big walls, ramparts, buttresses, towers and a sturdy central keep, and panoramic views out over the surrounding countryside.

(*www.np-krka.hr;110kn/90kn/30kn summer/spring & autumn/winter*) The 72km Krka River and waterfalls are a popular rival to the Plitvice Lakes further north, and are essentially a result of the same travertine process which formed (and is continuing to form) Plitvice (page 172). Krka makes a great excursion from Šibenik, and is offered as a day trip by any number of tour operators all the way from Zadar to Split, though it's easy enough to visit under your own steam, too.

Krka is the most popular national park in Croatia after the more famous Plitvice, with a huge number of visitors annually. In fact there's arguably more to see here than at Plitvice, and a far greater water flow. The biggest falls, Skradinski Buk (where you can swim in summer), see an average of 55m^3 per second all year round, rising to a splashy 350m^3 per second after heavy rains inland.

After much wrangling between the proponents of hydro-electricity and conservationists, the middle and lower parts of the Krka River were finally declared a national park in 1985, and the park's recently been extended pretty much all the way to the river's source, near Knin. The two most impressive waterfall systems are Roški Slap to the north and Skradinski Buk to the south, separated by a wide section of river on which you'll find the islet of Visovac and a Franciscan monastery. There are also archaeological remains to be seen at Burnum. For the last 20km downstream from Skradinski Buk, the Krka is at sea level, with a mix of salt and fresh water.

GETTING THERE AND AWAY If you're not on an excursion, you can easily reach Krka National Park on the **bus** that runs half-a-dozen times a day from Šibenik to the western entrance at Skradin, stopping on the way at the eastern Lozovac entrance (timetables at http://atpsi.hr). If you have your own wheels there's plenty of parking at both. Out of season you can usually drive the 4km into the park from the Lozovac entrance, while in summer you have to take the park bus.

Access from Skradin to the waterfalls is by national park **boat**, included in the 110kn entrance fee, which leaves the quay every hour on the hour and takes around 25 minutes. Both the park bus from Lozovac and the boat from Skradin only run from April to October, so if you're on public transport in winter you need to factor in a good 45-minute walk at either entrance – the entry fee is reduced to 30kn as compensation. You can also sail straight to Skradin from the sea, tying up just downstream from the Skradin bridge.

Inside most of the park itself – from the Skradin bridge upstream – you're restricted, quite properly, to the national park boats and footpaths. If you want to see the **Krka Monastery** (Orthodox Monastery of the Holy) towards the northern end of the park (⊕ *Apr–Oct; 100kn*), or Visovac island with its 15th-century Franciscan monastery (⊕ *Mar–Nov; 130kn*), you can join one of the organised boat trips which can be booked through the national park office. For further information, or for reservations on any of the boat-rides upstream of the first waterfalls – highly recommended in summer, as the boats do fill up – contact the **national park office** in Šibenik (\ *022 201 777; www.npkrka.hr*) or the **information centre** in Skradin (\ *022 771 688*).

WHERE TO STAY AND EAT Skradin – a pretty, leafy town with cafés along the waterfront – is worth visiting in its own right now that it has recovered from being pummelled by both sides during the homeland war. There's a nice place to stay, in the shape of the **Hotel Skradinski Buk** (*Burinovac bb;* \ *022 771 771; www.skradinskibuk.*

Krka Monastery †

↗ Knin

Laškovica

Roški Slap

Visovac
Monastery †

Drniš ○

↗ Knin

Zadar

Skradin

Krka

Watermill
Museum

A1

Lozovac ○   Skradinski Buk

N

Bradt

0 _____ 5km
0 _____ 5 miles

Šibenik ↙

hr; **€€€**), which has a very pleasant terrace restaurant, serving excellent, reasonably priced food. Alternatives in Skradin include **Guesthouse Ankora** (*Mesarska 5a;* m *095 910 7068;* **€€**) and **Guest Accommodation Žura** (*Grge Vatavuka 6;* m *099 213 5107;* **€€**), each of which offers six apartments. In Lozovac there's the **Hotel Vrata Krke** (*Lozovac bb;* ☏ *022 778 091; www.vrata-krke.hr;* **€€€€**). Contact the **tourist office** for more information, including a list of private accommodation (*Trg Male Gospe 3;* ☏ *022 771 329; www.skradin.hr*).

WHAT TO SEE AND DO The national park has a rich variety of plant life (some 860 species and sub-species), as well as 18 different kinds of fish, including 10 species endemic to the Krka River. A diverse range of amphibians and reptiles, more than 200 species of bird, and 18 species of bat – some practically extinct elsewhere in Europe – make the park an important wildlife sanctuary. Dragonflies and butterflies are spectacular – 34 species of the former, and almost 200 of the latter have been recorded in the park (to put that latter figure into context, it's well over three times the total number of butterfly species in the UK as a whole).

In terms of attractions for the visitor, the first and most obvious sight is **Skradinski Buk**, the largest of a series of waterfalls dropping down towards Skradin in 17 steps. As at Plitvice, wooden walkways and forest paths lead you around the waterfalls, in this case from bottom to top and back again, with a full leisurely tour taking a couple of hours. At the bottom there's an excellent opportunity to swim at the base of the falls, so if you're here in summer bring your beachwear. After crossing the long footbridge below the thundering Skradinski buk, follow the trail up to the small **church** and **ethno village**. Here you'll find interesting ethnographic displays, including a blacksmith's workshop, an interactive area for kids and a **watermill museum** – in the past the power of the falls was harnessed for milling, rolling and pounding, and there are demonstrations during the season, included in the park entry fee. There's a small café here, too. Before reaching the church you'll pass the former site of the **Krka Hydro-Electric Dam**, which went into operation here in 1895, and was only the second such hydro-electric power station in the world (the first, at Niagara Falls in the USA, went into operation just two days earlier). After the watermill museum, follow the road for a short distance (towards the Lozovac entrance) then turn left and follow boardwalks through the forest and across water channels and pools, before descending on the far side of Skradinski buk to the base of the falls again, for that well-earned swim.

From April to October, you can also take a variety of national park boat excursions – buy your ticket on arrival if you haven't reserved ahead, and then visit Skradinski Buk while you're waiting. The most popular excursion is the two-hour boat ride up to the ridiculously picturesque island of **Visovac**, where you'll be given half an hour to explore the Franciscan church and monastery. Started in the 14th century, it now houses a small museum and a precious library.

A bigger excursion (four hours) takes in Visovac and then heads upstream through a gorge to the **Roški Slap** waterfalls, which may not quite be a match for Skradinski Buk, but make for a delightful hour's wander all the same.

From the upper end of Roški Slap, it's a further 100kn, two-hour excursion by boat up to the fine Orthodox Krka Monastery, dating from 1359, though much rebuilt over the succeeding 400 years.

Also within the confines of the national park are some excellent ruined medieval castles and important archaeological remains; ask for directions and a map when you buy your entry ticket, if you're interested.

PAG

Pag, stretching some 60km alongside the coast north of Zadar, is one of the most barren of the Adriatic's big islands. It supports fewer than 10,000 people (and rather more sheep) in a handful of villages, and it can be a torpid, stifling place in the dog days of August, with the general lack of trees (barring some ancient olive groves in the north, and some stunted figs) being maddening and oppressive.

Nonetheless, it's very popular as a holiday destination, with an interesting old town and some fine sandy beaches, and wonderful lace-making tradition of Pag town remains charming rather than touristy. Tourism is Pag's sole source of real prosperity, nevertheless apart from a few weeks at the end of July and the beginning of August in Novalja – Croatia's answer to Ibiza, with club owners and entire clubs coming down from Zagreb for the season – Pag is still far from crowded.

Pag's reputation in the past was tied to salt, and there are still big saltpans in the centre of the island, but today its fame rests primarily on Paški Sir, the distinctive hard cheese that is one of the highlights of Croatia's indigenous cuisine. The unique flavour is a combination of the sheep's diet – mainly salt grasses and sage – and the way it's matured, rubbed with olive oil and ash. Even here, it's relatively expensive, and harder to find than you'd expect, but it's worth making the effort (there's a

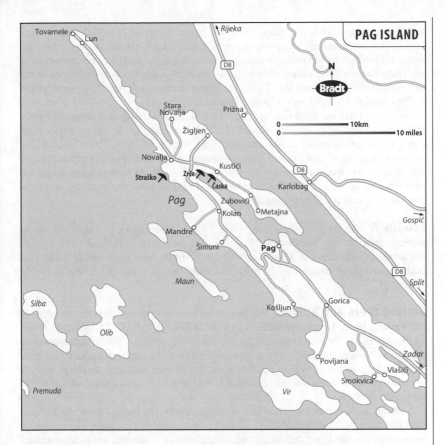

shop selling Pag cheese on Od Špitala, a few doors along from the tourist office). The factory where the cheese is actually made is on the main road on the southeast outskirts of Pag town (*www.paskasirana.hr*).

HISTORY It's hard to believe now, but Pag was covered with woods when it was first settled by the Illyrian tribes, and was still forested through its Roman occupation, the arrival of the Slavs in the 7th century, and the feuding of the bishops of Zadar and Rab (back when Rab had a bishop) over the island's salt-pans in the late Middle Ages.

It was the Venetians who did the damage, here and all the way around the Kvarner Bay and throughout northern Dalmatia, cutting down the trees wholesale for shipbuilding (it has to be said that the locals were usually quick enough to sell the precious wood). The scrub grasses and roots that were left behind were then over-cropped by sheep, and the bura winds blew away whatever topsoil was left. The land has never recovered, even now supporting little more than a few herbs and salt grasses.

Pag fell under Austro-Hungarian control after the fall of Venice, and became Yugoslav after World War I, though neither left much of a mark on the island until the bridge connecting it to the mainland was built in 1968.

GETTING THERE AND AROUND Access to Pag from the south is across the road bridge, while from the north you're better off taking the **ferry** from Prižna

Northern Dalmatia PAG

7

to Žigljen (6km across the island from the main resort of Novalja), which runs hourly in winter and continuously in summer (day and night). Note that when the bura's a-blowing, however, especially in winter, the ferry might not be running at all. There's also a daily **catamaran** from Rijeka to Novalja via Rab during summer (*www.jadrolinija.hr*), and a small passenger boat running to Lun at the northern tip of the island from Rab (*www.rapska-plovidba.hr*).

Six **buses** a day run between Novalja, Pag and Zadar during the summer, slightly fewer off season, and two daily Rijeka–Zadar buses run via the island rather than along the coast, stopping at Novalja and Pag town on the way. Three buses a day run from Zagreb to Novalja and Pag, and there's also a daily bus from Novalja and Pag to Split. Most of these routes are run by Antonio Tours (*www.antoniotours.hr*) or Autotrans (*www.autotrans.hr*). Pag town is under an hour from Zadar, 3½ hours from Rijeka, and 5½ hours from Zagreb.

PAG TOWN The attractive, partially walled old centre of Pag you see today is in fact the new town – the original Pag was 3km south of here, and you can still see some of the ruins at Stari Grad. The new town was founded in 1443 and built according to designs by Juraj Dalmatinac, the man behind Šibenik's lovely cathedral.

Getting there and around The bus stops just west from the old town, near the Pagus Hotel. **Tourist information** (*Od Špitala 2;* \ *023 611 301/286; www. tzgpag.hr*) is on the southern side of the old town, towards the bridge across to the old salt warehouses (one of which now houses the interesting Salt Museum (page 294), another of which has been converted into a disco), and has a good reversible map of the town and the island. Shame about the website, which is not very user friendly.

You can book excursions from the usual agencies – the best of these are the day trips out to the Kornati archipelago. Meridijan also rents out bicycles, a great way of exploring the island, but make sure you have plenty of water and are well protected with sunblock – there's no real shade anywhere to speak of.

Where to stay and eat *Map, page 293*

Meridijan (*Ante Starčevića 1;* \ *023 612 162; www.meridijan15.hr*), by the bus stop, is a travel agency handling a growing supply of private rooms– expect to pay around €40 for a decent double. Another travel agency handling private accommodation is Mediteran (*Golija 41;* \ *023 611 238; www.mediteranpag.com*), also just around the corner from the bus station as you're walking towards the old town. It's also highly likely you'll be approached by old women when the bus arrives, and given Pag's small size it's worth going and having a look.

The nearest **campsite** is 8km away, at Šimuni (\ *023 697 441; www.camping-simuni.hr*; €€€–€€), on an attractive bay on the western side of the island, halfway to Novalja, which offers wooden bungalows as well as pitches – buses stop here, and there's a popular marina, too.

Pagus (117 rooms) A Starčevića 1; \ 023 492 050; www.hotel-pagus.hr. 4-star place right by the bus stop, with its own concrete beach & sea-view dbls, with balconies. €€€€€

Biser (20 rooms) A G Matoša 46; \ 023 611 333; www.hotel-biser.com. Across the bay, a 30min walk from the old town, the 3-star Biser has its own rather nicer beach. €€€€

Meridijan (45 rooms) A Starčevića 1; \ 023 612 162; www.meridijan15.hr, Centrally located, with rooms decorated in vintage Biedermeier style. Restaurant & pool. €€€€

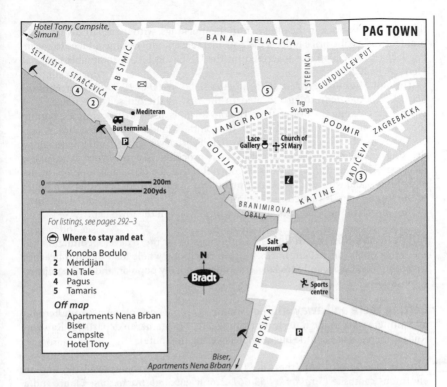

Hotel Tony, Campsite, Šimuni

BANA J JELAČIĆA

A STEPINCA

GUNDULIĆEV PUT

ŠETALIŠTEA STARČEVIĆA

A B ŠIMIĆA

Mediteran

Bus terminal

VANGRADA

GOLIJA

Trg
Sv Jurga

PODMIR

ZAGREBAČKA

Lace
Gallery

Church of
St Mary

RADIĆEVA

0   200m
0   200yds

KATINE

BRANIMIROVA
OBALA

Salt
Museum

For listings, see pages 292–3

Where to stay and eat

1   Konoba Bodulo
2   Meridijan
3   Na Tale
4   Pagus
5   Tamaris

Off map
    Apartments Nena Brban
    Biser
    Campsite
    Hotel Tony

N

Bradt

Sports
centre

PROSIKA

Biser,
Apartments Nena Brban

✳🏠 Apartments Nena Brban (6 apts)
Ljudevita Gaja; ☏023 600 252; m 095 598 8599.
Spotless apts just a 10min walk west of the old
town. Recommended. €€€

🏠 **Hotel Tony** (20 rooms) Dubrovacka 39;
☏023 611 370; www.hotel-tony.com. Welcoming,
well-priced family hotel, with own restaurant. €€€

🏠 **Tamaris** (3 rooms, 1 apt) Križevačka 2;
☏023 612 277; http://tamaris-pag.com.hr. Small

family-run place just west of the old town, with its
own, popular restaurant. €€€

✕ **Konoba Bodulo** Van Grada 19; ☏023 611
989; ⊕ noon–midnight daily. Low-key, family-run
konoba just outside the old town. €€€

✕ **Na Tale** Stjepana Radića 4; ☏023 611 194;
www.ljubica.hr. Popular bistro serving Pag & other
Dalmatian specialties. Apts available. €€€

What to see and do A regular grid of old narrow streets meets at the town's main
square, Trg Kralja Krešimira IV, which contains the **Church of St Mary** (meant to
be a cathedral), the **Duke's Palace**, and the unfinished **Bishop's Palace** – Pag never
quite got its act together on becoming a bishopric.

The church has a fine, simple front, with a carved Gothic portal, four unfinished-
looking saints, and a Renaissance rosette window. Inside, there are lovely Romanesque
arches with Corinthian capitals (at the far right-hand end check out the cavorting
dolphins), while on the ceiling there's a huge plaster relief of St George and the Dragon.
The solid bell tower, behind and to the left, looks firmly rooted in the 16th century.

Given the town's heritage, it would be madness not to pop into the tiny **Lace
Gallery** (*Galerija paške čipke;* ⊕ *Jun–Sep*), on one side of the square, which has a
small collection of intricate work. Pag has been famous for its lace for centuries,
with each piece being unique; after being closed for decades the lace school here
was reopened in the late 1990s. If you want to buy genuine lace, your best bet is
to purchase directly from the lace museum or the women making it – you'll see

7

them dressed in black in the old town in the mornings, with their hair distinctively braided. The asking price reflects the considerable amount of time it takes to make. Pag lace (Paška čipka) was inscribed on the UNESCO List of Intangible Cultural Heritage in 2009.

The **Salt Museum** (*Sol Muzej;* ⊕ *Jul/Aug 10.00–13.00 & 19.00–23.00 daily, Jun/ Sep 10.00–13.00 daily; 10kn*), located in the first of the old salt warehouses you reach after crossing the bridge from the old town, is also worth seeing, explaining the history and tradition of salt production on the island over the centuries.

Also revived has been the **Pag Carnival**, in February, a cheerful affair with lots of dressing up, folk music, dancing, parades and processions, and performances of the local play *The Slave Girl of Pag*. It's so much fun that the carnival is repeated at the end of July – and why not? On **Assumption Day** (Velika Gospa, 15 August) a statue of the Virgin Mary is carried in a solemn procession from a shrine in the old town to the Church of the Assumption of the Virgin Mary in the town centre.

NOVALJA AND NORTHERN PAG Much busier and far more developed than Pag is the resort of Novalja, 20km north. Within reach of a whole load of good beaches (notably **Zrče**, **Časka** and **Straško**), it's understandably popular, and well equipped for visitors

Getting there and away The bus station is on the edge of town. From here it's a 15-minute walk to the waterfront from where the catamaran departs for Rab and Rijeka (there's also a shuttle bus service covering the route).

Where to stay and eat There are thousands of private rooms available, and an enormous campsite (*Straško;* ☏ *053 661 226; www.kampstrasko.com;* €), around a third of which is given over to naturists. The sleepier old town, Stara Novalja, is a few kilometres to the north. For something decidedly more upmarket, go for the boutique **Hotel Boškinac** (*Škopaljska ulica 220;* e *info@boskinac.com; www. boskinac.com;* €€€€) in a lovely location about half way between Novalja and Stara Novalja, with its own restaurant and winery. Hotels in Novalja itself include the 14-room **Terra** (*Slatinska 51;* ☏ *053 661 815; www.hotel-terra.hr;* €€€€), and Villa Marija (*Bok bb;* ☏ *053 662 155; www.sanko-novalja.com;* €€€) which has five modern apartments. For more on Novalja, and accommodation contacts, go directly through the Novalja **tourist office** (*Trg Briščić 1;* ☏ *053 661 404; www. visitnovalja.hr*). Expect to pay around €40 for a double room in summer.

What to see and do Two kilometres south of Novalja, just off the main road to Pag town, is the beach of **Zrče**, a kilometre or so of shingle that has become one of Croatia's hippest summer night-time playgrounds, with clubbing until dawn (*http://zrce.eu*). There are three main bars/clubs operational through the summer; the original is **Calypso**, but offshoots of well-known Zagreb clubs – and notably **Aquarius** – have long been setting up camp here, too. There's a shuttle bus from Novalja if you don't fancy the walk.

Also close to Novalja are the meagre ruins of the Roman town of **Cissa** (now Časka), with the best bits being underwater, as the coast sank here. The main attraction is the underground Roman aqueduct, constructed in the 1st century AD, and visitable for around 150m of its length – further excavations are under way.

The island of Pag ends in the narrow 20km-long **Lun Peninsula**, famous for its ancient olive groves (the few trees not cut down by the Venetians), and ending in the quiet fishing village of **Tovarnele**.

SILBA, OLIB & PREMUDA

North of Dugi Otok and Ugljan and west of Pag, the Zadar archipelago ends in the cluster of small islands including Silba, Olib and Premuda. Though little visited by overseas tourists they are a lovely area, far from the madding crowds of Hvar, Brač and other better-known islands, but easily accessible by catamaran and ferry from Zadar, Pula and Mali Lošinj. If you were to ask the updater his favourite Croatian islands, his answer would very likely be Silba (and Vis).

SILBA Silba is the nicest of the three, a lovely, traffic-free oasis home to clean seas and uncluttered beaches, with a good range of private rooms and apartments to choose from. Silba, the main village, is a small place pinched at the centre of the island's hour-glass shape, with only a 5–10-minute walk to the ferry dock and the beaches on either side of the island. Which side of the island you choose to swim on depends as much on the weather as anything else – if the seas are slightly rough on one side, you'll probably find them calm on the other. The **tourist office** (\ *023 370 010; www.tzsilba.hr*) can supply you with a small map and other information.

Getting there and away Silba is connected to Zadar by fast catamaran (*1hr; www.miatours.hr*) and by slower ferry departing from Zadar's Gaženica terminal and continuing to Mali Lošinj (*5hrs; www.jadrolinija.hr*). Another fast catamaran connects Silba with Pula (*3hrs 20mins; http://lnp.hr*), also calling at Mali Lošinj and continuing to Zadar.

🏠 **Where to stay and eat** The village has everything you really need for a week's stay, including a small supermarket, a well-stocked fruit and vegetable stall, and several restaurants and cafés. There's a list of **private accommodation** on the tourist office website (*www.tzsilba.hr/en/iznajmi-apartman*). The owner of your apartment will usually arrange to meet you from the catamaran or ferry, with a small hand-pulled cart on which they'll transport your bags and show you to your accommodation. As well as private accommodation, there's one small pansion,

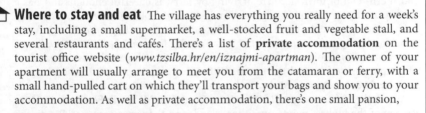

✳🏠 **Fregadon** (6 rooms) \ 023 370 104; www.pansion-silba.com. This small pansion provides an alternative to the private accommodation on the island. Also houses the best restaurant in Silba (€€€–€€) – it is open to non-guests but you need to make a reservation the previous day. A 3-course set meal will set you back around 90knpp excluding drinks. €€€

✕ **Konoba Žalić** ⏲ 11.00–14.00 & 17.00–23.00 daily. Nice little konoba, though not as memorable as Fregadon. €€€–€€
✕ **Leggiero** ⏲ 11.00–23.00 daily. Opposite the supermarket, this does decent pizzas & grills, usually – though the service & food can be quite hit & miss. €€€–€€
🖥 **MIK** ⏲ 07.30–23.00 daily. Just off the main square, this is the best place for a coffee.

UGLJAN AND PAŠMAN

Just a few kilometres offshore from Zadar are the pretty islands of Ugljan and Pašman. Like Cres and Lošinj in the Kvarner Bay, they were originally a single island, but while Cres and Lošinj have been separate for millennia, the (much larger) channel between Ugljan and Pašman was only dug during the 19th century, to help sea traffic on its way.

Most visitors are locals, as neither island has yet been really developed as a package destination. As a result, Ugljan and Pašman are better geared up for individual visits rather than groups, though they're far from empty, with Ugljan being the most densely populated island in the Adriatic (it's practically a suburb of Zadar).

GETTING THERE AND AROUND There are frequent car **ferries** over to Preko on Ugljan from Zadar's Gaženica ferry terminal (*25mins*), with passenger services also running from Zadar's old town (*25mins*); and from Biograd to Tkon on Pašman (*20mins*) (all *www.jadrolinija.hr*). A regular **bus** service runs the length of the two islands – timetables can be found on the Ugljan Tourist Office website and at http://navadriatic.com.

UGLJAN The island of Ugljan is largely dedicated to the cultivation of olives, and some of Croatia's best olive oil comes from here, although it's rarely commercially available. Many of the rest of the inhabitants work in Zadar, while there are lots of mainlanders' second homes on the island, meaning it can get pretty busy on summer weekends.

Preko Just half an hour away from Zadar, Ugljan's main settlement is Preko, an unpretentious little town focused more on day-to-day life than anything like a tourist industry. Ferries come across roughly every hour, all year round, and alternate ones are met by buses heading north up to the town of Ugljan or south to Pašman, passing through Kali and Kukljica on the way. See http://navadriatic.com for bus timetables.

The **tourist office** (*Magazin 8;* \ *023 286 108; www.preko.hr*), towards the far (northern) end of town if you're arriving by ferry, is cheerful enough, and has a list of private rooms (expect to pay around €40 for doubles). Otherwise, for private rooms and apartments, contact either the Rušev agency (*Duga Mocira 12;* \ *023 286 266; www.croadria-rusev.com*) or Nav Travel (*Magazin 5;* \ *023 286 730; http://navadriatic.com*), from where you can also rent out bicycles and boats – great ways of getting yourself around the island. **Villa Eden** (*Jaz 18;* m *098 1652 165; www.eden.hr;* **€€€**) has apartments by the beach at Jaz, around 500m from town.

Worth the 90-minute uphill hike is the trip up to **St Michael's Fortress**. At 250m it's one of the highest points on either island, and the views across to Pag to the north, Dugi Otok to the west, the Kornati archipelago to the south and over to the Velebit massif on the mainland can be absolutely breathtaking. Dating from the early 13th century, the fortress is very much ruined, mostly by time, but also more recently by the Serbs shelling it in 1991. Most of the walking is on asphalt road and it can get extremely hot, so take a hat and water. The nicest hike on the island is the rocky path to the top of the tongue-twisting Šćah, the highest point on the island at 286m, from the village of Turkija.

After your exertions you'll definitely deserve a swim, and Preko has a nice enough town beach, but under 100m offshore is the lovely little wooded island of Galovac, with a 15th-century monastery and the best local beaches. In summer it's easy enough to find a taxi-boat to whisk you across.

Ugljan village The village of Ugljan, 10km north of Preko, is a forgotten sort of place, though it has a lovely beach and a Franciscan monastery you can visit. Ask at the **tourist office** (\ *023 288 011; www.ugljan.hr*) about private rooms, or stay at the **Hotel Ugljan** (*Ugljan 16;* \ *023 288 024; www.hotel-ugljan.hr;* **€€€**), which has reasonable doubles right on the harbour. You can also rent bikes and boats at the hotel. Alternatively, try **Apartmani Galius** (*Gaj 9;* \ *023 288 314; www.apartmaniugljan.com;* **€€€**), which also has its own restaurant.

Kali and Kukljica Heading south from Preko it's not far to the active fishing village of Kali, and a further 5km on to Kukljica, which is a fishing village as well, but also the nearest thing Ugljan has to a holiday resort. The **tourist office** (*Svetog Lovre 2;* \ *023 282 406; www.kali.hr*) can help you find private accommodation; the **Zelena Punta** (\ *023 492 050; www.zelenapunta.hr;* €€€€) tourist settlement consists of apartments and bungalows, which tend to be block-booked months in advance. From here it's barely 2km to the bridge leading over to Pašman.

PAŠMAN Pašman is a smaller, less densely populated, even less developed version of its northern neighbour, and although the number of visitors has been growing every year, that's from a pretty low base.

The island is a popular weekender for locals from Biograd on the mainland, and there are 11 ferries a day all year round (13 in summer) across to **Tkon**, the main settlement in the south of the island (*20mins*). Tkon has a couple of reasonable beaches and a naturist campsite, **Sovinje** (\ *023 285 541; www.fkksovinje.hr*), 2km to the south, with one of the few sandy naturist beaches in Croatia.

Not far from Tkon, on Mount Ćokovac, is the monastery of **Kuzma i Damjan**. Originally a Venetian fortress, built in 1125, it became an important Glagolitic centre, and is today the only active Benedictine monastery in Croatia. The church here was built from 1369 to 1419, and has a fine 14th-century crucifix.

A few kilometres north, on the way to the village of Pašman, at **Kraj**, there's a solid, defensive Franciscan monastery dating from 1390, though much remodelled in the 16th century. The Renaissance cloisters here are lovely, and there's an interesting little museum housing several valuable religious works.

The village of **Pašman** itself, 6km north of Tkon, is the last place of any significance heading towards Ugljan – after that it's one sleepy fishing hamlet after another. There are a handful of private rooms available – there's a list on the website of the **tourist office** (\ *260 260; www.pasman.hr*) – and a couple of pleasant beaches from which to swim.

Between Ugljan and Dugi Otok lies the sheltered island of Iž, which is little more than two harbour settlements – **Mali Iž** and **Veli Iž** – connected by what passes for a road in these parts. There's one hotel on the island, in Veli Iž, the **Korinjak** (\ *023 277 064; http://korinjak.com;* €€€€–€€€ HB), which has 80 fairly simple rooms.

In the past Veli Iž was famous for its pottery, supplying large parts of the coast with clay cooking pots. Local lore has it that potters threw unsold goods into the sea on the homeward voyage, rather than face the shame of having failed to sell them. There's a daily ferry to Iž from Zadar (*40mins*) – don't bother bringing the car.

DUGI OTOK AND THE KORNATI ARCHIPELAGO

Dugi Otok (literally 'long island') and the Kornati archipelago, stretched in a 75km line marking the outer ridge of the Adriatic's submerged mountains, are among the most dramatic and spectacular places in Croatia.

The endless indentations and extraordinary shapes of the islands are a magnet for sailors in summer, and although there's almost nothing as such to do, the wild scenery alone makes for a remarkable visit.

It's easiest to visit the Kornati archipelago as part of an excursion – these are offered from Zadar and Šibenik, and as far away as Trogir and Split, but are best from Murter (page 300), which is home to the park office. Bear in mind that some excursions – from Zadar in particular – only go as far as Dugi Otok's Telašćica Bay (nevertheless a very beautiful nature park) not into Kornati National Park itself. Far and away the finest way to see them, however, is from the deck of your own boat, and the archipelago is understandably popular with nautical tourists, although the sheer number of islands means you'll never find them even the least bit crowded.

DUGI OTOK Dugi Otok is nearly 45km long but never as much as 5km wide. All the attention goes to the two lobster-clawed ends of the island. The tiny resort and harbour of **Božava** is in the northwest, while the island's capital, **Sali**, is in the southeast – this is the closest town to the remarkable Telašćica Bay, a nature park which blends imperceptibly into Kornati National Park at its southern end.

The island has no fresh water supply at all, so it relies on collected rainwater, and in hot summers drinking water has to be ferried over from the mainland; it's not a place to leave taps running. The north is moderately fertile, while the southern end of the island (like most of the Kornati archipelago) is more dramatically barren.

There are a few diving schools on Dugi Otok, including **Kornati Diver Diving Center Eric Šešelja** in Zaglav (m *098 169 3107;* e *info@dive-dugiotok.com; www. kornati-diver.com*) and **Diving School Božava** (☏ *023 318 891;* m *099 591 2264; www.bozava.de*) in Božava – see the Dugi Otok tourist office website, www. dugiotok.hr.

Getting there and around There are two different ferry routes to Dugi Otok from Zadar. The **car ferry** runs three or four times a day, all year round, and takes about 1½ hours to reach Brbinj. There's really nothing much here, in spite of the sometimes busy port and surrounding olive groves, so if you're not driving yourself, try not to miss the connecting bus which meets the ferry and makes the 15km run north to Božava. There's no bus south from Brbinj to Sali, around 20km distant. There is, however, a small **passenger ferry** running three times daily, all year round from Zadar either to Sali or Zaglav (*http://gv-zadar.hr*), 3km north – when it goes to Zaglav there's a bus onwards to Sali – and a catamaran running the same route. In summer there are also various privately operated hydrofoil and ferry services from Zadar to the island.

Dugi Otok's settlements are connected by a single road, although if you're here without your own wheels you'll soon discover there's only one bus a week which connects north with south; and if you do bring your own car, remember there's only one petrol station (at Zaglav). If you want the flexibility to visit both ends of the island and you don't have own wheels (car or bike), you can call on the services of a local **taxi** operator – Taxi Frka (m *098 891 036; www.taxidugiotok.com*) can be highly recommended. Alternatively, begging, borrowing or renting a boat is still one of the best ways of visiting.

Božava and around The fishing village of Božava, with just 112 residents, is a (very) quiet place most of the time, though it's increasingly popular with Italian yachtsmen and women at the height of the season. There's even a mid-sized hotel complex, the eponymous Božava (☏ *023 291 291; www.hoteli-bozava.hr;* €€€€€) which consists of four hotels: the Maxim (the most upmarket), Agava, Lavanda and Mirta. Private rooms can be booked through the tourist office (☏ *023 377 607; www.dugiotok.hr*).

A couple of kilometres northwest of Božava is the even smaller village of **Soline**, at the head of **Soliščica Bay**, which has plenty of swimming opportunities on mostly rocky beaches, heading up towards **Veli Rat**, the northernmost settlement on the island. From here it's a few hundred metres north to the lighthouse, and some popular rocks from which to bathe. If you turn left down a gravel road halfway between Soline and Veli Rat, it's a kilometre or so south to **Sakarun**, a half-kilometre stretch of fine shingle on a truly lovely bay, facing south.

Sali Sali, with over 1,000 inhabitants, is Dugi Otok's social and economic hub. It still derives a good deal more of its revenue from fishing than tourism, though that balance is surely set to change, as more people are visiting every year. The town is understandably popular with sailors, who come here on their way to or from Telašćica Bay, the Adriatic's largest and most dramatic natural harbour, and the Kornati islands.

Sali's **tourist office** (*Obala Petra Lorinja bb;* \ *023 377 094; www.dugiotok.hr*) will help with finding you private rooms. There's also the **Hotel Sali** (\ *023 377 049; www.hotel-sali.hr;* €€€), 300m across the headland to the north, set in pine woods, which rents out bikes – just what you need to cruise over to Telašćica Bay, around 8km each way. **Apartmani Šošterić** (*4 apts;* \ *023 377 050;* m *098 987 5989;* €€), the pink building right beside where the ferry/catamaran from Zadar sets down passengers in Sali, is clean, comfortable and good value.

The tourist office will also point you in the right direction for one of the dive centres here, as well as organising boat trips for you around the island and into the Kornati archipelago – by far the best way of seeing the dramatic scenery. But before you let yourself be whisked off to the Kornati islands, don't miss the spectacular **Telašćica Bay** (*http://pp-telascica.hr; 25kn, valid for 1 day*), a nature park which is just as beautiful (and more easily accessible, if you're already on Dugi Otok) as its more famous neighbour. If you're arriving by sea with your own boat, you can find ticket prices at http://pp-telascica.hr/cjenik.php. Although you can walk the 3km west to the head of Telašćica Bay, it is the farther end of the bay you really want to get to – and most of the walking is on asphalt, so it's really more pleasant to hire a bike or take a taxi (page 298), the latter costing about 70kn per person for the drive out from Sali to the car park at the end of the road, and a pickup at an arranged time. Taxis also take passengers from Sali out to the beach at Saharun and pick them up at the end of the day.

In the southwestern pincer, about 8km from Sali, but still within Telašćica Bay, there is a small string of cafés, and just south of these, a 5-minute walk up through the trees, are some spectacular sea cliffs, some of the highest on the Adriatic. Beyond the cafés is **Mir Bay** ('bay of peace'), which harbours a saltwater lake, connected to the sea by underground karstic channels. The rocks around here are popular with naturists. Donkeys roam this area, but you are not advised to feed them – they have been known to become quite aggressive and bite.

KORNATI NATIONAL PARK (*www.np-kornati.hr; entry per boat per day: 150kn up to 11m, 250kn 11–18m, 450kn 18–25m; per boat for 3 days: 300/500/900kn; per boat for 5 days: 450/750/1350kn*) Eighty-nine of the 140-odd islands, islets and reefs of the Kornati archipelago were declared a national park in 1980, with the boundary also including the spectacular Telašćica Bay on Dugi Otok. It's understandably popular with yachting types, and a great place to learn to sail.

The park is managed from the town of **Murter**, on the island of Murter, connected to the mainland by a drawbridge. As it's the closest place to the national park it's also the best starting point for an excursion – you'll see much more if you're not spending most of the day schlepping your way up the coast from Split or down from Zadar.

Murter's also the place to start if you want to stay on one of the Kornati islands and experience so-called 'Robinson Crusoe tourism'. This represents quite an investment; as you can't normally stay for less than a week, you need to pay for transport as well as accommodation, and it doesn't make much sense not to have your own boat while you're out there.

On the other hand, there are few places in Europe that offer you this much isolation or privacy with such a great climate. In some cases there's no electricity, let alone shops or restaurants, and the cottages have just the bare essentials, though twice a week a supply boat will come and deliver you staples (food, not office supplies), as well as the gas which powers the fridge, cooker and lights. Catching your own fish, grilling it over an open fire, and watching the sun plunging into the sea on a sultry evening is a sure cure for urban stress.

Local house owners with a contract from the national park office authorising them to provide private accommodation are listed on the national park website (*www.np-kornati.hr/en/tourism/accommodations*).

Otherwise, you could try talking to the locals in Murter and negotiating your way out to one of their own houses on the islands – the archipelago is actually the property of the people of Murter, and there's still a certain amount of fishing and agriculture that goes on. Your chances with this particular strategy will be greatly enhanced if you speak Croatian and can handle your rakija.

Even if you're only here on a day trip, you'll see some of the most extraordinary scenery in Europe. Most of the islands are covered in sage and feather grasses, or low scrub, turning the grey karst green, though some also permit the cultivation of figs, grapes and olives.

Where the islands face the open sea, to the southwest, dramatic cliffs plunge into the water. Known locally as 'crowns' (you'll have your wrist slapped if you say 'cliff'), they rise up to around 80m tall, and extend underwater almost as far. The crowns are the most obvious sign of the fault zone running down the Adriatic, the result of sudden tectonic movements in the past.

The highly varied submarine flora and fauna, along with the unusual geomorphology, also make for excellent diving and snorkelling.

Murter

Murter is about 25km up the coast from Šibenik, and is served by half a dozen daily buses (timetables at http://atpsi.hr) – change in Vodice if you're coming from the north. The town itself is nothing special, though there are some pretty good beaches on the island if you have some time to while away.

The **national park office** (*Butina 2;* ℡ *022 435 740; www.np-kornati.hr*) will sell you entry tickets (per boat per day: 150kn up to 11m, 250kn 11–18m, 450kn 18–25m; per boat for 3 days: 300/500/900kn; per boat for 5 days: 450/750/1350kn), an annual fishing licence (something of a bargain at 1kn!), a diving permit (100kn per person, which includes entrance fee – note that diving is strictly controlled and you can only dive as part of an organised diving tour) and good maps, as well as letting you know who's authorised to offer excursions into the park. Note: these are prices for tickets bought outside the park; tickets bought within the park itself cost almost double. There's a list of places selling tickets on the national park website.

There are a number of **agencies** in town who can arrange both day trips and longer stays on the islands, and costs generally include the park entrance fee. Coronata (*Zrtava ratova 17;* ℡ *022 435 933; www.coronata.hr*) and KornatTurist (*Hrvatskih vladara 2;* ℡ *022 435 855; http://murter-active.holiday*) are both reliable.

8

Central Dalmatia

Telephone code 021 (+385 21 from abroad)

Central Dalmatia is wonderfully rich both in cultural sights and the great outdoors – whether it be the stark severity of the **Biokovo massif** above Makarska, or the green islands of **Šolta**, **Brač**, **Hvar** and **Vis** offshore, with their innumerable beaches, bays, coves and fishing villages. Unmissable are the Emperor Diocletian's palace in **Split**, the medieval island town of **Trogir** and the Renaissance elegance of **Hvar** town – along with the extraordinary shingle spit of Zlatni Rat, at **Bol**, and the Blue Cave on **Biševo**, just offshore from the island of Vis, itself only open to tourists since 1989.

TROGIR

UNESCO World Heritage listed Trogir – just 26km up the coast from Split – is one of the most attractive stops in Dalmatia, with the old town being not just excellently preserved but also delightfully car-free. Come here to soak up a pleasantly uncorrupted medieval atmosphere, where stone-carved balconies overhang the narrow streets, and Renaissance and Gothic palaces compete for your attention with the ancient cathedral.

HISTORY Trogir started out in the 3rd century BC as Tragurion, an offshoot of the Greek colony of Issa (on Vis), before being developed as a key port under the Romans. Later overshadowed by Salona (page 315), Trogir grew in importance once again during the 7th century, when Salona was sacked and its refugees came north to Split.

Relative peace under the Croatians and Hungarians came to a sudden halt in 1123, when the Saracens pretty much demolished the city, but prosperity soon returned, and the 12th–14th centuries were a golden age for the town. From 1420 onwards Venice ruled, while from 1797 to 1918 the Austro-Hungarians were in charge – with a short break for Marshal Marmont and the French, from 1806 to 1814. The rest, as they say, is Yugoslavia – until Croatia won independence in 1991.

GETTING THERE AND AROUND Trogir is on the main coast road, so it's easy to reach by **bus** from Zadar (*2½hrs*) or Šibenik (*1hr*) to the north, or Split to the south. It's also the terminus for the local #37 bus from Split – buy a four-zone ticket at a kiosk or on the bus (21kn)– which runs half-hourly, making Trogir an easily feasible day trip from Split (*40mins*) – see www.promet-split.hr for a timetable and click on 'Linije, cienik i vozni redovi'. An even quicker alternative is the regular **coach** that leaves from the Split ferry terminal. (The reverse is also true – if you can get in at one of the private rooms or small hotels in Trogir itself, it's a really attractive option as a base from which to visit Split.)

Split airport is just 10km east of Trogir. There's a shuttle bus from Split (30kn; see www.ak-split.hr for timetables as the airport website and that of the shuttle bus

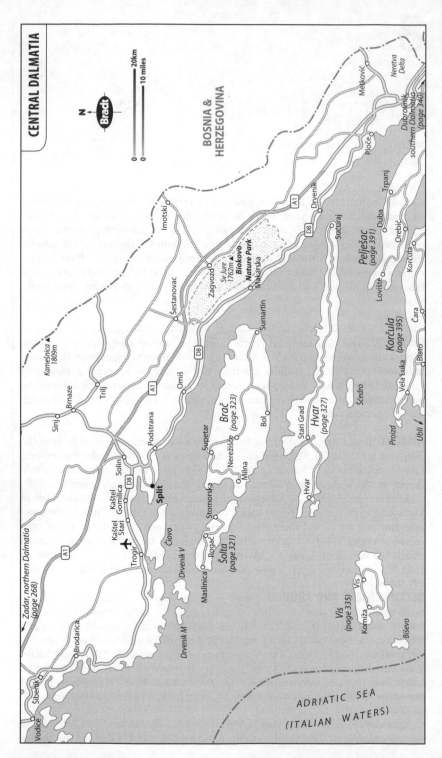

N

Brač

0 ___ 20km
0 ___ 10 miles

BOSNIA &
HERZEGOVINA

ADRIATIC SEA
(ITALIAN WATERS)

Kamešnica ▲
1809m

Imotski

Šibenik

Vodice

Brodarica

Sinj

Brnaze

Trilj

Šestanovac

Omiš

Podstrana

Solin

Split

Kaštel
Gomilica

Kaštel
Stari

Trogir

Čiovo

Drvenik V

Drvenik M

Maslinica

Rogač

Stomorska

Šolta
(page 321)

Supetar

Nerežišće

Milna

Bol

Brač
(page 323)

Sumartin

Zagvozd

Sv Jure
1762m ▲

Biokovo
Nature Park

Makarska

Drvenik

Sućuraj

Stari Grad

Hvar
(page 327)

Hvar

Šćedro

Vis
(page 335)

Komiža

Vis

Biševo

Proizd

Ubli

Vela Luka

Blato

Čara

Korčula
(page 395)

Korčula

Lovište

Pelješac
(page 391)

Orebić

Duba

Trpanj

Ploče

Metković

Neretva
Delta

Dubrovnik
southern Dalmatia
(page 340)

Zadar, northern Dalmatia
(page 268)

A1

D8

D8

D8

A1

A1

operator annoyingly don't bother to include them), and the #37 bus will also drop you off near the airport. A taxi from the airport to Trogir is cheaper than one to Split, but will still cost you well upwards of 100kn. For details of airlines flying to Split, see page 34.

Your only problem might be in leaving, if you're heading north in summer – the coastal buses from Split often arrive here full on their way to Zadar. It's not unheard of to take the #37 back to Split, make an onward reservation, and spend some time sightseeing before heading north again.

Trogir's bus station (more of a bus stop; there are no left-luggage facilities) is right by the stone bridge leading on to the island containing the old town. Just beyond the bridge – and indeed on it – you'll find a colourful local market selling everything from fruit, vegetables and flowers to homemade liquor.

If you're coming in by **car** out of season then cross the stone bridge and immediately turn right along the quay – there's a certain amount of paid parking along here, and the location's perfect. In summer don't even think about this – traffic snarls up a treat. Instead, stop a few hundred metres west of the bridge on the main road into town, and park in one of the several car parks along here.

Once you're in town you'll find it charmingly small – the whole place, connected to the mainland by the stone bridge and to the island of Čiovo by a drawbridge, is barely 500m long and under half that width.

For all things Trogir, have a look at www.trogironline.com.

WHERE TO STAY AND EAT *Map, page 304*

The **tourist office** (✆ 885 628; *www.tztrogir.hr*), on the front facing Čiovo, is friendly and has a map for you. For private rooms head for one of the many agencies in town – try **Sea Gate** (*Kneza Trpimira 133;* ✆ 885 951; *www.sea-gate.net*) or **Kairos** (*Obala Bana Berislavica 23;* ✆ 796 290; *www.kairos-trogir.com*). Rooms in or very close to the old town get snapped up quickly, with doubles going for around €40–60 a night, and there's a 30% surcharge for stays of under five nights here.

Concerning hotels, Trogir has some excellent small, family-run places – but Trogir's a popular place, and you need to book well ahead.

You can also camp, either at **Rozac** (*Okrug Gornji;* ✆ 806 105; *www.camp-rozac. hr*; €) on the island of Čiovo, or **Seget** (*Hrvatskih zrtava 121;* ✆ 880 394; *www. kamp-seget.hr*; €), which is a couple of kilometres west of town, and has all the usual facilities, including windsurfing.

Eating in Trogir is as easy as falling off a log. Practically every square has its own terrace set up in summer for alfresco dining, and the only hard thing is to choose which one suits you best. Booking is essential in high season.

🏠 **Concordia** (11 rooms) Bana Berislavića 22; ✆ 885 400; www.concordia-hotel.net. On the southwestern corner of the front, the lovely Concordia is near the fortress, & great value. €€€€

🏠 **Fontana** (14 rooms) Obrov 1; ✆ 885 744; www.fontana-commerce.htnet.hr. Right by the front in the old town is the reliable Fontana, which boasts nice accommodation; the best room is the top-floor apartment, which is great for families or a couple looking to splash out. Has its own restaurant, with a diverse menu. €€€€

🏠 **Pašike** (13 rooms, 1 suite) Sinjska bb; ✆ 885 185; www.hotelpasike.com. Small, family-run hotel in the old town, with its own restaurant. Free airport transfers with web bookings. €€€€

🏠 **Tragos** (12 rooms) Budislaviceva 3; ✆ 884 729; www.tragos.hr. Small, family-run place with lovely stone-walled interior, right in the heart of the old town, with its own restaurant. €€€€

🏠 **Vila Sikaa** (10 rooms) Kralija Zvonimira 13; ✆ 881 223; www.vila-sikaa-r.com. Across the drawbridge on the Čiovo front, facing back towards Trogir (a lovely view), is the Vila Sikaa, with very

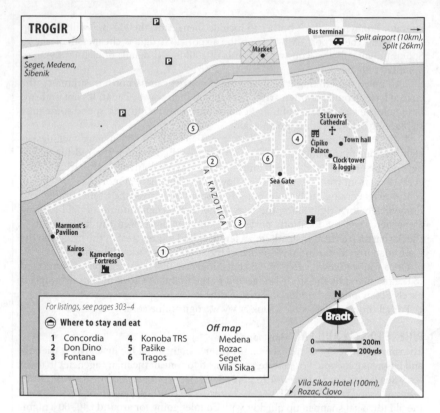

TROGIR

P

Bus terminal · Split airport (10km), Split (26km)

Market

Seget, Medena, Šibenik

P

P

⑤

St Lovro's Cathedral

④ Čipiko Palace · Town hall

② ⑥ Clock tower & loggia

A KAZOTICA

Sea Gate

③

Marmont's Pavilion

Kairos · Kamerlengo Fortress

①

For listings, see pages 303–4

🍴 **Where to stay and eat**

1	Concordia	4	Konoba TRS
2	Don Dino	5	Pašike
3	Fontana	6	Tragos

Off map
Medena
Rozac
Seget
Vila Sikaa

N

Bradt

0 ———— 200m
0 ———— 200yds

Vila Sikaa Hotel (100m), Rozac, Čiovo

---

nice rooms, including superior dbls with spa jets. €€€€

🏠 **Medena** (630 rooms) ✆880 588; www. hotelmedena.com. If Trogir itself fails you – or if you want to swim – then head 4km west to this resort, where you'll find a rocky beach & hundreds of rooms. To get there catch the Medena bus, which runs about hourly; otherwise it's a dullish 50min walk. €€€€–€€€

🍴 **Konoba TRS** Matije Gupca 14; ✆796 956; www. konoba-trs.com; ⏱ 11.00–23.00 daily. Dalmatian specialties cooked with a modern twist by renowned Croatian chef Dragan Grbić. €€€€–€€€

🍴 **Don Dino** Kazotica 8; ✆882 656; www. dondino.hr; ⏱ 11.00–23.00 daily. Popular family-run restaurant in the heart of the old town. €€€

WHAT TO SEE AND DO The old town is entered through a 17th-century gate – hook left and right from here and you'll find yourself on the pretty main square, Trg Ivana Pavla II, home to most of the famous sights, including **St Lovro's Cathedral** (⏱ *09.00–noon & 16.00–19.00 daily; 10kn*).

The cathedral's portal, dating from 1240, is the stunning work of truthful but far from bashful local boy Radovan (look for the inscription above the door: '*per raduanum cunctus hac arte praeclarum*' – 'all of this was made most excellently by Radovan'). Adam and Eve stand apparently appalled at their nakedness, atop two superb Venetian lions. The inner pillars, resting on the shoulders of medieval bugbears (Turks and Jews), frame graphic scenes from the calendar year (labours of the summer and winter months), while above it all sits a superb Nativity.

Inside, the cathedral's a cluttered, sombre place, still used by older local women every morning for prayers. The most important thing to see here is the extraordinary

Ursini Chapel, in the north aisle, which is arguably the most beautiful Renaissance monument in Dalmatia. Sculpted by Nikola Firentinac (Nicholas of Florence) at the end of the 15th century, it's here you'll find those torch-bearing cherubs featured in the tourist board's promotional literature. Other sights within the cathedral include the elaborately carved 15th-century choir stalls, and an octagonal 13th-century pulpit.

Outside, have a good look at the campanile – the first floor's 15th-century early Gothic, the second's pure Venetian Gothic, and the third is late 16th-century Renaissance.

Opposite the entrance to the cathedral is the Venetian **Čipiko Palace** complex, now home to the Čipiko tourist agency. Pop into the hallway and check out the giant wooden cockerel on the wall, a trophy from the prow of some long-forgotten Turkish warship. Across the square is the **town hall** – in the courtyard, you'll see the coats of arms of the ruling families of Trogir.

Completing the square are the town's 15th-century **clock tower** and **loggia**. Both feature more work by Nikola Firentinac, while the loggia also has a large Meštrović bas-relief. Behind the loggia is the oldest surviving pre-Saracen church (**St Barbara's**), dating from the 11th century.

It's a short walk south from here to the Riva and the few remaining preserved parts of the city walls – Marshal Marmont, the Napoleonic administrator in the region from 1806 to 1814, had the rest torn down in an attempt to introduce sea breezes as a cure for malaria. Draining the swampy western end of the island a century later was a far more successful strategy.

Along the lovely Riva you'll find the huge **Kamerlengo Fortress** (⊕ *summer 09.00–19.00 daily; 10kn*). Beyond that Trogir peters out with a football pitch and a small car park, but have a look at **Marmont's Pavilion**, if you're up here – it's a small (and sadly graffitied) memorial to the man who really did try to do his best for Napoleon's short-lived Illyrian Provinces.

Finally, if you want to visit the nearby islands of **Drvenik Veli** and **Drvenik Mali** (they both have some nice beaches), you should ask at the tourist office on Riva (page 303) – there are ferries, but the times aren't always convenient for day trips, and there's nowhere to stay. Both islands are emerging as something of a favourite with foreign second-home owners.

SPLIT *Telephone code 021*

Croatia's second biggest city is a brash and captivatingly energetic hub, with a population of over 200,000 – but the old centre is surprisingly compact and easily manageable on foot. The main draw is Diocletian's Roman palace, just along the Riva from the port where you're likely to arrive – still stunning after more than 1,700 years of builders' alterations. Diocletian no doubt had a monster ego (being emperor has that effect), but even he can't have imagined his retirement home would be so well worth visiting in the 3rd millennium.

Split's a lively, friendly city, and although it wasn't the victim of a Dubrovnik-like siege during the 1991–92 war (just one casualty was sustained here), it suffered the effects of large numbers of refugees coming in and a huge drop in tourism, and unemployment is still high. Happily, that doesn't stop people from having a good time, and the café terraces along the front are packed, practically all year round. Split has also long been a voice of political dissension, and was home to the weekly *Feral Tribune*, a bitingly satirical magazine (and regular thorn in the side of politicians) which was published between 1984 and 2008.

With the fanatically supported local football team, Hajduk Split, enjoying some recent success (and its 100th anniversary in 2011), a modern motorway that connects the city to Zagreb, and several budget airline connections to the UK, not to mention some exceptionally swish hotels which have opened in recent years, Split is clearly on the up and up.

HISTORY Although previously inhabited, Split only officially came into existence when Diocletian retired here in AD305, after 21 years as Roman emperor. The palace – started halfway through Diocletian's reign, in AD295 – was built on a vast 170m-by-190m ground-plan, with walls 2m thick and up to 26m high, making it the largest private residence in antiquity.

Post-Diocletian, the palace continued to be used on and off as a sort of upmarket hotel for the elite, until the Roman Empire finally collapsed. After the Avars burned Salona in 614, refugees moved in permanently, converting chambers into houses, and corridors into streets, using the huge defences to good effect against invading hordes from the north.

Byzantium, the Ottomans, the Austro-Hungarians, the Venetians and Napoleon all left their mark on Split, but it was the Scottish architect, Robert Adam, who practically created it as a tourist destination overnight. Having seen Palladio's drawings, Adam and his team of draughtsmen stopped over in Split for five weeks in 1757, at the tail end of his 'Grand Tour' (tours really were grander then), and made hundreds of drawings and surveys of the palace. Published to huge acclaim in 1764, they came to dominate Georgian architecture, and influenced the future shape of whole tracts of London, Bath, Bristol and Edinburgh.

The name Split is itself relatively recent – the town was probably originally called Aspalatos (after the yellow broom still common round here), before metamorphosing into Spalatum, Spalato and Spljet, and finally settling down as Split.

GETTING THERE AND AROUND Split's international **airport** is 20km/half an hour west of town, almost at Trogir, and flights are met by Croatia Airlines buses, which will run you into town for 30kn (for details of airlines flying to Split, see page 34). Shuttles return to the airport from the air terminal (near the passenger ferry terminal and bus station) 90 minutes before flight departures. For timetables, see www.plesoprijevoz.hr. If you miss the shuttle, local bus #37 also runs half-hourly from Split to the airport and on to Trogir – buy a four-zone ticket on the bus. A **taxi** to or from the airport will set you back around 250kn, though some hotels offer to pick up guests from the airport.

Just to the east of the old town, in a row, you'll find the passenger **ferry** terminal, the train station, the bus station and the car ferry terminal.

Ferries run frequently from Split not just to the local islands of Šolta, Brač and Hvar, but also to Vis, Korčula and Lastovo, as well as up and down the coast to Rijeka and Dubrovnik, and across the Adriatic to Ancona (*11hrs*) – see individual islands for details of ferry and catamaran services. If you're planning on taking your car by ferry anywhere in the summer, reserve as far ahead as you can, or expect a long wait. There are good, cheap left-luggage facilities next to the ferry terminal.

The **train** station is effectively the only coastal railhead south of Rijeka, though the new high-speed rail link to Zagreb is certainly not as high speed as you might expect (*6hrs*). Timetables are available at www.hzpp.hr.

Split's incredibly well connected with everywhere by **bus** – at least a dozen a day go to each of Dubrovnik (*5hrs*), Rijeka (*8hrs*) and Zagreb (*5hrs*). There are also international departures several times a week to destinations in Germany and elsewhere in Europe. Again, book ahead if you can, as buses fill up fast, especially in summer. The bus station has timetables on its website (*www.ak-split.hr*) and a left-luggage office with long hours (⏰ *04.30–22.00 daily*).

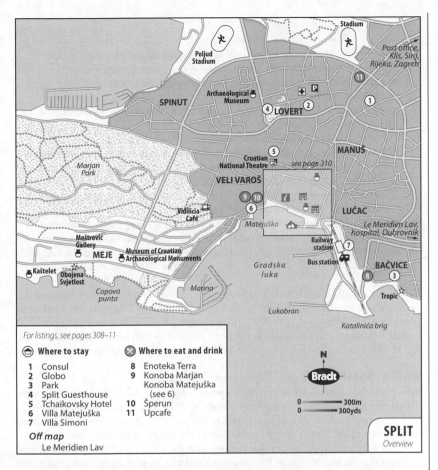

For listings, see pages 308–11

🏠 **Where to stay**

1 Consul
2 Globo
3 Park
4 Split Guesthouse
5 Tchaikovsky Hotel
6 Villa Matejuška
7 Villa Simoni

Off map
   Le Meridien Lav

🍴 **Where to eat and drink**

8   Enoteka Terra
9   Konoba Marjan
    Konoba Matejuška
    (see 6)
10 Šperun
11 Upcafe

SPLIT
Overview

0 ————— 300m
0 ————— 300yds

If you come in by **car** you'll discover that Split has its fair share of traffic problems, and parking can be a major hassle in summer. The best-located **car park** is right on the Riva in front of Diocletian's Palace (10kn for 1 hour, then 15kn/hour after that), but you'll be lucky to find a spot in season. The car parks on Svačićeva and Zr Frankopanska, just north of the old town, are cheaper at 7kn per hour. For more information on car parks and parking, see www.promet-split.hr (Croatian only) and click on 'Parkirališta'.

Once you've arrived, everything's easily reached on foot, though you may end up taking local bus #12 if you're going to the two galleries west of town, or on to the Marjan Peninsula – Split's huge hilltop park, and home to the nearest beaches. Tickets cost 11kn on the bus, less if bought in advance from a kiosk.

Split's main **tourist information** office is located on the Riva (*Obala Hrvatskog Narodnog Preporoda 7;* ✆ *348 600; www.visitsplit.com*). Nearby, the Turist Biro (*Obala Hrvatskog Narodnog Preporoda 12;* ✆ *347 100; www.turistbiro-split.hr*) is just one of the many travel agencies that organises private rooms, and can also give you more detailed information on excursions, etc. Both offices will sell you the **Split Card** for €5– and it's free if you're staying in town for three days or more. This gives you 72 hours' worth of free access to some of the city's museums, half-price access to others, 20% off selected car hire, 10% off your bill at the Park Hotel, 5% off at the

In its heyday the palace must have been extraordinary. At over 30,000m², it included everything from vast reception chambers to temples, arcaded corridors, baths, huge storerooms, extensive private apartments and an entire barracks. No expense was spared in its construction, with materials shipped in from Egypt and Greece, though it was built in a terrible rush, as it had to be ready for the emperor's retirement.

It's thought that Diocletian's wife and daughter never joined him here, in spite of their having lavish residences within the palace, and it's not clear whether he eventually had them killed – or indeed whether or not he himself committed suicide, was murdered, or died a natural death. What is known is that he passed his retirement years in Split having Christians captured, tortured and put to death – so many were martyred, in fact, that Diocletian holds the individual record for saint creation. Fighting Christianity was a losing battle, however – only two years after his death, in AD316, the Milan edict legitimised the religion. Ironically the site of his former tomb is now the city's Christian cathedral.

Bellevue, Consul, Marjan and Split hotels, and 5% off at a number of restaurants. There's also a tourist information kiosk inside Diocletian's Palace, by the cathedral (*Peristil;* ☎ *345 606*).

Last but not least, if you need a laundrette, there's Modrulj Laundrette, at Šperun 1 (☎ *315 888*), just beyond the western end of the marina next to the Šperun restaurant.

 WHERE TO STAY   *Map, page 310, unless otherwise stated*
Split these days has plenty of accommodation options, with several boutique-style **hotels** opening in recent years within the walls of the palace, as well as the five-star Meridien south of the city, which opened late in 2006. Staying in – or anywhere near – Diocletian's Palace doesn't come cheap, especially in season.

There's a good supply of **private rooms**, and these can most easily be arranged through the Turist Biro (page 307) on the Riva, just west of the palace. You'll pay the usual surcharge of 30% for three nights or fewer.

If you come in by boat, train or bus you'll also be offered rooms on arrival – these can be a great deal (bargain assiduously), but bear in mind that Split's a big city and some rooms can be far, far away. Even as seasoned a traveller as Dervla Murphy was caught out here, when she was researching her book *Through the Embers of Chaos* – perhaps ripped off by the same woman as the author a decade earlier when he was researching *Yugoslavia: The Bradt Travel Guide* back at the end of the 1980s. Check the location carefully, and for a realistic idea of where the place actually is, double the time or distance you're told. If you leave your bag at left luggage, you'll have the freedom to reject a room that's too far away, too expensive, or not up to scratch – you'll be back down in this area soon enough anyway. Or just go the simple route and use the Turist Biro.

There are no **campsites** near Split – the closest is 26km southeast, at Omiš.

Luxury

🏠 **Globo** [map, page 307] (33 rooms)
Lovretska 18; ☎ 481 111; www.hotelglobo.com.
Smart 4-star near the Consul, renovated in 2007.
€€€€€

🏠 **Jupiter Heritage Hotel** (14 rooms)
Grabovčeva Širina 1; ☎ 786 500; www.lhjupiter.
com. Once the #1 cheapie backpacker hostel within the palace, now revamped as a boutique luxury hotel. €€€€€

🏠 **Le Meridien Lav** [map, page 307] (381 rooms) Grljevačka 2A; 📞 500 500; www. lemeridienlavsplit.com. Down the coast, 8km south of the city, this 5-star hotel immediately became Split's swankiest on opening at the end of 2006. Smart rooms, excellent service, pools, a spa, restaurant & cocktail bar are just some of the hotel's facilities. There's a hotel shuttle running into town, & a taxi will set you back less than 100kn. €€€€€

🏠 **Park** [map, page 307] (54 rooms) Hatzeov perivoj 3; 📞 406 400/406; www.hotelpark-split. hr. If your budget stretches that far, the renovated 4-star Park is one of the nicest & best located of the town's hotels, just round the headland from the ferry terminal, & set above Bačvice beach, a 10min walk from the old town. Noisy summer Sat night festivities can go on until dawn. €€€€€

🏠 **Peristil** (12 rooms) Poljana Kraljice Jelene 5; 📞 329 070; www.hotelperistil.com. A great option tucked within the walls of Diocletian's Palace right by the peristyle. The staff are genuinely welcoming & will go out of their way to help you. €€€€€

🏠 **Piazza Heritage Hotel** (7 rooms) Kraj Svete Marije 1; 📞 553 377; http://piazza-heritagehotel.com. Boutique luxury in the old town. €€€€€

🏠 **Slavija** (25 rooms) Buvinina 2; 📞 323 840; www.hotelslavija.com. Once the sole preserve of backpackers & students, the Slavija has been reborn with a flash new lobby & cleaned up façade, though the admittedly clean rooms are still relatively basic. A good palace option. €€€€€

🏠 **Vestibul Palace** (7 rooms) Iza Vestibula 4; 📞 329 329; www.vestibulpalace.com. Smart 4-star boutique hotel just up the stairs from the peristyle. Spend the night in the shadows of a Roman emperor on the 2nd tier of Dicoletian's Palace. One of Croatia's only 2 hotels listed on Small Luxury Hotels of the World. High on atmosphere, with stylish, modern, tastefully furnished rooms. €€€€€

Mid-range

🏠 **Adriana** (14 rooms) Obala Hrvatscog Narodnog Preporoda 8 📞 340 000; www.hotel-adriana.com. 3-star with central, waterfront location. €€€€

🏠 **Bellevue** (50 rooms) Bana Jospia Jelačića 2; 📞 345 644; www.hotel-bellevue-split.com. On the western side of the elegant Trg Republike (a minor copy of St Mark's Square in Venice) & a stone's throw from the old town, is a hotel in serious need of a revamp. It was here that President Mitterrand stayed in 1992, during peace talks. €€€€

🏠 **Consul** [map, page 307] (15 rooms) Tršćanska 34; 📞 340 130; www.hotel-consul.net. 10mins' walk north of the old town & palace, with spacious dbls. €€€€

🏠 **Kaštel B&B** (8 rooms) Mihovilova Sirina 5; 📞 343 912; www.kastelsplit.com. Overlooking the Riva at the southwest corner of the palace. €€€€

🏠 **Villa Matejuška** [map, page 307] (6 apts) Tomića stine 3; 📞 321 086; m 098 222 822; www. villamatejuska.hr. Nice & very good-value apts just a few mins' walk from the palace, towards Marijan. Below the apts there is a very highly rated konoba (page 311). €€€

Budget With just a few exceptions, those after 'budget' accommodation in Split will need to aim for private rooms & hostels (for a list of hostels see http://visitsplit.com/en/hostels).

🏠 **Design Hostel** Morpurgova Poljana 2; 📞 510 999; http://gollybossy.com. Large, central, spotlessly clean (& painted bright yellow) modern hostel. *Dbl* €€€€, *dorm* €

🏠 **BASE Rooms** (3 rooms) Kraj Svetog Ivana 3; 📞 317 375; m 098 361 387; www.base-rooms. com. Very good value, right next to the Temple of Jupiter. €€€

🏠 **Villa Simoni** [map, page 307] (7 rooms, 4 apts) Zlodrina Poljana bb; 📞 488 780; m 098 979 0757; www.sobesimoni.com. First-rate place, conveniently located just behind the railway station, on the far side of the tracks – clean, efficient, friendly & a bargain at 400kn for a dbl in summer. No credit cards. €€€

🏠 **Split Guesthouse** [map, page 307] (20 beds) Lovretska 1; m 091 303 0105; www. splitguesthouse.hostel.com. Popular and homely, centrally located hostel with dbl, 4- and 6-bed dorms, 400m from the National Theatre. €

🏠 **Tchaikovsky Hostel** [map, page 307] (20 beds) Ulica Petra Ilíča Čajkovskog 4; 📞 317 124; m 099 195 0444; http://tchaikovskyhostel.com. Popular centrally located hostel with 4- and 6-bed dorms, 20 minutes' walk from the bus station just beyond the National Theatre. €

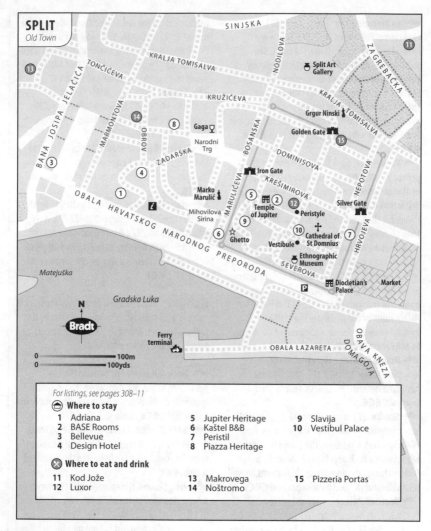

SPLIT
Old Town

SINJSKA

KRALJA TOMISLAVA

TONČIĆEVA

KRUŽIĆEVA

NODILOVA

ZAGREBAČKA

Split Art Gallery

KRALJA TOMISLAVA

Grgur Ninski

BANA JOSIPA JELAČIĆA

MARMONTOVA

OBROV

ZADARSKA

Gaga

Narodni Trg

BOSANSKA

Golden Gate

DOMINISOVA

Pizzeria Portas (15)

Iron Gate

NEPOTOVA

Marko Marulić

MARULIĆEVA

KREŠIMIROVA

Temple of Jupiter

Peristyle

Silver Gate

Mihovilova Sirina

Ghetto

Vestibule

Cathedral of St Domnius

HRVOJEVA

Ethnographic Museum

OBALA HRVATSKOG NARODNOG PREPORODA

SEVEROVA

Diocletian's Palace

Market

Matejuška

Gradska Luka

N

Bradt

OBALA LAZARETA

OBAVA KNEZA DOMAGOJA

Ferry terminal

0 ———— 100m
0 ———— 100yds

For listings, see pages 308–11

🛏 **Where to stay**

1	Adriana	5	Jupiter Heritage
2	BASE Rooms	6	Kaštel B&B
3	Bellevue	7	Peristil
4	Design Hotel	8	Piazza Heritage

9 Slavija
10 Vestibul Palace

✖ **Where to eat and drink**

11	Kod Jože	13	Makrovega	15	Pizzeria Portas
12	Luxor	14	Noštromo		

✖ WHERE TO EAT AND DRINK *Map, above, unless otherwise stated*

There are relatively few really good restaurants in Split's tourist-oriented old town, though this is compensated for by some very good eateries elsewhere. If you're looking for your own ingredients there's an excellent daily market just to the east of the palace, while on the west side of town you'll find the famous fish market. The smell here has more to do with the sulphur spa next door than the fish itself, which is guaranteed super-fresh.

✖ **Enoteka Terra** [map, page 307] Braće Kaliterne 6; 📞314 800; www.vinoteka.hr; ⊕ 10.00–midnight Mon–Sat, 11.00–midnight Sun. A cosy option, set below street level in a candlelit cellar just back from Bačvice. Feast on tapas-style Croatian dishes, such as spicy kulen sausage from Slavonia, pršut from the Dalmatian hinterland & truffle-infused mushroom bruschetta, before moving on to more substantial dishes. A highlight is the excellent English explanations of the various wines on offer. €€€€

🍴 **Noštromo** Kraj Sv Marije 10; m 091 405 6666; www.restoran-nostromo.hr; 🕘 11.00–23.00 daily. Upscale restaurant adjacent to the fish market, with some of the best seafood in town, including dependable grilled fish & generous fish platters. €€€€–€€€

★🍴 **Kod Jože** Sredmanuška 4; ☎ 347 397; 🕘 10.00–midnight Mon–Fri, noon–midnight Sat/Sun. On the far side of the park behind the palace, hidden down a side street, this homely, well-priced konoba does excellent seafood, as well as other dishes such as rich & authentic gnocchi with game. Recommended. €€€

🍴 **Konoba Marjan** [map, page 307] Senjska 1; m 98 934 6848. Popular konoba at the bottom of Senjska. €€€

🍴 **Konoba Matejuška** Tomića stine 3; ☎ 355 152; m 095 909 9131; www.konobamatejuska.hr; 🕘 08.00–23.00 daily. Below the guesthouse of the same name (page 309), traditional Dalmatian dishes in a rustic interior. €€€

★🍴 **Šperun** [map, page 307] Šperun 3; ☎ 346 999; 🕘 09.00–23.00 daily. Bags of character just off the Riva in Varoš. Choose between the handful of tables outdoors or descend into the main body of the restaurant, which is awash with bric-a-brac & Croatian flags. Mainstays include fresh fish simply grilled, seafood risotto & some hearty meat dishes. Excellent value. Recommended. €€€

🍴 **Upcafe** [map, page 307] Domovinskog rata 29a; www.upcafe.hr; 🕘 07.00–21.00 Mon–Fri, 07.00–20.00 Sat, 08.00–20.00 Sun. Another refreshingly healthy option, under the same ownership as Makrovega. €€€

🍴 **Makrovega** Leština 2; ☎ 394 440; www.makrovega.hr; 🕘 09.00–20.00 Mon–Fri, 09.00–17.00 Sat. Essential calling point for vegetarians travelling in Dalmatia, or anyone else who wants a refreshing break from seafood & grills. €€€–€€

★🍴 **Pizzeria Portas** Kod zlatnih vrata 1; ☎ 482 888; 🕘 08.00–23.00 daily. Formerly called Pizzeria Grgur, this is still the place to go for reliable pizzas in the old town, with a lovely terrace. Just around the corner from the Golden Gate. Recommended. €€€–€€

☕ **Luxor** Kraj sv Ivane 11; 🕘 09.00–midnight daily. Arguably the most atmospheric location for a coffee in Split, with cushions outside on the 2,000-year-old stone slabs of the peristyle itself.

ENTERTAINMENT AND NIGHTLIFE Split is certainly not short on bars and clubs. **Gaga** (*Iza Lože 5; 🕘 until 02.00*) is the city's favourite cocktail bar, located in the open market near the palace. Inside the palace walls, **Ghetto** (*Dosud 10; 🕘 until midnight*) is Split's coolest club, with an underground, bohemian feel, and as popular with locals as it is with tourists. Outside the palace walls, Split's answer to Ibiza is the ever-popular **Tropic** (*Bačvice; f Tropic Club; 🕘 until 05.00*), at Bačvice beach; a less well-known alternative is **Obojena Svjetlost** (*Šetalište Ivana Meštrovića 35; 🕘 until 03.00*), near the Meštrović Gallery on Kasuni beach.

For something more sedate, there's the **Croatian National Theatre** (*Trg Gaje Bulata 1; ☎ 306 908; www.hnk-split.hr*).

OTHER PRACTICALITIES Split's main **hospital** with an accident and emergency department is at Spinčićeva 1 (*Clinical Hospital Firule; ☎ 556 111; www.kbsplit.hr*). For a list of **pharmacies**, see www.visitsplit.com/en/236/pharmacies. The main **post office** is at Hercegovačka 1.

WHAT TO SEE AND DO The main draw is clearly the former palace, on the Riva, though what you see now, inside the old walls, is an entire town, centred on Diocletian's peristyle. Around 3,000 local people still live within the walls – barely fewer than in Dubrovnik's much bigger old town – so you'll find the cafés and bars catering to a healthy mix of both visitors and residents.

Enter the old town from the Riva, which is actually reclaimed land – the gate you go through (known as the Brass Gate) was originally on the sea. It was built to be used as an emergency escape route for Diocletian in case of trouble, but may also have seen service as a delivery entrance. The gate leads through a semi-underground chamber, now a small crafts market, flanked by chambers you can visit before climbing some worn steps up into the peristyle.

The peristyle The peristyle (*peristil*), an open, colonnaded square, was the public heart of Diocletian's Palace, and is still an extraordinary place to sit and wonder. Everything off to the south (towards the sea, behind you) was originally Diocletian's imperial quarters, while to the north were servants' lodgings and soldiers' barracks.

The pink granite columns are Egyptian, while their capitals are Corinthian. You can see that even originally there were four antique columns too few, with local marble pillars making up the difference. The cracked black sphinx dates back to the reign of Thutmosis III, who ruled Egypt from 1504 to 1450BC (though how anyone knows these things for certain beats me), and was originally one of ten imported for Diocletian from the land of the Pharaohs. Another four survive, in varying states of repair – one in the underground chambers, one in the Temple of Jupiter and two in the Archaeological Museum.

The streets out of the peristyle lead to the palace's other three gates – north, to the Golden Gate (the main entrance, coming in from Salona), east, to the Silver Gate, and west, to the Iron Gate. On the peristyle itself you'll find the **Vestibule** (above the podrum – see page 313), the **cathedral** (actually Diocletian's mausoleum), and off down an alley to the other side the Baptistery of St John (the **Temple of Jupiter** – Diocletian reckoned he was Jupiter's son). Inside the barrel-vaulted temple (also known as the Temple of Aesculapius) you should be able to see a couple of classical statues, an interesting 11th-century baptismal font, and a statue of John the Baptist by Meštrović.

The Vestibule was the main entrance hall to the imperial quarters. The domed roof has long gone, along with the ornate mosaics that would have lined it, but it's worth walking through here and circling round to the left, back to the cathedral, for some idea of where Diocletian lived – this was originally the dining halls and Roman baths. There are some mosaics here, hidden under protective sand, awaiting restoration.

The Cathedral of St Domnius (*Sv Duje;* ⊕ *08.00–19.00 Mon–Sat, noon–18.00 Sun; 15kn*) In a move that must have had Diocletian whirling in his sarcophagus, the emperor's mausoleum was long ago converted into one of Christianity's smallest cathedrals, honouring one of his own victims, St Domnius.

The main structure, including the dome, is original, dating from AD300, but the choir is a 17th-century addition. The entrance doors, with 28 excellent carved wooden panels describing the life of Christ, date from 1214 – the lower four panels have been damaged by centuries' worth of being pushed open by booted feet.

At the base of the dome there's a pagan-looking frieze, and what are said to be medallions of the heads of Diocletian and his wife. Diocletian's ahead of you as you come in, while his wife is two medallions to the left. Down below, the 13th-century pulpit may be a Romanesque masterpiece by Radovan (he of Trogir fame), but to my eye it's too big for the space it's in. The Baroque 17th-century chapel is the one housing the Domnius relics; the other two chapels are 15th-century Gothic. Finally, the choir itself may be 17th-century, but the stalls are around the same age as the cathedral doors, and are a fine example of early Dalmatian woodcarving.

Take the time to climb up inside the campanile for an excellent view over the palace and out to sea – this version dates from 1908, following the collapse of the original, which was built in stages from the 13th to 17th centuries.

Underneath the cathedral is the spooky circular crypt, dedicated to St Lucy, patron saint of the blind (legend has it that Diocletian put her eyes out). The function of this chamber in antiquity isn't known – it's unlikely that it would have been a prison, being under a mausoleum, but large numbers of human bones were found here, and it is the kind of damp, gloomy, airless place you could imagine being used as a dungeon. Ask in the cathedral if you want to see the crypt – it's not always open.

The basement halls (*podrum*) Don't miss the chance to see the huge semi-underground chambers that provided the foundations for the imperial quarters above. The only whole rooms remaining from the original palace, they give some idea of the sheer scale and size of Diocletian's ego. Remarkably, these chambers only survive because of sewage – during the Middle Ages, people simply threw their slops down holes in the floor, and it accumulated here, protecting the rooms from future squatters.

After World War II, the western rooms were cleared out and opened to the public, while the eastern wing wasn't excavated until 1997 – at various points you can see the original waste chutes coming in from above, along with the foundations of medieval houses. The halls are now used for temporary exhibitions, but look out for a few original curiosities, including some mosaics that clearly pre-date the palace – they run underneath Diocletian's walls – and a marble *mensa*, a Roman table with raised edges for resting your forearm on.

Beyond the palace Just outside the Golden Gate you can hardly fail to spot Meštrović's monumental 1928 statue of **Grgur Ninski**. Originally standing in the peristyle (which looked pretty wild – there's a photo in the first edition of Rebecca West's *Black Lamb and Grey Falcon*), the statue commemorates the 10th-century Bishop Gregorius of Nin, who tried (but failed) to introduce Croatian instead of Latin into the liturgy. According to local tradition, touch his big toe and your wish will come true – which explains why it's been worn golden.

Walk west a block and head down Marulićeva Bosanska, the narrow street separating the palace from the rest of the old town. This is the least well-preserved wall of the palace, with an unbroken row of houses built into the original fortifications. On the left-hand side, unmarked, is Split's first **synagogue** – Europe's third, after Prague and Dubrovnik.

Halfway down the street is the palace's **Iron Gate**, which leads out into the old town's main square, Narodni Trg (also known as Pjaca, pronounced piazza). Palazzi from different periods surround the square, with a Venetian Gothic town hall standing on one side and an Austrian Secessionist palace dominating the square's west end. The next square to the south, just off Riva, has an excellent statue of **Marko Marulić**, the father of Croatian literature, who died in 1524 but is still widely celebrated, and indeed read. Yes, you guessed – it's by Meštrović.

The old town's western boundary is the elegant shopping thoroughfare of Marmontova, named after Napoleon's Marshal Marmont, the captain of his Illyrian Provinces, and the man responsible for both the Riva – Narodni Trg had got too small to function as a collective town square – and Trg Republike, now used for summer concerts.

West of the town you'll find the popular old quarter of **Veli Varoš**, which leads up the slopes of the 182m **Marjan Peninsula**, Split's own city park, featuring woods, picnic areas and beaches – a great place to get away from the crowds, though very popular with the locals at weekends. Stop in at **Vidilicia Café** for a cooling drink with a view over Split under a relaxed terrace, as the city unfolds below and the islands beckon in the distance.

Central Dalmatia SPLIT

8

Museums and galleries Split has several museums and galleries of particular note, one within the palace, two about a 15-minute walk north (head up Zrinko Frankopanska, from the top of Marmontova), and two a 20-minute walk west on to the Marjan peninsula – or a short hop on local bus #12 from Trg Republike.

Archaeological Museum (*Arheološki Muzej; Frankopanska 25;* ✆ *329 340; www. armus.hr;* ☉ *Jun–Sep 09.00–14.00 & 16.00–20.00 Mon–Sat, Oct–May 09.00–14.00 & 16.00–20.00 Mon–Fri, 09.00–14.00 Sat; 20kn*) Heading north the secessionist Archaeological Museum houses Croatia's biggest collection of remains from antiquity, and especially is strong (unsurprisingly) on artefacts from Salona (see box, page 315). The Roman findings include excellent glass, jewellery, ceramics and statues, featuring some extraordinarily rich sarcophagi. There's also an extensive collection from very early Christianity.

Ethnographic Museum (*Etnografski Muzej; Iza Vestibula 4;* ✆ *344 164; www. etnografski-muzej-split.hr;* ☉ *Jun–Sep 09.30–20.00 Mon–Sat, 09.30–13.00 Sun, Oct– May 09.00–16.00 Mon–Fri, 09.00–13.00 Sat; 15kn*). Now moved from Narodni trg to the Vestibule, with a good collection of folk costumes.

Split Art Gallery (*Galerija Umjetnina Split; Kralja Tomislava 15;* ✆ *350 112; www.galum.hr;* ☉ *10.00–19.00 Tue–Sat; 20kn*) Has a terrific collection of paintings from the 14th century onwards. Unless you're an expert on Croatian art you won't recognise many of the names, but make the effort to come here and you'll find a rich tradition of painting which is especially strong on late 19th- and early 20th-century works, including a couple of masterpieces by Vlaho Bukovac (see box, page 378).

Museum of Croatian Archaeological Monuments (*Muzej Hrvatskih Arheoloških Spomenika; Stjepana Gunjace bb;* ✆ *323 901; www.mhas-split.hr;* ☉ *09.00–13.00, 17.00–20.00 Mon–Fri, 09.00–13.00 Sat; free*) Heading west from the old town, a 15-minute walk will get you to this unusual and fascinating collection of Croatian artefacts from the 7th century on, housed in a wonderfully airy modern building. Around 5,000 items are on display (from a collection of more than 20,000 in total), running from old jewellery and stone inscriptions to a unique series of monuments from early Croatian churches, including gables, friezes, altar canopies and baptismal fonts. Worth buying the English guide for full information.

Meštrović Gallery (*Galerija Ivana Meštrovića; Šetalište Ivana Meštrovića 46;* ✆ *340 800; www.mdc.hr/mestrovic;* ☉ *May–Sep 09.00–19.00 Tue–Sun, Oct–Apr 09.00–16.00 Tue–Sat & 10.00–15.00 Sun; 30kn*) Five minutes west of the Museum of Croatian Archaeological Monuments is this vast mansion built by the sculptor between 1931 and 1939, and intended both as a museum and as his retirement home – instead, he emigrated to the USA, dying there in 1962. If you're even remotely interested in Meštrović – and you should be – then this comprehensive collection is the best anywhere. Outside is the sculpture garden; indoors, the full range of the sculptor's work can be seen, from family portraits to religious tableaux, to allegorical works.

Kaštelet (*Meštrovićeve Crikvine Kaštilac; Šetalište Ivana Meštrovića 39;* ✆ *340 800; www.mdc.hr/mestrovic;* ☉ *May–Sep 09.00–19.00 Tue–Sun, Oct–Apr by appointment*) The same entry ticket for the Meštrović Gallery is also valid here, just down the road at number 39, which Meštrović bought to house one of his most important works, a series of large wooden friezes dedicated to the life of Christ, and which (pre)occupied the sculptor on and off from around 1916 until its completion in 1950.

AROUND SPLIT

Klis Just 9km north of Split, on the road to Sinj, are the magnificent monumental ruins of the fortress at Klis (Tvrđava Klis), situated along the length of a 340m hill. It was captured by the Turks in 1537 and remained in their hands for just over a century until the Venetians got their own back in 1648. Today there's not a great deal to see, but the ruins are highly atmospheric and make for a superb picnic spot. Look out also for the trio of informal restaurants that dish up first-rate local lamb simply served with crusty bread. You can reach Klis either by taking the #34 or #36 bus to Klis–Megdan (where you'll find the fortress entrance), or by taking the Sinj bus to Klis–Varoš, and hiking up the hill from there. By car, take the old road from Solin (rather than the new road from Split to Sinj), and turn left at the Tvrđava sign.

Sinj Thirty kilometres out of Split is the town of Sinj, famous mainly as the scene for the annual **Sinjska Alka**, a festival celebrating the 1715 victory over numerically superior Turks. Taking place over three days leading up to the first Sunday in August, with the main tournament on the Sunday itself, the Alka is a knightly tournament in which metal rings suspended on a wire have to be speared at full gallop by chaps in traditional costume. It's all very noisy and colourful, and one of only two places where the time-honoured Tilting at the Ring still takes place (the other is in the village of Barban, in Istria – see page 220). The other main event is the huge procession and pilgrimage, on the **Feast of the Assumption** (Velika Gospa, 15 August), of the Madonna of Sinj – the 15th- or 16th-century painting with which the victory of 1715 is popularly associated.

Half-hourly buses from Split will bring you to Sinj in under an hour.

SALONA

If you know your archaeology, a trip out to Salona (now called Solin) might interest you – though be warned that anything which could be carried off has been carried off (some of the best pieces are in the Split Archaeological Museum), meaning you'll need to rely heavily on your imagination if you're going to people the dusty fields here with temples, houses, markets and an amphitheatre capable of seating nearly 20,000 people.

Salona is 5km north from the centre of Split, and is best reached on the #1 bus, which drops you off at the Caffe Bar Salona, at the entrance to the site. There's a small archaeological museum here (an offshoot of the one in town), called Tusculum, where you can pick up a local map – after which you're on your own to wander across the worn grass and traces of the extensive ruins of the city, home to around 60,000 people in the 1st century AD.

The amphitheatre is the most impressive ruin, though there's very little left beyond the foundations. The Venetians carted off most of the stone in the 17th century, and used it for local building works and fortifications, claiming the dismantlement was only to prevent the Turks from using the amphitheatre as a hideout.

If you've come this far, the quickest way back to Split is on the #37 city bus. Cross the new highway using the underpass, and walk towards Solin centre until you get to the bus stop.

Where to stay and eat The **Hotel Alkar** makes a good place to stay in Sinj (*Vrlička 50;* ☎ *824 474; www.hotel-alkar.hr;* **€€€**), otherwise the friendly and helpful tourist office (*Put Petrovca 12;* ☎ *826 352; www.visitsinj.com*) has details of private rooms available. Accommodation can be hard to find during the Alka, so book far ahead if you can. For a town its size, Sinj has a lot of bars and cafés on the cobbled streets around the Church of the Miraculous Madonna of Sinj – and you can expect all of them to be full to bursting point after the Alka.

The two best places to eat are **Konoba Ispod Ure** (*Istarska 2;* ☎ *822 229;* ⊕ *07.00–23.00 Mon–Sat, 10.00–23.00 Sun;* **€€€–€€**) and **Konoba Potkova** (*Alkarsko trkalište 22;* ☎ *822 792;* ⊕ *07.00–23.00 Mon–Sat, 10.00–23.00 Sun;* **€€€–€€**), both of which have delicious food and friendly service in a low-key, rustic setting.

MAKARSKA/BIOKOVO

The 100km or so of coast south of Split, to **Drvenik**, is a long string of pebbly beaches, broken only by the **Cetina Gorge** which cuts through the mountains to emerge at **Omiš**, once home to audacious pirates but now a rather half-hearted resort, given over as much to industry as to tourism. Rafting trips are also possible in the gorge, ask at Omiš **tourist information** (*Trg Kneza Mislava;* ☎ *861 350; www.visitomis.hr*) for details.

Twenty kilometres beyond Omiš, **Brela** marks the start of the 60km-long **Makarska Riviera**, a series of cheerfully touristy villages and beaches sheltered by the solid mass of Biokovo to the northeast. If you want to stay in Brela, try **Abuela's Beach House** (*Jardula 20;* ☎ *619 003;* 📱 *091 155 5044; www.abuelasbeachhouse.com;* **€€€€–€€€**), which has four spacious, colourfully decorated apartments with balconies and sea views, 3km outside the town centre and just 50m from the sea.

MAKARSKA At the heart of the Makarska Riviera is Makarska itself, a small but busy town, tastefully restored in stone after the devastating 1962 earthquake. With a lovely palm-studded front and a 2km beach across the Sveti Petar headland, it's a perfect sunny stop if you're travel-weary and footsore. If you don't have sore feet, then Makarska's also the gateway to some of the most spectacular hiking in Croatia, on the Biokovo massif, home to four rare species of eagle (golden, imperial, grey and snake) and culminating in one of the country's highest peaks, Sveti Jure, at 1,762m.

Getting there and away Without your own wheels, you'll be arriving in Makarska either by bus or ferry. Ferries come in from Sumartin, on the eastern end of Brač, four times a day in winter and five times in summer, while at least ten daily buses stop in on their way from Split to Dubrovnik, and vice versa. There are direct buses to both Rijeka (*9hrs*) twice daily, and Zagreb (*6½hrs*), several times daily.

Where to stay and eat From the bus station, on Ante Starčevića, the main road running above the town, it's a 5-minute walk downhill to the front, where you'll find everything you need. The **tourist office** (*Kralja Tomislava 16;* ☎ *612 002; www.makarska-info.hr*) has maps and information and can put you in touch with any number of agencies handling rooms and excursions, including the Turist Biro (*Kralja Tomislava 2;* ☎ *611 688; www.turistbiro-makarska.com*). **Private rooms** (doubles) go for €30–50 depending on level of comfort and location, with the usual 30% surcharge for three nights or fewer. The nearest **campsite** is at Camp Jure (*Ivana Gorana Kovačića bb;* ☎ *616 063; www.kamp-jure.com; 2 people plus pitch around €30*), on the northwestern edge of town, which also has bungalows and mobile homes which sleep four to six people for €117–128. Most of the big **hotels** in Makarska are on the town's long pebble beach, across the headland to the northeast of town. Makarska has no shortage of **eateries** along the front, where terraces spill out across the pavement, and slightly cheaper places a block or two back from the sea. There's also an excellent daily market, if you're looking for picnic food, just up from the town's only old square, Kačićev Trg.

🏠 **Porin** (7 rooms) Marineta 2; ☎613 744; www.hotel-porin.hr. Lovely 19th-century building, once the local library, renovated & converted into a hotel in 2002. €€€€€

🏠 **Biokovo** (55 rooms) Kralja Tomislava; ☎615 244; http://holidaymakarska.com. Right on the waterfront in the middle of town. With any number of busy late-night terraces on the Riva below it, you may be glad of the AC & double-glazing. €€€€

🏠 **Maritimo** (19 dbls, 1 suite) Put Cvitačke 2a; ☎619 900; www.hotel-maritimo.hr. Recently opened small, beachfront boutique hotel, towards the northwestern edge of town. €€€€

🏠 **Meteor** (270 rooms) Kralja Petra Kresimira IV; ☎564 200; www.hoteli-makarska.hr. The triangular front gives most rooms a generous sunny balcony, & the hotel has a good pool. €€€€

🏠 **Osejava** (10 rooms) Šetaliste Dr Fra Jure Radića bb; ☎604 300; www.osejava.com. Built on the same waterfront location as what was once Makarska's most famous hotel back in the 1920s, this is a new boutique number. €€€€

🏠 **Pension Batešić** (3 rooms) Kipara Meštrovića 25; ☎612 974; m 095 821 3105; http://batosic.com. Small, family-run pansion with a breakfast terrace, all rooms with AC, balcony and en suite. Dinner & boat trips available. Excellent value. €€–€

What to see and do Makarska isn't a place you come to for culture – it's a town with a great beach and even better hiking up in the mountains – so the sights can be comfortably counted off on the fingers of one hand. On Kačićev Trg there's the 18th-century St Mark's Church (usually closed), while at the eastern end of town you'll find Croatia's finest **malacological museum** (*Franjevački put 1;* ☎ *611 256;* ⊕ *09.00–13.00 & 17.00–20.00 daily; 15kn*) – that's seashells, to you – housed in the cellars of the Franciscan Monastery. The collection of more than 3,000 shells from around the world was put together by one of the Franciscan monks, Jure Radić, and opened in 1963. Radić also founded the botanical gardens in Kotišina (page 319).

A couple of kilometres along the coast to the north there's a curious shrine at the **Vepric Cave** (Vepric Špilja). Inaugurated in 1908, on the 50th anniversary of the apparitions in Lourdes, the sanctuary was founded by Bishop Carić (who was buried here on his death in 1921) and dedicated to Our Lady of Lourdes. It is popular with pilgrims, and is especially busy on 11 February, 25 March, 15 August and 7–8 September.

Finally, if you're here in May, don't miss Makarska's spectacular rowing regatta, which proves the town hasn't entirely forgotten its Venetian legacy.

BIOKOVO The Biokovo massif rises up steeply above the Makarska Riviera in three ever-more steep shelves, providing hiking at all levels and fabulous views, but if you're coming here to head up into the mountains don't underestimate them, and start out as early in the day as you can. The weather can change very quickly, there's no water or food to be had once you're out, and the karst limestone is hard on even the toughest hiking boots. It's highly inadvisable to go out far if you're alone. If you run into trouble, it's unlikely anyone would find you, and – without wishing to sound alarmist – you should remember there are still wolves in the wild up here. A large part of the massif was designated a **nature park** in 1981.

Hiking in the Biokovo Nature Park (*www.pp-biokovo.hr; 50kn, tickets valid – rather meanly – for 1 day*) The two main summits reachable from Makarska are

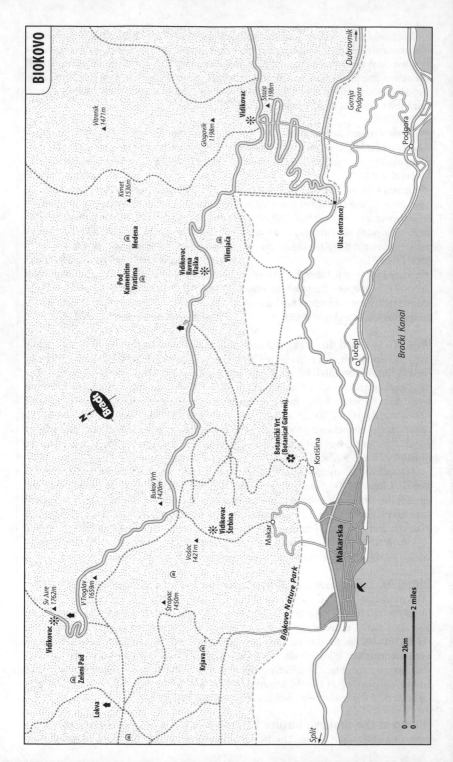

BIOKOVO

Vitrenik
▲ 1471m

Kimet
▲ 1536m

Glogovik
1198m ▲

Vidikovac
※

Staza
1198m ▲

Dubrovnik →

Gornja
Podgora

Podgora

Medena

Pod
Kamenitim
Vratima

Vidikovac
Ravna
Vlaska
※

Vilenjača

Ulaz (entrance)

Tučepi

Brački Kanal

Brač
N

Bukov Vrh
▲ 1420m

Botanički Vrt
(Botanical Gardens)

Kotišina

Vidikovac
Štrbina
※

Makar

Sv Jure
▲ 1762m

V Troglav
1659m ▲

Vošac
1421m ▲

Stropac
1450m

Makarska

Vidikovac ※

Zeleni Pad

Lokva

Krjava

Biokovo Nature Park

Split →

0 ——— 2km
0 ——— 2 miles

Vošac (1,420m or thereabouts; a 3½-hour hike one-way) and **Sveti Jure** (1,762m; allow a good 5 hours up and 4 hours back).

There are two paths up out of town leading to Vošac and on to Sveti Jure, one going via the village of **Makar**, and the other via the village of Kotišina. Once you get to either village the trail is well signed with red and white flashes, but pick up a map from the tourist office before you head out.

In either case, start off from Kačićev Trg, pass the church and market, and cross the main road, continuing up **Put Makra** until you reach the next main road, Dubravačka. For the Makar route you should then stay on the continuation of Put Makra until you reach the village. For Kotišina turn right after 200m up Put Mlinica, which leads to the village of **Mlinice**, from which you'll see signs for the path to Kotišina. Both Makar and Kotišina are at around 200m above sea level and take around 45 minutes to reach on foot from the seafront.

The village of Kotišina was definitively abandoned after the 1962 earthquake, but locals still keep weekenders up here. It's well worth a visit, not just because of the interesting **fortress** built right into the rock here, but also because of the **Botanički Vrt**, the botanical gardens founded by Jure Radić. Radić knew more than anyone about the flora of Biokovo and built the gardens here – more an oversized rockery – as a plant haven. Sadly, since his death in 1990, it has all fallen somewhat into disrepair.

From Makar or Kotišina it's a tough hike to the summit of Vošac, but the views once you get there are absolutely stupendous, way out across the sea and islands. Beyond Vošac, it's another hour and 45 minutes, the last part of it quite steep, to **Sveti Jure**, the highest point on the massif. At the top, there's a little church completely dwarfed by a TV transmitter.

There are several **mountain huts** on Biokovo, but most are only open by appointment and you should never assume they'll be open – contact the tourist office for details, or see the list of huts and contacts on the nature park website (*www.pp-biokovo.hr/en/72/park-lodging*).

Driving the Biokovo massif
If hiking's not for you, Sveti Jure isn't necessarily out of the question. There's a narrow road that goes up to the summit from Makarska, making for a 30km white-knuckle ride, best performed by jeep and with someone else at the wheel. The road is the highest in Croatia, positively vertiginous, and has no safety barriers.

From Vošac and the road to Sveti Jure, a marked trail heads northwest along Biokovo to **Sveti Ilija** (1,642m), with more wonderful views – but this is further than you'll be able to get in a single day. For more information on hiking or jeeping up the mountain contact the tourist office or **Biokovo Active Holidays** (*Gundulićeva 4;* \ *679 655;* m *098 225 852; www.biokovo.net*) – especially if you're travelling alone and would like the security of some company on the trail – or see Rudolf Abraham's *Walking in Croatia* (page 429).

Creveno Jezero and Modro Jezero
On the far side of the Biokovo mountains, tucked into the border with Bosnia & Herzegovina, and near **Imotski**, which is on the way to absolutely nowhere (a back road to Mostar or Sarajevo, conceivably), are two typically strange karstic phenomena, the so-called **Crveno Jezero** and **Modro Jezero** (the Red and Blue Lakes).

Each of the lakes was formed by the roof collapsing above a vast cave, and even though they're more than 20km from the sea as the crow flies, and on the wrong side of a major mountain range, the lakes are deep indeed – the bottom of Crveno

Jezero is a mere 19m above sea-level, with the lake depth itself varying between 280m and 320m. Modro Jezero, for its part, really is blue. With less steep sides than Crveno Jezero, it's used by local boys for swimming – when there's water in it at all – or as a football pitch when it's dried up.

ŠOLTA

The island of Šolta, easily accessible from Split and right next to the much larger Brač, is something of a mystery. It's pretty, it's wooded, it has old stone hamlets (it even has a couple of prehistoric and Roman ruins, and a sprinkling of medieval monuments), it has appealing coves, beaches and bays, and yet it's somehow off the main tourist map – it sees only around a tenth of the visitors of Brač or Hvar, and most of those check in at the increasingly large apartment complex at Nečujam. Come and stay in one of the 120 or so private rooms on the island and you'll never believe Split's under half an hour away on the catamaran.

Šolta is 20km long but less than 5km wide, and has a local population of under 1,500, mainly in a handful of settlements along the north coast and in the interior. The south coast, a crenulated maze of inlets, coves and tiny bays, is almost entirely uninhabited. Olives, figs, wine production and fishing still drive the part of the economy that isn't fuelled by tourism.

GETTING THERE AND AROUND Five ferries a day make the 1-hour crossing from Split to Šolta's port, **Rogač**, all year round (*www.jadrolinija.hr*); in summer, the frequency increases to six. There's also a fast catamaran service, which cuts journey time down to just 35 minutes (*www.lnp.hr*). More irregular crossings (aimed mainly at weekenders) are made in summer to **Stomorska**.

Regular ferries and catamarans are met by the bus which connects all the main settlements – if you miss the bus or want to get around the island at other times your options are limited to walking or calling Šolta Taxi (m *091 573 9983*). You can also get from port to port by local water taxi.

WHERE TO STAY AND EAT If you're staying here – you could also do a day trip from Split – accommodation is limited to private rooms and apartments, of which there are plenty. These can be sourced via the **tourist office** (*Podkuća 8;* \ *654 657; www.visitsolta.com*), or **Rina Tourism** in Stomorska (*Riva Pelegrin 29, Stomorska;* \ *658 169; www.rina.hr*). You could also try your luck on the spot at the tourist offices in Rogač, Nečujam or Maslinica, but you'd be far more sensible to try to book ahead, especially if you're planning on staying on the island in high summer. Private rooms come in at around €40 a night for doubles.

Alternatively, you can try the luxurious new **Martinis Marchi** (\ *572 768; www.martinis-marchi.com;* €€€€€) in Maslinica, or the much more homely and affordable **Villa Šolta** in Rogač (*8 rooms & apts;* \ *654 540;* m *091 520 4437; www.villa-solta.com;* €€€–€€), which has rooms and spacious apartments, and a good restaurant.

Apartments Funda (*3 apts;* m *091 505 3560; www.apartmani-funda.com;* €€€–€) offers apartments in Nečujam, each sleeping four to six and going for €70–80 in high season. **Apartments Skelin** (*4 apts & 1 dbl;* \ *650 013;* m *098 980 8484; www.necujam-apartments.com;* €), also in Nečujam, offers apartments sleeping up to four or five.

If you want to camp, try **Camp Mido** in Stomorska (\ *658 011;* m *099 832 3016;* ▪ *Camp Mido Solta*), which also has apartments and a restaurant.

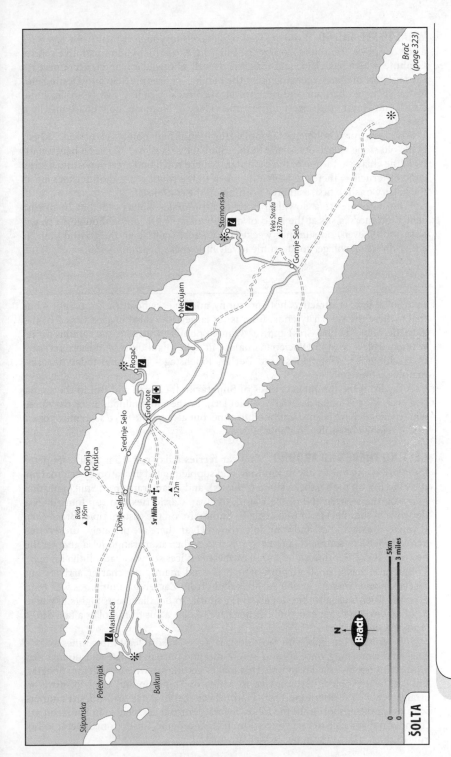

ŠOLTA

Brač
(page 323)

Stomorska

Vela Straža
▲237m

Gornje Selo

Nečujam

Rogač

Grohote

Srednje Selo

Donja
Krušica

Brda
▲195m

Donje Selo

Sv Mihovil
▲
212m

Maslinica

Stipanska

Polebrnjak

Balkun

N

Bradt

0
0

5km

3 miles

WHAT TO SEE AND DO If you are walking, make sure you have plenty of water – it's a hot, dry place. It's around 2km up the hill from Rogač to the administrative centre, **Grohote**, which has a shop and pizzeria, as well as a regular market. From here it's the best part of 8km west, passing by the hamlets of **Srednje Selo** and **Donje Selo**, to the sheltered harbour and beaches at **Maslinica**. Heading east from Grohote, it's around 7km to the once-upon-a-time village of Nečujam, now unashamedly a tourist resort.

Also 7km from Grohote, at the foot of the island's high point (Vela Straža, 237m), is the old stone village of **Gornje Selo**, 150m above sea level. There's a paved path from the village to the top of the mountain, where you'll find great views and a large concrete crucifix. There are footpaths down to the south coast, though stock up at the bakery or shop first, as there's nothing on the coast itself.

From Grohote it's a downhill 3km to **Stomorska**, Šolta's other main tourist centre. Stomorska sits at the head of a lovely narrow bay, and although it can get busy (noisy, even) on summer weekends, a short walk along the coastal path in either direction will get you to some lovely little rocky beaches.

BRAČ

Like Šolta, Brač is attractive, hot and sunny, and an easy boat trip from Split – but that's where the similarity ends. Brač is far larger (the third biggest island in the Adriatic, after Krk and Cres) and vastly more popular with tourists. Famous for its white marble – used in Diocletian's palace in Split in antiquity, and more recently in Washington's White House and Berlin's Reichstag – the island today depends mainly on tourism.

Away from the two main centres of **Supetar** in the north and **Bol** in the south, however, it's still often deserted, particularly in the mountainous interior, where whole villages have been abandoned to time, but also on the large sections of coast not developed or easily accessible by road.

GETTING THERE AND AROUND Nine car **ferries** a day run from Split to Supetar (*50mins*), rising to 14 a day in summer, and supplemented in season by catamarans direct to Bol on the southern shore (*70mins*), and catamarans from Split via Milna (*1hr*), on the western end of the island, to Hvar. Car ferries also run four times a day (five in summer) from Makarska to **Sumartin**, on the eastern tip of Brač (*1hr*). If you're already in Bol, and want to go on to Hvar, there are privately run services across to Jelsa in summer – otherwise, just take the catamaran to Jelsa and get the bus from there. For timetables for all of these services see www.jadrolinija.hr.

Brač also has a small **airport**, which is used mainly for charter arrivals but receives a once weekly Croatia Airlines flight from Zagreb in summer as well (*Sat; 50mins*). There's usually (but not always) a shuttle to Bol that meets flights. If you're heading onward to Supetar you'll either have to take a bus from Bol or a taxi direct from the airport.

Supetar is the **bus** hub, with most destinations served at least three times a day – once in the morning, once around lunchtime, and once in the late afternoon – and with about ten buses a day to Bol. This makes getting anywhere easy from Supetar, but can be a problem if you arrive in Milna or Sumartin and want to move on straight away. The afternoon ferry from Makarska, in particular, doesn't connect with onward transport until the following day. Fortunately people in Sumartin are friendly and will help to find you a room if you need one. Buses from Supetar to Bol run 18 times a day in summer (fewer in winter).

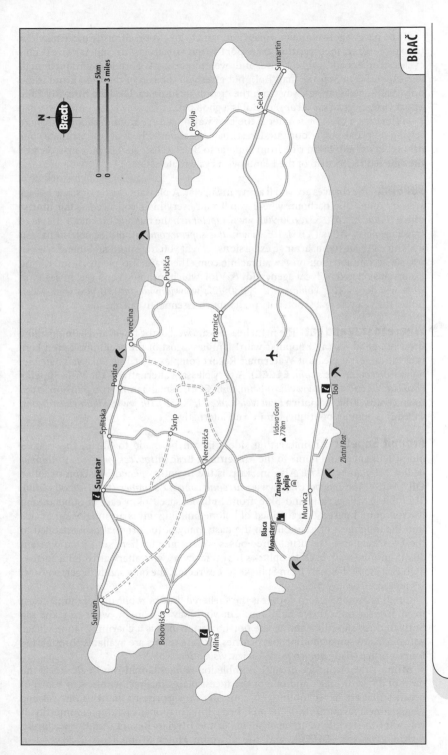

If you haven't got your own wheels and want to give yourself vastly more freedom to explore Brač, then **renting transport** is the way to go. In Supetar you'll find cycles, scooters and cars for hire, and even motorboats. Hire isn't cheap (though less expensive in Supetar than Bol), but gives you the run of the island, and is the only real way of getting away from the crowds in summer. For bike hire, **Big Blue Sport** (*www.bigbluesport.com*) in Bol is a good bet.

Ultimately, a cycle or scooter is the best way of getting around, though if you're relying on pedal-power don't underestimate the summer heat or overestimate your fitness – it's a hilly 40km ride from Supetar to Bol. Cyclists should pick up a copy of the detailed HGSS map of the island, with cycle routes.

SUPETAR The chances are you'll arrive in Supetar. A pleasant cluster of stone houses spreads round the harbour, where you'll find everything you need – the **tourist office** (*Porat 1;* ✆ *630 551, 630 900; www.supetar.hr*), the bus station, and a couple of travel agencies. **Atlas** (✆ *631 105; www.atlas-supetar.com*) should be able to fix you up with a private room, arrange excursions, or rent you transport, and there's a list of private accommodation on www.bracinfo.com. There are also plenty of interesting excursions offered by local agency **Idi & Vidi**, which means 'go and see', in case you were wondering (*Ive Vojnovića 2;* ✆ *630 427; www.idiividi.com*). If you want a car, rather than a cycle or a scooter, it's pretty much essential to call ahead.

🏠 **Where to stay and eat** The main beaches are west of the town, and being shallow these are good for (and popular with) families. Most of the accommodation here is at the large but pleasant **Waterman Resort** complex (*Put Vele Luke 4;* ✆ *640 253; www.watermanresorts.com;* €€€€€). A very pleasant alternative is the **Villa Supetar** (*Bračka 2;* ✆ *630 894; www.villasupetar.com;* €€€), a small family-run pansion in the town centre. **Villa Adriatica** (*Put Vele Luke 31;* ✆ *755 010; www.villaadriatica.com;* €€€€€) is another boutique, family-run alternative.

Around Supetar An interesting side trip can be made to **Škrip**, the island's oldest settlement and home to the **Museum of Brač** (*http://czk-brac.hr;* ☼ *summer 08.00–20.00 daily; 15kn*). Also in Škrip is the recently opened **Museum of Olive Oil** (*Muzej Maslinovog Ulja; www.muzejuja.com;* ☼ *summer 09.00–20.00 daily*). The hilltop village is inland 3km from **Splitska**, itself 6km east of Supetar, and the museum, housed in a fortified old stone building, gives an interesting glance into the toughness of island life in the past; many of the original residents fled to the USA long ago. The usual three buses a day come up here, and it's a pleasant 30–45-minute walk back to Splitska if you fancy a swim afterwards. It's a further 4km east along the coast from Splitska to **Lovrečina**, the only sandy beach on Brač. It's no secret, believe me.

On Brač's southwestern corner is the sheltered little port of Milna, around 20km from Supetar on a thrice-daily bus. On your way you might want to come via **Sutivan**, the last settlement on the north coast, which is a charming stone village with access to some good pebble beaches. Private rooms are available through the **tourist office** (*Blato bb;* ✆ *638 357; www.visitsutivan.com*).

Milna – the birthplace of 2001 Wimbledon winner Goran Ivanišević – is at the head of a narrow inlet, and one of the nicest places in Brač, within easy reach of beaches that are never too busy. It comes as no surprise to find this once sleepy village now a favourite with the well-heeled international yachting community. If you want to stay, there are apartments at the **Illyrian Resort** (✆ *636 566; http://illyrianresort.com;* €€€€€), and the 25-room **Hotel Milna** (✆ *636 283; www.*

hotelmilna.com; €€€€€), or you can get private rooms through the **tourist office** (✆ *636 233*). At Gornji Humac, halfway across the island between Supetar and Bol, **Konoba Tomić** (m *091 225 1199; www.konobatomic.com;* €) is a lovely place with a restaurant using ingredients from its own farm, and private accommodation in nine rooms.

BOL

Brač's biggest draw by far is Bol – or more accurately the extraordinary spit of fine shingle called **Zlatni Rat**, the Golden Cape. Featuring in every Croatian tourist promo, the tip of the south-facing 500m triangular spit shifts west or east depending on the season, and the beach attracts around 50,000 visitors a year. It's not the only place to swim near Bol – the town, sheltered by the mass of **Vidova Gora** behind it, is at the heart of a 15km stretch of beaches – but it's certainly the most popular.

Zlatni Rat is a pleasant half-hour stroll west of Bol, which is a pretty little fishing harbour surrounded by old stone houses. New developments spread up the hill, but the centre itself is compact and charming. It's far too small to accommodate all the people who want to see it, however, so be warned ahead if you're crowd-phobic.

The **tourist office** (✆ *635 638; www.bol.hr*) has a good supply of maps, which you'll find useful if you're exploring the surrounding area.

Where to stay Accommodation mainly consists of the Bluesun resort hotels near Zlatni Rat (€€€€€–€€€€): the **Bonaca** (*www.hotelbonacabol.com*), **Borak** (*www.brachotelborak.com*) and **Elaphusa** (*www.hotelelaphusabrac.com*). There's not much to choose between them – they're all similarly priced (from around €160–250 for a double at the top of the season) and well located – though the Bonaca is best for families (one child aged 13 and under stays free) and the Elaphusa's a bit more upmarket than the others. All three can be booked either through the individual hotel websites or centrally through the Bluesun Hotels company (✆ *01 3844 288; www.bluesunhotels.com*).

Otherwise, for most of the town's 3,000 or so beds in private rooms and apartments, you'll need to go through an agency – **Adria Tours** (*Bračka cesta 10;* ✆ *635 966; www.adria-bol.hr*), **More** (*Vladimira Nazora 28;* ✆ *642 050; www.more-bol.com*) and **Bol Tours** (*Vladimira Nazora 18;* ✆ *635 693; www.boltours.com*) are all in the middle of town (and can also organise the usual excursions and hire). Expect to pay €50 or so for a double in season, and a surcharge of 20% for three nights or fewer.

There are also a few smallish hotels and apartments in Bol itself:

Hotels

Villa Daniela (18 rooms, 5 suites) Hrvatskih domobrana 19; ✆ 635 660; www.villadaniela.com. Boutique luxury up towards the back of the town. €€€€€

Hotel Ivan (30 rooms) David 11a; ✆ 640 888; www.hotel-ivan.com. Stone hotel with a swimming pool, though there have been reports of poor service. €€€€€–€€€€

Hotel Kaštil (32 rooms) Radića; ✆ 635 995; www.kastil.hr. Nice place right on the fishing port, with sea-view rooms. €€€€€–€€€€

Villa Giardino (10 rooms) Novi put 2; ✆ 635 900; e villa.giardino@st.t-com.hr; www.dalmacija.net/bol/villagiardino. Small, family-run place with a lovely garden. €€€€

Villa Daniela (30 rooms) Domovinskog rata 54; ✆ 635 959; www.villadaniela.com. Centrally located with its own pool. €€€€–€€€

Apartments

Zlatni Bol Apartments (4 apts) Ivana Gundulićeva 2; m 091 2244 700; www.zlatni-bol.com. Apts sleeping 2 to 4 people. €€€€

Alpeza Apartments (16 apts) Ivana Mažuranića 2; m 098 346 029; www.alpeza-apartments.com. A range of stylish, good-value apts sleeping 2 to 6 people. €€

✕ Where to eat and drink There's no shortage of places to eat out in Bol – try **Restaurant Ranč;** (*Hrvatskih Domobrana 23;* ✆ *635 635;* ⏰ *18.00–23.00 daily;* €€€) or **Mendula** (*Hrvatskih Domobrana 7;* ⏰ *11.00–23.00;* €€€). **Arguola** (*Vladimira Nazora 6;* €€–€) does good, well-priced sandwiches.

What to see and do Once you've had your fill of beach life, one of the best side trips you can make is to head to the top of **Vidova Gora**. At 778m it's not just the highest point on Brač, but the highest point on any Adriatic island, and the views are terrific – down on to Zlatni Rat far below, and across to the island of Hvar to the south. The easy way up is to travel by road, either with your own wheels or on an excursion, but the most satisfying way to reach the summit is by hiking up from Bol. It's a good 2½ hours of steady trekking, but it's well worth the effort – the path is well maintained, though walking boots are recommended. At the top there's a konoba that usually opens to coincide with the arrival of excursions.

Another interesting side trip you can make is to the **Dragon's Cave** (Zmajeva Špilja), above the little village of Murvica, to the west of Bol. It's a bit of a mystery as to who carved the wild beasts and mythological creatures here, but they're likely to date back to the 15th century at least. The cave itself is locked, and the once reasonably-clear path from near Zlatni Rat has been obliterated with the construction of the new asphalt road to Murvica – so you'll need to contact a local guide (*Zoran Kojdić;* m *091 514 9787*).

Finally, there's the extraordinary **Blaca Monastery**, which underwent restoration work in 2013. This is most easily visited on an excursion, though you can get there on your own (but check the opening times at Bol's tourist office) if you have wheels and fancy a hike. There are two routes; either take a boat trip to a bay below the monastery and hike up from there; or get there from the Vidova Gora road – turn right down a gravel track marked Blaca, and leave your car at the start of the marked footpath around 4km further along (this route's a three-hour round trip).

Set high up under a cliff, the imposing monastery served as a refuge from the 16th century on, and was still inhabited until the last monk, Niko Milčević, died here in 1963. It now houses a curious collection of astronomical instruments, old weapons and watches, and an exceptional library.

HVAR

Smooth, sultry and sexy, Hvar is the undisputed jewel in Croatia's Adriatic crown as far as Europe's cognoscenti and the local smart set are concerned. And indeed, the island, lying south of Brač and stretching finger-like towards the southern end of the Makarska Riviera, is one of the most pleasant in the Adriatic. It has an elegant 16th-century Venetian capital, plenty of beaches and great weather – it boasts 2,700 hours of annual sunshine and averages only eight snowy days a decade. In winter you'll find hotels offering 50% off your room rate for any day on which it rains for more than three daylight hours, and free board and lodging if it goes below freezing during the day.

Not surprisingly, along with Dubrovnik it is one of the Adriatic's worst-kept secrets – book well ahead if you want to stay in any of the hotels at the height of the season when the island is quite literally full. Or simply follow the example of Riccardo Mazzucchelli, the wealthy Italian businessman (and former husband of Ivana Trump, though at Bradt we wouldn't normally stoop to such tabloid gossip), who's bought himself a fabulous villa and grounds on the island.

Hvar town sits at the sheltered southwestern tip of Hvar, separated from the other main settlements of Stari Grad, Vrboska and Jelsa by the UNESCO-listed

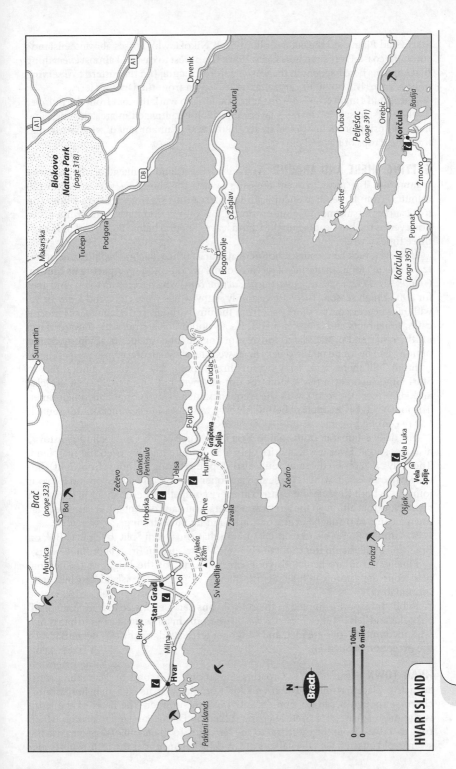

HVAR ISLAND

Stari Grad Plain, and the 600m bulk of Sveti Nikola, which rises above the island's southern coast. Hvar stretches nearly 70km from west to east, but almost everything that happens here happens in the western third, Sućuraj (on the eastern tip) serving only as an arrival point for car traffic on its way in from the Drvenik ferry.

The island's main crop – it won't take you long to work this out from the number of places it's on sale in Hvar – is lavender, which is cultivated in great swathes, and makes a spring break here a real treat. There's also a fair amount of wine made, and the usual crops of figs and olives.

GETTING THERE AND AROUND Arrival on the island is inevitably by **ferry** or **catamaran**. The most frequent crossing is also the shortest – it's only 5km (20 minutes) from Drvenik to Sućuraj, and the ferry runs six times a day in winter (up to 11 a day in summer). Count on doing this only if you have your own wheels, however, as the bus heading up the island leaves Sućuraj before 06.00, and only runs three times a week.

If you get stuck here, contact the **Sućuraj tourist office** (*Sućuraj bb;* ⧵*717 288; www. tz-sucuraj.hr*) for a smattering of private rooms or you could try **Apartment Modrić** (m *098 921 0432; www.hvar-apartment-sucuraj.com*) which sleeps up to five and goes for €90 in high season. There are certainly many worse places to spend a day or so, with nice beaches only a short walk from the tiny harbour, and a handful of cheerful cafés, restaurants and shops on hand. It's an option for arrival, with onward travel off the other end of the island. Much more on Sućuraj, including accommodation options, can be found on the cheery local website, www.sucuraj.com.

From Split there's a car ferry two or three times a day, all year round, direct to Stari Grad (actually a few kilometres out of town, but buses to Stari Grad, Jelsa and Hvar meet the ferry), with the frequency increasing substantially in summer. The journey takes a couple of hours. Reserve well ahead in summer on this route if you're coming by car.

The daily catamaran from Split to Vela Luka (on Korčula) and Ubli (on Lastovo) also stops in at Hvar town, and it's only a 50-minute journey from the mainland. The daily car ferry on the same route also stops by (taking 1½ hours from Split), but only twice a week in winter. These services offer you a good onward option for your journey, as both Korčula and Lastovo are very compelling destinations in their own right. Note that although the ferry carries cars, you can't disembark at car-free Hvar town – come in through Sućuraj or Stari Grad if you're driving.

In summer there's also a daily catamaran that runs from Split to Jelsa via Bol, on Brač, and a catamaran from Split to Hvar via Milna, also on Brač (*both 1hr 40 mins*).

Finally, if you are here with your **car**, especially at the height of the season, plan your departure carefully, as the queues to get off the island can be pretty intimidating.

Public transport is limited to the reliable **bus** service between Hvar, Stari Grad, Vrboska and Jelsa (timetables at www.cazmatrans.hr or www.stari-grad-faros.hr), – all incoming ferries are met, and outgoing ferries fed, by the bus network (with the exception of Sućuraj).

HVAR TOWN Hvar town is Croatia's St Tropez, and one of Dalmatia's most attractive places, rivalling Dubrovnik or Korčula with its Venetian Renaissance charm – though it can get oppressively busy in summer. The heart of the town is the main square, Trg Sveti Stjepana, billed as Dalmatia's largest piazza, which runs east–west from the cathedral to the harbour. To the north of the square is the swanky old quarter, with the palaces of **Grad** sheltering under the 13th-century city

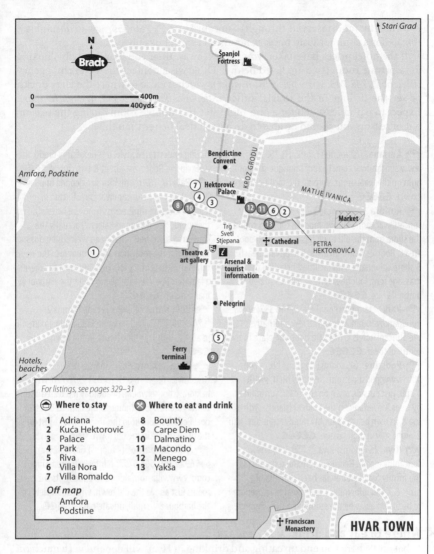

walls and overlooked by the fortress on the hill. To the south is the old residential town of **Burg**.

In the early 15th century, Hvar became the wealthiest town in Dalmatia, under Venice, as all ships to and from the republic stopped in here. What you see today, however (barring the mostly original city walls), is uniformly late 16th century, as the Turks razed it to the ground in 1571.

🛏 Where to stay *Map, above*

If you're planning to stay in a hotel in Hvar, be prepared to pay the price, which is pretty high in the package hotels spread along the coast (most are within 10–15 minutes on foot), and even higher at one of the few hotels right in town. Count on €130 a night for a decent double room with a view out of town, and anything from €200 to €450 a night in town. Almost every accommodation option in Hvar is owned by (and reserved through) Sunčani Hvar (\ *750 555; www.suncanihvar. com*) – for a summer visit, book as far ahead as you possibly can.

If the hotel prices have taken your breath away, then you'll probably be looking for a private room (two are listed below). Otherwise, contact the **Pelegrini** agency (*Riva bb;* \ *742 743; www.pelegrini-hvar.hr*), which is close to where the ferry docks; or see the listings in the **tourist office** (*Stjepana bb;* \ *741 059; www.tzhvar.hr*). Expect to pay at least €60 for a one-night stay in a double room during the season; out of season you should be able to do a great deal better than this.

⌂ **Adriana** (62 rooms) Fabrika; \ 750 200; www.suncanihvar.com. Luxury boutique spa hotel, right on the waterfront, with all the facilities you'd expect. €€€€€

⌂ **Amfora** Majerovica; \ 750 300; www. suncanihvar.com. This big, modern complex round the shore from the old town has a cascading pool area & Bonj les Bains, an attractive private beach & shore colonnade with facilities including private massage tent, lounge & terrace bar, & sun bed & umbrella hire. €€€€€

⌂ **Park** (15 rooms) Bankete; \ 718 337; www. hotelparkhvar.com. One of the few alternatives to the Sunčani hotels is this nice boutique place in the centre of town. €€€€€

⌂ **Podstine** (45 rooms) Podstine bb; \ 740 400; www.podstine.com. Recently built, swish 4-star, just outside town on the coast, surrounded by trees & overlooking the Pakleni Islands, with a spa & its own beach, & highly rated restaurant. Min 2-night stay in high season. €€€€€

⌂ **Riva** (54 rooms) Riva; \ 750 100; www. suncanihvar.com. Near to where the ferry docks, the former Slavija hotel has been done up big time, & if you remember the original then prepare to be blown away by the stunning refurbishment.

Oozing understated style, it is justifiably proud of its Exclusive Roots restaurant & bar/club. €€€€€

⌂ **Palace** (62 rooms) Trg sv Stjepana bb; \ 741 966; www.suncanihvar.com. Sitting in a prime location right across from the Arsenal, the appropriately named Palace – actually the converted town hall – has been welcoming guests since 1903. The reception area is built into the original 16th-century loggia, while upstairs there's a fabulous open terrace giving on to the harbour & main square. €€€€

⌂ **Villa Nora** (4 rooms) Frane Primija 2; \ 742 498; http://villanora.incroatia.info. Rooms in a 14th-century stone house in the town centre. €€€€

⌂ **Kuća Hektorović** (3 rooms) Petra Hektorovića 8; \ 718 083; m 091 7276 720; www. hektorovichousehvar.hr. Beautifully renovated 13th-century stone house (home to the famous Croatian poet Petar Hektorović in the 16th century), just off the main square in the old town. €€€

⌂ **Villa Romaldo** (4 rooms) Gojava 23; m 091 546 6929, 091 666 6767; e info@villa-romaldo. com; www.villa-romaldo.com. 2 nice apts & 2 rooms just above the old town, with good views of the harbour & a small, private garden. €€€

✕ Where to eat and drink *Map, page 329*

What and where you end up eating and drinking in Hvar will depend very much on what time of year you're here. In high summer there are dozens of restaurants and even more bars and cafés, and you can pick and choose to some extent – though the fare mostly sticks to the traditional seafood/pasta/pizza variety; hardly surprising, given Hvar's enduring popularity with Italians. Out of season it's a different matter altogether, and when I was here at Easter – notwithstanding the religious festivities going on – there were only two restaurants open in the whole town, and a mere handful of bars. In recent years, some exciting new restaurants have opened for business, and others have upped the ante.

✕ **Dalmatino** Banketi 1; m 091 529 3121; www.dalmatino-hvar.com; ⊕ May–Oct noon– midnight daily. Upmarket seafood & steakhouse. €€€€

✕ **Macondo** Petra Hektorovića; \ 742 850; ⊕ Apr–Nov noon–14.00 & 18.30–midnight Mon–Sat, 18.30–midnight Sun. Although a firm favourite with the locals, the service can be a bit hit & miss. Generally the seafood is excellent, but very pricey. €€€€

✗ Yakša Petra Hektorovića; ☎717 202; ⌚ summer 10.00–16.00 & 19.00–midnight, winter noon–1400 & 18.00–23.00 daily. Funky addition to the Hvar restaurant scene using fresh Croatian ingredients with some interesting twists. €€€€

✗ Bounty Pjaca; ☎742 565; ⌚ 11.00–midnight daily. Full marks to this place on the old harbour, which served up the best fish soup I ate

in Croatia on that trip, & offered the local Hvar house white wine at an all too reasonable 40kn a litre. In summer of course it's packed out & quite a bit more expensive; but well worth it all the same. €€€

✗ Menego Groda bb; ☎717 411; www. menego.hr; ⌚ Apr–Nov 11.30–14.00 & 17.00–midnight daily. Homely place specialising in Dalmatian dishes, all made with home-grown produce. €€€

Entertainment and nightlife

🍸 Carpe Diem Hvar Riva; ☎742 369; www. carpe-diem-hvar.com; ⌚ 09.00–02.00 daily. Hvar offers one of Croatia's hottest party scenes in summer, with a number of bars to choose from, but the action always inevitably focuses on Carpe Diem, the legendary lounge bar on the waterfront.

This is where Zagreb's movers & shakers come to pose & a certain Russian billionaire, popular in the west of London, is said to have been spotted here. Mere mortals can just come along & enjoy a siesta on the sumptuous outdoor sofas before partying the night away.

What to see and do The main sights are on or near the main square. The **cathedral** (actually a church, but let's not be pedantic) with its Renaissance trefoil façade is attractive enough (and the campanile, with its increasing number of windows on each storey, is lovely), but nothing particularly special inside, barring a fine 13th-century Madonna and Child, in striking contrast to the morbidly graphic Baroque paintings on the other altars. Check out the modern main doors, the work of the sculptor Kuzma Kovačić, the man also behind the design on Croatia's kuna and lipa coins. (If you're around on Maundy Thursday, just before Easter, don't miss the religious processions around the island, maintaining a 500-year-old tradition. The festivities reach a climax on Easter Monday, when the six big crosses from the island's main settlements are paraded around town.)

Also on the main square is the great hulk of the **Arsenal** – unusual indeed among naval buildings in having a theatre upstairs, and especially so in this case, as it was one of the first in the Western world open to all comers. The **theatre** was built in 1612, as you can see by the inscription outside saying '*Anno Secundo Pacis MDCXII*' – the peace referred to here was the ending of the century-long spat between commoners and nobs throughout the 16th century, following the 1510 uprising by Matija Ivanić, when 19 men were hanged from galley masts here.

Access to the theatre is through an adjoining **art gallery**, which has highly variable temporary exhibitions from Croatian artists. The theatre itself is charming, with just 86 seats and 28 pint-sized boxes, and is finally benefiting from long-awaited restoration.

On the other side of the square, dominating the main town gate, you'll find the so-called **Hektorović Palace**, an ornate but unfinished Venetian Gothic building, which has remained unroofed and overgrown since the 15th century. The 'palace' pre-dates the famous poet, in fact – and a more fitting memorial can be seen at his actual palace in Stari Grad.

Up the stepped street from here you'll find a small **Benedictine Convent**, where the few remaining nuns – they never leave the hallowed walls, and are bound to an oath of silence – spend their hours making the extraordinarily intricate lace which you'll find for sale around town (you'll know it's the real thing by the serious price tags). Just below the convent is a small, plain church, remarkable only for the portrait of Cardinal Stjepinac (page 116), bearing an even more alarming resemblance than usual to Vladimir Putin.

Continuing straight up the street brings you out into the park above town, and the path eventually winds its way up to the 16th-century **Španjol Fortress** (⊕ *09.00–20.00 daily*) at the top of the hill. With a wonderful view over the old town and across the Pakleni Islands – especially in the early evening – the place is understandably popular. Inside the fortress there's a collection of amphorae and other bits and pieces fished out from the sea and dragged up here.

South of the town (just follow the quay down past the ferry terminal) is the 15th-century **Franciscan Monastery**. Just two monks live here now, and the place serves as an endearing little museum, with old oil jars and a comprehensive numismatic collection dating back to Roman times. There are some interesting bits of modern sculpture (some of it by one of the monks) and a collection of mostly Venetian paintings. The biggest of these, taking up most of an end wall, is an especially rowdy Last Supper. It's said to be the work of a Venetian painter who was in quarantine here, with only a cat for company – the cat's on the left and the painter's on the right. On the other side of the cloisters is a curious and rather spooky church, which is a bit of a mish-mash architecturally, but has good 16th-century choir stalls and a couple of huge dark altarpieces by Leandro Bassano. Look out among the various tombs for that of the local writer Hanibal Lučić (1485–1553).

There are several rocky beaches close to town (notably in front of the big hotels), but serious bathers will want to take a trip out to the **Pakleni Islands**, just offshore, which is where all the best beaches can be found (you'll be told that the name Pakleni means 'devils', but it actually refers to the pine resin). Pick up information from the tourist office (page 330), and get there by taxi-boat from the harbour.

STARI GRAD Stari Grad, set around an elongated horseshoe harbour at the head of a long sheltered bay, was formerly the capital of the island, and the location of the 4th-century BC Greek colony of Pharos (the name Hvar comes from Pharos) – though these days you'll find it infinitely less frenetic than Hvar town. The town is on the south side of the harbour, with the northern shore occupied by a string of package hotels. If you're driving from Hvar there are two roads, the new fast route through the tunnel, or the picturesque old road over the hills, past the village of **Brusje**. Take the high road if you're not in a rush.

🏠 **Where to stay** The helpful **tourist office** (*Obala dr Franje Tuđmana 1;* ✆ *765 763; www.stari-grad-faros.hr*) is on the harbour, while private rooms can be arranged through **Hvar Touristik** (*Šiberija 31; 717 580; www.hvar-touristik.com*), close to where the bus stops.

🏠 **Heritage Villa Apolon** (6 rooms) Šetalište Don Šime Ljubića 7; ✆ 778 320; www.apolon.hr. Very swish boutique hotel housed in a beautifully restored old villa, with spacious, impeccably decorated suites & its own restaurant, right on the Riva. Given the price of a standard hotel room in Hvar town, or even at the Helios Faros complex, these represent tremendously good value, & the price drops dramatically outside the high season. €€€€€

🏠 **Arkada, Lavanda and Helios Apartments** ✆ 765 866; http://heliosfaros.eu. All part of the same complex, these do reasonable dbls with views, though some parts of the complex could really do with something of a makeover – a good 20min walk from the tourist office along the waterfront. €€€€€–€€€€

🏠 **Apartments Marinko** (10 apts) Domobranska 24; m 098 9397 490; www. ilovehvar.com. Good-value apts in the streets north of the harbour, about halfway out to Hotel Helios. €€€

🏠 **Hostel Sunce** (14 beds) Ulica don Mihovila Pavlinovica 2; m 097 6639 000; http://

hostelsunce.freshcreator.com. Centrally located about halfway between the bus station & the tourist office. Sgls, dbls & trpls for €17pp in high season, €20 with b/fast. €€

✘ Where to eat and drink

✘ **Antika** Kola bb; ⊕ 11.00–23.00 daily. Popular cocktail bar/restaurant just off the Riva. €€€

✘ **Konoba Kolumbić** Ul Mala Poica 2; m 091 7977 769; https://konoba-kolumbic.fullbusiness. com; ⊕ opening times may vary so call ahead to check. Nice little konoba near the summit of Sv Nikola, surrounded by vineyards, with its own wines. Order *ispod peka* dishes in advance. Makes a perfect place to stop for lunch if hiking or biking over Sv Nikola. Transport can also be arranged for groups. €€€

✘ **Nauta** Ive Dulcica 10; ⊕ 11.00–23.00 daily. Highly rated place out past Tvrdalj. €€€

✘ **Konoba Kokot** Dol Sv Ana; m 091 511 4288; ⊕ noon–22.30 daily. Highly rated local konoba in the village of Dol, with traditional local dishes prepared with locally grown & organic ingredients. Order ispod peka dishes in advance. €€€–€€

✳✘ **Marko** Trg Ploča bb; ☎ 765 889; ⊕ 10.00–23.00 daily. Consistently excellent little pizzeria, also serving grills, seafood, pasta & salads, in a pleasant stone-paved street just off Trg Stjepana Radića. Friendly service & very good value. Recommended. €€€–€€

What to see and do Little has survived from antiquity (barring a small section of the original walls, a few paving slabs, and some Greek gravestones in the museum at the monastery), but the town is nevertheless a small but agreeable hodge-podge of little streets and small squares. Head for the **Tvrdalj**, the summer house of one of Dalmatia's most famous poets, Petar Hektorović (1487–1572). The fortified house has undergone numerous facelifts since being started in 1520, but features interesting inscriptions on the walls from Hektorović's work, in Croatian, Italian and Latin, and a heavy cloister surrounding a fishpond – a memorial to the poet's love of fish, fishing and fishermen. There's also a **Dominican Monastery** (*Dominikanski samostan;* ⊕ *May–Oct 09.00–17.00*) to visit, with an interesting museum off the cloisters.

If you want to get out of town, it's well worth picking up one of the good local booklets from the tourist office that detail various **walks and cycle routes** in the area, including ones up to Svete Nikola and to Glavica, the hill overlooking the town. You can also rent bikes in Stari Grad, and the cycling round here is excellent, with quite flat terrain and very little traffic – in fact Stari Grad makes a better base for hiking and cycling on the island than Hvar town.

Stretching between Stari Grad and Vrboska is the UNESCO-listed **Stari Grad Plain**, where the ancient Greek system of land division is incredibly well preserved, and the cultivation of grapevines and olive trees appears to have changed remarkably little over the past two and a half thousand years. Best explored by bike – grab a free map from the tourist office.

Another great area to explore by bike is the **Kabal Peninsula** which stretches off to the northwest.

JELSA AND SURROUNDINGS The small town of **Jelsa** – mostly modestly 19th century, sitting on a pretty port – is today somewhat dwarfed by the hotel complexes on either side. Nonetheless it's an attractive place in itself, surrounded by pine forests and giving easy access to a number of beaches, including by taxi-boat to the best ones on the Glavica Peninsula, and across to the naturist island of **Zečevo**. Some of Hvar's cool crowd are increasingly looking towards Jelsa, which has an ever-improving range of bars and restaurants.

Jelsa also offers one of the very few routes across the island to the south coast. You'll need wheels, as the route winds 4km up to the old village of **Pitve** before entering the Vratnik Gorge, and a long tunnel, which comes out above the village of Zavala (around 7km from Pitve).

Zavala itself is a tiny fishing village, but it does have an excellent place to stay, the **Villa Stella Mare** (✆ *767 128; www.stellamare-hvar.com;* €€€€–€€€). There are seven apartments, and the friendly staff can even rent you a bike, a scooter or a boat if you want to explore the deserted coves and beaches along Hvar's south coast.

Three kilometres offshore is the island of **Šćedro**. Protected since 1972, the island doesn't see many visitors (the occasional sailing boat and motor cruiser), and has a resident population of just one. It makes for a lovely day trip from Zavala (or Jelsa), with its dense woods, sheltered inlets, and the remains of a 15th-century monastery.

From Jelsa it's only a 45-minute walk west along the coast path (or a short taxi-boat ride away) to **Vrboska**, a charming old village set along both sides of an inlet. Stone bridges connect the two halves, which are dominated by the fortified 16th-century **Church of St Mary** (Sv Marija), built after the Turks destroyed the place in 1571. You can climb up to the battlements for a nice view over the village.

East of Jelsa, Hvar becomes very empty indeed, and although there's plenty to explore if you have your own wheels, it's pretty much impossible otherwise. The **tourist office** (*Riva bb;* ✆ *761 017; www.tzjelsa.hr*) is on the Riva.

 Where to stay and eat Hotel accommodation in Jelsa is almost exclusively at the resort complexes which include the **Fontana** (✆ *761 810; www.resortfontana-adriatiq.com;* €€€€–€€€) and the **Hvar** (✆ *761 024; www.hotelhvar-adriatiq.com;* €€€€–€€€). Private rooms, however, are in good supply and considerably cheaper here than in Hvar town, and can be booked through Atlas (✆ *761 605*), just up from the tourist information office. There is also the nice little family-run **Pansion Murvica** (*Sv Roka;* ✆ *761 405; www.murvica.net;* €€), near the bus station (they also have a nice stone house available in the village of Humac).

There are some private rooms available in **Vrboska** – contact the Vrboska tourist office (✆ *774 137; www.vrboska.info*) for more details – and one hotel, the Adriatic (✆ *774 039; www.vrboska-hotel.com;* €€€€) out on a headland beyond the village.

VIS

The lovely hilly island of Vis is Croatia's farthest flung possession, and also its oldest recorded settlement, having been colonised by the Greeks (from Syracuse, on Sicily) at the beginning of the 4th century BC. The colony of Issa then went on to found its own colonies (notably at Trogir and Salona) before succumbing to Roman rule, and following much the same historical fate as most of the rest of Dalmatia – Venetians, Austrians, the French, Austrians again, and then Yugoslavia – with the notable exception that Vis was also a British possession, from 1811 to 1814.

The British came back here in 1944, when the island was briefly Tito's headquarters – after the war, when Vis was Yugoslavia's naval staff headquarters, the only foreigners allowed on the island for decades were British veterans, who came back every September for their annual reunion.

Since 1989, Vis has been open for business, and despite the growth in tourism over the past decade, remains pleasantly less busy than Hvar or Brač. The island is also the jumping-off point for trips to the famous Modra Špilja (Blue Cave) on nearby Biševo, but it's well worth visiting in its own right.

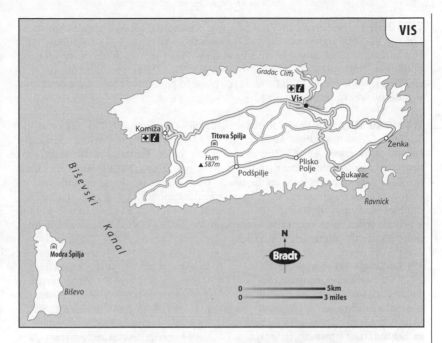

Vis has no freshwater sources, apart from a few springs near Komiža – water has to be brought in during the summer months by ship and stored in cisterns – so don't expect to be able to fill up here if you're sailing; head instead for Hvar and Korčula. The lack of water, however, doesn't stop the locals making excellent wine in great quantities, notably the red Plavac, and the dry (but sweet-scented) white Vugava.

The capital, Vis town, is in a sheltered inlet on the spectacular north side of the island (the cliffs at Gradac, nearby, rise 100m out of the sea), while Komiža, in a large bay facing west, is the other main settlement, closer to the island of Biševo.

The ferry journey out to Vis is one where you're quite likely to see dolphins alongside the boat.

GETTING THERE AND AROUND Two or three **ferries** a day come from Split all year round (*2½hrs*), stopping twice a week in Hvar, while in summer there's also a daily catamaran, which takes around 1½ hours from Split. Don't even think about trying to bring your car here in summer – rent a scooter or mountain bike on the island.

Public transport on Vis consists of the **bus** which runs several times daily between Vis town and Komiža, a short (15 minutes) but fairly spectacular ride along the northernmost of the two main roads across the islands. Another, less regular bus service covers the other, southern road. There's also a great network of tracks and **hiking** trails across the island, including to Titova Špilja (Tito's Cave), used as a base by the Partisan leader towards the end of the Second World War. Several hiking routes are described in detail in Rudolf Abraham's *The Islands of Croatia* (page 429), and there's an excellent detailed map of the island published by the HGSS. Active holidays can also be arranged through **WearActive** who run sea kayaking and other adventures with accommodation in a stone house in the village of Rukavac (*Gornji Rukavac 4;* m *098 1314 179;* e *croatia@wearactive.com; http:// wearactive.com*).

VIS TOWN Ferries arrive in Vis town, the diminutive capital, which consists of Luka to the west and Kut to the east, though the whole place is a 20-minute walk end-to-end, leading to the famous local quip, 'Vis town ain't big enough for the both of us'. The **tourist office** (↘ *717 017; www.tz-vis.hr*) has some local information and maps, while Ionios (↘ *711 532*) is the place to go to rent bikes and scooters – a wonderful way of seeing the island.

⌂ **Where to stay** The **Issa** (*130 rooms; Apolonija Zanelle 5;* ↘ *711 124*) and the **Tamaris** (*27 rooms; Obala Sv Jurja 30;* ↘ *711 350;*) hotels are priced identically (*www.hotelsvis.com;* €€€€). The rooms at the older Tamaris, in the middle of town, are considerably nicer than those at the newer Issa, but the latter does have the advantage of being right on the beach. Both hotels are closed from the end of October to the beginning of May; in the shoulder months, off-season, the price of doubles plummets by almost 50% to around the same as you'd expect to pay for a private room in town (available through the Ionios agency). More interesting, however, are the alternatives listed below.

⌂ **San Giorgio** (10 rooms) Hektorovića 2; ↘711 362; www.hotelsangiorgiovis.com. Beautiful little boutique hotel in Kut, with its own restaurant, Boccadoro. San Giorgio also arranges stays in the old stone lighthouse building on the island of Host at the mouth of the bay. €€€€€–€€€€

✳ ⌂ **Kuća Visoka** (sleeps up to 6) Vis; ↘(UK) 020 3287 0015; e enquiries@thisisvis. com; www.thisisvis.com. Beautifully restored old stone townhouse in a quiet part of the old town near the waterfront, owned by British couple Emma & Ben Heywood (who have subsequently repeated a similar venture in Montenegro). 2 dbl bedrooms plus 1 sgl, lounge, kitchen/diner, 2 bathrooms. €850/week or €130/night in high season, dropping to €800/week or €120/night in shoulder seasons & €700/week or €110/night in Apr/Oct – so even for 2 people taking the whole house, it's less than most hotel rooms, & with 4–6 people sharing it's an absolute bargain. Minimum 4-night stay. Highly recommended. €€€€–€

⌂ **Pansion Dionis** (8 rooms) Matije Gubca 1; ↘711 963; www.dionis.hr. Nice little family-run pansion/pizzeria in the town centre. Good value. €€€

✗ **Where to eat and drink** There's no shortage of places to eat in Vis – but for the best, head out to Kut along the eastern part of the bay.

✗ **Konoba Roki** Plisko polje 7; ↘714 004; www.rokis.hr; noon–23.00 daily. Out at Plisko polje, popular with tourists & expats, but the updater is not a fan – the food & setting are good, but being overcharged twice leaves a poor impression. Bookings essential. €€€€

✗ **Villa Kaliopa** Vladimira Nazora 32; ↘711 755; ⊕ Apr–Nov 13.00–16.00 & 17.00–midnight daily. Swanky place situated in the gardens of the fine 16th-century Renaissance Garibaldi Palace. Pricey but good, & increasingly popular with well-heeled Italians. No credit cards. €€€€

✗ **Karijola** Šetalište Viškog Boja 4; ↘711 433; ⊕ Jun/Sep 17.00–23.00 daily, Jul/Aug noon–midnight daily. Nice terrace, & the best pizzas on Vis, period. €€€

✳ ☐ ✗ **Konoba Vatrica** Petra Krešimira IV 13, Kut; ↘711 574; f Konoba Vatrica; ⊕ summer noon–23.00 daily, winter 17.00–midnight daily. Consistently good konoba on the waterfront in Kut. €€€

✳ ✗ **Pojoda** Don Cvjetka Marasovića 8, Kut; ↘711 575; ⊕ summer noon–01.00 daily, winter 17.00–midnight daily. Truly lovely seafood restaurant in a beautiful courtyard setting in Kut, the best restaurant on Vis & as far as the updater is concerned, one of the nicest anywhere in Croatia. Highly recommended. €€€

☐ **Lambik** Kut; ⊕ 07.00–02.00 daily. Great café/bar on the main square in Kut, with wicker sofas out front & a wonderful vine-covered courtyard at the back.

What to see and do There's not much to see in the way of Greek and Roman heritage, though the **Archaeological Museum** (*Arheološki Muzej;* \ *711 729;* ☺ *May–Oct 10.00–13.00 & 17.00–21.00 Mon–Fri, 10.00–13.00 Sat; out of season visits by appointment; 20kn*) housed in the old fortified battery (Gospinoj batariji) has a few treasures on show, including the famous 4th-century BC bronze head of a Greek goddess. There is also a useful leaflet detailing the sites of local ruins, though there isn't that much to see on the ground – the remains of the Greek cemetery and walls are really just vestiges, while what was once the Roman theatre has been firmly overbuilt by a Franciscan monastery.

More immediately evocative – especially to students of English history – are the remains of the imperial forts. Head up the hairpins behind the town then along the headland on the eastern side of the bay to the ruins of the **Wellington Fort** – though unfortunately the route takes you past the huge local rubbish heap, all going into landfill (a sobering reminder of the negative impact of buying plastic bottles of mineral water). On the northern headland, the once even more dilapidated **King George III Fort** was restored and converted into an art/music venue and bar in 2013 (*www.fortgeorgecroatia.com*) – which would have been great aside for the fact that you can now hear the bar, quite loudly, even in the otherwise quiet neighbourhoods of Kut and Lučica on the opposite side of the bay. Heading out past Kut takes you past a small **British cemetery**, just before the popular pebble beach, **Grandovac**. There are nicer beaches not far from town however – rent a bike and head out of town to **Stončica**, which is great for kids.

Finally, if you want to base yourself somewhere more remote than Vis town or Komiža, try WeAreActive in **Rukavac** (ⓜ *098 1314 179; http://wearactive.com*). Run by a Welsh couple, they offer a week's bed and breakfast including five days of activities (kayaking, hiking, cycling etc), three evening meals and four picnic lunches, together with transfers to/from Vis town (and restaurants when eating out), for €1,120–1,285 per person (late May–early Oct).

KOMIŽA Komiža, at the other end of the island, is a strong rival for Vis. Set under the bulk of Hum Mountain (587m), the town stretches in a lovely palm-studded sweep round the bay, and has plenty of appealingly run-down 16th- and 17th-century houses, as well as a fine 16th-century Venetian fortress, dominating one end of the harbour.

Behind the town, up the hill, is the austere fortified Benedictine **Monastery of St Nicholas** (Sv Nikole). On the saint's feast day, 6 December, the local fishermen drag a fishing boat up here and then set fire to it, in a display that certainly has nothing whatsoever to do with pagan rites.

🏠 **Where to stay and eat** Komiža's **tourist office** (*Riva Sv Mikule 2;* \ *713 455; www. tz-komiza.hr*) can fill you in on local sights, while **Blue Cave** (*Trg kralja Tomislava 10;* \ *713 752; www.visbluecave.com*) and **Darlić & Darlić** (*Riva Sv Mikule 13;* \ *713 760; www.darlic-travel.hr*) have private rooms for around €50. Plenty of eating and drinking goes on around Komiža's attractive main square, Škor, which is home to a handful of bars, cafés and restaurants, though the better and less touristy places tend to be those further north along the waterfront around Pol Kalafotovo beach.

🏠 **Villa Nonna** (7 apts) Ribarska 50; \ 713 500; ⓜ 098 380 046; www.villa-nonna.com. More atmospheric than the Biševo, this offers studio apts set in a renovated 400-year-old stone house. €€€€

🏠 **Biševo** (120 rooms) Ribarska 72; \ 713 279; www.hotel-bisevo.com.hr. The town's only hotel has a handful of pleasant rooms overlooking a pebble beach. €€€

✕ Konoba Jastožera Gundulićeva 6; m 099 670 7755; http://jastozera.eu; ⊕ Apr–Oct 17.00– midnight daily. Right on the waterfront, specialises in lobster & other seafood. €€€€

BLUE CAVE (MODRA ŠPILJA)

No trip to Vis seems to be complete without the obligatory visit to this cave, on the island of Biševo, 5km southwest of Vis (the island is now uninhabited, though families still tend the vines here, travelling back and forth by boat). And indeed, if you get there at the right time of day (between 11.00 and midday), and you have a moment in the cave to yourself, then it is surely one of the most beautiful sights on the planet. Sunlight filters down through the water and reflects off the pale sea-floor, giving a vibrant blue and turquoise shimmer to the cave. It's an absolutely incredible place to swim, especially if you've brought along a snorkel and mask.

Unfortunately, that's not the experience most people have. Out of season, access to the cave is often made impossible by choppy seas, while in July and August, on calm days, the cave gets almost as crowded as its namesake on Capri, and you'll be briskly ferried out to make room for the next boatload coming in.

The cave was discovered – and the entrance enlarged to allow boats in and out – in the 1880s. You can access the cave most easily via an excursion from either Vis or Komiža, though you can also easily charter your own boat. If you go, make sure you're wearing swimmers, and have a snorkel and mask if at all possible – even if your time in the cave is short you should manage a quick dip. Excursions usually then take you on to one of Biševo's many coves and beaches, and often feature the obligatory fish picnic.

Finally, spare a thought while you're here for the terribly endangered Mediterranean monk seal, the world's rarest pinniped; the islet of Brusnik, off to the west, near Svetac, is one of the very few places where it's recently been sighted in the past decade or so. Brusnik is also home to a charming endemic subspecies of the Dalmatian wall lizard, *Podarcis melisellensis melisellensis*.

9

Southern Dalmatia

Telephone code 020 (+385 20 from abroad)

The biggest draw in southern Dalmatia is the extraordinary walled city of **Dubrovnik**, but the area is unusually rich in other sights as well, and – in spite of some of the Adriatic's cleanest waters – there are fewer resorts and package destinations on the islands here than further north. The islands range from the quiet **Elaphites** (**Koločep, Lopud** and **Šipan**) and the near-perfection of **Mljet** (most of which is a national park), to popular **Korčula**, remote **Lastovo**, and Dubrovnik's own back garden, **Lokrum**. Onshore there's the long, straggly wine-growing peninsula of **Pelješac**, with oyster-rich **Ston** at its base, while against the Bosnian border you'll find the wetlands of the **Neretva Delta**.

DUBROVNIK

Dubrovnik is an extraordinary place. Vast walls, up to 25m high, come complete with fortresses, towers, crenellations and an ancient footpath along the entire 2km extent. The walls encircle an incredible stone-built red-roofed city, which juts out into the clearest, cleanest blue-green waters of the Adriatic. The streets are paved with time-polished pale marble, with the town's harmony owing as much to the 17th-century rebuilding programme following the Great Earthquake in 1667 as it does to Dubrovnik's remarkable history, stretching back well over 1,000 years.

Of course Byron's 'Pearl of the Adriatic' is no secret, with nearly half a million people a year staying at least one night, and even more coming in for the day on several hundred-odd foreign cruise ships every year. Nevertheless the city copes admirably with the influxes, and you'll find a place full of cheerful cafés, bars and restaurants, wonderful architecture, intriguing museums, atmospheric churches and a world-famous summer festival. The entire old city is a UNESCO World Heritage Site.

As if that weren't enough, Dubrovnik is blessed with an especially kind climate. Winter daily maximums rarely fall below 12°C, the sun shines reliably right through the summer, and there are plenty of beaches, with swimming popular from May to October. The city even has its own perfect forested island, Lokrum, just a few hundred metres offshore.

HISTORY Although some Roman, Illyrian and early Christian remains have been found in Dubrovnik, it was only at the beginning of the 7th century that the area was permanently settled. Survivors from the Roman colony at Salona (near Split), which had been taken over by avaricious Avars, teamed up with the remnants of the colony at Epidaurus (now Cavtat), which had been ravaged by Slavs, and settled on the rocky outcrop which is now the part of the old town south of Stradun. Doubtless scarred by their recent experiences, they started building fortifications right away –

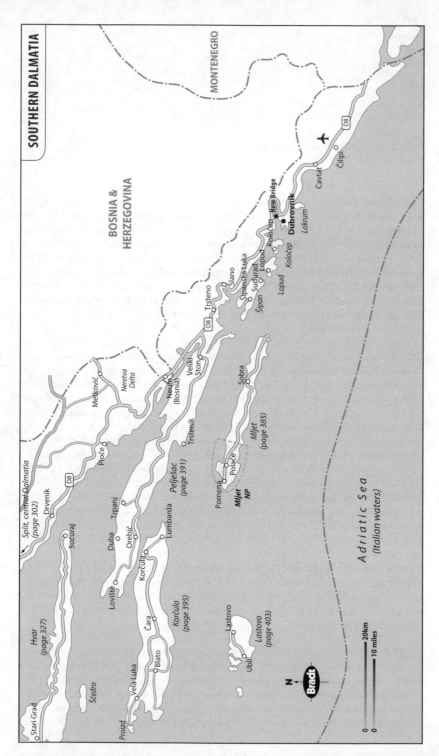

MONTENEGRO

BOSNIA &
HERZEGOVINA

D8

Cilipi

Cavtat

New Bridge

Koločep
Lopud
Sudurad
Šipanska Luka
Slano
Tsteno
Šipan
Lopud
Koločep
Dubrovnik
Lokrum

D8

Neum
(Bosnia)

Metković

Neretva
Delta

Veliki
Ston

Sobra

Ploče

Trstenik

Mljet
(page 385)

Pelješac
(page 391)

Polače
Pomena
Mljet NP

D8

Drvenik

Split, central Dalmatia
(page 302)

Sućuraj

Trpanj
Duba

Orebić

Lumbarda

Korčula

Lovište

Čara

*Korčula
(page 395)*

Lastovo

Blato

Vela Luka

*Lastovo
(page 403)*

Ubli

*Hvar
(page 327)*

Ščedro

Proizd

Stari Grad

*Adriatic Sea
(Italian waters)*

N

Bradt

20km
10 miles

0
0

and kept on doing so until the 16th century. They called their town **Ragusa**, which first shows up in print in the year 667.

Slavs, meanwhile, settled on the lower slopes of **Mount Srđ**, across the marshy channel that would become Stradun. Over the centuries the populations mixed, the channel was filled in, and the city walls grew to encompass both parts of the settlement. But even today there's a clear distinction between the steep narrow streets leading uphill from Stradun to the north and the palaces and churches and open squares that characterise the rest of the city to the south. To their dying day (which we'll get to in a little while) Ragusan patricians insisted they could trace their lineage back to Roman rather than Slav ancestors.

After switching between Byzantium and Venice and back again, and even throwing in its lot with the Normans on a couple of occasions at the end of the 11th century, Ragusa finally recognised that Venice was top dog in the Adriatic in 1205, and remained under Venetian sovereignty until 1358. It nonetheless kept its own currency and continued to develop its own institutions and culture.

Ragusa was also becoming a trading state of increasing importance, capitalising on its fortunate position between north and south and east and west. By the early 13th century favourable trading agreements were in place with many of the Italian city states and far inland into the Balkans. Over the years it developed a strong seafaring tradition, with trade routes eventually established all the way to Spain, Portugal and England. Dubrovnik sailors were even on board Columbus's ships when they discovered the West Indies in 1492.

Back at home the early 14th century saw a number of important developments. After a huge fire destroyed most of the city in 1296, a new urban plan was developed. Dominicans and Franciscans were allowed inside the city walls for the first time, on condition that they defended the two main land gates at either end of Stradun – where you'll still find their respective monasteries and churches today.

The city's first hospital was inaugurated in 1347, but a seriously nasty dose of the plague all too quickly followed in 1348, which reduced the population by 8,000. Soon, however, Dubrovnik was ready for its '**Golden Age**', which began when it escaped Venice's grasp in 1358 by formally becoming part of the Hungarian-

A NOTE ON CROSSING BOSNIA & HERZEGOVINA

Southern Dalmatia is cut off from the rest of Croatia by Bosnia's land corridor to the sea, and while for most visitors (including UK visitors and those from the rest of the EU, USA, Australia and New Zealand, all of whom can stay up to 90 days without a visa – see page 32 for visa requirements) this isn't a problem, for some other nationals it will mean getting a Bosnian visa – which is a serious hassle if this is all you need it for (it's not unknown for your passport to be sent to Sarajevo). If you're travelling by bus and don't plan on stopping in Bosnia, then you don't really need a visa as you can plead your transit case with the guards who board the bus – in the worst case you'll have to go around, via Pelješac, but we've never known the guards to insist on this.

If you're driving yourself, however, you do in theory need a visa (I have met people who've winged it successfully, but it's not recommended). Safer by far, and completely legitimate, is to get round the Bosnian section of road altogether by taking a ferry from Ploče to Trpanj (on Pelješac) and continuing south from there – though it does add at least a couple of hours to your journey. When the motorway is open this particular hassle will be a thing of the past.

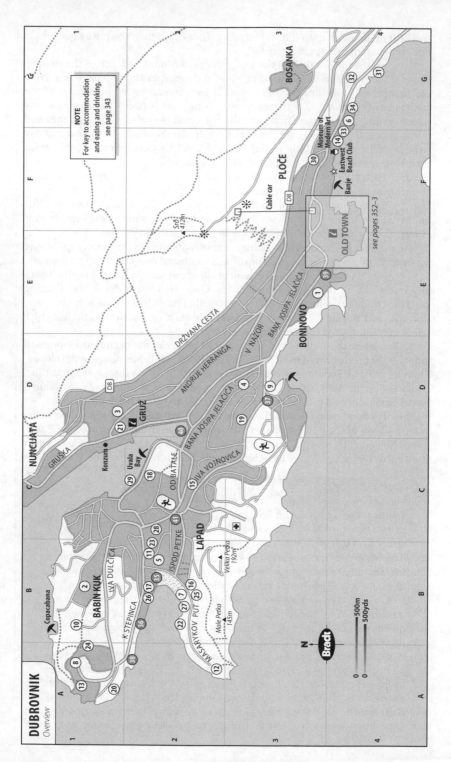

NOTE
For key to accommodation
and eating and drinking,
see page 343

BOSANKA

PLOČE

Museum of
Modern Art

Eastwest
Beach Club

Banje

Cable car

D8

Srđ
412m

OLD TOWN

see pages 352–3

BONINOVO

BANA JOSIPA JELAČIĆA

V NAZOR

DRŽAVNA CESTA

ANDRIJE HERRANGA

BANA JOSIPA JELAČIĆA

GRUŽ

NUNCIJATA

GRUŠKA

Konzum

Uvala
Bay

IVA VOJNOVICA

OD BATALE

LAPAD

ISPOD PETKE

Velika Petka
192m

Mala Petka
145m

MASARYKOV PUT

K STEPINCA

IVA DULČIĆA

BABIN KUK

Copacabana

N

Bradt

0   500m
0   500yds

Croatian kingdom. In exchange for paying Hungary 500 ducats a year, however, and providing armed forces when called upon to do so, the republic was allowed to do pretty much whatever it liked.

The first thing it liked to do, it seemed, was to frogmarch the Venetian rector, Marco Saranzo, off on to his state galley, thereby kicking off the best part of 500 years of tension between the two republics – a situation only resolved when Napoleon dissolved La Serenissima in 1797.

In 1365, just seven years after sorting things out with Hungary, Dubrovnik signed a treaty with Sultan Murat I – again with a 500-ducat-per-year price tag – which allowed the republic free-trading status across the whole of the occupied territories of the Ottoman Empire. By monopolising large chunks of the trade to and from the interior, Dubrovnik became hugely wealthy. Dubrovnik had freedom, liberty and independence – but it was *Libertas* (the republic's long-standing motto) bought with gold.

With money came territory, and during the Golden Age Dubrovnik's lands stretched from the town of Neum to the north (now in Bosnia) all the way to Sutorina, on the Bay of Kotor, to the south (now in Montenegro), a distance of around 120km. It included the Elaphite Islands (Koločep, Lopud and Šipan), the islands of Mljet and Lastovo, and the Pelješac peninsula.

At the beginning of the 15th century the remaining wooden houses in the town were demolished and rebuilt in stone. This was not so much for aesthetic reasons as to prevent fires from spreading. With many potential enemies, Dubrovnik had large stockpiles of munitions, and they had an unfortunate habit of going off – the Rector's Palace was destroyed by fire and explosions twice within a generation, in 1435 and then again in 1463.

The 15th century also saw Dubrovnik flourishing as a haven of liberalism. It offered asylum to refugees, including Jews, at times when many other cities turned them away at the gate. In 1416 slavery was definitively abolished, over 400 years ahead of Britain (1833) and America (1863). Many slaves subsequently had their

Southern Dalmatia   DUBROVNIK

9

freedom bought for them by Ragusan nobles. A public health service was in place as early as 1432, while the principle of education for all was established three years later, along with one of Europe's first orphanages and a free retirement home for the poor and elderly (it's still running, but no longer free).

The republic's wealth was also put to good use in a major building programme. The city walls were reinforced and defensive fortresses and towers constructed along their length. Onofrio della Cava, a bright engineer and architect from Naples, spent the six years to 1444 putting in place a sophisticated water supply (including an 8km aqueduct) which still works today and powers the two Onofrio Fountains on Stradun. In 1468 Stradun itself was repaved with marble, and in 1516 work began on the Customs House (formerly called the Divona and now known as the Sponza Palace).

Tragically an earthquake destroyed most of the city in 1520, and the plague returned in force in 1528, leaving 20,000 dead.

By the end of the 1520s, the Turks had pretty much defeated Hungary, and Dubrovnik was quick to change its allegiance from the Hungarian king to the Turkish sultan – now agreeing to pay an annual tribute of 12,500 ducats to keep the peace (that's inflation for you). The money was taken to the Sublime Porte every two years by envoys who then had to spend the next two years waiting there as effective hostages until they were relieved by the next cash-laden delegation.

In 1588 Dubrovnik joined the Spanish in their **'Invincible Armada'** and lost a dozen of its finest ships. As a result, trade with Britain was interrupted for the best part of two centuries. The battle neatly marks the beginning of the long, slow decline of the republic. New trade routes across the Atlantic made Britain, Spain and Portugal into wealthy nations, and Mediterranean shipping was never to regain its former importance.

Real disaster didn't strike, however, until 08.00 on the morning of 6 April 1667, the Saturday before Easter, when a **massive earthquake** destroyed Dubrovnik. More than 5,000 people – including the rector, the entire Minor Council and more than

WHAT'S IN A NAME?

For most of its extensive history – right from the 7th century through to 1918, in fact – Dubrovnik was known as Ragusa. The name was changed to Dubrovnik (according to Rebecca West, at least) only because Ragusa sounded too Italian by half.

The truth, as usual, is somewhat more complicated. Dubrovnik was originally not one place but two, divided by what's now the main street, Stradun. On the seaward side, which was originally almost an island, was Ragusa, populated by people of Roman origin. On the landward side, populated by Slavs, was Dubrovnik. Given that the nobles all came (or claimed to come) from Roman stock, Ragusa was the name which stuck – until the city was incorporated into the newly founded Kingdom of Serbs, Croats and Slovenes after World War I.

The name Ragusa is thought to be a corruption of the Greek word *lausa*, meaning rock, while the name Dubrovnik comes from the Croatian word for oak woods, *dubrava* – which were once plentiful on the hills above the town before being cut down and used to build Dubrovnik's impressive fleet of ships. (A fleet of ships that gave us another word, incidentally – argosy, a variant on the name Ragusa.)

half the Great Council – were killed. Only the Sponza Palace, the two monasteries, the bottom half of the Rector's Palace and the Revelin Fortress were left standing.

Seizing his opportunity, the Turkish sultan asked for a vast ransom to be paid if Dubrovnik wanted its freedom to continue as before. A delegation was sent in 1673 to the Porte to, well, 'talk turkey' with the Turks. Among the party were Nikola Bono and Marojica Koboga. Bono was to die in prison, but after the Turks were defeated at Vienna in 1683, Koboga came home to a hero's welcome. Dubrovnik had got away without paying the ransom, and was still free. It consolidated its position in 1699 by letting the Turks have chunks of land at either end of its territories – which is why today Neum is in Bosnia not Croatia, and Sutorina is in Montenegro. This meant that potential attacks from Venice could now only come from the sea and not overland.

Although Dubrovnik would never regain its former glories, the massive programme of rebuilding which went on through the early 18th century was to deliver the harmonious city you see today. Things started to look up for the republic, and by the end of the 18th century it had regained a considerable amount of its wealth and standing, and even boasted some 80 consulates in various cities across the continent.

Unfortunately, however, Napoleon was on the horizon, and on 26 May 1806 – as the only way to break a month-long siege by Russian and Montenegrin forces – the republic allowed a French garrison to enter the town. (Even now, clocks in the city's museums are often set to 17.45, the hour at which the troops entered.) Once installed, the French didn't leave, and on 31 January 1808 the republic was finally abolished. The following year it was absorbed into the newly created French 'Illyrian Provinces', which stretched all the way up the Adriatic coast to Trieste.

When Napoleon was defeated, Austria sent troops south and took control of Dubrovnik in 1814. Dubrovnik's noble families, in a terminal huff, took a vow of celibacy and swiftly died out. A century later Dubrovnik became part of Yugoslavia, but when Yugoslavia fell apart the city came under siege (see box, page 350).

GETTING THERE AND AWAY
With no train line, you'll most likely be arriving by plane, boat or bus, or in your own car.

Čilipi Airport is about 20km/half an hour south of town (see page 34 for flight details), and there's an airport shuttle that coincides with arriving flights (timetable at www.atlas-croatia.com – click on 'Transfers'). It returns to the airport from the Dubrovnik bus station around 2 hours before international departures, 90 minutes before domestic flights, and costs 40kn. Taxis (m 091 3322 022; www.taxidubrovnik.hr) cost around 250kn – if the meter's off make sure you've agreed and understood the fare with the driver before you set off.

All **ferries** come in to the city's port, Gruž, which is about 500m north of the bus station, itself just over 2km north of the old town (catch a local bus). There are also an increasing number of cruises featuring Dubrovnik; these too will bring you into Gruž harbour.

Long-distance **buses** come straight to the bus station [352 A2] (*Put Republike 19; 357 020*), past the port. If you're coming from the north you'll have driven across the fabulous, modern suspension bridge over the Dubrovačka Rijeka inlet, which cuts a welcome 15km off the journey. From one side you'll notice it labelled as the Tuđman Bridge, while from the other it's the Dubrovnik Bridge – telling you something useful about local politics. There's one direct bus a day from Frankfurt and Trieste, two from Sarajevo, eight buses a day from Zagreb (*8½–12hrs*), and 15 from Split (*4½hrs*) – for timetables see http://libertasdubrovnik.com and click 'Interurban timetable'. The bus station has Dubrovnik's only left-luggage facility (⊕ *04.30–21.00 daily*).

If you're coming in by **car**, be warned that parking in Dubrovnik can be both a problem and expensive. Hotel car parks tend to be overflowing, while street parking, especially in summer, is a non-starter. **Parking** operates in three zones (Zones 1 to 3, with Zone 1 being the closest to the old town), with automated payment possible through one of three corresponding phone numbers: Zone 1 ☎ 708 200; Zone 2 ☎ 708 202; Zone 3 ☎ 708 203 – simply send an SMS containing your vehicle's license plate number (no spaces) to the number for the appropriate zone; you should receive a confirmation, valid for one hour (you'll need to send another SMS for each subsequent hour when the first one is up). Alternatively you can buy a ticket from parking meters or nearby newspaper kiosks, and display these behind your windscreen. The closest car park to the old town is on Iza Grada, alongside the north wall (*Zone 1; 30kn/ hr, 15kn off season*), though it will almost certainly be full. A better choice is the larger car park at Gruž harbour (*Zone 3; 5kn/ hr, 85kn/day*). Probably the best option, however, is the huge 24-hour car park at Ilijina Glavica (*Zagrebačka ulica; not part of the Zone 1 to 3 parking system; 20kn/hr, 240kn/day, discount to daily rate if you tell the car park operator within 15mins of arriving that you want a day ticket*); there's a bus from there to the Pile Gate, or it's a 10-minute walk down a flight of steps through Baltazar Bogisic Park. More information on the Ilijina Glavica car park is available from Ragusa Parking (☎ 312 720); for information on parking within Zones 1 to 3 contact the local parking authority (☎ 640 134).

RAGUSA'S POLITICAL SYSTEM

Ragusa's political system was a variant on that of its rival Venice, though it was somewhat more subtle and complex. The main governing body was the Great Council, which consisted of all the male nobles over the age of 20; their main function was to elect the head of state, the rector, and supervise the Senate. The Senate comprised 45 nobles over the age of 40, though it had a purely consultative mandate. From the Senate, five men over the age of 50 were given a one-year term by the Great Council as Proveditores, keepers of the legal statutes and the constitution.

Executive power was wielded by the Minor Council, which consisted of 11 nobles appointed by the rector, with the youngest taking on the role of Foreign Minister. The rector had a term of office of just one month, during which he lived alone in the Rector's Palace, separated from his family and the rest of society. He was only allowed to leave the palace on state business or to attend church, and couldn't be re-elected within two years. In spite of all these restrictions he was merely a figurehead, wielding no power.

The political system was designed to concentrate power into the hands of a trusted few – in the 15th century there were only 33 noble families – but to avoid any one person or family being able to dominate, and for centuries it worked remarkably effectively.

The class system was rigidly enforced. Inter-marriage between classes was forbidden and social relations between them strongly discouraged – though that doesn't seem to have been necessary, given the divisions even within classes. The nobles defined themselves as Salamancans or Sorbonnais, named after the respective Spanish and French universities, with the former sympathetic to Spanish Absolutism and the latter with a liberal Francophile outlook. Apparently hostility was such that members of the two factions couldn't even bring themselves to greet one another in the street.

If you park illegally you can definitely expect your car to be towed away by the ruthlessly efficient 'Sanitat Dubrovnik' (✆ *640 136*; *www.sanitat.hr*) tow-away service. The number to call when this happens is ✆ 331 016, 24 hours a day, and the pound, where your car will have been taken, is on Lichtensteineov put, in Lapad. The nearest bus route is the #9; take it to the terminus (the hospital) and walk round to the left to find the top end of Lichtensteineov put.

GETTING AROUND Flat-fare Libertas **buses** cover the whole of Dubrovnik and most run from 05.00 to midnight (timetables for city routes at http://libertasdubrovnik. com/gradski-vozni-red, suburban routes at http://libertasdubrovnik.com/ prigradski-vozni-red). Tickets can be bought in advance from newspaper kiosks at 12kn apiece, or on the bus for 15kn – and you'll be expected to have the right money (except on the Cavtat bus). You can also get a day ticket (*dnevna karta*) valid for 24 hours from first use for 30kn – though the best value is just to get a **Dubrovnik Card**, which allows free transport on local buses (see box, page 349).

The main bus routes used by visitors are:

#1A and #1B	From Pile to the bus station & on to Gruž; about every half hour.
#3	From Pile to Gruž; about once an hour.
#4	From Pile to Lapad, passing many of the main hotels & terminating at the Dubrovnik Palace; 2 to 3 times an hour.
#5	From Pile to the Lapad post office & on to the Hotel Neptun on Babin Kuk; about once an hour. The return route goes round the one-way system, arriving at the Ploče Gate & then going round behind the old town walls to Pile.
#6	From Pile to the bus station, then up to the Lapad post office, terminating at the Dubrovnik President Hotel on Babin Kuk; about 4 times an hour.
#7B	From Gruž to the bus station & then up towards Lapad, passing the Hotel Bellevue & the Lapad post office before terminating at the Dubrovnik President Hotel on Babin Kuk; about once an hour.
#8	From Pile to the bus station, then on to Gruž where it goes into a one-way system, which ends by coming down the hill past the Ploče hotels to the Ploče Gate, & round behind the old town walls to Pile; 2 to 3 times an hour, but less frequently at w/ends.
#9	From the bus station up to the Lapad post office & on to the hospital before taking a shorter return route to the bus station; about once an hour.
#10	From the bus station to Cavtat; about once an hour. The fare to Cavtat is 15kn & you pay on the bus.

Notwithstanding the excellent local buses, Dubrovnik also has plenty of **taxis**, with stands at Pile, Ploče, Gruž, the bus station and Lapad (on Kralja Tomislava, just before the Lapad post office). You can also call taxis from any of the main hotels.

TOURIST INFORMATION The **tourist office** (*http://experience.dubrovnik.hr*) dishes out maps and various leaflets and can help you with booking concert tickets etc. There's an office just outside the Pile Gate [352 B3] (*Brsalje 5;* ✆ *312 011;* ⊕ *08.00–20.00 daily*) and another at Gruž [342 D2] (*Obala S Radića 32;* ✆ *417 983;* ⊕ *08.00–20.00 daily*), next door to the Jadrolinija ticket office. The website, however, is frankly infuriating and practical information on various sites can be fiendishly difficult to find.

You can also usually pick up maps and flyers from the various local tourist operators and agencies, though of late – particularly when a cruise ship arrives – they've taken to charging a token fee for maps.

🏠 **WHERE TO STAY** Dubrovnik's long been popular with visitors, with the first proper accommodation for them opening in 1347, and private rooms coming on-stream in the second half of the 14th century. The Grand Hotel Imperial, with 70 rooms just up from the Pile Gate, opened for business in 1897, but it was gutted by fire during the war in 1991. It reopened in 2005, as the Hilton Imperial, symbolic of a city once again ready for business.

During the siege of Dubrovnik (see box, page 350) the city lost around half of its total hotel stock, with damage being caused first by bombs and then by refugees flooding in afterwards. The scene improved fast, however, with most of the affected hotels now restored and reopened.

Your main accommodation options in Dubrovnik are hotels or private rooms – of which there is a plentiful and growing supply. There's also a youth hostel and a solitary campsite (pages 356–7). Private rooms offer the best value for money, but if you're in the mood to splash out there's certainly plenty of choice at the top end of the market too.

Hotel accommodation fills up fast in summer, so it's definitely recommended that you reserve well ahead of time, and confirm by email. Private rooms can be booked on the fly, though those in the best locations fill up well in advance.

Hotels In terms of location, Dubrovnik has just a couple of hotels in the old town (and one right by the Pile Gate); the rest are distributed around the smart suburb of Ploče just south of the old town, on the Lapad and Babin Kuk peninsulas, a few kilometres away, and in the port area of Gruž.

If you're coming to Dubrovnik out of season, shop around for serious reductions at almost all the hotels listed here – but especially those in Lapad and on Babin Kuk.

Most of Dubrovnik's accommodation is spread out around the **Lapad and Babin Kuk peninsulas**, and mainly caters to package tours. It has the advantage of being away from the bustle, and most of the hotels have access to a beach, but you may find yourself further away from the old town than you wish to be. That said, it's only a matter of 5km from the furthest point on Lapad to the old town, and there are regular buses (page 347). By taxi you're looking at a 10–20-minute ride, depending on the hotel location and traffic density.

Until recently, accommodation in the **old town** itself was limited to a handful of private rooms, but this is gradually changing as new boutique hotels open up for business. Bear in mind if you stay here that it can be stifling hot in summer, and views will be minimal – but on the other hand there's atmosphere in spades to be had from being inside the old walls.

If you can afford it, there's a lot to be said for staying in **Ploče**. The hotels overlook the sea and the island of Lokrum and have that view of Dubrovnik's old town walls and port. Seen in the light of early morning or late evening, it's a prospect to die for.

Old town

🏠 **Hilton Imperial Dubrovnik** [352 A2] (147 rooms) Marijana Blažića 2; 📞 320 320; www. hilton.com. It may not technically be in the old town, but it is right by the Pile Gate & offers jaw-dropping views of Dubrovnik's voluminous walls, the shimmering Adriatic & the towering hulk of Lovrijenac. The 5-star Hilton has thrown money into the impressive redevelopment of this grand old dame & she looks every bit as good, if not better, than she did in 1991 when she was shelled during the siege of the city. Be sure to

It's well worth getting a **Dubrovnik Card** during your stay (*www. dubrovnikcard.com*). Available for durations of 24 hours (*150kn*), three days (*200kn*) or seven days (*250kn*), this gets you free entry into eight of the city's top monuments and attractions – including the city walls, the Art Gallery, Marin Držić House, Rupe Ethnographic Museum and the Maritime Museum – as well as free use of public transport, and various other discounts. Considering a visit to the walls alone would otherwise set you back 100kn, and any of the above museums another 100kn (most museums now operate on a joint ticketing system, so it's 100kn whether you visit one or several) buying the card will almost certainly save you money. Buying the card online gets you 10% off these prices – just show proof of purchase at the tourist office and pick up your card on arrival. You can also buy the full price card at the tourist office, travel agencies, etc.

book a room with a sea view; some of the rooms & suites on the higher floors have balconies that you could throw a wedding reception on. Old-school grumpy Dalmatian service is out & smooth 5-star smiles are in, & facilities include a swimming pool & gym. An executive room is worth the extra as you can take b/fast & enjoy complimentary snacks & drinks, both alcoholic & non-alcoholic, throughout the day, in the lounge that also boasts a terrace overlooking the old city. €€€€€

🏠 **Pučić Palace** [353 E5] (17 rooms, 2 suites) Od Puća 1; ✆ 326 222; www.thepucicpalace.com. Fabulously located on the corner of Gundulićeva poljana, the heart of the action in the old city, the 5-star Pučić Palace is situated in a noble's luxuriously refurbished home. You could argue that the rooms – & particularly the bathrooms – have been over-restored, but you certainly couldn't complain about a lack of opulence. My favourite is the Ivan Gundulić room – though it's not the quietest, as it overlooks the square, which hosts both the early morning market & the late-night revelry spilling out from the back door of the Troubadur (page 361). As you'd expect it's not cheap, with doubles going for well over €500 in summer. €€€€€

🏠 **Hotel Stari Grad** [352 D3] (8 rooms) Od Sigurate 4; ✆ 322 244; www.hotelstarigrad. com. The 4-star Stari Grad (meaning 'old town') is situated between Stradun & Prijeko, only a couple of alleys in from the Pile Gate. It's a tiny establishment, with 4 dbls & 4 sgls in an ancient renovated house. Old stone, flagged floors &

tasteful furniture don't quite override the vague sense of unwelcome – or perhaps that was just the day I was there. You won't have any kind of view from your room (Od Sigurate is a narrow alley), but there is a 5th-floor terrace, with wicker furniture & fine views across the rooftops, where you can b/ fast in summer. €€€€€

🏠 **St Joseph's** [352 C4] (6 rooms) Sv Josipa 3; 📱 095 8223 740; www.stjosephs.hr. Boutique luxury hotel in a restored 16th-century property at the heart of the old town. €€€€€

🏠 **Fresh Sheets B&B** [353 E5] (6 rooms) Bunićeva poljana 6; 📱 091 896 7509; http:// freshsheetsbedandbreakfast.com. Lovely rooms in the old town near the cathedral. €€€€€– €€€€

Ploče

🏠 **Grand Villa Argentina** [342 G4] (162 rooms) Frana Supila 14; ✆ 300 300; www. adriaticluxuryhotels.com. In a very similar mould to the Excelsior, the Argentina consists of a 1920s stone-built hotel with a modern annexe grafted on. It was entirely renovated in 2002, & offers everything you'd expect from a 5-star hotel, including a small swimming pool & fitness centre. There are lovely gardens running down to the sea, & almost 2km of private beach. It's also well worth trying the Caravelle restaurant, which specialises in Croatian cuisine. €€€€€

🏠 **Hotel Excelsior** [342 F4] (nearly 200 rooms) Frana Supila 12; ✆ 300 300; www. adriaticluxuryhotels.com. For years after 1991 the 5-star Excelsior enjoyed an uninterrupted reign as

Dubrovnik's finest hotel. It may now have a string of competitors, but it has managed to raise its game, & no one can beat its views of the old town. Just 5mins walk uphill from the Ploče Gate, the Excelsior consists of a stone 1920s building & a largish glass & concrete annexe. It's unashamedly luxurious, with a private beach, a fitness centre, a great big indoor swimming pool with two jacuzzis, & wonderful terraces where you can sip cocktails & admire the views. The main restaurant, the Zagreb – which also serves as the b/fast room – is a bit too big for comfort, but the Taverna Rustica, set apart from the

THE SIEGE OF DUBROVNIK

In October 1991, with the war in full flow, the Yugoslav army laid siege to Dubrovnik, shutting off the water and electricity supplies, and raining shells down into the heart of the old town from air, land and sea.

The quick capitulation the Serbs expected never happened, mainly because of determined resistance, but at least in part because Onofrio's fountains – supplied by 15th-century plumbing – continued to function throughout the siege. Nevertheless, for three months there was no water for anything other than drinking, and no electricity or telephone service at all.

More than 100 civilians lost their lives in Dubrovnik, either when their houses were bombed or by snipers up in the hills, looking straight down Stradun – people simply didn't believe they were going to be shot in the sunny streets of Dubrovnik's old town. On one day alone (6 December 1991) the Serbs shelled the city from 05.00 to 16.10 with only a 15-minute break. In all the siege lasted from October 1991 to August 1992, though a ceasefire of sorts was in force at the beginning of 1992.

The material damage caused was enormous, with 70% of the old town's 800 houses sustaining direct hits, and more than 50 shells landing on Stradun alone. Many churches and monuments were targeted in spite of being clearly marked with UNESCO flags.

Dubrovnik's newly refurbished airport was completely destroyed, with the brand-new equipment being looted and taken back to Montenegro and on to Belgrade. Many people moved out, and not all have moved back – the old town's population, at 4,000, is still around 20% less than it was in 1990.

The damage sustained to Dubrovnik's reputation as a holiday destination was incomparably worse, and it took a full decade to bring back just half the visitors.

Yet Dubrovnik has made a truly heroic recovery from the war. Today, beyond a few pockmarked buildings, and acres of new tiles on the roofs, you'd never know there had been a terrible siege just two decades ago. (Ironically, some of the old tiles pulled off roofs during renovations were sent to villages further north to repair war damage there – only to be caught in the 1996 earthquake which destroyed much of Slano and Ston, at the base of the Pelješac peninsula.)

The only real reminder that the war happened at all – beyond the psychological scars – are the multi-lingual signs at each entrance to the old town, showing the 'City Map of Damages caused by the aggression on Dubrovnik by the Yugoslav Army, Serbs and Montenegrins, 1991–1992'.

Some justice has been done – in March 2004 a retired Yugoslav navy admiral, Miodrag Jokić, was sentenced to seven years in prison at The Hague for his part in shelling Dubrovnik. Most of the perpetrators, however, will never be brought to trial.

hotel up its own private path, has great atmosphere on its waterfront terrace & good regional cuisine. Some rooms have spectacular views. If you really want to splash out, try one of the lavish suites – the St Jacques suite, room 231a, has magnificent views of the old town through mirrored glass in the bathroom – as well as from the generous balcony. Great city breaks available, comprising 3 nights in a room with a sea view, a dinner at the Taverna Rustica & airport transfers. €€€€€

🏠 **Villa Dubrovnik** [342 G4] (56 rooms) Vlaha Bukovca 6; ⬚ 500 300; www.villa-dubrovnik. hr. Another 600m along the coast beyond the Argentina (turn off the main road just after the Villa Scheherazade) is the Villa Dubrovnik, refurbished in 2009–10. Walk down about 60 steps to get to reception, & you'll find the rest of the hotel below in terraces, dropping down to the rocky shoreline. The public areas are tastefully modern, light & airy, with white linen furnishings & rattan furniture, & the dining room & bar (& all the rooms) have gorgeous views back to the old town. In general, the amenities are excellent (all rooms have sea views & balconies), & it has its own rocky beaches & a boat to take you into the old town, as well as a lovely outdoor area called the Bistro Giardino, which is a perfect place for a pre-dinner drink. €€€€€

🏠 **Villa Orsula** [342 F4] (12 rooms) Frana Supila 14; ⬚ 300 300; www.adriaticluxuryhotels.com. Just 150m up the road from the Excelsior is the lovely 5-star Villa Orsula, under the same management (& connected to) the Argentina next door. The beautifully restored 1920s villa is somewhat dwarfed by the 2 big hotels on either side of it, but the rooms are delightful. All facilities are shared with the Argentina (page 349). €€€€€

🏠 **Villa Scheherazade** [342 G4] (5 rooms) Frana Supila 14; ⬚ 300 300; www. adriaticluxuryhotels.com. Further up the hill from the Argentina is the Villa Scheherazade. This Moorish-looking palace is a further luxury wing of the hotel. It certainly has plenty of atmosphere – it was formerly one of Tito's many residences, where (according to my trusty 1967 guide) the Marshal 'entertained Anthony Eden & many other world political figures'. €€€€€

Lapad, Babin Kuk & Gruž

🏠 **Grand Hotel Park** [342 B2] (248 rooms) Šetalište Kralja Zvonimira 39; ⬚ 434 444; www. grandhotel-park.hr. Situated between the Kompas

& the Komodor, & set back from the Uvala beach, is the boxy 3-star Grand Hotel Park. It has pretty good indoor & outdoor sea-water swimming pools, but make sure you go for a refurbished room; the older ones are really pretty tatty, making the sea-view dbl-room price tag (which you may be able to negotiate in winter) look a bit steep. €€€€€

🏠 **Hotel Argosy** [342 A1] (308 rooms) Iva Dulčića 41; ⬚ 446 100; www.valamar.com; ⏱ Apr–Nov. Behind the President is the Argosy, also owned by Valamar – a large hotel that is a step down in both facilities & price, though it still has access to the beach & tennis courts, etc, & boasts a decent-sized outdoor swimming pool. €€€€€

🏠 **Hotel Bellevue** [342 D3] (93 rooms) Pera Čingrije 7; ⬚ 300 300; www.adriaticluxuryhotels. com. The 5-star Bellevue has long enjoyed one of the best locations in Dubrovnik, just 15mins from Pile Gate on a cliff top overlooking its own beach &, fully refurbished in 2008, is now one of the city's finest hotels. Renata Štrok (the wife of the man behind the Adriatic Luxury Hotels group, Goran), herself a successful businesswoman with an eye for fashion, has personally overseen the creation of a unique hotel bathed in natural light that makes good use of local stone, wood & fabrics. As well as 2 bars & 2 restaurants the hotel boasts a presidential suite. To give you an idea of the clientele they're aiming at, there's a car lift that has been built to take 'Lamborghinis & Ferraris'. €€€€€

🏠 **Hotel Dubrovnik Palace** [342 A2] (308 rooms) Masarykov put 20; ⬚ 300 300; www. adriaticluxuryhotels.com. This 1st-rate hotel just can't seem to stop winning awards. Situated right at the end of the Lapad headland, Dubrovnik's biggest hotel reopened in 2004 after years of restoration & rebuilding. The 10-floor, 30,000m² complex boasts 3 outdoor swimming pools, rocky beaches & a diving centre, along with 2 indoor pools, 4 restaurants, 11 bars & a jazz club. Every room has a balcony & a sea view looking out towards the Elaphite Islands, & behind the hotel are lovely paths up into the woods leading to stone belvederes with views out to sea. The hotel is also home to a lavish health spa with signature hot stone massages, although many guests choose to while away hours in the pools & jacuzzi. Bus #4, which leaves from just outside the Pile Gate, takes you to the hotel; plans have also been mooted for a shuttle bus. €€€€€

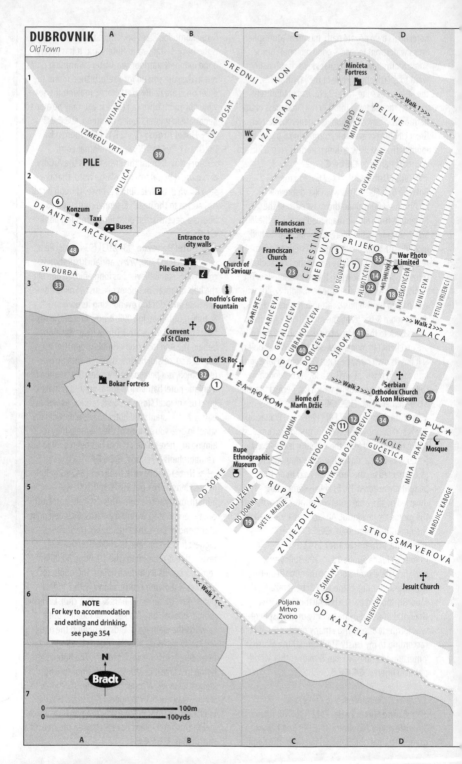

DUBROVNIK
Old Town

SREDNJI KON

Minčeta Fortress

>>> Walk 1 >>>

IZA GRADA

ISPOD MINČETE

PELINE

IZMEĐU VRTA

ZVIJAČICA

UZ POSAT

WC

PILE

39

PLOVANI SKALINI

PULIĆA

P

Franciscan Monastery

PRIJEKO

MEDOVIĆA

CELESTINA

6 Konzum

Taxi

Buses

DR ANTE STARČEVIĆA

Entrance to city walls

Franciscan Church

3

OD SIGURATE

7

15

War Photo Limited

48

Pile Gate

Church of Our Saviour

23

PALMOTIĆEVA

14

ANTUNINSKA

22

18

NALJEŠKOVIĆEVA

KUNIĆEVA

PETILO VRIJENCI

SV ĐURĐA

33

20

Onofrio's Great Fountain

GARIŠTE

>>> Walk 2 >>>

PLACA

Convent of St Clare

26

ZLATARIĆEVA

GETALDIĆEVA

ČUBRANOVIĆEVA

ĐORĐIĆEVA

40

ŠIROKA

41

Church of St Roc

32

1

OD PUČA

ZA ROKOM

>>> Walk 2 >>>

Serbian Orthodox Church & Icon Museum

27

Bokar Fortress

Home of Marin Držić

OD DOMINA

SVETOG JOSIPA

11

12

NIKOLE BOŽIDAREVIĆA

34

OD PUČA

NIKOLE GUČETIĆA

MIHA PRACATA

Mosque

Rupe Ethnographic Museum

OD RUPA

45

MAROJICE KABOGE

OD ŠORTE

PULIJEVA

OD DOMINA

19

SVETE MARIJE

44

ZVIJEZDIĆEVA

STROSSMAYEROVA

<<< Walk 1 <<<

Poljana Mrtvo Zvono

SV SIMUNA

5

OD KAŠTELA

CRIJEVIĆEVA

Jesuit Church

NOTE
For key to accommodation and eating and drinking, see page 354

N

Bradt

0 ——— 100m
0 ——— 100yds

352

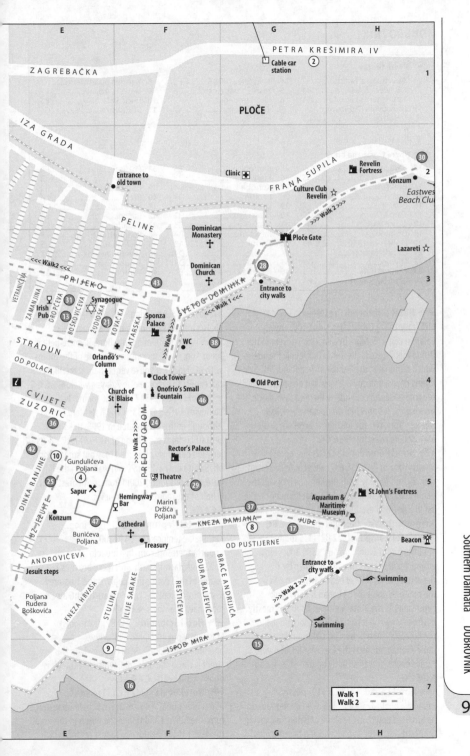

E | **F** | **G** | **H**

ZAGREBAČKA

PETRA KREŠIMIRA IV

Cable car station ②

PLOČE

IZA GRADA

1

Entrance to old town

Clinic ✚

Revelin Fortress

FRANA SUPILA

Konzum ●

㉚

Eastwes Beach Clu

2

PELINE

Culture Club Revelin ☆

Ploče Gate

Lazareti ☆

VETRANIĆEVA

<<< Walk2 <<<

PRIJEKO

Dominican Monastery ✝

Dominican Church ✝

⑱

Entrance to city walls

3

ZAMANJINA

DROPČEVA

Irish Pub

㉛

BOŠKOVIĆEVA

⑬

Synagogue ✡

⑳①

ŽUDIOSKA

KOVAČKA

ZLATARSKA

Sponza Palace

Walk 2 >>>

<<< Walk 1 <<<

SVETOG DOMINIKA

STRADUN

WC

㊳

OD POLAČA

Orlando's Column

Clock Tower

Onofrio's Small Fountain

Old Port

4

ℹ

CVIJETE ZUZORIĆ

㊱

Church of St Blaise ✝

㉔

PRED DVOROM

Walk 2 >>>

㊻

DINKA RANJINE

㊷

⑩

Gundulićeva Poljana

④

Rector's Palace

㉙

Theatre

⑤

St John's Fortress

㉕

Sapur ✗

Hemingway Bar

Marin Držića Poljana

Aquarium & Maritime Museum

Konzum ●

㊼

㉗

JUDE

Beacon ⚓

Cathedral ✝

KNEZA DAMJANA

⑧

⑰

Bunićeva Poljana

Treasury ●

OD PUSTIJERNE

ANDROVIĆEVA

DURA BALJEVIĆA

BRAĆE ANDRIJIĆA

Entrance to city walls

Jesuit steps

KNEZA HRVAŠA

STULINA

ILIJE SARAKE

RESTIĆEVA

Swimming

6

Poljana Rudera Boškovića

Walk 2 >>>

Swimming

⑨

ISPOD MIRA

⑮

⑯

7

Walk 1 ┄┄┄┄

Walk 2 ┄ ┄ ┄

E | **F** | **G** | **H**

⬅ Where to stay

1	Apartments Falkuša, Bracera & Galijan............B4	
2	Apartments Laptalo........G1	
3	Dubrovnik Old Town Hostel.....................C3	
4	Fresh Sheets B&B............E5	
5	Fresh Sheets Hostel........C6	
6	Hilton Imperial Dubrovnik.....................A2	
7	Hotel Stari Grad.............D3	
8	Karmen apartments.......G3	
9	Nevena Abjanić...............E7	
10	Pučić Palace.....................E5	
11	St Joseph's.......................C4	

✖ Where to eat and drink

12	Baracuda...........................D4	
13	Barba................................E3	
14	Buffet Škola.....................D3	
15	Buža I...............................G7	
16	Buža II..............................F7	
17	Carpe Diem......................G5	
18	Dolce Vita........................D3	
19	Domino.............................C5	
20	Dubravka 1836................A3	
21	Dundo Maroje..................E3	
22	D'Vino..............................D3	
23	Festival Café....................C3	
24	Gradska Kavana..............F4	
25	Kamenice......................... E5	
26	Klarisa..............................B3	
27	Konoba Dalmatino.......D4	
28	Labirint............................G3	
29	Lokanda Peskarija..........F5	
30	Maestoso.........................H2	
31	Malvasia...........................E3	
32	Mea Culpa.......................B4	
33	Nautika.............................A3	
34	Niko..................................D4	
35	Nishta..............................D3	
36	Pizzeria Olivia............... E4	
37	Pizzeria Storia................G5	
38	Poklisar........................... F4	
	Porat............................(see 6)	
39	Posat................................ B2	
40	Presa................................C4	
41	Proto................................D3	
42	Ražonoda.........................E5	
43	Rozario.............................F3	
44	Spaghetteria Toni...........C5	
45	Taj Mahal.........................D5	
46	Taverna Arsenal..............F4	
47	Troubadour......................E5	
48	Wanda..............................A3	

🏠 **Hotel Dubrovnik President** [342 A1] (180 rooms) Iva Dulčića 39; ☎ 441 100; www. valamar.com; ⏲ Mar–Dec. In a similar vein to the Dubrovnik Palace is the 4-star Dubrovnik President, which dominates the Babin Kuk headland. All rooms have a balcony & a view out across the sea to the Elaphite Islands, & there's a fairly large beach area. It's unashamed upmarket package-tour territory, but the location is excellent & the atmosphere cheerful. €€€€€

🏠 **Hotel Komodor** [342 B2] (63 rooms) Masarykov put 5; ☎ 433 637; www.hotelimaestral. com. Across the bay from the Kompas is one of the peninsula's oldest hotels, the 3-star Komodor – the 1st in a line of 5 establishments along Masarykov put run by the Maestral hotel chain. €€€€€

🏠 **Hotel Kompas** [342 B2] (115 rooms) Šetalište Kralja Zvonimira 56; ☎ 300 300; www. adriaticluxuryhotels.com. Right down by the attractive Uvala Bay beach, which marks the meeting point of the Lapad & Babin Kuk peninsulas, is the 3-star Kompas. Its rooms mostly have sea views, & it has its own indoor pool, but the hotel has seen better days. Now under the same management as the Excelsior & Dubrovnik Palace hotels, it was recently upgraded to 4-star. €€€€€

🏠 **Hotel Lapad** [342 C2] (157 rooms) Lapadska obala 37; ☎ 455 555; www.hotel-lapad. hr. Situated down on the shore of Babin Kuk, facing Gruž harbour, is the Lapad, which is based around a renovated old building with a modern annexe. There's a small swimming pool, & the nearest beach is about 600m up the shore. If you're here in Jul or Aug, make sure you ask for one of the rooms with AC. Finally, if you're vegetarian, & on HB, you can expect to eat omelette 7 days a week. €€€€€

🏠 **Hotel Lero** [342 D3] (160 rooms) Iva Vojnovića 14; ☎ 341 333; www.hotel-lero.hr. Although entirely renovated in 1998, the 3-star Lero still retains something of its 1971 feel – & its location on a busy main road may put some people off. But it's only a 15 or 20min walk from the Pile Gate, on a bus route, 200m from the nearest beach, & half of the rooms have sea views. €€€€€

🏠 **Hotel Neptun** [342 A1] (150 rooms) Kardinala Stepinca 31; ☎ 440 100; www. importanneresort.com. In a great location on Babin Kuk, facing south with rocky beaches & a couple of nice swimming pools, is the 10-storey 3-star Hotel Neptun. Its rooms are bright, airy & most have sea views. €€€€€

🏠 **Hotel Splendid** [342 B2] (59 rooms) Masarykov put 10; ☎ 433 633; www. hotelimaestral.com. Last of the bunch on this street is the 3-star Splendid, which like the Vis is right on the beach. €€€€€

🏠 **Hotel Uvala** [342 B1] (51 rooms) Masarykov put 6; ☎ 433 608; www.hotelimaestral. com. The newest addition to the hotels in this area, the 4-star Uvala 'health & wellness centre', which promises to pamper the guests in its rooms, most of which have sea views. €€€€€

🏠 **Hotel Villa Wolff** [342 B2] (6 rooms) Nika i Meda Pučića 1; ☎ 438 710; www.villa-wolff.hr. Right next door to the Kompas is the 4-star Hotel Villa Wolff. You wouldn't know it walking up the short flight of steep steps from the coastal path (next door to the Casa Bar), but above you is a charming little boutique hotel, with just 3 dbls; 1 junior suite, 2 suites with balconies & sea views. It has its own terrace & Mediterranean garden, complete with rosemary bushes, palms, cypresses & ancient olive trees, with a great view across the bay. €€€€€

🏠 **Kazbek** [342 C2] (12 rooms, 1 suite) Lapadska obala 25; ☎ 362 900/999; www.kazbekdubrovnik.com. New luxury boutique hotel in beautifully restored 16th-century noble's palace at Lapad. €€€€€

🏠 **Berkeley Hotel** [342 D1] (24 rooms & suites) Andrije Hebranga 116a; ☎ 494 160; www.berkeleyhotel.hr. Nice, good-value – & very popular – aparthotel in Gruž. €€€€

🏠 **Hotel Adriatic** [342 B2] (158 rooms) Masarykov put 9; ☎ 433 609; www.hotelimaestral.com. Just up the road from the Komodor is one of Dubrovnik's last-remaining 2-star hotels, the Adriatic. The beach is just across the street & it's a bargain (& almost invariably fully booked). But we have received negative reports from readers who have written in to say it's noisy, unwelcoming & that rooms aren't always up to standard. €€€€

🏠 **Hotel Club Dubrovnik** [342 B1] (338 rooms) Iva Dulčića 18; ☎ 447 100; www.valamar.com; ☀ Apr–Nov. Further into the Babin Kuk headland, & facing the islet of Daksa. Good family choice, within reach of one of Dubrovnik's most popular beaches, the Copacabana, where you can indulge your taste for water polo, water skiing, scuba diving, wind surfing, & banana rides. €€€€

🏠 **Hotel Dubrovnik** [342 B2] (22 rooms) Šetalište Kralja Zvonimira bb; ☎ 435 030; www.hoteldubrovnik.hr. A nice option is the 3-star Hotel Dubrovnik (not to be confused with the Villa Dubrovnik, the Dubrovnik Palace or the Dubrovnik

President), all of 100m away from Grand Hotel Park, which may have neither indoor nor outdoor pools, but does have clean, well-appointed rooms including 4 suites at reasonable rates, & a welcoming staff. €€€€

🏠 **Hotel Ivka** [342 C2] (76 rooms) Ulica od Sv Mihajla 21; ☎ 362 600; www.hotel-ivka.com. Small, decent value family-run place on Lapad. €€€€

🏠 **Hotel Petka** [342 D1] (104 rooms) Obala Stjepana Radića 38; ☎ 410 500; www.hotelpetka.hr. Situated right next to the main ferry-landing in Gruž, the 3-star Petka features AC in all rooms, 64 of which have balconies giving views over the picturesque port. It's nothing fancy, but gives easy access to the islands, & is only a short bus ride away from the old town. The prices offer good value by Dubrovnik standards. €€€€

🏠 **Hotel Sumratin** [342 B2] (40 rooms) Šetalište Kralja Zvonimira 9; ☎ 436 333; www.hotels-sumratin.com. Further inland is the 2-star Sumratin, which has neither sea views nor a swimming pool, but is simple, clean & good value for money. €€€€

🏠 **Hotel Tirena** [342 A1] (208 rooms) Iva Dulčića 22; ☎ 445 100; www.valamar.com; ☀ Apr–Oct. The Tirena is located between the Argosy & the Club Dubrovnik, & therefore also within reach of Copacabana beach, although only 28 of the rooms offer sea views. Its main advantage over the others is in being attached to the little local shopping centre. €€€€

🏠 **Hotel Vis** [342 B2] (152 rooms) Masarykov put 4; ☎ 433 605; www.hotelimaestral.com. Over on the seaward side of Masarykov, is the 3-star Hotel Vis, whose main attraction is being right on its own decent-sized beach. Like the Adriatic, it's very often full up. €€€€

🏠 **Hotel Zagreb** [342 C2] (22 rooms) Šetalište Kralja Zvonimira 5; ☎ 438 930; http://hotelzagreb-dubrovnik.com. Almost next door to the Sumratin is one of my favourites, the 2-star Zagreb. It offers clean dbls at reasonable prices in a lovely refurbished old building. €€€€

Private rooms/apartments Dubrovnik has a huge supply of private rooms available, and although they're more expensive here than most places in Croatia, they're still a good deal cheaper than the hotels, with most private double rooms going for around €60 a night, even in summer.

The obvious way of finding a private room is through one of Dubrovnik's ubiquitous travel agencies, who will generally welcome your business. There are also a number of online resources if you want to book/look ahead – over a hundred properties are listed at each of www.dubrovnik-apartments.com and www. dubrovnik-online.com/dubrovnik-private-acomodation, for example.

If you come in by ferry or bus, you're likely to be assailed on arrival by offers of private rooms. These may work out cheaper than anything you can get through travel agents, and unless the season's especially busy you can haggle – but check both the location and total price very carefully before accepting an offer.

🏠 **Apartments Laptalo** [353 G1] (2 apts) Petra Kresimira IV 13; ☎ 427 476; www. dubrovnikapartments-laptalo.com.hr. Nice, spacious apartments in Ploče with good views. €€€€

✱ 🏠 **Karmen apartments** [353 G3] (4 apartments) Bandureva 1; ☎ 323 433; m 098 619 282; e – the best way of reserving, for once – marc.van-bloemen@du.t-com.hr; www. karmendu.com. Of the places I've stayed at, the outstanding recommendation has to go to this place. The apartments are situated in an ancient stone building in a stunning location right on the old port. They're not cheap – but they're great value & perfectly located. 20% surcharge for stays of under 3 nights. €€€€

🏠 **Nevena Abjanić** [353 E7] (4 apartments) Ilije Sarake 8; ☎ 323 690; m 091 528 0091; www. abjanic.com. Another great recommendation goes to Nevena Abjanić, which has apartments just within the walls of the old town, all tastefully decorated & all with terraces. €€€€

✱ 🏠 **Villa Branko** [342 F3] (4 rooms) Put Petra Kresimira IV 33; e info@villabranko-

dubrovnik.com; www.villabranko-dubrovnik.com. Also highly recommended is Kathy Ljubojević's family-run villa. The house is high up in Ploče with a staggering view down on to the old town & across to Lokrum. The rooms are clean & tidy; the front 2 have balconies & stupendous views; ideal for small groups or families. €€€€

🏠 **Villa Odak** [342 G4] (2 rooms) Frana Supila 16; (UK) 020 8144 0215; http://villa-odak. dubrovnikhotelscroatia.net. Small place near Ploče. €€€€

🏠 **Apartments Falkuša, Bracera & Galijan** [352 B4] Ferićeva 1; m 098 455 847; www.dubrovnik4you.com.hr. 3 pleasant apartments for 2 or 4 people in the old town, just a short walk from the Pile Gate & Onofrio's Fountain. €€€€–€€€

🏠 **Apartment and room Lukre** [342 E3] (1 room, 1 apt) Don Frana Bulića 7; m 099 420 2066, 098 795 962; www.dubrovnikapartment-roomlukre.com. 2-min walk to the Pile Gate. €€€

Hostels These days Dubrovnik's hotels are rounded out by a decent range of hostels, providing budget accommodation in and around the old town.

🏠 **Fresh Sheets Hostel** [352 C6] Svetog Simuna 15; m 091 799 2086; www. freshsheetshostel.com. Small, award-winning family-run hostel opened in 2008, in the old town. 4- & 6-bed dorms & 1 dbl. €€€

🏠 **Dubrovnik Old Town Hostel** [352 C3] Od Sigurate 7; ☎ 322 077; www. dubrovnikoldtownhostel.com; ☺ Mar–Nov. With beds in 4- & 6-bed dorms plus some dbls & 1 sgl, for €15.50pp. €€

🏠 **Dubrovnik Youth Hostel** [342 D3] Vinka Sagrestana 3; ☎ 423 241; www.hfhs.

hr; Dubrovnik's youth hostel is in a pretty good location, about 20mins uphill from the bus station, just off Bana Jelačića, & for single people on a budget it's as cheap as you'll find in Dubrovnik, at €21–€27pp in Jul/Aug. That said, as you can imagine it's very hard to secure one of the 80-odd places, especially in summer, & for 2 or more people travelling together private accommodation can be not only more convenient – no daytime lockout, for example – but also competitive on price & location. 1 dbl, 14 quad- & 4 6-bed dorms. €€

Campsite Dubrovnik also has a solitary campsite, on the Babin Kuk Peninsula (managed by Valamar), but unless you're absolutely desperate to get under canvas, I can't really recommend it as an accommodation option for a short break. Having said that, if you are coming here with your tent, the **Auto-Camp Solitudo** [342 B2] (*Iva Dulčića 39;* ☏ *465 010, 448 686* e *camping@valamar.com; www.camping-adriatic.com*) offers 166 pitches, newly refurbished bathrooms and laundry areas, and charges roughly €27 per pitch and €11.50 per person in August. It also has mobile homes, and it's close to various beaches.

✖ **WHERE TO EAT AND DRINK** As you'd expect, Dubrovnik is brimming with places to eat, though with a few exceptions there's often surprisingly little to distinguish one place from another. Food in the old town tends universally towards grilled fish, meat and shellfish at the upper end of the spectrum, and pizza and pasta dishes in the mid-tier establishments.

Restaurants
Inside the walls Dubrovnik's busiest restaurant district is along Prijeko, the street running parallel to Stradun on the landward side for its entire length. Unfortunately, it's managed to get itself something of a bad reputation over the years, which hasn't been helped by the touts along Stradun trying to entice passing trade. While there's no doubt good food to be had, there's a level of unscrupulousness here that probably comes from knowing the chances are you won't be coming back, and tales of poor-quality food and routine overcharging are legion. It's a pity, as the location is perfect and the atmosphere ought to be first-rate. Two exceptions to the Prijeko rule are Nishta and Rozario – though, even at the latter, readers have reported offhand service. It's also worth noting that prices at restaurants and cafés on Stradun itself are usually significantly higher – as much as 50% – than elsewhere in the old town.

Expensive

✖ **Labirint** [353 G3] Svetog Dominika 2; ☏ 322 222; ⏰ 11.00–midnight daily. Set into the city walls near the Dominican Monastery, Labirint offers an upmarket restaurant as well as various bars, terraces & a discreet nightclub. The fish soup was excellent on my visit, while mussels are comparatively expensive, with mouth-watering scallops a much better deal. Expect meat dishes to cost upwards of 150kn & wine to set you back around 200kn or more a bottle. Booking essential in season & w/ends. €€€€€

✖ **Proto** [352 D3] Široka 1; ☏ 323 234; www. esculaprestaurants.com; ⏰ 10.00–23.00 daily. Proto is one of Dubrovnik's most famous landmarks & makes a big deal about having been in business since 1886 & having had Edward VIII & Wallis Simpson to dinner in the 1930s. In spite of the hype there's still a lot to be said for both the fish & meat dishes here, which are probably as good as anywhere in town – & the upstairs terrace is always packed in summer. Worth reserving ahead. €€€€€

Mid-range

✖ **Domino** [352 C5] Od Domina 3; ☏ 323 103; www.steakhousedomino.com; ⏰ 10.00–

midnight daily. At the top end of Od Domina, not far from the inside of the sea wall, Domino prides itself on its great steaks, but also has decent fish & seafood specialities, including a particularly good grilled squid. The outside terrace is enduringly popular. Check out its sister restaurant, Bistro Riva, on Lapad. €€€€

✳✖ **Konoba Dalmatino** [352 D4] Miha Pracata 6; ☏ 323 070; http://dalmatino-dubrovnik. com; ⏰ 11.00–23.00 daily. Traditional Dalmatian cuisine with a twist, & a good wine list. €€€€

✖ **Lokanda Peskarija** [353 F5] Na Ponti; ☏ 324 750; www.mea-culpa.hr; ⏰ 08.00–midnight daily. Absolutely my favourite place in Dubrovnik out of season, even if it does have one of the world's shortest menus – or perhaps because of it. Situated right on the old port, the establishment is tiny, with a bar downstairs & a handful of tables upstairs, though in fine weather it quickly spreads out across the quayside. The fried squid here can be outstanding, but standards tend to fall off somewhat during high season. The restaurant's homemade fish pâté or the marinated anchovy fillets are good choices. €€€€

✖ **Taverna Arsenal** [353 F4] Pred Dvorom 1; www.mea-culpa.hr/arsenal-gradska; ⏰ 10.00–

02.00 daily. Cavernous deep-red dining space in the old port, with wooden beams supposed to be evocative of an old Dubrovnik ship. During the day the interior is geared towards large groups, with other diners soaking up the old harbour views from the outdoor terrace. Veal kebabs are the standout among solid Dalmatian fare. At night the restaurant is transformed into a late-opening lounge bar, which stays open until 04.00. €€€€

✕ Dundo Maroje [353 E3] Kovačka; ☎ 321 021; ⏰ 11.00–midnight daily. On one of the tiny alleys connecting Stradun with Prijeko, Konoba Dundo Maroje comes highly recommended for its excellent & reasonably priced seafood dishes, & outsized plates of squid. No views whatsoever but a great atmosphere. €€€€–€€€

✕ Klarisa [352 B3] Paska Milečevića 1; ☎ 413 100; www.klarisa-dubrovnik.com; ⏰ summer 08.00–midnight daily, winter 11.00–22.00 daily. Formerly called Jadran, Klarisa had a facelift in 2011 & has a perfect location inside the old cloisters of the former Convent of St Clare (go through the alley to the right just after you come through the Pile Gate, past a sports shop on the right & a souvenir shop on the left). Dating originally from the 13th century, the convent became the republic's orphanage in 1432, & an open-air cinema after World War II. A lovely place to sit & while away an hour or two – especially if it's windy, as it's a well-sheltered spot. €€€€–€€€

✕ Poklisar [353 F4] Ribarnica 1; ☎ 322 176; www.poklisar.com; ⏰ 09.00–midnight daily. Poklisar has a great location right on the old port, next to the fish market (*riba* means fish). It has a lovely twin terrace & serves up the usual range of fish dishes as you'd expect, as well as reasonable pizzas – though you could argue that you're paying as much for the setting as for the food here. €€€€–€€€

✕ Mea Culpa [352 B4] Za Rokom 3; ☎ 323 430; www.mea-culpa.hr; ⏰ 09.00–midnight daily. Owned by the same people as Lokanda Peskarija (page 357), Mea Culpa is located at the other end of town, serving up large pizzas & simple seasonal salads. Tables spill out on to the street, & it's a popular place with locals & visitors alike, though the quality of the food can be a bit hit & miss. €€€

Budget

✕ Pizzeria Oliva [353 E4] Lučarica 5; 324 594; www.olivadubrovnik.com; ⏰ 10.00–23.00 daily. Often tipped as the best pizza in town. €€€–€€

✕ Pizzeria Storia [353 G5] Kneza Damjana Jude 6; m 091 2111 152; ⏰ 11.00–23.00 daily. Popular pizzeria/spaghetteria in the shadow of the old walls, on the south side of the old harbour. €€€€–€€€

✕ Rozario [353 F3] Prijeko 1; ☎ 322 015; www.konoba-rozario.hr; ⏰ noon–23.00 daily. Rozario has been open for around 40 years, & manages to break the Prijeko mould (see the introductory section, page 357), serving up unpretentious local Croatian fare in a nice setting near the Dominican Monastery. €€€€–€€€

✕ Baracuda [352 D4] Nikole Božidarevićeva 10; ⏰ 11.00–23.00 daily. Small place serving up tasty pizzas & very little else (there really isn't room). Situated just off Od Puča, near the Serbian Orthodox Church. €€€

✕ Kamenice [353 E5] Gundulićeva poljana 8; ⏰ 07.00–22.00 daily. Kamenice – literally small stones, but here meaning oysters – is a great place in a great location. It specialises in seafood, & in particular oysters. The menu is short but excellent, with the *frittura* (whitebait) & the squid particularly good, & the house wine affordable. The service can be a little slow and surly, & you'll probably have to queue for a table, but perhaps that's all part of the charm. €€€

✕ Nishta [352 D3] Prijeko 30; ☎ 322 088; www.nishtarestaurant.com; ⏰ 11.30–23.00 Mon–Sat. Great little vegetarian option on Prijeko, with plenty of vegan & gluten-free options – mains include smoked seitan burger with sweet potato sticks, fried rice noodles with tofu & ginger, spelt pasta tossed with capers, olives, sundried tomatoes & herbs. Definitely an exception to the general lacklustre quality of many Prijeko eateries. €€€

✕ Spaghetteria Toni [352 C5] Nikole Božidarevićeva 14; ☎ 323 134; www.spaghetteria-toni.com; ⏰ 11.00–23.00 daily. Just a couple of doors up from the Baracuda (see above) is Spaghetteria Toni, which serves up some of the best pasta in town (though 1 reader certainly didn't agree). Check out the vast homemade lasagne or the various pasta dishes with seafood sauces. Toni feels like an Italian trattoria, only this one serves thick Turkish coffee; it's cheerful, informal & highly popular with locals – last time I ate there the director of the Museum of Modern Art was having dinner with friends at the next table. €€€

✕ Taj Mahal [352 D5] Nikole Gučetica 2; www.tajmahal-dubrovnik.com; ⏰ 09.00–midnight daily. Just up the street from the mosque, this small restaurant serves up – in spite of the misleading name – excellent Bosnian food, including 1st-rate *ćevapčići* & spicy pies to the

Outside the old town walls

Expensive

✕ Maslina Tavern [342 A2] Masarykov put 20; ✆430 351; www.dubrovnikpalace.hr. Fine dining with great views out towards the Elaphite Islands – & service as smooth & food as mouthwatering as you'd expect from the Dubrovnik Palace Hotel. €€€€€

✕ Nautika [352 A3] Brsalje 3; ✆442 526; www. nautikarestaurant.com; ⏱ noon–midnight daily. For years the ritziest place in town, the Nautika trades heavily on having had Pope John Paul II to lunch on 6 June 2003, though it's hard to imagine the late pontiff scoffing his way through the 5-course menu on display. These days I'd personally rather eat at Labirint or Levanat if spending that kind of money, though Nautika does have an excellent location, on the water, right outside the Pile Gate, & a gorgeous pair of terraces, as well as smart dining rooms indoors. The food is excellent, as you'd expect for the price, & the service impeccable – but check your bill carefully as mistakes have been reported. Nautika also offers a 'Light Lunch' on the terrace outside, though I wasn't all that impressed. Reservations recommended. €€€€€

✕ Porat [352 A2] Marijana Blažića 2; ✆320 320; www.hilton.com; ⏱ 07.00–23.00 daily. The signature restaurant at the Hilton Imperial is a welcome addition to the dining scene, marrying as-good-as-it-gets Croatian food with international treats. Highlights on an ever-changing menu include the huge starter of lobster spaghetti & a great cheese board from Pag. You can't go wrong with the steak, or traditional Adriatic cuisine. Reservations recommended. €€€€€

✕ Levanat [342 A2] Nika i Meda Pučića 15; ✆435 352; www.restaurant-levanat.com; ⏱ 08.00–midnight daily. With an unbeatable waterfront location on Babin Kuk, Levanat is secluded, upmarket & pricey. It's easy to get to by walking along the footpath that starts at Casa (opposite) for about 10mins, or from the Babin Kuk or Neptun hotels; otherwise you might want to consider getting a taxi, as it's quite a schlep from

sounds of *sevdah* music. You can book a table online. A sister restaurant opened in Hotel Lero (page 354) in 2013. €€€–€€

the old town. The menu focuses on excellent – & by Croatian standards – original fish dishes. You can also come here just for a drink. Reservations recommended (not least to check it's open). €€€€€–€€€€

Mid-range

✕ Maestoso [353 H2] Put od Bosanke 4; ✆420 986; ⏱ 10.00–midnight. Well-known & popular restaurant just outside the Ploče Gate with a view across to the old town harbour. The fare is the traditional grilled meat & fish, but the place is (in this author's opinion) somewhat overrated. €€€€

✕ Orhan [342 E3] Od Tabakarije 1; ✆411 918; www.restaurant-orhan.com; ⏱ 09.00–midnight daily. Orhan serves up the same sturdy Adriatic staples – squid risotto, mussels & fish platters – that you find all over Dubrovnik, with the tempting addition of a self-service salad bar for just 15kn a bowl. The real reason to come here though is the stunning views over the city walls from the terrace, right underneath the Lovrijenac Fortress. There are also a few private rooms available. €€€€

✕ Wanda [352 A3] Prijeko 8; m 098 944 9317; www.wandarestaurant.com; ⏱ 11.00–22.00 daily. Along with Nishta & Rozario, this place is a cut above the rest in Prijeko. €€€€

✕ Casa [342 B2] Nika i Meda Pučića 1; ✆438 710; www.villa-wolff.hr; 09.00–23.00 daily. Billed as 'Bar & Ristorante', Casa has a great location right on the waterfront at Uvala Bay, just where the Babin Kuk & Lapad peninsulas meet. It's right under the Hotel Villa Wolff & next door to the Hotel Kompas, & marks the start of the path that goes clockwise around Babin Kuk. It only actually serves food in summer, & then more of the snack variety than the full meal, but it's an excellent place to sit, with the light bouncing off the water. €€€€–€€€

✕ Pantarul [342 C3] Kralja Tomislava 1; ✆333 486; www.pantarul.com; ⏱ noon–16.00 & 18.00–midnight Tue–Sun. Unpretentious but stylish new restaurant in Lapad, with an emphasis on local, seasonal produce. €€€€–€€€

Southern Dalmatia   DUBROVNIK

9

✘ **Otto Taverna** [342 D2] Nikole Tesle 8; m 095 8484 316; www.tavernaotto.com; ⏲ noon–16.00 & 19.00–23.00 Mon–Sat. Good-value taverna in Lapad, specialising in grilled meat & fish. €€€

✘ **Posat** [352 B2] Uz Posat 1; ☎ 421 194; ⏲ 09.00–23.00 daily. Well located outside the Pile Gate (just up and to the right) is the Konoba Posat,

which has a large & leafy terrace. It's as good a place as any for grilled meats. €€€

✘ **El Toro** [342 D3] Ivo Vojnovića 5; ⏲ 09.00–23.00 daily. Just up the road from the Hotel Bellevue, with a nice leafy high-up terrace, you'll find the Café Pizzeria El Toro, which is cheap & cheerful & serves up reasonable pizzas at a good price. €€

Buffets and snack bars If you're on a really tight budget there are plenty of buffets, snack bars and sandwich joints in town, some with a few tables, some take-away only. Here are three of the best, all in the old town.

✘ **Barb** [353 E3] Boškovićeva 5; ⏲ 10.00– midnight daily. New place billing itself as 'sea food street food'. Sandwiches (tuna with anchovies, octopus with marscapone, both around 30kn), pizza, salads (44kn), fried squid, etc. A few nice wooden tables inside. €€–€

✘ **Buffet Škola** [352 D3] Antuninska; ⏲ 10.00–midnight daily. On the left-hand side

heading up towards Prijeko. Terrific homemade sandwiches filled with cheese or pršut for 20–30kn. A few tables outside. €

✘ **Presa** [352 C4] Đorđićeva 2; ⏲ 10.00– midnight daily. No-nonsense cheapie with sandwiches, grills, & some good, fresh-looking salads (20kn). A few tables outside. €

Ice cream Dubrovnik's also great for ice cream. There's a flurry of establishments in the old town, with the best being **Dolce Vita** [352 D3], on Naljeskovićeva, one of the streets between Stradun and Prijeko, which serves quite the tastiest and freshest ice cream (and frozen yoghurt) in town. Also highly recommended is **Niko** [352 D4], on Od Puca, near the Serbian Orthodox Church

Cafés and bars With great weather and lots of visitors, there's no shortage of places to sit and have a drink in Dubrovnik, though fashions change quickly, and today's groovy hangout can all too rapidly become tomorrow's leftover. You can expect most of these places to stay open until midnight or later. Needless to say, Dubrovnik has its own life beyond that aimed at tourists, and there are a couple of areas where this goes on outside of the town walls, notably on Bana Jelačića, running up into Lapad, and on Iva Vojnovića, in the heart of Lapad. A new scene has sprung up here in just the last few years, with a clutch of eight trendy new bars which are hugely popular with the locals and rarely visited by foreigners.

Inside the walls

🍺 **Carpe Diem** [353 G5] Kneza Damjana Jude 4. Situated on the narrow street running down to the aquarium, & billing itself as an 'Art Caffe', Carpe Diem does a light b/fast in the morning & exotic cocktails in the evening. It's long, narrow, smartly decorated & popular late into the evening.

🍺 **Festival Café** [352 C3] Stradun; www. cafefestival.com. Benefiting from a perfect location on Stradun, the rather pricey Festival Café is especially popular through the day & in the early evenings, when it's a great place to see & be seen. Pull up a director's chair & watch the action unfold.

🍺 **Gradska Kavana** [353 F4] Pred Dvorom 1; www.mea-culpa.hr. In arguably the best location in town, next door to the Rector's Palace and opposite St Blaise's Church, the newly renovated Gradska Kavana (literally 'town café') has a spacious interior & a raised terrace, which is perfect for people-watching.

🍷 **D'Vino** [352 D3] Palmotićeva 4a; ☎ 321 130; http://dvino.net; ⏲ 10.00–02.00 daily. Largest selection of wines by the glass in Dubrovnik.

🍷 **Malvasia** [353 E3] Dropčeva 4; www. malvasija.com; ⏲ 18.00–02.00 daily. Good little wine bar, owned by a local wine producer.

Ražonoda [353 E5] Od Puča; www. thepucicpalace.com. Next door to the Pučić Palace hotel & under the same management, Ražanoda is a swanky, upmarket wine bar with a good list of the best Croatian wines – & price tags to match. It's just a shame it doesn't sell wine by the glass.

Troubadour [353 E5] Bunićeva poljana; summer 09.00–03.00 daily, winter 17.00–23.00 daily. Properly known as the Hard Jazz Café Troubadour, this is an excellent bar with a pub-like atmosphere & live music most evenings. The front door is on Bunićeva poljana & the back door on Gundulićeva poljana. The tables outside are made from old sewing machines, which is an unusual touch. The ambience has been somewhat ruined by the recent addition of a bright neon advertising sign right behind where the bands play. You can always choose to sit at one of a sprinkling of other bars with outdoor tables, & listen to the music from there.

Outside the old town walls

Buža I [353 G7] Situated on the rocks outside the western (seaward) walls of the city, Buža is the place to come if you want to watch the sun go down. The only sounds are the sea & the gulls, & it's gloriously informal – though arguably less so than it once was. The entrance is pretty well hidden – to get there, go up behind the Jesuit Church & out of the square on the opposite corner, & then turn left under the walls along Od Margarite. After a short while you come to a hole in the wall on your right (buža means 'hole') that leads out on to the rocks – & there you are. Seats are set out on the rocks that spill down to the Adriatic. This is a great place for taking a dip, too, so don't forget your togs. Only open – you'll see why – when the weather's fine.

Buža II [353 F7] Another hole-in-the-wall establishment, with a slightly different outlook

over Lokrum & a slightly more formal set-up, with more chairs, tables & parasols in a main bar area. Again the bar isn't permanent, so no hot drinks, & of course no draught beers. Follow the directions for Buža I (opposite) but turn right under the walls along Od Margarite, instead of left. Again, you'll quickly come to a hole in the wall, but this time it will be on your left.

Casa [342 B2] Nika i Meda Pučića 1; www. villa-wolff.hr. Casa has a great location right on the waterfront at Uvala Bay, under the Villa Wolff (page 355), & although the drinks are fairly pricey, the situation alone makes it worth the visit.

Cave Bar More [342 B2] Pucića 13; ☎494 200; http://cavebar-more.com. Stylish new bar set in a cave under Hotel More, with wonderful views from the waterfront terrace outside.

Dubravka 1836 [353 A3] Brsalje; ☎426 319; www.dubravka1836.hr. Occupying prime real estate right outside the Pile Gate, opposite Nautika, the Kavana Dubravka has a lovely terrace set overlooking the little bay between the Bokar & Lovrijenac fortresses. Inside, it's worth having a look at the photos on the walls of the old trams that used to ply their way up the hill from here. For a well-invested few kuna you can use the toilets – which are a whole lot nicer than the public ones over on the other side of the Pile Gate.

Sunset Lounge [342 A2] Masarykov put 20; ☎430 000; www.dubrovnikpalace.hr. The stylish Sunset Lounge at the Hotel Dubrovnik Palace (page 351) is firmly established as the place to watch sunset in Dubrovnik, through floor-to-ceiling windows that provide spectacular views over the Elaphite Islands & the Adriatic as the day draws to a close – even if prices are fairly high. Bus #4, which leaves from just outside the Pile Gate, will take you to the hotel.

Self-catering
If you're looking for picnic food, you'll probably be reliant on the Konzum supermarket – there's a branch on Gundulićeva Poljana [353 E5], and one outside each of the two main gates. There's also a huge new one down at Gruž, just past the ferry terminal [330 C1].

NIGHTLIFE
Though there's plenty of late-evening café activity and drinking going on in the old town, actual nightlife is decidedly thin on the ground in Dubrovnik, with most places closing up by 01.00. The newest addition to the nightlife scene is the wine/lounge bar at **Taverna Arsenal** [353 F4] (page 357), however, which does stay open until 04.00 year round, and during the season the

cocktail bar at the **Banje Beach Club** [342 F3] (*http://ew-dubrovnik.com*), located on the Branje beach just beyond the Ploče Gate, keeps going until up to 06.00 during the summer. In summer there are more chances to dance, but not a whole lot more. The best place is arguably **Lazareti** [353 H3] (*www.lazareti.com*), out past the Ploče Gate on Supila, which features DJs and probably the hippest music you'll find in the area – but Ibiza it ain't, and hours vary. There's also **Culture Club Revelin** [353 H2] (m 098 533 531; *http://clubrevelin.com*) on Svetog Dominika, near the Ploče Gate, with similar hours.

BEACHES The other way of entertaining yourself, of course, is with a trip to the beach. The nicest ones are out on the island of Lokrum, and it's well worth getting out there if you possibly can (page 375) – it's also the nearest naturist beach to the old town.

If you simply fancy cooling off after a hot walk around the city walls, walk just round the corner at the old port and there's a swimming area off the rocks, by the jetty.

The city's main public beach is at **Banje** [342 F4], just outside the Ploče Gate, facing the old port. It's recently been refurbished and you can now rent parasols and deckchairs here, and order yourself cocktails at the summer bar. In spite of being right next to the old port the water is beautifully clear.

Another option is the tiny beach underneath the Hotel Bellevue, half of which is public (the other half belongs to the revamped hotel). It's on a gorgeous little cove facing southeast, and hosts Dubrovnik's annual water-polo championships – each little beach and cove around the city has its own team.

For pure hedonistic beach-games and watersports you can't do better than the **Copacabana** beach [342 B1] on Babin Kuk, though in high season it does get mighty crowded with the package tours from the Babin Kuk hotel complex taking up most of the space. Finally, the **Uvala Bay** beach [342 C2], on Lapad, is the locals' beach of choice, and offers lovely swimming out to sea between Babin Kuk and Lapad.

OTHER PRACTICALITIES Dubrovnik's main general **hospital** (*Opća Bolnica*) is out at Lapad [342 C3] (*Dr Roka Mišetića 2;* \ 431 777; *www.bolnica-du.hr*). If you're looking for a list of pharmacies, unfortunately the chaotic tourist office website will be of no help at all, so it's useful to know that there's a **24-hour pharmacy** in the old town at Placa 4 [353 E4] (\ 321 133) and another in the main hospital at Lapad – one or the other will always be working, though they generally alternate so call to check. There's a **post office** in the old town at Široka ulica 8 [352 C4], and plenty of other branches including out at Lapad (*Ulica Miljenka Bratoša 21*) and towards Gruž, where you'll find the main post office at Vukovarska 16.

WHAT TO SEE AND DO The main sight of course is Dubrovnik itself, and the best way of seeing it is from the city walls, which are among the best preserved and most picturesque in the world. There's a promenade along their entire length, and you should make every effort to circum-perambulate at least once, as it really gives you the best possible perspective (physical and historical) of just what Dubrovnik really means. Another wonderful view can be had from the top of Mount Srđ (412m), the mountain looming above the city – you can take a cable car all the way up (page 375).

Once you've seen Dubrovnik from above, choose your time of day for the city itself with care; after 11.00 there's a predictable tendency towards more visitors and less atmosphere – though early evening is a lovely time, regardless of the crowds, with soft light treating old stone kindly.

There's a lot to see in the old city, but don't be too obsessive – not all of the 48 churches within the walls need a visit (or indeed are open), and the museums are mostly fairly low key. In any case, make sure you get a **Dubrovnik Card** (page 349) which will get you free admission to many of the museums and galleries, as well as the walls themselves.

The city is great for walking around – if you want to tap into the knowledge of a local guide then consider booking a place on one of the guided walks organised by **Dubrovnik Walking Tours** (✎ 436 846; *www.dubrovnik-walking-tours.com*). All tours leave from Onofrio's Great Fountain; ask at the tourist office for more detailed information.

The city walls (Jun/Jul 08.00–19.30, Apr/May & Aug/Sep 08.00–18.30, Oct 08.00–17.30, Nov–Mar 09.00–15.00; 100kn)

The walls surround the entire old town and run for a whisper under 2km. At their highest they're 25m tall, and at their fattest 12m thick. There are five fortresses and around 20 towers. Work started on the walls in the 8th century and continued more or less continuously until the 16th, though much more than you might imagine is also late 20th-century restoration – even before the Serb shells pounded the city in 1991–92. Indeed, when I was here in the 1980s, the promenade around the walls wasn't actually complete. Since the war, huge amounts of restoration have been done throughout the old city, including the complete repaving of Stradun – not that you'd know – and the replacing of most of the houses' roof tiles.

There are three places where you can get up on to the walls – on Stradun, right next to the Pile Gate (the busiest of the three); on Svetog Dominika, the road leading up to the Dominican Monastery; and on Kneza Damjana Jude, near the Aquarium. The earlier you get up on to the walls the less crowded you'll find them.

If you stop to take pictures (and you will), the whole circuit takes a leisurely hour or so – at least.

Inside the walls

The main sights are all close to one another – the main street, Stradun, is all of 300m long. The following itinerary starts at the Pile Gate and works its way back and forth across the old city, before ending at the Church of St Blaise. At a leisurely pace – and without stopping for any length of time to admire the attractions or visit museums and churches – it would take about 1½–2 hours. If you dip into a handful of the main sights you should count on a good half day; if you want a detailed visit to everything on the itinerary you'll need a couple of full days at least. If you do nothing else, visit the Rector's Palace, the two monasteries and the cathedral treasury.

The **Pile Gate** [352 B3], dating back to 1471, is approached across a wooden drawbridge which used to be pulled up every night. Set into a niche here is the first of many statues you'll see of St Blaise (Sveti Vlaho), the city's patron saint. Indeed, as you enter the gate you'll immediately see another – this time by Ivan Meštrović, Croatia's most famous sculptor.

Once inside the gate you come straight on to Dubrovnik's famous main street, Stradun, which is paved in marble (be careful when it's wet; it can be lethally slippery). This was originally the marshy channel which separated the Roman settlement of Ragusa on one side from the Slavic settlement of Dubrovnik on the other.

On the square inside the Pile Gate stands **Onofrio's Great Fountain** [352 B3], which was completed in 1444 by the Neapolitan architect Onofrio della Cava as part of the city's smart new plumbing. Unfortunately all the fancy ornamental work from the upper part of the fountain was lost in the Great Earthquake of 1667.

To your left as you come into the city is the tiny **Church of Our Saviour** (Sv Spasa) [352 B3]. It was completed in 1528 as a thank you from the survivors of the 1520 earthquake, and itself survived the far more dramatic quake of 1667 – a tribute to the building skills of the Andrijić brothers, from Korčula, who also worked on the Sponza Palace (page 366). The simple Renaissance trefoil façade and rose window are quietly pleasing, and hide a Gothic interior which is mainly used these days as a venue for candlelit concerts.

The Franciscan Monastery and Pharmacy [352 C3] (*Franjevačkog Samostana; Placa 2;* 321 410; ⊕ *summer 09.00–18.00 daily, winter 09.00–17.00 daily; 30kn*) Next door to Our Saviour is the Franciscan Church and Monastery. The church is entered from Stradun itself, where you'll find the south door crowned by a wonderful *pietà* – evocatively described by Rebecca West in 1937 as 'definite and sensible. The Madonna looks as if, had it been in her hands, she would have stopped the whole affair.'

The pietà survived the Great Earthquake, but the church itself was entirely gutted by fire and countless treasures were lost forever. What you see today dates from the 18th century onwards, which explains the Baroque nature of it all. The church is famous locally as the final resting place of Ivan Gundulić (page 368), though he's actually interred in a part of the church that is closed to the public – you can still pay your respects at a plaque on the north wall, however.

The rest of the monastery is accessed down a narrow passage next to Our Saviour. At the entrance you'll find the famous pharmacy, self-billed as the oldest in the world. Whether it is or not, it probably was one of the earliest to be open to the public, and it's still operating today, though from a 1901 refurbishment. The original pharmacy was established in 1317, and in the museum off the cloisters you can see an interesting collection of jars and poisons from the 15th century on, along with ancient pharmacopoeias. The museum also contains various religious artefacts, as well as a testy portrait of Ruđer Bošković, Dubrovnik's mathematical genius (see box, page 366), painted in 1760 in London. Most interesting of all, however, is a canvas showing the old town before the earthquake – note how much greater Onofrio's Great Fountain was before 1667.

The cloisters themselves are truly exceptional, consisting of rows of double octagonal columns with individualised capitals. They are the work of Mihoje Brakov, a sculptor from Bar (in what's now Montenegro), who died here of the plague in 1348. One of the capitals near the entrance, depicting a medieval man with terrible toothache, is said to be a self-portrait of the sculptor. Inside the courtyard are palm trees and well-trimmed box hedges, and it's a great place to get away from the heat in high summer.

Fans of the hit HBO TV series *Game of Thrones*, based on George Martin's epic series of best-selling novels, will know Dubrovnik by another name – King's Landing. Dubrovnik (along with Iceland, Ireland, Andalucía and Morocco) has been a key location for *Game of Thrones* – to the uninitiated, King's Landing is the capital of Westeros, site of the Red Keep and it's hotly (and bloodily) contested Iron Throne – since Series Two (prior to this, Malta was used as the location for King's Landing). Exact locations include the Bokar and Lovrijenac fortresses, the Minčeta tower (that's the House of the Undying to *Game of Thrones* fans), and the streets and cascading steps outside the Dominican Monastery.

Dubrovnik's city walls, fortresses, streets and palaces are not the only locations in Croatia to be used for filming *Game of Thrones*. Other major locations include the island of Lokrum (as the city of Qarth), Diocletian's Palace in Split (numerous street scenes) including its underground chambers (various scenes in Meereen, including chambers where Daenerys's dragons are kept), the ruined fortress at Klis (Meereen again, including the site outside the city where its former rulers are crucified), a section of old stone waterfront houses in Kaštel Gomilica (a village between Trogir and Split, which forms part of the CGI enhanced city of Braavos), the Arboretum at Trsteno (doubling as the palace gardens in King's Landing), and scenes have also been shot on Biokovo.

It was overseas tour operators who first began capitalising on the *Game of Thrones* connection – indeed by most accounts many local tour guides were initially rather peeved that their city's millennia-and-a-half-long history should have been apparently trumped by a fantasy TV series. But local operators have now waded in as well, and in any case the city's (already staggering) number of visitors has surged further, meaning that unless you visit in the shoulder seasons or off season you're likely to find Dubrovnik full to bursting point.

Stradun and Luža Square
Stradun itself (also known as Placa – pronounced platsa) continues in a widening straight line all the way to the Clock Tower at the far end. As you'll notice, the houses along the street are nearly identical; a result of the careful post-earthquake planning at the end of the 17th century. Note the distinctive '*na koljeno*' single-arched frame that combines the entrance door and window to provide a counter over which goods could be served to customers.

In Luža Square, at the far end of Stradun, you'll find **Orlando's Column** [353 E4], a statue of Roland symbolising the city's desire for freedom (*libertas*) and which has marked the centre of town since its erection in 1418. For centuries Roland's forearm was Ragusa's standard measure of length (the *lakat*, since you ask), a convenient 512mm long – you can see the reference groove at the base of the statue. All state declarations were read from a platform above the column in the days of the republic, and condemned criminals were executed at its base.

Behind Orlando's Column you can't miss the **Clock Tower** [353 F4], originally built in 1444, which features a complex astronomical clock, and a pair of green men (the *zelenci*) who strike the hour. The tower was rebuilt in 1929 (which is presumably when the digital clock was added), so the only thing that's really original now is the bell, dating from 1506, which weighs over two tonnes. The original clock mechanism and green men are in the Sponza Palace (pages 366–7). Next to the clock tower is **Onofrio's Small Fountain** [353 F4], dating from 1441.

Southern Dalmatia DUBROVNIK

9

The Sponza Palace [353 F3/4] (*Luža*) On the left-hand side of Luža square is the Sponza Palace, which functioned variously as a cistern, the customs house and the state mint. Today it houses the Memorial Room of the Dubrovnik Defenders, the original innards of the city clock, and the State Archives. It's one of the most charming buildings in Dubrovnik, boldly mixing pure Venetian Gothic and late Renaissance into a harmonious whole. It was built in 1522 to plans by the local architect Pasko Miličević, and features work by the Andrijić brothers, the master sculptors who were also responsible for much of Korčula Cathedral – as well as the Church of Our Saviour at the other end of Stradun. The Sponza was one of the few buildings to survive the Great Earthquake of 1667.

The entrance is through a wide-arched Renaissance portico, above which there's a lovely Venetian-Gothic first storey, topped with a row of four late-Renaissance windows and a statue of St Blaise in a niche. Inside there's a courtyard with a double cloister.

The name Sponza comes from the Latin word *spongia*, meaning sponge, as there was originally a cistern on this site. The Sponza's main purpose, however, was to serve as the republic's customs house (which is why it's also sometimes referred to as the Divona or Dogana). On the ground floor here goods were measured for duty, under the inscription '*Fallere Nostra Vetant et Falli Pondera Meque Pondero cum Merces Ponderat ipse Deus*' – which translates roughly as 'the scales we use to weigh your goods are the same scales used by God to weigh us'.

The ground-floor rooms originally served as warehouse space, while those on the first floor were used for literary and scientific meetings. Up on the second floor was the state mint, which issued Dubrovnik's currency (*perperae*, *grossi* and *ducats*) from 1337 until 1803.

After World War II, the Sponza housed the Museum of the Socialist Revolution, though of course that's disappeared following the more recent war. Instead you'll find the original 16th-century mechanism for the city clock here, along with the two green men, Maro and Baro, who struck the bell until 1928. The space is used for concerts during the Summer Festival.

The **Memorial Room of the Dubrovnik Defenders** (✆ 321 032; ☉ *summer 09.00–21.00 daily, winter 10.00–15.00 daily; free*), on the ground floor, is a commemoration of the tragic events here from 1 October 1991 to 26 October 1992, when more than 200 defenders and 100 civilians were killed. It's a terribly sobering place, with the remnants of the flag from the Imperial Fort on Srđ and the pictures and dates of all the young lives that were snuffed out during the siege. Many of the photos are the work of local photographer Pavo Urban, who was tragically cut down in his prime (aged just 23) by shrapnel just yards from the memorial room in December 1991.

The building also houses the **State Archives** (✆ *321 032;* ⊕ *daily; call or email in advance to visit*), which are among the most complete in the world, chronicling pretty much everything that happened during the 1,000-year history of the republic. Altogether there are some 8,000m of shelved documents, ranging from the 13th-century city statutes to Marshal Marmont's orders dissolving the republic in 1808.

The Dominican Monastery [353 F3] (*Dominikanskog Samostana; Sv Dominika 4;* ✆ *321 423;* ⊕ *summer 09.00–18.00 daily, winter 09.00–17.00 daily; 20kn*) The

winding street Svetog Dominika leads up to the Ploče Gate. On the way you can't miss the Dominican Monastery. Notice the way the steps on the way up are walled in, up to a height of about two feet to protect the modesty of travellers and save the monks from impure ankle-related thoughts.

The monastery was used by the occupying French troops from 1808 – you can see from the outside where windows were sealed up to make a Napoleonic prison, and the church itself was used as stables. In the cloisters you can still see the horse troughs which were hacked into the retaining walls by the cavalrymen.

The original church here was completed in 1315, but had to be rebuilt after the Great Earthquake of 1667. It was then paved with the coats of arms of all the noble families, but unfortunately was repaved in 1910 with plain marble. Today it's a vast, boxy place, and most of the best art has been moved to the museum – though not the greatest treasure of all, a terrific 5m-by-4m crucifixion by Paolo Veneziano, which was installed here in 1358. There's also an interesting painting of St Dominic by local boy Vlaho Bukovac, though it's not, frankly, the artist's best work – you can see some of this at the Museum of Modern Art (page 373) in Dubrovnik, and even more in the painter's home town, Cavtat (page 376).

The cloisters are a late-Gothic masterpiece, built to a design by the Florentine architect Maso di Bartolomeo, but with extra flourishes added by local stonemasons. In the courtyard oranges and lemons grow, and – like the Franciscan cloisters – it's a wonderfully cool, shady place on a hot day.

The monastery also houses an interesting museum and an extraordinary library; with over 16,000 works and 240 incunabula, it was one of the greatest European libraries of the Renaissance. In the museum you'll find a rare 11th-century Bible, along with a much-reproduced triptych featuring St Blaise with a model of pre-earthquake Ragusa in his right hand – still recognisable as Dubrovnik today, though both the Franciscan and Dominican monasteries sported bigger spires back then. Also of note is a marvellous altarpiece by Titian featuring Mary Magdalene with St Blaise and the Archangel Raphael – the chap on his knees is the member of the Pučić family who commissioned the work.

Up a couple of stairs there's a room full of votive gold – a fraction of what was here originally, as most of it was sold off after World War II to support the faculty of theology, unfunded in communist times. There's an interesting Flemish diptych here – with Jesus on the left while on the right there's a reversible panel, with love on one side and death on the other, usefully adaptable according to your moods and whims.

The synagogue [353 E3] (*Žudioska 5;* ☎ *321 028;* ⊕ *summer 10.00–18.00 daily, winter 10.00–15.00 daily; 20kn*) As you leave the monastery, turn right and you'll find yourself at the eastern end of Prijeko, which is best visited early in the day, before the eager restaurateurs can get their teeth into you, so to speak (page 357). Take a detour down Žudioska, and you'll find one of Europe's oldest (and smallest) synagogues. It's Europe's second oldest (after Prague) and in spite of restrictions placed on Jews here during World War II, it was the only European synagogue to function all the way through the war.

The synagogue – with original 17th-century furnishings – is on the second floor, while below it, on the first floor, there's a fascinating two-room museum, where you can see richly decorated Torah Scrolls and binders, and ancient Ark Curtains, as well as a copy of the letter signed by Marshal Marmont granting the Jewish community full emancipation from 1808. There's also a chilling selection of documents from 1941, issued by the fascist NDH (page 17), restricting the movement of Jews and ordering them to wear yellow ribbons and badges.

War Photo Limited [352 D3] (*Antuninska 6;* ☎ *322 166; www.warphotoltd.com;* ⊕ *Jun–Sep 09.00–21.00 daily, May/Oct 10.00–16.00 Tue–Sun, closed Nov–Apr; 40kn*) Continue down Prijeko for most of its length – or if it's already approaching lunchtime consider avoiding the touts by walking along the old city's uppermost street, Peline, which gives great views down the steep-stepped streets crossing Prijeko – and then turn left down Antuninska, where you'll find the extraordinary War Photo Limited.

It's one of Dubrovnik's most emotionally charged galleries, and I can't recommend a visit too highly. Specialising in first-rate temporary exhibitions by the world's greatest modern-war photographers, the gallery aims, as the New Zealand-born director, Wade Goddard, says: 'to strip away the Hollywood image of war, to replace the glamour, the heroic bravura, the "only the bad guys suffer" image of war, with the raw and undeniable evidence that war inflicts injustices on all who experience it'.

It would require a heart of stone to come away unmoved by the extraordinary (and often painful) images. In 2012 there was an exhibition of Tarik Samarah's images of the exhumation of the bodies from the mass graves at Srebrenica, in 70 stark black-and-white images. The collection is nothing if not eclectic, and has also taken in the troubled African continent in 2006 and Colombia in 2009, and more recently the crisis in Ukraine.

IVAN GUNDULIĆ – MASTER OF BAROQUE POETRY

Ivan Gundulić was born in Dubrovnik in 1589, and was famous even in his lifetime as a remarkable poet, churning out vast quantities of – perhaps excessively rhetorical? – Baroque verse. Coming from a prominent noble family, it's likely he would have eventually become rector, but he died in 1638, just a few months before the 50th birthday which would have made him eligible.

Gundulić played an important part in standardising the Croatian language, and was enthusiastically taken up by the Croatian Nationalist Movement in the 19th century – indeed it was only then that the great lyrical poem *Osman* was finally finished, with the last two chapters being penned by Ivan Mažuranić, who later went on to become the Ban of Croatia.

As well as being honoured by the statue in Dubrovnik, a fetchingly bewigged Gundulić also appears on the 50kn note.

To the Orthodox Church and Icon Museum On the other side of Stradun, a short walk along Gariŝte brings you to Za Rokom, where you'll find the little **Church of St Roc** [352 B4]. Round on the right-hand wall of the church is a fine piece of carved graffiti dated 1597 and reading '*Pax vobis memento mori qui ludetis pilla*' – which translates roughly as 'Peace be with you, but remember that you must die, you who play ball here', clearly the work of an irate adult, keen to warn off noisy, football-mad kids.

Continue along Za Rokom until you get to the end of the street, then turn left into Ŝiroka. On the right-hand side you'll find the house where Marin Drŝić (page 374) once lived [352 C4] – although unless you're a serious fan of the playwright's work, you won't get a great deal out of a visit. Equally, unless you have a lot of time on your hands you probably needn't visit the **Rupe Ethnographic Museum** [352 B5] (*Etnografski Muzej; Od Rupa 2;* 🕻 *323 018;* ☺ *summer 09.00–16.00 Wed–Mon; 100kn Dubrovnik Museums Ticket*), a block away – though the former granary building itself is interesting, as you can see some of the vast chambers which were dug into the rock to store grain back in the 16th century, keeping the food dry and cool.

Turning on to Od Puĉa, you'll find the Orthodox Church on your left, and (two doors down) the Icon Museum. This part of town is where most of the small remaining Serbian community lives and works. Just down Miha Pracata, on the left-hand side, you'll also find Dubrovnik's **mosque** [352 D4/5] (☺ *10.00–13.00 daily*), though there's really nothing special to see there.

The **Serbian Orthodox Church of the Holy Annunciation** [352 D4] (*Od Puĉa;* ☺ *09.00–16.00 daily*) is one of Dubrovnik's most recent, only being completed in 1877. A plain exterior shelters a rather spare interior, with a traditional iconostasis (with icons from the 15th to 19th centuries) separating the clergy from the congregation. The church was one of the last buildings in the old town – perhaps unsurprisingly – on which restoration work got underway after the end of the siege in 1992, but happily is now receiving both attention and funds; hopefully it will be fully restored in the near future.

Two doors down is the rarely visited **Icon Museum** [352 D4] (*Muzej Ikona; Od Puĉa;* 🕻 *323 283;* ☺ *summer 09.00–14.00 Mon–Sat, winter 09.00–14.00 Mon–Fri; 10kn*), upstairs, on the second floor (past a sign in Cyrillic saying СРПСКА – Srpska, or Serbian). It's a pity as the two-room collection brings together a wide range of icons from the 18th and 19th centuries, as well as some earlier ones from the 15th and 16th centuries. They come from all across the Balkans and Russia and the differences between the various schools are fascinating – the Russian icons featuring long noses; the ones from the Bay of Kotor having deep, dark shadows. In the second room there are also half a dozen dark, dark portraits of local 19th-century Serb notables by Vlaho Bukovac (see box, page 378), quite unlike anything else you'll see by the famous local painter.

To Gundulićeva poljana Continuing down Od Puĉa brings you past the Puĉić Palace Hotel and out on to Gundulićeva poljana – literally Gundulić's little field. In the centre of the square stands a **statue** of Ivan Gundulić himself (see box, page 368), which dates back to 1893. There's a marvellous allegorical vignette at the base of the statue; a bethroned Dubrovnik has both Turkey and Venice at her feet – with Turkey represented as the dragon on the left and Venice as the winged lion on the right. A certain irony, therefore, that the city's most expensive hotel, the Puĉić Palace, overlooking the very same square, should today be Turkish-owned.

The Jesuit Church [352 D6] (*Properly the Church of St Ignatius of Loyola, or Ignacija Lojolskog;* ☺ *08.00–19.00 daily*) Turn right out of Gundulićeva poljana and head up the great flight of steps – said to be modelled on the Spanish Steps in Rome – leading to the Jesuit Church, a massive structure clearly intended to make a point. It was built to plans by the Jesuit artist Andrea Pozzo, who had already done great works in Rome and would go on to design the cathedral in Ljubljana.

Completed in 1725, the church features a dramatic double-storeyed set of Corinthian columns lifting the façade skywards, and the church behind it is enormous, covering a surface of over 600m². Inside it feels very big and gloomy, as you'd expect, with the interior modelled on the Gesù Church in Rome and featuring lots of fabulous *trompe l'oeil*, Pozzi's speciality – he was the author of a seminal work on perspective, *Prospettiva de' pittori et architect*, which revolutionised painting in the 18th century and is still used today. The main attraction is the inside of the apse, which features spectacular scenes from the life of Ignatius, the founder of the Jesuit order, by the Sicilian painter Gaetano Garcia.

Altogether less spiritually uplifting – though popular enough with local devotees, it seems – is the 'Grotto of Lourdes', which was added in 1885.

To the Maritime Museum and Aquarium You can leave the rather tatty square in front of the Jesuit Church by the far corner and wind your way all the way along Ispod mira, the alley leading along the inside of the city walls. This is perhaps the quietest and shabbiest part of the town, with lots of buildings still unrestored after being badly damaged in an earthquake in 1979.

At the end of the line, so to speak, you'll find **St John's Fortress** [353 H5], which houses the Maritime Museum upstairs and the aquarium on the ground floor. Spread out over two floors, the **Maritime Museum** [339 H5] (*Pomorski Muzej; Damjana Jude 2;* ❧ *323 904; www.dumus.hr;* ☺ *summer 09.00–18.00 Tue–Sun, winter 09.00–14.00 Tue–Sun; 100kn Dubrovnik Museums Ticket*) covers the entire history of seafaring in the area, from the Golden Age of the republic through to the arrival of steam-powered ships. It's well worth a visit if you're into ships and sailing, with lots of maps, evocative old photos and models of various types of ship, along with bits of rigging and ships' supplies and cargoes.

Downstairs, you'll find Dubrovnik's dismal seawater **Aquarium** (❧ *323 125; www.imp-du.com;* ☺ *summer 09.00–21.00 daily, winter 10.00–13.00 Tue–Sun; 40kn*). Mostly it amounts to large Mediterranean fish (groupers, eels and the like) swimming listlessly round in tanks that are far from big enough. The whole bleak experience is epitomised by the solitary giant turtle which paddles its way to and fro miserably in a pond-sized pool – or these days, hardly moving at all – while school groups shower the benighted beast with small change.

The cathedral and treasury [353 F5/6] (*Poljana Marina Držića;* ☺ *summer 09.00–17.00 Mon–Sat, 11.00–17.00 Sun, winter 10.00–noon & 15.00–17.00 Mon–Sat, 11.00–noon & 15.00–17.00 Sun; treasury 15kn*) Heading back into the heart of the city, the first thing you come to is the cathedral. The former Romanesque number – said to have been bankrolled by a shipwrecked Richard the Lionheart (see box, page 372) – was demolished by the Great Earthquake in 1667, so what you get today is the Baroque replacement, completed in 1713 to plans by the Italian architect Andrea Buffalini. The statues of the saints along the eaves are rather fine, though notice that St Mark has been relegated to an inferior position – perhaps a none-too-subtle snub to Venice.

Surprisingly, for Baroque, the cathedral is a rather spartan affair inside, with a chunky modern altar and acres of whitewash – and it's curious in having a west-facing altar. The compelling attraction is the treasury, though if you're here it's nonetheless worth having a look at the impressive (school of) Titian altarpiece.

Altogether, there are well over 100 priceless relics in the **treasury**, many of which are carried around the town in a grand procession on 3 February, the feast day of Dubrovnik's patron saint. The most important of these is the Head of St Blaise himself, which was bought from Byzantium (along with the saint's arms and a leg) in 1026. The head is housed in a fine casing decorated with 24 Byzantine enamel plaques from the 12th century, featuring austere, intense portraits of the saints.

The treasury also includes one of John the Baptist's hands, a bit of the True Cross incorporated into a crucifix, one of Christ's nappies in a silver box, and a dark wooden lectern which once belonged to England's Henry VIII – after the Reformation, treasures from the dissolved monasteries went up for sale, and a small selection ended up in the hands of enterprising sailors from Lopud.

Over on the right-hand side is an extraordinary painting by Raphael, the *Madonna della Seggiola (Sedia)*, which is almost identical to the 1514 version in the Palazzo Pitti in Florence. Why there's a copy here – painted on what looks like the bottom of a barrel – is a mystery, but the painting itself is a pure wonder.

Last but not least is an extraordinary pitcher and ewer from the 15th century, prominently on display, which is an allegory of Dubrovnik's flora and fauna. Featuring snakes and tortoises, eels and lizards, and some pre-Dalí lobsters, along with alarming amounts of vegetation, it looks like it would be the very devil to clean. It's thought to have been made as a gift for the Hungarian king of the day, Matthias Corvinus the Just, but ended up here as the king died before he could receive the tribute.

It's always aroused a certain amount of passion. In 1929, Count Voynovitch, author of a handy little guide to the city, said: 'The basin is delightfully finished'. Just eight years later, however, (the ever-opinionated) Rebecca West was writing: 'Nothing could be more offensive to the eye, to the touch, or to common sense … it has the infinite elaborateness of eczema, and to add to the last touch of unpleasantness these animals are loosely fixed so that they may wobble and give an illusion of movement. Though Dubrovnik is beautiful, and this object was indescribably ugly, my dislike of the second explained to me why I felt doubtful in my appreciation of the first. The town regarded this horror as a masterpiece.'

And it's true; it does.

The Rector's Palace [353 F5] (*Knežev Dvor; Pred Dvorom 3;* ☎ *321 437;* ⊕ *summer 09.00–18.00 daily, winter 09.00–16.00 daily; 100kn Dubrovnik Museums Ticket*)

Diagonally opposite the cathedral is the Rector's Palace, with the municipal theatre next door. If you get the chance, pop inside and admire the charming, miniature version of the grand Austro-Hungarian opera houses and theatres – complete with gilded boxes and velvet seating, which date back to 1869.

The Rector's Palace was the seat of Ragusa's government. It would once have looked more like a castle than a palace, but after the original was accidentally blown up in 1435 (always a mistake keeping your gunpowder next to your government) it was rebuilt in the Venetian-Gothic style by Onofrio della Cava – he of the fountains' fame.

It wasn't to last, as the gunpowder went off again in 1463. This time the palace was restored by Michelozzo Michelozzi, who also did lots of work on the city's defensive fortresses, and Juraj Dalmatinac, who added various Renaissance touches.

You enter through a fine loggia topped with superb carved capitals on pillars of Korčula marble; the outer pairs are the original Gothic while the middle three are Renaissance. Most interesting of all is the rightmost capital, thought to portray Asclepius, the Greek god of healing, who was born in Epidaurus (now Cavtat).

Ask anyone about Dubrovnik's cathedral and it won't be long before Richard the Lionheart's name comes up. According to local legend, the English king ran into a terrible storm near here on his return home from the Crusades at the end of 1192, and vowed that if he survived he would build a church on the spot. Miraculously, he was saved, and washed up on Lokrum.

On hearing the news of the arrival of such an important – and apparently loaded – visitor, Dubrovnik sent over a welcoming party, who persuaded King Richard that his money would be better spent on building a cathedral in Dubrovnik. In exchange, the Ragusan nobles would build a votive church on Lokrum at their own expense. Richard agreed, and handed over 100,000 ducats, before continuing on his journey to Italy and – eventually – England.

In all probability, however, the Lokrum part of this charming tale is a Benedictine fabrication. The monks on Lokrum had good cause for inventing – or at the very least embellishing – such a story. Because of it, they enjoyed various privileges in Dubrovnik's cathedral, including the abbot of Lokrum being allowed to hold the Candlemas pontifical mass, which is celebrated on 2 February, the day before St Blaise's feast day. This mass apparently enraged successive bishops of Dubrovnik, who demanded the privilege be rescinded. In the end, in the 1590s, the Ragusan government had to resort to writing letters to the pope, who finally decided in favour of Lokrum's Benedictines – thereby legitimising the Lionheart story.

The main door leads into an atrium which is the (surprisingly small) venue for summer recitals. In here you'll find the only statue ever raised to an individual in Ragusa's long history. On dying in 1607, Miho Pracat (see box, page 382), a remarkable ship owner and adventurer from Lopud, left 1,000 shares in the Bank of St George in Genoa to the city. The city was suitably grateful – back then those shares were worth around 100 lira apiece, at a time when gold was fetching three and a half lira an ounce. The interest on the capital was used by the city to free slaves, and Pracat got his statue.

The ground floor of the palace was formerly a prison, handy for the courtroom off to the right, with a curious marble barrier and wooden bench being about all you can see today. Upstairs are the state offices and rector's chambers – from the day they were elected, rectors were effectively prisoners here, only allowed to leave with the senate's permission. Fortunately each only served a one-month term.

The main staircase was only used for the rector's inaugural procession on the first of the month, taking him upstairs to his confinement. Nobody ever came down the stairs unless the rector died in office – the hidden staircase behind was the way out. On your way up the main stairs notice the handrails, supported by realistic (if not entirely tasteful) carved hands.

At the top of the stairs, over the door which originally led into the Grand Council chamber, there's an inscription reading '*Obliti Privatorum Publica Curate*' – a quote from Pericles, reminding councillors to forget their private concerns and think of public affairs instead.

The upstairs rooms are a curious collection – mainly because the palace was plundered, first by the French in the early 19th century, and then again by Yugoslavia's King Aleksandar after World War I, for the Royal Palace in Belgrade. As a result they're for the most part furnished with private donations. You'll find an odd mix of Venetian repro, Louis XV copies, painted wood, Neapolitan ebony and marble veneer, along with an unusual collection of canvases featuring local bigwigs. Note also the keys to the city – the gates were locked every night and the keys were kept in the rector's office – and the candlelit clock.

The Church of St Blaise [353 F4] (*Sv Vlaho; usually* ⊕ *08.00–20.00 daily*) The original church on this site was built in the 14th century, and although it (mostly) survived the Great Earthquake in 1667, it was subsequently consumed by fire. Miraculously, the 15th-century gold and silver statue of St Blaise escaped unharmed.

The new Baroque Church of St Blaise was completed in 1717 to plans by the Venetian architect Marino Grapelli, who based the interior design on the Church of San Maurizio in his home town. It's even more unusual than the cathedral in its orientation, in having a south-facing altar.

The church is an elegant tribute to the city's patron saint, with a classic Baroque façade. Inside it's not as austere as the cathedral but not too over the top either. The main attraction is the altar, where you can admire the famous statue of St Blaise holding the city – which shows you what it looked like in about 1485.

Also worth your attention is the painting across the organ loft representing the Martyrdom of St Blaise, which was painted by local boy Petar Matejević in the early 18th century. Spare a moment too for the stained-glass windows, which depict Sts Peter and Paul and Sts Cyril and Methodius, the creators of the Glagolitic alphabet (a later variant of which, Cyrillic, is named after St Cyril). These are the work of Ivo Dulčić, one of Dubrovnik's most famous modern artists, who died in 1975.

Ploče and the Museum of Modern Art The Ploče Gate leads out from the old town into the expensive suburb of Ploče. The gate is a complex structure actually comprising several gates and bridges which were built in the 15th century – though the current design dates from 1628. There's the familiar statue of St Blaise, and a drawbridge leading out into what used to be a market square.

The main road leads up to the **Lazareti**, Dubrovnik's quarantine houses. Dubrovnik was one of the first ports in Europe to introduce quarantine restrictions, and if you wanted to visit you had to spend 40 days here first before being allowed in. These days the houses and courtyards are used as artists' studios and performance spaces.

A little further up the hill, on the left-hand side, is Dubrovnik's excellent **Museum of Modern Art** [342 F3] (*Umjetnička Galerija Dubrovnik; Put Frana Supila 23;* ✆ *426 590; www.ugdubrovnik.hr;* ⊕ *09.00–20.00 Tue–Sun; 100kn Dubrovnik Museums Ticket*). Even if there were no art to see, the building itself is magnificent and well worth a visit. Built in 1939 as the summer villa for a wealthy ship-owner, Božo Banac, it was designed in a Renaissance style reminiscent of the Rector's Palace and you wouldn't know it wasn't ancient. Since 1950 it has housed the museum's ever-expanding (and excellent) collection.

The permanent collection includes paintings and sculpture from Croatia's greatest artists as well as focusing on the burgeoning local scene. The works are rotated and there are usually temporary exhibitions, so what's on show at any one time varies. Look out for sculpture from two of Croatia's most representative and best-known sculptors, Ivan Meštrović and Frano Kršnić, as well as landscapes by Mato Celestin Medović and interiors and still lifes from Emanuel Vidović. The show is stolen, naturally, by Vlaho Bukovac (see box, page 378), and the gallery holds some of his very best work, including a number of gorgeous, complex portraits – though they're not always all on show. They have been undergoing restoration in various stages over the past few years.

Culture and the Dubrovnik Summer Festival Dubrovnik has a richly vibrant cultural scene, with its own symphony orchestra, theatre group and dance ensemble. Most performances take place during the season – broadly speaking from May to October – when there's usually something on every night, but most important of all is the annual **Dubrovnik Summer Festival**.

The festival is big, prestigious and serious, with every conceivable space in the old town – indoors and out – being turned into a performance-stage. The 45-day festival kicks off on 10 July with the performers being given the keys to the city and closes on 25 August with a fabulous firework display.

During the festival you can find everything from opera and classical concerts to chamber music and soloists, while theatre performances tend to concentrate on Shakespeare and local boy Marin Držić (see box, below). A festival standard is the traditional performance of *Hamlet* in the Lovrijenac Fortress, which is a wonderfully atmospheric setting for the play.

Tickets for the main events sell out well in advance, so if you're serious about attending check out the website (*www.dubrovnik-festival.hr*) or contact the organisers (℡ *020 326 100*) as soon as the programme becomes available (usually in April) – and make sure you get your accommodation sorted out way ahead of time, too. If you haven't got tickets in advance there are usually places available for the lower-key performances on site – you can buy these from the festival kiosks on Stradun and at the Pile Gate.

Even outside the festival there are plenty of opportunities to listen to classical music, largely thanks to the tireless **Dubrovnik Symphony Orchestra** (*www.dso. hr*), which puts on an astonishing range of concerts, all year round. The two most common venues – outside festival time – are the Revelin Fortress, just outside the Ploče Gate, and the Church of Our Saviour, just inside the Pile Gate, where there are regular candlelit performances.

Dubrovnik also has one of the country's most famous folk-dancing troupes in the form of the 300-strong Lindo ensemble. They're a regular mainstay of the festival, and also perform twice a week from May to October at the Lazareti, the old quarantine houses just up from the Ploče Gate. It makes for an amazing and authentic spectacle. Lindo's office is at Marojice Kaboge 12, two streets back from Gundulićeva poljana.

MARIN DRŽIĆ – DUBROVNIK'S REBELLIOUS PLAYWRIGHT

Born into a large family of merchants in 1508, Marin Držić was originally destined for the Church, and after being ordained at the age of 18 he was sent to Siena to study Church law. He was soon thrown out for his involvement with the theatre, and returned home to Dubrovnik, where he wrote his first plays. These weren't popular with the nobles, who rightly saw the Držić comedies for the political vehicles they were – and presumably weren't wild about being portrayed as inbred fools either.

The latter part of the playwright's life is somewhat of a mystery, though we know that he left Dubrovnik and took up something of a crusade against it. He even wrote a series of letters to the Medicis in Florence, asking them to help him overthrow the republic – though he never received an answer, and died in Venice in poverty in 1567.

Needless to say once Držić was safely out of the way his reputation was quickly rehabilitated, and today his plays – and in particular *Dundo Maroje* – form a central part of the Dubrovnik Summer Festival.

Mount Srđ Looming large above Dubrovnik, and visible from all over the city, is the mountain of Srđ. Up until 1991 there was a cable car that whisked visitors up to the top for the incredible view over the city and the islands, but it became one of the first victims of the war, dramatically destroyed by a Serb air raid.

A **cable car** runs to the top [353 G1] (*www.dubrovnikcablecar.com*; ⊕ *Jun–Aug 09.00–midnight, Sep 09.00–22.00, Apr/Oct 09.00–20.00, Feb/Mar/Nov 09.00–17.00, Dec/Jan 09.00–16.00; 108kn/50kn adult/child return*); however, if you decide to walk up instead, bear in mind that the path is long, steep, and entirely without shade for the last two-thirds. At first it's through pine trees, with butterflies and cicadas – magic and very cool. There's no water to be had, either on the way up or at the top, so take plenty with you. And although the path is perfectly safe, and the hillside is said to be clear of unexploded ordnance, you should stick to the main track just in case. Locals tend to hunt with shotguns here too, so be careful where you walk. The path climbs up from the main road running above Dubrovnik – referred to variously as Državna Cesta or Jadranska Cesta (and formerly Put Jugoslavenske Narodne Armije). Starting at the Pile Gate, turn right just after the bus stop and work your way up Zrinsko-Frankopanska. Cross over Zagrebačka and then Gornji Kono, then take the next right and follow this slip road under Jadranska Cesta. After this the footpath starts off to your left, from the highway. From the Pile Gate it will take you anything between 1 and 2 hours to the top of Mount Srđ, depending on how fit you are.

At the top you'll find the **Imperial Fort**, which was built by the French in 1810. In the 1970s it became a popular discotheque (rumours that your author was once seen strutting his stuff there many years ago are clearly without foundation). Today, the fort is still badly damaged but the plan is to house the **Museum of the Croatian War of Independence** (*Muzej Domovinskog Rata*; ⊕ *08.00–20:00 daily, with reduced hours in winter*; *20kn*) here – a small part of which has now been completed and can be visited. The main reason to come up here for most visitors however is for the magnificent views. There's a restaurant at the top.

There's a huge cross at the top, which now dominates the Old Town, especially when it's illuminated at night. As you come up, spare a thought for the mothers of those killed in the war who come up on foot as a pilgrimage for their sons, walking barefoot to the top and stopping to pray at each of the 13 crosses placed at corners along the way.

LOKRUM When you're in Dubrovnik, keep at least half a day free for a trip to sub-tropical Lokrum, the town's own offshore nature reserve. Said to have been visited unwillingly by Richard the Lionheart in 1192 (see box, page 372) the island is today just a 15-minute boat-ride away from the old town quay.

Lokrum remains undeveloped, and makes for a wonderful break from the crowds onshore. Even when the boats are arriving full, every half hour, the 2km-long island can easily absorb all comers, leaving an impression – away from a small central part – of calm and tranquillity, punctuated only by the cries of birds and the fluttering of butterflies.

A network of footpaths criss-crosses the island and provides access to the sea and into the dense woods. There are several rock beaches, and these are cleaner, fresher and less crowded than Dubrovnik's, as well as a warm **saltwater lake** (Mrtvo More, the Dead Sea), on the other side of the island from where the boat arrives. This has a 10m cliff which encourages the local lads to dive off it, apparently without harm. There's a **naturist beach** on Lokrum, too, on the southeastern end of the island, away from prying eyes – follow the FKK signs.

Lokrum's main attraction lies in its enormous variety of vegetation, which is all the more astonishing when you realise there's no fresh water supply – hence the absolute ban on making fires of any kind or even on smoking. When you're wandering the paths look out for numerous species of birds (including peacocks) and butterflies. On a visit here in June I saw white admirals, several sorts of fritillary and some skittish large yellows.

In the middle of the island, there's an old **botanical garden**, most of which seems like a series of wonderfully unmaintained secret gardens. Among slightly dilapidated walls you'll find palms with soft furry trunks, trellises of twisted vines and crippled trees supported on crutches, while broken cloches sprout thyme and basil and lettuce run to seed.

In the heavy silence and deep shade there's an agreeable air of mystery – which is shattered fairly unceremoniously when you round a corner and discover the restaurant and bar, and a small natural history museum, all within the structure of what was once a large Benedictine monastery.

On the summit of the island – a steepish 20-minute hike – there's a ruined **fort**. Built by the French in 1808, it gives great views out over Dubrovnik, and the nearby coast and the islands. Be careful here though – it's in a parlous state, and the steps leading inside and up to the lookout are on the point of collapse.

It was from the northern tip of Lokrum that I finally realised what it was I'd found vaguely make-believe about Dubrovnik all along: it's a film set. So many movies have plundered that fortified look – the big walls, the red-roofed houses nestled between them dominated by a smattering of palaces and churches – that it doesn't seem real. It looks like it's meant to be looked at, but could never really have been lived in.

To get to Lokrum, take the half-hourly boat (every day in season, less frequently out of season) from the old harbour, and make sure you know what time the last one is coming back. Tickets cost around 40kn return, less for children. If you're here on a weekday out of season just ask around at the harbour and you'll soon find someone willing to take you across. Expect to pay around 100kn a head, and make sure the skipper knows what time you want to be picked up.

SOUTH OF DUBROVNIK

From Dubrovnik, it's 40km south to the Montenegrin border. On the way there's a string of resorts (Kupari, Srebreno, Mlini, Soline and Plat) collectively known as the Župa Dubrovačka, which lead to the town of Cavtat (pronounced tsavtat), after which there's just Čilipi Airport and the ruggedly beautiful Konavle region (the latter just opening up to tourists) before you reach the border.

CAVTAT Situated just 16km south, the small, pleasant seaside town of Cavtat makes an excellent and easy excursion from Dubrovnik – and can even be considered as an alternative place to stay, with regular buses and ferries between the two and accommodation both cheaper and easier to find here. If you're visiting the area by car, Cavtat makes an ideal base, with nothing like the parking hassles you'll find in Dubrovnik itself.

Cavtat was originally the Greek and then Roman colony of Epidaurus, though there's nothing left at all from that era barring a few classical fragments built into houses – fishermen, in Rebecca West's nicely turned phrase, having 'taken what they would of sculptures and bas-reliefs to build up their cottage walls, where they can be seen today, flowers in the buttonhole of poverty'.

Getting there and away The #10 Libertas **bus** runs about once an hour from 05.00 to 01.30 from Dubrovnik (last reliable bus back from Cavtat 23.00, for timetables see http://libertasdubrovnik.com and click 'Suburban timetable'), and costs 15kn each way (pay on the bus). The standard **ferry** runs until 18.00 and costs around 80kn return (50kn single) – and docks conveniently in Dubrovnik's old town harbour. There's more than one ferry company running to different timetables. Rates are the same for all operators.

Where to stay If you want to stay in Cavtat, there are lots of private rooms available – just ask around or contact the **tourist office** (✆ 479 025; www.tzcavtat-konavle.hr). There are also a number of hotels, including one of Croatia's largest, the 5-star Hotel Croatia.

Hotel Croatia (482 rooms) Frankopanska 10; ✆ 430 830; www.adriaticluxuryhotels.com. This stunning multi-tiered, 5-star hotel does sea-view dbls. The hotel is happily sheltered from view by the headland, & has its own beaches (both standard & naturist). It's also home to the Feral Restaurant, which has live music every evening. €€€€€

Castelletto (13 rooms) Frana Laureana 22; ✆ 479 547; m 099 227 5160; www. dubrovnikexperience.com. Family-run place with spacious rooms, restaurant & outdoor pool. €€€€

Hotel Supetar (28 rooms) A Starčićeva 27; ✆ 300 300; www.adriaticluxuryhotels.com.The Supetar is stone-built with 3-star rooms right on the Cavtat quayside. €€€€

Villa Pattiera (12 rooms) Trumbićev put 9; ✆ 478 800; www.villa-pattiera.hr. Small, family-run boutique 4-star in the old town. €€€€

Villa Radović (10 rooms) Ljudevita Gaja 3; ✆ 479 021; e villaradovic@gmail.com; http:// villaradovic.weebly.com. Good-value place with simple, spacious en-suite rooms & use of a communal kitchen. Free airport transfers with direct bookings. €€€–€€

Where to eat and drink As well as the restaurants listed, there are several pizzerias – try **Kabalero** (*Put Tihe 14;* €€€).

Leut Trumbićev Put; ✆ 478 477; www. restaurant-leut.com; ⊕ 11.00–23.00 daily. One of the best of Cavtat's many restaurants is at the southern end of the town, right on the water. It's been in the Bobić family since 1971, and the food is excellent, as you'd expect for the price – though even an advance reservation won't necessarily guarantee they'll hold on to your waterside table here. €€€€

Taverna Galjia Vulčevića; ✆ 478 566; www. galija.hr; ⊕ 11.00–23.00 daily. If you lose your table at Leut, head here – it also serves first-rate seafood. €€€€

Bugenvila Obala A Starcevica 9; ✆ 479 949; http://bugenvila.eu; ⊕ 11.00–23.00 daily. A stylish & popular place with good food, wine & cocktails & a nice terrace. €€€

Konoba Toranj Obala A Starcevica 13; ✆ 479 577. Popular place with a reputation for very good food. €€€

What to see and do Cavtat (the name seems likely to be derived from the Latin word *civitas* (meaning state/citizenship) occupies a peninsula between two bays, and has a charming palm-studded front lined with cafés and restaurants. There's not a whole lot to do, though the Franciscan Monastery, at the end of the quay, hides a pair of lovely Renaissance paintings, and the Rector's Palace, at the other end of the waterfront, houses the **Baltazar Bogišić Collection**, part of which is on display there (*Obala A Starčićeva 18;* ✆ 478 556; ⊕ 09.00–13.00 Mon–Fri; 10kn) – notable in particular for a selection of excellent works by the local painter Vlaho Bukovac (see box, page 378).

Many more Bukovac paintings can be found at the artist's house, which is now the **Kuća Bukovac** (*Bukovčeva 5;* ✎ *478 646; www.kuca-bukovac.hr;* ⊕ *May–Oct 09.00–13.00 & 16.00–20.00 Tue–Sun, Nov–Apr 09.00–13.00 & 14.00–17.00 Tue–Sat, 14.00–17.00 Sun; 20kn*). More than 80 of the artist's oils, spanning his entire career, are on show here.

Right at the end of the peninsula, in a gorgeous hilltop location overlooking the sea and surrounded by cypresses, is the town cemetery. Here you'll find one of Cavtat's most important treasures, the **Račić Mausoleum** (*Trumbićev put 25;* ✎ *478 646;* ⊕ *10.00–noon & 18.00–20.00 Mon–Sat, 10.00–noon Sun; 20kn*). Its commissioning by a daughter of the ship-owning Račić family seems to have been their downfall. No sooner was the building underway than she, her father and her brother died in quick succession, and just as soon as the mausoleum was completed her mother followed them into it.

The mausoleum is one of the most important works by Croatia's most famous sculptor, Ivan Meštrović, with the white-marble Byzantine sepulchre dating from 1922. Topped with a cupola and featuring sculpted angels, dogs and eagles, along with the four Račić sarcophagi, it's a quite extraordinary work. It excited mixed feelings in Rebecca West when she was here in 1937: 'There are some terrible errors, such as four boy musician angels, who recall the horrid Japaneseries of Aubrey Beardsley … but there are moments in the chapel which exquisitely illustrate the theory that the goodness of God stretches under human destiny, like the net below trapeze acts at the circus.'

If you're after something a little less esoteric, there's a pleasant walk around the headland, with plenty of places where you can swim off the rocks, and regular trips across the bay for around 50kn to the tiny, almost barren island of **Supetar**, which boasts a simple restaurant.

Rather more strenuous are several local **hikes**. The shorter of these leads from Cavtat to Močiči and Čilipi, taking around 1½ hours. The other involves a 3–4-hour trek up the 'Ronald Brown Pathway' (Pjesačka Staza Ronald Brown) that starts from the main road above the town and leads up into the mountains to the cross commemorating the delegation led by the American Minister of Trade in 1996.

VLAHO BUKOVAC – VIRTUOSO PAINTER

Vlaho Bukovac was born in Cavtat in 1855, and showed prodigious talent from an early age. In 1877, he went to the Beaux Arts in Paris to complete his studies and a year later became the first Croatian painter to be accepted into the prestigious Paris Salon. Travelling widely around Europe, Bukovac nonetheless played a vital part in the development of Croatian art – not just by being enormously prolific himself (he left over 2,000 works), but by supporting younger artists as well.

In his forties, Bukovac spent five years living in Cavtat before accepting the post of Professor of Fine Arts in Prague, though he returned to his childhood home regularly until shortly before his death in 1922.

At their best, Bukovac's paintings are simply marvellous, combining an almost photographic realism with impressionistic touches, and some of his portraits are truly stunning. As a virtuoso painter, he seems to have had a penchant for technically difficult or daring compositions, and there's a wonderful picture of a woman coming in (or going out?) through a doorway, which is in the Museum of Modern Art in Dubrovnik, along with a brilliant portrait of his daughter.

There's a useful list of hiking and biking routes, including maps, on the tourist office website (*www.tzcavtat-konavle.hr*).

SOUTH TO THE MONTENEGRIN BORDER Past the airport of the same name you'll find the pretty village of **Čilipi**. After Sunday mass the locals put on a show of folk music and dancing in the main square here, so it's not surprising that it's become something of a Sunday-morning excursion from Dubrovnik and the nearby resort hotels.

Three buses a day (*#11; first bus from Dubrovnik 10.00, last bus back 18.30; timetable at http://libertasdubrovnik.hr*) run from Dubrovnik to Čilipi and on to **Molunat**, a sleepy resort which has sprung up around a tiny fishing village in a lovely cove right at the very end of Croatia. With just a handful of private rooms, and no hotels nearby, it's within an hour of Dubrovnik, and an utterly charming place to stay. To be honest, however, given the bus times and the minuteness of the place, you'd need to be in Dubrovnik on an extended visit to make the excursion worthwhile.

If you've got your own transport then it's also worth checking out the front-line trenches, bunkers and anti-aircraft gun emplacements at **Đurinići**; not to mention the remains of an old Illyrian hill fort. There's an English-language information board, but this is well off the tourist trail, so keep your eyes peeled for the Croatian flag flying above a small cattle shed.

✗ Where to eat and drink There are a couple of nice restaurants in the south towards the border:

✗ Konoba Konavle Vojski Do, Šilješki; m 098 674 363; ⏰ noon–midnight daily. This is a welcoming family restaurant housed in a stone building that used to be a railway station. Dine on homemade cheese, pršut & grilled meats from the station platform (peka-cooked dishes need to be ordered a day in advance) & soak up the views of Čilipi & the Konavle from this elevated position. The restaurant is signposted from the main Dubrovnik to Čilipi road, from where the road snakes up the mountainside, so keep your eyes peeled. €€€

✗ Konoba Vinica Ljuta; ☎791 054; m 099 2152 459; www.konobavinica.com. Inland from the main road in the village of Ljuta, this serves good, traditional local & Dalmatian dishes (including ispod peka dishes, *pašticada* & grilled trout) in a rustic setting, with a lovely riverside terrace. €€€

THE ELAPHITE ISLANDS (KOLOČEP, LOPUD, ŠIPAN)

The Elaphite Islands lie in a string north of Dubrovnik. These once-quiet islands have seen tourism well and truly arrive, with a growing number of day trip operators allowing much easier access to the islands.

The Jadrolinija ferry runs up and down the Elaphites from Dubrovnik four times daily all year round – if you're clever with the Jadrolinija timetables you can also use these ferries to combine the islands with a trip to Mljet (for timetables see www. jadrolinija.hr). There's also a fast G&V ferry (*www.gv-line.hr*) calling at Šipanska luka *en route* between Dubrovnik and Mljet.

Even with more tourism than there used to be, the Elaphites still make for a great excursion, getting you away from the crowds and into nature; there are no cars on Koločep and Lopud, and barely a handful on Šipan. If you're interested in staying in private rooms or apartments, it's well worth contacting **Meet Lopud** (☏ *021 864 498; www.meetlopud.com*), which specialises in accommodation on the islands.

KOLOČEP The first inhabited island in the Elaphites is Koločep, just 7km and 35 minutes away from Dubrovnik on the ferry, making it a very easy day trip. The ferry –

which costs just 12kn – docks at Donje Čelo, and although there's another settlement on the other side of the island, it's here that you'll find the main infrastructure.

Outside the tourist season Koločep has an official population of just 148, and the doctor only comes once a week. Indeed, if you come here before May, you'll find only a single shop and a post office open in the mornings, and nowhere on the island to eat or drink at all – so bring a picnic, and make sure you know what time the last ferry leaves.

Donje Čelo is spread around a gentle bay, and has a biggish and reasonably sandy beach. A concrete path heads up from the ferry landing and winds across the island, leading through lovely woods and dry-stone-walled fields to the settlement of Gornje Čelo on Koločep's southeastern shore – where you'll find a couple of bars in summer and nothing whatsoever in winter. Smaller paths head on into the scented woods, and the island's sufficiently large for you to lose sight of anyone else, but small enough for most people to avoid getting lost.

Where to stay and eat If you want to stay (from May to October), there's a single hotel in Donje Čelo, across the bay from the ferry landing, which had a makeover in 2014 and has changed its name to the **Kalamota Island Resort** (⌕ *312 150; www.kalamotaislandresort.com;* €€€€€). It is exclusively the domain of over 18s – which unfortunately means that for families it now makes more sense to skip Koločep and head for Lopud. When the hotel's open in summer there are also a handful of restaurants on the island – try **Villa Ruža** (m *098 443 382; www.villa-ruza.com;* €€€€) which specialises in seafood. There are also a handful of private rooms available – just ask on arrival if you haven't made prior arrangements.

LOPUD Twenty minutes – and a mere 10kn more on the ferry – beyond Koločep is the larger island of Lopud. Important in Ragusan times, it once had a population of 4,000 and harboured nearly 100 ships, as well as being home to Miho Pracat, the man whose bust sits in the Rector's Palace in Dubrovnik (see box, page 382).

Today the 4.5km-long island has a population of just 348 (though locals put the figure even lower, at barely half that). Everyone lives in one settlement, the eponymous Lopud, on a curved bay with a decent beach facing the village of Suđurađ on the next-door island of Šipan. There's no traffic, no pollution and no crime – and out of season nothing much open beyond a bar and a couple of shops. In summer, however, Lopud really comes into its own, and the village positively hums; it's a great place to come for the day or even for a holiday in its own right.

Where to stay and eat If you want to stay on Lopud, there are quite a few private rooms and apartments for rent (ask on arrival, or contact Meet Lopud – page 379). There are restaurants and bars all along the front, but it's also worth climbing up the street near the harbour to **Terrasse Peggy** (€€€), which does a great grill in summer and boasts breezy views out across the sea to the island of Šipan. Try its versions of limoncello and a curiously potent, nameless local drink made from honey and herbs. Pretty much everything, including all the hotels and most of the island's restaurants, closes from November to April.

Villa Vilina (20 rooms) Iva Kuljevana 5; ⌕759 333; www.villa-vilina.hr. A restored mansion that's been in the Vilina family since 1792 now houses Lopud's most upmarket accommodation

option (4-star), with nicely furnished sea-view dbls & a lovely suite with its own balcony. €€€€€

Glavović (12 rooms, 2 apts) Iva Kuljevana; ⌕759 359; www.hotel-glavovic.hr. The 3-star

Glavović was the island's 1st hotel, which opened in 1927 & was renovated in 2004. Even if it's comfortable enough, the accommodation is still fairly basic – though the sandy beach just outside is a bonus. €€€€

🏠 **Lafodia** (200 rooms) Iva Kuljevana; 📞 450 300; www.lafodiahotel.com. Located at the far end of the bay from the ferry terminal & harbour, the Lafodia is Lopud's main package tour hotel. Refurbished, with swish, spacious rooms with balconies & nice views. €€€€

What to see and do There's not a huge amount to see or do, but if you're here (and it's open) check out the church above the harbour, which has some fine 16th-century Venetian paintings and lovely 15th-century carved choir stalls. The church – one of 33 on the island – forms part of the Franciscan Monastery, which was dissolved by the French in 1808.

Also of interest are the small **town museum and treasury**, which are just off the quay opposite the end of the harbour, on Zlatarska. If they're closed – and they usually seem to be – pop through the gap between the two into a walled courtyard and seek out Lopud's priest, Don Ivan Vlašić, who holds the keys.

The treasury houses an assortment of ancient icons, vestments and sacred remnants, and a handful of very battered 9th-, 11th- and 12th-century frescoes. In the museum you'll find an extraordinary assembly of stuff ranging from Roman amphorae to 500-year-old pudding bowls to 19th-century English pottery. There's a nasty-looking French bayonet from 1806, a couple of pulleys from Miho Pracat's ship, and a cloak from the Giorgis, one of Dubrovnik's last noble families. Most curious of all is a shaving gown that belonged to King Charles V of Spain, which was a gift to Miho Pracat (see box, page 382).

Behind the museum you can see the crumbling ruins of the Dubrovnik **Rector's Palace**, testimony to the fact that even now there are far more houses on Lopud than there are people. Walk further along the quayside and there's a lovely park featuring tall pines and palms – each one planted, it's said, by grateful sailors who'd avoided shipwreck.

Just beyond the park, before the former Grand Hotel, there's a path leading up to the left which crosses the island and comes out half an hour later at **Šunj**, one of the loveliest beaches on the Adriatic. On the crest of the hill, on the left, there's a concrete monument to Viktor Dyk, the Czech poet, author and political journalist, who died unexpectedly of a heart attack while on holiday here in May 1931, aged only 53.

The sandy beach at Šunj has a lovely shallow descent into the water and a temporary bar/restaurant open in season. It's an ill-kept secret, however, with sizeable crowds of locals coming over from the mainland during summer weekends.

The name Šunj provides the clue to Lopud's apparently mysterious use of a snake swallowing a child on its coat of arms – something you're more likely to have seen as the right half of the Alfa Romeo logo. According to the legend, Otto Visconti was shipwrecked here in 1098, on his way back from the Crusades, and so grateful was he to survive that he had a votive church built on the hill above the bay. This was decorated with a copy of a shield which had been used by one of the defeated Saracens – featuring the snake and the child – and which subsequently became the Visconti crest. Over time the locale became known as *biscione*, the Italian for 'big snake', which was later abbreviated to Šunj.

The present **Church of Our Lady of Šunj** (Gospa od Šunja) above the bay – turn left just after the Dyk memorial, if you're coming from Lopud – dates from the end of the 15th century. If it's open (which sadly is not all that often) it's well worth looking in to see the marvellous carved wooden altarpiece featuring Mary and the Apostles. This, oddly enough, is English, from the 16th century. Lopud sailors –

arguably among the best in the world at the time – heard that Henry VIII was in conflict with the pope and busily dissolving the monasteries, so off they went to go and buy bargain relics and religious treasures. The background to the altarpiece shows the Lopud ship which brought the Madonna here.

There's a direct path leading back from the church into the town; off to the right of this, heading away from Šunj, there's a track leading up to a great ruined **fortress**. Built originally in the 16th century, it was reinforced and expanded by the French between 1808 and 1813. Today it's soulful and dilapidated, and there's nothing particularly special to see – though the views across to the island of Šipan are undoubtedly fabulous.

ŠIPAN Furthest away, largest and least-visited of the Elaphites, Šipan is lovely. Known as the 'Golden Island', it once had 300,000 olive trees and a sizeable population, but centuries of emigration have left it with fewer than 500 inhabitants and – like Lopud – with many more houses than people. During Dubrovnik's Golden Age, it was fashionable for wealthy nobles to spend the summer season on Šipan, and you'll come across their (mostly dilapidated) summer residences all over the island – along with a smattering of Roman ruins and a score of churches from the 11th century onwards, but the main reason to come here is very much to get away from it all.

It takes around 75 minutes to get to Šipan from Dubrovnik on the Jadrolinija ferry (and costs a princely 19kn one-way). On the fast G&V ferry this time is reduced to 40 minutes, but tickets are 35kn. The main centres – and the only places where you'll find anything at all to eat or drink – are **Šipanska Luka** (which is where the G&V ferry stops) to the northwest at the end of a deep inlet, and **Suđurađ**, which is where the Jadrolinija ferry stops, to the southeast, opposite Lopud. The two settlements are about 7km apart, and connected by an irregular minibus service run by Libertas. There's also a handful of other hamlets across the island.

Where to stay and eat Everything on the island is pretty much closed from November to April. In season, there are a few private rooms available at either end of the island, and you may find people touting these as you get off the boat – otherwise just ask around. There are also two hotels, one at each end of Šipan:

Hotel Božica (26 rooms) Suđurađ; ☎325 400; www.hotel-bozica.hr. A 4-star hotel with a good restaurant offering stunning views back from Suđurađ towards the Croatian mainland. €€€€€

Šipan (84 rooms) Šipanska Luka; ☎361 902; www.hotel-sipan.com. Enjoying a great location on Šipanska Luka's harbour, this hotel has fairly functional rooms but is good value. €€€

✗ Konoba Kod Marka Šipanska Luka; ☎758 007; ⊕ noon–22.00. Highly regarded konoba. No menus, the waiter will tell you what's on offer that day. €€€€–€€€

What to see and do An excellent excursion is to start from one end of the island and then walk across to the other, ie: Šipanska Luka to Suđurađ or vice versa. It takes a leisurely 2 hours by the most direct route, on Šipan's only paved road. The interior of the island is a fertile valley where you'll see grapes, figs and olives being grown, and there are plenty of places to stop and have a picnic and a bottle of wine.

You can also wander up any of the many tracks on the island (though stay well away from any remaining uncleared ordnance – well-marked signs mark the spots), which lead up to the island's two limestone ridges. Here you'll find abandoned olive groves surrounded by crumbling dry-stone walls, though above Šipanska Luka itself work is progressing apace on bringing some of the olive trees back into production. You may also come across the rooting-marks made by wild boar here. They're a recent arrival on the island, and something of a nuisance to the olive farmers, having swum across from the mainland after a forest fire at the end of the 1990s.

As you traverse the island, look out for the ruined Napoleonic fortress on the southern ridge, along with a hospital and barracks dating from the same era. There are also secretive military tunnels which dive into the hillside nearby, though for the time being these are off limits to the public.

If you're walking from Šipanska Luka to Suđurađ you'll pass a great fortress of a church dating from the 16th century, dedicated to **Sveti Duh** (the Holy Spirit), as you climb up out of the central valley. Just after this the road forks – if you go right it passes the local clinic and loops down to the port; if you go straight on it goes directly through Suđurađ itself before emerging at the harbour.

The dominating feature of Suđurađ is the summer residence of Vice Stjepović-Skočibuha, which is the only one of Šipan's 42 original mansions to be entirely preserved. It was built in 1563, with the tower being added in 1577, and is today used for conferences and functions. Other places to eat at this end of the island include an informal bar-restaurant on the waterfront and **Karmelo Cvjetković** (m *098 9145 756;* €€€), where Tomaš and his dad serve up fish soup, salad, homemade wine and homemade cheese or pršut at a fraction of Dubrovnik prices.

If you want to explore further afield, you'll find boats down on the harbour whose owners are happy to take you out to the uninhabited Elaphite islands as well as to delightful unspoiled coves and beaches on Šipan itself – if there's nobody around ask at the little bar along the harbour front, which is where most of the fishermen and seafaring types hang out.

MLJET

Mljet is one of the most attractive islands in the whole Adriatic. Despite being unusually beautiful, and entirely unspoiled by deforestation (it was never ruled by Venice, hence also the lack of towns of any size), it has hitherto remained relatively unvisited – though with the fast connection from Dubrovnik more people are coming every year. Nonetheless, the island is easily big enough, at over 100km², to absorb many more visitors without getting overcrowded.

The entire western end of Mljet is a national park, and features two gorgeous saltwater lakes, the larger of which has an island with a ruined monastery on it. It's easy to visit on a day trip from Dubrovnik, but if you want to stay longer there's a hotel and some private rooms, and the island has great walking, cycling and canoeing, along with a nascent (if rather casual) diving school, and the opportunity of learning to sail.

HISTORY Legend has it that Ulysses stopped here for seven years on his Odyssey, and while there's absolutely no historical basis for the assertion, it makes a nice story. More credence can be given to the theory that on his way to martyrdom in Rome, St Paul was shipwrecked here, not on Malta. It's not just the name (Mljet used to be called Melita), but also the snakes – St Paul was bitten by one soon after arriving, which would be improbable (then as now) on Malta, whereas Mljet was notoriously snake-infested until the 19th century.

What's sure is the island's use by the Illyrians and the Romans – the remains of the Illyrian fort can still be seen on the summit of Mali Gradac, near **Babine Kuče**, while the settlement of **Polače** is named after the ruins of the 4th- or 5th-century Roman palace there.

The next significant development was in 1151, when Mljet was given to the Benedictines, who built the monastery on St Mary's Island. They stayed on even though Mljet itself was handed over to Dubrovnik in 1333, and lived a peaceful life until the arrival of Napoleon's troops in 1808, after which the monastery was abandoned.

The administrative centre of the island, **Babino Polje**, dates from the Middle Ages, but apart from the monastery, nothing on the western end of the island reaches back beyond the late 18th century, and the new port of **Pomena** wasn't established until after World War II.

WILDLIFE Mljet is famous for being the only place in Europe where you can find mongooses in the wild. The **Indian grey mongoose** was introduced to Mljet in 1910, by the Austrians, in an attempt to eradicate the infestation of venomous snakes. This had been a problem since time immemorial – and was probably the reason why the Benedictines built their monastery on the island in the first place ('Never mind the beauty and the isolation, Brother Jacob, let's get away from those blasted snakes!').

Seven male and four female mongooses were introduced, and they adapted well to the Mljet lifestyle, proliferating and practically eradicating the snake population over the next 20 years. So successful were they, in fact, that they lost their statutory protection in 1949, and excessive numbers have proven difficult to curb. Small animals, as well as both resident and migratory birds, fall prey to the feral hunters, and they're not over-popular with the islanders, either.

Mljet's other fauna used to include the **Mediterranean monk seal**, though none has been spotted here since 1974. You may, however, see the **Turkish gecko**, the **sharp-snouted lizard**, or **Dahl's whip snake** (if the mongooses haven't got to him first), and there are now quite a few **fallow deer** in the forests – following their introduction in 1958.

GETTING THERE AND AWAY In summer you can take the 1½-hour crossing on the fast catamaran *Nona Ana* (*www.gv-line.hr*), which comes out to Mljet twice daily from Dubrovnik, in the morning and evening (the morning sailing continues to Korčula and Lastovo). Fares are 60kn Dubrovnik–Sobra and 70kn Dubrovnik–Polače. Alternatively, there's a fast catamaran between Split and Dubrovnik, calling

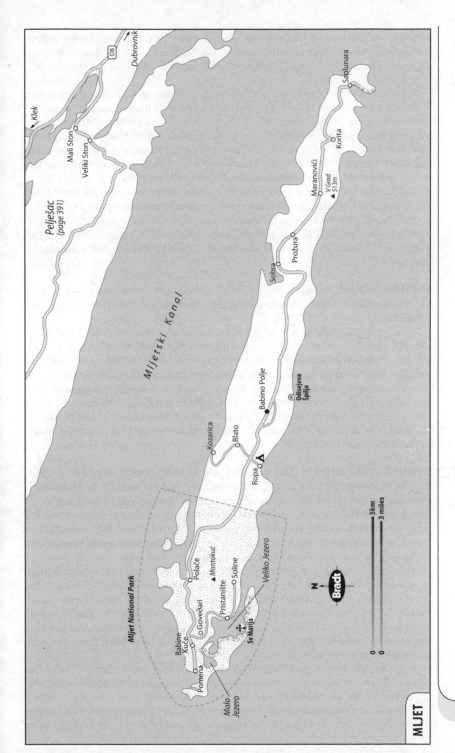

MLJET

at Milna (on Brač), Hvar, Korčula and Mljet, daily in the summer and three or four times a week in shoulder seasons (*www.krilo.hr*). There's also a car ferry five times daily in the summer between Prapratno on Pelješac and Sobra (*www.jadrolinija.hr*), which takes 45 minutes.

Ferries dock just east of **Sobra**, about a third of the way along Mljet's north shore, and are met by the local bus – but be warned that on busy days in summer there can be fewer buses than passengers, and if you're stranded your only realistic option is to rent a bike – at sellers' prices (and it's a long, hard, hot and hilly ride). To solve this problem the catamaran has taken to sailing on to **Polače**, and if you're on a day trip this is definitely the way to go. There's also a ferry linking Polače with Trstenik on the Pelješac peninsula between mid-July and mid-September.

The easiest way of seeing Mljet is by taking an all-inclusive package from Dubrovnik or Korčula (available from all the usual agencies – page 397). These go for around 250–400kn, and include the ferry fare, the entry fee to the national park, a trip out to the island on the lake, and (sometimes) a guided tour, as well as the chance to swim. Bring a bottle of wine and a picnic, and it makes a wonderful day out.

GETTING AROUND Apart from the local buses that run between Sobra and Pomena to coincide with the Jadrolinija ferry arrivals and departures, there's no public transport.

If you want to **cycle** on the island the best place to rent bikes is at the Hotel Odisej (page 387) in Pomena (check with the tourist office: www.mljet.hr), or by the lakes themselves. Rates run from around 40kn an hour to 150kn a day, and the paths around the lakes are absolutely perfect for cyclists. (There are several other places which rent out bikes too, if the stock at the Odisej's already out on loan, or if you haven't yet got as far as Pomena, including Sobra and Polače.) Even on the main roads, there's no traffic to speak of. You can rent buggies, cars or scooters outside the hotel, too, as well as at Sobra and Polače, with cars going from around 400kn a day, including fuel and 100km.

 WHERE TO STAY AND EAT The monastery on St Mary's Island served from 1960 to 1988 as the lovely Hotel Melita, but since it was handed back to the Dubrovnik bishopric it's fallen into ruin. Although restoration commenced in 2004, nobody's sure what will become of it – there's no doubt it would make the most wonderful boutique hotel, but there are also plans to turn it into a research or information centre, or to leave it as a visitor attraction. At present, there's just a modest restaurant serving the numerous visitors to the island throughout the day.

Although there's only one hotel, Mljet has a reasonable (and steadily increasing) supply of **private rooms**, but it's a very good idea to book ahead. This can be arranged through the **tourist offices** in Sobra (❧ 746 025; www.mljet.hr) and Polače (❧ 744 186; www.mljet.hr), or travel agents in Dubrovnik. Polače, a few kilometres away from the Hotel Odisej, but still within easy walking distance of the lakes, has good private rooms on the shore, and also has a bakery and a couple of cheerful restaurants.

There are two rather plain **campsites** on the island – one in Babino Polje, the other in Ropa. Other, more personal sites are run by private individuals – just ask around when you arrive at the port.

Half-a-dozen **restaurants** line the harbour, which is very popular with people from visiting yachts (as indeed is Polače), though food shopping is limited to the early morning bakery van, a couple of fruit stalls and the absolute basics.

🏠 **Odisej** (150 rooms) Pomena; ☎ 300 300; www.adriaticluxuryhotels.com; ☉ Apr–Oct. Mljet's only hotel rooms spread across a number of buildings, with sea-view dbls with balconies. €€€€€–€€€€

🏠 **Apartments Stražičić** (8 dbls, 4 apts) Pomena 14; ☎ 745 082; e marija.strazicic@du.htnet.hr; www.mljetpomena.com. Highly recommended private accommodation with its own restaurant. €€€–€€

🏠 **Holiday House Matana** (4 dbls, 6 apts) Pomena 10; ☎ 744 066; www.mljetvacation.com. €€€–€€

🏠 **Pansion Kiko** (5 rooms, 2 apts) ☎ 020 744 074; www.accommodation-mljet.com. Home to the Konoba Kiko restaurant, where the grilled lamb is highly recommended. €€

ACTIVITIES If you're here for more than a day trip, take advantage of the island's excellent **walking and hiking**. From the gentle paths around the lakes to the harder trails into the hills, Mljet's unspoiled beauty is overwhelming, and away from the lakes you'll pretty much have the place to yourself. Even on the lakeshore, you don't have to walk far to have almost total seclusion. There's a good marked trail from near Soline up Montokuč overlooking the lakes (the ascent takes around 40 minutes), with great views from the top. Rather than retrace your steps, you could return to Pristanište or continue to Polače or Goveđari. Within the park, trails lead to unexplored coves on the island's northwest tip, while even outside the park the ratio of nature to people is very high. If you're going to be walking or hiking here, or elsewhere in Croatia, it's well worth getting hold of *The Islands of Croatia* by Rudolf Abraham or *Croatia: Car Tours and Walks* by Sandra Bardwell, both of which do a great job of covering the country from a walker's perspective. There's a good new hiking map published by the HGSS (page 37).

The **Mljet Hiking Trail**, opened in 2012, is a 43km marked hiking route across the island, from Pomena to Sobra – via Goveđari, Blato, Babino Polje and Veliki Grad – and can be comfortably walked in 3 days. See www.mljet.hr for more details.

If it's watersports you're after, there's plenty of choice. Exploring by **kayak or canoe** makes for a great way of seeing the lakes at your own pace – they can be rented by the little bridge or at the hotel, with prices roughly the same as for bikes. **Windsurfers** can be rented out from the hotel, too, and there's also a sailing school based here, though it's a pity it doesn't have dinghies on hand. For **divers**, the local diving centre (*Aquatica-Mljet, based in Pomena; contact Mario Orlandini;* m *098 479 916;* e *info@aquatica-mljet.hr; www.aquatica-mljet.hr; or book through the hotel*) can take you out to a Roman wreck, complete with original amphorae, or to a defunct German U-boat. Expect to pay upwards of €50 for a dive with a guide, including equipment – though if you're a novice you might want to take heed of reports of a certain laxity in this department. Visits to either of the wrecks cost an additional €15.

WHAT TO SEE AND DO
Mljet National Park (☎ *744 041; www.np-mljet.hr; 100kn inc the boat ride to St Mary's Island (80kn without) in Jun–Sep, 90kn/70kn Oct–May*) Mljet's main draw is the national park, and specifically the two saltwater lakes, **Veliko Jezero** (with St Mary's Island and the crumbling monastery) and **Malo Jezero** – literally 'Big Lake' and 'Small Lake'.

Established in 1960, the national park is run from the settlement of **Goveđari**, roughly equidistant from both Pomena and Polače. Entry fees go to the upkeep of the park, so don't be tempted to try to avoid paying. Anyway, if you're caught without a ticket, you'll be charged – double. Detailed maps are available from the park office (on the shore of the main lake, at the locality called **Pristanište**) or from the kiosk selling tickets in Pomena, though the footpath network shown on these maps is none too accurate. There's another kiosk on the road in from Polače.

The national park is unusual among nature reserves in including the main villages, the hotel and the basic tourist infrastructure within its boundaries, but don't be lulled into a sense of false security. You're in an ecologically fragile area here, and it's important to follow the rules, especially relating to fire – in 1917 an accidental blaze destroyed much of the old forest and the restoration took decades. So don't light fires, don't smoke, don't camp – and do stay on the paths.

If you're on a day trip you won't have time to see a great deal else other than the lakes. As you'll probably guess – the saltwater's a bit of a giveaway – neither Malo nor Veliko Jezero is actually a lake. The sea feeds into the larger one, and that feeds into the smaller one. The tidal changes allowed the monks to run a useful watermill in the past, and although the mill's long gone you can still easily see which way the tide's headed from the bridge over the shallow channel between Malo and Veliko Jezero.

Unfortunately, the bridge originally spanning the seaward exit of Veliko Jezero was lost when the channel was widened and deepened in 1960 (under Tito's orders, so tourists could come in by ship straight to the former hotel), so you can't now do the full 12km circuit round the lake without getting wet. A word of warning: we advise you *not* to attempt to swim the 13.6m wide and 2.6m deep channel, or at least if you do, to be very sure which way the current's going, and how fast it's moving – there's an awful lot of water coming in and out of there, and it's frighteningly easy to be swept out to sea.

The boat out to **St Mary's Island** (Sv Marija) runs several times a day, and if you want to visit make sure you buy the national park entry ticket with the boat fare included (page 387). On the island itself there's not been much to see in recent years, but the monastery is currently being restored and the church is now open for services at 11.30 on Sunday. You can visit the monks' gardens, complete with lemon trees, in the original cloisters (if they're open). The island also has a couple of restaurants, which are highly popular as the luncheon venues for excursions, as well as ice-cream stopovers.

Take the 10-minute path around the little island and you'll see two other plain but evocative votive chapels dating from the 17th or 18th century. These were built by grateful sailors who'd survived shipwrecks or storms. If you're here in spring, you'll find lots of wild asparagus, while in summer you'll be overwhelmed by the noise of cicadas in the afternoon haze.

Beyond the national park
Three-quarters of Mljet is forest-covered, meaning good shade in the summer heat (but take plenty of water with you; there are no supplies at all), while the few settlements are rarely visited, and you'll be made to feel welcome by the locals. This is especially true on the 15km stretch of the island east of Sobra, where the settlements of **Prožura**, **Maranovići** and **Korita** are practically never visited by foreigners. Right at the far eastern tip, at **Saplunara**, are two sandy beaches, the only ones on the island. You'll need a car (or a bike, and strong legs) to get here as no buses run beyond Sobra. The first is below the village itself; the other, round the next bay, has a shallow and very sheltered lagoon, and is almost deserted. Debris washed in on the tide is a problem in parts at present, but with the current promotion by the tourist board, this – and the seclusion – are likely to change.

The highest point on the island (Veli Grad, 513m) is just above Mljet's diminutive administrative capital, **Babino Polje**, again practically unvisited.

Babino Polje sits on the side of the island's largest field system – the endless dry-stone walls here are the result of centuries of clearing stones from the fields. The main produce is olives and (surprisingly expensive but incredibly tasty) goat's cheese. Much of the island's very drinkable wine comes from the village of Blato, just outside the national park.

Directly south of Babino Polje is **Ulysses Cave** (Odisejeva Špilja), a good half hour's tough walk across fields and down the cliff, but well worth the effort. It's not suitable for young children, however – if you're travelling with the family take the boat trip from the Odisej, as it's a magical cave to explore in calm seas.

TRSTENO

Just 18km up the coast from Dubrovnik is the little village of Trsteno, which would be entirely unremarkable were it not for the wonderful arboretum here. Originally created as the summer residence and gardens of Ivan Gučetić, a Dubrovnik noble, in 1502, and expanded over the centuries, the estate was nationalised by the communists in 1948 and re-branded as the Arboretum of the Yugoslav (now Croatian) Academy of Arts and Sciences. Inexplicably it was subject to Serb shelling during the 1991–92 war.

Anyway, the gardens here are delightful, and make a charming excursion out of Dubrovnik. Buses #12, #15, #22 and #35 from Dubrovnik stop at Trsteno (*20mins*), and buses going up the coast to Split etc set down and pick up in the middle of the village, where the first thing you'll see is a splendid pair of huge 500-year-old plane trees. Beyond these, heading towards the sea in a series of terraces, is the **arboretum** itself (✆ *751 019;* ☉ *summer 07.00–19.00 daily, winter 08.00–16.00 daily; 40kn*).

There's nothing special to do other than to wander round the gardens, which vary from the formality of the oldest part, beneath the villa, with geometrical box hedges enclosing different planted areas, to the wilder areas off to the sides. There's a lovely orchard with citrus fruits, avenues of palms and firs, and all manner of exotic semi-tropical plants, most of them usefully labelled. There's even a rather fanciful 18th-century grotto, where you'll find Neptune with his trident presiding over a water-lily-strewn fishpond and playful water-spouting fountains in the form of dolphins.

PLOČE AND THE NERETVA DELTA

Roughly halfway between Split and Dubrovnik lies the industrial port of **Ploče**. Known during the 1980s as Kardeljevo, after one of Tito's pals, it still handles most of Bosnia & Herzegovina's sea-bound freight (the coastal town of Neum, actually in Bosnia's land corridor, is a dreary little resort with no proper port) and acts as a transport hub.

The re-established rail link to Sarajevo (a spectacular journey) starts from here, and there are Jadrolinija car ferries across to Trpanj, on Pelješac – three a day in winter, seven in summer. Otherwise there's no reason to break your journey.

South of Ploče is the extraordinary **Neretva Delta**. Long a marshy, malarial swamp, the pancake-flat river delta is now a series of fertile agricultural wetlands, producing Croatia's best citrus fruits (you'll see delicious tangerines for sale along the roadside), and providing shelter to waterfowl and wading birds, as well as spawning grounds for many species of fish, including eels.

Deep in the delta are six hard-to-find dedicated ornithological reserves. You'll need time, patience and your own transport – in which case you should keep a weather-eye on the main road for flying customs squads, on the lookout for Bosnian contraband and speeding tourists.

A total of 299 species of bird have been recorded in the delta, with 92 nesting here, including the pigmy cormorant, coots, crakes, warblers and shrikes, several species of heron and egret, all five species of European grebe and almost every species of European duck. In 1999, a government proposal was initiated to proclaim the entire delta as a nature park, but obstacles include various development and road-improvement plans.

Easily the best way of visiting is to persuade one of the locals to take you around in a punt (the indigenous *trupica* or *lad-a*), poling you along the reedy channels which separate the reclaimed market gardens, and giving you a chance to soak up the mysterious atmosphere. Far simpler, however, is to book yourself on a day-long excursion from Dubrovnik for around 300kn – this includes a comprehensively guided boat tour and is available from most local travel agencies. Take insect repellent with you – the mosquitoes here can be fearsome.

 WHERE TO STAY AND EAT

Hotel Restaurant Villa Neretva (8 rooms) Krvavac II, Metković; ☎672 200. The main reason to stop off here is for the photo safaris that take you by boat to the hotel's sister property Neretva House, which can only be reached by water; | Dalmatian cuisine dominates the menus at both restaurants. The photo safari costs 500kn/boat, so bring some friends. If you want to stay over, the rooms are simple, well priced & clean. €€

PELJEŠAC PENINSULA

An island in all but name, the 65km Pelješac Peninsula runs up from the isthmus at Ston to the island of Korčula. Never more than 7km wide, Pelješac is mountainous and rocky, an unlikely home to two of Croatia's best wines, the hearty Dingač and Postup reds.

Two buses a day travel up and down the main road from Dubrovnik to Ston and on to Orebić (*2½hrs*), the main departure point for Korčula, and buses also hook up with Trpanj, the arrival point for ferries from Ploče, on the mainland. But if you want to explore the dozens of small villages, or the myriad hidden bays and beaches, you'll definitely need your own wheels.

STON The land entrance to Pelješac is at Ston, which guards the isthmus with a series of remarkably well-preserved walls from the 14th century on. On the south coast is the village of **Veliki Ston**, while on the northern bay is **Mali Ston** – the two settlements are a 20-minute walk apart, should you get off the bus at the wrong stop.

The reason for a visit here is twofold – firstly to see (and clamber upon) the walls, which rival Dubrovnik's, and secondly to sample Croatia's best oysters, which are farmed here, as are mussels. The walls were built from the 14th century on, primarily to protect the salt-pans – the salt trade was one of the republic's biggest earners, and it's said that Napoleon was even keener to get his hands on Ston than Dubrovnik. Today 20 of the original 40 towers and some 5km of walls are still standing, and if you climb high enough up – the public access is from Veliki Ston – there are great views across to the island of Mljet (page 383).

The area was subjected to Serb shelling during the war and then badly hit by an earthquake in 1996, which destroyed many of the houses in both Veliki and Mali Ston, along with most of the town of Slano, further down the coast towards

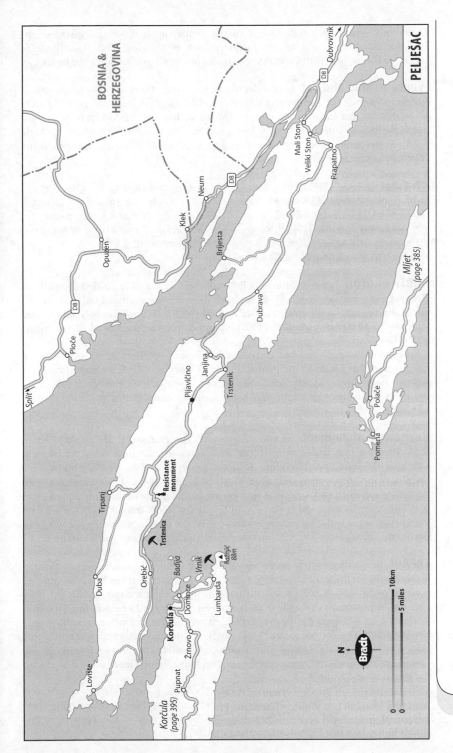

PELJEŠAC

BOSNIA &
HERZEGOVINA

Dubrovnik

D8

Mali Ston
Veliki Ston
Prapatno

D8

Neum

Klek

Brijesta

Opuzen

Dubrava

D8

Mljet
(page 385)

Ploče

Trstenik

Janjina

Split

Pijavičino

Polače

Pomena

Resistance
monument

Trpanj

Trstenica

Duba

Orebić
Badija

Vrnik
Ražnjić
88m

Korčula

Domince

Lumbarda

Žrnovo

Pupnat

Lovište

Korčula
(page 395)

N

Bradt

10km

5 miles

0

0

Dubrovnik – and even today some of the properties here remain boarded up. Nonetheless, Mali Ston's tourist infrastructure is thriving, and the village is increasingly popular with Croatian romantics on oyster-fuelled weekend breaks.

🏠 **Where to stay and eat** If you decide to stay over, there are two lovely small hotels in Mali Ston. The **tourist office** in Veliki Ston (*Pelješki put 1;* \ *754 452; www.ston.hr*) can also point you in the direction of the few private rooms available locally. Finally, there are two great restaurants on the harbour in Mali Ston: **Kapetanova Kuča** (same ownership as Ostrea; €€) and **Taverna Bota** (*www.bota-sare.hr;* €€).

🏠 **Ostrea** (9 rooms) \ 754 555; www.ostrea. hr. This is just inside the walls & is somewhat more upmarket than the Vila Koruna. €€€€€
🏠 **Vila Koruna** (6 rooms) \ 754 999; www. vila-koruna.hr. Just outside the old walls is the attractive hotel, which has simple dbls, & a great covered terrace of a dining room, right on the water. Three oysters plus a glass of wine goes for 40kn, while oysters, mussels & a glass of wine comes in at 55kn. The lobster is superb, though the price tag is eye watering. €€€

NORTH OF STON Between Ston and Trstenik there's a flat, tree-shaded campsite at **Prapratno** (*www.duprimorje.hr;* €) set back from a wide, secluded beach. Directly above, on the side of the road, the **Bella Vista** (\ *753 110; www.bella-vista.com.hr;* ☺ *Apr–Oct 10.00–midnight daily;* €€€) is a good stopover for a meal or just coffee and cakes.

The small holiday village of **Trstenik** on Pelješac's southern coast is of note for the summer ferry linking the peninsula with Polače on Mljet, a pleasant hour or so's trip away, from mid-July to mid-September. There's a sheltered beach here, with diving available through Mario on Mljet (page 387), and the nearby winery is open to visitors.

Resistance monument As you progress up the peninsula, about 40km from Ston, there's a huge monument to the Resistance, right where the road crests a hill, near the locality of Pijavičino. If you're under your own steam, stop here by the abandoned restaurant, and take a moment to look at the stylised bronze frieze depicting scenes from World War II, showing brutal oppression, firing squads, the first signs of resistance and uprising, and finally the joy of freedom. On the back of the curved walls is the seemingly endless list of the local dead, while the whole is dominated by a pair of curved concrete pillars stretching about 30m into the sky.

TRPANJ In a sweeping bay on Pelješac's north coast is the small town of Trpanj, arrival point for the ferries from Ploče (three a day in winter, seven a day in summer, with an extra service to Drvenik, further up the mainland coast, in season). The cheerful little town has a couple of cafés and restaurants, and a helpful **tourist office** (*Zalo 7;* \ *743 433; www.tzo-trpanj.hr*) hidden behind the Flok pizzeria on the front, which can arrange private rooms. Opening hours in winter are sporadic to say the least. The website has details of some short, easy local hiking and cycle trails. Buses connect with the ferries here, and take you to Orebić, which leads on to Korčula or back to Ston and Dubrovnik.

Trpanj has one hotel, the **Faraon** (*Put Vila 1;* \ *743 408; www.hotelfaraon-adriatiq. com;* €€€€€), with around 150 rooms, all with balcony and sea view, and obligatory full board. It sits right on the large pebble beach to the west of the harbour, facing across to the Biokovo massif on the mainland.

OREBIĆ Pelješac's best-known resort, Orebić, is an unpretentious little town with an excellent climate – it's protected by the mountains from the bura wind, giving it mild winters, early springs and long-lasting summers. The town is right across the strait from Korčula, and in summer 13 ferries a day go in each direction (seven in winter). To get back to the mainland the easiest routes are to either take the direct bus to Dubrovnik (three a day) or to catch the ferry to Korčula and then go on the next ferry to Split from there. Alternatively, you can catch the bus to Trpanj, and the ferry from there across to Ploče (or Drvenik, in summer).

To the west of Orebić are a series of resort hotels, on a mixture of nice sandy and pebble beaches, while 500m to the east you'll find the **Trstenica** beach, which ought to be one of the nicest little stretches of the Adriatic coast – it's backed by cacti and palms, and home to a row of fine 18th- and 19th-century villas – but it has been known to be filthy in the early summer, strewn with litter and beer bottles, and badly in need of a clean-up.

Where to stay and eat The **tourist office** (*Trg Mimbelli;* 713 718; *www. visitorebic-croatia.hr*) has walking maps (or see its website under 'Download') and a list of **private rooms** – to book private accommodation contact an agency such as Orebić Tours (713 367; *www.orebic-tours.hr*) or Croadria (714 214; *www. croadria-peljesac.com*).

Adriatic (6 rooms) Šetalište Kneza Domagoja 8; 714 488; www.hoteladriaticorebic.com. Boutique hotel with plenty of exposed stonework in a restored 17th-century building. €€€€€

Bellevue (80 rooms) Obala pomoraca 36; 797 500, 713 193; www.orebic-htp.hr. This 2-star hotel is the nearest to the centre, & faces on to a rocky beach. The Belleview Apartments work out slightly cheaper. €€€€

Indijan (50 rooms) Škvar 2; 714 555; www.hotelindijan.hr. This 4-star option is right on the beach. €€€€

Guesthouse-Restaurant Mimbelli (5 rooms) Trg Mimbelli 6; 713 636; m 098 1766 771; http://hotel-mimbelli.com. Nice rooms in a restored 19th-century sea-captain's house. Also has a terrace restaurant. €€€

What to see and do From the Bellevue, it's an uphill hike westwards to the 15th-century **Franciscan Monastery** which houses the icon known as 'Our Lady of the Angels' – for centuries sailors came here with votive gifts after being saved from shipwreck, storms or pirates. The terrace of the monastery, at 150m above sea level, looks down across the strait to Korčula town, a lovely view.

Even finer panoramas can be had from the 961m summit of Mount St Ilija. It's a steep hike, 4 hours up from Orebić including rests, and another two for the descent, but the simply wonderful views from the summit include the whole of the island of Korčula, Mljet to the south, and the gaunt karst mountains of the mainland to the north.

If you're **hiking** up here wear proper hiking boots (there are reported sightings of vipers), start very early (there's little or no shade), take plenty of water, and use common sense and the route markings as well as the map. Follow the path up to the monastery, and then continue to Bilopolje, after which the track bears off to the right, following red-and-white flashes to the summit. For further information see *Walking in Croatia* by Rudolf Abraham (page 429).

Some of Croatia's best **red wine** is produced not far from Orebić, in Pelješac's Dingač region, and some of the vineyards are open for wine tours – contact Orebić Tours (see above).

Finally if you're a windsurfer you'll want to head a few kilometres further along Pelješac to **Viganj**, one of the top **windsurfing** spots in Croatia – contact Water

Donkey in Viganj about courses and board rental (*www.windsurfing-kitesurfing-viganj.com*).

KORČULA

Like Hvar, Korčula has a lovely old town and lots of hard-to-reach coves and beaches. Like Hvar, too, Korčula's no secret, but it doesn't have nearly the visitor numbers of its northern neighbour (though Korčula's numbers are growing significantly faster, year on year).

The island is nestled up to the western end of Pelješac (less than 1.5km of sea separates them at the narrowest point) and stretches about 45km west into the Adriatic. On average it's about 6km across, from north to south, and has a mountainous spine rising to 568m just west of the village of Pupnat.

The main attraction on the island is the old town of Korčula itself, almost opposite Orebić (on Pelješac), though a close second has to be Korčula's powerful white wines, notably Pošip, Rukatac, and Lumbarda's Grk. Korčula also makes a pretty good base for exploring Pelješac, and offers easy excursions over to Mljet (page 383).

HISTORY Korčula's history stretches back as far as anywhere in Croatia, with Neolithic settlements here followed by the arrival of Greek colonists in the 6th century BC. The Greeks co-existed peaceably with Illyrians on the island for several hundred years before the Romans barged in during the 1st century BC, enraged by the island's propensity for harbouring pirates. Most of the population was either killed, exiled or enslaved, setting something of a pattern until the late Middle Ages, when Korčula went through the usual southern Adriatic tussle between Venice, Dubrovnik and the Turks.

In 1298, just off Lumbarda, a total of more than 180 galleys from the rival Venetian and outnumbered Genoan fleets clashed in one of the biggest sea battles of the Middle Ages. Genoa won the day, and took 7,000 prisoners, including a certain Marco Polo (see box, page 398), who was back in the Adriatic after more than 20 years in Asia with his father and uncle, and was on that day at the helm of one of the Venetian battleships.

Today, Marco Polo is unquestionably Korčula's most famous son, though some scholars now think he may have been born in Šibenik, further up the Dalmatian coast. Whatever the truth, Korčula does much more for Marco Polo than anywhere else, and the setting of the old town here is suitably evocative as the kind of place where he might have been brought up.

Recent history on Korčula has been dominated by tourism, though there's still a fish-processing factory in Vela Luka, at the western end of the island, and the wine business is increasingly important. Olive oil has also been a valuable source of revenue.

GETTING THERE AND AROUND Daily **buses** arrive on Korčula from Dubrovnik and Zagreb, rolling on to the car ferry from Orebić for the last couple of kilometres. The journey from Dubrovnik, up through the Pelješac Peninsula, takes a little under 4 hours; from Zagreb it's a 12- or 13-hour overnighter, and not particularly recommended.

From Korčula town to Vela Luka there are half-a-dozen buses a day, though fewer at weekends (timetables at www.autotrans.hr) – the ferries always connect with a bus, however. In summer, there's also a service (one to three times a day) from Drvenik direct to Korčula.

Car **ferries** from Orebić (arrive early if you're bringing your car) come in at Dominče, 3km south of Korčula town, 14 times a day in winter, more in summer. If

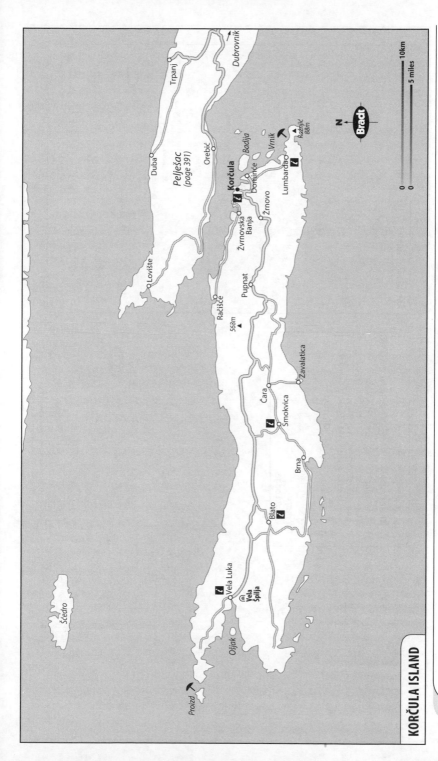

KORČULA ISLAND

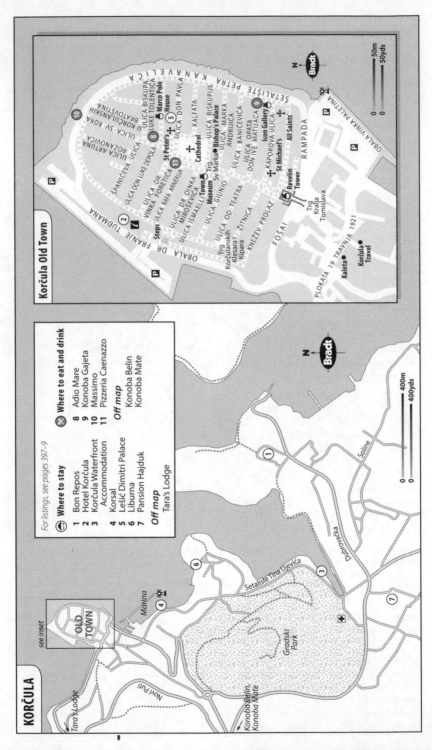

KORČULA

Korčula Old Town

Where to stay
For listings, see pages 397–9

1 Bon Repos
2 Hotel Korčula
3 Korčula Waterfront
   Accommodation
4 Korsal
5 Lešić Dimitri Palace
6 Liburna
7 Pansion Hajduk

Off map
   Tara's Lodge

Where to eat and drink

8   Adio Mare
9   Konoba Gajeta
10 Massimo
11 Pizzeria Caenazzo

Off map
    Konoba Belin
    Konoba Mate

OLD TOWN
see inset

Marina

Novi Put

Tara's Lodge

Konoba Belin,
Konoba Mate

Gradski
Park

Setalište Tina Ujevića

Soline

Dubrovačka

ULICA BISKUPA
LUKE TOLENTIĆA

Marco Polo
House

ULICA SV ROKA
U KORCULANSKIH
BRATOVŠTINA

ULICA ARTUNA
ROŽANOVICA

ŠPANIĆEVA ULICA

ULICA DON LUKE DEPOLA

St Peter's

ULICA DR
VINKA FORETICA

Steps ULICA RAFA ARNERIJA

ULICA DR DINKA
MIROŠEVICA

ULICA ISMAELI

Trg
Korčulanskih
Klesara I
Kipara

ULICA OD TEATRA

KNEZEV PROLAZ

ULICA GUNIO

ULICA GUNIO

ŽITNICA

Town
Museum

Trg
Sv Marka

Cathedral

Bishop's Palace

KALFATA

ULICA DON PAVLA

ULICA BISKUPIJE

ULICA MARKA
ANDRIJIĆA

ULICA BANIĆEVICA

ULICA OPATA
DON IVE MATIJACA

KAPOROVA ULICA

St Michael's

Icon Gallery

All Saints

Revelin
Tower

FOSAI

Trg
Kralja
Tomislava

PLOKATA 19 TRAVNJA 1921

Kaleta

Korčula
Travel

RAMPADA

ŠETALIŠTE PETRA KANAVELIĆA

KANAVELIĆA

OBALA VINKA PALETINA

OBALA DR FRANJE TUĐMANA

Bradt

Bradt

0   400m
0   400yds

0   50m
0   50yds

N

N

you're not on the bus already you can avoid the hike into town by hopping on to one of the hourly buses from Lumbarda to Korčula, though don't rely on this service at weekends. As a foot passenger, you're better off taking the smaller boat which runs from Orebić directly to Korčula town's west harbour (seven a day in winter, at least 13 in summer).

A daily ferry service runs from Split to Vela Luka, at the western end of Korčula (and on to Lastovo), taking around 3½ hours; the same journey can be done in just over 2 hours on the daily catamaran.

There's a daily catamaran (*3 hours, www.jadrolinija.hr*) from Split to Korčula town itself, departing Korčula early in the morning and returning from Split in the afternoon (the journey is shortened to 2 hours 40 minutes in winter, when the catamaran doesn't call at Prigradica). The Rijeka–Dubrovnik ferry also calls in at Korčula town, as does the summer catamaran (*www.krilo.hr*) from Split to Dubrovnik via Milna (Brač), Hvar and Mljet.

If you're reliant on **public transport** you'll be pretty much limited to Korčula town, the sandy beaches of Lumbarda, 6km southeast (roughly hourly buses; flaky weekend service), a few buses to the village of Račišće along the north coast of the island, and the regular bus service along the main road to Vela Luka, via Blato and Smokvica (timetables at www.autotrans.hr) – for access to Korčula's many hidden beaches and coves, which tend to be at the end of long gravelly roads, you'll definitely need your own wheels.

A great, liberating option is to rent a **bike**, which you can do from many of the tour agencies in town – try Korčula Travel (✆ *711 806; www.korcula-travel.com*) or Kaleta (✆ *711 282; www.korcula-rooms.com*), which have mountain bikes from 100kn per day. The **tourist office** (✆ *715 701; www.visitkorcula.eu*) has superb maps of the town, the island and its bike routes, and its website has a list of suggested bike routes.

If you don't have your own transport and can't face biking, you might consider taking an **organised tour** (from Korčula Travel or Kaleta in Korčula town, or Mediterano in Vela Luka; page 402) to get more of a feel for the island's hidden charms. On offer are anything from a fish picnic to an island tour, to boat trips round the local islands, to an excursion to Mljet or Dubrovnik, or wine tours on Korčula or Pelješac. Alternatively you can negotiate with one of the water taxis at the eastern harbour of Korčula town to take you to one of the local islands or remoter beaches, and pick you up a few hours later.

🏠 WHERE TO STAY *Map, page 396*

If you're on a budget or the options below don't suit, there are plenty of good **private rooms** and apartments available – especially along the waterfront west of the town (*Put Sv Nikole*). Try Kaleta (see above), and expect to pay at least €40 for a double, with a 30% supplement for stays of three days or less. If you come in by boat or bus, you'll be met by people offering you rooms, and while these can be better value, check the agencies as well, especially if you're staying for four or more days. It's worth checking out the website at www.korcula.net for private rooms and apartments online.

🏠 **Hotel Korčula** (20 rooms) Obala Franje Tuđmana; ✆ 711 078; www.hotelkorcula.com. The rooms themselves aren't anything to write home about, but the location, right on the old town's western harbour, is perfection itself – so book ahead. This was a popular café in 1871, & became the town's first hotel (the Hotel de la Ville) in 1912. €€€€€

🏠 **Korsal** (10 rooms) Šetalište Frana Kršinića 80; ✆ 715 722; www.hotel-korsal.com. Smart designer 4-star at one end of the marina, about a 5-min walk from the old town, with sea views &

hardwood floors. Much better value than the old Hotel Korčula. €€€€€

🏠 **Lešić Dimitri Palace** (13 rooms) Don Pavle Poše; ☎715 560; www.lesic-dimitri.com. 5-star luxury option, occupying an 18th-century bishop's palace & five medieval cottages. €€€€€

🏠 **Liburna** (110 rooms) Put od Luke; ☎726 006; www.korcula-hotels.com. Located a 15min walk east of the old town by Hotel Park & newly remodeled in 2015, this place offers a swimming pool, tennis courts & private car park. More importantly some of its rooms have stunning views back over Korčula, but book ahead to get these. €€€€€

🏠 **Tara's Lodge** (14 dbl, 3 suites) Žrnovska Banja; ☎721 555; www.taraslodge.com. Swish modern rooms in a bay around 25mins' walk west of the old town. €€€€€

🏠 **Korčula Waterfront Accommodation** (5 apts) Šetaliste Tina Ujevića 33; m 098 9370 463, 098 674 167; www.korcula-waterfront-accomodation.com. Beautiful, modern 1- & 2-bedroom apts sleeping up to 3 & 5 respectively, each with private balcony, just a 10min walk southeast of the old town. €€€€

🏠 **Bon Repos** (370 rooms) Dubrovacka cesta 19; ☎726 880; www.korcula-hotels.com. Traditional tourist comfort in an enormous establishment 3km out of town towards the departure point for the car ferry to Orebić, which is best reached by taxi-boat. The Hotel Park, closer to town, has similar prices. €€€€–€€€

🏠 **Pansion Hajduk 1963** (15 rooms) Ulica 67/6; ☎717 267; m 098 287 216; www.hajduk1963.com. Small family-run guesthouse a short walk south of the old town, with simple but very good-value rooms, & there's a nice restaurant. €€

✖ WHERE TO EAT AND DRINK *Map, page 396*

While in Korčula town, make sure you pop into the excellent **Cukarin**, a traditional cake shop with plenty of delicious things to buy (*www.cukarin.hr*).

✖ **Adio Mare** Marka Pola 2; ☎711 253; www.konobaadiomare.hr; ⊕ noon–23.00 Mon–Sat, 17.00–23.00 Sun. Korčula's best restaurant serves up delicious fish dishes in a nautically themed setting. €€€€

✖ **Konoba Belin** Žrnovo; m 091 503 9258; ⨍ Konoba Belin; ⊕ 10.00–14.00 &19.00–midnight daily. Small, family-run konoba in the village of Žrnovo. €€€

IL MILIONE – THE BIRTH OF TRAVEL WRITING

While he was in prison in Genoa, Marco Polo's stories were written down by a Pisan romance writer who was sharing the same cell as the great explorer. Published in Franco-Italian, *Divisament dou Monde* (*Description of the World* – now better known as *The Travels of Marco Polo*) was received with widespread disbelief. But it was too late – modern travel-writing had been born. The book soon became known as *Il Milione*, possibly because it was seen as a million fables rather than a travelogue – whoever heard of paper money? Or nuts the size of a human head (coconuts)?

Because the book came out before printing was invented, it circulated as a series of hand-copied manuscripts, and more than 100 different versions still exist (but no original), in several languages, making it even harder than it might otherwise have been to know exactly what Marco Polo actually did or saw.

What's important, however, is that he inspired people to travel and explore foreign lands, and was the first Westerner to describe the east in any detail. Controversy still reigns over how much of *Il Milione* is true – how can Marco Polo have missed out the Great Wall, for goodness sake? – but it remains one of the great classics of travel writing all the same, and is one of the reasons I ended up travelling (and writing about it) myself.

Konoba Gajeta Šetalište Petra Kanavelića; ⏱ 10.00–midnight daily. Good, unpretentious restaurant serving a range of reasonably priced dishes, overlooking the water on the east side of town. €€€

Konoba Mate Pupnat; ☎717 109; www. konobamate.hr; ⏱ 11.00–14.00 & 19.00–midnight daily. Small, family-run konoba in the village of Pupnat using fresh, locally grown produce including vegetables from their own garden. No credit cards. €€€

Massimo Šetalište Petra Kanavelića; ⏱ 18.00–02.00 daily. The place to enjoy a sundowner atop a stone tower that was once part of the city's fortifications. Not for those with vertigo (or if you've had a few) as you have to climb up/down a ladder to get there. Seeing your drink hauled up on a pulley is all part of the fun. €€€

Pizzeria Caenazzo Trg Sv Marka; ⏱ 10.00–23.00 daily. Excellent, well-priced pizzeria on the square in front of the cathedral. €€€–€€

✳ Vinum Bonum ⏱ summer 11.00–14.00 & 18.00–midnight daily. Great little wine bar serving local wines from Korčula & Pelješac. To find it, go across the road from the old town, & walk down the narrow streets beyond Korčula Travel – it's just round the corner from Sv Justine. Highly recommended.

WHAT TO SEE AND DO Korčula's top draw is the old town itself, set on a tiny peninsula jutting north into the Pelješac channel. The medieval walls have largely disappeared (Austria wouldn't pay for the upkeep), but there are still towers and buttresses here and there, and the old quarter is a harmonious mix of 15th-century Gothic with 16th-century Renaissance trimmings. The leaf-veined network of narrow streets was designed to keep the place cool in summer yet sheltered in winter – the roads to the west are straight, allowing in the summer sea breezes, while those to the east are curved, to minimise the effects of the nasty winter bura. The arched entrances to the old cellars were built that way to ease the passage of barrels, a reminder of Korčula's long-standing importance as a centre of wine production.

In various places around the town you'll see sculptures by Frano Kršnić, who was born in Lumbarda – they're softer and gentler than the works of Ivan Meštrović, with more than a passing nod to Rodin, and a tribute to Korčula's centuries-old tradition of stone-carving.

The obvious access to the old town is through the southern land gate and the 15th-century **Revelin Tower**, which has a small Moreška exhibition inside, and excellent views from the top. The sweep of stone steps leading up to the gate was only added in 1907, replacing the drawbridge. On the left-hand side as you come in through the gate there's a fine loggia (and a pleasant café). The main street then leads straight to **St Mark's Cathedral** (Sv Marko; like Rab's and Hvar's, actually a church, since the island long ago lost its bishopric, but who's quibbling?). It's crammed into a space that's manifestly too small, and is one of around 150 churches still used on the island.

Over the main door there's a throned statue of St Mark, flanked by a pair of fine Venetian lions on buttresses, the early 15th-century work of Bonino, the Italian sculptor. Supporting the lions are a wonderfully primitive, cowering Adam and Eve, while the blind pillars feature unusual carved clove-hitches halfway up. Inside, at the end of the curiously skewed nave (look at the ceiling), there's a famous but frankly rather heavyweight altar canopy from the late 15th century and a couple of paintings attributed to Tintoretto – the altarpiece featuring St Mark, and an Annunciation in the southern nave. Also inside you'll find halberds from a 1483 battle and cannonballs from the Battle of Lepanto in 1571. Near these is a rare and celebrated 14th-century icon which came from the monastery on Badija; it's due for return to the Franciscans there once restorations have been completed.

On the left-hand side of the church is the large chapel dedicated to Roc, the patron saint of the plague; here you'll find a convincing St Blaise by Meštrović and a dusty sculpture over the doorway of St Michael killing Lucifer. If you're in town on 29 July, you'll see the relics of the cathedral's co-patron, St Theodore, being carried in a procession around town.

Next door to the cathedral is the **Bishop's Palace**, which houses an impressive treasury, though it's really more of a museum. It's an extraordinary collection, covering everything from ancient kitchenware to contemporary art. There are collections of coins, church silver, relics from the Roman catacombs, medieval ballot boxes and a birth register from 1583. Strangest of all is a statue of Mary Queen of Scots, carved in ivory in the early 17th century – her skirts open to reveal a tiny triptych. The last room is lined with antique ecclesiastical robes, which get an airing on ecclesiastical shoulders during the Easter processions.

Opposite the treasury is the **Town Museum** (*Gradski Muzej;* ⟍ *711 420; www. gm-korcula.com;* ⊕ *Apr–Jun 10.00–14.00 daily, Jul–Sept 09.00–21.00 daily, Oct– Mar 10.00–13.00 daily; 15kn*), on several floors of a nice old building. It's in need of restoration, however, and the collection's a bit piecemeal to say the least – but there are some interesting bits of sculpture on the ground floor, where you'll also find the (reproduction – the original's in Zagreb) Greek tablet known as the Lumbarda Stone, which lists the names of the families who lived on Korčula around 2,300 years ago. Upstairs there's a replica of an old-fashioned kitchen, a section on shipbuilding and a re-creation of an elegant 18th-century salon. Most evocative of all, however, are the black-and-white photos on the stairs, showing the arrival of the likes of Fitzroy Maclean during World War II, bringing British aid to the partisans (Maclean's widow, Veronica, still spends part of every year in Korčula).

Heading away from the centre of town you'll find the so-called **Marco Polo House**, which has been bought by the town council and will eventually become a Marco Polo Museum. There are great views from the top of the small tower upstairs. There are also plans to build a full-scale reproduction of the galley he used in the famous battle in 1298, and if you're here in May or September you'll definitely want to take part in the **Marco Polo Days**, when everyone dresses up to stage a minor re-creation of the battle in which Marco Polo was captured by the

MOORISH DANCES – THE MOREŠKA

For around 400 years the people of Korčula have been dressing up and performing the Moreška, a famous sword dance which continues a tradition once common across the whole of Europe. Few of the dances retain anything remotely Moorish about them (least of all Britain's morris dancers), but the name has stuck fast. Korčula is special, however, in still using real swords in what is effectively a war dance.

Originally an annual festival, the Moreška is now performed around twice a week (in a much condensed version – 40 minutes instead of the original 2½ hours) in Korčula town in summer, and makes for a spectacular evening show. The plot's pretty simple – bad king runs off with good king's squeeze; good king's soldiers fight bad king's soldiers; squeeze is saved from bad king's embraces – but none the less enjoyable for all that. Mind the flying, broken swords in the front row …

In other villages on Korčula they perform a similar dance, the Kumpanija (the main difference being that it's sabres rather than swords which are used), particularly in Blato, towards the western end of the island. These are hard to get to without your own transport.

Genovese. The festivities culminate with the great 'local' explorer being given a triumphant welcome home.

In the southeastern corner of town there's an interesting **Icon Gallery** (*Muzej Ikona;* ⊕ *summer 10.00–14.00 & 17.00–20.00 daily; 15kn*) – and entry to this also gives you access to **All Saints' Church** (Svih Sveti), across the little bridge which is still used on special occasions by the local Brotherhood, or Guild. Indeed, the Guilds play an important part in Korčula life, with most people belonging to one or another – the Guild of All Saints was founded in 1301, that of St Roc in 1571, and that of St Michael in 1603. In the icon museum check out the huge candles which are paraded around on feast days, and a fine two-sided cross for use in processions, which dates back to 1430. The church itself was originally the town's cathedral, and features an altar canopy similar to the one in St Mark's, along with a fine carved wooden altarpiece.

Beyond the main sights it's really worth getting up at dawn and walking round the outside of the old town and through the narrow streets, when the place is practically deserted. The pale light of early morning does wonders for the old stone – most of which was quarried locally, on the island of **Vrnik**, just behind **Badija**. Vrnik also provided stone for the walls of Dubrovnik, for the Parliament in Vienna, and for Stockholm's Town Hall. To the west of town, just around the headland, are the attractive **Monastery and Church of Sv Nikola**.

It's also well worth taking one of the regular taxi-boats from Korčula's eastern harbour to the island of **Badija**, just offshore, as it has the best (and closest) beaches to Korčula town, including one reserved for naturists. You have to wonder what the Franciscan monks – who've now been given back the monastery (currently undergoing restoration) that was used as rather spartan tourist accommodation in the socialist era – think of the naturists. Or indeed vice versa.

LUMBARDA Even without your own transport, it's easy enough to get to Lumbarda – there are hourly buses in the week, and a restricted service at weekends. But if you're heading for the seaside, and not the unassuming village itself, you're much better off either hiring a bike or taking a taxi-boat, and negotiating to be dropped right at the beach.

Lumbarda sits on the north shore of Korčula's southeastern peninsula, and the sandy soil here makes not just for the excellent local Grk wines, but also for some of the island's best beaches, all around the Ražnjić headland.

Where to stay and eat

🏠 **Hotel Borik** (60 rooms) \01 3646 601; www.hotelborik.hr. Clean, simple dbls with HB, just across the road from the beach. €€€€€–€€€€

🏠 **Pansion Bebić** (30 beds in apts & rooms) \712 505; www.bebic.hr. Just out of Lumbarda, with its own restaurant & offering HB. €€€€–€€€

🏠 **Agroturizam Bire** (10 rooms) m 098 344 712; www.bire.hr. Nice apts in a vineyard with views down to the sea. It also has its own wine, & frequent tasting sessions. €€€

🏠 **Pansion Lović** (4 rooms) \712 052; www.lovric.info. Small family-run pansion. €€€

VELA LUKA Right at the other end of the island is Korčula's largest town, Vela Luka. It's much maligned, and in the past was known only for its shipyard and fish-processing factory, but with a great situation, at the head of a well-sheltered bay, and industry slowing down, the town is increasingly a tourist destination in its own right. It has a cheerful heart, a handful of good places to stay, brilliant beaches on nearby offshore islands, and good transport connections. Direct buses come from Dubrovnik and Korčula town, and it's also on the main ferry and catamaran lines running from Split to Hvar to Vela Luka to Lastovo.

The helpful **tourist office** (☏ *813 619; www.tzvelaluka.hr*), on the front, can provide you with maps and local information.

🏠 **Where to stay and eat** If you want a private room then the place to go is the excellent and very helpful **Mediterano Tourist Agency** (*Obala 3;* ☏ *813 832; www.mediterano.hr*), which will sort you out in a jiffy – expect to pay around €30–40 for a double room in summer. Mediterano is also the place to head if you want to rent a car or scooter, or arrange an excursion.

🏠 **Korkyra** (58 rooms) Obala 3/21; ☏601 000; www.hotel-korkyra.com. Modern designer 4-star, with smart rooms, spa & an enormous pool. Centrally located on the south side of the harbour. €€€€€

🏠 **Dalmacija** (14 rooms) ☏812 064; www. humhotels.hr. Situated right on the waterfront, with clean if rather plain, but good-value rooms. €€€

🗶 **Konoba Bata** Ul 56/1; ☏812 457; ⊕ noon–15.00 & 17.00–23.00 daily. Popular little place hidden away in the backstreets – a reservation might be wise in the evenings. €€€

🗶 **Pizzeria Alfa** Obala 2; ☏813 710; ⊕ 11.00–23.00 daily. Best bet in town for a decent pizza, though meals can take a while to arrive. On the waterfront. €€€

What to see and do If you're here for any time, it's well worth making the effort to walk out of town to an impressive **Neolithic cave**, Vela Špilja ('Big Cave' in local dialect; Vela Luka means 'Big Bay') – check with the tourist office for visiting times (*www.velaspila.hr*).

If you're feeling more hedonistic, an attractive alternative is to take one of the thrice-daily boats to the lovely little island of **Proizd**, right off Korčula's northwestern tip. This has several pebble beaches and some of the clearest waters I've ever swum in. There's a cheerful restaurant operational between the first and last boats, and a couple of naturist beaches, if that's your thing. Otherwise just enjoy the sea and sunshine – there's absolutely nothing else to do here. There are also boats from the quayside in Vela Luka out to the even closer island, Ošjak, which is almost within Vela Luka's harbour – it has lovely beaches and is popular with romantic couples, from which it had gained the nickname 'island of love'.

LASTOVO

A dozen kilometres south of Korčula is the island of Lastovo, barely 10km long. Like Vis (page 334), it was off-limits for half a century and only opened up in 1989. In 2006 Lastovo and its archipelago gained the status of a nature park. Tourists are still comparatively few and far between, though numbers are growing steadily.

It's a low-key destination, with (as yet) only one large(ish) hotel – in Pasadur at the western end of the island – and nothing remotely like nightlife. But if you like lobster, fresh white wine, a chance to meet the local people, and peace and quiet, hiking trails and remote chapels, then Lastovo's your place – unless you come during the carnival, when it goes berserk in a small-town sort of way, especially on Poklad's Tuesday (page 404).

GETTING THERE AND AWAY Lastovo is the last stop for the daily ferry and catamaran from Split via Vela Luka (on Korčula), with boats arriving at Ubli in the early evening and leaving at the crack of dawn (before 05.00), effectively meaning you can't 'do' the island in less than two nights. It takes over 5 hours for the ferry to come from Split (75 minutes from Vela Luka), but just over 3 hours on the catamaran (55 minutes from Vela Luka).

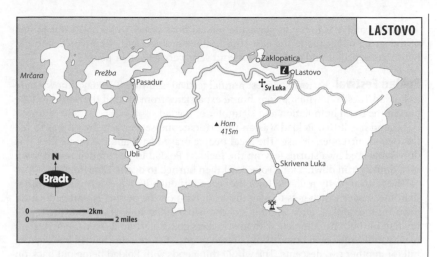

A minibus meets the incoming boats in Ubli, and takes you the 10km to the village of Lastovo, spread out on a steep hillside facing away from the sea and sheltered from the bura. The helpful **tourist office** (☏ 801 018; http://tz-lastovo.hr; ⊕ summer 08.00–20.00 daily, winter 08.00–15.00 Mon–Fri) is right where the bus stops. It has some good maps and brochures on the island, including one on the old chapels and churches scattered across the island.

WHERE TO STAY AND EAT If the options below don't suit, the tourist office (see above) can fix you up with a private room. You can also try www.lastovo.net and www.lastovoapartments.com.

Hotel Solitudo (72 rooms) Uvala Pasadur; ☏802 100; www.hotel-solitudo.com. Out at Pasadur, & so is less convenient if you don't have your own wheels & want to explore the island, though they pick up guests from the ferry, & are currently the only place on the island offering bike rental. €€€

Λ Camp Skriveni Skrivena Luka; ☏801 189; m 095 573 41 02, 099 288 8757; www.camp-skriveni.com. 6km from Lastovo near Skrivena Luka, this has pitches below twisted branches in a small, peaceful olive grove. There are delicious homecooked meals available, with fresh seafood caught that day by the owner & prepared by his wife, which you may just decide is one of the best seafood meals you have in Croatia. The beach

at Skrivena Luka is 500m away, though there's another, more secluded beach slightly closer & only accessible by foot. Highly recommended. €

✕ Konoba Augusta Insula Zaklopatica; ☏801 167; www.augustainsula.com; ⊕ noon–23.00 daily. Serves up excellent dishes at Zaklopatica, in the north of the island. You can also rent scooters from them. €€€€

✕ Konoba Bačvara ☏801 131; ⊕ 17.00–23.00. A lovely welcoming little place towards the bottom of the many flights of steps leading down through Lastovo itself, with delicious local specialities such as chickpea stew – highly recommended. €€€–€€

WHAT TO SEE AND DO There's nothing much to see in town – a handful of small 15th- to 17th-century churches pretty much sums it up – but do make the hike up to the ruined French fort right at the top of the hill, dating from 1810. It's now a weather station, with fabulous views.

There are some lovely hiking trails on the island to several of the chapels and churches on the island, including the 11th-century Sv Luka, the lighthouse at Struga (the oldest on the Adriatic) and the summit of Hom.

Southern Dalmatia LASTOVO

9

An alternative is to try to persuade a local boat owner to take you out to one of the string of islands to the east (the Lastovo archipelago). Here you'll find old lighthouses, pebble and rock beaches, and very, very few other people.

Poklad Festival Lastovo's biggest annual festival is Shrove Tuesday (known here as Poklad Tuesday), which brings home expatriates from around the world to take part in the ritual humiliation and slaughter of Poklad.

Legend has it that Poklad was an unfortunate messenger sent by pirates to tell Lastovo to surrender, or else. The local people prayed hard and the pirate fleet was duly scuppered by a storm, leaving the luckless Poklad to be paraded round town on a donkey, run down a long rope, and then burned to death. Charming.

The festival pretty much follows the legend, though it's a luckless puppet rather than messenger which gets to play the lead. First off the puppet is paraded round town on the donkey, after which it's slid down a 300m-long rope from the top of town to the bottom, complete with firecrackers going off from its feet. On arrival it's met by uniformed men brandishing drawn swords, before being hauled back up the hill for another two descents. The whole thing ends with Poklad being put back on the donkey before being speared and burned à la Guy Fawkes – though you won't see the Lastovo sword dances on bonfire nights in Britain. It's an extraordinary spectacle.

10

Diving in Croatia

Thammy Evans

With almost 4,000 miles of coast, Croatia hosts 1,185 islands, islets and reefs, which are home to some stunning marine wildlife, beautiful underwater vistas, as well as wrecks dating from 3–4BC to World War II and later. The island of Vis and the peninsula of Istria have the highest concentration of wrecks, with Vis being a more compact location for diving as well as boasting better visibility

Over 50,000 divers visit Croatian underwater sites annually, as diving here is easily accessible and offers warm waters from May to October. Water temperature averages 21–29°C at the surface during summer and 7–10°C in the winter. At 20–30m the water temperature remains a constant 16–19°C from the summer until the end of the diving season in November. Visibility is best in spring, autumn and winter, when summer plankton and spawning algae clouds are completely absent.

Home of the International Centre for Underwater Archaeology (ICUA), opened in Zadar in 2007, Croatia is leading the world marine community in conservation and preservation. It is also an excellent place to start an interest in wreck diving. Numerous sites lie close to the coast and in PADI open-water or advanced open-water dive depths (up to 30m). Many dive centres along the coast offer diving courses at all levels, and some offer wreck diving speciality courses. At the end of this chapter you'll find ten of some of the best introductory wreck and cave dives in the country, as well as one of the top ten house-reef dives in the world.

PLANNING THE DIVE

DIVE COSTS AND PACKAGES Diving costs with a dive centre range from as little as 50kn for a beach dive to 150kn for a boat dive, and up to 350kn for a wreck dive. A dive guide will be an extra 75kn and an accompanying instructor up to 350kn extra. Many places will do packages, such as a discount for two dives in a day, or up to ten dives in a week, sometimes with limitless shore dives.

All the dive centres offer diving courses at most levels, usually in PADI (Professional Association of Diving Instructors) or with SSI (Scuba Schools International) and sometimes with CMAS (Confédération Mondiale des Activités Subaquatique) or VDST (Verband Deutsche Sport Taucher). BSAC (British Sub-Aqua Club) instruction and certification is available at three centres, all listed on page 406. Again prices vary, so it is worth comparing websites for up-to-date prices: a Discover Scuba afternoon comes to around 450kn, while a PADI Open Water Diver (OWD) course is around 3,500kn. Some centres also offer wreck diving speciality courses for around 2,000kn.

RULES AND REGULATIONS As with elsewhere around the world, diving in Croatian waters is regulated by several laws. These are overseen by the Croatian

Diving Federation (Hrvatski Ronilački Savez; *www.diving-hrs.hr*), which grants diving concessions to qualified centres, clubs and individuals. Qualified individuals wanting to dive independently of the dive centres and of local clubs must apply for a concession via the local harbour master.

Wreck-salvage laws in Croatia are very strict and very simple: nothing may be removed from a wreck. All battlefield casualty wrecks in Croatian waters are war graves, and thus also deemed cultural monuments. Diving to most Croatian wrecks therefore also requires a special permit, which usually costs €10 and is organised by the local dive centre that has permission to take divers there. Not every dive centre is allowed to go to every wreck.

Wildlife and natural habitat is also protected. It is illegal to even swim in some marine habitats, such as the Limski Kanal (diving and swimming is permitted at the mouth of the Limski Kanal only) and a permit is required to dive around some national parks, such as the Brijuni Islands and Kornati archipelago. Some of the dive centres which have permission and permits to dive at restricted sites are listed in this chapter.

EQUIPMENT All diving centres will have the basic equipment that you find in most dive centres around the world, and in Croatia they tend to be in good condition. Female wet suits are increasingly common, but female BCDs (buoyancy control devices) are rare, as are BCDs with integrated weight systems. Even in the summer, diving is usually done in a 5mm full wet suit, with boots and strap fins. Only some centres have Nitrox, and fewer still have Trimix. An increasing number of dive centres now sell a small range of diving equipment; otherwise you can find the following dedicated stores dotted along the coast (but note that prices in Croatia will often be more expensive than the big specialist diving stores elsewhere in the world). From northwest to southeast:

Oceanic Slovenia Polje 21, 6310 Izola, Slovenia; +386 (0)5 640 1100; m +386 51382-313, +386 41 854 118; e info@oceanik-trgovina. si; www.oceanic.si; ⊕ 10.00–18.00 Mon–Fri, 09.00–13.00 Sat. Set in the industrial zone on the east outskirts of town, this warehouse type shop has a bit of everything, & is still cheaper than the few options in Croatia. Its website is only in Slovenian.

Pop Valmade 58, 52100 Pula; 052 214 185; e pop@cressi-sub.hr; www.cressi-sub.hr; ⊕ 10.00–17.00 Mon–Fri. Distributor for Cressi, but does not service gear. Also has a small shop on Ciscuttijeva 9 around the back of Pula's old town. Pop's English website is often several months out of date compared with the Croatian version. Also runs an online store: www.divestore.hr.

Di-Nautika Uvala Baluni bb, 21000 Split; 021 322 005; e info@di-nautika.hr; www. di-nautika.hr; ⊕ 10.00–17.00 Mon–Fri, 09.00–13.00 Sat. Right on the bay, this little shop is the showcase of its bigger version on the west side of town on Kralja Zvonimira 85. Offers a good range of equipment for both recreational diving and fishing as well as professional diving trades. Also services equipment.

SAFETY Diving safely is the responsibility of every diver. In general, if you've not dived for three years or more, most dive centres will want you to do a refamiliarisation dive or scuba tune-up with an instructor (for around €80). If you've not been diving over the winter, or for a year or so, then your first dive of the season should always be a check dive, especially if you have your own equipment, to ensure that you and your equipment work as you expect them to. Check dives are usually done from the shore in front of the dive centre, as these are the cheapest, and it is easy to go back to the centre if something's not working. Croatia's hyperbaric chambers are, from northwest to southeast, at:

Poliklinik Oxy Kochova 1/a, 52100 Pula; ☎052 215 663; e polilkinika@oxy.hr; www.oxy.hr. In case of emergencies (24/7) m 098 219 225 – Dr. Mario Franolić. You can also get recreational oxygen top-ups here, & get equipment serviced.
Poliklinik Oxy Gajevo šetalište 21, 51260 Crikvenica; ☎051 785 229; e poliklinika.ck@oxy.hr
Mobile Hyperbaric Chamber Obala kneza Trpimira bb, 23 000 Zadar; ☎023 332 954;

in case of emergencies (24/7) m 098 254 207 – Damir Velimir. The chamber is part of the Zadar Underwater Activities Club.
Split Hyperbaric Decompression Chamber Šoltanska 1, 21000 Split; ☎021 354 511 – Dr Nadan Petri
Poliklinik Oxy Dr. Roka Mišetića 2, 20000 Dubrovnik; ☎020 431 687; in case of emergencies m 098 381 685 – Dr. Davor Romanović.

WRECK DIVING With hundreds of shipwrecks strewn along the coast, Croatia is a great place to go wreck diving. Most sites are within 90–100 minutes boat ride from a dive centre, and many lie within Croatia's stated recreational dive limit (40m). That said, diving at 20m+ in Croatia is not like diving in the clear blue waters of the tropics or off Egypt, Malta or some of the Pacific islands. Planning the dive and diving the plan is essential in waters that can have low visibility, even when you are outside of the wreck. Navigational and decompression skills are a must, as is a Nitrox qualification if you want to stay down long enough to make the descent worthwhile.

As a result of the higher skillset required to dive wrecks, most centres will require that you are qualified to at least CMAS 2* level (equivalent to PADI Rescue Diver, SSI Advanced Open Water Diver (AOWD) +40 dives, or having taken the BSAC Dive Leader course even if you have not qualified with all the dives). Many will also require that you show a current (within the last year) fit-to-dive medical certificate. If you have not brought one from your usual doctor, then sometimes these can be obtained through a private doctor in Croatia. Your dive centre will be able to tell you where if there are any indications that you need one.

If the dives listed at the end of this chapter whet your appetite, there are even bigger, better, deeper dives for you techies out there, including the 120m *Numidia* off the west coast of Istria, the 150m *Columbia* near Dubrovnik, and numerous American B-24 Liberator fighter planes around the island of Vis. Most recently, a very rare Junkers Ju 87 Stuka was found off the island of Žirje by the Croatian Department of Underwater Archaeology.

DIVING CENTRES

There are some 140 diving centres in Croatia. The ones listed here are chosen for their spread along the coast and for their access to some of the best dive sites. An almost up-to-date list of dive centres can be found at www.divingcroatia.net. Most dive centres are open from May to September unless otherwise listed. Key staff at the centres all speak English (as well as Croatian, German and Italian). For those wanting to know more about diving for the disabled, see www.iahd-adriatic.org. From northwest to southeast:

DIVING CENTER POREČ (*Brulo bb (parking at Hotel Diamant), 52440 Poreč;* ☎*052 433 606;* m *(Olwyn) 091 452 9071, (Miloš) 091 452 9070;* e *info@divingcenter-porec.com; www.divingcenter-porec.com;* ⊕ *Apr–Nov; see ad, page 420*) Olwyn (from Newcastle, England) and her husband Miloš pride themselves on providing fun and safe dives, catering particularly for the beginner end of the market during the high season. As a result, the centre's PADI courses are very reasonably priced, and its shore and boat dives are the cheapest in Istria. Perfect English, Croatian and Dutch is spoken at the centre, as well as German and Italian. Their house shore dive is a real gem at night, with

10

The Adriatic is a rich, fascinating and unique body of seawater. It is unique largely because no more than 4% of the water-flow of the northern Adriatic around the Istrian peninsula escapes into the southern Adriatic (beyond Dubrovnik). Over 75% of the Adriatic's water-flow, which is anti-clockwise, recycles around at Split. On its way around, the water-flow picks up more polluted waters from the eastern Adriatic coast and organic matter from the main Mediterranean basin and mineralises it through a system of combination with the clean karst-rock waters from Croatian rivers.

As a result of all this, the Adriatic is home to over 70% of all the fish species to be found in the whole Mediterranean, and over 30 of these are found only in the eastern Adriatic due to the karst rock formations of the region and their abundance of fresh spring water. Seven of the species of fish found in the Adriatic are endemic to the waters (ie: found nowhere else in the world). Sadly, however, overfishing in the last 50 years threatens the extinction of 64 fish species found in the Adriatic.

COMMON SIGHTINGS Crabs, moray eels, goby, cleaner shrimp, and lobsters are very common. Others include:

Alcyonacea Soft corals, particularly gorgonian sea fans and sea whips, are common in waters with higher nutrient value (and therefore lower visibility) where they filter-feed off plankton as well as through some photosynthesis in a symbiotic relationship with algae. A large gorgonian colony can be over a metre high and wide, but only some 10cm thick. They will be oriented across the current to maximise access to food. Those unable to photosynthesise are more brightly coloured.

Chromis chromis Juvenile damselfish are deep lightning blue in colour and only 2–3cm in length. Shoals of 20 or 30 are common at 3–4m. Adults are dark brown or black.

Conger conger The European conger eel, like the moray eel family, is found in cracks and crevices. European congers are grey, while moray species tend to be more colourful. Neither species is poisonous or dangerous unless provoked (although the flesh of morays if eaten can be poisonous if the eel itself has eaten something else poisonous). The European conger can grow up to 3m in length (morays up to 4m).

Hermodice carunculata Growing up to 15cm long, bearded fireworms are poisonous to touch, causing sharp irritation where bristles enter the skin, and there have been reports of dizziness and nausea in severe cases. Bristles can be successfully extracted using sticking plaster, and the irritation can be relieved by applying neat alcohol or white spirit.

Nudibranchia These amazing tiny shell-less molluscs, often only 1cm long, are abundant for those with the patience to see them. A torch helps in order to highlight their colours in lower visibility. Flabellina affinis (fuschia pink) and Janolus christatus (electric blue) are especially common.

PROTECTED FLORA AND FAUNA

Aphanius fasciatus The Mediterranean killifish, also known as the south European toothcarp, is a locally protected species which is more abundant elsewhere in the Mediterranean. It is becoming rare in Croatia due to the destruction of its preferred lagoon habitat.

Asteroides callycularis Orange stony coral are best seen on a night dive when their colours show up brightly in a torch's rays, and when these primitive animals feed on the likes of tiny brine shrimp.

Caretta caretta The loggerhead turtle is an extremely rare sight along the built-up and shallow shores of the northern Adriatic, but the clean waters of the eastern Adriatic are their preferred choice.

Gerardia savaglia Sometimes better known as 'black' tree-coral, this fast-growing branchy primitive animal is beige-yellow when alive and leaves behind a brown-black skeleton. Found below 15m depth and as low as 120m, it is has been a popular souvenir leading to its destruction.

Hippocampus ramulosus The long-snouted seahorse, like all seahorses, is a protected species. It is particularly vulnerable because of its commercial value in traditional Chinese medicine (to counter weak constitution in children, adult male impotence and bed-wetting!) and for aquariums, for which over 25 million are caught wild every year. Slow moving because of their tiny fins, the creatures are very shy and tend to hide in sea grass, which they cling to with their tails to prevent being swept off by sea currents. Sea horses have been seen at Lanterna dive site near Novigrad, and Karbula near Poreč. In some instances they have been known to grow up to 15cm in length.

Ophidiaster ophidianus The long-armed purple starfish grows to 15–40cm in length. Usually found below depths of 5m, they can sometimes appear red or orange

Pinna nobilis This is the largest bivalve mollusc in the Mediterranean, and can grow up to 1m in height. Often found among seagrass at shallow depths. Take great care not to touch it, so watch your buoyancy in its vicinity.

Posidonia oceanic Endemic to the Mediterranean, Neptune grass only grows in very clean waters. It is thus of course on the decline. It tends to grow in meadows on sandy beds and can reach up to 1.5m in height. Lesser Neptune grass (*Cymodocea nodosa*) is also protected but can be found outside the Mediterranean.

Tethya aurantiacum This sea sponge looks exactly like an orange. I love this quote by Barnes, Fox and Ruppert (2004): 'some are known to be able to move at speeds of between 1mm and 4mm per day'.

For a full list of protected sea flora and fauna see www.aquarium.hr/eng/species-list. The aquariums at Rovinj and Pula jointly run a turtle rescue centre, excellent information on which can be found at www.aquarium.hr/eng/marine-turtle-rescue-centre, including what to do if you find a stranded turtle.

regular sightings of octopus, plaice, red mullet and feeding Pinna nobilis. Labyrinth is another truly excellent dive of theirs. It's a 10-minute walk from the parking at Hotel Diamant to the dive centre (head left down the path by the tennis courts along the back of the hotel grounds). Off-season it's possible to drive to the dive centre.

PUNTIŽELA (*Autocamp Puntižela, 52100 Pula;* ✆ *052 517 474 15 Apr–15 Oct, +49 9188 305 415 Nov–Mar;* m *098 903 3003;* e *info@relaxt-abgetaucht.de; www.relaxt-abgetaucht.de*) This is the only dive centre with access to Rt Peneda dive site at Brijuni Island. Almost all the centre's dives are within a 10–20min boat ride away, and so it often succeeds in providing up to four dives in a day (including a night dive). Offers Nitrox, and SSI and CMAS courses.

MARINE SPORT (*Hotel Marina, Aleja Slatina bb, 51417 Moščenička Draga;* m *(Robert) 091 515 7212, (Darko) 091 293 2440;* e *info2@marinesport.hr; www. marinesport.hr*) On the east coast of the peninsula, this dive centre has access to some fantastic wall and drift diving, including one of the top ten house-reefs in the world. Offers Nitrox, and teaches PADI courses.

DIVE CITY (*Brace Buchoffer 18, Crikvenica;* ✆ *051 784 174;* m *091 572 4776;* e *info@ divecity.net; www.divecity.net;* ⊕ *daily Apr–Oct, rest of the year by reservation for groups of six or more*) About 30km southeast of Rijeka, this diving centre accesses a wide range of sites around the nearby islands of Krk, Lošinj and Creš. The centre stocks a small range of equipment, and offers PADI, SSI and CMAS courses. Boris, who runs the centre, is also a BSAC Advanced Instructor, although the centre no longer runs BSAC courses. Offers Nitrox and Trimax.

BOUGAINVILLE (*Put Kumenta 3, Biograd na moru;* ✆ *023 385 900;* m *098 783 738;* e *info@bougainville.nl; www.bougainville.nl;* ⊕ *24 Apr–1 Nov*) Based on the mainland, this dive centre is easy to get to and has good access to many of the dive sites in the underwater Kornati National Park (page 299). The centre can also organise a variety of other outdoor activities, including hiking, biking, rafting and yachting. Offers BSAC, CMAS, PADI, SSI and TDI courses, as well as Nitrox and Trimix.

DIVE DUGI OTOK (*Zaglav, 23281 Sali, Dugi Otok;* m *098 169 3107;* e *info@dive-dugiotok.com;* ⊕ *May–Oct*) Set up by Eric Šešeja, a Canadian-Croatian, this dive centre is the place to dive the Kornati National Park. Great package rates. PADI courses only.

DUPIN DIVE CENTRE (*Hotel Mon Repos, 20260 Korčula Island;* ✆ *020 711 342;* m *098 812 496;* e *croatia_diving@hotmail.com; www.croatiadiving.com*) Run by a British couple who managed their own diving and yachting centre in the UK before moving to sunny Croatia. Dupin hosts the UK West Midlands BSAC Regional Expedition Diving Scheme (REDS) archaeology dive expedition every other year, and 2017 is the next expedition. A premier BSAC diving school (#393), it offers a 10% discount for ten dives or more.

TROGIR DIVING CENTRE (*Pod Luka 1, Trogir, 21223 Okrug Gornji;* ✆ *021 886 299;* m *091 5241 856;* e *mail@trogirdivingcenter.com; www.trogirdivingcenter.com;* ⊕ *1 Apr–1 Nov*) Northwest of Split, near the ancient town of Trogir, this diving centre is popular, not least because it also has its own on-site tavern cooking excellent food for centre divers only, including breakfast, lunch and dinner if required. With five boats the choice of dives for the day is wide. Offers CMAS courses only. Nitrox available.

ISSA DIVING CENTRE (*Komiža, 21485 Vis Island;* \ *021 713 651;* m *091 2012 731;* e *info@scubadiving.hr; www.scubadiving.hr*) ISSA Diving Centre is a haven for wreck divers as it is located on the most wreck-abundant island in Croatia. As a result it is fully equipped for technical diving and offers TDI as well as SDI diving courses. The centre has three boats at its disposal and offers Nitrox and Trimix.

DUBROVNIK DIVING AQUARIUS (*Šetalište M. Maroneca 27; 20207 Mlini;* m *098 229 572;* e*info@dubrovnik-diving.com; www.dubrovnik-diving.com;* ☉ *Apr–Oct*) Located 7km south of Dubrovnik in the heart of the village of Mlini, this dive centre also has great access to diving at Cavtat, where a number of wrecks of Roman seafaring vessels are located. While little of the boats themselves can be seen to the untrained eye of the average diver, many valuable amphorae can be spotted. These sites are under Croatian cultural preservation, and require a special permit for diving. Two boats (a 19m catamaran, including toilet, kitchen, sun deck and wheelchair access for disabled divers; and a 9.5m speedboat) offer access to a variety of dives including the *Taranto* wreck and the 150m-long *Columbia*, which was bombed and sunk during World War Two. Offers PADI courses. Nitrox and Trimix available.

TOP TEN DIVE SITES IN CROATIA

1 HMS *CORIOLANUS*

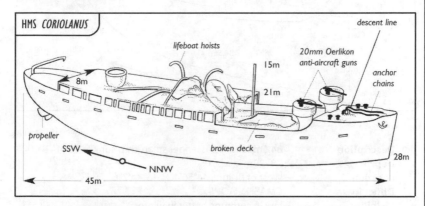

Description	45m British Royal Navy minesweeper sunk in 1945
Depth	15–28m
Location	West of Novigrad, 45°19'239"N 13°23'406"E
Difficulty	CMAS 2*, AOWD
Visibility	low in summer, better in winter
Dive centre	Diving Centre Poreč, Starfish

Interestingly, German guidebooks on this wreck site describe the *Coriolanus* as a radio-monitoring ship, whilst British and Croatian descriptions of it state it was a minesweeper, and some hint that it was a 'spy' ship. Clearly a trip to the British

10

National Archives is in order to get to the bottom of this story. Nonetheless, the *Coriolanus* was sunk on 5 May 1945 when it hit a floating mine which had been laid as part of the German defence line.

Although visibility is low to moderate during the main dive season, on a good day the top of the wreck can be seen from the surface. It's possible to dive the entire outside of the *Coriolanus* in a 25-minute bottom time, so it is quite a good introduction to wreck diving. As she lies on a sandy bottom at 28m, there is also no fear of going over the safe recreational diving limit of 40m, and a visit to the propeller is usually possible.

Overall, the wreck is in relatively good condition, save for the mine explosion hole in its starboard, and its missing mast and bridge, which were possibly mined after it was sunk so that it would not snag sea traffic. Two mounts with 20mm Oerlikon guns are aft, and one is on the stern of the upper deck. She also carried a 12 pounder anti-aircraft gun. She is thickly encrusted with shells and coral and the roof of her mid-deck has caved in. Entry into the wreck is not recommended for sport diving.

2 BARON GAUTSCH

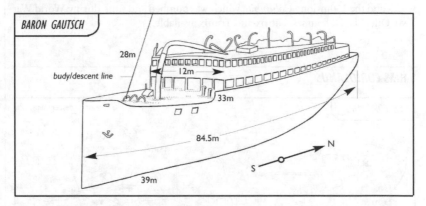

Description	84.5m luxury passenger steamship sunk in 1914
Depth	28–39m
Location	West of Brijuni, 44°56'4"N, 13°34'7"E
Difficulty	CMAS 2*, AOWD
Visibility	low in summer, better in winter
Dive centre	Starfish Vrsar, Valdaliso Rovinj

Built in Scotland's Dundee shipyard by Gourlay Brothers, this Austro-Hungarian passenger steamship was launched in 1908 and became the pride of the Austro-Hungarian shipping fleet Austrian Lloyd (today's Italia Marittima) based in Trieste. She sailed the Trieste–Kotor route (in Montenegro), and was leased by the Austro-Hungarian Navy in World War I to transport military personnel to Kotor. On a return trip on 13 August 1914, laden with civilian passengers and refugees, the ship hit a mine and sunk west of Brijuni islands.

Accusations were levelled against the crew for mismanagement (including lifejackets locked away to prevent third-class passengers using them to sleep on), and Austrian Lloyd was sued in the Viennese courts by dependents. Riots in Vienna in 1925 torched the court house records of the case, and later in 1939 the offices of the defending lawyer Dr Shapiro, who was Jewish, were ransacked in progroms. As a result the only remaining official record of the event lies in Rovinj's city archives.

The wreck is a war grave and has been looted extensively in previous years. After almost 100 years, the wreck today is quite decayed but the overall structure retains its shape. The wreck is marked by a buoy and, as visibility can be low, descent and decompression is by the buoy line. This can get busy in the summer. A double wreck dive trip to this and to the nearby torpedo boat *Guiseppe Dezza* is offered by Starfish Dive Centre.

Further information on the *Baron Gautsch* can be found at www.adventuredives. com/barong.htm.

3 HOUSE REEF BISER

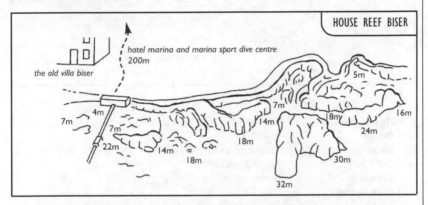

Description	House reef in front of Marine Sport
Depth	0–33m
Location	Moščenička Draga, 45°10'11"N, 14°14'14"E
Difficulty	OWD
Visibility	good
Dive centre	Marine Sport

The east coast of Istria does not quite have the depths of the southern Adriatic, but the drops on this side are much more significant than on the eastern side of Istria, thus harbouring far clearer waters and a greater variety of wildlife. The house reef in front of Marine Sport Dive Centre might not even be the best place to witness this drop, but for those starting out in diving, or taking their first dive after a long break, this is an excellent first dive of the season. The house reef of any dive centre is an important place; it is the one probably most dived at the centre because of its immediate location and thus the ease with which it can be used for refresher dives and night dives.

House reef Biser has been voted into the top ten house-reefs in the world by *Tauchen* dive magazine of Germany, ranking alongside the house reefs of the great diving meccas of Egypt, the Maldives and others. Apart from ease of access, Biser

10

gives a great range of easy and interesting diving conditions in great visibility. The reef descends gradually to 30m and holds up to that depth a labyrinth of karst formations for 100m along the northern side of the coast. These hide and house many shoals of different fish, including the famous John Dory, as well as red Gorgonia and feather star corals.

4 PELTASTIS

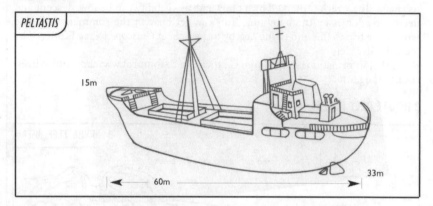

Description	60m Greek freight ship wrecked in 1968
Depth	15–33m
Location	northern side of Krk island, 45°09′37″N, 14°30′1″E
Difficulty	CMAS 2*, AOWD
Visibility	good
Dive centre	Dive City

Being underwater for less than 50 years, this wreck is relatively intact. The bridge is large enough to dive inside, although care needs to be taken to prevent snagging. The wreck is known for being the permanent home of conger eels in the cargo, as well as to lobsters. Encrusted with wildlife, shoals of fish also swarm the wreck in pursuit of food lingering on this man-made 'reef'.

The ship went down in the early hours of 8 January 1968 during very heavy storms in which her anchorage just north of Crikvenica was not enough to hold her. Drifting towards the island of Krk, she foundered on the rocks and went down with her crew of 12. Four were saved, seven were subsequently found dead, but the captain, Teodoris Belesis, was missing. An official search dive down to the boat was not conducted, even after local divers knew that a corpse was to be seen standing in the ship's bridge. Only after an Austrian tourist took a photo of the corpse did media attention to the issue prompt a full official search dive, to find that the captain had indeed gone down with his ship. Captain Belesis, well preserved in the cold waters at depth, was brought up and, after an autopsy confirming death by drowning, was buried in Kozala cemetery in Rijeka on 11 November 1968.

Descent is usually via the mast, the top of which is at approximately 8m depth. The bow end of the deck lies at 15m, from which most dive plans descend along the side of the ship to the propeller, which lies partially buried in the mud at 35m. Back up at the stern's deck, the dive continues to the bridge, which may be penetrated. Penetration of the main cargo area and particularly the engine room are ill-advised due to the thick sediment, which can reduce visibility to less then 5cm and cause severe disorientation. Above the bridge, an ascent can be made up the stern masts and along the buoy line.

5 TIHANY

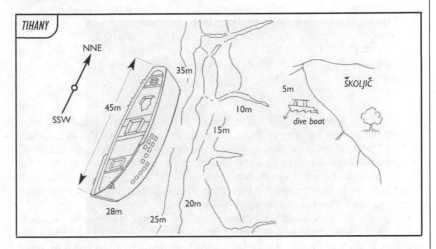

Description	45m cargo ship stranded and sunk in 1917
Depth	28–35m
Location	Near Unije island, 44°38'10"N, 14°13'49"E
Difficulty	CMAS 2*, AOWD
Visibility	low in summer, better in winter
Dive centre	Orca

The *Tihany* was a cargo ship that served as part of the Austro-Hungarian navy during World War I. On 12 February 1917 a navigational error caused her to founder on the islet of Školjić. The navy spent five days attempting to rescue her, but to no avail, finally sinking to her present location on 17 February, complete with her cargo of 129 tonnes of coal and ten tonnes of oil. Thankfully, all of the crew survived the ordeal.

Only the metal structure of the ship remains after some 96 years of being under water, making the *Tihany* light and open to dive. She is usually dived as part of the reef where she lies. Anchoring off the western tip of Školjić islet, the dive descends west to the sandy bottom of the reef and then southwest towards the wreck site. She lies tipped on her port side with her bow partially buried in the sandy sea floor. Coal can still be found in her hold and one of the propellers is also still to be seen.

Well encrusted over the years, the *Tihany* is home to an abundnce of underwater wildlife including scorpion fish, Sabella fan worms, lobsters and damsel fish. Less than 10m to the west of the site can also be seen broken pieces of amphorae from a Roman ship wrecked in the same location some 2,000 years ago. A return northeast

10

gradually ascending the reef reveals further wildlife and a cascade of colourful sponges. The reef plateaus just above 10m, rising gently up to your anchor line and the boat near Školjić.

6 MODRA ŠPILJA

Description	large cave dive, accessible by boat and diving
Depth	0–12m (length 24m)
Location	Near Biševo island, 42°58'97"N, 16°01'2"E
Difficulty	OWD
Visibility	best light shows just before midday
Dive centre	ISSA

The glimmering Modra Špilja (Blue Cave) is the best cave dive in Croatia, comparable with other caves of the same name in more famous diving locations such as Malta. This 15m-high cave within the small island of Biševo has a small opening that allows a concentrated ray of light to penetrate to the water under the cave for about an hour before midday. The cave's fame, and the beauty of diving it, come from the almost fluorescent-blue light which radiates throughout the water during this time, making objects under the water look silver.

Originally the cave could only be accessed by a small underwater entrance, but in 1884 a new entrance was created in the side of the cave in order to allow boats in. It has now become a popular tourist boat destination, so you'll be vying with onlookers when you start the dive. The dive's exit is via the natural entrance underwater which opens on to a sponge-rich exterior wall with crevices and fissures teaming with fish.

This dive usually starts and ends with a boat ride from nearby Vis island. Southeast of Vis, on the very small island of Ravnik, another similar light phenomenon occurs in Zelena Špilja (Green Cave). The cave gets its name because of the apparent green water caused by the reflection of light against green algae, which colonise the shallows of the entrance to the cave. This effect is magnified further by the concentrated lighting effect of a small shaft of light piercing through the roof's cave all the way to the shallow bottom of the waters at 3–7m. Diving in and out of the lightshaft is reminiscent of scenes in *Pirates of the Caribbean – The Curse of the Black Pearl*. Outside the cave, the dive can descend to 30m.

7 VASSILIOS

Description	104m cargo ship sunk by its own crew
Depth	25–55m
Location	Near Vis island, 43°00'24"N, 16°03'56"E
Difficulty	CMAS 2*, AOWD
Visibility	usually good even in summer
Dive centre	ISSA

The *Vassilios* has an interesting history. It was built by Nitta Ship Builders in Osaka, Japan for the US Shipping Board (USSB) and its construction was completed in

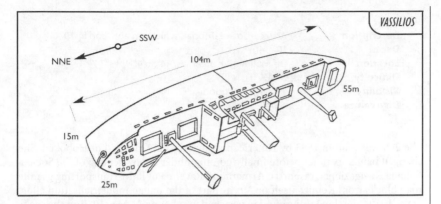

SSW

NNE

104m

55m

15m

25m

1920. Originally named *Eastern Temple*, it was sold to a Greek cargo company in 1938, when it was used to transport coal bought by fascist Italy from coal mines in Wales to supplement the coal already being mined in nearby Istria. On one of her regular voyages from Swansea to Venice, her rudder failed just off Vis on 19 March 1939, while navigating up the Adriatic. Hitting the shore, she quickly sank, but all the crew survived. It was not uncommon in those days for owners to sink their own ships in order to collect insurance money. At the time the ship was worth almost eight million Royal Yugoslav dinar, with 1.25 million dinar of Welsh coal aboard.

The wreck is so close to the coast, just 25m from the Rt Stupišće lighthouse, that it can be dived from the shore. Most diving expeditions come by boat, however, and anchor just off the light house. From there a descent to 15m starts to reveal this huge vessel below, with the starboard side of the bow reached at 25m. The ship lies completely on her port side. Her interior is easy to access through the bulkheads and corroded deck, with chinks of light coming through the increasingly corroded hull. Her cargo of coal is difficult to discern as it is now so covered in sediment, but the coal and many other items on the ship can still be seen.

This is a big ship to dive, and so Nitrox or Trimix is recommended for advanced divers to increase bottom time and shorten decompression time. It is a great dive for novice technical divers, and with the usually good visibility of the northeastern Adriatic. Open Water Divers can also get much out of the dive from the starboard side of the ship.

8 *TETI*

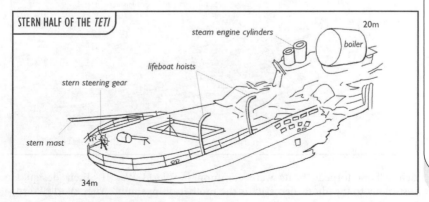

STERN HALF OF THE *TETI*

steam engine cylinders

20m

boiler

lifeboat hoists

stern steering gear

stern mast

34m

Diving in Croatia   TOP TEN DIVE SITES IN CROATIA

10

Description	72m cargo steamboat, which ran aground in 1930
Depth	10–34m
Location	Off Mali Barjak, near Vis, 44°56'4"N, 13°34'7"E
Difficulty	OWD
Visibility	usually very good
Dive centre	ISSA

The *Teti* was built in 1883 by American shipyard John Cockerill of Hoboken. She changed hands six times before finally coming under the ownership of the Societa Italiana Navigazione Trasporti e Armamenti Ravenna of Italy. Transporting granite road blocks from Komiza itself on Vis as part of the Italian industrialisation effort of the 1930s, the ship ran aground in very bad weather on 23 May 1930 on the rocky shores of the island of Mali Barjak. The incident is well documented in the local archives, due to the rescue efforts of the local islanders, who saved all the crew and were officially thanked by the Kingdom of Italy for their bravery.

With the wrecked bow of the boat lying in only 10m of water and the almost intact stern gradually descending to 34m, this is an excellent introduction to the thrills of wreck diving. The relatively low depth of the boat allows for a reasonable bottom time on air for those without a Nitrox qualification and there is usually little current, making for easy diving. Visibility is almost always very good, and the ship is small enough that almost the entire boat can be seen from one end or the other, and the whole ship can be explored in one dive (although subsequent dives are always interesting). Descent to and ascent from the wreck is directly down and up the gradient of the shoreline, making it additionally easy to refind your dive-boat in the event of separation.

The steam boiler and engine cylinder can be explored, and the rear steering wheel, completely intact and thoroughly barnacled, makes for excellent photo opportunities. For those with AOWD and enough experience, the cargo area of the stern can be entered through the bulkhead and exited through an additional port hatch further down the stern.

9 *S57* TORPEDO BOAT

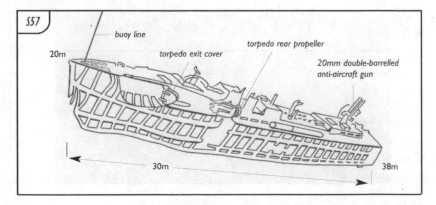

Schnellboot torpedo boats were common in World War II. Their design is testimony to the idiom 'necessity is the mother of ingenuity'. After World War I,

Description	S57 German torpedo boat wreck
Depth	20–38m
Location	Near Vis island, 42°51′21″N, 17°29′37″E
Difficulty	CMAS 2*, AOWD
Visibility	low in summer, better in winter
Dive centres	Žuljana, S-57, Abyss

Germany's re-industrialisation was curbed in the Treaty of Versailles in an effort to ensure that she did not build excessive war-fighting capability. However, this only resulted in effective and efficient developments under different circumstances. Instead of big and obvious, Germany went for small and fast. The resulting schnellboote (known as 'E-boats' in English) were less than 35m in length, with high sides and of lightweight construction (steel frame with a mahogany hull). Armed with torpedos, fired from two ports on either side of the bow, they were fast and deadly. They were also quick to make in only four months, aiding their proliferation.

The *Schnellboot-57* first saw service in October 1940 in the North Sea. She was transferred to duties in the Adriatic in early 1944. During the early morning of 19 August that year she was engaged in a battle with British motor torpedo boats (MTBs). *S57* was hit and caught alight. Neither the crew nor those of her accompanying schnellboote could put out the fire. So having towed her in vain as far as the shores of Pelješac, her crew detonated an explosive in her hull, which broke her bottom and she sank.

The *S57* is well-preserved. There is much to see from the outside through her metal frame, which is no longer cased in its wooden hull, having rotted early on. Of particular interest to most are her remaining torpedos, her anti-aircraft guns, and the bridge control panel. Only three dive centres (see above) have the permits to dive this site.

Further information on Schnellboote can be found at http://www.bmpt.org.uk/boats/S130/index4.htm.

10 SVETI ANDRIJA

Description	Steep cliff dive below the island's high lighthouse
Depth	3–80m
Location	Sv Andrija island, near Dubrovnik, 42°38′08″N, 17°57′03″E
Difficulty	OWD
Visibility	excellent
Dive centre	Abyss, Aquarius

A number of Croatia's islands have lighthouses atop them. The one on Sv Andrija was built in 1873. It presides over a particularly sharp cliff drop on the southwest side of the island and which continues into the sea for another 80m depth. This makes for one of the best and sheerest wall dives in all Croatia. The wall is a firework of colour and activity, although you'll need a torch at lower depths. Rare red Gorgonia coral grow here, as well as Clavelina red sea-potatoes, and other

10

Mediterranean sponges. With the greater depths available immediately below, the location is host to larger fish, such as greater amberjack, groupers and the odd ray. Closer to the wall are shoals of electric-blue baby damsel fish in early summer, and pink swallowtail sea perch. At 12m depth a small cave in the wall makes for a convenient first decompression stop for those who have gone deep.

Other lighthouse-topped dives, which are even more spectacular but more difficult to access, are Sušac, and Palagruža. Sušac is only 13 nautical miles from Lastovo, but 19 nautical miles from the nearest harbour. Here an inland lake surrounded on all sides by high cliff walls can only be accessed underwater. Palagruža, at 37 nautical miles from Vis, is Croatia's most southernmost land point. Although Palagruža islands stand tall like towers, the water at their feet is a mere 10m, making them a warm harbour for an abundance of fish. The lighthouse here provides accommodation (*www.uniline.hr/croatia/lighthouses.php*). Diving these locations is an adventure for the journey there itself and, once there, their remote nature offers wildlife opportunities that are hard to find closer to the mainland coast. Arranging diving here is also difficult and expensive because of the long travel times. Try ISSA and Abyss for arrangements.

Appendix 1

LANGUAGE

The official language is Croatian, written using a Latin alphabet. For 98.5% of the population, this is their mother tongue. Croatian is a tough language to learn, but words are nothing like as difficult to pronounce as you'd think, since every letter always has a unique pronunciation – albeit often not the same as in English. Although you're unlikely to have time to learn much Croatian, grab at least a handful of words and phrases to take with you – the effort will be richly rewarded.

The language comes from the group usually described by linguists as Serbo-Croat, meaning that Serbs, Croats and Bosnians can readily understand each other – not that you'd necessarily know this, judging by the strife of the past 20 (or even 200) years. Within Croatia itself, there are also regional variations and dialects, with the one you'll most likely notice being the three different ways Croats have of saying 'what?'. The official version – used in the media – is the Slavonian '*Što?*', but in the Zagreb you'll hear '*kaj?*' and along the coast it's invariably '*ča?*'.

The use of the Latin alphabet is largely to do with religion, and the east–west division of the Roman empire – it was in Croatia in the 9th century that Sts Cyril and Methodius invented the Glagolitic alphabet (see Glagolitic Alley, in Istria), which was converted by St Clement, in Ohrid (now in the Former Yugoslav Republic of Macedonia), into the Cyrillic alphabet, variants of which are now used throughout the Orthodox world. You won't see Cyrillic – unless you happen into an Orthodox or Greek Catholic church, or you're travelling on into neighbouring Serbia, Bosnia or Montenegro.

Most people – especially in the capital and along the coast – speak at least one foreign language, with German very widely spoken, and English being increasingly taught and popular among the young. Italian is understood by many on the coast and islands.

PRONUNCIATION Croatian words aren't anything like as hard to pronounce as you might expect them to be – just concentrate on pronouncing each letter the same way every time, and you won't go far wrong.

A	as in **party**	Đ, đ	as in **George**, **jam**	J	as in **yet**
B	as in **bed**		(sometimes written	K	as in **kept**
C	as in fa**ts**, ba**ts**		Dj, dj, to help non-	L	as in **leg**
Č, č	as in nur**ture**,		natives)	M	as in **mother**
	cul**ture**	E	as in **pet**	N	as in **no**
Ć, ć	as in **chew**, **chump**	F	as in **free**	O	as in **hot**
D	as in **dote**	G	as in **goat**	P	as in **pie**
		H	as in **hat**	R	as in **air**
		I	as in **feet**, **pizza**	S	as in **sand**

421

Š, š	as in **sh**ovel, **ch**ampagne	U	as in l**oo**k	Ž, ž	as in trea**s**ure
T	as in **t**oo	V	as in **v**ery		
		Z	as in **z**oo		

WORDS AND PHRASES
Courtesies

hello/bye (informal)	*bok* (only used in Zagreb – even more familiar is *bok bok* – in other areas *bog*)
cheers!	*živjeli!* [**zhi**-vel-ee]
good morning	*dobro jutro* [**dob**-ro you-tro]
good day	*dobar dan* [**dob**ber dan]
good evening	*dobra večer* [**dob**-ro vetch-air]
good night (on leaving)	*laku noć* [**la**koo notch]
good luck (as a salutation)	*sretno* (old miners' greeting) [**sret**-no]
how are you?	*kako ste?* [ka-ko stay]
I'm fine, thank you	*dobro, hvala* [**dob**-ro, hfar-la]
please/thank you	*molim/hvala* [mo-**leem**/hfar-la]
thank you very much	*hvala lijepo* [hfar-la lee-**ye**po]
excuse me	*oprostite/sori* [o-pros-ti-te/sorry]
goodbye	*doviđenja* [**doe**-vee **jen**-ya]

Basic words

yes/no	*da/ne* [dar/**nay**] (*nema* = emphatic no) [nay-ma]
that's right	*tako je* [ta-ko yay]
OK	*OK* [okay]
maybe	*možda* [mozh-da]
large/small	*veliko/malo* [veli-ko/mar-lo] (*velika/mala* are feminine forms)
more/less	*više/manje* [vee-sh/man-ye]
good/bad	*dobro/loše* [**dob**-ro/lo-sh]
hot/cold	*toplo/hladno* [top-lo/hlad-no]
toilet	*zahod* [zar-hod] (also *toalet* [toe-a-let], *WC* [vay-say])
men/women	*muški/ženski* [moosh-kee/zhen-skee]

Numbers

1	*jedan*	9	*devet*	60	*šezdeset*
2	*dva*	10	*deset*	70	*sedamdeset*
3	*tri*	11	*jedanaest*	80	*osamdeset*
4	*četiri*	12	*dvanaest*	90	*devedeset*
5	*pet*	20	*dvadeset*	100	*sto*
6	*šest*	30	*trideset*	1000	*tisuća*
7	*sedam*	40	*četrdeset*		
8	*osam*	50	*pedeset*		

Questions

how?	*kako?* [ka-ko]
how much?	*koliko?* [ko-lee-ko]
what's your name?	*kako se zovete?* [ka-ko say zov-et-e]
when?	*kada?* [ka-da]
where?	*gdje?* [gud-ee-ya]
who?	*tko?* [teko]

why?	zašto? [za-shto]
do you speak English?	govorite li engleski? [gov-or-itay lee en-gleski]
how do you say in Croatian?	kako se to kaže na hrvatskom?
	[ka-ko say toe ka-zhay na hair-vat-skom]
can you tell me the way to…?	možete mi reći put do …?
	[mo-zhet-e mee retchi put doe]
how do I get to…?	kako mogu doći do …?
	[ka-ko moe-goo do-tchi doe]
is this the right way to…?	je li ovo pravi put do …?
	[yay lee ovo prar-vee put doe]
is it far to walk?	je li daleko pješice …?
	[yay lee dal-ecko pyay-shee-tzay]
can you show me on the map?	možete mi pokazati na karti?
	[mo-zhet-ay mee pocka-zarti na kar-tee]

Getting around

bus/bus station	autobus/autobusni kolodvor
	[out-o-boos/out-o-boosnee kolo-dvor]
train/express train	vlak/brzi vlak [vlack/berzee vlack]
main train station/	glavni kolodvor/željeznički kolodvor
railway station	[glav-nee kolo-dvor/zhel-yez-neetchki kolo-dvor]
plane/airport	avion/zračna luka or aerodrom
	[av-ion/zratch-na loo-ka or air-o-drom]
car/taxi	auto/taxi [out-o/taksi]
petrol/petrol station	benzin/benzinska stanica [ben-zin/ben-zinska stan-itza]
entrance/exit	ulaz/izlaz [oo-laz/iz-laz]
arrival/departure	dolazak/odlazak [do-laz-ak/odd-laz-ak]
open/closed	otvoreno/zatvoreno [otvo-ren-o/zatvo-ren-o]
here/there	ovdje/tamo [ov-dee-ye/tar-mo]
near/far	blizu/daleko [bleezu/dal-ecko]
left/right	lijevo/desno [lee-yeh-vo/des-no]
straight on	ravno [rav-no]
ahead/behind	naprijed/iza [nap-ree-yed/eeza]
up/down	gore/dolje [go-reh/dol-yeh]
under/over	ispod/preko [iz-pod/precko]
north/south	sjever/jug [syeh-vair/yoog]
east/west	istok/zapad [iz-tok/zap-ad]
road/bridge	cesta/most [tzesta/most]
hill/mountain	brežuljak/planina [breh-zhul-yak/plan-eena]
village/town	selo/grad [seh-lo/grad]
waterfall	slap [slap]

Accommodation

reservation	rezervacija [rez-air-vatz-eeya]
passport	putovnica [put-ov-nitza]
bed	krevet [krev-et]
room	soba [so-ba]
key	ključ [kl-youtch]
shower/bath	tuš/kada [toosh/ka-da]
hot water/cold water	topla voda/hladna voda [top-la vo-da/hlad-na vo-da]

Miscellaneous

tourist office	*turistički ured* [tooris-**titch**-kee u-red]
consulate	*konzularni ured* [kon-zoo-larnee u-red]
doctor	*liječnik/doktor* [lee-**yetch**-nik/doktor]
dentist	*zubar* [**zoo**-bar]
hospital/clinic	*bolnica/klinika* [bol-**nitza**/klin-icka]
police	*policija* [**pol**-itz-ee-yah]

Time

hour/minute	*sat/minuta* [sat/min-**oota**]
week/day	*tjedan/dan* [**tjeh**-dan/dan]
year/month	*godina/mjesec* [god-eena/mee-**yeh**-setz]
now/soon	*sada/uskoro* [sa-da/oos-koro]
today/tomorrow	*danas/sutra* [da-nas/**soo**-tra]
yesterday	*jučer* [**you**-tchair]
this week/next week	*ovaj tjedan/slijedeći tjedan*
	[ov-eye **tyeh**-dan/sli-**yeh**-detchi tyeh-dan]
morning/afternoon	*jutro/poslije podne* [**you**-tro/poz-**lee**-yeh pod-nay]
evening/night	*večer/noć* [**vetch**-air/notch]

Monday	*ponedjeljak* [pon-ed-**yeh**-lee-yak]
Tuesday	*utorak* [**oot**-or-ak]
Wednesday	*srijeda* [sree-**yeh**-da]
Thursday	*četvrtak* [**tchet**-ver-tak]
Friday	*petak* [**pet**-ak]
Saturday	*subota* [**soo**-bo-ta]
Sunday	*nedjela* [ned-yeh-la]

January	*siječanj* [**si**-yeh-tchan-yeh]
February	*veljača* [**vel**-ya-tcha]
March	*ožujak* [o-zhu-yak]
April	*travanj* [trav-anya]
May	*svibanj* [svee-banya]
June	*lipanj* [lip-anya]
July	*srpanj* [ser-panya]
August	*kolovoz* [kolo-voz]
September	*rujan* [**roo**-yan]
October	*listopad* [lis-toe-pad]
November	*studeni* [**stoo**-den-ee]
December	*prosinac* [pro-seen-atz]

spring	*proljeće* [pro-**lyeh**-tcheh]
summer	*ljeto* [lyeh-toe]
autumn	*jesen* [yeh-sen]
winter	*zima* [zeema]

Food and drink

bon appetit!	*dobar tek!* [**dob**-bar-tek]

Essentials

breakfast	*doručak* [do**roo**-tchak]

lunch	*ručak* [roo-tchak]
dinner	*večera* [**vetch**-air-a]
water	*voda* [**vo**-da]
beer	*pivo* [**pee**-vo]
draught beer	*točeno pivo* [totch-**ay**-no **pee**-vo]
wine	*vino* [**vee**-no]
white wine	*bijelo vino* [bee-**yello vee**-no]
white wine and soda	*špricer* (1dl)/*gemišt* (2dl) [spritzer/gem-**isht**]
red wine	*crno vino* [**tzair**-noe **vee**-noe]
rosé wine	*roze vino* [rozay **vee**-no]
house wine	*domaće vino* [dom-**atch**-ay **vee**-no]
spirit (generic)	*rakija* [**rak**-ee-ya]
spirit (from herbs)	*travarica* [trav-**are**-itza]
brandy	*lozovača* [lozov-atch-ka]
pear spirit	*kruškovača* [kroosh-kov-atch-a]
cold	*hladno* [**hlad**-no]
hot	*vruće* [**vroo**-tchay]
bread/bakery	*kruh/pekarnica* [kroo/pek-**are**-nitza]
jam	*džem* [d-zhem] (some say *pekmez* [**peck**-mez])
coffee	*kava* [ka-va]
tea	*čaj* [tchai – rhymes with 'try']
tea with milk	*crni čaj s mlijekom* [tzair-nee tchai soo mil-yeh-kom]
	(ask for black, otherwise you get fruit tea with milk …)
tea with lemon	*čaj s limunom* [tchai soo lee-**moon**-om]
sugar	*šećer* [**shetch**-air]
salt	*slan* [slun]
cheese	*sir* [seer]
soup	*juha* [**you**-ha]
thick soup/bean soup	*ragu/grah* [ra-**goo**/grar] (not a vegetarian dish!)
egg (eggs)	*jaje* (*jaja*) [**ya**-yay/(ya-ya)]
ham	*šunka* [**shoon**ka]
air-dried ham	*pršut* [per-**shoot**]
fish	*riba* [**ree**ba]
chips	*pomfrit* [pom-freet]
meat	*meso* [**may**-so]
vegetables	*povrće* [pov-air-tchay]
fruits	*voće* [**vo**-tchay]
homemade	*domaće* [dom-**a**-tchay]
grilled	*sa roštilja* [sar rosh-til-ya]
baked	*pečeno* [petch-**ay**no]
fried	*prženo* [per-**zay**no]
boiled	*kuhano* [**koo**-hano]
stuffed	*punjeno* [**poon**-yayno]

Fish

sardines	*sardina* [sar-**dee**na]
mackerel	*skuša* [skoo-sha]
bass	*lubin/brancin* [loo-ben/bran-tsin]
grey mullet	*cipal* [tzi-pal]
red mullet	*barbun* [bar-boon]
bream	*zubatac* [zoo-ba-tatz]

A1

tuna	*tuna* [toona]
trout	*pastrva* [pas-ter-va]
salmon	*losos* [loss-oss]
perch	*grgeč* [gerg-etch]
zander/pike-perch	*smuđ* [smoodge]
catfish	*som* [som]
pike	*štuka* [shtooka]
squid	*lignje* [lig-nyeh]
mussels	*dagnje/školjka* [dag-nyeh/shkol-yeka]
	(in general – there are other variants)
oysters	*oštrige/kamenice* [osh-trig-eh/kam-en-itz-eh]
prawns/crayfish	*škampi* [shkampi]
crab	*rak* [rak]
lobster	*jastog* [yah-stog]
spicy fish stew	*fiš paprikaš* [fish pap-rik-ash]

Meat

beef	*govedina* [**gov**-ed-eena]
pork	*svinjetina* [**svin**-yet-eena]
lamb	*janjetina* [**yan**-yet-eena]
mutton	*ovčetina* [**ov**-tchet-eena]
veal	*teletina* [**tel**-et-eena]
chicken	*piletina* [**pil**-et-eena]
spicy smoked sausage	*kulen* [**kool**-en]
goulash	*gulaš* [**gool**-ash]
wild boar	*divlja svinja* [**div**-lee-yah **svin**-yah]
meat stews	
pepper and tomato	*sataraš* [**sat**-a-rash]
rice and tomato	*đuveč* [**joo**-vetch]
beef with dumplings	*pašticada* [pash-titz-arda]
stuffed vine leaves	*sarma* [sar-ma]

Vegetables and side-dishes

potatoes	*krumpir* [krum-**peer**]
rice	*riža* [**ree**-zha]
green peppers	*paprika* [pap-**reeka**]
onion	*luk* [look]
garlic	*češnjak* [tchesh-nyak]
asparagus	*šparoge* [shpar-o-gay]

Salads

salad	*salata* [sal-ata]
green salad	*zelena salata* [**zel**-ena sal-ata]
cucumber	*krastavac* [krasta-vatz]
cabbage	*kupus* [koo-poos]
tomato	*rajčica* [rai-tch-itza]
	(*paradajz* [para-dize] is sometimes used)
mixed	*miješana* [me-**yeh**-sha-na]
with chillies and cheese	*grčka* [**gertch**-ka]
with tomatoes and cheese	*šopska* [**shop**-ska] (many also use name *grčka*)

Fruit

orange	*narandža* [na-**rand**-zha]
	(or *naranča* [na-rand-tcha])
lemon/s	*limun* [lee-**moon**]
plums	*šljive* [shl**yee**-vay]
melon	*dinja* [din-ya]
pears	*kruške* [kroosh-kay]
peaches	*breskve* [**bresk**-vay]
cherries	*trešnje* [tresh-nee-yeh]
strawberries	*jagode* [yag-o-deh]
apples	*jabuke* [ya-**boo**-keh]
bananas	*banane* [ba-na-neh]

Appendix 2

FURTHER INFORMATION

BOOKS Many of the books listed here are long out of print, but most can be found second-hand – either by trawling through old bookshops, or online at places like Abe Books (*www.abebooks.com*).

History/politics

Bracewell, Catherine Wendy *The Uskoks of Senj: Piracy, Banditry and Holy War in the Sixteenth-Century Adriatic* Cornell University Press, 1992. The definitive account of the history of the Uskoks.

Curta, Florin *Southeastern Europe in the Middle Ages 500–1250* Cambridge University Press, 2006. Good regional account of the medieval period.

Glenny, Misha *The Fall of Yugoslavia* Penguin, 1996, 3rd edition. Former BBC correspondent's account of how it all fell apart – compelling, if depressing, reading.

Goldstein, Ivo *Croatia: A History* C Hurst & Co, 1999, 2nd edition. Well-balanced Croat historian's view of Croatian history from Roman times to the present day. Hard to find, however, in spite of its relatively recent publication.

Harris, Robin *Dubrovnik – A History* Saqi, 2003. Solid doorstop of a tome with a wealth of fascinating insight and wonderful illustrations – but quite a dent in the wallet at 25 quid.

Hawkesworth, Celia *Zagreb: A Cultural and Literary History* Signal Books, 2007

Macan, Trpimir, and Šentija, Josip *The Bridge – A Short History of Croatia* Journal of Croatian Literature, Zagreb, 1992. Notwithstanding the rather fanatical introduction by Yale professor Ivo Banac, this is an excellent history of Croatia in two sections, the first up to 1941, and the second from 1941 to 1991, with semi-official status. Hard to find, however.

Margaritoni, Marko *Dubrovnik, Between History and Legend* Dubrovnik State Archives, 2001. Lots of wonderful tales and legends by a local author. Order the book for 200kn from the man himself, at marko.margaritoni@du.htnet.hr.

Mesić, Stipe *The Demise of Yugoslavia: A Political Memoir* Central European University Press, 2004

Rheubottom, David *Age, Marriage and Politics in 15th-century Ragusa* Oxford University Press, 2000. Intriguing – if at times weighty – insights into the inter-relationships between politics, kinship and marriage in the republic. Expensive, however, even secondhand.

Silber, Laura et al *The Death of Yugoslavia* Penguin, 1996. Tie-in with the BBC series, and while it's not wholly successful without having seen the programmes it's still a frightening blow-by-blow account of the events of the war.

Tanner, Marcus *Croatia: A Nation Forged in War* Yale University Press, 1997. An excellent and detailed history of Croatia, by the *Independent*'s correspondent during the conflict – probably the best book currently available.

Travel and travel literature

Abraham, Rudolf and Evans, Thammy *Istria. The Bradt Travel Guide* Bradt, 2013. The essential guide to doing Istria in depth from food and culture to cycling and diving.

Abraham, Rudolf *Walking in Croatia* Cicerone, 2016, 3rd edition. The most detailed and comprehensive guide to hiking in Croatia available in English, covering the main ranges (Velebit, Gorski kotar etc) as well as islands and areas further inland.

Abraham, Rudolf *The Islands of Croatia* Cicerone, 2014. Award-winning new guide to hiking on Croatia's islands, including in depth coverage of Krk, Rab, Korčula, Hvar, Vis and others, and detailed local hiking maps and information on wildlife, etc.

Abraham, Rudolf *The Mountains of Montenegro* Cicerone, 2015, 3rd edition. Detailed guide to hiking in Montenegro.

Abraham, Rudolf *Peaks of the Balkans* Cicerone, 2016. Guide to hiking this spectacular long-distance trail through the borderlands of Montenegro, Albania and Kosovo.

Abraham, Rudolf *Alpe Adria Trail* Bradt, 2016. Guide to hiking the 750km Alpe Adria Trail through Austria, Slovenia and Italy.

Bardwell, Sandra *Croatia: Car Tours and Walks* Sunflower, 2006. Excellent guide aimed at walkers and hikers, and covering the coast and islands as well as the Plitvice Lakes.

Bridge, Ann *Illyrian Spring* Chatto & Windus, 1935. Rather fey (very 1930s) novel about a lady painter working her way down the Adriatic coast in search of inspiration and love – but great descriptions of Pula, Split, Dubrovnik etc.

Clancy, Tim *Bosnia & Herzegovina: The Bradt Travel Guide* Bradt, 2013, 4th edition. Comprehensive guide to this newly accessible Croatian neighbour.

Coyler, William *Dubrovnik and the Southern Adriatic Coast from Split to Kotor* Ward Lock & Co, 1967. Delightfully dated mini hardback with lots of black and white photos.

Cuddon, J A *The Companion Guide to Jugoslavia*. Collins, 1986, 3rd edition.

Delalle, Ivan *Guide to Trogir* Trogir Tourist Board, 1963. Brilliant black-and-white pocket guide to the city first published in 1936; full of words like 'historiography'.

Evans, Thammy *Macedonia: The Bradt Travel Guide* Bradt, 2012, 4th edition. The essential companion if you're going on to Macedonia – the author lived there for five years.

Goldring, Patrick *Yugoslavia* Collins Holiday Guides, 1967. Marvellous pocket guide featuring mainly Croatia – and a splendid peasant smoking a roll-up on the cover.

Gray, William *Travel with Kids* Footprint, 2012. Great source of inspiration for family travel.

Kaplan, Robert *Balkan Ghosts* Picador, 1994. The author uses his 1990 odyssey through the Balkans to explain the conflictual politics across the region in depth. Relatively easily available secondhand.

Kastrapeli et al *Dubrovnik Tourist Guide* Minčeta, 1967. Classic 1960s mini guide – gushing prose, black and white photos.

McClain Brown, Cody *Chasing a Croatian Girl. A Survivor's Tale* Algoritam, 2014. Often hilarious anecdotes on life in Croatia by this popular blogger, an American expat living in Croatia. Particularly amusing for those with some familiarity with Croatian habits and customs.

McKelvie, Robin and McKelvie, Jenny *Slovenia: The Bradt Travel Guide* Bradt, 2008, 2nd edition. The essential companion if you're going on to Slovenia.

Mitchell, Laurence *Serbia:. The Bradt Travel Guide* Bradt, 2013, 4th edition. The best guidebook available on Serbia.

Murphy, Dervla *Through the Embers of Chaos – Balkan Journeys* John Murray, 2002. Brilliant account of a long cycle tour through the Balkans, including Dubrovnik, Split, Zagreb etc. Truly a wonderful, inspirational book.

Phillips, Adrian and Scotchmer, Jo *Hungary: The Bradt Travel Guide* Bradt, 2010, 2nd edition. You couldn't look for a better guide if you're heading on to Hungary.

Rellie, Annalisa *Montenegro: The Bradt Travel Guide* Bradt, 2015, 5th edition. Essential reading if you're digging deeper into Montenegro.

Thompson, Trevor and Dinah *Adriatic Pilot: Croatia, Slovenia, Montenegro, East Coast of Italy, Albania* Imray, 6th edition, 2012. Benchmark sailing guide.

Voynovitch, Count Louis *A Historical Saunter through Dubrovnik (Ragusa)* Jadran, 1929. Nearly impossible to find, but marvellous short guide to the city from a 1929 perspective. It's amazing how little has changed in spite of both a world and a local war.

West, Rebecca *Black Lamb and Grey Falcon* Canongate Books, 1993. Without question the most comprehensive (1,200pp) and best-written account of Yugoslavia in the 1930s. Rebecca West travelled widely in Croatia (and the other republics of the former Yugoslavia) in 1936 and 1937, and spent five years researching and writing this book. Fatally flawed in places, and terribly naïve in its conclusion, it's nonetheless by turns funny, passionate and tragic – and always brilliantly opinionated. If you come across the original two-volume hardback from the 1940s, go for it; there are excellent black-and-white photographs.

Natural history

Gorman, Gerard *Central and Eastern European Wildlife* Bradt, 2008. Excellent all-round introduction, well illustrated.

Mitchell-Jones, A J et al *The Atlas of European Mammals* Academic Press, 1999. Heavyweight guide to nearly 200 species, with distribution maps and a real wealth of detail.

Polunin, Oleg *Flowers of Greece and the Balkans* Oxford, 1980. The definitive guide to the flora of southeast Europe.

Still, John *Butterflies and Moths of Britain and Europe* Collins, 1996. Handy guide for lepidopterists.

Svensson, Lars *Collins Bird Guide* Collins, 2010, new edition. Simply excellent guide to European birds, with truly wonderful illustrations. The many Collins field guides (trees, flowers etc) are also highly recommended.

Tolman, Tom and Lewington, Richard *Collins Butterfly Guide* Collins, 2009. The definitive guide to the butterflies of Europe.

Art and culture

Abraham, Rudolf *Croatian Miscellany* Blurb, 2016. Photography book – an intimate, personal portrait of Croatia beyond the tourist sites.

Beretić, Dubravka *Art Treasures of Dubrovnik* Jugoslavija Guides, 1968. Obscure guide dating back to the communist heyday – still remarkably accurate, however.

Čošić, Stjepan et al *Croatia: Aspects of Art, Architecture and Cultural Heritage* Frances Lincoln, 2009. Large coffee table book with essays on various aspects of Croatian art and history, and an introduction by John Julius Norwich.

Crnković, Vladimir *The Art of the Hlebine School* Croatian Museum of Naïve Art, 2005. Definitive snapshot of Croatia's naïve art scene and the people and places behind it, by the curator of the museum in Zagreb himself.

Pavičic, Liliana and Pirker-Mosher, Gordana *The Best of Croatian Cooking* Hippocrene Books, 2000. You're back home and missing those Croatian dishes? This is the book for you.

Radovčić, Jakov *Gorjanović-Kramberger and Krapina Early Man* Školska Knjiga Zagreb, 1988. Fascinating biography of the man who discovered and created the Krapina Man collection, by the current curator and the man responsible for the new museum opening in Krapina.

Susnjar, Ante *Croatian-English/English-Croatian Dictionary and Phrasebook* Hippocrene, 2000. Good, helpful reference guide to the language.

WEBSITES There's a mountain of information and a wealth of resources concerning Croatia on the web. Here's a selection:

General

www.croatia.hr The National Tourist Board's exemplary website, with a huge amount of practical information and the phone number of most hotels, travel agencies and campsites across the country.

https://croatianmiscellany.wordpress.com Croatia in black and white.

www.dalmacija.net Dalmatia's own tourist information site, with online hotel bookings etc. See opposite for the sailing section.

www.diving-hrs.hr Croatian Diving Federation. Small (the English part, anyway) but useful site listing the rules and regulations for scuba diving.

www.eudict.com Excellent English-Croatian and Croatian-English dictionaries, though you need to have some idea of context as the responses are provided without separate definitions (the word 'set' gives you 41 different responses, for example).

www.hfhs.hr Croatian Youth Hostel Association. Gives the latest situation concerning youth hostels across the country, and works as a central reservation office, though make sure you have your confirmation with you when you actually show up at the hostels.

www.hr The so-called 'Croatian Homepage', an English-language site featuring 7,500 links in hundreds of categories, all about Croatia. You can spend many hours here.

www.mdc.hr Muzejski dokumentacijski centar, with details of most museums in Croatia.

www.meteo.hr Croatian Meteorological Service. Click on the flag for English and find out everything you ever wanted to know about Croatia's weather, including forecasts.

www.tportal.hr/imenik Croatia's online phone directory (including an English-language option). Just what you need when it turns out the phone number listed in this guide has already changed.

www.uhpa.hr Association of Croatian Travel Agencies. A good way of finding out what can be organised for you.

http://zablogreb.blogspot.com Humorous blog by American expat.

www.zagreb-touristinfo.hr The official site of the Zagreb Tourist Board. Excellent, detailed information about just about everything you'd want to know.

Transport

www.akz.hr Zagreb bus station, mostly in Croatian. Nonetheless excellent site with all arrivals and departures, including costs – go to Vozni red (timetable) from the homepage.

www.hak.hr Hrvatski Autoklub (Croatian Automobile Club). In Croatian only, though it does have an interactive traffic snarl-up area in English.

www.hzpp.hr National Railway. Even in Croatian you'll be able to find your way round the timetables, and the standard fares are displayed when the times come up – online booking is a bit trickier.

www.ina.hr The state-owned oil company. Complete with fuel prices and the locations and opening hours of every petrol station in the country.

www.jadrolinija.hr, www.krilo.hr, www.lnp.hr, www.miatours.hr, www.rapska-plovidba.hr, www.snav.it, www.triestelines.it, www.venezialines.com The main ferry companies plying the Adriatic.

Government and media

www.dzs.hr Croatian Bureau of Statistics. Everything you ever wanted to know.

www.hic.hr/english/index.htm Another news portal (also available in Croatian and Spanish).

www.hrt.hr Croatian national TV and radio (in Croatian).

www.mint.hr Ministry of Tourism. More statistics and all the forms you'll need if you're planning on starting a business in the Croatian tourist industry.

www.mvp.hr Ministry of Foreign & European Affairs. Everything you need to know about visa requirements etc.

www.tportal.hr Big customisable portal in Croatian from the main telecoms provider, with daily news bulletins, weather, traffic, entertainment etc.

Hiking and cycling

www.dinaridestrails.org Dinarides Trails. Plenty of information on mountain bike routes throughout Croatia, as well as hiking (in Croatian).

www.hps.hr Hrvatski planinarski savez (Croatian Mountaineering Association)

Sailing

www.aci-marinas.com Adriatic Croatia International Club homepage, with full details of everything ACI offers.

www.dalmacija.net An excellent section on sailing is included on the Split & Dalmatia County Tourist Information Service, with lots of information on marinas, regulations for foreign boats, where to get charts, weather, safety etc.

www.itinerances-dalmates.com Excellent French site with lots of rentals and good information on sailing, winds, guides etc. In French, of course.

www.portfocus.com/croatia Site providing links to harbours and ports in Croatia, as well as weather and satellite photos.

Index

Page numbers in **bold** indicate main entries; those in *italics* indicate maps

INDEX OF ADVERTISERS